THE BASEBALL BOOK
1992

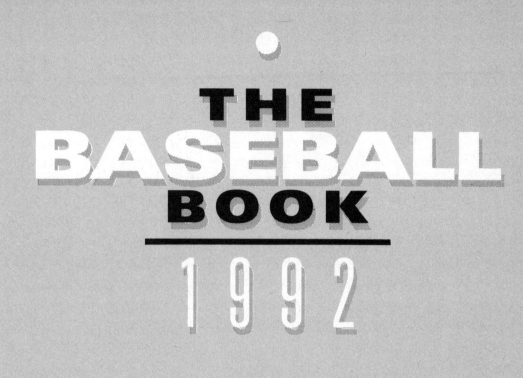

THE BASEBALL BOOK 1992

BILL JAMES

VILLARD BOOKS | NEW YORK | 1992

Published in the United States by Villard Books, a division of Random House, Inc.,
New York, and simultaneously in Canada by Random House of Canada Limited, Toronto.

ISSN: 1055-1433

Designed by Robert Bull Design

9 8 7 6 5 4 3 2

First Edition

DEDICATION

This book is for Mike Kopf. Some of Mike's work is included in the book, and I am uncertain whether this is a reason I should not dedicate the book to him, but I am of a mind to begin dedicating my books to my friends, and I don't want to start in the middle of the list.

PREFACE

OK, if you haven't thought about baseball all winter, here's what you need to know. The 1991 season was full of surprise heroes. The Atlanta Braves and the Minnesota Twins, neither of which teams had won a game for several years, met in the World Series. It was a great series and the Twins won. A lot of people still say that the Pittsburgh Pirates were the best team in baseball, but there you go; in time they'll stop saying it.

Terry Pendleton and Cal Ripken were the MVPs, and then there was a winter with a bunch of trades and free agent signings and stuff, and now we're ready to start over.

INTRODUCTION

Hi.

FOREWORD

Ahem.

THANKS

Now, I acknowledge that I have had a lot of help with this book. I even admit this, and confess it. In English the word "acknowledge" is often paired with "grudging" (the questioning of the DA elicited a grudging acknowledgement that between four and six million dollars could not be accounted for), or sometimes with an *implied* grudge (the school superintendant today acknowledged that there were problems with the training of bus drivers). Among the set of words which imply recognition "acknowledgement" is one of the least friendly, ahead of "admission" or "confession", but behind "appreciation", "thanks", and "gratitude":

1) Bill James *confessed* today that he had help in writing this book.
2) Bill James *admitted* today that he had help in writing this book.
3) Bill James *acknowledged* today that he had help in writing this book.
4) Bill James *recognized* today that he had help in writing this book.
5) Bill James *appreciates* the help he has had in writing this book.
6) Bill James *is grateful* for the help he has had in writing this book.
7) Bill James *wants to thank people* for the help he has had in writing this book.

I've always thought that what I wanted to say here was more along the lines of *thanks*, rather than *acknowledgement*.

Well, anyway, my full-time help is Rob Neyer. It is Rob's job to find out everything I need to know and don't know, which when you don't really know anything and are pretending to be some kind of a frigging expert can be quite an extensive list. In addition to Rob I confess that this book also includes articles by Mike Kopf and Jack Etkin, and I'm grateful for that. There's an article by Eddie Epstein.

I admit that the statistical section of this book is compiled by John Dewan and the folks at STATS, Inc., including but not limited to Sue Dewan, Dick Cramer, Ross Schaufelberger, Bob Mecca, Steve Moyer, Art Ashley, Bob Meyerhoff, Jim Musso, Chuck Miller, Jonathan Forman, Nadine Jenkins, Marge Morra, Suzette Neily and Dave Pinto, all of whom are greatly appreciated.

In compiling the teams in a box I talked to everybody I know at least twice, including but not limited to Paul Bauer, Allen Barra, Frank Kern, Lloyd Johnson and Don Zminda, as well as many of the people acknowledged before.

Susan McCarthy is my wife and greatest helpmate, and also an artist who supplied some of the drawings which highlight the *Biographic Encyclopedia*. John Sprengelmeyer is a young cartoonist; his work is included here, and I certainly don't deny that.

At least two people at the Hall of Fame were helpful, Bill Deane and Tom Heitz. David Jenkins provided some information for an entry in the *Bio En*.

For more than ten years Liz Darhansoff has been my agent and Peter Gethers my editor; I appreciate their continued support. Peter is not in the Villard offices any more, so I work through Stephanie Long, Dennis Ambrose, and Leta Evanthes. Grace McQuade, Villard publicity, is responsible for the fact that you know who I am. Well, that may be a bit of an overstatement, but when I was self-publishing I would sell about 2,000 copies a year and now I sell more than that on a good day, so you can see that publicity makes a difference. This book was designed by Bob Bull, whose contributions were indispensable. Thanks to all, and to R, I, S, I, B, A, D, T, B and the S and LF. Most grateful, most grateful.

Damn, I forgot to thank the goldfish.

CONTENTS

PART ONE

THE TEAMS

THE MINNESOTA TWINS
• IN A BOX •

1991 Won-Lost Record: 95–67 .586

Rank among 26 teams: 2nd
Over Last Five Years: 423–385 .525
Rank over Five Years: 5th
In Last Ten Years: 784–836 .484
Rank over Ten Years: 22nd

Best Player: Kirby Puckett

Weak Spot: The 1991 Twins did not have a particular weak spot, although of course some positions were not as strong as others. Probably the weakest spots looking ahead to 1991 are the left side of the infield (third base and shortstop) and catcher if Harper leaves as a free agent. In 1991 what most distinguished the team, rather than any particular strong point, was the absence of a conspicuous non-producer.

Best Pitcher: Jack Morris, if he stays.

Staff Weakness: Allan Anderson

Best Bench Player: Tom Kelly uses a professional bench, a group of players whom he has kept around for several years. They had a very good year in 1991. Randy Bush, coming off the bench with a .401 on-base percentage, was the best.

Best Young Player: Chuck Knoblach

Ugliest Player: Greg Gagne

Most Pleasant Surprise, 1991: Shane Mack

Biggest Disappointment, 1991: Allan Anderson

Best Minor League Prospect: Paul Sorrento

Who Is: A left-handed hitting first baseman, now 26 years old; he's had almost 200 major league at bats and was on the World Series roster. There's no spot open for him with Hrbek at first, so Sorrento is basically cooling his heels. I don't believe Sorrento is a *better* hitter than Hrbek, but I think he is almost as good. If he doesn't get a job this year he's the Don Mincher of the 1990s.

Other Prospects: If the Twins have anyone in their roster who has superstar potential, I've missed it. In addition to Sorrento they have **Pedro Munoz,** an outfielder who, like Sorrento, can hit the hell out of the ball but doesn't do other things well enough to push people out of the way. Munoz is listed at 23 years old (born September 1968) but has been in pro ball for seven years; he does run well. If he's really 23 years old he's going to have a good major league career. If Dan Gladden doesn't return and Munoz has to play, in my opinion this will improve the team.

Their top pitching prospects are **Denny Neagle,** a left-hander who reached the majors last August, and **Pat Mahomes,** a right-handed starter with a fastball and a curve. I like both quite a bit. Mahomes is a power pitcher who has been consistently healthy for several years, and may be finding his control. Neagle shot through the minors with a 32–10 won-lost record and outstanding strikeout/walk ratios. Perennial prospect **Willie Banks** is still trying to develop a breaking pitch.

Designated Malcontent: None

Park Characteristics: Loud and Ugly

The Park Helps: All hitters. Kirby Puckett appears to have a larger home-field advantage, over a period of years, than any of the other long-term Twins.

The Park Hurts: No one. The Twins over the last six years have a winning percentage 144 points better at home than on the road (.582 at home, .438 on the road.) This is the third-largest home field advantage in baseball, behind Boston and Houston.

ORGANIZATIONAL REPORT CARD

Ownership:	A
Upper Management:	C−
Field Management:	A
Front-Line Talent:	B−
Second-Line Talent:	B+
Minor League System:	C

TEAM LEADERS:

Batting Average: Kirby Puckett, .319

Last Ten Years (Season): Kirby Puckett, 1988, .356
Last Ten Years (Total): Kirby Puckett, .320

Doubles: Chili Davis, 34

Triples: Dan Gladden, 9

Home Runs: Chili Davis, 29

Last Ten Years (Season): Kent Hrbek, 1987, 34
Last Ten Years (Total): Kent Hrbek, 242

Extra Base Hits: Chili Davis, 64

RBI: Chili Davis, 93

Last Ten Years (Season): Kirby Puckett, 1988, 121
Last Ten Years (Total): Kent Hrbek, 885

Stolen Bases: Chuck Knoblach, 25

Runs Created: Chili Davis, 107

Runs Created Per 27 Outs: Chili Davis, 7.1

Secondary Average: Chili Davis, .418

Wins: Roger Erickson, 20

Last Ten Years (Season): Frank Viola, 1988, 24
Last Ten Years (Total): Frank Viola, 112

Winning Percentage: Roger Erickson, .714

Strikeouts: Jack Morris, 163

Last Ten Years (Season): Frank Viola, 1987, 197
Last Ten Years (Total): Frank Viola, 1214

ERA: Kevin Tapani, 2.99

Saves: Rick Aguilera, 42

League Leaders: Kirby Puckett in 1991 hit .407 against left-handed pitchers, highest in the major leagues.

Stat of the Year: Kirby Puckett has a career batting average of .349 in the Metrodome.

1991 SEASON

Background: After outstanding years in 1987–1988 the Twins spun their wheels for two years, finishing under .500. In 1990, as most of you know, they finished last in the American League West.

Outlook: There was no obvious reason, as the Twins headed into the 1991 season, to expect dramatic improvements. The mid-winter signing of veterans Chili Davis (.265 with 12 homers, 58 RBI) and Jack Morris (15–18, 4.51) seemed, at the time, pointless attempts to bolster an aging team. Many people, including me, picked the Twins to finish last again.

Getaway: Dismal. The Twins opened the season at Oakland, and after coming home for a three-game series went back to the West Coast to play Seattle and California. They dropped nine of their first eleven games, putting them in last place, five games behind Chicago. Rumors circulated that Tom Kelly's job was in trouble.

Low Point of the Season: April 20, Twins dropped to 2–9.

Stretch Drive: The Twins rallied quickly, blowing away Seattle in a four-game series in late April and reaching .500 on May 7 (13–13). Stagnant through most of May, they ignited on a trip to Texas and Kansas City, won 18 of 19 games between May 28 and June 16. They never experienced another significant letdown after June 1.

High Point of the Season: Game Seven of the World Series.

Most Exciting Game of the Season: Probably Game 6 of the World Series.

Major Injuries: The Twins did not suffer any really serious injuries during the 1991 season.

Offense: The Twins have a high-average offense which led the majors in batting average (.280 as a team) but didn't do anything else particularly well. They were in the middle of the pack in home runs, walks and stolen bases, and finished fourth in the league in runs scored.

Defense: The addition of Chuck Knoblach at second base cemented a defense which at times had struggled. A good summary of most of the defense would be "they're slow but they execute". The notable exception to that are left fielder Dan Gladden, who isn't slow, and catcher Brian Harper, who doesn't throw.

Starting Pitching: Three things happened to vault the Twins starting pitching suddenly from an apparent weakness to an outstanding strength. One was the signing of Jack Morris. Second was the sudden development of Scott Erickson, and third was the less striking but still impressive development of Kevin Tapani.

Bullpen: Aguilera and Willis were outstanding, and created generally good stats for the bullpen as a whole, although the bullpen depth was not good. Twin relievers saved 53 games in 66 opportunities, the best percentage in the league, and were charged with only 16 defeats.

Best Game by a Starting Pitcher: Jack Morris, Game 7

The best regular-season pitching performance was probably a 2-hitter by Erickson against the Red Sox on May 1 (9 2 0 0 1 7, Game Score 87).

Indicators for 1991 were: Up 4.1

Number of regulars having good seasons by their own standards: Only Three

1991 Over-Achiever: Chili Davis

1991 Under-Achiever: Dan Gladden

Infield: Above Average, not spectacular. Hrbek is among the better players at the position, but not among the *best;* he's not Cecil Fielder or Rafael Palmeiro. Knoblach was very good, Gagne very ordinary and the platoon combination at third avoided being a liability.

Outfield: Above average. Two regular outfielders (Puckett and Mack) were .300 hitters, and one (Gladden) is defensively outstanding for his position.

Catching: Strong. Harper doesn't throw well, but a catcher's throwing arm is one of the most over-rated things on a baseball team. The man can hit.

Percentage of 1991 Offense Accounted for by:

Young Players:	15%
Players in their Prime:	35%
Veterans:	50%

Team Age

Everyday Players:	29.1
Pitchers:	28.5
Overall:	28.85

In retrospect, the critical decisions were:

I would say there were three key personnel decisions which converted the 1991 Twins from tail-enders to champions. All three worked out spectacularly well. Those were:

1) Signing Chili Davis as a free agent,
2) Signing Jack Morris as a free agent, and
3) Bringing up Chuck Knoblach from AA to play second.

In addition, there are several "non-decisions" which need to be cited. The Twins *didn't* fire Tom Kelly in April, when they got off to a 2–9 start following 1990's last-place finish.

When the Twins traded for Steve Bedrosian, there was talk about putting Rick Aguilera back in the rotation and making Bedrosian or Rich Garces the closer. I thought this was an outrageous idea, and ripped it in last year's book—but the Twins didn't make the move. They left Aguilera in the bullpen, where they needed him.

THAT AND THE OTHER

Lookalikes: Scott Erickson and Jose Canseco

Hall of Fame Watch:

The Twins have two players who are good Hall of Fame candidates, and almost no one else of any interest to Cooperstown at this time. **Jack Morris** did more to improve his Hall of Fame position in 1991 than any other major league player. Entering the season with 198 career wins and two straight losing seasons, he would have had to be considered a Hall of Fame longshot. He left the year as a very solid candidate.

Kirby Puckett's accomplishments have reached the point at which his Hall of Fame induction seems almost inevitable. It doesn't seem possible, but Kirby already has 1,602 major league hits, meaning he is more than half-way to the big number. Even if he were to become an ordinary player tomorrow, he would probably clear 2,500 hits before gravity pulled his career to earth.

Chris Berman, Have You Considered: Scott (Would Your Sister) Leius

Throwback: Dan Gladden

Attendance Trend: Has been downward in recent years. The 1991 team drew 2.3 million, more than 700,000 fewer than they drew in 1988. One would expect another attendance spurt following the World Championship.

Players with a Chance for 3000 career hits:

Kirby Puckett	37%
Kent Hrbek	1%
Chili Davis	1%

Kirby also has an estimated 1% chance to get *4000* hits in his career.

Probably Could Play Regularly For Another Team: Paul Sorrento and Pedro Munoz

Best Fundamental Player: Al Newman. The Twins are probably the best fundamental team in baseball.

Worst Fundamental Player: No one sticks out.

Best Defensive Player: Probably Gladden, for his position

Worst Defensive Player: Brian Harper

Best Knowledge of the Strike Zone: Kent Hrbek or Knoblach

Least Command of the Strike Zone: Greg Gagne

Fastest Runner: Jarvis Brown. Knoblach is probably the fastest among the regulars.

Slowest Runner: Brian Harper

Note: Like many championship teams, the 1991 Minnesota Twins had very little team speed, and in fact were almost certainly the slowest team in the American League West. Four Minnesota regulars—Harper, Hrbek, Pagliarulo and Chili Davis—are among the slowest in the league at their positions. No Twin regular was among the fastest men at his position, and the Twins led the majors in grounding into double plays.

However, while the Twins are slow, they run the bases exceptionally well. They go first-to-third on a single as well as any team in baseball, and they tag up on a fly and advance *more* often than any other team, despite their lack of speed. As they do in some other ways, the Twins substitute intelligence for athletic ability, and wind up ahead on the deal.

Best Baserunner: Dan Gladden

Most Likely to Still be Here in 2000: Kirby Puckett

Best Fastball: Willie Banks

Best Breaking Pitch: No one sticks out

Best Control: Kevin Tapani

Never Going to be As Good as the Organization Thinks He Is: Willie Banks

Most-Comparable Players:

to C Brian Harper, Terry Steinbach
to 1B Kent Hrbek, probably Pedro Guerrero
to 2B Chuck Knoblach, Delino DeShields
to 3B Mike Pagliarulo, Brook Jacoby
to SS Greg Gagne, Shawon Dunston
to LF Dan Gladden, Kevin Bass
to CF Kirby Puckett, See Note
to RF Shane Mack, Felix Jose
to DH Chili Davis, George Bell

Most Fun to Watch: Kirby Puckett is as much fun to watch as anybody in the game. Scott Erickson was a lot of fun when he was on his game early last year—unique, gritty. Al Newman and Dan Gladden are fun to watch.

Least Fun to Watch: Tom Kelly

Managerial Type: Knoblach

Town Team:

C—Terry Steinbach
1B—Kent Hrbek
2B—Gene DeMontreville
3B—Paul Molitor
SS—Jerry Terrell
LF—Jim Eisenreich
CF—Dave Winfield
RF—Rip Repulski
SP—Jack Morris
SP—Chief Bender
SP—Jerry Koosman

Post-Season Transactions: None to date

What Needs to Be Done For 1992: The Twin team, despite the World Championship, has obvious shortcomings. They have to decide now whether they want to try to keep it going, or close the book on the Hrbek/Gaetti/Puckett era, and rebuild.

Outlook for 1992: None so far. At this writing Jack Morris, Dan Gladden and Brian Harper are unsigned, and the Twins may lose any or all three of them.

Index of Leading Indicators for 1992: Down 20.3
The Twins leading indicators for 1992 are the most negative for any major league team.

Positive Indicators: None worth mentioning.

Negative Indicators:

1. Plexiglas Principle.
2. Tendency of all teams to move toward .500
3. Team Age

Due for a better season: Mark Guthrie

Likely to have a worse season:

Chili Davis
Roger Erickson
Shane Mack

1992 Won-Lost Record will be: 82–80

SEVENTH GAME STORIES

Once in awhile they play one game on which the whole season rests. In 1991 it was a great game. In watching that game I thought about the rare beauty of it, to have at one time a great game, and a game of such supreme importance. This led me to reflect on seventh games in general, and from that I realized how much there was I didn't know. Such as:

How often does this happen?

Thirty-two times in history, or a little more than once every three years. If the two teams are even and there is not assumed to be any law of competitive balance operating, a mathematician would expect there to be a seventh game of the World Series five times in each sixteen years. The actual historical frequency has been just a little higher than that.

How often does that turn out to be a great game?

There are ten seventh games in baseball history that I think we would all agree were great games, classic games. Those were the games of:

1912 (Snodgrass' muff)
1924 (Ground ball bounces over Lindstrom's head in the 12th inning)
1925 (Peckinpaugh's eighth error of the series undermines Walter Johnson in the eighth inning)
1926 (Alexander strikes out Lazzeri)
1946 (Slaughter beats Pesky's throw to the plate)
1955 (Amoros' catch; Podres shuts out Yanks)
1960 (Mazeroski's homer)
1962 (Ralph Terry beats the Giants, 1–0)
1975 (Less remembered than Game Six, but great in its own right.)
1991 You probably remember it

There are other games you can argue for. Cardinal fans will insist the 1964 game was a classic, but it wasn't.

The two most-overlooked Game Seven classics are the games of 1971 (Pittsburgh over Baltimore) and 1972 (Oakland over the Reds.) Baseball was in a down cycle then; the perception that football was the game of the future was at its peak. The games of 1971 and 1972 didn't seem to stick in the public's mind as great games, but if you read the play-by-play . . . well, there's a lot there. Same with the seventh game of the 1940 series, Cincinnati over Detroit.

And how often is the seventh game a blowout?

There have only been five times in history when a seventh game was a rout—1909, 1934, 1945, 1956 and 1985. Two of those resulted in famous on-field melees, the 1934 Medwick fruit-throwing incident in Detroit, and the 1985 Andujar incident in Kansas City.

What's the greatest game by a pitcher in the seventh game? Was it Morris's?

You can argue that it was. I ran Game Scores for all the starting pitchers in Game Seven. The highest Game Score in a seventh game was by Sandy Koufax in 1965; Koufax pitched a three-hit shutout and struck out ten men, for a Game Score of 88. The second-highest Game Score is now Morris's (84), and the third-highest is 83, by Ralph Terry in 1962. Terry had stopped the Giants, a formidable hitting team, without a baserunner through five and two-thirds, the perfect game broken up by the opposing pitcher.

Of course, the Game Score is just a number, and the method doesn't consider everything. Morris deserves extra credit for pitching in such a tense game, a nothing-nothing game for nine innings. But Terry's game was 1–0, and Koufax had a tough job, too; he had only two runs to work with (a 2–0 game), and he was working on two days rest. He had pitched an equally spectacular game just three days earlier. Here's a formal list of the highest Game Scores:

	IP	H	R	ER	BB	SO	
Sandy Koufax, 1965	9	3	0	0	3	10	88
Jack Morris, 1991	10	7	0	0	2	8	84
Ralph Terry, 1962	9	4	0	0	0	4	83
Dizzy Dean, 1934	9	6	0	0	0	5	80
Bob Gibson, 1967	9	3	2	2	3	10	80
Johnny Kucks, 1957	9	3	0	0	3	1	79
Saberhagen, 1985	9	5	0	0	0	2	79
Steve Blass, 1971	9	4	1	1	2	5	78
Babe Adams, 1909	9	6	0	0	1	1	75
Lew Burdette, 1957	9	7	0	0	1	3	75

The best *relief* appearance in a seventh game, by far, was by Joe Page in 1947—five innings, one hit, no walks, no runs. The best effort by a losing pitcher was by Mike Cuellar in 1971, losing to Blass 2–1. The best effort by a no-decision pitcher was by Smoltz, last year.

What's the *worst* game by a pitcher?

The lowest Game Score is 26, by Walter Johnson in 1925 and Roger Craig in 1956. I wouldn't choose either one as the worst performance ever. Johnson's manager left him on the mound to allow 15 hits and 9 runs, an unusual thing for a World Series Game Seven. In a relief appearance, Craig gave up a Grand-Slam homer without getting anybody out, but that game was probably lost before he made his appearance.

Subjectively, I might choose Vic Aldridge's start *opposite* Walter Johnson in 1925 as the worst ever. Aldridge got one man out and put the Pirates in a 4–0 hole, but they rallied to win.

What's the best game by a hitter?

Maybe Willie Stargell, 1979. A left-handed hitter facing a left-handed starter who was having a fine game otherwise, Stargell singled in the second, doubled in the fourth, homered in the sixth, and doubled again in the eighth, although he did ground into a double play in the ninth, after the Pirates had broken it open a little bit.

The other two guys you might choose are Max Carey and Yogi Berra. In 1925 Carey went four-for-five against Walter Johnson with three doubles, a stolen base, three runs scored and two RBI. In 1956 Yogi hit two-run homers in the first and third innings, sparking the Yankees to a rout of the Dodgers.

The only other guys who had four hits in a seventh game were Ripper Collins (1934) and George Brett (1985), but both of those games were blowouts. Nobody else has homered twice in Game Seven.

Those guys are all Hall of Famers. Who's the *unlikeliest* Game-Seven hero?

At the time, Babe Adams was a longshot, a rookie sixth starter who got hot and dominated the 1909 World Series. He turned out to be a fine pitcher. Paul Richards, a weak-hitting catcher better known as a manager, drove in four runs in the seventh game in 1945, but that was the war years, and unlikely heroes were likely then.

The answer might be Darryl Motley, 1985. Motley hit a two-run homer to break the Royals loose, added two more singles and another RBI. He was a marginal player not having a particularly good year by his own standards.

Campy Campaneris, a shortstop who hit like a shortstop, had a great seventh game in 1973 (4 2 3 2). Campy started the scoring that day with a two-run homer, and built on it. He should have been the MVP of that series.

Was anybody ever the star of Game Seven more than once?

Not really, no. You can argue for Bob Gibson.

Who played in Game Seven the most times?

Mantle played in the seventh game of a World Series eight times, or one-fourth of all the seventh games ever played. Berra and Elston Howard played in seven each, and Moose Skowron and Gil McDougald in six. All Yankees, in other words, although Howard's last one was with the Red Sox.

Some of those guys must have had good games more than once?

Oh yes; many players have had *good* games in Game Seven more than once. It's just that nobody is *dominant*; nobody leaps out at you.

Moose Skowron holds the record for RBI in Game Seven, with nine, and is tied for the record in home runs, with three. The most RBI in a seventh game are four, and that's been done five times—but by only three different players. Paul Richards did it once, Skowron did it twice, and Berra did it twice.

In six Seventh Games, Skowron went 7-for-25 (.280) with a double, three homers, five runs scored and nine RBI. That might seem to make him the all-time Game Seven star, but when you look at it a little closer I'm not so sure. He hit a double against Podres in 1955, but a two-out double with nobody on in the second inning, so that didn't mean a whole lot. He hit a Grand Slam homer in 1956, after Yogi's two homers had already decided the game.

In 1958 Skowron's four RBI were monsters, critical to the 6–2 victory. In the second inning, Yankees down 1–0, Skowron tied the score with a ground ball. Then in the eighth inning, two out, two on, score tied 2–2, Skowron hit a three-run homer to break the game open.

Then in 1960, Game 7, Yankees trailing 4–0, Skowron hit a solo home run to ignite the first Yankee comeback. It's an impressive record, and if you want to say Skowron was the greatest Game-Seven star of all time, I won't argue with you.

Yogi Berra hit just .200 in Seventh Games, but may be the number one Game-Seven performer anyway. He was 5-for-25 career, but the five hits were three homers and two doubles, and he drove in eight runs. He and Skowron are the only guys with three Game-Seven homers.

Rizzuto in three games was 5-for-11, three runs scored.

Mantle was good in his eight games, going 9-for-30 (.300) with a double, two homers and seven RBI.

Del Crandall played in the seventh game twice, and homered both times.

Lou Brock was five-for-eleven with a double, a homer and three stolen bases.

Doc Cramer appeared in seventh games twice, fourteen years apart. As a young bench player in 1931, he appeared as a pinch hitter and hit a two-run single for the A's only two runs of that game. At the other end of a fine career in 1945, he got into the series with Detroit and went three-for-five in Game Seven (5 2 3 1) with a stolen base.

Campaneris, in addition to his great performance in 1973, was 2-for-4 in 1972.

Lonnie Smith in three games has gone six-for-twelve with three doubles and a stolen base. He has scored four runs.

Keith Hernandez in two games drove in five runs.

Dan Gladden in two games has had four hits including three doubles, one of which may well be the greatest double in baseball history. I couldn't believe he made second on that ball, and after all it was only the ballgame, the World Series and the season which hung in the balance.

Any pitchers?

The only pitcher to start the Seventh Game three times in his career was Bob Gibson, and many people would name Gibson the outstanding Game-Seven performer of all time.

I can't bring myself to agree.

Gibson completed all three of his starts, 27 innings, in which he struck out 27 batters. That's impressive. He won two of the three games.

The problem is that he just didn't pitch that well. He allowed eleven runs in the 27 innings, a 3.67 ERA.

The overall ERA for all pitchers in all seventh games is 3.27. Gibson was pushing it up.

He won the seventh game in 1964, but the Cardinals scored seven runs. Gibson allowed five runs, including two solo homers to weak hitters in the ninth inning, but staggered to the line.

In 1967 he pitched great in the seventh game, a super game. He didn't pitch as well as Jack Morris, but he pitched super.

In 1968 he pitched well, but he lost 4–1.

His three complete games are more attributable to the fact that he was BOB GIBSON than to how he pitched. It's hard to believe that anyone else would have been allowed to finish the game, as Gibson was in 1964, after giving up home runs to Clete Boyer and Phil Linz in the ninth inning. More incredible than that is 1968, when Gibson was allowed to stay in and bat for himself in the eighth inning, trailing 3–0. Red Schoendienst elected *not* to pinch hit for Gibson, down three runs and one inning away from final defeat. That seem a little strange to you? Sure, he's a .170 hitter, and sure, it's the eighth inning and we're three runs down, and sure, it's the Seventh Game of the World Series, but hey, he's *Bob Gibson*. He'll pull us out of this if anybody can.

Gibson pitched 17 innings more in the World Series than Jack Morris has (27–10) and allowed 11 more earned runs (11–0). That's a residual ERA—the difference between what Gibson did and what Morris has done—of 5.82. I can't see how it makes him the greatest Game-Seven performer of all time.

The only other guys who have *started* the Seventh Game of the World Series more than once are Lew Burdette and Don Larsen, who were matched against each other in 1957 and again in 1958. Neither one of them has an argument.

What about Whitey Ford?

Remarkably, *Whitey Ford never appeared in the seventh game of a World Series.* Ford started the *first* game of a World Series eight times in his career (I'd like to see somebody break **that** record), but never the seventh one. And he never appeared in the seventh game in any capacity—reliever, pinch runner, anything.

I found this to be so astonishing that I thought maybe we should recount how this came to be. The Yankees played seven-game series eight times between 1950, when Ford came up, and 1964, his last World Series.

In 1952 Ford was in the Army, and didn't pitch.

In 1955 Ford started the first game in Yankee Stadium, and won 6–5. Ebbets Field was a tough place for a left-hander to pitch, however, and Ford had been hammered in his only start there, during the 1953 World Series. Stengel elected not to start Ford in Ebbets Field, but brought him back in Game Six in Yankee Stadium. He won Game Six, setting up Tommy Byrne to start Game Seven against Podres.

In 1956 Ford started the first game in Ebbets Field and was hit hard again. He was out early, so he came back to pitch Game Three in Yankee Stadium, where he won. Ford had been brilliant that year (19–6, league-leading 2.47 ERA), and would seem to be the logical selection to start Game Seven. Stengel, however, chose his other ace for that season, Johnny Kucks (18–9, 3.86). According to *Slick*, by Whitey Ford with Phil Pepe:

> Now we were tied, three games apiece, and the seventh game was in Ebbets Field, and everybody was speculating again on who Casey was going to start in the final game.
>
> I knew it wasn't going to be me for two reasons—my record in Ebbets Field and the fact that I had warmed up for four innings during Larsen's [perfect] game.

Still seems pretty weird to me.

In 1957 Ford started the first game of the series, beat Warren Spahn, rested four days and came back for Game Five, which he lost 1–0 to Lew Burdette. But while Burdette came back on two days rest to start (and win) Game Seven, Stengel started Don Larsen, who pitched badly.

In 1958 the scenario was similar: Ford started Game One against Spahn, and pitched pretty well (no decision). He rested three days and started Game Four against Spahn; Spahn beat him three-to-nothing.

Down three games to two and facing elimination, Stengel brought Ford back with two days rest to start again in Game Six, 1958. He was knocked out in less than two, confirming Stengel's belief that Ford didn't pitch well on short rest. The Yankees rallied to win Game Six, and Stengel started Don Larsen, for the second straight year, in Game Seven. Larsen gave up a run early and left early, but the Yankees rallied to win the seventh game behind Bob Turley.

In 1960 Ford didn't have a good year (12–9), and Stengel elected not to pitch Ford in Game One in Forbes Field, which was a right-hander's park, or anyway people said it was. Ford started the first game in Yankee Stadium (Game Three), shut out the Pirates, and came back to shut them out again in Game Six—in Forbes Field. But he wasn't available for Game Seven, which was cited by some people as contributing to Stengel's firing. Stengel had risked the series by failing to position Ford so that he could pitch three times. He limited Ford to one start in Yankee Stadium and one in Pittsburgh, when he could have had one in Yankee and two in Pittsburgh.

In 1962 Ford started the first game in San Francisco, and won. He came back in Game Four, and pitched well. But then three game days were eliminated by rain, and with the travel day Ford had six days rest by Game Six. Ford started Game Six, which he lost—setting up Bill Terry's sterling performance in Game Seven.

In 1964, finally, Ford started the first game, and was hit hard. According to *Slick:*

> . . . Mike Shannon hit a two-run homer and Tim McCarver followed with a double. Now Elston Howard threw me the baseball and I went to take it out of my glove and I suddenly didn't have the strength to grab the ball. My arm just lost all of its strength, just like that.

He didn't pitch again during the 1964 series, his last.

So while Bob Turley pitched three times in seventh games (in relief) and Tommy Byrne twice and Ralph Terry twice and Don Larsen *started* twice, Whitey Ford never came into the seventh game of a World Series.

Who was the most *un*-likely pitcher selected to start the Seventh Game of the World Series?

By far, the most improbable selection to start the Seventh Game of a World Series was Hal Gregg, who started the Seventh Game for the Dodgers in 1947. Gregg's record that year was 4–5, his ERA 5.88—not the man you would ordinarily choose to pitch the biggest game of the year. Not only that, but Gregg had pitched seven innings only three days earlier, so he was starting on two days rest. He was ineffective, and the Dodgers lost.

But wait a minute. If you look at it in context, you'll realize that Burt Shotton (Dodger manager) really didn't have any better option. Here's how it happened.

Gregg had been the Dodgers' best pitcher in 1945, the last War year, when the talent was scarce. A big, powerful 23-year-old with a deferment of some kind, he had gone 18–13. When the *real* major leaguers came back in 1946 he continued to pitch well, posting a 2.99 ERA in 26 games, so he was in the rotation at the start of the 1947 season.

He pitched badly that year, as I said, so by the World Series he was just hanging around. The Dodgers' top four starters in 1947 were Ralph Branca (21–12, 2.67 ERA), Joe Hatten (17–8, 3.64), Harry Taylor (10–5, 3.11) and Vic Lombardi (12–11, 2.98). They were all four good, they included two left-handers and two right-handers, and they were young, although as luck would have it none of the four survived to play a key role among the Boys of Summer except Branca, whose role there was not a happy one. By October the fifth starter was Rex Barney (5–2, 4.96 ERA).

Well, Ralph Branca started Game One of the World Series, and he was hammered, giving up five runs in four innings.

Vic Lombardi started the second game and he was hit as hard as Branca, giving up five runs in four innings.

Joe Hatten started the third game, and he was hit even harder, giving up six runs in four innings.

Harry Taylor started Game Four. He didn't get anybody out. He loaded the bases and walked DiMaggio, after which Hal Gregg came in.

Yet somehow, by luck, hitting and the bullpen, the Dodgers had it tied up at two games apiece, despite having four starters in succession pasted to the outfield wall. While Hatten had been miserable in Game Three, the Dodgers had gotten to Yankee pitching for a 9–8 victory. After Taylor made an early exit in Game Four, Hal Gregg pitched seven extremely fine innings in long relief, allowing the Dodgers to stay close. Hugh Casey pitched brilliantly in late relief, got the win in both games, and the Dodgers broke up Bevens' no-hitter in the ninth to knot the series at two all.

Rex Barney started Game Five. On top of everything else, the starting pitching for the Dodgers was so bad that Shotton was forced to use his starters in long relief, leaving him unable to rest Branca and give him another shot at it. He didn't do anything in long relief that suggested he *deserved* another shot at it. Branca, incidentally, had also started the first game of the three-game playoff against the Cardinals for the 1946 pennant and had also been creamed in that one, so even then he didn't have a reputation as a big-game pitcher, and it was Rex Barney's turn in Game Five.

Barney lasted four and two-thirds innings, and walked nine men.

The Dodgers lost.

Shotton tried Lombardi again in Game Six.

Lombardi was shelled again, giving up five hits and four runs in less than three innings.

The Dodgers scored eight runs, however, and beat the Yankees 8–6, forcing it to the seventh game. Who was to start?

The logical answer is now "Hal Gregg". Everybody else on the staff had failed miserably. Gregg pitched seven strong innings. Who are you going to try?

Well, Hal Gregg gave up three runs in three and two-thirds innings, so the Yankees won the Series. It's an astonishing sequence of events. The Dodgers had one of the better starting rotations in baseball that year, yet in a seven-game series they had not a single starting pitcher last as long as five innings. For the series, the seven Dodger starters pitched a total of 23 and a third innings, giving up 26 runs, 25 of them earned. They put 53 runners on base by hit or walk—two and a half per inning—and had an ERA for the series of 9.64. The situation was so bad that

Hank Behrman, a relief pitcher with a 5.48 ERA, was called upon to pitch in five of the seven games.

There are a couple of other strange selections to start the Seventh Game, although none on the same level as Hal Gregg. In 1952 the Dodgers started Joe Black, a relief pitcher who had only started two games all season, three times during the series, which included the seventh game. He isn't the only pitcher to start more times during the series than he had during the season. Two years earlier the Phillies had started Jim Konstanty, the MVP reliever who hadn't started a game all season, in the first game of the World Series. As the Phillies had with Konstanty, the Dodgers figured that Black was the best pitcher they had, so they'd ride him as far as he could carry them.

There is one other improbable seventh-game starter story. You will remember that in the sixth (and final) game of the 1990 NL Championship Series, Jim Leyland started Ted Power, a reliever. This was done to deprive the Reds of the platoon advantage. Leyland apparently hoped to start Power, a right-hander, force the Reds to start a left-handed lineup, and switch to his left-hander, Zane Smith.

I wrote about this in last year's book, in the Ted Power comment:

> [This] was an old table-game strategy come to life . . . I've seen managers do that in table game leagues for years—the strategy is not well thought of—and I've *heard of* managers doing it in the majors. Leo Durocher supposedly did it a few times, but I've never actually seen it done, and certainly never seen it done in the final game of a championship series.

Well, several alert readers wrote or called me to tell me that this in fact *had* happened before. Specifically, it happened in the Seventh Game of the 1924 World Series.

Bill Terry was a rookie in 1924, and hadn't done anything during the season, hit .239 in limited playing time. He got hot during the World Series, however, and was in danger of becoming the decisive player of the series, hitting .500 (six-for-twelve) with a triple and a homer.

Terry was a left-handed hitter, and didn't normally play against left-handed pitchers. Washington manager Bucky Harris didn't want him in the game. So what he did was, he started his sixth starter, a rookie *right*-hander named Curly Ogden. Terry was in the lineup. Harris let Ogden get one man out, and then replaced him with a left-hander, George Mogridge.

John McGraw let Terry face the left-hander twice, in the second and in the fourth. He was 0-for-2 with a strikeout. When Terry came up in the sixth, however, two men were on base and the Giants trailed by a run. McGraw had to act. He sent up a right-hander, Irish Meusel, to pinch-hit for Terry.

Presto. Harris switched back to a right-hander, and Terry was out of the game.

Both managers got what they wanted out of it. Meusel hit a sacrifice fly to tie the game, and the Giants took the lead in the inning. But Washington came back to win the game.

Is there anything which typifies seventh games, as a whole?

There are two things which dominate seventh games: Great pitchers, and great pitching.

Remember, we're talking about just 32 games here, albeit 32 games which have a huge impact on the history of baseball. That's 64 starting pitchers. I don't know how many of those 64 are Hall of Famers or are going to be, but it has to be around 30. Look at the names—Christy Mathewson, Walter Johnson, Waite Hoyt, Jesse Haines, Dizzy Dean, Sandy Koufax, Bob Gibson three times, Jack Morris, Frank Viola, Bret Saberhagen. And the non–Hall of Famers in the group are guys like Lew Burdette and Mike Cuellar, who were pretty damn good. It's not what you see in your typical 32 games.

And because of that, and also because of the weather in late October, seventh games tend to be dominated by pitching. Last year (1991) was extreme, the best pitcher's duel ever in a seventh game—but many of those 32 games have been pitcher's duels. There have been four relatively high-scoring games to decide the championship of the world—1925 (Pittsburgh 9, Washington 7), 1960 (Pittsburgh 10, New York 9), 1964 (St. Louis 7, New York 5) and 1986 (New York 8, Boston 5). As mentioned before, there were also five blowouts, in which one team scored a lot of runs but the other team didn't. But there have been about a dozen seventh-game pitcher's duels.

Let me summarize that with two stats. The overall batting average of all batters in seventh games is .237. The overall ERA is 3.27.

Another thing which contributes to this, of course, is that managers are very quick to go to the bullpen in seventh games, and they will use *anybody* who hasn't pitched six innings in the last 24 hours.

What's the greatest GAME in the ultimate contest? Was the 1991 championship game the greatest ever?

I listed earlier ten candidates for that distinction. From that list, I think you can eliminate four games—1925, 1955, 1962 and 1975. Any of the other six games—1912, 1924, 1926, 1946, 1960 and 1991—I think you can argue for.

Forced to choose, I'd take the 1960 game, in which each team fought back *twice* from long odds to set up Mazeroski's homer, as the greatest Game Seven ever played.

If not, in fact, the greatest game of baseball ever played.

TWIN BROTHERS

The Theory of the "Most-Comparable Players" lists is this. Suppose that any player, or each player, *had* to be traded for some reason. Suppose that Kirby Puckett, let us say, developed an inflammation of the ear drums which gave him splitting headaches at noise levels over 80 decibels, and *had* to be traded. Who could you trade him for without *really* changing the team? Who is there, somewhere in the major leagues, who plays the same position, is about the same age, is of about the same value, and who would play the same offensive role on the team?

Sometimes there's a good answer to that question; sometimes there isn't. Some guys are a dime a dozen. You can trade Gene Larkin or Randy Bush for any of a dozen guys who are just like him. Some guys have *one* almost perfect comp, somewhere in the major leagues. Gary Gaetti and Tim Wallach. Ryne Sandberg and Cal Ripken, although you have to flip-flop at second and short.

Kirby Puckett is a unique player, and consequently not closely comparable to anyone. The player with the most comparable 1991 and career batting record is **Julio Franco,** but Franco is not what you would call a *good* comp for Kirby even as a hitter, and it is awkward to compare a center fielder to a second baseman. The most comparable all-around player is probably Andy Van Slyke, but again, Van Slyke is not truly comparable; he's merely *more* comparable than anybody else.

A player who is comparable to Brian Harper in a different way is **Jerry Willard,** who surfaced last year with Atlanta. Willard is only a few months younger than Harper, so the odds are that he will never get another shot, but he is exactly what Harper was for so many years—an excellent hitting catcher who would be very valuable to a major league team in the right role, but whose career got side-tracked due to defense and other problems.

THE CHICAGO WHITE SOX
• IN A BOX •

1991 Won-Lost Record: 87–75 .537

Rank among 26 teams: 6th
Over Last Five Years: 398–410 .493
Rank over Five Years: 17th
In Last Ten Years: 815–803 .504
Rank over Ten Years: 13th

Best Player: Frank Thomas

Weak Spots: Right Field, Depth of starting pitching

Best Pitcher: Jack McDowell

Staff Weakness: Only one quality starter

Best Bench Player: Ron Karkovice

The White Sox have the best bench in the American League, which is one reason I pick them to win the division. Backup catcher Karkovice is the best backup catcher in baseball, and probably played better than Fisk last year. Both Karkovice and Fisk had slugging percentages of .413, but Karkovice had a better batting average and on-base percentage. Defensively, Fisk threw out 41% of opposition base stealers, which is very good, and Karkovice threw out 43%, which is sensational. The staff had an ERA of 3.95 with Fisk catching, 3.66 with Karkovice.

You don't judge a player on one-year performance, particularly when the differences are minuscule, so I'm certainly not advocating that Karkovice should play ahead of Fisk. Karkovice has played well for three straight years, but Fisk played better the other two.

Anyway, the rest of the White Sox bench is also terrific. In the infield they have Joey Cora, an excellent second-string infielder, and Craig Grebeck, who may have played himself into first-string status. In the outfield are Warren Newson, a Gary Redus type, and Mike Huff. Then there's Dan Pasqua, an extra hitter with the signing of Bo, and Matt Merullo, who I don't know anything about but he played alright, and Rodney McCray, pinch runner. One hell of a bench.

Best Baseball Name: Estaban Beltre

Best Young Player: 1. Frank Thomas
2. Robin Ventura

Best Looking Player: Frank Thomas

Ugliest Player: Ron Karkovice

Most Pleasant Surprise, 1991: Warren Newson

Biggest Disappointment, 1991: Alex Fernandez

Best Minor League Prospect: Johnny Ruffin

Who Is: A right-handed pitcher. He was a fourth-round draft pick out of high school in 1988, made slow progress for a couple of years but throws very hard. He was 11–4 at Sarasota last year, peripheral stats not spectacular.

Other Prospects: **Derek Lee,** a 25-year-old, left-handed hitting outfielder is capable of hitting .280 in the majors with 50–70 walks and a lot of doubles. The Sox have a pitcher named **Bob Wickman** at AA who lost the tip of his index finger in a farming accident, and apparently has been able to get an unusual spin on the ball because of the distinctive digit. He didn't have a great record at Birmingham but is well thought of.

In the Cory Snyder deal the White Sox acquired a reliever named **Jeff Carter,** who has pitched well at times. He's a marginal prospect.

Designated Malcontent: Melido Perez

Park Characteristics: New Comiskey appears to be a great park for hitters, especially right-handed hitters. Both Frank Thomas (right-hander) and Robin Ventura (left-hander) hit much better in Comiskey than they did on the road. Thomas hit .371 in Comiskey, as opposed to .271 on the road, and hit 24 home runs at home, 8 on the road. His slugging percentage was almost three hundred points higher at home than on the road (.708 to .411). Ventura hit only eleven points higher at home than on the road, but hit 16 of his 23 home runs at home.

The Park Helps: Obviously, the park is going to make Thomas appear to be an even greater hitter than he is, but I wouldn't want to make too much of this yet. My feeling is that Thomas really *is* a very impressive hitter, and this his 1991 home/road disparity is at least half just random chance.

ORGANIZATIONAL REPORT CARD

Ownership: A−
Upper Management: B+
Field Management: Unknown
Front-Line Talent: B+
Second-Line Talent: B
Minor League System: B−
Comment: See article, "Home Office"

TEAM LEADERS:

Batting Average: Frank Thomas, .318

Last Ten Years (Season): Frank Thomas, 1991, .318
Last Ten Years (Total): Harold Baines, .293

Doubles: Frank Thomas, 31

Triples: Lamar Johnson, 13

Home Runs: Frank Thomas, 32

Last Ten Years (Season): Carlton Fisk, 1985, 37
Last Ten Years (Total): Carlton Fisk, 203

Extra Base Hits: Frank Thomas, 65

RBI: Frank Thomas, 109

Last Ten Years (Season): Harold Baines, 1985, 113
Last Ten Years (Total): Harold Baines, 729

Stolen Bases: Tim Raines, 51

Walks: Frank Thomas, 138

Runs Created: Frank Thomas, 145

Runs Created Per Game: Frank Thomas, 9.7

Frank led the major leagues in both runs created (145) and runs created per 27 outs (9.7).

Secondary Average: Frank Thomas, .483

Wins: Jack McDowell, 17

Last Ten Years (Season): Lamarr Hoyt, 1983, 24
Last Ten Years (Total): Richard Dotson, 74

Winning Percentage: McDowell, 17–10 .630

Strikeouts: McDowell, 191

Last Ten Years (Season): Floyd Bannister, 1985, 198
Last Ten Years (Total): Floyd Bannister, 759

ERA: Jack McDowell, 3.41

Saves: Bobby Thigpen, 30

League Leaders: Charlie Hough made an average of 2.4 throws to first per baserunner last year, almost twice as many as anyone else in the American League.

1991 SEASON

Background: Stumbling through the 1980s in the wake of the Harrelson era, the White Sox won only 67 games in 1989. In 1990 they made the great leap to respectability, winning 90 games.

Outlook: Of course when a team improves dramatically in one season many people will expect further improvement the next, although this is not entirely realistic. Most people a year ago picked the Oakland A's to continue to rule this division, but most of those who did not picked Chicago.

Getaway: The White Sox won their first six games in 1991—all of them on the road—and stayed well over .500 through April (11–6). They left on May 10 for a road trip to Toronto and Boston, lost a couple of close games, and limped through May, dropping to 20–23 by May 30. They didn't get hot until late June.

Stretch Drive: On June 21 the White Sox rallied for a 6–5, eleven-inning victory over Texas, igniting a seven-week stretch in which they played as well as a team can play.

High Point of the Season: Wilson Alvarez no-hitter, August 11. Between June 21 and August 11 the White Sox won 35 games and lost only 12 to pull within one game of first place.

Low Point of the Season: Bret Saberhagen's no-hitter, August 26.

The White Sox second major slump began, again, on a trip East. It began the very day after Alvarez' no-hitter. Losing the last game of a series in Baltimore, the White Sox flew to Detroit, where they lost three out of four, and then to New York, where they lost two of three. They came home to face Detroit on August 19, still very much in the race at 67–54, but lost three straight to Detroit in Chicago. They flew to Cleveland—and lost three straight. From there it was on to Kansas City, where Saberhagen no-hit them in the first game of a three-game sweep.

Most Exciting Game of the Season: Two games of the 1991 White Sox stick out. On July 31, late in their drive into contention, the White Sox took a 4–1 lead against Texas. The Rangers fought back on homers by Palmer, Palmeiro and Sierra and led 8–5 in the eighth, 8–6 heading into the bottom of the ninth. Two out, bases loaded, ninth inning. Robin Ventura hit a grand slam, his second home run of the game, to deliver victory from the fly swatter of defeat.

The other memorable game was on September 20, at home against California. The Angels led 2–0 in the ninth, Mark Langston working on a shutout until Bo Jackson hit a pinch-hit, two-run homer. The White Sox won it in the eleventh.

Major Injuries: None

Offense: Frank Thomas is so strong in all three of the basic elements of offense (hitting for average, power, and walks) that he makes the White Sox offense all-around above average. Take away Frank and the offense, at least in 1991, isn't much.

Defense: Excellent. Up the middle—Fisk, Guillen, Grebeck and Johnson—the White Sox couldn't be much better than they are.

Starting Pitching: Weak, the weakest part of the team. The signing of Charlie Hough kept the bottom from dropping out.

Bullpen: Thigpen, brilliant in 1990, was unimpressive in 1991, and the White Sox blew 24 save opportunities, as many as anyone in the league. Radinsky, Pall, Patterson and Melido Perez gave the White Sox excellent relief in the middle innings.

Best Game by a Starting Pitcher: Alvarez' no-hitter (9 0 0 0 5 7, Game Score 89).

Indicators for 1991 were: Down 23.3

Number of regulars having good seasons by their own standards: Three

1991 Over-Achiever: Robin Ventura

1991 Under-Achiever: Tim Raines

Infield: Above average, very good if Thomas is considered the first baseman. He usually was DH.

Outfield: Not enough offense. Raines is a good leadoff man, Johnson a fine center fielder, and Pasqua a good enough bat in right, but none of the three is a legitimate third- or fourth-hitter.

Catching: Outstanding.

Percentage of offense created by:

Young Players:	49%
Players in Their Prime:	31%
Past Their Prime:	20%

Team Age:

Age of Non-Pitchers:	27.7
Age of Pitchers:	26.6
Overall:	27.25

In retrospect, the critical decisions were:

The critical decision of the 1991 season was made June 5, 1989, when the White Sox drafted Frank Thomas.

THAT AND THE OTHER

Lookalikes: They don't look a lot alike, but one day late in the year, after Bo started working out with the team, Tim Raines put on Bo's uniform and gave several interviews with out-of-town reporters, at least one of whom went to press with his story without ever realizing that he'd been talking to Raines.

Hall of Fame Watch: Carlton Fisk is a Hall of Famer. It's too early to even talk about Thomas or Ventura or McDowell.

Chris Berman, Have You Considered: Brian (Three-Act) Drahman

This is Really What They Call Him: Lance (One Dog) Johnson

Throwback: Scott Fletcher

Most Emotional Player: Joey Cora

Attendance Trend: With a new park and a better team, of course, the White Sox attendance has vaulted far beyond previous highs.

Players with a Chance for 3000 career hits:

Tim Raines	17%
Ossie Guillen	10%

Best Interview: Jack McDowell

Definitely Could Play Regularly For Another Team: Ron Karkovice

Best Fundamental Player: Robin Ventura

Worst Fundamental Player: Bo Jackson

Best Defensive Player: Lance Johnson

I asked three die-hard White Sox fans who their best defensive player was. All three said Lance Johnson, and none thought Guillen was on the same level. One of the three did think that Karkovice was as impressive defensively as Johnson.

Worst Defensive Player: No one stands out

Best Knowledge of the Strike Zone: Frank Thomas

Least Command of the Strike Zone: Sammie Sosa

Fastest Runner: You could get a heck of a footrace among Raines, Lance Johnson, Joey Cora and Sammie Sosa. Raines used to be the fastest man in baseball other than perhaps Willie Wilson, but he's 32. All four of those guys can move.

Slowest Runner: Carlton Fisk

Best Baserunner: Tim Raines or Sammie Sosa

Most Likely to Still be Here in 2000: Frank Thomas

Best Fastball: Scott Radinsky

Best Breaking Pitch: Melido Perez, if you count the forkball as a breaking pitch, and Charlie Hough if you count the knuckleball. Wilson Alvarez has the best curve on the team.

Best Control: Don Pall

Most Overrated Player: Bo Jackson

Most Underrated Player: Warren Newson or Scott Radinsky

Oddest Collection of Abilities: Ozzie Guillen is one of those players, like Rob Deer, who is either first or last on any list you make. Ozzie probably creates as few runs as any .270 hitter in baseball history.

Never Going to be As Good as the Organization Thinks He Is: Sammie Sosa

Why is this man in the Major Leagues: Don Wakamatsu

Best Local Sportswriter: Bob Verdi

The Most Knowledgeable People About Local Baseball History Are:

1. Richard Lindberg
2. Jerome Holtzman

Local Neanderthal Sportswriter:

1. Bill Gleason
2. Jerome Holtzman

Most-Similar Players:

to C Carlton Fisk, Gary Carter
to 1B Dan Pasqua, Ivan Calderon
to 2B Scott Fletcher, Jose Uribe
to 3B Robin Ventura, Carlos Baerga
to SS Ossie Guillen, Jose Lind
to LF Tim Raines, Rickey Henderson
to CF Lance Johnson, Steve Finley
to RF Sammie Sosa, Bernie Williams
to DH Frank Thomas, Albert Belle

Most Fun to Watch: Ozzie Guillen

Least Fun to Watch: Charlie Hough

Managerial Timber: Terry Bevington (Third Base Coach)

Among the All-Time Team Leaders: Carlton Fisk is the White Sox All-Time Leader in Career Home Runs.

Ozzie Guillen will begin moving onto the White Sox all-time leaders this year.

Town Team:

C—Ray Schalk
1B—Bill Skowron
2B—Marty McManus
3B—Bob Kennedy
SS—Lou Boudreau
LF—Johnny Groth
CF—Kirby Puckett
RF—Jesse Barfield
SP—Denny McLain

Post-Season Transactions:

December 6, Signed Brad Komminsk to a minor league contract

December 7, Re-signed Carlton Fisk

What Needs to Be Done For 1992: Solidify the starting rotation

Outlook for 1992:

I'm picking the White Sox to win the division, with grave misgivings. The White Sox do some strange stuff. Nobody really knows why they signed Bo Jackson; to most of us the probability of Jackson developing into anything special seems remote. Still, who knows, so if they wanted to sign him . . . but then why did they keep Dan Pasqua? Signing Bo forces Thomas out of the DH spot and back to first base, so why do you sign Dan Pasqua?

Answer: for exactly the same reason we re-signed Greg Walker two years ago.

Then there's the pitching staff, which still seems to be about three quality starting pitchers short of a rotation. If I thought the division would be strong again, as it was last year, I suppose I would pick someone else.

But the White Sox have something going here. While the A's and Angels have no really good young players and Kansas City has one maybe, the White Sox have Thomas and Ventura. They have Jack McDowell, Bobby Thigpen and Scott Radinsky. They are the youngest *real* team in baseball, the youngest team that didn't push the average age down by dumping everybody making money. They have the great bench; they have Guillen and Fisk. While the starting rotation is suspect, there are two young pitchers (Alex Fernandez and Wilson Alvarez) who have the obvious potential to turn it around in a hell of a hurry. Maybe three, if you count Ramon Garcia. If the starting rotation is just decent, Big Frank can pull them to a pennant.

Index of Leading Indicators for 1992: Mixed (Down 9.3)

Positive Indicators: 1. Team Age

Negative Indicators: 1. Poor Play Late in season

Due for a better season: Sammie Sosa

Likely to have a worse season: Don Pall

1992 Won-Lost Record will be: 90–72

FRANK THOMAS AND THE TRIPLE CROWN

I was asked several times last summer about Frank Thomas' chance of winning a triple crown some time in his career, and so I began trying to think through this issue. From 1920 to 1967 the winning of a triple crown was not a spectacularly uncommon event. Two players won triple crowns in the 1920s (or actually, one player twice), four players did it in the 1930s, two more in the 1940s, one player in the fifties and two in the sixties. It happened every once in a while, anyway, but then since 1967 it hasn't. Why? Has leading the league simultaneously in home runs, RBI and batting average actually become more difficult, and thus moved off into the reaches of history with thirty-win seasons and .400 batting averages, something that we probably won't see again unless the game changes? Or has there simply been an accidental 24-year hiatus, such as might easily happen at random in an event which only occurs once or twice a decade?

Parenthetically, there is a fascination with the triple crown which I find somewhat inexplicable. Although no one has won a triple crown in 25 years, I am frequently asked about it on the air—much more frequently than I am asked about, let us say, Roger Clemens' chance of winning 30 games, or Jose Canseco's chance to hit 62 homers. Just after I started this article the December, 1991, issue of *Baseball Digest* arrived, containing two articles related to the issue ("Winning the Triple Crown, An Elusive Goal for Hitters" and "Some Words of Hitting Wisdom for Jose Canseco", subtitled *If A's home run slugger would shorten his stroke on occasion, he'd be a genuine Triple Crown threat.*) I see it all the time—each issue of each publication seems to bring it up at least once.

Anyway. The question confronting me was this: how can we determine whether there is a *cause* for this 24-year interruption in triple crown honors, or whether it is an accident of history?

I found the answer to that question in this manner. Step One: If there was a cause, what might it be? Focus on an element of the larger question: what might be *one* cause of the decline?

Step Two: The most obvious cause would be the expansion of the leagues. In 1956, Mickey Mantle had to beat all the other players on *eight* teams; Frank Thomas will have to beat all the other players on *fourteen* teams, which is obviously more difficult.

More difficult, but *how much* more difficult? Would this make triple crowns 20% less common? 60% less common? What?

Thinking about this, I realized that the exact collections of teams which form a league are not inevitable, and, so long as a reasonably constant set of norms prevail, need not be treated as inevitable. Step Three: re-cast the leagues. Let's look at Carl Yastrzemski, 1967, the last Triple Crown winner. Yastremski had to beat all of the players on ten teams in all three categories, but what if it had been fourteen teams? What if he had had to beat, let us say, all the players on the Cardinals, Cubs, Phillies and Braves as well? Would he still have been the triple crown winner?

No, he would not have; Tony Gonzales of Philadelphia would then have been the batting champion, with a .339 average, and no triple crown for Yastrzemski. What if the American League had included Houston, San Francisco, Cincinnati and Pittsburgh? Would he then have been the triple crown winner?

No, he would not have; the batting title would have gone to Roberto Clemente. What if the American League had included Los Angeles, the Mets, St. Louis and the Cubs?

Still no triple crown; in that case the batting championship would have gone to Curt Flood of St. Louis, at .335.

It is *possible* to pick four National League teams to add to the American League without taking the batting championship from Yastrzemski, but, since four of the NL teams have players with batting averages higher than Yaz's, it is relatively difficult. There are 210 different ways to choose four teams from ten, but only 15 of those 210 combinations do *not* include a player with a batting average higher than .326; thus, if you choose four teams at random from the National League, 93% of the time you're going to make a new league in which Yastrzemski is *not* the triple crown winner.

Is this unusual? Let's try the same with Frank Robinson, the 1966 American League triple crown.

Robinson has a slightly better chance than Yastrzemski; Robinson has to skate around five players who have higher batting averages and also one with more RBI, but those six players are concentrated on three teams. That improves his chance of winning the 14-team triple crown from 7% to 17%.

Mickey Mantle, 1956, is another kettle of fish; Mantle leads not only the American League in all three categories, but also the major leagues. No matter what six teams you add to his "league", he still wins—as long as you stick to 1956. If you add teams from 1955 or 1957, then it's no longer inevitable.

It is apparent through this exercise, however, that **making larger leagues very significantly impacts on the likelihood of a player's winning a triple crown.**

Now, this seems fairly obvious having approached it from this angle, but I have to say that it was a new realization to me. I had of course realized that it would be *somewhat* more difficult to lead a larger league, but had assumed that this wasn't a big deal. When you start putting it together in concrete terms, you realize that it is a big deal, that the larger leagues in fact make it *much* more difficult to lead the league in all three categories.

Step Four: Model the problem so as to estimate the extent of this one distortion.

And in trying to figure out a solution to that side problem, that *element* of the problem, I accidentally discovered the solution to the larger problem. I entered into a small program the triple crown stats for all the regulars in a few years from different eras in history—1930–1932, 1950–1952, 1959–1961, 1970–1972, and 1989–1991. Then I started re-casting leagues from those groups of teams, and seeing how often I wound up with a triple crown winner. Let us take, for example, 1930–1932; there are 48 major league teams in that era. I programmed the computer to choose eight-team leagues at random from those 48 teams.

There are 15 trillion ways to choose an eight-team league from 48 teams. Obviously, I didn't check all 15 trillion; I set the computer to check a thousand "leagues" and stop. This enables us to remove from the discussion two complications. First, in real life we had only eight-team leagues in 1930 and have only larger leagues today, but in the study we can make up eight-team leagues for 1991 or fourteen-team leagues for 1960, and in that way we can isolate the effects of the larger leagues from any *other* causes which might be contributing to the disappearance of triple-crown winners. Second, because we have hundreds of "leagues" to study, we avoid the problem of separating real changes from accidents of history. All of baseball history from 1968 to 1991 is only 48 leagues, which is a small sample. I can replace that with a sample of a thousand leagues, and thus *know* whether something has really changed.

When I made eight-team leagues from 1959–1961 data I would wind up with a triple-crown winner about 17% of the time. The best triple-crown candidate in those three years, fifty teams, is Norm Cash, 1961 (41 homers, 132 RBI, .361 average.) He didn't win a triple crown, but obviously he *could* have, with those numbers. When I recast the leagues, sometimes he does—and sometimes Hank Aaron does, 1959 season, and sometimes Mickey Mantle does, 1961, and once in awhile somebody else will, like Frank Robinson. The 17% from this era, because of Cash's super year, is higher than the test figures from the other eras, which tended to be around seven percent.

But when I expanded the leagues to 14 teams, the percentage of triple-crown winners dropped from 7% to 2%, actually slightly less than two percent. This leads us to our first significant conclusion in this research: **the expansion of the leagues from eight to fourteen teams, absent any other contributing causes, would cut the number of triple crown winners to less than one-third of what it previously was.**

Why is the difference that large? Because you're dealing with an *extreme* phenomenon, in which only the extreme outlying data is of interest. Intuitively, it had seemed to me that a player who leads *eight* teams in batting average probably would lead six more as well, but that's not right; that's not how it works. A better intuitive logic would be this: that winning a triple crown is enormously difficult anyway, even with eight teams. Anything that you add to that task pushes it to the range of being almost impossible.

Now, let me tell you where I *thought* I was going with this. I *thought* that I would find that the *only* thing that had really changed was the size of the leagues. I thought I would wind up reporting to you that we would still have triple crown winners, in the 1990s and beyond, but merely at a decreased frequency because of the larger leagues. I thought that when I compared the frequency of triple crown winners in theoretical six-, eight-, ten- or fourteen-team leagues, I would find that that frequency was the same in our era as it was in 1930–1932, 1959–1961, etc.

But it isn't. It's dramatically less. I can't really tell you why; I don't know. But it is less.

The smallest unit here is the one-team league. Obviously, a player can't win a triple crown unless he leads his own *team* in home runs, RBI and batting average. For some reason, the percentage of players leading their own team in home runs, RBI and batting average has nose-dived in the last twenty years. In the first group in my study (1930 to 1932), 15 players led their own *teams* in all three categories, which is 31%. This figure—31% of players leading their team in the triple crown categories—remains almost exactly the same through the other samples in the study, except the last one. **In the last three years only 13 players have led their own *team* in the triple crown categories; 13 of 78.** That's 17%—completely different from the 31% level of the earlier studies. Although 1987 and 1988 weren't part of the general study, I also checked them to see if I was dealing with a fluke. The data is the same—9 of 52, 17%.

I checked all the combinations—one-team leagues, two-team leagues, three-team leagues, etc.—and compared the 1989–1991 data to the earlier samples. The 1989–1991 data is lower all along the spectrum, as obviously it would be starting out at a level so much lower.

The question I can't answer is, why has the percentage of players leading their own team in the triple crown stats dropped so dramatically? The first thought is "specialization"; in modern baseball we have power hitters and singles hitters, but not both.

A look at the data, however, tells you quickly that that isn't it, and that in fact a better explanation is *de*-specialization, the *lack* of specialists. In the 1930s, and to a lesser extent in the 1950s and 1960s, each team might have only two or three real hitters, and each team might have only one power hitter, if that. The competition for the league lead in home runs and RBI, realistically, might be among just three or four players.

Players today *don't* specialize offensively, to the degree they did earlier. Rather than a cleanup hitting first baseman, a .245-hitting shortstop and a base-stealing outfielder, what we have now is a fleet-footed outfielder who is *also* a power hitter, and the .245-hitting shortstop might very well lead the team in home runs. And I can't really tell you why that is, other than simply that the distance between the good players and the average players isn't nearly as great as it used to be.

I also wish I could tell you exactly how often we could expect to see a triple crown winner in modern baseball. I can't, for two reasons. First, the assumption that the standards are constant so leagues can be re-divided, while it is a workable assumption, is not a perfect assumption. Second, what I can't tell you from this study is how often a player in modern baseball might produce stats so tremendous—Mickey Mantle, 1956—that he would override the odds.

But in my simulation, players under modern conditions won the triple crown *less than one percent of the time even when grouped into eight-team leagues*, and not at all when grouped into fourteen-team leagues. In a sample of 1,000 fourteen-team leagues made up of teams from 1989–1991, no one won the league's triple crown, although it could have happened. Cal Ripken's stats last year—34 homers, 114 RBI, .323 average—might be good enough to win a triple crown in exactly the right circumstances.

I also did another computer run here, which I'll throw in since it doesn't fit anywhere else. I compiled a list of all the seasons in baseball history which meet these three standards:

1) 40 Home Runs
2) 120 RBI
3) .320 Batting average.

You do that exactly and you still *probably* won't win the triple crown, but at least you're in the competition.

There are only 42 such seasons in baseball history. The first was by Babe Ruth in 1920. He did it several more times, and several others of his generation also joined him; altogether there were 12 such seasons in the 1920s and 17 in the 1930s. Then there were only two in the 1940s, six in the 1950s, three in the 1960s, two in the seventies, and there have been none since 1977 (George Foster). So that's also related—17 such seasons in the 1930s, none in the 1980s. Of course that's potentially misleading, because league-leading standards have changed.

Frank Thomas may be capable of having a better year than that—let's say, 45 homers, 130 RBI, .340. Ken Griffey Jr. could win a triple crown.

But it isn't going to happen very often unless something changes dramatically in baseball. You and I may never again see a triple crown season.

HOME OFFICE

The White Sox' minor league system appears almost empty right now, and evaluated by what it figures to produce in the next two years would receive a lower grade than I gave it. On the other hand, the White Sox number one draft picks from 1987 through 1990 were Jack McDowell, Robin Ventura, Frank Thomas and Alex Fernandez. It would be misleading to suggest that there was something seriously wrong with a farm system which produces those results. If the White Sox' number one draft pick from 1989 was now a hot prospect, that would be considered a positive for the farm system. We can't mark them down because he is already an MVP candidate.

The ownership of the Chicago White Sox is a hands-on ownership. When Jerry Reinsdorf and Eddie Einhorn bought this team from Bill Veeck they inherited a front office run by Roland Hemond, a long-time baseball executive who now runs the Orioles. They built on what they had there and things went well until the mid-eighties, when the White Sox suddenly moved Hemond out, and hired Ken Harrelson to be their General Manager.

Harrelson is a likeable, dynamic man who knows a lot about baseball, and Einhorn and Reinsdorf overlooked just one thing when they hired him: he's not an executive. He made decisions by the seat of his pants, without any real respect for input, process and review—all of that boring stuff that distinguishes companies which stay in business from those which don't. He wasn't a system-builder, and I think that they knew that, but I think they figured that since *they* were system-builders, and since *they* were there in the office, what they needed to build in was baseball experience.

So that didn't work, and they replaced Harrelson with Larry Himes, now GM of the Cubs. Himes was a good executive, and quickly began to restore the talent base and re-build the system. In a perfect world he would probably have been able to stay and see the White Sox win a pennant, but some silly mistakes were made—fighting with the team over petty stuff—and his support eroded.

The performance of the White Sox front office in the Himes and post-Himes eras has been extremely solid. There doesn't seem to be a strong central authority here, below the ownership. The White Sox are run by Ron Schueler, who is the "Senior Vice-President, Major League Operations", and Dan Evans, who is the "Director of Major League Operations", and Jack Gould, who is the "Senior Vice-President, Baseball", and a few other people. These titles are no doubt meaningful to the people who have them, but don't explain much to the rest of us.

But in the end the White Sox put a good product on the field, and they sell it well. The departure of Jeff Torborg, who did a fine job as field manager, is certainly a matter of concern, but

a) I don't recall that there was any tremendous demand for Jeff Torborg's services three years ago, and

b) he didn't win all those games by himself.

The Sox are going to be alright.

THE TEXAS RANGERS
• IN A BOX •

1991 Won-Lost Record: 85–77 .525
Rank among 26 teams: 7th
Over Last Five Years: 396–413 .489
Rank over Five Years: 19th
In Last Ten Years: 755–862 .467
Rank over Ten Years: 23rd

Best Player: Ruben Sierra

There are people who believe that Ruben Sierra is the best player in baseball. I don't agree, but I do concede that there's an argument to be made there.

Weak Spot: Starting Pitching

Best Pitcher: Nolan Ryan

Staff Weakness: Constant Walks (See *Kremlin Watch*)

Best Bench Player: Geno Petralli

Best Young Player: 1. Juan Gonzalez
2. Ivan Rodriguez
3. Dean Palmer

Best Looking Player: Juan Gonzalez

Ugliest Player: Kevin Reimer

Most Pleasant Surprise, 1991: Brian Downing

Biggest Disappointment, 1991: Bobby Witt

Best Minor League Prospect: Rob Maurer

Who Is: A left-handed hitting first baseman, now 25 years old. Maurer isn't going to run Rafael Palmeiro off first base, but he is a fine major league hitter, a .270 hitter with some homers and lots of doubles, quite a few walks. His name rhymes with "power" and he was a college teammate of Andy Benes. As a hitter I'd describe him as Rance Mulliniks with more paurer.

Other Prospects: **Monty Farriss** is a middle infielder, hits pretty well for a middle infielder but can't play short and offense isn't a big asset as a second baseman. He could have a future, but didn't help himself last year. **Jose Hernandez** is a shortstop, will probably never hit enough to be a regular.

ORGANIZATIONAL REPORT CARD

Ownership:	B+
Upper Management:	B
Field Management:	C
Front-Line Talent:	A+
Second-Line Talent:	C
Minor League System:	A

TEAM LEADERS:

Batting Average: Julio Franco, .341
Last Ten Years (Season): Julio Franco, .341 in 1991
Last Ten Years (Total): Julio Franco, .318

Doubles: Rafael Palmeiro, 49

Triples: Ruben Sierra and Gary Pettis, 5 each

Home Runs: Juan Gonzalez, 27
Last Ten Years (Season): Larry Parrish, 32 in 1987
Last Ten Years (Total): Larry Parrish, 149

RBI: Ruben Sierra, 116
Last Ten Years (Season): Ruben Sierra, 119 in 1989
Last Ten Years (Total): Ruben Sierra, 586

Extra Base Hits: Palmeiro, 78

Stolen Bases: Julio Franco, 36

Walks: Rafael Palmeiro, 68

Runs Created: Rafael Palmeiro, 129

Runs Created Per Game: Julio Franco, 7.7

Secondary Average: Rafael Palmeiro, .325

Gary Pettis had a secondary average of .355 as a part-time player.

Wins: Jose Guzman, 13
Last Ten Years (Season): Charlie Hough, 18 in 1987
Last Ten Years (Total): Charlie Hough, 133

Winning Percentage: Nolan Ryan, 12–6 .667

Strikeouts: Nolan Ryan, 203
Last Ten Years (Season): Nolan Ryan, 301 in 1989
Last Ten Years (Total): Bobby Witt, 951

ERA: Nolan Ryan, 2.91

Saves: Jeff Russell, 30

League Leaders:

1. Julio Franco led AL in batting average.
2. Nolan Ryan led the majors in fewest hits/nine innings and fewest baserunners/nine innings.
3. Jeff Russell led the American League in Blown Saves, with ten.

Stat of the Year: The two most important offensive stats for a hitter are on-base percentage and slugging percentage. Ryan led the majors in both opposition on-base percentage (.263) and opposition slugging percentage (.285).

1991 SEASON

Background: From 1972 until the mid-1980s the Rangers were an up-and-down organization, and an up-and-down organization will have more down years than up years. In the late 1980s they began to show some consistency.

Outlook: No different than this year. A few people expected them to win, some expected them to fade.

Getaway: The Rangers season can be divided into four parts:

1. Early malaise
2. The 14-game winning streak
3. Letting the league get even
4. The rest of the year.

The first three phases were over by June 10th, and after that they were just letting the clock run.

1. Early malaise The Rangers lost their first four games, at home. For a month they would win a few, lose a few; by May 11 they were 11–14.

2. The streak Pounding out 19 hits in Fenway on May 12, the Rangers triggered a 14-game winning streak, during which they hit .348 as a team. Their pitching was mediocre even during the streak.

3. Letting the league get even The Minnesota Twins came to town on May 27, floundering. They lost the first game, which was the Rangers' 14th straight win.

One would never have known it at the time, but the game of May 28, 1991 was the turning point of the season for both the Twins and the Rangers. Scott Erickson shut out the Rangers with an inning of relief help from Rick Aguilera, igniting a two-week hot streak through their competitors which left the Twins in control of the race. The loss by the Rangers, combined with two injuries to their starting rotation, plunged them into a two-week slump which took them back to .500, or actually one game over (26–25) by June 11.

4. Playing out the string Although they played good ball for the next month and were 44–33 at the All-Star break, very much in the race, the Rangers never got *really* hot again, and drifted gradually out of contention.

Most Exciting Game of the Season: September 11, wild 12-inning game in Anaheim, won 11–9.

Major Injuries: The Rangers continue to be undercut by injuries to their pitching staff, as they have been throughout the Tom House/Bobby Valentine era. In late May, as the Rangers were near the end of their fourteen-game winning streak, two of their young starting pitchers were placed on the disabled list, both expected to be back by mid-season, but both, as it turned out, gone in effect for the rest of the year. On May 26, **Scott Chiamparino** was placed on the DL with a sore right elbow. The next day, May 27, **Bobby Witt** went on the DL due to a partially torn rotator cuff in his right shoulder. He had won his last two games, but was out until August and ineffective then.

Nolan Ryan battled a sore back and stiff shoulder most of the year, and went on the disabled list July 29 with "a recurring ache in his shoulder." In fact, if you'll notice, the one thing that Ryan has conceded to time is that he doesn't pitch nearly as *much* as he used to. In his three years with the Rangers he has averaged 205 innings per season. In his first three years with California (1972–1974) he averaged 314 per year, and the average has declined steadily since then.

Gerald Alexander missed a month after pulling his groin. **John Barfield** fractured a rib and strained his left shoulder, and missed the last two months.

Offense: Awesome. The Rangers led the majors in runs scored, 829, and were above average offensively in every area except stolen bases and at every position except catcher and shortstop.

Defense: Improved, still not championship quality. They still don't really have a shortstop, Julio Franco isn't a glove man at second base and Gonzalez doesn't have the speed of a Devon White or a Lance Johnson in center field.

Starting Pitching: Awful.

Bullpen: Below average. Jeff Russell was fair as a closer, not one of the league's best. Nobody behind him was consistently good, or even consistently OK.

Best Game by a Starting Pitcher: Nolan Ryan's no-hitter du jour, May first (9 0 0 0 2 16). The Game Score, 101, was the highest for any major league game in 1991.

Indicators for 1991 were: Down 9.9

Number of regulars having good seasons by their own standards:

Seven (All the Texas Regulars had good years by their own standards except Ivan Rodriguez, who had never played before and therefore had no previous standards.)

1991 Over-Achiever: Julio Franco

1991 Under-Achiever: Gary Pettis

Infield: Excellent offensively, fair defensively.

Outfield: Excellent offensively, fair defensively.

Catching: Weak offensively, solid and sometimes brilliant defensively.

Percentage of offense created by:

Young Players:	53%
Players in Their Prime:	33%
Past Their Prime:	14%

Team Age:

Age of Non-Pitchers:	27.2
Age of Pitchers:	29.7
Team Age:	28.23

In retrospect, the critical decisions were:

Taking a chance on young talent generally has worked out well for the Rangers in the development of a lineup, to which in 1991 the Rangers added Gonzalez, Rodriguez, Palmer and Reimer. It hasn't worked out for the pitching staff. The young pitchers have just gotten hurt, so that as each next year arrives, instead of a crop of second-year starters, they just have another crop of rookies and guys trying to come back from injuries.

THAT AND THE OTHER

Lookalikes: Brian Downing and Christopher Reeve

Hall of Fame Watch: Nolan Ryan is an obvious Hall of Famer. Ruben Sierra will be a Hall of Famer if he continues to play the way he is playing now for another seven or eight years. It's too early to talk about Palmeiro and Gonzalez.

The intriguing one here is Julio Franco. Nobody *thinks* of Julio Franco as a Hall of Fame type player, and in the ballplayer stock markets you can buy his rookie card for almost nothing. But the fact is that he is *going* to get 2500 hits, and may very well get 3000, so he'll have to be taken seriously by the Hall of Fame voters.

Chris Berman, Have You Considered: Rafael (Relax, You're Soaking in) Palmeiro

Throwback: Ivan Rodriguez

Attendance Trend: Solidly and *consistently* upward

Players with a Chance for 3000 career hits:

Julio Franco, 44%
Ruben Sierra, 35%
Rafael Palmeiro, 24%

In addition, Franco, Sierra and Palmeiro all show a theoretical chance to get *4000* hits in their careers—a 7% chance for Sierra, 5% for Franco and 1% for Palmeiro.

Both Sierra and Franco have more hits than anyone else their age—in fact, both men are their age-group leaders by margins of more than 300. Sierra has 993 hits at age 25, Franco 1,605 at age 29. Sierra also leads his age group in home runs, and has almost twice as many career RBI as any other player of the same age.

Record Watch: At this time, the only two major league players who would appear to have any chance to break Pete Rose' career record of 4,256 hits are Ruben Sierra and Roberto Alomar. Sierra's chance to break that record is between two and three percent, while Alomar's is less than one percent.

Probably Could Play Regularly For Another Team: Rob Maurer

Best Defensive Player: Gary Pettis

It was Steve Buechele, but he's gone

Best Knowledge of the Strike Zone: Brian Downing

Least Command of the Strike Zone: Ivan Rodriguez

Fastest Runner: Gary Pettis

Slowest Runner: Kevin Reimer

Best Baserunner: Pettis

Most Likely to Still be Here in 2000: Gonzalez

Best Fastball: Ryan or Witt

Best Breaking Pitch: Nolan Ryan

Best Control: John Barfield

Most Underrated Players:

1. Julio Franco
2. Brian Downing
3. Gary Pettis

Oddest Collection of Abilities: Gary Pettis

Best Local Sportswriter: Tracy Ringolsby

Most-Similar Players:

to C Ivan Rodriguez, no one
to 1B Rafael Palmeiro, Mike Greenwell
to 2B Julio Franco, Steve Sax
to 3B Steve Buechele, Kelly Gruber
to 3B Dean Palmer, Luis Gomez
to SS Jeff Huson, Rene Gonzales
to LF Kevin Reimer, Darrin Jackson
to CF Jose Gonzalez, Ken Griffey Jr.
to RF Ruben Sierra, Barry Bonds
to DH Brian Downing, Jack Clark

Most Fun to Watch:

1. Nolan Ryan
2. Pudge
3. Ruben Sierra
4. Franco
5. Palmeiro

Actually, when you think about it, the Rangers are a fun team. Rob Neyer posted a write-in vote for Gerald Alexander as the most fun to watch because "he's short, has a funny face and he pitches weird." Brian Downing is one of my all-time favorite players.

Least Fun to Watch: Bobby Valentine

Managerial Type: Jeff Huson

Town Team:

C—Dave Duncan
1B—Ernie Banks
2B—Rogers Hornsby
3B—Pinky Higgins
SS—Spike Owen
LF—Bibb Falk
CF—Tris Speaker
RF—Ruppert Jones
SP—Burt Hooton
SP—Greg Swindell

Post-Season Transactions:

December 5, Signed minor league free agent Tom Drees to a contract with Oklahoma City (see Tom Drees comment).

December 8, Re-signed Brian Downing and Geno Petralli

What Needs to Be Done For 1992: I have never seen a major league team for which it was more obvious what needed to be done. For as long the Grieve/Valentine/House triumvirate has been here, the Rangers have been pissing away ballgames by using young pitchers who don't know what they're doing. Well, that was one thing two years ago, when the A's were in the seventh house and Jupiter aligned with Mars and the Rangers weren't going to win anyway. It's a different thing now. This is a helluva ballclub, the best eight-man lineup in the American League, if not in baseball. They can't afford any more Kenny-Rogers-as-a-starting-pitcher type experiments. They've got a great everyday lineup, and they've got Nolan Ryan. What they need behind that is four starting pitchers who don't *lose* the game for them. They need to bolster the starting pitching with three or four guys like Scott Sanderson or Bill Gullickson or Bob Tewksbury who pitch 220 innings and walk 35 men. Those guys are around, available. They're not available cheap *after* they win twenty games, but they are before then. If the Rangers can find a couple of those guys, they're ready to win this division.

Index of Leading Indicators for 1992: Minus 6.4

Positive Indicators: 1. Young Lineup

Negative Indicators: 1. Poor AAA team

Due for a better season: Gerald Alexander

Likely to have a worse season: Julio Franco

1992 Won-Lost Record will be: 88–74

DELTA BURKE AS A GUNFIGHTER, ARNOLD SCHWARZENEGGER IN A DRESS

I did a search to try to identify the *most miscast* offensive player in the major leagues. What I was looking for was a player who had a HIGH run element ratio, but a LOW ratio of runs scored to RBI, or vice versa. Run element ratio is (Walks Plus Stolen Bases) divided by (Extra Bases on Hits), the theory being that a player who has a HIGH run element ratio—more walks and stolen bases than power—is most valuable **early in the inning,** to set the table or create the opportunity for a run, while a player who has a LOW run element ratio—more power—is most valuable **late in the inning,** to drive in the run. Eighty percent of major league players *are* used in roles accommodating their skills in this way—that is, guys who walk and steal bases but don't have power are used to lead off or bat second—and most of the exceptions are trivial, guys who are plus three one way but minus one the other way. What I was looking for was the exceptions—leadoff men used in RBI situations, or RBI men used high in the order.

My conclusion was that the most miscast major league player of 1991 was Rafael Palmeiro of Texas. Despite a very low run element ratio (his skills are those of an RBI man, not a leadoff hitter), Palmeiro batted second almost all year, and wound up the season with 115 runs scored, only 88 RBI.

In a sense, this validates the method, since everyone who covered the Rangers was aware that Palmeiro was being used in a somewhat odd way offensively, due to the nature of his team. The Rangers have three cleanup hitters but no natural leadoff man except possibly Julio Franco, who for some reason they don't want to lead off. Palmeiro had 78 extra base hits, second-highest total in the majors, but is relatively slow, so he's not what one ordinarily looks for in a number two hitter, and Texas fans were very aware of this.

The other most-miscast players were:

2) Devon White, Toronto. White was used as a leadoff man by Toronto (and did a fine job) even though he doesn't walk a lot and also had 67 extra base hits (40 doubles, 10 triples, 17 homers). As in the Texas case, I am *not* criticizing the manager; merely pointing out that a player was forced into a role which was somewhat unnatural for him.

3) Jay Bell, Pittsburgh. Like Palmeiro, Bell hit second for a powerhouse offense although he is not fast (10 stolen bases) and has significant power (32 doubles, 8 triples and 16 homers).

4) Mike Devereaux, Baltimore. Basically the same story.

5) Barry Bonds, Pittsburgh. Bonds is the opposite. Because of his power he hits in an RBI spot, although his walks (107) and stolen bases (43) would make him a formidable early-in-the-inning type player.

This is **not** a method which should be taken very seriously, or a method which could be used as the basis for any really significant research in any way that I can see. I just thought it was kind of a fun thing to play around with.

DYNAMITE

Take a group of mediocre teams, .500 teams or thereabouts. Some of this group are outstanding one way (offense or defense), but so poor the other way that it negates the strong point. The rest of them are just average all around.

The Rangers, of course, are the former; they led the majors in runs scored, but also allowed more runs than any other team.

I can't prove it, but it has always *seemed* to me that a team like this (or like the Angels, the opposite) was a much better bet to improve dramatically and leap into the pennant race than a team which was just average both ways. I can cite testimonial evidence in support of that:

• The 1961 San Francisco Giants finished in the middle of the pack (third) although they led the National League in runs scored. The next season, patching the starting rotation with veterans Billy Pierce and Billy O'Dell, they again led the league in runs scored—and won the pennant.

• The 1964 Minnesota Twins finished under .500 (79–83) although they led the American League in runs scored. The next season, patching the starting rotation with veterans Mudcat Grant and Jim Perry, they again led the league in runs scored—and won the pennant.

• The 1969 Cincinnati Reds finished in third place despite leading the major leagues in runs scored. The next season, patching the rotation with a pitcher acquired in trade and one returning from an injury, they failed to lead the league in runs scored—but won the pennant.

• The reason the 1970 Reds didn't lead the league in runs scored was the 1970 San Francisco Giants, who scored a tremendous number of runs (831) but allowed almost as many (826) to finish third. The next season, getting a comeback year from Juan Marichal, the Giants won the National League West.

• The 1974 Boston Red Sox led the American League in runs scored (696) but finished near .500 due to their usual problems. The next season, adding vet Rick Wise to the staff, the Red Sox won the pennant.

• The 1980 St. Louis Cardinals finished way under .500 (74–88) despite leading the league in runs scored. That was the winter Herzog shook up the team in mid-winter, adding Bruce Sutter to the bullpen, and the Cardinals had the best record in the NL East in 1981, although they didn't get the title due to the split season. They did win the World Series in 1982.

The 1987 Mets and 1989 Red Sox also led the league in runs scored while finishing as also-rans, and came back to win divisional titles in the following seasons. Obviously, this doesn't *always* happen, but it does happen a lot.

A team with this kind of an offense knows it can win if it can just get OK pitching, and knowing you can win if . . . well, that's half the battle. I don't have a lot of confidence in Tom House's ability to make a pitching staff out of anything, but if the Rangers can just add a couple of serviceable veterans to Guzman and Ryan, they've got a real shot to have a big year in 1992. This team is dynamite; they just need a blasting cap.

KREMLIN WATCH

As I was writing here I was watching the Bill Gates hearings on television. Gates, you may remember, is the new head of the CIA, and is being interrogated closely by Congress, which wants to know why, as the CIA's top Soviet Intelligence Analyst, Gates failed to foresee the breakup of the Soviet Union.

Right. Like you guys woulda had this all figured out, I'm sure.

Anyway, I was thinking that, with glasnost now beyond glasnost, trying to figure out what is going on in a modern baseball front office is kind of like Kremlin watching. For thirty years an academic industry grew up studying the chair alignments at the May Day parade in Red Square, and selling the reports to the CIA so they could interpret them and leak the results to Morley Safer.

The Ranger engine has idled with the team a little over .500, and Ranger fans may think I am being generous in my grading of the management. I think you have to focus on the situation as it was when Tom Grieve came here, and the situation as it is now. Before Grieve the Rangers were winning about 70 games a year—77 in 1983, 69 in 1984, 62 in 1985. They've had three straight years now over .500, and that's progress. They have as much young talent as any team in baseball.

I would also point out this: that two trades made by Grieve several years ago now look very good in retrospect. In December, 1988, the Rangers traded Mitch Williams and a package of five other players for Rafael Palmeiro and two others. Palmeiro is now far more valuable than anyone else in that trade. A few days later, they traded Pete O'Brien, Oddibe McDowell and Jerry Browne for Julio Franco. I didn't like the trade at the time, but Franco is the only player in the trade who now has any value, and he's the batting champion.

Grieve's philosophy is easy to read at a certain level: he believes in commitment, consistency and patience. He believes in moving slowly, cautiously, and being certain that you know what you're doing before you do it. He's looking at the long haul, rather than short-term payoffs. It is, to me, not strange that he has refused to fire Bobby Valentine after almost seven years of pulling teeth. It is somewhat strange that he has refused to move out *either* Valentine or Tom House despite:

a) Five years of injuries in the pitching staff, and

b) The fact that House and Valentine apparently don't care too much for one another.

Apparently, I say; Kremlin watchers used to tell us that Gorbachev was Andropov's stooge.

The Rangers always lead the league in walks. They led the league in walks in 1986, 1987, 1988 and 1989. They didn't lead in 1990, as Detroit walked more, but they were back in the lead last year.

I don't want to sound like Frankie Frisch, but you can't overstate the seriousness of that. The Rangers have been walking four-plus men a game for so long that they think that's normal. As long as the Rangers lead the league in walks it is almost certain that they're going to be below average in ERA. As long as they're in the bottom half in ERA, it's almost impossible for them to win. If any team can win anything walking 650 men a year, this would be the team, but that's a tough assignment.

I don't think that the Rangers are playing as well as they're capable of playing. Unless they start moving forward again, there is a danger that they'll miss their moment, that the team will start breaking up before they have the big seasons that they should have with Franco, Palmeiro, Sierra and Gonzalez in the lineup.

Half of me thinks that this is the Rangers' year, that after seven years of building, and building, and building, they're going to become an overnight sensation in 1992. The other half thinks that if they can't win with seven regulars having good years in 1991, then they're never going to win. A couple of guys will have off years, a key player will get hurt, they'll win seventy games and the entire ruling class will be thrown from the Kremlin windows. That's what they play the season for, to figure out which theory is half right.

TOM DREES

The signing of Tom Drees, although not a lot can be made of it, could turn into a steal for the Rangers. Drees, you will remember, is the starting pitcher who pitched two straight no-hitters and three in a season in 1989. The White Sox never believed in him as a prospect, and his stock shrunk even further when he had shoulder surgery in 1990, so he never received a serious major league trial.

Although Drees signed a minor league contract, he will no doubt be at the major league camp, and he'll be in camp with a team that desperately needs starting pitching. He pitched extremely well at Vancouver in 1991, posting a 3.52 ERA for a team which had a staff ERA of 4.88. The scouts don't believe that he can pitch in the majors, and the scouts may be right 90% of the time, but sometimes they're dead wrong, too. I hold to the belief that a man who pitches well at AAA has got a *chance* to pitch well in the majors until proven otherwise.

NO-HITTERS

I realized last summer that I really don't know a lot about no-hitters. I've never seen one, for one thing, not live, and I have no idea in the world why we have been having this run of them during the last two seasons. Why now? Is something causing this to happen?

I assume, of course, that it's just a random event—what else would you assume, until you could show something else?—but nonetheless I got to thinking about how often one should *expect* to see a no-hitter.

If everybody was average, this would be a fairly simple problem. The major league batting average last year was .256. Suppose that every hitter was a .256 hitter and that every pitcher was average. If that was the case, the chance of seeing a no-hitter in any game would be .744 to the 27th power, which is .00034, or one in every 2,934 starts by a pitcher. That would mean there would be, in a typical season, 1.4 no-hitters in the major leagues.

That's in the right *range* of frequency; no-hitters occur more than 1.4 times a season, but not a hundred times more often or even ten. It's in the right range, but it's not *right*, so how can you make it right?

The fact that every hitter is not average makes the no-hitter *less* likely than the first estimate. If you're a pitcher, your chance of getting out a .200 hitter and then a .300 hitter is less then your chance of getting out two straight .250 hitters. However, while this aspect of non-randomization makes the no-hitter *less* likely, there are many other aspects of non-randomization, and almost all of the others make the no-hitter *more* likely. For example:

1. The quality of the pitcher. If the batting average against a pitcher was twenty points under the league average, that pitcher would be *twice as likely* to pitch a no-hitter. If the batting average against him was twenty points over the league average, that would make the no-hitter *half as likely*. That makes 2.5 no-hitters where there should be 2.0, so that makes no-hitters more common than they would otherwise be.

In real life this effect is larger than that. Nolan Ryan may allow a batting average sixty points less than the league average or even more, while another pitcher might be forty points over the league average and still be able to stay in the rotation. This makes no-hitters much more common than the 1.4 per season which we would otherwise expect.

2. The quality of the opposing team. If a team has a batting average twenty points better than the league average, the chance of a no-hitter against them is cut in half. But if the batting average of a team is twenty points less than average, the chance of a no-hitter against them is doubled. Again, this helps to make no-hitters more common than they otherwise would be.

3. The characteristics of the ballpark. Same thing, but at a lower level; a no-hitter is much more likely in the Oakland or Dodger Stadium than in Wrigley Field or Fenway. On balance, this increases the odds on a no-hitter.

4. The weather.

5. The home plate umpire.

All of these things and who-knows-what else might make a no-hitter more likely than it would otherwise be.

I was trying to establish a method to estimate the probability of a no-hitter in any start—a start by Trevor Wilson against St. Louis in Candlestick in August, let us say—and I realized that several of the pieces were missing. I simply didn't *know* things that I needed to know in order to work through the problem. It seems to me, for example, that a greatly disproportionate number of no-hitters are pitched in the last few days of the season, when the weather begins to turn cold. But is that true?

Are most no-hitters pitched against bad teams? Who knows?

Announcing Mark Gardner's sort-of no-hitter on local news, a sportscaster said "there was another no-hitter in baseball today, and as usually seems to happen it was thrown by a pitcher whose record up to now has been nothing to brag about." Is that true? I always thought that most no-hitters were thrown by good pitchers, but who knows?

A very basic piece of information that I was missing: how many batter's outs does it take to pitch a no-hitter? We assume it's 27, but there are going to be *some* games when it is less because a batter walks and is thrown out stealing or another one grounds into a double play. Just a few of those plays can significantly change the odds. If you can get a no-hitter with 25 outs, that's about 40% easier than getting one with 27 outs.

If *I* don't know this stuff, who would? So I decided to find out. I studied the last 100 no-hitters. For simplicity's sake, I decided to use only nine-inning, complete-game no-hitters. I looked for anything that might help us understand *why no-hitters occur where and when they occur.* Rob Neyer rounded up the information I wanted on the last one hundred no-hitters, and Robbie Getz entered that into a computer, and I studied it. Here's a few of the questions and answers from the study:

How often do no-hitters occur, over time?

The list of the last 100 no-hitters goes back to July 12, 1951, when Allie Reynolds no-hit the Indians in Cleveland. Since that time there have been about 73,000 major league games, give or take a few. That means that there are 100 no-hitters in 146,000 pitcher's starts, or one in each 1,460. Stated the other way, that's a frequency of .00068 as opposed to the theoretical .00034. In other words, no-hitters occur almost exactly twice as often as they would if all players were of the same skill. In that case, there would be 1.4 no-hitters per season; in reality, there are 2.9.

Could the rash of no-hitters over the last two years occur by random chance?

Easily. Using the Commissioner's new definition of a no-hitter, there were six no-hitters in the major leagues in 1990, and five more in 1991. These are not extraordinary figures.

Assuming that each game has a .00068 chance of being a no-hitter and that there are 4,212 starts in a season, there would be five or more no-hitters in 17% of all seasons. This is the full schedule:

Likelihood of	
0 no-hitters	6%
1 no-hitter	16%
2 no-hitters	23%
3 no-hitters	22%
4 no-hitters	16%
5 no-hitters	9%
6 no-hitters	4%
7 no-hitters	2%
8 no-hitters	1%
9 no-hitters or more	1%

So to have six in one year and five the next . . . well, that's not extraordinary. The zero no-hitters of 1989 is actually more improbable than the six no-hitters of 1990, but when nobody throws a no-hitter, there's no story, so nobody says anything about it. The six no-hitters of 1990 *seemed* remarkable because it followed the zero no-hitters of 1989, but it really isn't some sort of off-the-wall fluke.

This chart will become obsolete when the NL expands. The chance of a season with no no-hitters will drop from 6% to 5%, etc.

Are most no-hitters thrown by quality pitchers?

The overwhelming majority of no-hitters are thrown by quality pitchers. Very, very few no-hitters are thrown by rumdums and yahoos. Sometimes they're thrown by guys you've never heard of *before* that time, but very rarely are they thrown by guys who really aren't *good.*

Of the 100 no-hitters:

69 were thrown by pitchers who had 100 or more career wins

24 were thrown by pitchers who had 200 or more career wins

12 were thrown by pitchers with 300 or more career wins

79 were thrown by pitchers who had career winning percentages over .500.

The *average* of career wins by no-hit pitchers was 147.

The aggregate career winning percentage for no-hit pitchers is .550.

Those are awesome numbers for a large group of pitchers. A hundred wins—that's a tough standard. How many pitchers win a hundred games in their careers? As a percentage of major league pitchers, damn few. A .550 aggregate winning percentage—that's unbelievable. There are a bunch of guys in the Hall of Fame who have career winning percentages around .550—Don Drysdale, .557, Gaylord Perry, .542, Robin Roberts, .539. We won't even talk about Eppa Rixey (.515), Ted Lyons (.531) and Red Faber (.544).

But wait a minute—there are two more points to be made. Many of these figures are going to go *up* yet. Since many of the pitchers who have thrown no-hitters are still active, in the end *more* than 69 of the no-hitters will be thrown by guys with a hundred or more career wins, and more than 24 will have been thrown by pitchers who won 200 games. No-hitters have been thrown by Wilson Alvarez, Tommy Greene, Terry Mulholland, Randy Johnson and Dave Righetti, none of whom has won a hundred games *yet.* The career average of 147 wins will be well over 150 by the time the records of these pitchers are complete.

Second, many of the no-hitters thrown by pitchers with less than 100 career wins were still thrown by quality pitchers. Len Barker pulled up lame with only 74 career wins, but he was a quality pitcher at that time, good enough to win 19 games for the Cleveland Indians, having winning records for three straight years and leading the league in strikeouts twice in a row. Jim Colborn won only 83 games in his career, but he was good enough to win 18 games that year and 20 another. John Montefusco won only 90 games in his career, but he certainly wasn't a bad pitcher at the time he threw the no-hitter, on his way to a 16-win season with a 2.85 ERA. Dick Bosman won only 82 games in his career, but he was good enough to lead the league in ERA. Steve Busby threw two no-hitters and won only 70 games, but he was a hell of a pitcher until he hurt his arm. Bob Moose, Ray Washburn, Ken Johnson, Jack Kralick, Jim Wilson—these guys were decent pitchers, and they're in the *bottom one-fourth* of the pitchers who pitch no-hitters.

On the other end, most of the truly outstanding pitchers of the last forty years show up on the list—Jim Bunning (twice), Warren Spahn (twice), Hoyt Wilhelm, Sandy Koufax (four times), Juan Marichal, Catfish Hunter, Gaylord Perry, Jim Palmer, Vida Blue, Bob Gibson, Nolan Ryan (seven times), Phil Niekro, Bert Blyleven, Tom Seaver, Fernando Valenzuela, Bret Saberhagen. Only a few comparable pitchers, in truth, have *failed* to throw no-hitters. Roger Clemens hasn't thrown one, yet, or Dwight Gooden.

Behind them are the *very good* pitchers, who throw the great bulk of the no-hitters. Allie Reynolds, Virgil Trucks, Sam Jones, Carl Erskine, Mel Parnell, Sal Maglie, Don Cardwell, Lew Burdette, Earl Wilson, Bill Monboquette, Jim Maloney, Sonny Siebert, Don Wilson, Dean Chance, Joel Horlen, Ken Holtzman, Dock Ellis, Bill Singer, Rick Wise, Burt Hooton, Milt Pappas, Larry Dierker, John Candelaria, Dennis Eckersley, the Forsch brothers, Jerry Reuss, Mike Scott, Tom Browning, Dave Stewart, Dave Stieb, Dennis Martinez—these are the kinds of pitchers who account for the great bulk of no-hitters. They're not Hall of Famers, but they're very, very good.

About ten of the one hundred no-hitters were pitched by pitchers who truly could not be described as quality pitchers. These include no-hitters thrown by Juan Nieves, Joe Cowley, Mike Warren, Don Nottebart, Bo Belinsky, Bob Keegan and Bobo Holloman, and a few other guys who were just a little better than these seven.

Did these pitchers tend to be having especially good seasons at the time of the no-hitters?

Not dramatically, no. No-hit pitchers are by and large very good pitchers, and they tend to be having good seasons for that reason, but they don't tend to be having any better seasons at the time they throw their no-hitters than through the rest of their careers.

This is the average season's record of a pitcher pitching a no-hitter:

G	GS	IP	W-L	Pct	H	ER	SO	BB	ERA	CG	ShO
33	30	213	14-10	.574	182	75	152	75	3.18	10	3

That's an awfully good record; if you show that record to a GM and say "do you want this pitcher for next season?", 26 general managers out of 26 are going to reach for their pens.

But it's not a lot better than what these pitchers typically do. Taking out the no-hitters themselves, the aggregate won-lost record of no-hit pitchers is 1283–1025, a .557 winning percentage. That's just a few points better than their career winning percentage.

Thirteen pitchers in that period won 20 games the year they pitched the no-hitter, and 39 had ERAs below 3.00.

Did the no-hitter tend to come *early* in these pitchers careers, when the pitchers throw hardest?

No, the no-hitters had no particular tendency to come early or late in the careers of the pitchers. The average record of a no-hit pitcher at the time of throwing the no-hitter is 72–57; his career record after that is about the same. Well, they do tend to throw the no-hitters *a little bit* before the middle of their careers, but it is certainly common for a pitcher to get his no-hitter quite late in his career, as Spahn did, and Bob Gibson, and Seaver and Allie Reynolds and Virgil Trucks.

Do these pitchers tend to be especially hot at the time of the no-hitters?

Not at all. The aggregate record of no-hit pitchers in the start *prior* to their no-hitters was 40–40 with a 3.59 ERA. No-hitters had a slight tendency to follow off games.

How do no-hit pitchers do in the start *after* the no-hitter?

Quite well, much better than in the start before. The aggregate record of the 100 no-hit pitchers in their next starts was 43–33, an ERA of 3.00.

Many of the no-hit pitchers pitched brilliant games in the start following their no-hitter.

Are most no-hitters thrown against bad teams?

Surprisingly, *no-hitters have virtually no tendency to be thrown against bad teams.* A first-place team is essentially as likely to be victimized by a no-hitter as is a last-place team.

Look at the no-hitters over the last two years. Five of the eleven no-hitters were thrown against quality teams—one against Oakland in 1990 (Nolan Ryan), one against Toronto in 1990 (Dave Stewart) and another one in 1991 (Nolan Ryan), one against the Dodgers last year (Dennis Martinez) and one against the White Sox (Saberhagen). Those are all good teams.

By contrast, only *three* no-hitters of the eleven were thrown against poor teams, one against the Cardinals in 1990 (Fernando Valenzuela), and one last year against Montreal (Tommy Greene) and Baltimore (Wilson Alvarez).

In the period of the study, 17 of the 100 no-hitters were

thrown against championship teams. No-hitters were thrown against the Yankees in 1952, when they won the World Championship, and again in 1958, when they won it again. Gaylord Perry no-hit the Cardinals in 1968, when the Cardinals won the National League. No-hitters were thrown in 1969 against the Braves, who won their division, and the Mets, who won 100 games and the World Championship. No-hitters were thrown against the Oakland A's in 1973 and 1974, when they won the World Series both years. A no-hitter was thrown against the Phillies in 1978, a division champion. A no-hitter was thrown against the Dodgers in 1981, when they won the World Series. A no-hitter was thrown against the White Sox in 1983, when they won 99 games and a division championship.

While the California Angels of 1986 were in the stretch run, September 19, Joe Cowley pitched a no-hitter against them. They still won the division. When the Dodgers were dashing to the World Championship two years later, Tom Browning pitched a perfect game against them. When the A's won 103 games in 1990, they were victimized by a no-hitter.

The Mets were victimized by no-hitters in 1962 and 1964, when they were an awful team—but then the Giants, an offensive powerhouse and one of the best teams of that era, were victimized by no-hitters in 1961 and 1963. **A bad team is no more likely to be victimized by a no-hitter than is a good team.**

The average record of a losing team in a no-hit season was 79 wins, 80 losses. Throw out the no-hitter itself, and the average was 79 and 79.

That doesn't make sense, does it?

Not initially, but remember that the key thing here is not whether a team is *good*, but whether they have a high team batting average. There is not an exceptionally close correlation between the two.

Teams which lost no-hitters *did* have a very significant tendency to have low batting averages, and had even more of a tendency to strike out. Of the 100 losing teams, 59 had season's batting averages below the league average, and 63 struck out more often than the league average.

What happens quite a bit is that high-strikeout, power teams are victimized by power pitchers. The classic would be the game that Nolan Ryan pitched against the Oakland A's on June 11, 1990. The A's were a great team, but their team batting average (.254) was five points *below* the league average, and they struck out a lot—992 times, which is about 10% more than the league average.

Facing Nolan Ryan on a night when Ryan obviously had something working, Ryan struck out 14 men, which leaves only 13 balls in play. None of the 13 eluded the fielders.

Are almost all no-hitters thrown by power pitchers?

Not "almost all", no; most, but many are not. Of the 100 no-hitters, 63 were thrown by pitchers who were over the league average in strikeouts, but 37 were not. *The strikeout tendencies of the losing team appear to be just as important in determining when a no-hitter will occur as the strikeout tendencies of the pitcher.*

A complete breakdown of the matchups is:

Strikeout pitcher against high-strikeout team:	38
Strikeout pitcher against non-strikeout team:	25
Non-strikeout pitcher against high-strikeout team:	25
Non-strikeout pitcher against non-strikeout team:	12

So if a strikeout pitcher is facing a strikeout team, a no-hitter is three times as likely as in the opposite situation.

At first glance it seemed odd to me that the strikeout tendencies of the team were as important as those of the pitcher, because the strikeout tendencies of teams are much less extreme than those of individuals. If the league strikeout rate is 5.5 per game, you'll have a pitcher or two who strike out 9 per game or even 10 per game, and others around 3 per game—but no *team* will be close to those extremes; all the teams will be between 4 and 7.

The reason this works out, though, is that a team that strikes out 6.5 times per game will play 162 games, and will be facing an increased risk of a no-hitter *every game*, while Nolan Ryan only starts 30–35 times a year. Used to, anyway.

In fact, though, most of the 37 pitchers who were under the league strikeout rate weren't that far under it. From the standpoint of strikeouts, the most improbable match for a no-hitter in the hundred was Bob Forsch against the Montreal Expos in September, 1983. Forsch was not a strikeout pitcher—56 men in 183 innings that year—and the Expos as a team struck out less than any other National League team that year. Forsch struck out six, though, got the other 21 out somehow and had his second career no-hitter.

On the other end of that, the most "high probable strikeout" games in the no-hit field were these:

Nolan Ryan against Oakland, 1990
Nolan Ryan against Toronto, 1991
Sandy Koufax against the Mets, 1962

Ryan struck out 14 A's in 1990 and 16 Blue Jays in 1991, while Koufax struck out 13 Mets in his first no-hitter. These figures really are not much above what one would expect of these pitchers and teams in a nine-inning game.

How many strikeouts are there in a typical no-hitter?

Seven and a half. In the 100 no-hitters there were 753 strikeouts.

There were 10 or more strikeouts in 26 of the 100 no-hitters.

What's the most improbable matchup for a no-hitter?

I haven't mentioned this yet, but 90 of the 100 pitchers—90%—allowed less than one hit per inning pitched. This makes sense, obviously; a guy like Tommy John, no matter how good a pitcher, is not a good candidate to throw a no-hitter. Still, 90 of a hundred is a very high percentage.

The chance of a no-hitter in any given start depends on the expected batting average in that start. I estimated the expected batting average in every actual no-hitter in the study, based on

1) The batting average against the pitcher in his *other* appearances that season, not including the no-hitter,

2) The batting average of the team in their other games that season, not including the no-hitter, and

3) The league batting average.

The most *im*-probable premise for a no-hitter, by far, is the famous one, Bobo Holloman's 1953 no-hitter in his first major league start. Holloman was facing a poor-hitting team that day, the Philadelphia A's, but Holloman himself was so ineffective the rest of the year that the expected batting average against him was way over .300. Holloman on the year faced 251 major league hitters, 50 of whom he walked, 3 of whom bunted and one of whom he hit with a pitch. That means that he had about 197 opposition at bats—and he allowed 69 hits. That's a .350 average—*including* the no-hitter. If you take out the no-hitter it goes to .404.

So the expected batting average against him that day, based on other information, would have been somewhere over .350—and yet the hitters went 0-for-26.

The most-improbable situations for a no-hitter were

1. Bobo Holloman
2. Fernando Valenzuela against the Cardinals, 1990
3. Charlie Lea against the Giants, 1981
4. Ken Forsch against the Expos, 1983
5. Ken Holtzman against the Reds, 1971

Fernando Valenzuela was once a great pitcher, but by 1990 not too much was left of him; he had a 4.59 ERA that year, and allowed 223 hits in 204 innings. The Cardinals team batting average was about the league average, so Fernando got no help there, although he did have the advantage of playing in Dodger Stadium, which I didn't factor into this equation. Anyway, he got them all out.

On the other hand, the most-*probable* situations for a no-hitter were these:

1. Nolan Ryan against Toronto, 1991

This shows up as number one on the list simply because Ryan himself was so un-hittable last year, allowing only 102 hits in 173 innings (102 in 164, not counting the no-hitter.) The Blue Jays also had a team batting average three points below the league norm. At his current rate of improvement, I figure in five years Ryan will be throwing a no-hitter every third start.

2. Sandy Koufax against the Cubs, 1965

Koufax was having one of the greatest seasons of all time, and the Cubs hit .238 as a team, so he was a threat to throw a no-hitter anytime he started against them. Well, not really, but the probability of a no-hitter in this game was about .0083, or about twelve times greater than normal.

3. Mike Scott against the Giants, 1986

Scott was pretty awesome at that time, too; this was the pennant-clinching no-hitter.

4. Sandy Koufax against the Mets, 1962
5. Vida Blue against the Twins, 1970.

What's the role of ballparks in creating no-hitters?

The ballparks have changed so much over the last 40 years that it is difficult to get precise information on this, not that a hundred no-hitters is enough to get precise information on anything.

The three best hitting parks in baseball, based solely on their effect on batting average, appear to be Fenway Park, Fulton County Stadium and Wrigley Field. The three worst are the Oakland Coliseum, Tiger Stadium and Candlestick Park.

All six of those parks have been in baseball since at least 1967, although their characteristics have changed some. I counted the number of no-hitters pitched in those six parks since 1967. There have been eleven no-hitters pitched in the bad hitting parks, and five in the good hitting parks.

Those numbers are so small they're of little use, so I decided to study the issue with models and math, rather than history. The best-hitting parks increase batting averages in the games played there by fifteen to twenty points; the worst ones cut batting averages by the same amount. That's a 35-point difference.

I figured the theoretical chance of a no-hitter at 35-point intervals—that is, the chance of getting 27 straight outs with a .215 batting average, a .250 batting average, a .285 batting average. A 35-point decrease in batting average makes the no-hitter *three to four times* more likely. Thus, a no-hitter should be three to four times more likely in the Oakland Coliseum than it is in Fenway Park, given the same teams and pitchers.

Aren't there a greatly disproportionate share of no-hitters pitched in September, particularly the last few days of the season?

A disproportionate share, yes, but not nearly as much of an effect as I was expecting. This is the breakdown of no-hitters by month:

April	11
May	17
June	20

July	12
August	16
September	23
October	1

We didn't use Larsen's no-hitter in the study; we stuck to regular season. The one no-hitter in October was Bill Stoneman's in 1972.

Anyway, seven of the no-hitters occurred in the starting pitcher's *last* start of the season. That's disproportionate, but it's not *grossly* disproportionate, not so disproportionate that it couldn't have just happened. In fact, none of the month-by-month data carries any certain meaning.

How many batting outs does a pitcher normally need to get to make a no-hitter? Is it 27? Is it more than 27, because of errors? Is it less than 27, because of runners put out on the bases?

It's less than 27—26.73, to be exact. There were 2,673 at bats in the 100 no-hitters.

This fact makes no-hitters eight percent more common than they otherwise would be.

In the 100 no-hitters there were:

285 walks,

14 hit batsmen,

44 errors,

15 runners caught stealing,

43 ground ball double plays, and

901 innings pitched, the extra inning being by Jim Maloney on August 19, 1965.

This is the record of the 100 pitchers who threw no-hitters, along with their records in their previous start and their next start:

	GS	IP	W	L	Pct	H	R	ER	SO	BB	ERA
Previous	97	641	40	40	.500	602	293	256	454	233	3.59
No-Hitter	100	901	99	1	.990	0	5	2	753	285	0.02
Next	93	680	43	33	.566	563	254	227	488	215	3.00

The pitcher who lost his no-hitter was, of course, Ken Johnson of Houston, who lost on an un-earned run. The two pitchers who allowed earned runs in their no-hitters were Joe Cowley and Dean Chance.

Do no-hit pitchers benefit from exceptional defense?

If they do you can't prove it by me. The fielding percentage of teams for which no-hitters are thrown is exactly average.

Is there anything else we should note about no-hitters, before we move on?

When collecting the data I noted whether the no-hitter was thrown at home or on the road, not for any particular reason but just because it was there. To my surprise, this revealed a substantial split in the data; 64 of the 100 no-hitters were thrown at home, and only 36 on the road.

Backtracking on this from the accidental realization, I see that it's not so surprising. In modern baseball the batting average of teams at home is usually nine or ten points higher than the batting average of teams on the road. A ten-point reduction in batting average makes a no-hitter 43% to 46% more likely, depending on where you start.

This becomes important because, like team strikeout tendencies but unlike most of the other things we can study, it's *always there*, every game.

If there were 43 to 46% more no-hitters at home than on the road, then over time 59% of no-hitters should be pitched at home. 59% is not a long way from 64%, the actual data.

Another thought was that perhaps no-hitters happen at home in part because of the candidates for the Dick Miller award, the official scorers. (Dick Miller once provoked a press box controversy by scoring an error on an obvious hit to protect a Nolan Ryan no-hitter.) The official scorers might give a hometown pitcher a break when he's going for a no-hitter that they wouldn't give to some guy from Altoona.

This could be true—it's consistent with the data—and could have helped move the 59% to 64%. I checked the error rates of teams behind no-hit pitchers at home and on the road. In 64 no-hitters at home there were 30 scored errors, or .47 per game. In 36 no-hitters on the road there were 14 scored errors, or .39 per game. That's not enough of a split in the data to reach any conclusion.

I studied one other thing, and this turned out to be a bit of a shock. I recorded the won-lost records of the losing teams *in the previous five games.*

I didn't expect to find anything. Searches for streak effects, in the past, have virtually always been unsuccessful, so unsuccessful that by and large we reject the whole idea of hot and cold hitters as an illusion created by random fluctuations in performance.

But this time I did find something. The teams which lost the no-hitters had, in fact, been playing very badly in their previous five games. The teams which were no-hit had a winning percentage of .448 in their previous five games. They were .500 teams for the season, remember (actually .499)—but they had been playing like sixth-place teams.

My first thought was that maybe this was created because they were on the road, 64% of them, but in working through the percentages I quickly saw that that's impossible; the fact that 64% of the teams were on the road could, by itself, create a winning percentage about .494 over the last five games (as opposed to .500), but nowhere near .448. I also checked out the last-five-games winning percentage in "home" no-hitters and 'road'' no-hitters, and confirmed that that wasn't the problem. The teams which were no-hit on the road had been playing .423 ball; the teams which were no-hit at home had been playing at a .492 clip. Both figures are well below what we would expect, although not equally.

My next question was whether it could have been random data, the "last five" won-lost log of 219–270. It's unlikely. The actual winning percentage of the losing teams, excluding the no-hitters, was .499, so I figured the chance that a .499 team would go 219–270 in 489 games. It's right on the border of what we might consider a reasonable possibility, being almost exactly a 1% chance.

SUMMARY

So when should you most expect to see a no-hitter?

The number one factor in determining where and when a no-hitter occurs is the quality of the pitcher on the mound. That's the number one thing—not the weather, not the ballpark, not the losing team, not anything else but the man on the mound. 79 of 100 no-hit pitchers had winning records in their careers. 90 of 100 no-hit pitchers allowed less than one hit per inning in their no-hit season. That's the one thing that sticks out above everything else.

Pondering the rest, I remember a story that Mike Shannon once told at a SABR convention. Shannon said that one of his best moments in a baseball uniform was Ray Washburn's no-hitter against San Francisco in 1968. It was a nothing game, a crowd of less than 5,000 in the park with the pennant race already decided. What made it special was that Gaylord Perry had thrown a no-hitter *against* the Cardinals the day earlier.

The day before that, you see, the Cardinals had clinched the pennant, and they went out and celebrated a good part of the night. Gaylord Perry pitched a no-hitter against them, and a writer for the San Francisco paper belittled the Cardinals' efforts in the Perry game, implying that they weren't really in the game. Shannon was furious. Pennant race or no pennant race, he didn't want any goddamned sportswriter writing that the Cardinals didn't care about the game they were playing. When Washburn no-hit the Giants the next day that evened the score, and became one of his sweetest memories.

Thinking about that, I remembered several other incidents which were not that dissimilar. I won't recount the details because this article is too long anyway, but I remember a team flying home from California one night, and being no-hit in their home park the next day. I remember the White Sox flying into Kansas City late one night, having to get up and face Bret Saberhagen a few hours later, and coming away with nothing. I remember the Cardinals flying to Pittsburgh to play a make-up game on what was supposed to be a day off, then flying to LA that night, and being no-hit by Fernando Valenzuela the next day. Maybe I'm making too much of it, but I think that's the missing link here: a lot of teams get no-hit when they're draggin' ass. I think that's why 64 of the 100 no-hitters happened *to* teams that were on the road. I think that's why a lot of them happened to teams which had been playing poorly. I think that's why almost a dozen no-hitters were pitched in the last week of the season.

In fact, if you look again at the pattern of no-hitters by month, you can see an explanation:

April	May	June	July	Aug	Sept
11	17	20	12	16	23

The pattern you see is teams getting tired. As the teams get more tired, the number of no-hitters builds up. Then there's the All-Star break and the hitters gather their wits, and then it starts over again. At the end of the season they're beat.

Of course that's a dangerous logic; as likely as not the month-by-month data doesn't mean a damn thing. But I suspect that if we checked, we'd find that a disproportionate number of no-hitters happen *late* on a road trip.

If you're looking for the perfect game for a no-hitter to happen, here's where you look:

1) Quality pitcher.
2) Power pitcher. Start with Nolan Ryan. If he's busy look for David Cone or the Rocket.
3) Pitching at home.
4) In a pitcher's park.
5) Against a tired team.
6) That strikes out a lot.
7) And may have a low batting average.
8) And may have been in a slump.
9) In September.

Unless Nolan Ryan signs with the Oakland A's, you're never going to get the perfect setup for a no-hitter.

THE OAKLAND A'S

• IN A BOX •

1991 Won-Lost Record: 84–78 .519
Rank among 26 teams: Tied for 8th
Over Last Five Years: 471–339 .581
Rank over Five Years: 1st
In Last Ten Years: 843–777 .520
Rank over Ten Years: 7th

Best Player: Jose Canseco or Rickey Henderson
I've always been a big fan of Rickey Henderson, but Canseco has probably become the A's best player.

Weak Spot: Third Base

Best Pitcher: Dennis Eckersley

Staff Weakness: Fourth starter

Best Bench Player: Lance Blankenship

Best Baseball Name: Todd Van POPpel

Best Young Player: No one.
Mike Bordick, if you held a gun to my head.

Best Looking Player: Rick Honeycutt

Ugliest Player: Terry Steinbach

Most Pleasant Surprise, 1991: None

Biggest Disappointments, 1991:
1. Mark McGwire
2. Young Pitchers
3. Dave Stewart

Best Minor League Prospect: Van Poppel

Who Is: A twenty-year-old right-handed pitcher, still three years away from finding his control.

Designated Malcontent: Rickey Henderson

Park Characteristics: Very poor hitters park, lowers batting averages and ERAs.

The Park Hurts: Canseco and McGwire more than anyone else.

ORGANIZATIONAL REPORT CARD

Ownership:	A
Upper Management:	A–
Field Management:	A
Front-Line Talent:	B
Second-Line Talent:	D
Minor League System:	D

TEAM LEADERS:

Batting Average: Harold Baines, .295
Last Ten Years (Season): Carney Lansford, 1989, .336
Last Ten Years (Total): Rickey Henderson, .295

Doubles: Dave Henderson, 33

Triples: 3 players with 4

Home Runs: Jose Canseco, 44
Last Ten Years (Season): Mark McGwire, 1987, 49
Last Ten Years (Total): Jose Canseco, 209

RBI: Jose Canseco, 122
Last Ten Years (Season): Jose Canseco, 1988, 124
Last Ten Years (Total): Jose Canseco, 647

Extra Base Hits: Canseco, 75

Stolen Bases: Rickey Henderson, 58

Walks: Rickey Henderson, 98

Runs Created: Jose Canseco, 116

Runs Created Per Game: Canseco, 7.0

Secondary Average: Rickey Henderson, .487

Wins: Mike Moore, 17
Last Ten Years (Season): Bob Welch, 1990, 27
Last Ten Years (Total): Dave Stewart, 104

Winning Percentage: Mike Moore, 17–8 .680

Strikeouts: Moore, 153
Last Ten Years (Season): Dave Stewart, 1987, 205
Last Ten Years (Total): Dave Stewart, 973

ERA: Moore, 2.96

Saves: Dennis Eckersley, 43

League Leaders:
1. Jose Canseco tied for the league lead in homers, with Henr Aaron's number.
2. Rickey Henderson once more led the American League ir stolen bases, with 58.
3. Joe Klink allowed only 15% of the runners who were o base when he entered the game to score, the best percentage ir baseball. **This was the second straight season that Klink had le the American League in this category.**

1991 SEASON

Background: After dominating the American League over th last three seasons, the Oakland A's entered the 1991 campaig trying to build on their credentials to be considered among th all-time great teams.

Getaway: The A's opened the season red hot (8–1), and continue to play well through the first one-third of the season. On June their record was 33–20.

Stretch Drive: The A's began to spin their wheels in June, an played basically .500 ball through the middle of the season. Al though the expectation of another 100-win season was slippin away, the A's remained in position to win through early August

High Point of the Season: From August 5–11 the A's won si straight games, lifting their record to 64–48. The A's were seve good weeks away from their fourth divisional title.

Low Point of the Season: The A's went to Seattle on August 12, where they lost four straight games, and from there on to Minnesota, where they lost three more. Only a week after surging near the top of the division, the A's found themselves staggering near the edges of the pennant race.

Major Injuries: The snow-mobile accident of **Carney Lansford** opened up a hole at third base, and began the process of questioning in the A's. The A's later suffered major injuries to **Walt Weiss, Gene Nelson, Todd Burns** and **Rick Honeycutt,** and all of these contributed to their poor 1991 season, as did nagging injuries to **Rickey Henderson.**

Offense: The A's have a low-average, power-and-walks offense, and despite the injuries in the off season it remained one of the best in the league. They were fifth in the league in runs scored (760), and playing in another park that total (and rank) would have been higher.

Defense: Fair. Gallego was brilliant at second, and McGwire at first is always good. That pretty much exhausts the A's defensive strengths.

Starting Pitching: Terrible. Scott Sanderson was sold to New York, and the A's attempted to replace him with Eric Show. Show stunk; the back end of the starting rotation was turned over to a series of pubescent apprentices. Then the number one and two starters, Bob Welch and Dave Stewart, began losing regularly.

Bullpen: Eckersley remained terrific, but the support for him was not up to the standard of previous years.

Best Game by a Starting Pitcher: Dave Stewart at Texas, July 3 (9 3 0 0 2 4, Game Score 83).

Worst Game by a Starting Pitcher: The three worst were all Bob Welch games:

	IP	H	R	ER	BB	SO	
May 5 vs Cle	4⅔	13	11	8	2	4	Game Score: 2
June 28 vs KC	3	9	9	8	3	1	Game Score: 5
August 17 At Minn	5⅔	11	9	9	4	1	Game Score: 8

These three games lifted Welch's ERA for the season from 3.79 to 4.58.

Indicators for 1991 were: Down 20.3

Number of regulars having good seasons by their own standards: Four (Baines, Canseco, Dave Henderson, Gallego)

1991 Over-Achiever: Gallego

1991 Under-Achiever: Mark McGwire

Infield: Gallego at second base was truly very good, but the rest of the infield was indescribably awful. For the season, A's first basemen hit .199, their third basemen .219 and shortstops .223. The defense at third and short were not good, either.

Outfield: Probably the best in baseball. The three outfield spots—primarily Henderson, Henderson and Canseco—hit 81 home runs and scored 329 runs among them.

Catching: Pretty good. Steinbach was OK, Quirk OK.

Percentage of offense created by:

Young Players: 18%
Players in Their Prime: 32%
Past Their Prime: 51%

Team Age:

Non-Pitchers: 30.1
Pitching Staff: 31.5
Overall Age: 30.71

Among the most curious decisions of 1991 was the A's willingness to systematically accumulate older players. Facing natural aging as players like the Hendersons, Lansford, Stewart, Welch and Eckersley moved into their mid- and late-thirties, the A's needed to blend in some younger players if they were to have any chance to sustain their dominance for more than another month or two. Instead, they seemed to concentrate on trying to get as many old guys on the roster as they possibly could—Harold Baines (added late 1990), Jamie Quirk, Willie Wilson, Eric Show, Brook Jacoby, Ernest Riles, Vance Law, Ron Darling.

In retrospect, the critical decisions were:

If you had to cite one, the decision to sell Scott Sanderson to New York rather than try to accommodate his salary demands would be the one. The absence of Sanderson set the stage for the degeneration of the A's starting staff.

THAT AND THE OTHER

Hall of Fame Watch:

Rickey Henderson is a Hall of Famer.

Jose Canseco will be a Hall of Famer if he continues to play the way that he has so far.

Harold Baines, Dave Stewart and Bob Welch are Hall of Fame candidates, but all pretty marginal as of this moment.

The most interesting Hall of Fame candidate on the team is Dennis Eckersley. The only Hall of Fame relievers are Hoyt Wilhelm and Rollie Fingers, so it's hard to say what the Hall of Fame standards for a reliever are. Eckersley's career totals are not impressive. His won-lost record is just 174–144, his ERA 3.47, his saves total 188—yet we all know that Eckersley has pitched as well over the last four years as any reliever has ever pitched, and was also a top-flight starter at one time.

Attendance Trend: Strongly upward in recent years, but down slightly in 1991.

Players with a Chance for 3000 career hits:

Rickey Henderson	20%
Harold Baines	13%
Jose Canseco	2%

Record Watch:

Jose Canseco is the only major league player who has established a chance to break Henry Aaron's career record for home runs, 755. Canseco's chance to break the record is approximately 8%, which is the best chance that anyone has had in several years.

By age 26 (1991) Canseco already has 209 career home runs. He not only has more home runs than anyone else his age, but also more than anyone who was 27 or 28 in 1991. On the other hand, Aaron at the same age had 236 career home runs.

My assumption has been that Canseco's back and antics will keep him from seriously threatening Aaron's record.

Rickey Henderson, of course, already holds the career record for Stolen Bases, now 994. I have believed for many years that Henderson would probably wind up with 1,300 to 1,500 stolen bases in his career, and that range still appears reasonable.

In last year's book I wrote about Henderson's chance of breaking Ty Cobb's career record for runs scored, which is 2,245. Henderson started last year 33 runs behind Cobb at the same age, 1,323 to 1,290. By scoring 105 runs he gained thirteen on Cobb, who scored 92 at the same age; Henderson now trails the record holder 1,415 to 1,395 at the same age. His chance of breaking that record, which I estimated to be 17% a year ago, would appear to be almost exactly the same now as it was then.

Rickey also has a chance to become the greatest power/speed combination of all time, supplanting Willie Mays, who had a career power/speed number of 447.1. With his thousand-plus stolen bases, Henderson will need to hit about 275 home runs in his career in order to have a higher power/speed number than Mays. He now has 184 career home runs.

Best Defensive Player: Mike Gallego

Best Knowledge of the Strike Zone: Rickey Henderson

Least Command of the Strike Zone: Terry Steinbach

Fastest Runner: Rickey Henderson

Slowest Runner: Mark McGwire

Best Baserunner: Rickey Henderson

Best Fastball: Van Poppel

Best Breaking Pitch: Dennis Eckersley

Best Control: Dennis Eckersley

Most Underrated Player: Mark McGwire

Oddest Collection of Abilities: Mark McGwire

Most-Similar Players:

to C Terry Steinbach, B.J. Surhoff
to 1B Mark McGwire, Kal Daniels??
to 2B Mike Gallego, Casey Candaele
to 3B Brook Jacoby, Mike Pagliarulo
to SS Walt Weiss, Kevin Elster
to LF Rickey Henderson, Tim Raines
to CF Dave Henderson, Kevin McReynolds
to RF Jose Canseco, Barry Bonds
to DH Harold Baines, George Bell

Most Fun to Watch: Rickey Henderson
Dave Henderson
Jose Canseco

Least Fun to Watch: Brook Jacoby

Managerial Type: Mike Gallego

Among the All-Time Team Leaders:

The A's count their team records from 1968, when they moved to Oakland; they don't count the records from Philadelphia or Kansas City. Rickey Henderson and Carney Lansford are prominent among the Oakland all-time leaders, among the top five in most categories, and Canseco is also climbing the lists. In career home runs Canseco is second, behind Reggie, and McGwire is fourth.

Town Team:

C—Ernie Lombardi
1B—Willie Stargell
2B—Joe Morgan
3B—Cookie Lavagetto
SS—Chris Speier
LF—Rickey Henderson
CF—Vada Pinson
RF—Frank Robinson
SP—Dave Stewart
MGR—Billy Martin

What Needs to Be Done For 1992:

The A's must make a decision by the first of June as to whether the salad days are over, or whether, with a few moves, the A's can be pushed back to the top of the league. This will be the most critical decision the organization has made in several years. If the A's decide to bail out and re-tool, they have enough talent left that they can probably get back in the race by 1994—but not if they don't decide to do it quickly. If, on the other hand, they make the judgment that they can still win and are proven to be wrong, then they'll make the upcoming down cycle deeper and longer than it needs to be.

Outlook for 1992: My own opinion is that the A's probably cannot get back to the top of the division in 1992, but will continue to drift further out of contention.

Index of Leading Indicators for 1992: Down 12.6

Positive Indicators: 1. Plexiglas Principle

Negative Indicators:

1. Team Age
2. Team did not play as well last year as won-lost record would indicate
3. Played poorly late in the season
4. Poor AAA team

Due for a better season: Mark McGwire

Likely to have a worse season: Dave Henderson

1992 Won-Lost Record will be: 78–84

SO WHAT IS A DYNASTY?

The recurring argument about what constitutes a "dynasty" in sports has only one possible use, that being to illustrate for the young the term "semantic debate". The A's have done exactly what they have done. Nothing is at issue here except the word that we choose to apply to it: was it or was it not a dynasty? When I mentioned this to George Will on *Sunday Sports America*, George said that many of our national debates are essentially semantic, like "What is justice?" and "What is liberty?" When one argues about what is justice, however, there is an unstated assumption that we should try to **do** what is just, and so there is always a consequence to the definition. This, however, is *truly* a semantic debate; If we call the A's a dynasty it doesn't add a single win to the W column of their glorious summers, or remove a single loss from October.

For what it's worth, my resolution of this is as follows:

Q) What is a dynasty, literally?

A) A dynasty, literally, is a series of rulers—kings or emperors or something—from the same family or clan.

Q) What then should be a sports dynasty?

A) Obviously, a series of championships from the same team.

Q) Have the A's won a series of championships?

A) Obviously they have.

While the literal interpretation of the term makes its meaning fairly clear, the term has acquired connotations which make it sit uncomfortably upon the shoulders of a real and present competitor. Tony LaRussa, asked if the Oakland A's are a dynasty, shivers violently and draws away as if he were being fitted for a leopard-skin jockstrap; for LaRussa to say that yes, by Golly, the A's ARE a dynasty, would be tantamount to admitting that yes, by Gosh, he IS a genius. "Dynasty", as it applies to a baseball team, has become vaguely synonymous with "great".

As I write this, June, 1991, there is some company running a silly contest to come up with a new term for "handicapped"—coin the best word and you win a free trip somewhere. There are already a million terms for handicaps. The problem is, we're not supposed to use them anymore. Our language has a thousand terms for people who don't learn very well—idiot, moron, imbecile, dumb, stupid, retarded, developmentally delayed. Almost all of these terms were first applied not in the attempt to be cruel, but in the attempt to be kind. Educators began calling children "retarded" just a couple of generations ago so that they wouldn't be labelled stupid or any of the other things. By the end of the first day, I would guess, the other kids were taunting the retarded as "tardos", and so retarded was replaced by developmentally disabled, dysfunctional, *special*. Each of these was discarded in the language in a futile flight from the painful connotations which inevitably gather around the chosen sound.

I find the following distinction to be useful in discussing great teams:

A *minor dynasty* is a series of championships won by an organization *with one group of players*. There are many minor dynasties in baseball history, and the A's success over the last three years is another one.

A *major dynasty* is a series of championships won by *different personnel* in the same organization over a period of time longer than a player's career. There are only four major dynasties in baseball history—that of the Yankees in the American League and those of the Giants (1904–1924), Cardinals (1926–1946) and Dodgers (1947–1966) in the National League.

RICKEY

Dear Bill,

Why do you always make such a big deal about Rickey Henderson supposedly being the greatest leadoff man in baseball history? Throughout baseball history the best hitters have always hit third and fourth. Ty Cobb, Honus Wagner, Willie Mays, Joe Morgan and many others would have been more effective in a leadoff role than Henderson, if they had been used that way. If the A's batted Henderson eighth, would you make a big deal out of his being the greatest number eight hitter ever? Research has always shown that batting-order effects are of minimal importance in determining how many runs are scored; what counts is how good the players are. So why make such a big deal about where Henderson hits?

To realize exactly how great a player Rickey Henderson is, consider these things:

Rickey Henderson had an injury-plagued 1991 season, missing 28 games with an assortment of complaints.

When in the lineup, he didn't play well by his own standards. He hit .268, his lowest average in five years. His batting average, on-base percentage, slugging percentage and stolen base percentage were all below his career norms.

He plays in one of the toughest hitter's parks in baseball.

The team for which he plays had a miserable year.

He still scored 105 runs.

Anybody else, even the best leadoff men in baseball, 105 runs scored is a hell of year. For Rickey, everything goes wrong and he *still* scores 105 runs.

Anyway, the letter above is *not* a real letter. I got a real letter just like it, from a friend of mine whom we'll call RW, and the real letter provoked me to do about a week's research, but I've lost the real letter so I can't reprint it or use my friend's name, sorry RW.

On a certain level I reject the entire premise of the letter. To say that Willie Mays *would have been* a better leadoff hitter than Rickey Henderson is like saying that he would have been a better second baseman than Rogers Hornsby, or like saying that Walter Johnson would have been a greater relief pitcher than Rollie Fingers if he had just been used as a relief ace. The speculative creation of a greater leadoff man does not diminish the fact that Rickey Henderson *is* the greatest leadoff man. Nobody would have used Willie Mays in his prime as a leadoff man, since this is an apparently inefficient use of his skills, while Rickey Henderson *is* a leadoff hitter because it is an obviously effective use of his skills.

The bit about the most effective number eight hitter is a red herring, because being a number eight hitter isn't a distinct offensive role. It's a place where they put the guy who isn't good enough to hit seventh. Batting leadoff is a distinct offensive role.

I also have to say, RW, that the inclusion of Joe Morgan on your list won't stand review, since if you look at their numbers, you'll realize that there's no way Morgan would have been a better leadoff man than Henderson. A great leadoff man, yes, but not as great as Rickey. Ty Cobb, I'll give you, as well as a couple you didn't mention, Ted Williams and Babe Ruth.

But Willie Mays? I'm not so sure that Willie Mays, used as a leadoff man, would have been more effective than Rickey Henderson.

To study this problem, I programmed a computer to play 100 simulated seasons under each of the following conditions:

1) With Rickey Henderson (career stats through 1990) leading off, and a lineup of eight fairly typical hitters coming up behind him. Not a statistical composite of a typical number four hitter, but a number four hitter who seems reasonably typical of the slot—Kent Hrbek, to be specific. 100 seasons of that, full lineup simulation.

2) With exactly the same lineup, only with Willie Mays (career stats) in the leadoff spot instead of Henderson.

3) Same lineup, but with Steve Sax leading off. Sax seemed to me to be a reasonably typical leadoff man, and thus an appropriate contrast to the Henderson/Mays comparison.

4) Same lineup, but with Steve Sax leading off and Rickey Henderson batting third.

5) Same lineup, but with Steve Sax leading off and Willie Mays batting third.

Here's the basic conclusion. Assuming that their career stats represent their abilities, Rickey Henderson is a better leadoff man than Willie Mays. The assumption that Mays, had he been a leadoff man, would have been more effective than Henderson is unfounded; he would not have been, unless perhaps he had adjusted his talents to the different role, and had a higher on-base percentage but less power.

In a simulation a player plays 162 games a year without ever coming out, so the raw numbers of at bats are a little unrealistic. What counts is the *comparison* between Mays and Henderson, with the same lineup coming up behind them. This chart compares their stats in an average 162-game season:

	AB	R	H	2B	3B	HR	RBI	BB	SO	SB	CS	Avg
Rickey	644	144	189	31	5	19	56	114	85	116	25	.293
Willie	679	134	205	32	9	42	89	80	96	23	6	.302

Looking at those stats, you might guess that Mays was the more effective leadoff man. Because of his walks and stolen bases Henderson scored ten more runs, but because of his power Mays drove in 33 more runs. Even from a leadoff man, 33 RBI might be considered worth more than ten runs scored.

I can't exactly tell you why, but it doesn't work out that way. The ultimate test of which would be the more effective leadoff man is not individual totals but the effect on the team. In a typical season the Sax simulation, Sax leading off, scored 708 runs and won 81 games, 81–81.

The substitution of Mays as the leadoff man improved their runs scored to 736, and their won-lost record to 83–79.

But the substitution of Henderson as the leadoff man improved the team runs scored to 745, and the won-lost record to 84–78.

But the study yielded an even bigger surprise when I substituted both Mays and Henderson into the *third* spot in the batting order, replacing the default player who was there (George Brett, 1987). These were their individual stats from the third slot:

	AB	R	H	2B	3B	HR	RBI	BB	SO	SB	CS	Avg
Rickey	607	119	178	29	5	17	96	107	80	99	21	.293
Willie	638	119	192	30	8	40	130	75	89	21	6	.301

Hitting third, Mays scored just as many runs as Henderson and drove in far more—yet the Henderson team scored just as many runs and won just as many games. Each team averaged 708 runs per season. Henderson's team, over the course of the hundred seasons, won 18 more games (8058 to 8040).

This probably tells us something about the relative attention that should be paid to runs scored and RBI counts, but I'm not precisely sure what, so I'm going to pass on that.

What the study *does* show, however, is the following:

1) The assumption that batting-order effects are minimal, while it is *generally* true, has limits.

2) The assumption that runs scored and RBI reflect offensive value, while it may be generally true, has limits.

3) The assumption that stolen bases are of minimal team value, while it may be generally true, has limits.

We shouldn't be too confident about the things we think we know.

4) The most important offensive statistic, by far, is on-base percentage. Henderson's extremely high on-base percentage, combined with his other offensive skills, puts him in a class with the greatest offensive players in baseball history.

I undertook one more exercise, while I was doing all this. In one simulation, with Sax batting leadoff and Mays third, I converted all of the outs into strikeouts. One question that I have worked on for many years from different angles is, what exactly is the cost of a strikeout as opposed to another out, an "undescribed" out. If *all* of your batting outs are strikeouts, as opposed to a mixture of ground balls, fly balls, line drives outs, strikeouts, what do you lose?

This team lost 27 runs per year. That is on an increase of 3,477 strikeouts, from 774 per team to 4,251. The team went from striking out 4.8 times per game to 26.2; this cost them one run every six games. The number of sacrifice flies per season went from 42 to 0—but the number of ground-ball double plays also went from 123 to 0. The net loss on strikeouts is tiny—but there is a net loss of approximately .01 run per strikeout.

THE SEATTLE MARINERS
• IN A BOX •

1991 Won-Lost Record: 83-79 .512

Rank among 26 teams: Tied for 13th
Over Last Five Years: 379-430 .468
Rank over Five Years: 22nd
In Last Ten Years: 730-889 .451
Rank over Ten Years: 25th

Best Player: Ken Griffey Jr.

Weak Spot: Designated Hitter

The Mariners last year had three first basemen in spring training, in Pete O'Brien, Alvin Davis and Tino Martinez. They sent Martinez back to Calgary, played O'Brien at first and Davis at the DH spot.

It wasn't a great solution for anybody. Martinez, one of the Mariners' most valuable properties, didn't do anything for his career by having another good year at Calgary. O'Brien, still trying to figure out why the Mariners signed him, had his third straight sub-standard season, although he did drive in 88 runs. He scored 58, which is an awful total for a man with 560 at bats. And Alvin Davis, a born DH, wiped about 15 points off his career batting average with a miserable .229 season.

Best Pitcher: Erik Hanson

Best Bench Player: Henry Cotto

Best Young Player: Ken Griffey Jr.

Best Looking Player: Tino Martinez

Ugliest Player: Randy Johnson

Most Pleasant Surprise, 1991: Bill Swift

Biggest Disappointment, 1991: Alvin Davis

Best Minor League Prospect: Roger Salkeld

Who Is: A 21-year-old right-handed pitcher. In 368 minor league innings, he has struck out 402 and walked 161. A #1 draft pick in 1989, Salkeld will probably pitch this season at Calgary, but will move into the rotation if he pitches well there and a hole opens in the Seattle rotation.

Other Prospects: **Marc Newfield** is a big (6-4, 205), young (19), power-hitting outfielder. *Baseball America* listed him as the #2 prospect in the California League last summer, just behind Pedro Martinez of the Dodgers.

Designated Malcontent: Jeff Smulyan

Park Characteristics: Two years of adjustments to the dimensions have left the Kingdome essentially a neutral park, having no obvious tendency to favor the hitter or pitcher. It may still be a slightly above-average home run park.

The Park Helps: Harold Reynolds has done very well here.

The Park Hurts: Jay Buhner has hit poorly in Seattle for the last two years.

ORGANIZATIONAL REPORT CARD

Ownership: D
Upper Management: C
Field Management: Unknown
Front-Line Talent: B−
Second-Line Talent: C+
Minor League System: B

TEAM LEADERS:

Batting Average: Ken Griffey Jr, .327

Last Ten Years (Season): Griffey Jr., 1991, .327
Last Ten Years (Total): Phil Bradley, .301

Doubles: Ken Griffey Jr., 42

Triples: Harold Reynolds, 6

Home Runs: Jay Buhner, 27

Last Ten Years (Season): Gorman Thomas, 1985, 32
Last Ten Years (Total): Alvin Davis, 160

RBI: Ken Griffey Jr., 100

Last Ten Years (Season): Alvin Davis, 1984, 116
Last Ten Years (Total): Alvin Davis, 667

Extra Base Hits: Ken Griffey Jr. 65

Stolen Bases: Harold Reynolds, 28

Walks: Edgar Martinez, 84

Runs Created: Ken Griffey, 118

Runs Created Per Game: Ken Griffey, 8.0

Secondary Average: Jay Buhner, .384

Wins: Brian Holman and Randy Johnson, 13 each

Last Ten Years (Season): Mark Langston, 19 in 1987
Last Ten Years (Total): Langston, 74

Winning Percentage: Bill Krueger, 11-8 .579

Strikeouts: Randy Johnson, 228

Last Ten Years (Season): Mark Langston, 1987, 262
Last Ten Years (Total): Mark Langston, 1078

ERA: Bill Krueger, 3.60

Saves: Bill Swift, 17

League Leaders: Harold Reynolds, as he did in 1990, led the major leagues in the number of offensive outs made, with 510. Reynolds had 471 batting outs, plus 14 bunts, six sacrifice flies, 11 grounded into double play and eight caught stealing. His stolen base percentage, historically poor, was very good last year (78%). The major league leaders in outs made:

1. Reynolds, 510
2. Jay Bell, 498
3. Brian McRae, 496

Stat of the Year: The Mariners last year turned 187 double plays, the most of any major league team since 1986, when the Mariners themselves turned 191. It was the first time that a team with a winning record had led the majors in double plays since 1987.

1991 SEASON

Background: Since their creation in 1977 the Mariners have fought a long battle to field a competitive team. Since the mid-1980s the Mariners' talent has not been obviously inferior to the other teams, and there has been no apparent reason for them to continue to lose.

Outlook: My own experience, which I think is fairly typical, is that I picked the Mariners to show improvement annually from 1983 on, and stopped doing so in the late 1980s simply because after several years I got tired of saying "the Mariners are going to be better this year". The Mariners were generally picked fourth to sixth in the American League West.

Getaway: The Mariners lost their first six games, then won their next eight.

High Point of the Season: In early May the Mariners won 12 of 13 games, pushing them into first place on May 18, a half-game ahead of Oakland. They were 22-14 at the time.

Low Point of the Season: September 8. The Mariners stayed over .500 and in the race until early July, when a five-game losing streak dropped them to 39-39, then to 40-42. They rallied quickly, and remained over .500 through most of July and all of August.

In early September the Mariners lost seven straight games to the Red Sox and 16 of 21 games overall, dropping them out of contention. A 17-6 loss in Fenway on September 8 completed the second Red Sox' sweep, and also kicked the Mariners under .500 for the first time since early July.

Stretch Drive: Seattle played well the last four weeks of the season to finish with their first winning record ever.

Major Injuries: As usual, Scott Bankhead had shoulder problems, and missed a few months. When he did pitch he was horrible. Henry Cotto, in the midst of a career season, went on the DL August 3 with a torn right rotator cuff and didn't play again. Erik Hanson twice missed two weeks with tightness in his right elbow. Rob Murphy missed the last month of the season after spraining his right ankle on September 8.

Offense: Fair to poor. Had Alvin Davis had his normal season the Mariner offense would have been above average. As it was they scored 702 runs against a league average of 727.

Defense: Strong, very strong up the middle. Valle (C) is outstanding, Reynolds (2B) is outstanding, Griffey (CF) is above average. Vizquel (SS) is a bit of a mystery and you can get an argument about his defense, but he looks good to me.

Pitching: Good

Best Game by a Starting Pitcher: A one-hitter by Randy Johnson at Oakland, August 14 (9 1 0 0 3 12 Game Score 94).

Worst Game by a Starting Pitcher: Rich DeLucia gave up nine runs in less than three innings on September 8 ($2\frac{2}{3}$ 7 9 9 5 1 Game Score 4)

Indicators for 1991 were: Down 0.6 (Basically Neutral)

Number of regulars having good seasons by their own standards: Five (Griffey, Martinez, Buhner, Reynolds, Vizquel)

1991 Over-Achiever: Henry Cotto

1991 Under-Achiever: Alvin Davis

Infield: Slightly above average

Outfield: Slightly below average

Catching: Poor. Valle's defense doesn't compensate for

a) Valle's offense
b) Bradley's offense, and
c) Bradley's defense.

Starting Pitching: Very good—among the best in the league

Bullpen: In 1991, very good. The Mariners for several years have been counting on Mike Schooler as their relief ace, to the point of being stubborn about it. Schooler wasn't available most of last year and Mike Jackson, second in line, lost the closer job, so a lot of people have written that the Mariner bullpen was weak. They're dead wrong. The Mariners blew only 16 save opportunities in 1991 (they were 48 for 64), had a winning record in the bullpen (23-20) and had a bullpen ERA of 3.16, third-best in baseball. Billy Swift was brilliant, Jackson wasn't *that* bad, and the third-line support was better than average.

Percentage of offense created by:

Young Players:	46%
Players in Their Prime:	43%
Past Their Prime:	11%

Team Age:

Age of Non-Pitchers:	27.6
Age of Pitchers:	27.3
Overall Age:	27.5

The Mariners are a young team.

In retrospect, the critical decisions were: The failure to sort out the three-men-on-first mess in a productive way left the Mariners short of talent at other positions. This would be the one thing I would cite which could have helped the Mariners to a better 1991 season, understanding that modern contract arrangements sometimes make it difficult to reshuffle the deck.

THAT AND THE OTHER

Hall of Fame Watch: The Mariners' only Hall-of-Fame type player, Griffey, is only 22. At this point the list of things he has done which would be typical of a Hall of Famer—hit .300, drive in a hundred runs—are the kinds of things a player has to do with great consistency to make a Hall of Fame career. The chance that he will be that good a player rests on his either doing things that he hasn't done yet, or doing what he has done the last two years every year for the next fifteen years.

Chris Berman, Have You Considered: Greg (The Life of) Briley

Throwback: Jay Buhner

Attendance Trend: Showing solid growth. The Mariners' 1991 attendance total (2.15 million) is somewhat misleading, because a group of Seattle businesses got organized to buy up tickets to pre-empt the possibility of the Mariners' leaving Seattle through an attendance clause in their lease.

However, the Mariners' attendance has grown sharply in recent years—from 1.02 million in 1988 to 1.30 million in 1989 and 1.51 million in 1990. Combining this with the improved play of the team, baseball in Seattle, despite the headlines about Smulyan wanting to leave, is *not* on its last legs.

Players with a Chance for 3000 career hits: Ken Griffey Jr. 24%

Record Watch: The Kid, of course, is his age-group leader in everything. At his age, this doesn't make him a serious candidate to break any records.

Best Fundamental Player: Pete O'Brien

Worst Fundamental Player: Edgar Martinez

Best Defensive Player: Harold Reynolds or Dave Valle

Worst Defensive Player: Alvin Davis

Best Knowledge of the Strike Zone: Alvin Davis

Least Command of the Strike Zone: Jay Buhner

Fastest Runner: Harold Reynolds

Slowest Runner: Dave Valle

I wonder how fast Ken Griffey Jr. really is. I don't know if you've ever noticed this, but Griffey has large, heavy legs for a young man. He also doesn't do a lot of things in a baseball game which are indicative of speed. He hasn't stolen 20 bases in a season yet, nor is his stolen base percentage terrific. He hit only one triple last year and grounded into ten double plays. He has a speed score of 5.1.

People talk about Griffey being fast, so maybe he is; the stats don't *always* tell. My guess is, though, that Griffey's speed may keep him from being in the Willie Mays class of player. He certainly runs well now, but I'm not so sure he will in five years.

Best Baserunner: Henry Cotto

Most Likely to Still be Here in 2000: Ken Griffey Jr.

Best Fastball: Randy Johnson

Best Control: Erik Hanson

Most Underrated Player: Edgar Martinez

Oddest Collection of Abilities: Dave Valle

Never Going to be As Good as the Organization Thinks He Is: Tino Martinez

Most-Similar Players:

to C Dave Valle, Darren Daulton
to 1B Pete O'Brien, Kevin McReynolds
to 2B Harold Reynolds, Ozzie Guillen
to 3B Edgar Martinez, Todd Zeile
to SS Omar Vizquel, Terry Shumpert
to LF Greg Briley, Joe Orsulak
to CF Ken Griffey Jr., Juan Gonzalez
to RF Jay Buhner, Greg Vaughn

Most Fun to Watch: Griffey Jr.

Least Fun to Watch: Pete O'Brien

Managerial Type: Scott Bradley

Among the All-Time Team Leaders: Of thirteen positive offensive categories listed in the Mariners media guide, Alvin Davis is the all-time team leader in nine of them: games, at bats, runs, hits, doubles, home runs, runs batted in, total bases, extra-base hits, and walks.

Town Team:

C—Sammy White
1B—Earl Torgeson
2B—Ryne Sandberg
SS—Mick Kelleher
3B—Ron Santo
LF—Woody Jensen
CF—Bill North
RF—Earl Averill
SP—Fred Hutchinson

Post-Season Transactions:

October 29, Bill Plummer named manager.

December 11, Kevin Mitchell and Mike Remlinger to Seattle for Bill Swift, Mike Jackson, and Dave Burba. After the trade several people associated with the Giants made a special effort to badmouth Mitchell.

What Needs to Be Done For 1992: With the loss of Swift and Jackson, the M's will need to re-construct their bullpen. Also, they need to sort out their first basemen.

Outlook for 1992: Mixed. Team could play well but the calibre of management is uncertain.

Index of Leading Indicators for 1992: Up 1.4

Positive Indicators: 1. Youth

Negative Indicators:

In a formal sense, there are no large negative indicators here. In an informal way, the Mariners' failure to retain Jim Lefebvre, their battles with the city and their underlying financial weakness are large, looming omens.

Almost nothing can undermine a ballclub as much as the perception of betrayal from above. Sports abound in cliches about group effort, about individuals submerging their own goals to those of the team. Those cliches are around because a sports team requires them. A sports team *needs* to have that "We're all in this together" attitude. To win a pennant requires a tremendous concerted effort from many people. Without that attitude, the effort required becomes impossible to sustain, and the team dissolves into a collection of individuals pursuing selfish goals only obliquely related to the team.

When a team perceives that there is no commitment to winning at the top, the team will almost never win—in fact, I don't believe I've ever seen a team in a situation like this pull out a championship in any sport. So, unless the ownership situation can be clarified, I will be very surprised if this team can do anything.

Due for a better season: Erik Hanson

Likely to have a worse season: Bill Krueger

1992 Won-Lost Record will be: 77-85

COLLOQUY

The Baseball Book: Senator, as I understand it, you have some ideas you wanted to put forward here about laws which could be passed that you feel would benefit the American sports fan.

Senator: Yes, sir.

The Baseball Book: Well, what are those ideas?

Senator: There are about eight proposals under consideration. Where do you want to start?

The Baseball Book: You pick.

Senator: I'll start at the top. Probably the most important legislation we could pass to benefit sports fans, as well as the public at large, is the Captive Audience Law.

The Captive Audience Law would require that whenever more than a thousand people were assembled in a public place such as a ballpark or theater, access must be provided for competing vendors. In essence, the law would end the practice of charging a "hidden admission" to public events by fixing exorbitant prices for concessions.

The Baseball Book: How do you regulate the cost of a hot dog?

Senator: We're not going to regulate the cost of a hot dog. We're going to let the market regulate the cost of the hot dog.

The Baseball Book: How's that?

Senator: A baseball team can charge $3.00 for a hot dog because they control the market; if you want the hot dog, you have to buy it from the team or a single vendor licensed by the team, so that vendor can set the price. They have a captive audience, and therefore they have a responsibility to deal fairly with that audience.

What this legislation would do is require the team—or the concert promoter, or whoever—to allow vendors access to the facility. The team can license the vendors and can regulate their activities in reasonable ways—you can't yell "POPCORN" during the third act of Hamlet, you can't sell peanuts to the on-deck hitter—but it cannot prevent vendors from operating at the event. This creates competition among vendors, and that creates reasonable prices for beer and hot dogs.

The Baseball Book: Isn't there a danger in that?

Senator: A danger in reasonable prices for beer and hot dogs?

The Baseball Book: Well, yes.

Senator: Which is?

The Baseball Book: Baseball in the last ten years has made real progress, maybe even remarkable process, in controlling reckless drinking at ballgames. It's easy to imagine free-lance vendors, competing to work a crowd, abandoning those controls and pandering to the element which goes to ballgames to drink and raise hell. It's hard to imagine how you can control that if you can't control the vendors.

Senator: We're talking about big money here. You go to a game, what do you spend for two beers, a hot dog and some peanuts? Maybe $12? Let's say ten. $10 a head for 20,000 people, that's $200,000 an event—for concessions which should cost maybe three dollars a head. A baseball team—or somebody—is ripping off the public for roughly $100,000 an event, 81 events a year. That's not $100,000 taken in; that's a $100,000 difference between the reasonable value of the foodstuffs, and what they are sold for. You're telling me that that's necessary so that a team can control excessive drinking at their ballgames?

Look, for fifty years baseball teams *promoted* reckless drinking at their games. OK, so ten years ago they developed a degree of social responsibility. That doesn't entitle them to milk millions of dollars a year out of the public on the pretense of protecting the public morality.

The Baseball Book: So how *do* you control the vendors?

Senator: Exactly the same way they're controlled now. We're not going to say you can't make a rule ending sales of alcohol after the sixth inning. We're only saying that the team can't monopolize the market; if *they* sell beer after the seventh inning, they have to allow properly licensed vendors to sell beer after the seventh inning. We're not saying that you can't prohibit selling beer to a man who is already intoxicated.

Besides, it's a silly argument. Who the hell appointed a baseball team to be the hall monitors of public drinking? That's not their job; that's not their privilege. Hell, my opinion is that most people don't even *want* to drink beer at a ball game. I think most people would be happy to drink Coke, or Pepsi, or Diet Cream Soda or some damn thing, but the Lemonade vendor don't come around. The club doesn't send anybody around pushing iced tea; they send guys around selling beer because they think that's where the money is. Then you're going to let them plead that they have to control the vendors so they can control the beer?

The Baseball Book: How do you justify the government intervening in this way between a baseball owner and his customers? Isn't it rather unusual for the government to intervene in the market this way?

Senator: What's unusual is that we *don't* regulate it. For a hundred years it has been the policy of our government to prevent a powerful company from establishing an economic monopoly, and exploiting that monopoly to fix prices. The policy of allowing a baseball team or a football team to do exactly that—to establish a monopoly and exploit it absolutely without shame to charge unreasonable prices—is an anomaly.

The Baseball Book: But isn't there a difference between regulating an open market in the public, and requiring a team owner to operate an open market on his own property?

Senator: What are you talking about, his own property? How many owners do you know who own their own parks?

The Baseball Book: Can the teams afford to lose . . .

Senator: Wait a minute. We're talking about *public* property here. We're talking about places that were built with your tax money and my tax money. Why do we *have* to concede to teams the right to use that public property in a way that is clearly taking advantage of those very same taxpayers.

The Baseball Book: Can the teams afford to lose this revenue? We already hear that the Seattle Mariners and the Cleveland Indians are fighting bankruptcy. If we eliminate a source of revenue for them, aren't we pushing them into receivership?

Senator: When baseball's revenues go up, their expenses, such as the salaries of the players, expand to consume the available money. If their revenues go down, their expenses will contract for the same reason.

Besides, I'm not at all certain that their revenues *will* go down *in those cities.* I think there are many people who don't go to games because they don't want to buy three-dollar warm beers and four-dollar cold hot dogs. It's not clear to me that eliminating these rip-offs will result in a net loss of income to the teams. In Boston, where the number of people who want to go to the games exceeds the number of seats, there will be a loss of revenue.

The Baseball Book: OK, I'll buy it. *The Baseball Book* officially endorses the Captive Audience Law. What else ya got?

Senator: Another piece of legislation which I plan to introduce this session is the Federal Right of Ticket Resale.

The Baseball Book: The Federal Right of Ticket Resale?

Senator: When you buy a ticket, you have a right to resell it, period.

The laws in this area are very confused right now, uneven from one jurisdiction to another, and not respected anywhere.

The Baseball Book: In essence, you want to legalize ticket scalping?

Senator: Well, the term "scalping" is loaded. It's a biased remnant of the campaigns to legitimize these laws. The term "scalping" implies that tickets are being bought for $10 and resold for $50, when in reality the much more common situation is that tickets are resold *below* their face value, not above it. What we're talking about is brokering tickets.

The Baseball Book: Why should the laws be changed?

Senator: On one level, for exactly the same reason the Captive Audience Law should be adopted: to allow a free market to operate. The real question is, who do these laws protect?

These laws were passed because the wealthy men who control baseball and other sports also were able to control, or at least were able to influence, state and local legislatures. The teams don't *want* you to be able to buy a ticket and resell it—in fact, Marge Schott is involved right now in a campaign to get Cincinnati and Covington to adopt laws to that effect.

If you buy a ticket and then find you can't use it, you should be able to sell that ticket back to the team or re-sell it to somebody else. But if you can't re-sell it to a third party—a broker—then the team is able to force anybody else who wants a seat to buy it from them. In effect, they are selling more tickets than are used for the game by taking advantage of the people who buy seats but can't attend the games.

The Baseball Book: If you legalize ticket scalping, though, aren't you allowing somebody to take advantage of the public by buying up tickets to a popular event and re-selling them at inflated prices? Don't you set up a situation in which all of the tickets to the big events—the World Series, etc.—are bought up by scalpers and sold for exorbitant prices?

Senator: Look, if the *team* sets the ticket price at $100 a ticket—and they do sometimes—we don't prohibit that, do we? We say if the ticket is worth a hundred dollars, sell it for a hundred dollars. And that's what we *should* say; hell, if a ticket is worth a hundred dollars, it isn't the business of the government to force it to be sold for ten dollars.

But as I've said before, that *isn't* the common situation. Most games aren't World Series games. The common situation is that a guy buys four season tickets, and finds in practice that he can only use about half the tickets—some days he can only use two of them, some days none. What does he do with the extras?

What he *should* be able to do with them is sell them, sell them openly, sell them publicly and sell them to the highest bidder, which is normally going to be about about half the face value. If there's a broker involved, the broker's going to buy a $10 ticket for $4 and sell it back to the next guy for seven. The teams have used this idea of "exploiting" the public with exorbitant ticket sales to prevent the poor sap who has extra tickets from getting his money back.

The Baseball Book: But that happens anyway, doesn't it? I mean, these laws against ticket scalping aren't strictly enforced, are they?

Senator: One more reason to get rid of them. It breeds disrespect for the law to have regulations on the book that we can't or don't enforce.

The Baseball Book: Well, my point was that we can and do enforce them against blatant offenders. If a guy tries to buy a ticket for $10 and re-sell it for $100, then we might use the law to discourage that. But in the ordinary case, where a $10 ticket is being resold for $7 to $15, we can just ignore it.

Senator: *Sometimes* we ignore it—in some states, in some places. The fact that the law is on the books gives the teams an authority that they shouldn't have. It gives them the right to harass the ticket brokers. Perhaps most importantly, the existence of these laws inhibits the development of an orderly market, and prevents us from regulating the market which does in fact exist.

When I go to baseball games, I *usually*, most of the time, buy tickets from the "scalpers", because that's where you can usually get the best ticket at the best price—

The Baseball Book: You realize that you just confessed to dealing with an illicit business.

Senator: That's alright; I'm not a real Senator. This is a one-shot thing; I don't have to run for re-election. Anyway, many people are reluctant to deal with these guys because what they are doing is technically illegal, and people feel that they're going to be taken advantage of. And, in fact, that's not an unreasonable fear; the fact that the business is extra-legal *does* tend to prevent honest, straight-up businessmen from getting involved with it, and does tend to draw a certain number of sleazy people into the business. If you don't know what you're doing, don't know the stadium or the value of the ticket, you can be taken advantage of.

By making the business legal—absolutely, clearly legal in all fifty states—we acquire the ability to regulate it. First, we bring a better class of people into the business of being ticket brokers. Then we can set up booths on the event site where the business is conducted. A guy who has a ticket to resell can go by that booth and sell it. If he doesn't like the offer from one guy, one broker, he can move on to the next. And the individual buying the ticket has the same option; he doesn't have to chase guys with wind-breakers and sunglasses all over the parking lot looking at what they have; he just goes to the ticket re-sale booth.

The Baseball Book: Can the worst extremes of ticket scalping—World Series tickets being sold for a thousand dollars, that sort of thing—can those still be prohibited?

Senator: There isn't any reason they *can't* be. Myself, I don't see why they should be. I mean, if somebody has a great seat to a World Series game and wants to sell it, my idea is that it *ought* to go to somebody who really wants it. But if the team insists on selling it for $20, you know what happens? It goes to somebody who has pull. It winds up going to some politician or some TV executive who hasn't been to three games all year, who gets a great seat to the World Series for $20 because he's got an angle.

The Baseball Book: OK, we'll think about it. We'll watch the course of this legislation with interest. I heard something about a law prohibiting baseball games from being played on artificial turf?

Senator: That's under consideration, yes. We haven't made a decision on it.

The Baseball Book: It sounds good to me, but what's the justification for it? Isn't that pretty intrusive . . .

Senator: The justification for the Natural Surfaces Act is worker safety. The law does not normally permit an employer to knowingly expose his workers to unnecessary health risks so that he can make extra money. There's a good argument that artificial turf is a textbook example of that which is normally prohibited in other fields. In order to prevent an occasional rainout—and thus, in order to maximize their own revenues—the teams require their employees to play the games on a hard, unnatural surface which risks injuries, even long-term damage.

The Baseball Book: Such a law would have considerable public appeal.

Senator: For the wrong reasons. The public doesn't like artificial turf for esthetic reasons, but we don't want to put the government in the business of supervising esthetic decisions.

The Baseball Book: Is that why you're going slow on this one?

Senator: No. I mean, I'm not a populist, but I'm also not going to refuse to do something which is in the public interest just because it is too popular. The problem with the legislation is that we can't really prove that artificial turf represents a health risk to the players.

The Baseball Book: The players say it is.

Senator: We know that the players hate it, and that's a vote against it, but there really aren't any studies which show that artificial turf shortens careers or increases injuries—in fact, the only studies which have been done on the issue tended to suggest that artificial turf did *not* increase injuries or shorten careers in baseball. I'm told that the turf does create injuries in football, and as an individual I'm prepared to accept that, but it's not a basis for legislative action. How many injuries are we going to be preventing, and at what cost? What are the injuries? Are there other things we could do at the same cost which would have more value in protecting the public? Are we setting a precedent of interfering in the private business of sports teams for trivial advantages? We have to *know* the answers to those questions before we start down the path to legislation.

The Baseball Book: It doesn't really affect that many people anyway, does it? I mean, how many professional athletes are there to be affected by this?

Senator: Numerically, the largest effect is on amateurs. If the pros have artificial turf, the colleges think they have to have it, too, and then the high schools. There are high school football teams with artificial turf now; twenty years from now there will be more of them. Unless we decide not to go that way.

The Baseball Book: Should the government make that decision?

Senator: No, but neither should the government allow the people who have money to make that decision in a way that is ultimately dangerous to the people who don't have money.

The Baseball Book: Isn't there a danger, in all of this, of extending government regulation into an area of our lives where we just don't want it?

Senator: Well, let's look at the three proposals that we have considered to this point. One of them—the Federal Right of Ticket Resale—is a proposal to *eliminate* government regulation. We're saying that state and local governments *can't* pass regulations to tell the police to act, in essence, as agents of the local sports team. Another of the three proposals I haven't advocated; it's merely under study. The third would regulate not the public, but the teams. So in reality, we're talking about changing the laws in a way that creates a net *loss* in the regulation of public conduct.

Besides, do you really believe that the public *wants* to pay $3 for a hot dog? Do you think the average man values that freedom from government regulation?

The Baseball Book: What else is under consideration?

Senator: At this time, the professional sports leagues all have laws preventing the public from buying stock in their component companies, the teams. I have no idea why the law allows these bizarre policies to exist; there certainly is no public benefit in them, and the only other legislation that I am prepared to advocate at this time is a public ownership law.

The Baseball Book: I'm not getting you. Isn't there some public ownership involvement in the Expos and the Green Bay Packers?

Senator: No no, not *municipal* involvement. *Public* ownership. At this time, all of the major league sports franchises are privately owned, and all of the leagues have policies preventing them from being sold to the public. Suppose that Jeff Smulyan wanted to ease the financial pressures on the Seattle Mariners' ownership group by selling stock in the Mariners to the public. In other words, he clears the appropriate regulatory hurdles of the ICC and FTC, expands the stock base and issues 200,000 shares of stock in his team, selling for $100 a share, thereby raising $20 million in operating capital. It's commonly done in other industries.

The Baseball Book: But it isn't done in baseball.

Senator: It *can't* be done in baseball, because the leagues have an internal regulation prohibiting it.

The Baseball Book: Why?

Senator: You tell me.

The Baseball Book: I don't know . . . because there is some sort of danger in it?

Senator: For *them*, yes, there's a danger in it. The danger is that they will have to respond to the interests of the public. The danger, for the teams, is that they will have to consider the public interest in making their decisions. The public will get to understand their business a lot better.

You see, if you sell shares to the public, then you have to deal with the public in an open, above-board way. You have to publish a profit and loss statement. The management is open to challenge from the shareholders; if one group does a poor job, another group can come in and push them out.

The Baseball Book: So in essence, the public would be looking over Bill Plummer's shoulder.

Senator: Or offering him a shoulder, whichever way you want to look at it.

The Baseball Book: They'd be *involved*, one way or the other. I listen to the call-in shows on the radio. Every time the team loses half the public wants to fire the manager. Every time a player makes an error half the people want to run him out of town on a rail. Do you really want those people to have the right to go to board meetings and conduct the same kind of debates there that they do at 4:00 every afternoon on AM radio? Wouldn't that reduce the management structure of professional teams to chaos?

Senator: Look, baseball managers get fired, on the average, every two years or so. The public is looking over Bill Plummer's shoulder anyway. Allowing the public to put their money where their mouth is isn't going to change that; managers are going to get fired every two or three years.

We're getting ahead of ourselves here; we're discussing the possible end products of the legislation, when we haven't discussed the reasons for it or the purposes of it. There are a million possible end products; the idea is to choose carefully among the things that we *could* do.

The Baseball Book: Make your case.

Senator: We have to begin by asking the question: why do the sports leagues prohibit the public from being involved in their ownership? Do they do this to protect the public, do you think, or do they do this to protect their own interests? The restrictive covenants in the league agreements exist for the explicit purpose of keeping the public in the dark about the business of professional sports. On the simplest level, that cannot be in the public interest.

For a hundred years, baseball teams have operated as feudal monopolies, owned entirely by the wealthy and operated entirely for the benefit of the wealthy. It has been this way for so long that people have lost the ability to see that it doesn't have to be that way, that baseball teams could be owned and operated exactly the way that other businesses are owned and operated. By keeping the public ignorant about the business of baseball, the owners protect their ability to put out self-serving bullshit about the balance sheet. The teams can pretend to be marginal businesses on the verge of bankruptcy, while in reality they may be raking in multi-million dollar profits.

By keeping the public ignorant about the *real* state of their finances, the teams protect their ability to pose as quasi-charitable public utilities while negotiating contracts for stadiums and other public facilities.

By excluding the public from all conferences where the business of baseball is discussed, the teams protect their ability to act in a manner which is contrary to the public interest—in fact, that, in one sentence, is precisely why they exclude the public from their business: to protect their ability to act in a manner which is contrary to the public interest. That should be reason enough for the government to require that the public be allowed to buy into the teams.

The Baseball Book: Contrary to the public interest, such as . . .

Senator: Let us say that the reality might be that the Seattle Mariners are in fact making money hand over fist. I'm not saying that it is; I'm saying that we don't *really* know. The only evidence we have that they're losing money is that they say they're losing money, and after all, fifteen years ago Bowie Kuhn put his hand on a bible and swore to Congress that if the player salaries went up 50% all the teams would go bankrupt. Let's say that the Mariners are making money, but that they want to force Seattle to build them a new stadium, which God knows they need; it's tough to sell tickets to a mausoleum. But in order to negotiate with the city of Seattle, it may well be that they have adopted the pretense that they're about out of money, and they're about to move—when in reality they have plenty of money and they're not going anywhere. If the public *knew* what their balance sheet was, they might lose a degree of leverage with the city in their negotiations, so they might lie to the people to protect their negotiating position. Maybe. All I'm saying is that it cannot be contrary to the public interest for the public to have access to the facts.

The Baseball Book: Well, OK, but let's deal with the end result a little bit. Do we *really* want to carry public empowerment to the point of the public being able to tell Bill Plummer when to bunt, or for that matter being able to fire him if he doesn't bunt when people think he should? I don't mean to sound elitist, but the quality of the public discussion as evidenced on radio shows and in letters to the editor is just not very good. A great deal of extremely sloppy logic is used to buttress irrational conclusions, and it is common for people to take strong emotional positions on sports issues when they don't understand the facts. Is it a good idea to give those people the power, however indirectly, to actually chart the course of the team?

Senator: A man behaves irresponsibly when he has no responsibilities. You say the public will be telling Bill Plummer when to bunt, but let me ask you: did you ever design the tail lights on a Buick? You have the right to invest in General Motors—but that doesn't mean that you or I or anyone else has the right to tell GM what kind of cars to build.

The Baseball Book: Then what does it mean?

Senator: It means that GM is ultimately answerable to their stock holders.

Look, teams are still going to have professional management—in fact, their management will obviously become *more* professional, not less. A manager or General Manager now is often hired on the whim of an owner; you'll have a much more orderly process, and much more effective competition for the good jobs, if the General Manager is selected by a Board of Directors which answers to a stock-holding public.

The Baseball Book: The public is emotional about player salaries . . .

Senator: Yes.

The Baseball Book: Let's say that the Cleveland Indians are purchased by an assemblage of 70,000 Cleveland Indians fans. Are those fans going to be willing to put out a $25 million guarantee for a four-year contract for a top free agent?

Senator: Well, what if they aren't?

The Baseball Book: The Cleveland Indians can't compete.

Senator: So what's new?

The Baseball Book: Bad example. Let's say that the Cincinnati Reds are purchased by a group of 70,000 Cincinnati Reds fans . . .

Senator: Well, you shouldn't assume that the people who call in to call-in shows will be typical of the people who invest real money in the teams. People who have money to invest will tend to think in economic terms, in terms of the economic value of the player's service, rather than the moral justification for his salary. But assuming you're right, some teams will win, and some will lose. That's alright. Some teams may refuse to pay million-dollar salaries. That's alright. That's not our problem. Believe me, they're going to find people willing to play baseball for $500,000 a year.

The Baseball Book: What do you think are the prospects for that legislation?

Senator: We're not ready to move on that one yet. For one thing, as I explained earlier, I'm not real; I'm just a figment of Bill James' imagination. For another thing, I haven't really worked out yet exactly how the transition from private to public ownership should be effected.

The Baseball Book: You're not just going to require the teams to be sold to the public . . .

Senator: Oh, no, nothing like that. The most radical proposal under consideration would be one which would require that each team must be offered to the public the next time that they are sold. In other words, when Ted Turner dies, the Braves have to be sold to the public, rather than being sold to another rich guy on an ego trip.

The Baseball Book: And what would be the most modest proposal?

Senator: The most modest proposal would simply order the leagues to abandon their policy of prohibiting public ownership, and *allow* a team, if it so desires, to sell shares to the public. In between that would be legislation abolishing the prohibitions against public ownership and also requiring that, in compensation for the one hundred years or so of operating outside the restraints of the anti-trust laws, twenty percent of the stock of each team or more must be sold to the public within the next five years. Ultimately, I think it makes no difference; I think that if the public *can* buy the baseball teams, they will. But it might be thirty years before the process is completed.

Another possibility is that the action might not require legislation, at all; we could probably accomplish the same thing by passing a sense-of-the-congress resolution stating that the anti-trust laws should apply to all professional sports. We really need to think through the specifics of how we get from here to there.

Philosophically, I am opposed to doing anything which would send an unnecessary shock through the system. I think that *gradual* changes, allowing the structure to adapt to the new reality as it develops, are less likely to damage the sport in some unintended way.

Speaking of Bill James, didn't he make a similar argument a few years ago in *The Baseball Abstract?*

The Baseball Book: Vaguely similar. There was an article a few years ago called *Revolution*.

Senator: Right.

The Baseball Book: The core argument of *Revolution* was that the system which tied baseball teams together, particularly the minor leagues and the major leagues, was corrupt and should not be permitted by anti-trust laws.

Senator: I remember. I read it.

The Baseball Book: Do you agree with that?

Senator: Certainly, but I don't think that that alone provides a basis for legislation. The system which has allowed major league teams to seize the teams in smaller cities and hold them as slaves is an unfortunate one. The fact that minor league teams charge admission to a sporting event while making no honest effort to win is appalling and shameful—but the truth is that the public knows of this system and approves of it.

The Baseball Book: Meaning that it's alright?

Senator: No, but meaning that it should be opposed in a different way. We should take every opportunity to point out to the public what is wrong with this system, and why it should ultimately be dismantled—but we don't want to ram undesired legislation down the throats of a public. It is not the function of government to destroy an existing industry in the hope that something better will sprout in its place.

The Baseball Book: There is no public outcry in favor of competing vendors at baseball games, yet you feel it's important to protect the public from being taken advantage of. I don't understand the difference. Isn't minor league baseball just as much of a ripoff?

Senator: Yes, it is, but the public *knows* it is being ripped off when it buys the concessions at a ballgame, and would rejoice at the end of the existing system. A man who pays $3 for a beer knows that he is being ripped off. People accept minor league baseball for what it is, because they've never really thought about what it should be. That is the difference.

The Baseball Book: James believes that the use of public money to support professional sports teams in any way, shape or form is wrong, and should be prohibited.

Senator: Exactly.

The Baseball Book: And therefore believes that, for example, any team which plays in a public stadium should be required to pay a fair rent for that stadium.

Senator: Yes. And so do I.

The Baseball Book: Is that a new law?

Senator: It's just an amendment to existing legislation. The ways in which public money can be used for the benefit of private interests are restricted by dozens if not hundreds of existing laws. We propose to extend those limitations to include the direct and indirect support of major league baseball.

The Baseball Book: But if I, as a citizen of Seattle, refuse to build a new stadium for the Mariners, the reality is that somebody else will. Tampa, or Phoenix, or New Orleans, or Buffalo, or some other city will build that stadium if I refuse to.

Senator: Which is why federal legislation is required. Tampa won't do any such thing if we tell them, by law, that they can't.

Look, philosophically I am opposed to expanding the role of the federal government. I absolutely believe that most of the functions of the federal government could be handled better by the states, that most of the functions of the states could be handled better by the cities, and that most of the functions of the cities should be handled by precincts. But there are places where federal legislation is needed, and this is precisely that type of place.

The Baseball Book: Why?

Senator: Because that which is in the best interests of each city is not in the best interests of the nation as a whole.

Professional sports leagues have figured out that they can extort money from cities by pitting one city against another in threatened or actual stadium wars. There are a limited number of major league teams, and an unlimited number of cities which would like to have them. OK, a much greater number. This places the major league teams in the position of being competed for, of being able to say to Cleveland or Seattle, "If you don't build us a stadium, we're going to move out. We're going to take away your status as a major league city." This, in effect, forces the taxpayers of that city to give major league baseball a $100 million gift—and that's appalling. For the ordinary, $30,000-a-year wage earner to be forced to pay higher taxes to support the millionaires who run major league baseball is abominable.

The Baseball Book: So what does that legislation say?

Senator: Very simple: it says that the use of public money to support professional sports in any way, shape or form is prohibited.

The Baseball Book: But you're not pushing for that.

Senator: It's a lower priority.

The Baseball Book: Why?

Senator: For one thing, the amount of public money taken in this way, even though it is substantial, is less than the amount of money lost to exorbitant concession prices. More than that, this legislation is perceived as being negative, anti-sports, even though that isn't its purpose.

Being perceived as negative doesn't make the legislation bad in all cases, but it does make it controversial, and that makes it a poor place to start. It's a lot easier to build a consensus against inflated concession prices than it is to convince the cities to stop throwing money at professional sports teams.

The Baseball Book: Before we end this colloquy . . . by the way, what exactly is a colloquy?

Senator: It's a conversation when the meter is running. It's hard to charge a client $150 or $200 an hour to have a "conversation" with another lawyer, or a "discussion" or even a "dialogue". But a "colloquy"—well, hell I can understand that.

The Baseball Book: Is this actually a colloquy?

Senator: No, I just like the word.

The Baseball Book: Before we end this conversation, then, are there any other proposals that you wanted to discuss? I understand your working group a couple of years ago put forward a proposal that would have limited the salaries of professional athletes?

Senator: Yeah, that's been discussed.

The Baseball Book: Are you in favor of it?

Senator: No.

The Baseball Book: It has popular appeal.

Senator: I'm not a populist.

The Baseball Book: Why should a ballplayer get $5 million a year?

Senator: What difference does it make to me if a ballplayer gets $10 million a year?

The Baseball Book: Let me try again: is it in the best interest of the public for an athlete to be paid $5 million a year?

Senator: It's an economic reality. That is what the market has determined his value to be.

The Baseball Book: Is it in the public interest?

Senator: Probably not. Let's say, for the sake of argument, that it is not.

The Baseball Book: Then why should it be permitted?

Senator: On what grounds should it be prohibited?

The Baseball Book: It is not in the public interest.

Senator: If the public interest is defined that broadly, it becomes a justification for government regulation of every element of our lives. TV shows that glorify violence? They're not in the public interest. Beer commercials with women in G-string bikinis? They're not in the public interest. T-Shirts saying "Just Do It"—what's the public value of those?

The Baseball Book: Are you saying there is nothing that can be done about these obscene salaries.

Senator: Oh, no, we could do something about them.

The Baseball Book: What?

Senator: We could simply prohibit them. We can simply pass a law that says that the maximum salary that can be paid to any individual for a year's work is a million dollars, whether you're a movie star or the president of General Motors. Or, for that matter, we can single out professional baseball players for a separate tax rate.

We can pass that law, and we can enforce it. We can say that the tax rate for income in excess of a million dollars a year is 125 percent; you don't pay it, and you deal with the IRS. You think that won't get somebody's attention in a hell of a hurry?

The Baseball Book: Wouldn't that be unconstitutional or something?

Senator: Why?

The Baseball Book: You can't just limit a man's earnings that way, can you?

Senator: Sure we can. We've done that lots of times. Remember the 90% tax brackets? It hasn't been that long since the top tax bracket wasn't 36%, it was 97%. We can do all kinds of things. During the Korean War we froze salaries. That 90% tax bracket can come back—in fact, I would argue that in the long sweep of history it is inevitable that it *will* come back, at some time.

Twenty years of Republican administrations have fixed in law the notion that excessive tax rates destroy the incentive to develop the economy. To be honest, that is something the Republicans can be proud of, because they're right: the 90%

tax bracket was a disgrace. It was that kind of thing that undermined the Democratic party.

But it's also *this* kind of thing—$6 million salaries for baseball players—that will eventually bring the 90% tax brackets back to life. Nothing gives energy to the impulse to level society like a few conspicuous examples of naked, unvarnished greed. The real significance of the $6 million baseball salaries—and the attention paid to them—is that they make the concept of confiscatory taxes more acceptable to the public.

The Baseball Book: But not to you?

Senator: But not to me.

The Baseball Book: Let me try this one more time. Do you think it is desirable for an athlete to earn more than a million dollars a year?

Senator: Do I?

The Baseball Book: Do you.

Senator: No, I don't.

The Baseball Book: Does it have any social value for an athlete to earn more than a million dollars a year?

Senator: None.

The Baseball Book: Does it even *really* do the athlete any good? Is there anything you can buy with the second million dollars that you can't buy with the first?

Senator: Nothing you need. Nothing that it does you any good to own.

The Baseball Book: Could we, by simply passing a law, put an end to these salaries?

Senator: We certainly could.

The Baseball Book: So why don't we?

Senator: The policies that we establish for athletes will eventually apply to all of us.

The Baseball Book: We're all going to make a million dollars?

Senator: You might be surprised. Let's say that we establish a confiscatory tax rate—99%—at a million dollars a year. This discourages players from asking for $6 million salaries, which they wouldn't be able to collect anyway.

This, however, isn't the end of the process. Every two or three years Congress has a budget crisis. The government runs out of money, and they start to nibble. They establish a 90% tax rate, starting at $800,000 a year. And then the next time, two years later, they establish an 85% tax group, starting at $400,000 a year.

And at the same time as this is happening, inflation is changing the meaning of the money. Historically, the value of a dollar is cut in half every ten or fifteen years by inflation. Twenty-five years from now, $100,000 a year is going to be a starting salary for a school teacher. So a million dollars a year—that sounds like it has nothing to do with you and me, but it does. If we establish the principle that the government has the right to determine how much money a man is entitled to earn, it is inevitable that that principle will eventually be applied to you and me.

The Baseball Book: I suppose it could happen.

Senator: No, it *will* happen. Not precisely that way, of course, but it will happen. Before you and I retire, the phenomenally progressive tax rates of the 1960s will return.

The Baseball Book: Is it really this easy to change the world?

Senator: It's a life's work to trim the world's fingernails. To make any *real* changes, by oneself, is impossible.

The Baseball Book: The difficulty . . .

Senator: The process. It's easy to think about how the world could be better than it is. What is amazing to me, that being the case, is how much time and energy are devoted to inarticulate battles about the process of change, and how little time is spent thinking about how the world could be better than it is.

The Baseball Book: What's next on your list?

Senator: There's a ballgame tonight.

The Baseball Book: See you at the park.

THE KANSAS CITY ROYALS
• IN A BOX •

1991 Won-Lost Record: 82-80 .506
Rank among 26 teams: 15th
Over Last Five Years: 416-392 .515
Rank over Five Years: 9th
In Last Ten Years: 836-782 .517
Rank over Ten Years: 8th

Best Player: Last year, Danny Tartabull.
The Royals team as it was in 1991 no longer exists, and it's anybody's guess what kind of team they will have in 1992. I'm going to fill in the remaining information here based on the 1991 team, even though that team is now scattered to the four winds.

Weak Spot: Second Base/Shortstop

Best Pitcher: Bret Saberhagen

Staff Weakness: The Royals staff weakness over the last two years has been that they have had to carry two players who were completely unproductive (the two Davises) because they had signed them to large contracts. The Royals *have* good pitchers—good starters, good relievers, good numbers—but they have worked shorthanded for two years because they had two dead spots on the staff.

Best Bench Player: Bill Pecota

Best Baseball Name: Flash Gordon

Best Young Player: Brian McRae

Best Looking Player: Brent Mayne

Ugliest Player: Kirk Gibson works at looking ugly, but isn't. Jim Eisenreich has an odd, stiff look and strange features, but an apparent dignity that saves him. Mike Macfarlane has a pencil neck and a weak chin that make him look odd to me, but women swoon over him and they're the experts. I could pick on Steve Crawford, who looks kind of like a scrubbed-up biker, but the Royals have released him.

Most Pleasant Surprise, 1991: Brent Mayne

Biggest Disappointment, 1991: Kevin Seitzer

Best Minor League Prospect: See article, "Royal Prospects"

Designated Malcontent: Danny Tartabull

Park Characteristics: Royals Stadium was the toughest home run park in the American League until the Indians moved their fences, but it has a fast turf which gives up doubles and triples, making the park neutral in terms of favoring the offense or the defense.

The Park Helps: Brian McRae

The Park Hurts: Kirk Gibson

ORGANIZATIONAL REPORT CARD

Ownership: C
Upper Management: D
Field Management: B+
Front-Line Talent: D
Second-Line Talent: B
Minor League System: D
Comment: See "Ewing Kauffman"

TEAM LEADERS:

Batting Average: Danny Tartabull, .316
Last Ten Years (Season): George Brett, 1985, .335
Last Ten Years (Total): George Brett, .300

Doubles: George Brett, 40

Triples: Brian McRae, 9

Home Runs: Danny Tartabull, 31
Last Ten Years (Season): Steve Balboni, 1985, 36
Last Ten Years (Total): George Brett, 187

RBI: Danny Tartabull, 100
Last Ten Years (Season): George Brett, 1985, 112
Last Ten Years (Total): George Brett, 838

Extra Base Hits: Danny Tartabull, 69

Stolen Bases: Brian McRae, 20

Walks: Kirk Gibson, 69

Runs Created: Danny Tartabull, 116

Runs Created Per Game: Tartabull, 9.0

Secondary Average: Tartabull, .424

Wins: Bret Saberhagen and Kevin Appier, 13 each
Last Ten Years (Season): Bret Saberhagen, 1989, 23
Last Ten Years (Total): Bret Saberhagen, 110

Winning Percentage: Bret Saberhagen, 13-8 .619

Strikeouts: Tom Gordon, 167
Last Ten Years (Season): Bret Saberhagen, 1989, 193
Last Ten Years (Total): Bret Saberhagen, 1093

ERA: Bret Saberhagen, 3.07

Saves: Jeff Montgomery, 33

League Leaders: Tartabull led the AL in slugging percentage with a .593 mark. Mike Boddicker tied for the league lead in hit batters with thirteen.

Stat of the Year: Kevin Seitzer was 11-for-20 as a pinch hitter, a .550 batting average which led the majors by more than a hundred points. In fact, I wonder what the record is for pinch hitting average, ten or more pinch hits.

1991 SEASON

Background: After winning the World Championship in 1985, the Royals got trapped in a cycle of short-term gambles intended to drain one more championship out of the George Brett era.

These gambles pushed them further and further away from contention from 1986 to 1990.

Outlook: The Royals were generally expected to have a better year than 1990, when they finished with only 75 wins. The Oakland A's had been so dominant in the previous years, and the Royals were so far from first place, that few people expected them to be serious contenders.

Getaway: The Royals opened unspectacularly (4-6), muddled along for a while, then lost ten of eleven. On May 8 they were 9-17.

The Royals' manager was John Wathan. There were constant rumors about who would replace him and when. The front office didn't want to fire Wathan, but after a certain point every loss became another argument against him. The Royals didn't fire him even after starting out 9-17—but after that point he was swimming upstream, and only a serious hot streak could have saved his job.

On Monday, May 20, the Royals played one of those games in which they looked like they would never win again. They lost to Seattle, 6-8, blowing a dozen scoring chances and handing out a hundred. They didn't look like they knew what they were doing. They didn't look like they cared. That game, one of the worst I've ever seen, finally sealed Wathan's fate. The Royals began negotiating with Hal McRae a few hours later.

Low Point of the Season: After the hiring of Hal McRae the Royals continued to lose. On June 22 Tom Gordon pitched brilliantly against Baltimore, but lost 1-0 when the Royals were stopped on three hits by the great Bob Milacki.

The Oriole series continued with a double-header on June 23. In the opener the Royals took an 8-4 lead into the ninth, but Chris Hoiles hit a grand slam to tie it, and the Orioles scored three more in the tenth for an 11-8 victory. In the second game the Orioles led 8-3 into the bottom of the ninth. The Royals scored five to tie, 8-8, but lost the game in twelve innings.

At the All-Star break the Royals were 36-44.

High Point of the Season: In last place throughout July, the Royals began to gain gradually on the division leaders. On August 4 they moved out of last place, ahead of the Angels. By August 7 they were 55-51, only eight and a half out of first place. On August 14, at 60-52, they had pulled to five and a half out of first place, fourth place, and were very much a part of the pennant race.

Stretch Drive: The Twins got hot at about that point, and the Royals were essentially eliminated by the end of August. They stumbled through September playing more or less as they had before the All-Star break.

Most Exciting Game of the Season: See article, "June 6"

Major Injuries: On July 15, Mike Macfarlane's left knee was destroyed in a home plate collision with Joe Carter. At the time, Macfarlane was having a Johnny Bench season, offensively and defensively, but the injury effectively ended his season. Brett, Saberhagen and Gubicza each missed a month.

Offense: Not good, but surprisingly productive. They scored more runs than they should have.

Defense: Very Poor

Pitching: Fair

Best Game by a Starting Pitcher: Bret Saberhagen had two tremendous games in August, August 4 against Cleveland (9 3 0 0 0 9 Game Score: 90) and a no-hitter against Chicago August 26 (9 0 0 0 2 5 Game Score: 90).

Worst Game by a Starting Pitcher: Tom Gordon, June 8 vs. Chicago ($4\frac{2}{3}$ 10 10 10 2 4 Game Score: 6)

Indicators for 1991 were: Up 19.7

Number of regulars having good seasons by their own standards: Three

1991 Over-Achiever: Tartabull

1991 Under-Achiever: Brett

Infield: The Royals infield in 1991 was probably the worst in the major leagues. George Brett was injured and moved off of first base, abandoning the position to Carmelo Martinez, who was terrible. Martinez was traded for Todd Benzinger, who played at an MVP level for three weeks, and then went back to being Todd Benzinger. At second base they had OK defense but no offense (Shumpert) and at third base and short they had disappointing offense and no defense.

Outfield: The Royals' outfield was reasonably productive at bat but weak defensively. McRae scored 86 runs, Gibson 81 and Tartabull 78; you can do worse. But only McRae can actually play the outfield.

Catching: The strongest element of their team, with Mike Macfarlane playing brilliantly the first half of the season, and Brent Mayne playing well enough the second half.

Starting Pitching: Didn't live up to advance notices. Two starters were good (Appier and Saberhagen), one was fair (Boddicker) and Gubicza, coming back from an injury, struggled.

Bullpen: Fairly good, thin because of the need to carry the two Davises. Montgomery pitched extremely well except for one sinking spell. Aquino, Gordon and Magnante provided decent support.

Percentage of offense created by:
Young Players: 24%
Players in Their Prime: 35%
Past Their Prime: 41%

Team Age:
Age of Non-Pitchers: 29.2
Age of Pitching Staff: 27.5
Overall Team Age: 28.52

In retrospect, the critical decisions were: On July 6, the last game before the break, McRae replaced Seitzer and Stillwell with Pecota and Howard. This wasn't the most critical decision of the year, but it was the most interesting, the most hotly debated. You'd have a hard time proving the latter two are better players than the men they replaced, but the Royals did play better ball the second half.

THAT AND THE OTHER

Lookalikes: Jim Eisenreich and Honus Wagner

Hall of Fame Watch: Brett, of course, is as good as in. Saberhagen has about 50% of a Hall of Fame career—two Cy Young seasons, a big World Series.

Chris Berman, Have You Considered: The Deaf Frenchman

Throwback: George Brett

Attendance Trend: Slightly downward. The Royals 1991 attendance of 2.16 million was their lowest in several years.

Players with a Chance for 3000 career hits: George Brett, 97%

Record Watch: Brett is 10th on the all-time doubles list, and should pass Paul Waner and Hank Aaron this summer.

Best Interview: Hal McRae

Best Fundamental Player: Bill Pecota, by far

Worst Fundamental Player: In 1991, Danny Tartabull, by far

Best Defensive Player: Brian McRae

Worst Defensive Player: The 1991 Royals were a pretty bad defensive team. Tartabull was the worst, but with him gone the distinction would probably pass to Kurt Stillwell, who is probably gone, too. That would leave Kevin Seitzer next in line if he's still here, and then there's Kirk Gibson, who hustles and makes some fine plays, but can't throw and often has trouble reading the ball.

Best Knowledge of the Strike Zone: Bill Pecota

Least Command of the Strike Zone: Brian McRae

Fastest Runner: McRae

Slowest Runner: George Brett

Best Baserunner: Bill Pecota

Most Likely to Still be Here in 2000: Brian McRae

Best Fastball: Saberhagen

Best Breaking Pitch: Tom Gordon

Best Control: Saberhagen

Most Underrated Player: Luis Aquino

Oddest Collection of Abilities: Kevin Seitzer

Manager's Pet Strategy:

1. Bringing the infield in for a play at the plate in the second inning.
2. Issuing an intentional walk to load the bases.

As an in-game manager there appears to be very little difference between McRae and the man before him, John Wathan.

Why is this man in the Major Leagues: Mark Davis

Gets Ahead of the Hitters Most Often: Saberhagen

Gets Ahead of the Hitters Least Often: Mark Davis

Best Local Sportswriter: Jack Etkin, but I'm prejudiced

The Most Knowledgeable People About Local Baseball History Are:

1. Bill Carle
2. Hal Dellinger

Most-Similar Players:

to C Mike Macfarlane, Pat Borders
to 1B Wally Joyner, John Kruk
to 2B Terry Shumpert, Mark Lemke
to 3B Bill Pecota, Casey Candaele
to SS Kurt Stillwell, Luis Rivera
to LF Kirk Gibson, Hubie Brooks
to CF Brian McRae, Ray Lankford
to RF Danny Tartabull, Kevin Mitchell

Most Fun to Watch:

1. Brian McRae
2. Bill Pecota
3. Brent Mayne
4. Terry Shumpert

Least Fun to Watch: Kurt Stillwell

Managerial Type: Pecota

Among the All-Time Team Leaders:

George Brett is, of course, by far the best player in Kansas City baseball history, and holds almost all of the team records.

Town Team:

C—Johnny Kling
1B—George Stovall
2B—Frank White
SS—Joe Tinker
3B—Ken Boyer
LF—Fred Clarke
CF—Bob Allison
RF—Zack Wheat
SP—Walter Johnson
MGR—Casey Stengel

Post-Season Transactions:

December 9, Signed Free Agent Wally Joyner

December 11, Traded Bret Saberhagen and Bill Pecota to the Mets for Gregg Jefferies, Kevin McReynolds and Keith Miller

December 11, Traded Storm Davis to Orioles for Bob Melvin

December 11, Traded Todd Benzinger for Chris Gwynn and Domingo Mota

What Needs to Be Done For 1992: See "Lost Generation"

Index of Leading Indicators for 1992: Down 6.8

Positive Indicators: 1. Played better late in the season

Negative Indicators: 1. Team Age
2. Plexiglas Principle

Due for a better season: Mark Gubicza

Likely to have a worse season: Mike Macfarlane

1992 Won-Lost Record will be: 77-85

THE LOST GENERATION

Sitting in the stands in the opening days of the 1989 season, I had the odd realization that anyone on the field for the Royals could potentially be a Hall of Famer. This is spring logic, of course, more desire than memory, yet as I look back on it I cannot see where I was wrong. Catching was Bob Boone, whose career is close to Hall of Fame standards, and who may well reach that place. At first base was George Brett, virtually a certain Hall of Famer. At second was Frank White. White had hit 61 home runs from 1985 to 1987; had he been able to come back with one or two more strong seasons, his Hall of Fame argument would have been strong. He didn't, but even so there are some people who feel he had a Hall of Fame career, and it is not inconceivable that he might one day stand on that platform.

At third base was Kevin Seitzer, who at that time had never failed to hit .300 in professional baseball. Twenty-six years old, he had a lifetime .315 batting average through two-plus years. At short was Kurt Stillwell, one of the more problematic Hall of Fame cases, to be sure, but not nearly so much as you might think. Just 23 years old, Stillwell was coming off a very creditable 1988 season (28 doubles, 10 homers, .251). *Baseball America* said he had the best arm of any American League infielder. Make a list of all the players in history who

a) establish themselves as major league regulars by the age of 22,
b) can play shortstop, and
c) have some pop in their bats.

You'll find that in the first place there *aren't* very many of them, and in the second place, a significant portion of those that there are go on to Hall of Fame careers. At 23, he didn't look very much different from a 23-year-old Alan Trammel or Dave Concepcion.

In left field was Bo Jackson, with his awesome un-connected skills, and the almost unshakable perception of unlimited potential, all newer then. In center field was Willie Wilson, a lifetime .292 hitter, a batting champion, the holder or co-holder of numerous major league records (at bats, season; stolen base percentage, career; hits, switch hitter, season). In a clear pattern of decline, he needed to snap back to form to have any chance, but it seemed possible. He had talked through spring training about taking more pitches, drawing more walks. Then 33 years old, he had almost 1800 career hits.

And in right was Tartabull, 25 years old and with three major league seasons behind him. In the first he had driven in 96 runs despite a mid-season illness. In the second he had hit .309 with 34 homers and 101 RBI. In the third he had driven in 102 runs.

What happened, of course, is that *all* of their chances took a turn for the worse over the next three years, all except Brett. Of the four young players who might have developed into stars—Seitzer, Stillwell, Jackson and Tartabull—three saw their careers degenerate with the implacable steadiness of Arnold Schwarzenegger pursuing a target, and the fourth (Tartabull) failed to overcome his early weaknesses.

One of my favorite things, and I can't tell you why I like this, is to watch the development of team records, all-time records. In their first fifteen years the Royals were an absolute delight for this indulgence. By 1989 the Royals' career leader boards, starting in 1969, were already more impressive than those of some of the teams which had been around since 1901. The Cleveland Indians' all-time leader in games played is Terry Turner, with 1,617. On the Royals' list that number would stand in sixth place, behind Brett, White, Otis, McRae Sr. and Willie Wilson. Comparing them in 1989, all of the Royals' records except career batting average and slugging percentage were already beyond Cleveland's, generally far beyond.

In early 1989 one could see the next wave coming up behind them—Seitzer, Stillwell, Jackson, Tartabull. Young players, good players; one could see them taking their place on the bottom of the Royals list and mounting up, until in another ten years the Royals' team batting lists could have been the third-most impressive in the American League, better than any team except Detroit or the Yankees.

Well, of course, it didn't happen. The four veterans faded at the pace of old players; the young players wilted beside them as if October had arrived in June. Jackson, Seitzer, Stillwell, Tartabull . . . none ever took a step forward. An entire generation of young Royals passed away with hardly a mark or memory.

The Royals now must face the fact that after four years of re-building they have nothing going for them; they are at the *beginning* of a re-building cycle, not the middle nor the end. And that is what will be hard for them and for their fans—to accept that what is gone, is gone. It looked good, but it didn't work, and nothing now can be saved from it. While anyone may be a year away from a miracle, they must face the fact that they are not a year away from having a good team, but three years. They need to face the fact that *they need to start over*. The trade of Saberhagen for Jefferies may be the first sign that the organization has reached that point.

EWING KAUFFMAN

At one time Ewing Kauffman was as good an owner as any major league team ever had. Kauffman did four things for the Royals, which propelled them to tremendous success in their first seventeen seasons:

1) He provided the money that the organization needed to pursue its goals.

2) He established for the organization an expectation of excellence. Without being Steinbrenner, he accomplished for the Royals what George Steinbrenner did for the Yankees in his early years: he conveyed the message that he *expected* first-rate performance.

3) He surrounded himself with quality baseball people, and allowed the baseball people to make the decisions. The high-level front-office people built up the lower levels of the organization.

4) He was *innovative* and *flexible* in trying to push the organization to excellence, focusing the organization on long-term goals and getting people to try new and different things to reach those goals.

As the organization has matured, and in the wake of his unhappy partnership with Avron Fogelman, three of these elements have been lost. To Kauffman's credit, he *has* continued to provide the organization with the financial support that they need. While other so-called "small markets" have whined about TV revenues and the impossibility of competing in a small market, Kauffman has continued to lay out whatever funds were needed to stay in the game, and has never forced the Royals' management to operate on a shoestring.

But that's it. The rest of it has gotten away from him.

2) Kauffman, who once insisted on excellence, has tolerated mediocrity, and accepted excuses for years of under-achievement.

3) The quality of the help has declined from bottom to top, and Kauffman, out of loyalty to men who by now he has known for twenty years, has failed to clean house and start over. The Royals' scouting department, one of the best in baseball from 1969 through 1982, has been gutted by retirements and defections, and the Royals have failed to rebuild it.

4) The Royals' *goals* since 1982 have become short-term and limited, and in consequence of that their approach, which was once so innovative and open, has become narrow and focused. Every year they sign a free agent and expect a better year next year, and when it doesn't happen they back up the next year and sign another one.

In my opinion there should be a support group for teams like the Royals called "Free Agents Anonymous", where guys could go and stand up and say "Hi. My name is Herk and I haven't signed a free agent in almost two months." The problem is that baseball teams get *immediate positive feedback* by signing free agents. The fans are happy right away, the call-in shows jingle, you may even sell a few tickets. For two weeks people treat you as if you were a successful person and had actually *accomplished* something, had actually "won" something, because you "won" the battle for Wally Joyner or the battle for Mark Davis or the battle to be the idiot who signs Storm Davis's checks for the next three years. The down side of the deal doesn't arrive until several months later.

Anyway, the Royals have a new General Manager now, their old GM having moved on to Atlanta and become a genius. I always figure a new man deserves the opportunity to make his own mistakes, rather than being criticized for the mistakes he inherited. The new man is Herk Robinson—a nicer man than Schuerholz, less arrogant. The fact that his background is in non-personnel areas doesn't really bother me, because the best GM the Royals ever had was Cedric Tallis, and he had about the same background. Robinson's mid-winter moves—the signing of Joyner, his first big trade—were good moves. The selection of Hal McRae as a manager is hard to fault. Schuerholz and Fogelman dragged Ewing Kauffman away from his roots, and got the organization away from the things they had done well. Perhaps Robinson can learn from history, and take Ewing Kauffman back to the pinnacle from which he has fallen.

ROYAL TRANSACTIONS

In four days in December, the Royals restructured their team so that only two regulars who were playing regularly at the end of the 1991 season (Brian McRae and George Brett) seem a good bet to return as regulars in 1992. This began with the signing of Wally Joyner on December 9.

The signing of Joyner was an opportunity that the Royals saw to be too good to pass up. Joyner, to his own surprise and disappointment, found the market for his services limited, and made the decision to sign a one-year deal and try to improve his value. Facing the loss of their best hitter to free agency, the Royals saw a chance to control the criticism and control the economic risk at the same time. They also needed a first baseman.

There is every reason to believe that Joyner will help the Royals. This made Todd Benzinger expendable, and Benzinger was traded to the Dodgers for Chris Gwynn, who was declared the starting right fielder.

Then the big trade, Saberhagen to the Mets for Gregg Jefferies, Kevin McReynolds and Keith Miller. This trade was initiated and pursued by the Royals, and was a trade to which the Mets, having signed two free agents to reduce their need for bodies, eventually acquiesced.

For most of my life, I am utterly puzzled by how it is that I am able to make a living doing what I do. There are only occasional moments when I understand why it is that I am able to make a living writing baseball books. One of those epiphanies occurred on the morning of December 13, when a local sports columnist wrote, as an off-hand, everybody-in-the-know-knows-this type of comment, that the key player acquired by the Royals was Kevin McReynolds.

Of course this represents incredible ignorance for a professional sports writer, but then that's what I was saying: I am so lucky as to be able to do this, I occasionally realize, because a great deal of my competition is incredibly ignorant. McReynolds is 32 years old, and coming off a poor season. It is unlikely that he will ever have another good year.

The Royals announced at the time of the trade that their scouts all thought that McReynolds had "several good years left", which is what you would expect them to say. As I said, it is in fact unlikely that McReynolds has any good years left, and *extremely* unlikely that he has more than one good year left. I ran a short "Kevin McReynolds study", looking for information on that question. What I did was, I looked for the major league players who were most comparable to Kevin McReynolds *two years ago*. In other words, who was exactly where Kevin McReynolds is *now* two years ago?

The players who were most nearly where McReynolds is now two years ago were Hubie Brooks, Gary Gaetti, Tim Wallach and Peter O'Brien. This chart compares McReynolds to Gary Gaetti, who I think is really the most comparable player:

Kevin McReynolds Now
Age 32

Year	G	AB	Run	H	2B	3B	HR	RBI	SB	Avg
1989	148	545	74	148	25	3	22	74	15	.272
1990	147	521	75	140	23	1	24	75	9	.269
1991	143	522	65	135	32	1	16	65	6	.259
Life	1232	4519	615	1215	226	29	183	695	82	.269

Gary Gaetti Then
Age 31

Year	G	AB	Run	H	2B	3B	HR	RBI	SB	Avg
1987	154	584	95	150	36	2	31	109	10	.257
1988	133	468	66	141	29	2	28	88	7	.301
1989	130	498	63	125	11	4	19	75	6	.251
Life	1207	4412	585	1144	225	20	185	673	68	.259

Wallach and O'Brien are almost equally comparable.

What you have in Gaetti, Brooks, O'Brien and Wallach, of course, is four guys who haven't done doodly over the last two years. Wallach had a good year in 1990, and that's it; one good year, seven bad ones. What you have in these players is four guys about whom for two years their announcers have been saying that he was only 32 so he was sure to start hitting again pretty soon. Every time Gary Gaetti or Pete O'Brien has appeared on ESPN for two years the announcer has said something like "he's struggling with the bat again this year. I don't know what's happened to him. He's still young and he's always been a good hitter, but he just hasn't been able to get it going with the bat for the last couple of years." The other guys who were most comparable to McReynolds were basically the same—Tom Brunansky, Jesse Barfield. That's exactly what people are going to be saying about Kevin McReynolds in 1992 and 1993: he's stopped hitting, and we don't know why. What these people don't understand is that when a player like this stops hitting at age 31, that's not the exception, *that's the rule*. Players like McReynolds stop hitting enough to justify their salaries when they're 31; the ones who *don't* stop hitting are the exceptions. These guys think it isn't a big deal whether a player is 31 or 29, but they're dead wrong—it *is* a big deal.

I have a count here, of the number of major league players playing regularly at each age. "Regularly" just means 100 games or 250 at bats; it's not too demanding. Here's the 1991 count:

Age 30: 31
Age 31: 16
Age 32: 14
Age 33: 9
Age 34: 8

What's that tell you? What that tells you is that half of the major league players who are 30 years old now are going to be out of a job in two years. And of the half that stay, half of those are going to be out of a job in two more years.

And if you carried it out two more years, half of those would be gone; at age 36 the count is 3.

And it *ain't* hard to figure out which half is which. The half which are good, stay. The other half goes. The guys who create six runs a game, they slip down to creating five runs a game, so they're fine. The guys who create five runs a game, they slip to creating four, so they're marginal; if their defense is good and somebody likes them, they'll stay. If not, the team can find somebody else just as good. But the guys who create four runs a game—they're out of here.

Further, McReynolds is probably the steadiest, most consistent player of our generation. He has never had a year when he didn't do what he was capable of doing. His slugging percentages since 1986 are .504, .495, .496, .450, .455 and .416—a clear and constant pattern of decline, *as is normal for a player of his age*, although usually with less consistency.

So when a player is 31 years old *and* has always been consistent *and* takes another step toward mediocrity at age 31, why in the world would you think that the year was just an aberration? It doesn't make sense. It wasn't an aberration for Pete O'Brien, it wasn't an aberration for Gary Gaetti, it wasn't an aberration for Jesse Barfield, and it isn't an aberration for Kevin McReynolds.

Kevin McReynolds is 32—turned 32 during the World Serious. He has already *proven* that he is in the "good" half; he's already survived the first cut. He created 5.5 runs a game, slipped to 4.5, he's survived. He *may* survive the next cut—in the way that Hubie Brooks did—that is, that by age 34 his productivity has not completely extinguished his playing time. He's going to hit .260 this year with 12 homers and 73 RBI, so he *may* not be out of a job by 1994. I wouldn't bet on even that much, but if he is playing at all by then, he'll be horseshit. Because if he wasn't horseshit at 34, he'd still be playing at 36, and the only guys in his age group who are still going to be playing at 36 are Cal Ripken and Ryne Sandberg and Kirby Puckett and one or two others.

So anyway, McReynolds is basically a throw-away at this point in his career, a player who isn't good enough to play regularly for the Mets anymore, so they've just dumped him and the Royals figure he's worth taking a chance on. There is always the *chance* that he'll be challenged by the trade, lose some weight, hit the weights and come back to have a good year in 1992. In my opinion he is too slow to play the outfield on artificial turf, even if he does. The trade is essentially Bret Saberhagen for Gregg Jefferies.

The Kansas City fans hated the trade. Emotionally, I hated the trade. Saberhagen was fun, and in the last few years he has been, at times, the only good thing on the team. The fan reaction was that the Royals have finally done it: they've gotten rid of the only good player on the team.

But as the emotions fade, I see the logic of it, and I have to say honestly that if this was a Strat-O-Matic league and I had Bret Saberhagen and could trade him for Gregg Jefferies, I'd do it in a heartbeat.

In structure, the trade is almost identical to one of the best trades ever made: Ernie Broglio for Lou Brock. Saberhagen is now essentially what Broglio was then, a quality pitcher with a tendency to bounce up and down. Broglio in 1963 was 18-8, 2.99 ERA, 27 years old. That wasn't his best season; in 1960 he had gone 21-9, 2.75 ERA. In between (1961–62) he hadn't been too good. That's Bret Saberhagen.

Lou Brock, at the time of that trade, was a young player who had always been regarded as having great potential, but whose production had been disappointing. He hadn't been *bad*, he just hadn't been as *good* as he was supposed to be. The Cubs had asked him to play center field, and he couldn't do that, so he was regarded as a butcher in the field and a disappointment with the bat. We gave him two-plus years to hit, he hasn't hit, let's give up on him—and that's exactly what Gregg Jefferies is now.

What Jefferies has hit for the Mets *isn't* bad—in fact, it's damn good for a player of his age. He was 24 last August. Most guys at that age are just getting to the majors. Only three or four players in Jefferies' age group have done more than he has (Ken Griffey, Frank Thomas, Roberto Alomar and arguably Juan Gonzalez.) He'll do better than that in Kansas City because:

a) it's a better hitter's park,
b) he will mature as a hitter, and
c) he desperately needed to get away from the Shea circus.

There may be a (d) and an (e) there, too. (D) is Hal McRae, probably the game's best hitting coach. (E) is that the Royals *may* have sense enough to find a defensive position he can handle, and leave him alone. Put it all together, and there's very little doubt that Jefferies is going to give the Royals better years than he gave the Mets.

Will he do as well as Brock did for St. Louis? I wouldn't bet against it. He doesn't *have* to do that; he doesn't *have* to be a Hall of Famer. I love Bret Saberhagen, but he's 18-17 over the last two seasons. To get Gregg Jefferies for Bret Saberhagen, at this point in their careers, is a hell of trade.

ROYAL PROSPECTS

The Royals in the Schuerholz administration liked to sign *athletes*, rather than *baseball players*. The Royals for years would sign somebody like Hugh Walker or Anthony Clements, and announce that he was a great athlete and they were going to teach him to hit. Of course you can't teach anybody to hit, and this was just organizational arrogance, but as a consequence of this and the lack of top-quality scouts, the Royals over the last ten years have produced very few position players.

They have finally broken with this practice, and begun to sign baseball players, rather than athletes. Brent Mayne, the number one selection in 1989, is already in the majors. **Joe Vitiello**, the number one pick of 1991, is an outfielder/first baseman, believed to be a hitting prospect.

The Royals top two prospects of recent years, **Jeff Conine** and **Bob Hamelin**, have been slowed to a crawl by injuries, and are both borderline prospects at this point. Both are first basemen.

A better prospect now is **Joel Johnston**, a big right-handed relief pitcher who was a third-round draft pick in 1988. His career didn't seem to be going anywhere because of serious control troubles, like a walk an inning. He began to get ahead of the hitters at mid-season in Omaha, then pitched brilliantly in 13 games with the parent club in September (0.40 ERA).

Two others who stand out are **Phil Hiatt** and **Joe Randa**. Both re third basemen and both spent last summer in A ball. The couts rave about Hiatt, but Randa is a better hitter at this point.

Harvey Pulliam, who played a few games last year, is a good thlete and a decent hitting prospect, although not as good as his 991 major league stats might make you think. I'd compare him hysically to Ron Jones of Philadelphia.

I COULDN'T HAVE SAID IT BETTER MYSELF

Royals' General Manager Herk Robinson, reflecting on the re-tructured team after the winter meetings:

"We're solid at every position, even though some of those ositions may be in question."

JUNE 6

t was a weekday afternoon. The Royals had been experimenting with the schedule, playing an occasional afternoon game with the world at work, just to see if it would draw. On this afternoon Nolan Ryan was scheduled to pitch against Bret Saberhagen. Susie and I quit work early and headed to the game, but half of he country seemed to have the same idea, resulting in a massive raffic jam. They parked us in a parking lot that I didn't even know existed, out behind a highway somewhere. I paid $30 to a scalper for two tickets. We didn't get there until the third inning, just in time to see the last 15 and a half innings.

Saberhagen and Ryan were fine but gone by 4 o'clock. Carmelo Martinez, in a terrible slump and booed every time he moved, which fortunately wasn't very often, hit a solo home run in the ninth to send it into extra innings. Everything happened at least twice in extra innings. Twice the Royals loaded the bases with none out, but failed to score. Twice Kevin Reimer set up Royal innings by misplaying balls in left field. Twice the Rangers tried to win it with a suicide squeeze, and twice failed. Twice Ruben Sierra kept the game alive with fabulous throws to the plate, once to hold a runner and once to nail him.

The Royals in the game were 2 for 19 with men in scoring position; Texas was 2 for 15. Ruben Sierra, who came into the game with the longest hitting streak in the majors, failed in nine trips to the plate to extend it. The two teams left 45 men on base in the game, tying a major league record. Twice the Royals tried to make a play at third on a ball hit to the mound, and twice failed, bringing McRae from the dugout. The second time he complained so bitterly that he was ejected from the game for the first time in his brief career, fined and suspended for three games for bumping an ump. Three times Susie called the baby sitter, explaining that the game was running long but we would be home in an hour or so.

The Royals eventually won it, 4-3 in 18 innings, on a wild throw to third base. It was the second time in extra innings that the Rangers had tried unsuccessfully to make a play at third on a bunt. The Rangers had walked thirteen men in extra innings. One of them had to score eventually.

THE CALIFORNIA ANGELS
• IN A BOX •

1991 Won-Lost Record: 81-81 .500

Rank among 26 teams: 16th

The 1991 Angels, as you probably know, had the best record of any last-place team in history, 81-81.

Last year 11 of the 14 American League teams were at .500 or better. This is not as improbable as you might think. Over time more teams play .500 or better ball than .500 or less ball. There often is, as there was in 1991, a cluster of teams with records a little bit above .500.

If eleven of fourteen teams in a league are at .500 or better, the chance that one entire (seven-team) division will be at .500 or better is 19%.

Over Last Five Years: 402-408 .496
Rank over Five Years: 15th
In Last Ten Years: 828-792 .511
Rank over Ten Years: 10th

Best Player: With the loss of Wally Joyner no one stands out

Weak Spot: Middle Infield

Best Pitcher: Chuck Finley

Staff Weakness: Kirk McCaskill

Best Bench Player: It was Dave Gallagher, now with the Mets

Best Baseball Name: Jim Abbott, but only if the Angels pick up John Costello.

Best Young Player: Polonia, I suppose. The Angels don't really have a player who is both good and young.

Best Looking Player: Chuck Finley

Ugliest Player: Gary Gaetti

Most Pleasant Surprise, 1991: Mark Eichorn

Biggest Disappointment, 1991: Dave Parker

Best Minor League Prospect: Troy Percival

Who Is: A right-handed starting pitcher. The Angels' sixth round draft pick last June, Percival struck out 63 Northwest League batters in only 38 innings.

Other Prospects: **Don Barbara**, a left-handed hitting first baseman, hit .362 for Midland last year, hitting ten homers in 63 games. He was a 24th round draft pick in 1990, but has come on strong. **Lee Stevens**, now 24, is also a first baseman, and also a great big guy, as is Barbara. In the past I have been skeptical about Stevens' abilities as a hitter. However, he has made very signif cant progress, and I now believe he could hit .270-.280 with som power.

Designated Malcontent: Junior Felix

Park Characteristics: The Big A is a good home run park particularly at night, when for some reason the ball seems t travel better. However, the outfield area is small, and with a gras field the park sharply reduces the number of doubles and triple hit, triples by 40%. Also, the visibility here is poor, so strikeout are up. On balance, the park is better for a pitcher than for hitter.

The Park Helps: Power pitchers—Finley, Abbott, Langstor Harvey.

The Park Hurts: Line drive hitters.

Over the last six years the Angels have had a homefield advar tage of only three games per year. This is the second-smalles home field advantage in the American League.

ORGANIZATIONAL REPORT CARD

Ownership:	B
Upper Management:	B
Field Management:	A−
Front-Line Talent:	C
Second-Line Talent:	C
Minor League System:	C

TEAM LEADERS:

Batting Average: Wally Joyner, .301

Last Ten Years (Season): Rod Carew, 1983, .339
Last Ten Years (Total): Rod Carew, .310

Doubles: Wally Joyner, 34

Triples: Luis Polonia, 8

Home Runs: Dave Winfield, 28

Last Ten Years (Season): Reggie Jackson, 1982, 39
Last Ten Years (Total): Brian Downing, 192

RBI: Wally Joyner, 96

Last Ten Years (Season): Wally Joyner, 1987, 117
Last Ten Years (Total): Downing, 659

Extra Base Hits: Dave Winfield, 59

Stolen Bases: Luis Polonia, 48

Walks: Dave Winfield, 56

Runs Created: Wally Joyner, 98

Runs Created Per Game: Joyner, 6.6

Secondary Average: Dave Winfield, .320

Wins: Mark Langston, 19

Last Ten Years (Season): Mark Langston, 1991, 19
Last Ten Years (Total): Mike Witt, 101

Winning Percentage: Mark Langston, 19-8 .704

Strikeouts: Langston, 183

Last Ten Years (Season): Mike Witt, 1986, 208
Last Ten Years (Total): Witt, 1208

ERA: Jim Abbott, 2.89

Saves: Bryan Harvey, 46

League Leaders:

1. Mark Eichorn led the American League in Holds, 25, and
2. Bryan Harvey led in Saves, 46.

Stat of the Year: Jim Abbott, who was 18-11 last year, led the majors in tough losses, with eight. Combining the games of April 17, April 22, June 8, July 6, July 13, August 2, September 13 and September 24, Abbott was 0-8 although he pitched an average of almost eight innings per start with an ERA of 2.97.

1991 SEASON

Background: Throughout their history the Angels have neglected the fundamentals of solid team construction, and opted to build by composites of players in mid-career. Their "teams", using the term loosely, have tended to be nothing more than one or two good players, surrounded by collections of once-outstanding players hanging on for a few more paychecks. With star players but no organizational fundamentals and no long-term commitment, they generate perpetually high expectations with over-rated, fading stars, and fire their managers every couple of years for failing to deliver.

The Angels hired Gene Mauch in 1981 and again in 1985, and for a while Mauch was able to lift them above their perpetual mediocrity, winning 90 games with the Angels in 1982, 1985 and 1986. But Mauch resigned after an off season in 1987, and the Angels have lapsed into the pattern which has characterized them since 1962.

Outlook: Most projections for the Angels a year ago were for another year of fair-to-middling performance.

Getaway: The Angels won five of their first six games, all at home, but cancelled the gains immediately when the home stand was over. The Angels were 10-10 on April 30, 16-16 on May 14.

High Point of the Season: The Angels pulled five games over .500 in late May, went 15-12 in June and won their first three in July. On July 3 they beat the Royals to take over first place in the AL West, a single percentage point ahead of Minnesota on the morning of the fourth of July.

Low Point of the Season: On the fourth of July the Royals beat them 12-5. Flying to Texas, the Angels lost 8-0, 4-3 and 7-0. Back home to face the Yankees, the Angels scored one run in three games, losing 2-0, 2-1 and 2-0. By July 13 the Angels had dropped to fifth place.

Stretch Drive: The Angels never got hot enough again to get back in the race. After reaching .500 on August 4 the Angels never got more than a few games above or below the break-even mark, with the top of the division gradually sliding out of reach.

Major Injuries: Junior Felix, acquired in mid-winter in a trade with the Blue Jays, was troubled most of the year by a calf muscle, and played only 66 games.

Offense: Very weak. The Angels' secondary offensive skills—the things they do *other* than hit singles—are extremely limited. Four California regulars or near-regulars had secondary averages below .200—Gary Gaetti (.198), Dick Schofield (.171), Dave Gallagher (.170) and Luis Sojo (.118). Three of those also didn't hit much for *average*, so that leaves three pretty big holes in the offense.

It's also hard to see what the mid-winter acquisitions will do to improve this. Von Hayes does have good secondary offensive skills (career secondary average of .338), but he's 33 years old, and he will replace one of the two Angels of 1991 who *did* put some runs on the scoreboard (Joyner or Winfield). Hubie Brooks could help a little in a platoon role, but he's not going to substantially change the offense.

Defense: Very ordinary. Parrish still throws extremely well but he can't get out of his own way. No other projected regular is significantly better than average defensively.

Pitching: See article, "Angel Arms"

Best Game by a Starting Pitcher: Chuck Finley pitched a two-hitter against Minnesota on April 19, beating them 2-0 (9 2 0 0 2 9 Game Score 90)

Worst Game by a Starting Pitcher: In mid-June the Angels had two awful games, one by Chuck Finley on June 15

(0⅔ 6 7 7 3 1 Game Score 10) and one by Joe Grahe on June 18 (0 5 7 7 2 0 Game Score Also 10).

Indicators for 1991 were: +8.8

Number of regulars having good seasons by their own standards: Two (Joyner and Gallagher. You can argue for Polonia.)

1991 Over-Achiever: Gallagher

1991 Under-Achiever: Gaetti

Infield: Poor. Without Joyner first base is in the hands of Hayes or Stevens, either of whom is alright but unexciting. The keystone combination of Sojo and Schofield is fair to good defensively, doesn't do anything to put runs on the scoreboard. Gaetti is still trying to spit out one more good year.

Outfield: Fair to poor. The Angels have released Dave Winfield, apparently counting on a free agent to replace him. To this point the free agent hasn't signed, and the Angels' only outfielder who can hit is Luis Polonia, a good singles hitter with no arm.

Catching: Poor. Parrish still hits for power, but he's a .216 hitter, the slowest runner in the league and strikes out three times as much as he walks. He's backed by Orton, who can't play at all, and Ron Tingley, a 33-year-old career minor leaguer.

Starting Pitching: Brilliant

Bullpen: Outstanding.

Percentage of offense created by:

Young Players:	24%
Players in Their Prime:	36%
Past Their Prime:	40%

Team Age:

Age of Non-Pitchers:	30.7
Age of Pitchers:	27.4
Overall Team Age:	29.34

THAT AND THE OTHER

Lookalikes: Gary Gaetti and Mike Scioscia

Hall of Fame Watch: No Angel now on the roster is a good candidate for the Hall of Fame. Any of the three top starters (Langston, Abbott and Finley) could emerge as a Hall of Fame candidate, but none of the three has done enough yet to be thought of in that way.

Trivia Time: Based on 100 games or more, who is the Angels' all-time ERA leader?

Throwback: Gary Gaetti

Attendance Trend: Fading. Angels attendance is off ten percent since 1986.

Players with a Chance for 3000 career hits: Luis Polonia 3%

Best Interview: Jim Abbott

Best Fundamental Player: Gaetti

Worst Fundamental Player: Polonia

Best Defensive Player: Parrish

Worst Defensive Player: Polonia

Best Knowledge of the Strike Zone: Wally Joyner

Least Command of the Strike Zone: Gaetti or Parrish

Fastest Runner: Luis Polonia

Slowest Runner: Lance Parrish

Best Baserunner: Dick Schofield

Most Likely to Still be Here in 2000: Jim Abbott

Best Fastball: Langston or Harvey

Best Breaking Pitch: Jim Abbott

Best Control: Mark Eichorn

Trivia Answer: The Angels' career ERA leader is a short reliever, but it's not Bryan Harvey. Bob Lee, who had three excellent years in the mid-sixties, had a career ERA (with the Angels) of 1.99.

Most Overrated Player: Gary Gaetti

Most Underrated Player: Mark Eichorn

Manager's Pet Strategy: Rodgers will occasionally hit and run with the bases loaded.

Why is this man in the Major Leagues: John Orton

Gets Ahead of the Hitters Most Often: Bryan Harvey

Gets Ahead of the Hitters Least Often: Mike Fetters

Most-Similar Players:

to C Lance Parrish, Gary Carter
to 1B Wally Joyner, Ivan Calderon
to 2B Luis Sojo, Mickey Morandini
to 3B Gary Gaetti, Tim Wallach
to SS Dick Schofield, Spike Owen
to LF Luis Polonia, Dave Martinez
to CF Dave Gallagher, Lance Johnson
to RF Dave Winfield, Dwight Evans

Most Fun to Watch: Jim Abbott

Least Fun to Watch: Dick Schofield

Managerial Type: Ron Tingley

Among the All-Time Team Leaders: **Wally Joyner**, now with Kansas City, had worked his way up to seventh on the Angels' list of career games played (846), and was among the leaders in almost everything else. His career batting average, .288, is third-best in California history, behind Rod Carew and Johnny Ray. With his departure the only Angel regular among the team leaders is **Dick Schofield**, who is fourth in games played and lower in everything else.

Among pitchers, **Kirk McCaskill** is fourth in career wins, with 78, and **Chuck Finley** is closing fast behind him (66). **Bryan Harvey** holds the franchise record for career saves (113).

Town Team:

C—Earl Battey
1B—Cecil Fielder
2B—Joe Gordon
SS—Tim Foli
3B—George Brett
LF—Barry Bonds
CF—Len Dykstra
RF—Bobby Bonds
SP—Bob Lemon

Post-Season Transactions:

October 24, released/disposed of Jeff Robinson, Kent Anderson and Barry Lyons

November 14, re-signed Scott Bailes for one year

December 8, traded Kyle Abbott and Ruben Amaro Junior to Phillies for Von Hayes

December 9, Wally Joyner signed with Royals

December 10, traded Dave Gallagher to the Mets for Hubie Brooks

December 10, sent Mike Fetters and a minor league pitcher to the Brewers in exchange for Chuck Crim

What Needs to Be Done For 1992:

To convert a roster laden with over-age, over-paid, under-motivated has-beens into a vibrant, vital ballclub may not be an overnight undertaking. Herzog, at this writing, has already pushed out of the nest Dave Winfield and Dave Parker, and others are sure to follow—Gaetti, Parrish, Venable. The Angels may be in contention by the end of 1992, but a more realistic goal would be simply to get the team re-focused on team goals, rather than individual profits.

Outlook for 1992: They can win. The pitching is terrific; the division won't be nearly as strong this year as it was last year. It's not likely, but they could win.

Index of Leading Indicators for 1992: Down 13.1

Positive Indicators: None really

Negative Indicators: The Team Age is by far the largest.

The Angels indicators are extremely negative, but I like them better than that might suggest for reasons I have already explained—Whitey Herzog and the pitching. I think this is a case in which the indicators may *not* predict the direction of the team's movement.

Due for a better season: Junior Felix

Likely to have a worse season: Eichorn has up-and-down history

1992 Won-Lost Record will be: 82-80

ANGEL ARMS

It was often written that the Angels of 1991 had the best pitching of any last-place team in history. I don't know exactly how one would figure that, but I'll buy it. With a big three of Abbott (18-11, 2.89), Langston (19-8, 3.00) and Finley (18-9, 3.80) backed by two relievers who pitched 137 times between them with ERAs in the ones, the Angels' staff, at a glance, seems more likely to have been in first place rather than last.

The record of the staff *other* than the big three was obviously not good. It was 26-53. Kirk McCaskill was 10-19, and that was *better* than the other guys (16-34). This was only half their fault; the offense supporting them was reported missing in mid-summer.

A few other last-place teams which included some quality pitching included:

1902 New York Giants

Staff included Christy Mathewson (14-17, but 2.11 ERA and led the league with eight shutouts), Joe McGinnity (joined the team in mid-season, had 2.06 ERA), and Dummy Taylor (7-15, but 2.28 ERA). The Giants won the National League title two years later, with those three pitchers winning 89 games among them.

1924 Chicago White Sox

Sloppy Thurston pitched as well as anyone in the league, finishing 20-14 with a 3.80 ERA. Behind him in the rotation were two Hall of Famers, Ted Lyons and Red Faber. The White Sox jumped over .500 the next couple of years, although they were never serious contenders.

1957 Pittsburgh Pirates

The Pirates finished last with a staff including Bob Friend, Bob Purkey, Vern Law, Ron Kline, and Roy Face, all quality pitchers. They led the Pirates to the World Championship three years later.

1966 Chicago Cubs

The Cubs lost 103 games with a staff containing numerous pitchers who had brilliant careers behind them (Robin Roberts, Curt Simmons, Larry Jackson, Bob Buhl) and several others who had brilliant careers ahead of them (Ferguson Jenkins, Ken Holtzman, Ted Abernathy.) They had the Cubs in contention the next year.

1971 San Diego Padres

Three quality starters (Clay Kirby, Dave Roberts and Steve Arlin) gave the Padres one of the best rotations in the league. They lost 100 games anyway, and the staff broke down and broke up before the Padres got into contention.

1974–75 California Angels

Nolan Ryan and Frank Tanana were young and threw beans, and were backed by Bill Singer, Andy Hassler and Ed Figueroa. They led the league in strikeouts both years, in shutouts in 1975. The Angels were on the way up, but it took a long time.

Actually, in the last seventeen years you have to look a long time before you find *one* eighteen-game winner on a last-place team, let alone three. The pattern of these teams is by and large encouraging.

THE COWBOY AND THE WHITE RAT

The Angels most important transaction of the winter occurred in the closing weeks of the 1991 season, when the Angels signed Whitey Herzog to make talent decisions in the front office.

Whitey Herzog, in my opinion, is *precisely* what the Angels needed to get Gene Autry into a pennant race. Autry's long stewardship of the Angels has been undermined by his failure to comprehend this simple fact: that once a player peaks, he fades. Autry has always been unable to deal with this: that pennants are by and large *not* won by established stars or established players, but rather by young men with ability who are anxious to move into that class.

Perhaps I should not dwell on this, because it's a lesson of life and either you've learned it or you haven't, but when a man has it made he tends to a certain extent to lose his drive, and to a much greater extent to lose his flexibility. A 24-year-old kid can be told to execute this play that way *exactly* and now go practice it a thousand times, and he'll do it because he desperately wants to be a part of that charmed circle. A 30-year-old millionaire—this has nothing to do with money—can be told the same thing and he's not going to do it because that's not the way he was taught by his last manager and he's got too damned many things to do to go practice some stupid drill a thousand times, and underneath it all there is no fear of failure and rejection. This is not about millionaires. We have all known beautiful young girls who, upon marriage, turned overnight into sluggish, heavy-limbed matrons.

Whitey Herzog, more conspicuously than anyone else in baseball, has always understood this.

Gene Autry, more conspicuously than anyone else in baseball, has always failed to understand this.

When John Mayberry put on weight and stopped hustling, Whitey Herzog insisted that the Royals' get rid of him—even though this was a tremendously unpopular thing to do.

When Keith Hernandez' hat size got to be bigger than his home run total, Whitey Herzog traded Hernandez for nothing, even though this was a tremendously unpopular thing to do.

When Fred Lynn was tired of being the best center fielder in the American League and wanted to get paid for it, Gene Autry signed him to a mega-buck contract.

When Reggie Jackson had battled and ego-tripped his way out of pinstripes, Gene Autry brought him to the Angels to collect the largest paychecks of his career.

When Reggie's replacement in New York, Dave Winfield, reached the same point in his career, guess who wanted him?

For twenty years, Herzog has pushed veterans out of their comfortable jobs and replaced them with kids. For thirty years, Autry has cashed in kids to trade for, and later to buy, comfortable veterans.

Autry looks *backward*, at what players *have done*, and indulges himself in the generous but misguided belief that if you pay them enough money they will do it again.

Herzog looks *forward*, at what players *can do*, and tells them that if they want to get rich they had damned well better do it.

Further, Herzog is strong enough, independent enough, to *tell* Autry what he needs to hear—that Dave Parker can't play anymore, that Dave Winfield can't play the outfield anymore and isn't going to be any better a year from now than he is now.

Having written this, I must say that there is no evidence of it in Herzog's first few moves of mid-winter. The acquisitions of Von Hayes and Hubie Brooks seem more Autry-esque than Herzogish. Two explanations are offered for this:

1) That Herzog, working for Autry, has succumbed to Autry's perpetual desire for immediate payoffs, or
2) That Herzog sees in the Angels a team whose pitching staff is so strong that they can win immediately if they just get a few guys having good years.

You never know whether combinations of talent will explode or go fizz. That's what we call chemistry, a word for the unknown. Whitey Herzog is what Gene Autry needed in 1975, in 1980 or 1985. We can only hope that it isn't too late for either one of them, that they still have the time and energy, with Autry's desire and Herzog's intelligence, to make the terrific team that they once could have been.

OUR GENERATION

No All-Star game is complete without a reflection on the giants of yesterday; someone is sure to run by us a box score with the names of Mays, Mantle, McCovey, Koufax, Brock and Brooks Robinson, and to marvel a moment about how many great players there used to be. To diminish the present is not only the effect of this but its purpose, and maybe, under control, it is a useful purpose. It works against the arrogance of the young.

What I always wonder, though, is how the players of today *really* match up against the comparables of other eras. I am old enough to remember the 1965 All-Star game, and one of the things I remember is those giants being diminished compared to the generation before them—Williams, Musial, DiMaggio, etc.—who in their day were derided by comparison to Ruth and Cobb. The comparison is always weighted against the active players because the last generation can be admired for what they accomplished over a twenty-year career, while the active players can only be evaluated by what they have done so far. But how do they *really* compare; if you compare Roger Clemens to Tom Seaver **at the same age**, what do you get?

My rule for this is that I only compare players in the age group 27-35. The natural comp for Ruben Sierra is Roberto Clemente, and if you would compare Sierra to Clemente at the same age, you would find Sierra far, far ahead. This is misleading, however, because Clemente didn't really *become* Clemente until he was about Sierra's age, and then he played better and better and better for a decade. We can't assume that Sierra will do the same, and a comparison of Sierra to Clemente, which would imply that Sierra is likely to outperform Roberto, would be misleading. The same is true of Ken Griffey Jr. and Willie Mays; compared at Griff's age, Griffey would be far ahead, but this is of no particular value because Willie Mays didn't really arrive as Willie Mays until 1954, when he was the age Griffey will be in 1992. Almost any young pitcher, compared to Sandy Koufax at the same age, will look good because Koufax wasn't a very good pitcher at a young age. This isn't a helpful comparison. By not comparing players at an age before maturity, we avoid that problem.

After the age of 35, on the other hand, a player has done what he is going to do. There is no point in comparing George Brett to Stan Musial at the same age, because George Brett is George Brett. He's accomplished more than most Hall of Famers already. You don't need comparisons to suggest what he might accomplish.

OK, let's start with **Roger Clemens** and **Tom Seaver**. Clemens turned 29 years old in August, which means he compares to Seaver through 1973, when Seaver turned 29 in November. Seaver at that time had seven full seasons in the major leagues; Clemens has six full seasons and two partial seasons. These are their stats:

	G	IP	W	L	Pct.	SO	BB	ERA
Clemens	241	1784	134	61	.687	1665	490	2.85
Seaver	251	1931	135	76	.640	1655	493	2.38

As you can see, Seaver and Clemens are extremely comparable at the same age; Seaver had a better ERA, but that's about the same in the context of his league and park, and Clemens has a better winning percentage, but that is also probably about the same in the context of his team. Their strikeout/walk data is almost exactly the same, although Seaver had done this in a few more innings. Seaver, incidentally, had completed the most productive phase of his career at this age; he had an off year in 1974 (11-11), recovered with outstanding seasons in 1975 and 1977, and then stayed around for ten more years at a different level.

Clemens and Seaver are an obvious match—two right-handed power pitchers with high strikeout totals and twenty wins a year. I didn't, incidentally, look for statistical "matches" in this case; I just compared modern players to the guys that they reminded me of. Sometimes you have to reach for a comparison, and wind up with one which isn't so obvious, like Wade Boggs. Who was the Wade Boggs of the last generation?

There wasn't one, but the best comparison I can come up with is **Pete Rose**, who like **Wade Boggs** was a singles hitter without much power or outstanding speed. Rose played some third base—in fact, he was a third baseman at Boggs' age and a leadoff hitter, so there's a general comparison.

Boggs turned 33 in June, so he can be compared to Rose through 1974, when Rose was 33:

	G	AB	R	H	2B	3B	HR	RBI	BB	SO	SB	AVG
Boggs	1482	5699	1005	1965	400	43	78	637	930	439	15	.345
Rose	1860	7559	1217	2337	394	91	117	701	872	723	94	.309

Boggs' batting average is more than thirty points higher than Rose's, despite which, due to his late start, he is still several hundred hits behind Rose, and also behind in most other cumulative categories. They're comparable, though; you don't tend to look at those lines and think that this guy Rose is twenty times better than the Boggs character. Of course, the comparison between Margo and a few months of involuntary confinement is too obvious to belabor.

If you add speed to Wade Boggs you get Tony Gwynn, and if you add speed to Pete Rose you get Rod Carew, so the logical match for **Tony Gwynn** is **Rod Carew**:

	G	AB	R	H	2B	3B	HR	RBI	BB	SO	SB	AVG
Gwynn	1335	5181	765	1699	248	72	53	550	460	275	246	.328
Carew	1405	5363	801	1777	260	72	62	613	500	626	232	.331

Gwynn was born in May (1960) and Carew was born in October (1945). If you compare Gwynn to Carew through 1976 you give Gwynn a five-month head start, and if you compare Carew through 1977 you give Carew seven extra months. I decided to split the 1977 season, which was Carew's best year, in half, and give him his totals through 1976 plus one-half of 1977.

Anyway, as you can see, these two guys are about as close as they could be at the same age; they are within a few points in batting average, a few home runs, runs scored, doubles, etc. Gwynn doesn't strike out nearly as much and has a few more stolen bases. Speaking of which, **Rickey Henderson** has already broken **Lou Brock's** stolen base record, but how do they compare as complete players?

	G	AB	R	H	2B	3B	HR	RBI	BB	SO	SB	AVG
Rickey	1742	6483	1395	1888	311	51	184	679	1191	869	994	.291
Brock	1604	6518	1047	1904	322	101	123	558	463	1198	533	.292

Henderson was born on Christmas and Brock in June, so once again we have to split Brock's 1972 season in half to get him as close as possible to the right age.

Brock's best stolen base year, 1974, was still ahead of him at this age, so the comparison may even out a little as they age, but as you can see Brock was not an all-around offensive player to be compared to Henderson. Henderson not only has stolen more bases than Brock would ever steal, but also has hit more home runs and drawn more walks.

Here's a small point but maybe worth making: note the difference in triples between Brock and Henderson—a big advantage for Brock, in lines which are otherwise comparable. You might think that this is because Brock played on artificial turf and Henderson has played on grass, but actually it's not—in fact, at this point in their careers Henderson has played about as many games on artificial turf as Brock had. It's because Brock was a left-handed hitter and Rickey's right-handed. Whenever you compare a left-handed hitter and a right-handed hitter of about the same skills, the left-hander will hit many more triples, because the balls that the left-hander pulls into the corner require the fielder to make a 350-foot throw to third, which means they require:

a) Jesse Barfield,
b) Mark Whiten
c) Roberto Clemente, or
d) a relay from the cut-off man.

The balls the right-hander pulls into the corner require a 230-foot throw to third base. Big difference. We've also lost a few triples over the years to balls hopping over the fences for ground-rule doubles, and of course they are individuals; some guys are just more determined to get to third base than other guys.

Actually, it's kind of unfair to Brock to compare him to Rickey Henderson; Rickey's the best ever of that type. It's probably more fair to compare him to Tim Raines:

	G	AB	R	H	2B	3B	HR	RBI	BB	SO	SB	AVG
Raines	1560	5914	1036	1761	293	87	101	602	858	631	685	.298
Brock	1528	6208	1007	1808	309	97	122	537	440	1152	502	.291

Raines, born in September, has a three-month disadvantage in this one, since I compared him to Brock through 1971. Raines, a switch hitter, has 90% of Brock's triples, amidst generally comparable records. Here's where Brock's late-in-life base stealing exploits are more important; Raines has a 183-stolen base lead on him and probably will steal more than 938 bases, pushing Brock to third on the list, but it is also possible that he won't.

One of the most obvious comparisons of players today to the last generation is **Freddie McGriff** to **Willie McCovey**. McGriff has been compared to McCovey almost daily since he was in the minor leagues, and it has proven to be a valid comparison: McGriff is, in fact, exactly the kind of player McCovey was.

	G	AB	R	H	2B	3B	HR	RBI	BB	SO	SB	AVG
McGriff	731	2472	432	687	118	9	156	411	457	630	25	.278
McCovey	792	2477	420	673	92	22	165	441	332	493	10	.272

McGriff was 27 years old at the end of the 1991 season, so I've compared him to McCovey through 1965, when Willie was 27.

McCovey had a complicated career from the time-line standpoint. He came up at 21, earlier than McGriff, and battered NL pitching senseless for a third of a season. He fell into a slump his second year, however, and the Giants had a problem, in that they had both Cepeda and McCovey and no DH rule, so McCovey became a platoon player for several years, losing a few hundred at bats. In 1963 he won a job and tied for the NL lead in home runs, but in 1965 he began to have problems with his feet, which would trouble him for the rest of his career.

The year that McCovey became a regular, 1963, the rules committee expanded the strike zone, and pitched all major league hitters into a six-year funk. McCovey, the top power hitter of that era, would have had much more impressive batting stats if he had played in almost any other era. When the strike zone was restored in 1969 McCovey had a couple of tremendous seasons, the best of his career, before age and injuries began to slow him down. Despite the injuries, he kicked along for another ten years, hitting another 200 or so home runs.

I guess what I'm saying, in short, is that McCovey had an upside potential, never realized, that was just awesome: this guy could have had stats like Jimmie Foxx. I'm not sure that McGriff has the same upside potential that McCovey had, but he also doesn't have the injury problems that McCovey had, and I doubt that he ever will. The general rule is that the "new" anybody will never turn out to be as good as the original; each "new" Willie Mays seems to slip a notch from the previous one. But this may be an exception: the new Willie McCovey may, in time, surpass the accomplishments of the original.

Andre Dawson may not be **Willie Mays**, but among the pretenders he is probably the closest we have:

	G	AB	R	H	2B	3B	HR	RBI	BB	SO	SB	AVG
Dawson	2167	8348	1199	2354	417	92	377	1335	522	1279	304	.282
Mays	2446	9130	1763	2812	446	129	587	1654	1137	1147	299	.308

Dawson is 37, so I violated my age-35 rule here, and compared him to Mays through 1968. Since Mays began to fade we have had a long series of "new Willie Mayses", like Bobby Bonds, Reggie Smith, Darryl Strawberry and Eric Davis, none of whom have really approached the standards of *the* Willie Mays. Perhaps the only Hall of Fame argument you need to make for Andre Dawson is this: that after 14 years in the major leagues, you can still compare him to Willie Mays. Mays had a little more power and his average was 25 points higher, but take 25 points and a little power away from Willie and he's still a hell of a player.

I always thought it might be kinder, when you see a new Willie Mays, to compare him instead to Bobby Bonds. Then, when he moves past Bonds, you can start comparing him to Willie—but make him earn that with five good years first. Maybe the most interesting of the "new Bobby Bondses" would be Barry Bonds:

	G	AB	R	H	2B	3B	HR	RBI	BB	SO	SB	AVG
Barry	870	3111	563	837	184	41	142	453	484	521	212	.269
Bobby	864	3480	668	961	168	34	165	481	345	745	222	.276

This compares Barry to Bobby through 1973, which was Bobby's best year. During the NL Playoff Jerry Coleman said that "Barry's father, Bobby, was a good ballplayer. Barry is a great ballplayer." Actually, as you can see, Barry doesn't quite match the numbers his father put up at the same age.

This stuff is only interesting, of course, with the very best players of an era, because ordinary players can be compared to their contemporaries. If you're looking for a comp for Pete Incaviglia, you need look no further than Rob Deer. I suppose the most-comparable player of the last generation to **Jose Canseco** would be **Reggie Jackson**, who in his day was another one of the "new Willie Mayses":

	G	AB	R	H	2B	3B	HR	RBI	BB	SO	SB	AVG
Canseco	853	3216	540	867	156	8	209	647	370	870	122	.270
Reggie	928	3251	533	858	156	22	189	536	447	891	101	.264

This also is Reggie through 1973; Jose and Barry Bonds are the same age and Reggie and Bonds were the same age and all four are vaguely comparable, so if you prefer you can compare Barry to Reggie and Jose to Bobby, or for that matter Jose to Barry and Reggie to Bobby; what the hell, you bought the book, make up your own rules. Anyway, as you can see, Canseco is probably a little better player, taking all things, than Reggie was.

Of course, there were players of the 1960s and 70s who have no peers today, like Willie and Hank Aaron. Aaron, when asked about the players of today, says that there are players who have great years now, but they don't put great years one after another after another the way he and Willie did. In his day they *had* to perform every year, because all they had was one year on a contract. Aaron is full of shit, of course; the players of today are not any less consistent than the players of twenty years ago. What, you're telling me Wade Boggs isn't consistent? Roger Clemens isn't consistent? Tony Gwynn doesn't consistently have great years? Ryne Sandberg doesn't? Give me a break. Of course there were players then who aren't matched today, but you can't expect all of the great players in baseball history to be replicated in today's game. There's no Mickey Mantle today, but then there was no Mickey Mantle of the 1920s, either. There are also players today who weren't matched then, like Ryne Sandberg and Cal Ripken. Who was the Cal Ripken of the 1960s? Who was the great power-hitting shortstop of the 1960s?

You can make matches, but they don't really fit. The best match for **Ryne Sandberg** would have to be **Joe Morgan**, which I guess it wouldn't hurt to look at:

	G	AB	R	H	2B	3B	HR	RBI	BB	SO	SB	AVG
Sandberg	1547	6093	976	1753	288	59	205	749	551	875	297	.288
Morgan	1492	5406	983	1501	252	73	142	594	1063	594	445	.278

Morgan and Sandberg were both born in September; this compares Ryno to Morgan through 1975, his first MVP year. It's a better match than I would have guessed; Sandberg doesn't match Morgan in walks and stolen bases, but will roll well past him in the basic career categories like hits and home runs. The natural match for **Ripken**, if we're determined to have one, would be **Ernie Banks**.

	G	AB	R	H	2B	3B	HR	RBI	BB	SO	SB	AVG
Ripken	1638	6305	970	1762	340	33	259	942	688	747	28	.280
Banks	1293	4975	794	1437	220	62	316	910	467	612	40	.289

I gave Banks half of the 1962 season in this comparison. Banks was a better hitter than Ripken, or at least, because of Wrigley Field, *appeared* to be a better hitter, but Ripken will probably pass by Banks in all career totals except possibly home runs and stolen bases. Even Ripken's batting average is a good bet to wind up ahead of Banks', which dropped to .274 before he quit. Ripken will probably play almost as many major league games as anyone ever has.

I'm not sure I would describe **Howard Johnson** as the new **Mike Schmidt**, but I don't want to compare him to Pie Traynor:

	G	AB	R	H	2B	3B	HR	RBI	BB	SO	SB	AVG
Hojo	1179	3959	624	1014	206	17	197	629	521	812	191	.256
Schmidt	1234	4261	778	1104	208	39	283	787	778	1077	129	.259

Mike Schmidt is through 1980, his first MVP year. Johnson's 1991 season (38 home runs, 117 RBI, .259) is statistically inseparable from a Mike Schmidt season, but Schmidt at this age had had a few more of those years than Johnson has. **Darryl Strawberry**—I don't know who I would compare him to, other than the guys I've already used, Reggie Jackson and Bobby Bonds. Maybe I'll throw in Frank Robinson and do comparisons to all of them through age 29:

	G	AB	R	H	2B	3B	HR	RBI	BB	SO	SB	AVG
Darryl	1248	4408	748	1159	209	34	280	832	655	1085	201	.263
Reggie	1231	4350	714	1154	220	26	254	733	600	1129	143	.265
Bonds	1159	4576	858	1249	214	45	218	637	529	1016	293	.273
Frank	1424	5236	988	1587	301	47	307	952	663	749	154	.303

I gave Frank Robinson half of the 1965 season; Reggie and Bonds are through 1975. Obviously, Robby is a bit strong for that qualifying heat, but Strawberry compares well to the other two. Strawberry has more home runs and RBI than Reggie had at the same age.

Let's see, who else could I do . . . Ozzie Smith is most-comparable to Luis Aparicio. There are two problems with that—

1) Ozzie is past age 35, where the cutoff is, and

2) Neither Ozzie nor Aparicio is defined by his hitting stats, the way an outfielder or first baseman is. Still, I'm curious what it will show:

	G	AB	R	H	2B	3B	HR	RBI	BB	SO	SB	AVG
Ozzie	2076	7569	1006	1955	327	55	22	650	890	490	499	.258
Looie	2232	8804	1176	2316	328	88	76	658	632	638	484	.263

This is Aparicio through 1970; he played three more seasons. I hadn't realized that there was that much of a difference in power between them, but I guess five homers a year add up if you do it long enough. I would still assume that Aparicio was the most-comparable player in history to Ozzie.

Kirby Puckett, there's a tough one. Looking for the **Kirby Puckett** of the 1960s, I draw a blank. I could reach back farther and compare him to Joe Medwick or Earl Averill, but I don't think I will because I'm not really interested in what the comparison would show. Their body types are so different that it is a little disconcerting, but maybe the most similar *player* in that generation was **Vada Pinson**:

	G	AB	R	H	2B	3B	HR	RBI	BB	SO	SB	AVG
Kirby	1222	5006	716	1602	266	47	123	675	275	639	100	.320
Vada	1376	5511	873	1652	299	84	172	733	393	802	191	.300

I gave Pinson half of 1967, since Kirby was born in March and Vada in August. Pinson was listed while active as having been born in 1938, but is now listed as hailing from 1936, which is a problem with this stuff; you're never **really** sure that a player's known age would tally with his mama's memory. Pinson, even assuming he was born in 1936, was a better player in his twenties than Roberto Clemente or a good many other Hall of Famers, but didn't age well. Puckett probably won't either.

Mark McGwire compares in a general way to **Harmon Killebrew**, Twins slugger of the sixties.

	G	AB	R	H	2B	3B	HR	RBI	BB	SO	SB	AVG
McGwire	777	2656	417	647	106	5	178	504	437	592	6	.244
Killebrew	995	3427	573	890	115	12	272	670	469	717	7	.260

Killebrew was 27 years, three months and two days older than McGwire, so I compared McGwire to Killebrew through the end of the 1964 season, which oddly enough ended almost on the day that McGwire was born. Killer came to the majors at eighteen and had six full seasons plus several partials by the time he was McGwire's age, so he had built up a lead.

I was talking about McCovey and McGriff. When McCovey came up he had to battle for playing time for several years with another equally awesome hitter, that being Orlando Cepeda. Oddly enough, the same thing happened to McGriff. At more or less the same time that the Blue Jays brought up McGriff, they also came up with a player named Cecil Fielder. In San Francisco the Giants initially liked Cepeda better than they did McCovey, so McCovey was forced into a platoon role for several years, whereas in Toronto the Blue Jays liked McGriff, and so the competition worked to the disadvantage of Cecil Fielder. It would be neat if we could also compare Fielder and Cepeda, but they're really not comparable types of players. In fact, I can't find a Cecil Fielder-type player from that generation, at least not without re-using Killebrew. Roy Sievers? Rocky Colavito? Ralph Kiner? I think I'll pass.

More in the tradition of **Cepeda** would be **Don Mattingly**; they're not physically similar and one's a left-handed batter, one right-handed, but they're both line-drive hitters with power, as opposed to true power hitters or power/speed combinations. Mattingly turned 30 in mid-season, 1991, so he compares to Cepeda through mid-season, 1968:

	G	AB	R	H	2B	3B	HR	RBI	BB	SO	SB	AVG
Mattingly	1269	5003	719	1570	323	15	178	827	388	300	11	.314
Cepeda	1466	5493	843	1680	300	23	276	972	376	828	116	.306

Eddie Murray may be more comparable to Cepeda than Mattingly is, but Eddie is 35 and has already hit more homers and driven in more runs than Cepeda would, so he doesn't fit the prerequisites for this bit. A couple of other first basemen, while we're on the subject, would be **Kent Hrbek** and **Boog Powell**. Again, we're comparing a right-hander to a left-hander, but they are comparable players, both had trouble keeping their weight down.

	G	AB	R	H	2B	3B	HR	RBI	BB	SO	SB	AVG
Hrbek	1431	5132	757	1484	270	17	243	892	660	657	28	.289
Boog	1596	5383	733	1434	223	9	286	991	794	1012	18	.266

Hrbek is 31 years old; I compared him to Powell at mid-season, 1973. Powell came up young and was virtually finished at that time; he had only one good year, one "comeback year", left in him.

Well, I'm down now to comparing non-Hall of Famers to guys who aren't going to be in the Hall of Fame, either, so I suppose it's time to stop this, or I'll be comparing Mariano Duncan to Eddie Bressoud in no time. *Whitaker* and *Trammell* can be compared to each other; there are probably comps for them from a few years ago, but I don't know who. Paul Molitor, again, doesn't immediately remind me of anyone from my youth, and Yount is too good to be paired with anyone I can think of. On the way out I'll also run comparisons of these guys' records in seasonal notation.

	Years	IP	W L	Pct.	SO	BB	ERA
Clemens	6.3	281	21-10	.687	263	77	2.85
Seaver	6.6	292	20-12	.625	251	75	2.38

	Years	AB	R	H	2B	3B	HR	RBI	BB	SO	SB	AVG
Boggs	9.1	623	110	215	44	5	9	70	102	48	2	.345
Rose	11.5	658	106	204	34	8	10	61	76	63	8	.309

	Years	AB	R	H	2B	3B	HR	RBI	BB	SO	SB	AVG
Gwynn	8.2	629	93	206	30	9	6	67	56	33	30	.328
Carew	8.7	618	92	205	30	8	7	71	58	72	27	.331

	Years	AB	R	H	2B	3B	HR	RBI	BB	SO	SB	AVG
Rickey	10.8	603	130	176	29	5	17	63	111	81	94	.291
Brock	9.9	658	106	192	33	10	12	56	47	121	54	.292

	Years	AB	R	H	2B	3B	HR	RBI	BB	SO	SB	AVG
Raines	9.6	614	108	183	30	9	10	63	89	66	71	.298
Brock	9.4	658	107	192	33	10	13	57	47	122	53	.291

	Years	AB	R	H	2B	3B	HR	RBI	BB	SO	SB	AVG
McGriff	4.5	548	96	152	26	2	35	91	101	140	6	.278
McCovey	4.9	507	86	138	19	5	34	90	68	101	2	.272

	Years	AB	R	H	2B	3B	HR	RBI	BB	SO	SB	AVG
Dawson	13.4	624	90	176	31	7	28	100	39	96	23	.282
Mays	15.1	605	117	186	30	9	39	110	75	76	20	.308

The Bondses

	Years	AB	R	H	2B	3B	HR	RBI	BB	SO	SB	AVG
Barry	5.4	579	105	156	34	8	26	84	90	97	39	.269
Bobby	5.3	653	125	180	32	6	31	90	65	140	42	.276

	Years	AB	R	H	2B	3B	HR	RBI	BB	SO	SB	AVG
Canseco	5.3	611	103	165	30	2	40	123	70	165	23	.270
Reggie	5.7	568	93	150	27	4	33	94	78	156	18	.264

	Years	AB	R	H	2B	3B	HR	RBI	BB	SO	SB	AVG
Sandberg	9.5	638	102	184	30	6	21	78	58	92	31	.288
Morgan	9.2	587	107	163	27	8	15	64	115	64	48	.278

	Years	AB	R	H	2B	3B	HR	RBI	BB	SO	SB	AVG
Ripken	10.1	624	96	174	34	3	26	93	68	74	3	.280
Banks	8.0	623	99	180	28	8	40	114	59	77	5	.289

	Years	AB	R	H	2B	3B	HR	RBI	BB	SO	SB	AVG
Hojo	7.3	544	86	139	28	2	27	86	72	112	26	.256
Schmidt	7.6	559	102	145	27	5	37	103	102	141	17	.259

Strawberry's Field

	Years	AB	R	H	2B	3B	HR	RBI	BB	SO	SB	AVG
Darryl	7.7	572	97	150	27	4	36	108	85	141	26	.263
Reggie	7.6	572	94	152	29	3	33	96	79	149	19	.265
Bonds	7.2	640	120	175	30	6	30	89	74	142	41	.273
Frank	8.8	596	112	181	34	5	35	108	75	85	18	.303

	Years	AB	R	H	2B	3B	HR	RBI	BB	SO	SB	AVG
Ozzie	12.8	591	79	153	26	4	2	51	69	38	39	.258
Looie	13.8	639	85	168	24	6	6	48	46	46	35	.263

	Years	AB	R	H	2B	3B	HR	RBI	BB	SO	SB	AVG
Kirby	7.5	664	95	212	35	6	16	89	36	85	13	.320
Vada	8.5	649	103	194	35	10	20	86	46	94	22	.300

	Years	AB	R	H	2B	3B	HR	RBI	BB	SO	SB	AVG
McGwire	4.8	554	87	135	22	1	37	105	91	123	1	.244
Killebrew	6.1	558	93	145	19	2	44	109	76	117	1	.260

	Years	AB	R	H	2B	3B	HR	RBI	BB	SO	SB	AVG
Mattingly	7.8	639	92	200	41	2	23	106	50	38	1	.314
Cepeda	9.0	607	93	186	33	3	30	107	42	91	13	.306

	Years	AB	R	H	2B	3B	HR	RBI	BB	SO	SB	AVG
Hrbek	8.8	581	86	168	31	2	28	101	75	74	3	.289
Boog	9.9	546	74	146	23	1	29	101	81	103	2	.266

THE ATLANTA BRAVES
• IN A BOX •

1991 Won-Lost Record: 94-68 .580

Rank among 26 teams: 3rd
Over Last Five Years: 345-460 .429
Rank over Five Years: 25th
In Last Ten Years: 740-874 .458
Rank over Ten Years: 24th

Best Player: Terry Pendleton was their best player last year. For 1992, I'd take Ron Gant.

Weak Spot: No glaring weakness in 1991; catcher was probably the weakest.

Best Pitcher: Tom Glavine

Staff Weakness: None—the starters are young, the bullpen is stocked

Best Bench Player: Keith Mitchell

Best Young Player: Dave Justice

Best Looking Player: Ron Gant

Ugliest Player: Juan Berenguer

Most Pleasant Surprise, 1991: Terry Pendleton

Biggest Disappointment, 1991: Sid Bream

Best Minor League Prospect: Ryan Klesko

Who Is: A left-handed hitting first baseman, will turn 21 in June. His career minor league batting average is .309, slugging percentage .475. If he came to the majors in 1992 I think he would hit around .275 with a slugging percentage in the low .400s, but in view of his age he probably has substantial growth in front of him.

Other Prospects: **Keith Mitchell**, Kevin's second cousin, hit in the .320s at AA and AAA last year before being called up to pinch hit. He hit .318 in the majors, and that may not be an aberration; he may be a .318 hitter.

The Braves had the second pick in the first round of the draft last year, and selected **Mike Kelly**, an outfielder who many thought should have been the number one pick. Kelly went to Durham, where he played fairly well (29 runs scored in 35 games), but struck out a lot.

Park Characteristics: Atlanta-Fulton County Stadium is a tremendous park for a hitter, and is one of four or five parks in the majors which so dramatically alters the statistics of those who play there that it interferes with our ability to evaluate the players accurately. The Braves (as a team) hit .273 at home, .243 on the road. They hit 83 home runs at home, 58 on the road.

Brave pitchers allowed a batting average of .254 in Atlanta, .226 on the road. They allowed 73 home runs in Atlanta, 45 on the road.

The Park Helps: All hitters, although **Ron Gant** has never hit much better in Atlanta than he has on the road.

The Park Hurts: All pitchers.

ORGANIZATIONAL REPORT CARD

Ownership:	C
Upper Management:	B−
Field Management:	A
Front-Line Talent:	C
Second-Line Talent:	B+
Minor League System:	A

TEAM LEADERS:

Batting Average: Terry Pendleton, .319

Last Ten Years (Season): Pendleton, 1991, .319
Last Ten Years (Total): Lonnie Smith, .295

Doubles: Ron Gant, 35

Triples: Terry Pendleton, 8

Home Runs: Ron Gant, 32

Last Ten Years (Season): Dale Murphy, 1987, 44
Last Ten Years (Total): Dale Murphy, 279

Extra Base Hits: Ron Gant, 70

RBI: Ron Gant, 105

Last Ten Years (Season): Dale Murphy, 1983, 121
Last Ten Years (Total): Dale Murphy, 845

Stolen Bases: Otis Nixon, 72

Walks: Ron Gant, 71

Secondary Average: Ron Gant, .431

Runs Created: Terry Pendleton, 107

Runs Created Per Game: Dave Justice, 6.9

Wins: Tom Glavine, 20

Last Ten Years (Season): Glavine, 1991, 20
Last Ten Years (Total): Rick Mahler, 71

Winning Percentage: Steve Avery, 18-8 .692

Strikeouts: Glavine, 192

Last Ten Years (Season): Glavine, 1991, 192
Last Ten Years (Total): Rick Mahler, 698

ERA: Glavine, 2.55

Saves: Juan Berenguer, 17

League Leaders: Terry Pendleton, Batting Average, .319

Stat of the Year: Ron Gant has a *career* batting average of .159 in April. In a typical year he goes 9-for-57 in April, with one home run.

1991 SEASON

Background: The Braves had endured a series of tough years. In a six-team division the Braves finished sixth in 1986, fifth in 1987, sixth in 1988, sixth in 1989 and sixth in 1990.

Outlook: Everyone knew that the Braves had young talent, and there was general optimism about the chance of improvement. But certainly very few people expected or predicted the sudden, dramatic improvement which was actually to occur.

Indicators for 1991 were: Strongly Positive (+15.0). The Braves' 1991 Indicators were the most positive for any National League team.

Getaway: The Braves won ten of their first twenty; as of July 11, they had won forty of eighty. This was considered remarkable progress at the time, but at that point, with Dave Justice unavailable, there was no reason to think the Braves would contend.

Low Point of the Season: April 20, Braves dropped to 3-6, casting doubt on whether 1991 would be any better than previous years.

Stretch Drive: Atlanta won 55 games after the All-Star break, five more than any other team. Starting on September 27 they won eight in a row before clinching.

High Point of the Season: October 5, Smoltz beat Houston 5-2 and the Braves clinched the title.

Most Exciting Game of the Season: The Braves played two great games against the Reds in the thick of the pennant race. On August 21 in Cincinnati the Braves capped an unlikely comeback with three runs off Rob Dibble to tie the game in the top of the ninth, and won the game, 10-9, with a run in the thirteenth. Braves' relievers Randy St. Claire, Mark Wohlers, Mike Stanton and Tony Castillo held the Reds scoreless the final eight innings.

Equally improbable was the Braves win in Cincinnati on October 1. Leibrandt spotted the Reds six runs in the bottom of the first—but that was all they would score. The Braves came up with two in the fourth . . . here, I'll run the line score:

000	210	202	— 7
600	000	000	— 6

Dave Justice hit a two-run homer in the ninth inning. A loss would have put Atlanta two games behind L.A. with four games to play, an almost untenable position, so this might be judged the Braves' most important win of the season.

Major Injuries: Dave Justice missed a third of the season with a sore back, and Sid Bream had knee surgery in June and missed two months. Their replacements, Otis Nixon and Brian Hunter, both played well.

Juan Berenguer, the Braves' ace reliever, went out in mid-August with a stress fracture in his right forearm, an injury which could have cost the Braves the pennant had not Schuerholz acted quickly to acquire Alejandro Peña from the Mets.

Offense: Fairly good. The Braves were second in the league in runs scored, 749, and 13% above the league average. Most of that advantage is attributable to the park, but even with park adjustments the Braves' offense was above average.

Defense: Unimpressive/below average. Rafael Belliard solidified the defense at short as long as he could stay in the lineup, but up the middle the team remained unimpressive—fair catching, different combinations at second and short, a hitter in center field. Free agents improved the defense at first and third, but the wing men in the outfield (Lonnie Smith and Dave Justice) are pretty awful outfielders. Of course, Otis Nixon gave the Braves two center fielders in the outfield until he was suspended.

Pitching: Spectacular. Even with the park working against them, the Braves had a staff ERA of 3.49, third-best in the league. That breaks down as 3.81 in Atlanta, but 3.17 on the road. This is a wonderful pitching staff.

Best Game by a Starting Pitcher: Tom Glavine threw a four-hitter at the Dodgers on April 23, Game Score 89 (9 4 0 0 0 10).

Number of regulars having good seasons by their own standards: Five (Pendleton, Otis Nixon, Gant, Treadway, Blauser)

1991 Over-Achiever: 1. Terry Pendleton
2. Otis Nixon

1991 Under-Achiever: Sid Bream

Infield: Fair. The offense was good at two positions (second and third) and the defense good at three (all except second.) Pendleton was a legitimate MVP candidate if not a legitimate MVP, but Braves' first basemen hit only .234.

Outfield: Outstanding. With two base stealers in the outfield (Nixon and Gant) the Braves had 128 stolen bases from the outfield. With two power hitters (Gant and Justice) they had 67 homers from the outfield. With outstanding backup outfielders, the Braves were able to withstand injuries. Their three outfield spots produced 324 runs scored (108 apiece) and 281 RBI (94 apiece).

Catching: Fair. The Braves' catchers were Olson, Heath and Cabrera, with a game each from Berryhill and Willard. They didn't throw very well and hit .239, but they did drive in 74 runs.

Starting Pitching: Extremely strong.

Bullpen: Brilliant. The Braves for the season as a whole blew only eleven save opportunities, the fewest of any major league team. Berenguer was very good until his injury; he was replaced by Peña, who was nearly perfect. Supporting them were Mercker, Stanton and Freeman, all very good.

Percentage of offense created by:

Young Players:	43%
Players in Their Prime:	40%
Past Their Prime:	17%

Team Age:

Age of Non-Pitchers:	28.3
Age of Pitching Staff:	26.8
Overall Team Age:	27.67

In retrospect, the critical decisions were: A year ago, in the winter of 1990–1991, John Schuerholz decided to broaden the Braves' talent base by adding to the team a number of free agents of modest accomplishment, such as Sid Bream, Terry Pendleton, Otis Nixon and Rafael Belliard.

At the time, I didn't like these moves, and I'm sure that anything I wrote about these actions a year ago would have been unfavorable. Despite the Braves' success in 1991, I am still absolutely opposed to the philosophy which guided these decisions, and I still believe that it is a philosophy which is ultimately destructive to the organization. Nonetheless, what must be said about short-term gambles is that they sometimes pay off in the short run, and these short-term gambles paid off, in 1991, in spades. Nixon and Pendleton, and to a lesser extent the other two, played a key role in catapulting the Braves out of last place.

The most significant in-season decision was the trade for Alejandro Peña, who saved eleven games in five weeks.

THAT AND THE OTHER

Lookalikes: Charlie Leibrandt looks a little like James Caan.

Hall of Fame Watch: The Braves' four best Hall of Fame candidates are Gant, Justice, Glavine and Avery. None of the four has yet completed 20% of a Hall of Fame portfolio.

Throwback: Tom Glavine

Attendance Trend: Until last year, lower and lower. The Braves in 1991 more than doubled their attendance, from 980 thousand to 2.14 million. This trend will continue upward because

1) Championship seasons build attendance in subsequent years, and
2) Schuerholz understands marketing.

Players with a Chance for 3000 career hits: Terry Pendleton, 2%

Record Watch: Ron Gant has a 9% chance to hit 500 career home runs.

Best Interview: Smoltz's shrink

Probably Could Play Regularly For Another Team: Jeff Blauser

Best Fundamental Player: Rafael Belliard

Worst Fundamental Player: Lonnie Smith

Best Defensive Player: Terry Pendleton

Worst Defensive Player: Lonnie Smith

Best Knowledge of the Strike Zone: Jeff Treadway

Least Command of the Strike Zone: Brian Hunter

Fastest Runner: Otis Nixon

Slowest Runner: Greg Olson

Best Baserunner: Nixon

Most Likely to Still be Here in 2000: Dave Justice

Best Fastball: Smoltz or Avery

Best Breaking Pitch: Smoltz's Slider

Best Control: Leibrandt

Most Overrated Player: Sid Bream

Most Underrated Player: Mike Bielecki

Oddest Collection of Abilities: Jeff Treadway

Never Going to be As Good as the Organization Thinks He Is: Deion Sanders

Manager's Pet Strategy: If the law allowed him to have two wives and platoon the redhead and the blond, I'm sure he'd give it a try.

Why is this man in the Major Leagues: Damon Berryhill

Gets Ahead of the Hitters Most Often: Glavine

Gets Ahead of the Hitters Least Often: Bielecki

Most-Similar Players:

to C Greg Olson, Tom Pagnozzi
to 1B Sid Bream, Candy Maldonado
to 2B Jeff Treadway, a slow Bip Roberts
to 3B Terry Pendleton, Tony Phillips
to SS Jeff Blauser, Bill Spiers
to SS Rafael Belliard, Felix Fermin
to LF Otis Nixon, Mike Felder
to CF Ron Gant, a fast Matt Williams
to RF Dave Justice, Jay Buhner

Most Fun to Watch: Dave Justice

Least Fun to Watch: Lonnie Smith

Managerial Type: Terry Pendleton

Among the All-Time Team Leaders:

The Braves list their franchise records from the beginnings of the team in Boston in the 19th century, so the competition is stiff. The only current Brave that I note among the team leaders in anything is Ron Gant, tenth on the career stolen base list, with 99. The best candidates are in the specialty areas, like home runs and stolen bases. Gant will join the Braves' top ten in home runs this year, while Otis Nixon with another 70-steal season would vault to the middle of the leaders in career stolen bases.

Have you noticed the extent to which the National League is beginning to dominate the South? With the new team in Miami the National League will have the only two true Southern cities in the majors, plus most of the "borderline South" cities like Cincinnati, St. Louis and Houston.

Town Team:

C—Josh Gibson
1B—Bill Terry
2B—Tony Phillips
SS—Marty Marion
3B—Luke Appling
LF—Suitcase Simpson
CF—Ty Cobb
RF—Mack Jones
SP—Spud Chandler

Post-Season Transactions: December 12, re-signed Otis Nixon for three years

What Needs to Be Done For 1992: Need to remain aggressive about correcting problems.

Outlook for 1992: Because they're a young team and the champions, most people will probably pick the Braves to repeat. I don't.

Index of Leading Indicators for 1992: Down 19.7

For 1992 the Leading Indicators for the Braves are the most negative for any National League team.

Positive Indicators:

1. Team played well late in season.
2. Slightly younger-than-average team.

Negative Indicators:

With the exception of the two cited above, all of the indicators are negative. The most important negative is the Plexiglas Principle, which tells us that teams which rise quickly often fall quickly.

Due for a better season: Mark Lemke

Likely to have a worse season: Otis Nixon, Terry Pendleton

1992 Won-Lost Record will be: 82-80

A MIRACLE MORE OR LESS

No one in Atlanta was crushed by the Twins' Seven-Game defeat of the Braves. It remained a great season, a miracle season, and if that alone were not enough of a cushion for defeat, there was still the future, and in the unwritten future a general expectation that more good years are to come. One ESPN analyst, in summarizing the series, virtually conceded the NL West to the Braves for several years to come. The Braves have a good young ballclub, and a system loaded with prospects.

Miracle teams, however, are always young teams, are they not? The Braves may well win this division; I'm not saying they won't. But before we decide that, let's look at what has happened to other miracle teams:

1. The 1914 Braves

The Boston Braves of 1909–1913 were the worst team in baseball. In 1909 they finished 45-108, in last place. In 1910 they finished 53-100, last again. In 1911 they were 44-107, last again and more than twenty games behind the seventh-place team. In 1912 they finished 52-101, last again. In all four seasons they finished more than fifty games out of first place.

In 1913 they looked a little better, finishing 69-82, a mere 31 and one-half games out of first place.

In 1914 they won it. It was a miracle. They were in last place in July, but only 9 and a half out, and then they got back in the race, and then they got hotter than anybody else. They won the pennant; they beat the heavily favored Athletics in a four-game series.

The Braves of 1914 were regarded, and rightly, as a tribute to the managerial genius of George Stallings. Stallings in 1914 was the first manager to platoon at more than one position over a long period of time, and the first to platoon as a positive strategy, rather than as a protective maneuver to hide a player who couldn't hit left-handers.

The Braves were also a very young team—in fact, the youngest team in baseball in 1914. Four regulars were 22 years old or younger, and of the fourteen Braves appearing in 50 games or more, only *one* was older than 27. They were kids.

But they never won again.

Their two ace pitchers developed arm trouble.

The other teams learned that they could platoon, too.

The young players didn't develop much.

A couple of trades were made, but didn't help the team.

The Braves slipped to second in 1915, to third in 1916, to sixth in 1917, to seventh in 1918.

After the 1920 season Stallings was fired.

It was 34 years before the Braves got back to the World Series.

2. The Whiz Kids

For as long as anyone could remember, the Philadelphia Phillies had been the dregs of the National League. Even in 1930, when Chuck Klein drove in 170 runs for them, they still finished last. They lost a hundred games in 1938, in 1939, in 1940. They lost 111 games in 1941, 109 in 1942.

The war came; it didn't help. They finished last in 1944, again in 1945. In 1945 they lost 108 games. The war ended; they continued to finish 20, 25 games under .500 every year.

In late 1948 Eddie Sawyer was hired to manage the team. He brought to the job a new enthusiasm, a new outlook—and all the young players he could find. Kids, kids, everywhere; he surrounded himself with players too young to realize they were doomed to lose. Richie Ashburn's parents came to Philadelphia and set up a rooming house, where many of the young players lived like brothers. *Major leaguers.*

In 1949 they struggled over the .500 mark (81-73), and then in 1950 lightning struck. Curt Simmons, 4-10 in 1949, went 17-8 in 1950. A heavy-set, bespectacled 33-year-old relief pitcher who had been a career minor leaguer until rescued by Sawyer had an MVP season. The Phillies, the Whiz Kids as they were known, won the National League title in 1950.

The Yankees destroyed them in the World Series, but everybody knew they'd be back. They had to be back; time was on their side. Their top starting pitcher, Robin Roberts, was only 23 years old, and destined for the Hall of Fame. Their number two starting pitcher, Simmons, was 21. Del Ennis, who led the team in home runs (31) and batting (.311) and led the *league* in RBI (126)—he was only 25. Their other .300 hitter, the brilliant Richie Ashburn, was only 23. Their number two power hitter, third baseman Willie (Puddin' Head) Jones, was only 24. Shortstop Granny Hamner, perhaps their best all-around player, was 23. They were embarking on a glorious era.

But it never came.

They never won again; they never came close again.

Curt Simmons had to go in the Army for a couple of years, and they couldn't replace him.

Ennis, Ashburn, Hamner, Jones—they all stayed where they were. They were all very good for many years, but none of them took that step forward into greatness.

The kids got married, and one by one moved out of the Ashburns' boarding house.

The chunky reliever who had had the MVP year went into a free-fall in 1951.

Sawyer was fired early in 1952.

The Phillies didn't see October again for 26 years.

3. The 1961 Reds

In the mid-1950s the Cincinnati Reds were a ferocious power-hitting team, arguably the best-hitting team in baseball, although of course Crosley Field had a lot to do with their batting stats. They didn't have the pitching to support the lineup, and so finished as an also-ran behind Brooklyn, the Giants and the Braves.

In the late fifties, as the Reds' offense began to break up, the team dropped toward the bottom of the league. By 1960 the Reds were in sixth place at 67-87, 28 games out.

And then in 1961 everything worked. Driven by manager Fred Hutchinson and MVP Frank Robinson, the Reds won 93 games and the National League pennant. They were not a *terribly* young team, but they were young, younger than the Braves of 1991. Their two best players, Frank Robinson and Vada Pinson, were 25 and 24 years old, and their two best pitchers were the same. Gordy Coleman and Gene Freese, who hit 26 homers apiece and drove in 87 runs apiece, were 26 and 27. The bench contained three brilliant young prospects—catcher Johnny Edwards (23), shortstop Leo Cardenas (22) and pitcher Jim Maloney (21). All three would go on to find major league careers. The farm system burgeoned with prospects—Tommy Harper, Pete Rose, Vic Davallilo, Cookie Rojas. The Reds wiped out in the World Series, but looked forward to more chances.

Which never came.

The two young pitchers, Joey Jay and Jim O'Toole, were good for a couple of years and then weren't.

Coleman and Freese couldn't hold their ground, and the organization couldn't replace them.

The Reds slipped to third in 1962, to fifth in 1963.

Hutchinson died.

Robinson was traded away, then Pinson.

The team was entirely re-built before they won again, nine years later.

4. The 1967 Red Sox

Ted Williams had been retired for seven years. In Williams' last half-decade the Red Sox had faded toward the second division, and then into the second division. In 1964 they lost 90; in 1965 they lost a hundred. In early 1966, when the Red Sox traded for a veteran center fielder named Don Demeter, a sportswriter wrote that the Red Sox had taken out a twenty-year lease on the second division. In 1966 they finished ninth, at 72-90.

In 1967 they won the pennant.

The Red Sox hired a new manager, Dick Williams. He was a tough guy, no-nonsense. He took a group of kids and spelled out the rules for them, rudely, roughly.

They didn't win the World Series—Bob Gibson and Lou Brock beat them—but they came close. They'd be back. The 1967 Red Sox were the youngest team ever to win a pennant. Of the eight regulars, six were 24 or younger, one was 25, and the other, the MVP, was 27. Their best pitcher, Jim Lonborg, was 25.

But they never won again, not with that team. Lonborg went skiing that winter, hurt his knee. Bad. George Scott, who had hit .303 with 19 homers in the championship year—he was 23—hit .171 with 3 homers in 350 at bats. Without a number-one pitcher and dragging an obelisk at first base, the 1968 Sox won 86 games, but not enough.

Dick Williams decided they hadn't worked hard enough. That was his philosophy; if you lost, it was because you didn't work hard enough or because you wussed out. He pumped up the volume. The players revolted.

The league split into two divisions in 1969, but the Sox into warring camps. Lonborg failed to come back. Scott came only part-way back. A trade worked out poorly. Williams was fired late in the 1969 season.

Only two members of the 1967 team were still around when the Sox won again, eight years later.

5. The 1969 Mets

The 1969 New York Mets have become the most famous miracle team of all time. From their birth in 1962 the Mets were a joke. Their first four years they finished last, losing well over a hundred games a year. In 1966 they got out of the basement for a year, but in 1967 they were back, losing 101.

In 1968 they hired a new manager, Gil Hodges. He was tough, too, but in a quieter way. His players loved him, and struggled to a 73-89 record, a ninth-place finish. That was their best record up to then, by far.

And, of course, they won then, with timing and arms. They had the best starting core in the league, with Tom Seaver (25 years old, 25-7), Jerry Koosman (26 years old, 17-9) and Gary Gentry (22 years old, 13-12). Relief ace Tug McGraw was 24. Tommy Agee at 26 was Ron Gant, one of the best outfielders in the league. Nolan Ryan was 22 then, and he won only six games but oh, could he bring it.

The magic stayed with them through the World Series, as they humiliated an Oriole team that was about 20 games better than they were.

But in 1970 the magic was gone.

The pitching remained great but the timing, the big hit always there when you need it—it wasn't there. Agee traded speed for weight. Ryan was erratic.

Years went by, 1970, 1971, 1972. Ryan struggled with his control, and they traded him. Gil Hodges died.

The Mets did win another pennant with that team, another little miracle in 1973. All the good teams were in the other division, and the Mets won the title with an 82-79 record. That was their future.

6. The Cubs of '84

The Mets won in 1969 by blowing by the Cubs, who . . . well, blew it. The Cubs had been out of contention for twenty years before Leo Durocher came, and when Leo left they were out of contention again in six minutes. It's unfortunate that Durocher's time in Chicago is remembered by his mistakes, but that's life.

After Durocher they were neither good nor interesting. From 1979 to 1983 they never finished better than fifth in a six-team division. That was their frame of reference; sixth place was a bad year, fifth place a good year.

And then they won.

1984. Ryne Sandberg was unbelievable. Jim Frey took over as manager, a positive thinker. It caught on. Three veterans were brought in who knew about pennant races—Larry Bowa, Ron Cey, Gary Matthews. Good players.

In mid-summer they traded kids for a starting pitcher, Rick Sutcliffe. Sutcliffe had one of the most amazing seasons in history. He won the Cy Young Award in a half-season in the NL, 20 starts. He was 16-1.

Nobody ever thought this team would be a dynasty, and everybody was right for a change: they weren't. They were back under .500 the next year, and back in fifth place the year after that, and back in sixth place the year after that.

They had another little miracle in 1989. Sutcliffe and Sandberg got enough help to take to another divisional title, and then they went back to the second division again.

These six, in my opinion, are the only *real* miracle teams in baseball history before 1991, or at least the only ones since 1900. Baseball is different now than it was in the 1960s, and very different than it was in 1914. The distance between the top of the league and the bottom is less than half what it once was. Last-place teams can go to the top a lot quicker than they could, and for that reason short-term strategies prevail in the front office. If a team loses three years in four but wins big the fourth year, general managers get to keep their jobs.

Also, what happened to the Boston Red Sox after 1967 was not inevitable fate; it is merely what happened. The fact that no miracle team has yet been able to move from one-year-wonder to consistent excellence doesn't mean that the Braves *won't* be able to.

But it ain't going to be easy. It's not going to follow from 1991 as the night follows the evening, but more in the way that a marriage follows a wedding. They're going to have to *make* it work.

THE GOOD-YEAR GUYS

One of the ways that we explain championships in modern baseball is that a team wins when a bunch of guys have good years at the same time. I have never been attracted to this explanation. To say that you win by getting eight guys having good years at the same time says, in essence, that logic, reason, patience, training and talent will not avail you if your timing is wrong: it's luck. You've got to get enough guys having good years at the same time.

I don't like the logic, but then, that's Ecclesiastes; the race goes not to the swift, nor the battle to the strong, nor riches to men of understanding, but time and chance happen to them all. That I don't *like* that explanation doesn't mean that it doesn't contain an element of truth.

Anyway, after the 1991 season I did a study which relates to this issue. I compared each player's 1991 offensive production to his career batting performance. If a player hit better in 1991 than he had before, then he's in the plus column; if he hit less than he had in his previous seasons, that puts him in the negative category. True rookies are at zero, since their 1991 batting performance *is* their career performance.

The major league over-achiever of the year in 1991 was—this is not a surprise—Terry Pendleton. Pendleton was about 43 runs better as a hitter in 1991 than he had been before. A major league "All-Guys-Having-Career-Years" Team:

C—Mickey Tettleton	+22
1B—Paul Molitor	+33
2B—Julio Franco	+40
3B—Terry Pendleton	+43
SS—Cal Ripken	+36
LF—Barry Bonds	+21
CF—Devon White	+28
RF—Danny Tartabull	+27
DH—Chili Davis	+31

A couple of position options here. We could move Tony Phillips (+26) to left field, bumping Bonds, but Bonds is one of two National Leaguers on the team, anyway. Molitor was really a DH, so we could put him at DH and put Rafael Palmeiro (+29) at first base. I reckon you'd win the pennant no matter who you chose from this group. The nine players above hit a composite .260 in 1990, with an average of 15 home runs and 65 RBI apiece, which is about what they'll do again in 1992. In 1991 they hit a composite .306 with 25 homers and 90 RBI. They created 4.9 runs per 27 outs in 1990, 7.1 in 1991.

Anyway, the real point here was that while I was figuring that I also figured team totals for each major league team. Simple idea;

I don't know why it took me fifteen years to reach this point, but the data was intriguing. The *best* team total in the National League was +80, for the Atlanta Braves. The second best team total was +52, for the Pirates. In other words, the teams which won the divisions were the teams which had the most guys having good years.

In the American League the division winners weren't the teams with the *best* team totals, but they were close. The Twins were +17, and Toronto +32. Both teams received major help from mid-winter acquisitions who made the list above, Chili Davis of Minnesota and Devon White of Toronto.

Well, I thought that data was so intriguing—maybe there *is* something to this idea that you win by having good years together—that I immediately decided to run the same data for 1990.

In 1990 the most-fortunate teams in the NL were Pittsburgh (+80) and Cincinnati (+48). Once more, the teams which had the most guys having good years *did* win in the National League—but didn't in the American League. In the American League the Red Sox won in 1990 although their collective offense was 107 runs under expectations, and the A's although they were minus two, two runs under.

I don't have a big finish here; the only real point I was making was that the Braves did win in 1991, in part, because they had players playing over their head. Pendleton was +43, Otis Nixon +16, Gant +11, Treadway +8, Blauser and Belliard each +5—while no one was having an awful year. If we pursued this line of study further, we *might* find some systematic knowledge which would be useful in analyzing a pennant race. We might find a leading indicator. It is reasonable to think that teams which didn't have a lot of players having good years last year might be expected to do better this year. But there would be all kinds of biases to adjust for before we reached that point.

CRITICAL LIST

When a major league player is released his teammates say he died.

Suppose we draw up a list of the number of major league players by age . . . how many 23-year-olds, 24-year-olds, etc. This is the list for 1991 from ages 26 to 36; this includes all players who played 100 games or batted 250 times.

26	27	28	29	30	31	32	33	34	35	36
31	29	23	21	31	16	14	9	8	11	3

I guess this is self-evident; there were 31 major league regulars or semi-regulars in 1991 who were 26 years old, 29 who were 27, etc. You will remember that earlier, in a part of the Kansas City comment, I focused on just a part of this spectrum:

At age:	30	31	32	33
Number of players:	31	16	14	9

What this tells us is that there are a whole bunch of major league players born about 1960 or 1961 who are going to kick the bucket in the next two years. As a player moves into his thirties his skills begin to slip. For a really good player—Cal Ripken or Ryne Sandberg—this isn't a big deal. Take twenty points and a little power away from Ryne Sandberg, and you've got a .280 hitter with 25 homers a year. Take twenty points and a little power away from Sid Bream, and you've got a first baseman who hits .240 with eight homers a year.

So who are they? It can't be that hard to figure, can it? If we take all major league players at age 30 or 31, we can figure that half of them—the ones who are good—are still going to be here in about two years, and the other half aren't. Who does this affect? What major league teams are going to be most affected by these losses?

I took a list of players by age. The obvious conclusion is that the two teams which will be *most* affected by having not-particularly-good players move into the twilight zone in the next two or three years are the two teams which met in the World Series—Minnesota and Atlanta. A list:

			1991	
Player	Born	HR	RBI	BAvg
G Gagne	November, 1961	8	42	.265
Belliard	October, 1961	0	27	.249
G Olson	September, 1960	6	44	.241
Bream	August, 1960	11	45	.253
A Newman	June, 1960	0	19	.191
Pagliarulo	March, 1960	6	36	.279
O Nixon	January, 1959	0	26	.297
D Gladden	July, 1957	6	52	.247

Incidentally, people assume that Greg Olson is young because he's only been in the majors a couple of years. He's 21 months younger than Mike Scioscia. He's older than Darryl Strawberry.

Anyway, probably no other major league team has an equal number of regulars and near-regulars who will need to be replaced within the next two seasons. A year ago, Terry Pendleton's career would also have been on the endangered list; now, it doesn't appear that way.

Well, I've written three articles here explaining what's wrong with the Braves, and you probably think I'm down on them. I'm not; they're an exciting team, and they may have another great season. I wish them well. My analysis doesn't say that this team should be the division favorite in 1992, and I wanted to explain why.

LASORDA'S LAMENT

In the last two weeks of the season Tommy Lasorda was reportedly upset because he did not feel that the Reds and Astros had made an effort to start their best pitchers against the Braves, whereas everyone in general and the Giants in particular were going all-out to stop the Dodgers. The Dodgers, he felt, were being treated unfairly by the rest of the league.

This reminded me that a few years ago Garry Templeton made a similar remark, that the Padres after winning the division in 1984 had faced all the best pitchers in 1985. To evaluate this I devised a simple test of the quality of opposition starting pitching, which I'll describe in a minute. What I found at that time (1986 *Abstract*) was that there *were* significant differences in the quality of pitching faced by different teams, which *don't* even out over the course of a season. The differences, however, appeared to be random, rather than organized for some particular purpose like pitching the best pitchers against the best teams.

I decided to repeat this study, and compare the quality of pitchers faced by the Dodgers and Braves not just over the season's last two weeks, but over the season as a whole. I graded every starting pitcher in the National League as an "A", a "B", a "C", or a "D". They are graded according to how many performance standards they have met, such as a winning record, 200 innings, an ERA better than the league norm, etc.

The "A" quality pitchers are the best pitchers in the league. There aren't a lot of these; the entire list of Grade A starting pitchers in the NL for 1991 is Steve Avery, Tim Belcher, Andy Benes, David Cone, Doug Drabek, Tommy Glavine, Pete Harnisch, Bruce Hurst, Charlie Leibrandt, Greg Maddux, Dennis Martinez, Ramon Martinez, Mike Morgan, Terry Mulholland, Jose Rijo, John Smiley, and Zane Smith. Atlanta, Los Angeles and Pittsburgh have three Grade-A starting pitchers apiece, and basically everybody else has one, who is the guy you hope doesn't start against you in a three-game series.

The "B" quality pitchers, of course, are the guys who just missed being "A" quality pitchers, and the "D" quality starting pitchers are the guys who started only a few times or pitched very badly, or both. There are lots and lots of D-quality pitchers, but as a group they only account for about as many starts as the A-quality pitchers.

Anyway, cut to the chase. **The quality of the starting pitchers faced by the Atlanta Braves over the course of the season was not weaker than the quality of starting pitchers faced by the Los Angeles Dodgers. It was stronger.** The Braves did face twelve D-quality starting pitchers after the first of September, whereas the Dodgers faced only five. Since both teams won almost all of those games, when they faced a weak starter down the stretch, this was a significant factor in Atlanta's ability to pull ahead of LA in the closing weeks. Lasorda no doubt picked up on this, and that was the basis of his complaint.

However, over the course of the entire season the picture is very different. **Over the course of the entire season the Braves faced significantly more high-quality starting pitchers than did the Dodgers.** This is the data:

Quality of Opposition Starters

	A	B	C	D
Atlanta	45	33	37	47
Los Angeles	39	30	40	53

The Braves faced 45 Grade-A starting pitchers in their drive to the title; the Dodgers faced only 39.

The Braves faced 78 Grade A or B starting pitchers; the Dodgers faced only 69.

The Braves faced more "A's" and more "B's"; the Dodgers faced more "C's" and more "D's".

The advantage derived from this by the Dodgers is not huge; it amounts to about one and a half games. (The winning percentage of Grade-A starting pitchers is about 220 points higher than that of Grade-D starting pitchers. There's a six-game swing there, which gives the Dodgers an edge of 1.32 games.) Essentially, the Dodgers started out the 1991 pennant race with a one-and-a-half game lead.

I doubt that there is a reason for this; I suspect it's just random. I do think that the issue would warrant further study, if only young sabermetricians would take the time and effort to study stuff like this rather than beating their heads against the wall trying to convince the world that they have developed a better way to rate the hitters. You might find, for example, that teams which play in hitters' parks tend to face better quality starting pitching because the opposition is afraid to experiment with the rotation in Wrigley Field or Fulton County Stadium. I doubt it, but you never know unless you look.

In any case, the Dodgers faced 38 poor-quality starting pitchers last year between opening day and the end of July; the Braves faced only 25. The Dodgers faced only three really good starting pitchers in August, 1991; the Braves faced seven. On balance, the league went easy on the Dodgers.

THE LOS ANGELES DODGERS
• IN A BOX •

1991 Won-Lost Record: 93-69 .574

Rank among 26 teams: 4th
Over Last Five Years: 423-384 .524
Rank over Five Years: 7th
In Last Ten Years: 849-768 .525
Rank over Ten Years: 5th

Best Player: Brett Butler

Weak Spot: Shortstop

Best Pitcher: Ramon Martinez

Staff Weakness: Bullpen Closer

Best Bench Player: Mike Sharperson

Best Baseball Name: Darryl Strawberry

Best Young Player: None

Best Looking Player: Tom Candiotti

Ugliest Player: John Candeleria

Most Pleasant Surprise, 1991: Juan Samuel's first half

Biggest Disappointment, 1991: Juan Samuel's second half

Best Minor League Prospect: Pedro Martinez

Who Is: Ramon's brother. Pedro, not as tall as Ramon but just as skinny, blew through three levels of competition last summer. He was 8-0 at Bakersfield, 7-5 with a 1.76 ERA at San Antonio, and pitched fairly well at Albuquerque. He doesn't turn 21 until July, but would seem to have a decent chance of breaking into the rotation this season if Ojeda or Gross falters.

Other Prospects: **Eric Karros,** a 24-year-old first baseman, may get some playing time left behind by Eddie Murray. He should hit OK, but I'm not predicting greatness. **Dave Hansen,** still only 23, is regarded as one of the best third base prospects around. **Jose Offerman,** last year's hot prospect, is the same age and still has a future at short. **Carlos Hernandez,** 25, is a fine-looking catcher, and in my opinion perhaps the best of the lot. **Henry Rodriguez,** who had a fine year at San Antonio in 1990, didn't do much with Albuquerque in 1991.

Designated Malcontent: Darryl Strawberry

Park Characteristics: A great pitcher's park, reduces the numbers of doubles, triples and home runs all substantially.

The Park Helps: All pitchers.

The Park Hurts: All hitters.

ORGANIZATIONAL REPORT CARD

Ownership:	A
Upper Management:	B
Field Management:	B+
Front-Line Talent:	C+
Second-Line Talent:	B−
Minor League System:	B

TEAM LEADERS:

Batting Average: Brett Butler, .296

Last Ten Years (Season): Pedro Guerrero, 1987, .338
Last Ten Years (Total): Pedro Guerrero, .310

Doubles: Eddie Murray, 23

Triples: Juan Samuel, 6

Home Runs: Darryl Strawberry, 28

Last Ten Years (Season): Pedro Guerrero, 1985, 33
Last Ten Years (Total): Guerrero, 150

RBI: Darryl Strawberry, 99

Last Ten Years (Season): Pedro Guerrero, 1983, 103
Last Ten Years (Total): Guerrero, 496

Extra Base Hits: Darryl Strawberry, 54

Stolen Bases: Brett Butler, 38

Walks: Brett Butler, 108

Runs Created: Brett Butler, 93

Runs Created Per Game: Darryl Strawberry, 6.3

Secondary Average: Darryl Strawberry .394

Wins: Ramon Martinez, 17

Last Ten Years (Season): Orel Hershiser, 1988, 23
Last Ten Years (Total): Fernando Valenzuela, 126

Winning Percentage: Mike Morgan, 14-10 .583

Strikeouts: Tim Belcher, 156

Last Ten Years (Season): Fernando Valenzuela, 1986, 242
Last Ten Years (Total): Valenzuela, 1563

ERA: Tim Belcher 2.62

Saves: Jay Howell, 16

League Leaders:

1. Eric Davis has a career stolen base percentage of 87%, which is the highest in major league history.

2. John Candelaria had 19 "Holds" in 1991, the most in the National League.

Stat of the Year: Ramon Martinez has a career won-lost record of 29-9 from April through July, but 15-17 from August 1 to the end of the season.

1991 SEASON

Background: Throughout the free-agent era the Dodgers have followed a pattern of "gearing up" for periodic drives to the title, while attempting to remain constantly competitive between chosen years. After finishing fourth in 1989 and second in 1990, the Dodgers felt it was time to make a major push again in 1991, and signed free agents Darryl Strawberry and Brett Butler (among others) to add impetus to that push.

Outlook: The signing of Strawberry made the Dodgers one of the favorites to take the division. Some people picked Cincinnati, some Los Angeles, but most of us picked one or the other.

Getaway: The Dodgers normally play *more* games than most of the other teams in April, and (perhaps for that reason) over a period of years have played extremely well early in the season, better than at any other time of the year. They didn't do it, in 1991; they were 11-12 on the morning of May 5.

High Point of the Season: The Dodgers went 28-12 between May 8 and June 20, and appeared to be in absolute command of the race at that time. The Reds, the co-favorite, were six games behind, in second place. The Giants, the other team the Dodgers feared, were playing awful. The Braves, who nobody took seriously anyway, were seven games out.

Stretch Drive: The Dodgers lost the pennant in August, when they went 13-16 to allow the Braves to slip a game ahead of them. There is no real reason for the slump. The Dodgers were at home most of the month, didn't have an unusual rash of injuries and, as I pointed out in the Atlanta comment, faced only three Grade-A starting pitchers during the entire month. They just played a lot of sloppy, ineffective baseball, and were beaten by some very ordinary pitchers, starting with a three-game series in which they were swept by the Houston Astros.

Once they realized that the Braves could actually beat them, the Dodgers did respond to the challenge. Everyone knows that the Braves played well down the stretch. So did the Dodgers. From September 1 on, the two teams had identical records, 22-9. The Dodgers started September one game back, and they wound up one game back.

Low Point of the Season: Elimination day, October 5. Despite being three time zones apart, the Dodgers-Giants and Braves-Astros games were played concurrently. Trevor Wilson stopped the Dodgers with a two-hit shutout, as the Braves were beating Houston 5-2.

Most Exciting Game of the Season: September 21, a classic pitching duel in the thick of the pennant race and in Dodger Stadium. The Dodgers scored one in the eighth and one in the ninth to beat the Braves, 2-1. The Dodgers collected six hits against Leibrandt and Stanton, the Braves only four against Hershiser, Gott and McDowell. The win put the Dodgers in first by a half-game.

Major Injuries: The biggest loss was Jay Howell, who the Dodgers insist is their relief ace although he hasn't had a healthy year since 1985. Howell was on the disabled list from June 20—the high point of the season—until July 23 because of a sprained ligament in his right elbow, and also didn't pitch from September 3 to October 6 because of the elbow problem.

Jeff Hamilton missed the better part of the season with a torn ligament in his knee, but he probably wouldn't have beat out Lenny Sharperson anyway. Strawberry missed a few weeks with a sore shoulder he sustained while making a catch at the wall. Kal Daniels was bothered by aching knees and shoulders, and didn't play as well as he is capable of playing.

Offense: Very good. The Dodgers scored an above-average number of runs (665, league average 663) despite playing in a poor hitter's park.

Defense: Better than in recent years, still not good. The addition of Brett Butler in center field improved the outfield defense, although the other two guys were not good outfielders. Samuel played better at second than he had in the past, Griffin was at short for his glove, such as it is, Murray at first was a good defensive player and Harris does some things well at third.

Pitching: Good. The Dodgers' ERA was 38 points better than any other team in the majors, and even in Dodger Stadium, that's pretty good.

Best Game by a Starting Pitcher: Tim Belcher threw a four-hitter at the Cubs on August 30, Game Score 89 (9 4 0 0 0 10).

Worst Game by a Starting Pitcher: Ramon Martinez, September 15 against the Braves. The line score was bad (2 4 7 5 3 2 Game Score 21), and it was also a critical game.

Indicators for 1991 were: Down 9.7

Number of regulars having good seasons by their own standards:

Two (Brett Butler, Len Harris). This is a misleading query for the Dodgers, because the Dodgers

a) are almost entirely built out of veteran players acquired from other teams, and
b) play in a terrible park for a hitter.

The great majority of players over the age of 29 are going to perform below their career standards in any season. When you put those players in a poor hitters' park, that makes it even more unlikely that they will match their career norms. So in any season it's going to be very unlikely that more than one or two Dodger hitters will have good years by their own standards, unless they start using some young guys.

Dodger Stadium may not be a bad park for Brett Butler, because Butler rarely hits drives to the outfield anyway. Butler bunts a great deal, which makes the condition of the infield grass critical to him.

1991 Over-Achiever: Harris

1991 Under-Achiever: Kal Daniels

Infield: Average/Below Average. Dodger shortstops in 162 games scored only 40 runs, drove in only 36 runs and made 38 errors. The Dodgers were eighth in the league in turning double plays.

The other three infield positions were fairly good, all things considered, but none of them were outstanding; nobody was a candidate for the post-season All-Star team. So you've got one big hole and no bright spot.

Outfield: Very good, even with the defense. Butler was an MVP candidate, and Strawberry drove in 99 runs despite an injury. Dodger outfielders hit .270, scored 284 runs and drove in 230.

Catching: Good. Scioscia was good, as he always is, and Carter played well.

Starting Pitching: Excellent, would have been best in the majors if Martinez had pitched as well as he did in 1990. The Dodgers had three Grade-A starters (Belcher, Morgan and Martinez), plus Ojeda was OK.

Bullpen: Fairly good. The Dodgers blew 16 save opportunities, more than Atlanta (11) or Cincinnati (15). Their bullpen ERA was 3.08, the best in the National League, and they had 54 Holds, the most in the National League.

Percentage of offense created by:

Young Players:	11%
Players in Their Prime:	44%
Past Their Prime:	45%

Team Age:

Age of Non-Pitchers:	31.0
Age of Pitching Staff:	30.0
Overall Team Age:	30.56

The 1991 Dodgers were the oldest team in the National League.

In retrospect, the critical decisions were: Obviously, there were a lot of *good* decisions made to get the Dodgers to 93 wins. The decisions to sign Brett Butler and Darryl Strawberry worked out well. The decision to move Juan Samuel back to the infield helped, at least in the first half of the season, and the trade for Bobby Ojeda in December, 1990, was a good trade.

Lasorda, trying to make 1991 a pennant year, chose to go entirely with veterans, and not to risk anything on rookies and young players. If I were to find fault with any particular decision of the 1991 Dodgers, it would be that I believe they went too far in this direction. At shortstop the Dodgers would have been better off with Offerman full time than Griffin, Offerman, Harris and Sharperson. That's a minor thing and might not have made a positive difference, but I also believe the Dodgers should have made more use of some of the young arms available to them, such as Dennis Cook, John Wetteland and Jim Poole, rather than relying entirely on veterans.

THAT AND THE OTHER

Hall of Fame Watch: See article, "Through a Plaque"

Chris Berman, Have You Considered: Jose (Jack) Offerman

Throwback: Brett Butler, to the dead ball era

Attendance Trend: Still solid and growing

Players with a Chance for 3000 career hits:

Brett Butler	9%
Darryl Strawberry	1%

Best Interview: Roger McDowell

Probably Could Play Regularly For Another Team: Mike Sharperson

Best Fundamental Player: Brett Butler

Worst Fundamental Player: Juan Samuel

Best Defensive Player: Brett Butler

Worst Defensive Player: Kal Daniels

Best Knowledge of the Strike Zone: Butler and Scioscia are both among the best in baseball.

Least Command of the Strike Zone: Juan Samuel

Fastest Runner: Juan Samuel

Slowest Runner: Mike Scioscia

Best Baserunner: Eric Davis

Most Likely to Still be Here in 2000: No obvious candidate. I think we can rule out John Candelaria.

Best Fastball: Ramon Martinez

Best Breaking Pitch: Tom Candiotti's knuckleball

Best Control: Tim Crews

Most Overrated Player: Eric Davis

Most Underrated Player: Mike Scioscia

Oddest Collection of Abilities: Juan Samuel

Best Local Sportswriter: I'll stay with my childhood hero, Jim Murray, but the Los Angeles area may have more quality sportswriters than any other city.

The Most Knowledgeable Person about Dodger history is: Tot Holmes

Most-Similar Players:

to C Mike Scioscia, Tony Peña
to 1B Eddie Murray, Dale Murphy
to 2B Juan Samuel, Tony Fernandez
to 3B Lenny Harris, Charlie Hayes (?)
to SS Alfredo Griffin, Rafael Ramirez
to LF Kal Daniels, Dan Pasqua
to CF Brett Butler, Willie McGee
to RF Darryl Strawberry, Joe Carter

Most Fun to Watch: Brett Butler

Least Fun to Watch: Kal Daniels

Town Team:

C—Del Crandall
1B—Eddie Murray
2B—Bobby Doerr
SS—Arky Vaughn
3B—Jackie Robinson
LF—Ralph Kiner
CF—Duke Snider
RF—Tony Gwynn
SP—Don Drysdale
MGR—Sparky Anderson

Post-Season Transactions:

November 15, Let Gary Carter go on waivers

November 27, Traded Tim Belcher and John Wetteland for Eric Davis and Kip Gross

Also November 27, Eddie Murray left as a Free Agent

December 2, Lost Mike Morgan as Free Agent

December 3, Signed Tom Candiotti as Free Agent

December 6, Signed Mitch Webster to a minor league contract

December 11, Traded Chris Gwynn and Domingo Mota to Kansas City for Todd Benzinger

What Needs to Be Done For 1992: See article, "So What Happens Now?"

Outlook for 1992: See article

Index of Leading Indicators for 1992: Down 18.2

Positive Indicators: 1. Good AAA team

Negative Indicators: 1. Team Age

Due for a better season: Kal Daniels

Likely to have a worse season: Lenny Harris

1992 Won-Lost Record will be: 82-80

SO WHAT HAPPENS NOW?

Kal Daniels has battled injuries for most of the last three years, and in 1991 did not play as well as has been his habit. His teammates, or at least some of them, have begun to question his commitment to the game, and so in late November Darryl Strawberry decided to take charge of the situation. "Somebody has to finally say something about him, and I'll be the guy," Strawberry told the *Los Angeles Times*. "Trade Kal. If he doesn't want to play, get him out of here."

Let's think this through. If the Dodgers intended to trade Kal Daniels, then Strawberry's statement is a pain, because it makes it much more difficult for the Dodgers to trade Daniels for value. He's being traded with a scarlet J on his chest, for Jakin' It.

If, on the other hand, the Dodgers intended to *keep* Daniels, then Strawberry's decision to speak out isn't exactly a great idea, either; now Strawberry has to share a clubhouse with a player he has ripped in public.

Within a few days it became apparent what the plan was, as the Dodgers traded Tim Belcher to Cincinnati for Eric Davis. The trade gave the Dodgers four star outfielders, or 2.3 if you go by playing time. Eric Davis and Darryl Strawberry, as I'm sure you know, are childhood buddies as well as terrifying hitters. Combining these two incidents, the impression is created that Darryl Strawberry is to be named the Dodgers' acting General Manager, as soon they can fit the extra duties into their budget. And if you want to fully boggle your imagination, consider the possibility that the Dodgers may actually put Eric Davis in left field, and trade somebody *else* because the other guy gets hurt so much that the Dodgers don't feel they can count on him.

In the last ten years the Dodgers have periodically picked out a season, geared up for a major one-season push, won the division title or more, and then backed off and re-tooled. Last year, for the first time, the Dodgers geared up for a major push and *didn't* win, so what happens now? Do they have the stomach to back off and re-load, understanding that this may put six years between their last championship and their next one? Or will they, as George Steinbrenner did, become so frustrated by their failure to meet expectations that they will try instead to increase the pressure so they can accomplish this year what they should have done last year?

The decision to let Eddie Murray go can be seen as evidence that the Dodgers are realists, while the trade for Eric Davis is not on the other hand, and the signing of Tom Candiotti a few days later puts the issue to rest. I wonder if the Dodgers in the next few years may begin to re-enact the history of their once most hated rivals? The Dodgers are a rent-a-player organization, as the Yankees were, and they're about where the Yankees were in 1985.

They'll pull out of it. My father used to say that a dictatorship was the best form of government as long as you had a good man at the top, a man who wanted to do things to help the people. In his generation this was not an uncommon belief. My father was a good man, but not what you'd call politically sophisticated. The problem with a dictatorship is, what happens when the dictator is wrong? In Steinbrenner's case, what happened was that he destroyed himself and his little fiefdom trying to prove that he wasn't. The Dodgers will pull in their horns before that happens.

Or then, maybe they'll win. If there's a good team in this 1992 division, I haven't seen it yet. Lasorda will be 65 in September. The Dodgers want to send him out a winner.

ONE DOLLAR SHORT

Years ago I wrote a short story, never published, about a bank teller who was one dollar short at the end of a day. The dollar didn't amount to anything, but a co-worker thought that he had seen the unfortunate man taking a dollar out of the drawer during the course of business, and mentions this to a supervisor. The teller, having a few drinks at a bar at the end of the day, hears from another co-worker that he (the teller) is being investigated by the bank, not knowing that the investigation involves only the missing dollar. The teller, slightly under the influence and depressed by troubles at home, bolts the county. Warrants are issued for his arrest; the story hits the papers. Two days later he realizes that he has acted irrationally and returns, but his job is gone and his wife has been humiliated by the scandal. Eventually she takes the kids and moves out. His life is ruined by the missing dollar.

The number of games a team will win in a season is a function of runs scored and runs allowed. The ratio between wins and losses will be almost the same as the ratio between the square of runs scored and the square of runs allowed; this is known as the Pythagorean Theory of wins and losses. If a team scored three runs per game for a season and allowed only two, their ratio of wins to losses would be 9 to 4.

Because deviations from this expectation are not predictable, they are believed to result from luck. There are two reasons for saying this: first, that the deviations don't correlate with any other skill at a meaningful level, and second, that deviations from expected wins and losses have *no* tendency to be consistent from year to year. True *abilities* in baseball, on a team or individual level, are consistent from year to year; a team which plays well in any phase of the game in 1991 will tend to play well in the same phase of the game again in 1992. Since this *isn't* true of over- or under-production of wins from runs, we tend to believe that it is not a true ability. Also, abilities form clusters. All skills are related to some other skills—teams which hit a lot of home runs tend also to draw walks, etc. Teams which hit doubles tend also to hit triples. Teams which hit triples tend also to steal bases. Since winning more games than expected by the Pythagorean Method doesn't correlate with any other skill, it doesn't appear to be a true ability in itself. It's luck.

If every team in the NL West had won *exactly* the number of games expected in 1991, these would have been the final standings:

	W	L	Pct.
LA	94	68	.580
Atl	93	69	.574
Cin	81	81	.500
SD	80	82	.494
SF	75	87	.463
Hou	67	95	.414

With the exception of Cincinnati, which had terrible luck in the close games, all of the other discrepancies in the projections are insignificant, like the missing dollar. The Dodgers, who should have won 94 games, won 93. The Braves, who should have won 93, won 94.

If they don't come back and win it this year, that tiny little shortfall will haunt some of them for the rest of their lives.

THROUGH A PLAQUE, BUT DARKLY

One of the questions I ask myself near the end of a baseball season is "What major league player has done the most this year to help himself get into the Hall of Fame?" Thinking about this a week from the end of the 1991 season, I concluded that there were three candidates—Paul Molitor, Jack Morris and Brett Butler.

Of course, when the shooting stopped the answer was obviously Jack Morris. Morris' fine season and brilliant seventh-game performance, in all likelihood, will one day put him in the Hall of Fame. The 1991 season changed him from a longshot to an odds-on favorite for eventual recognition.

Molitor helped himself, too; he still has a battle, but he'll be taken very seriously for the Hall of Fame if he gets close to 3,000 hits, and the 1991 season means that he will get close to 3,000 hits. He already has more than 2,000.

Butler, on the other hand . . . well, he needed help. He's probably not going to get 3,000 hits, and while he has always done *some* things which would be characteristic of a Hall of Famer, he has never been able to hit the biggies. With a week to go in the 1991 season, he was in position to score big. He was hitting over .300, and leading the league in hits, walks and runs scored. He had done for Los Angeles what Terry Pendleton had done for Atlanta, and he could very well have been the MVP. Then he's in post-season play, and who knows; he could have been the guy who got hot at the right time.

It didn't happen, of course. At the wire he dropped under .300, lost the league lead in hits, and the Dodgers lost a race they should have won. Pendleton got the MVP, and Morris was the star of the series. Butler was a longshot for the Hall of Fame a year ago, and he's a longshot now. If it was 15 to 1 against him a year ago, it's 10-1 now. Give him a couple of breaks, and he could have been even money.

THE SAN DIEGO PADRES
• IN A BOX •

1991 Won-Lost Record: 84-78 .519

Rank among 26 teams: Tied for 8th
Over Last Five Years: 396-413 .489
Rank over Five Years: Tied for 18th
In Last Ten Years: 816-803 .504
Rank over Ten Years: 12th

Best Player: Fred McGriff

Weak Spots: Left Field and Third Base

Best Pitcher: Andy Benes

Hurst and Benes had comparable records last year, 15 wins apiece with similar stats. Ordinarily I would pick as their best pitcher the one who had a better record over a period of years, which would be Hurst. However, I've always believed in Benes, and always thought he would eventually be a star. With Benes' tremendous finish (11-1 with a 1.86 ERA in his last fourteen starts) and Hurst's so-so finish (one win in his last eight starts) I have to think Benes is now the ace of the staff.

Staff Weakness: Relief ace

Best Bench Player: Thomas Howard

Best Baseball Name: Scott Coolbaugh

Best Young Player: Benito Santiago
(See Hal Morris comment, Cincinnati)

Best Looking Player: Thomas Howard

Ugliest Player: Derek Lilliquist

Most Pleasant Surprise, 1991: Darrin Jackson

Biggest Disappointment, 1991: Presley and Coolbaugh

With Jim Presley on hand and Scott Coolbaugh also picked up from Texas, the Padres thought they had the third base problem not only solved but double-solved, solved and protected. It didn't work. Presley stunk, Coolbaugh froze and the job fell in the lap of Jack Howell, who hit .207. For the season, San Diego third basemen hit .194.

Best Minor League Prospect: None

San Diego Prospects: See article, "Padre Future"

Designated Malcontent: Benito Santiago

Park Characteristics: Low-average, good home run park, on balance favors the pitcher more than the hitter.

The Park Helps: No one to a great extent.

The Park Hurts: Same.

ORGANIZATIONAL REPORT CARD

Ownership:	D
Upper Management:	C+
Field Management:	I don't know
Front-Line Talent:	B+
Second-Line Talent:	C
Minor League System:	D

TEAM LEADERS:

Batting Average: Tony Gwynn, .317

Last Ten Years (Season): Tony Gwynn, .370 in 1987
Last Ten Years (Total): Tony Gwynn, .328

Doubles: Gwynn and Fernandez, 27 each

Triples: Gwynn, 11

Home Runs: Fred McGriff, 31

Last Ten Years (Season): McGriff, 31 in 1991
Last Ten Years (Total): Terry Kennedy, 74

RBI: Fred McGriff, 106

Last Ten Years (Season): Joe Carter, 115 in 1990
Last Ten Years (Total): Tony Gwynn, 550

Extra Base Hits: Fred McGriff, 51

Stolen Bases: Bip Roberts, 26

Walks: Fred McGriff, 105

Runs Created: Fred McGriff, 107

Runs Created Per Game: McGriff, 7.2

Secondary Average: McGriff, .422

Wins: Hurst and Benes, 15 each

Last Ten Years (Season): Andy Hawkins, 18 in 1985
Last Ten Years (Total): Eric Show, 99

Winning Percentage: Bruce Hurst, 15-8 .652

Strikeouts: Andy Benes, 167

Last Ten Years (Season): Hurst, 179 in 1989
Last Ten Years (Total): Eric Show, 929

ERA: Benes, 3.03

Saves: Lefferts, 23

League Leaders: STATS Inc. maintains "zone ratings" for defensive performance. The field is divided by letters and numbers, and when each hit occurs the STATS scorer, in the press box, notes the direction and distance where the ball was hit. The fielders can be evaluated, among other things, by the percentage of balls in their zone which they convert into outs.

Thomas Howard last year played 188 innings in left field and 321 innings in center field. He had the highest zone rating in the major leagues at *both* positions, getting to 98% of the balls in his zone while in left field, and 91% in center field.

Stat of the Year: The 1991 Padres cut their staff ERA month by month. They had an ERA of 4.25 in April, cut it to 4.20 in May, cut that to 3.47 in June, to 3.45 in July, to 3.35 in August and to 2.92 in September. In October it went back to 3.27, but that's just four games, and 3.27 is still good. Their pitching staff was rolling at the end of the year.

1991 SEASON

Background: The Padres since 1984 have been bedeviled by front office confusion. Starting with battles between Dick Williams and Jack McKeon and working through the family troubles of the Kroc/Smith era and then some guy who wanted Roseanne Barr to sink the National Anthem, the Padres haven't been able to lay out an organizational plan and build on it. At times they haven't seemed to know who was in charge. The teams on the field have reflected the turmoil in the front office.

Outlook: The Padres won only 75 games in 1990, and while most of us anticipated a better year, no one expected any dramatic improvement in 1991. The off-season discussion centered around the effects of the big trade, Roberto Alomar and Joe Carter for Fred McGriff and Tony Fernandez.

Getaway: The Padres won six of their first seven games, keeping them at or near the top of the division through April.

Low Point of the Season: After the quick start the Padres played stuttering, inconsistent baseball for four months, keeping them within a few games of the .500 mark. They were at .500 on May 11 (15-15), on May 22 (20-20), on June 1 (25-25), on June 14 (31-31), and on June 27 (37-37).

Through July they began to lose more than they won, and so when they lost the first two games of a series in the Astrodome on August 5 and 6, they fell to 50-56. And even the Astros were beating them.

High Point of the Season: Andy Benes began to win every start beginning about July 28, and this had a positive effect on the entire team. Winning ten of fourteen, the Padres were back to .500 on September 6 (68-68), and continued to win, getting to 73-70. They weren't *really* in the race, but then they weren't really out of it, either.

Stretch Drive: The Padres continued to play fairly well until the end of the season. They wound up the year six games over .500, which was their high-water mark for the year.

Most Exciting Game of the Season: October 2, San Diego scored six runs on seven singles and an error in the top of the eighth. San Diego won, 9-4, and dropped the Dodgers into a tie with the Braves. Lasorda said that if he lived to be a thousand he would never forget the top of the eighth.

Major Injuries: The biggest injury was the loss of Ed Whitson. Whitson, a brilliant pitcher for two years, posted a 3.73 ERA through seven starts before developing tendinitis in his right elbow. After the tendinitis cleared up he had a bone spur on the elbow—probably he had it all along—and went back to the DL.

Larry Andersen was troubled throughout the season by ruptured, herniated and bulging discs in his neck.

Offense: Poor. The Padres as a team hit for a very low average (.244), are just average in power, below average in speed and below average in walks.

Defense: Fair. Santiago and Fernandez are talented, but take criticism for their intensity and consistent performance. The Padres don't have a Gold Glove at second or in center, and don't have a third baseman at all. Gwynn and McGriff are good defensive players.

Pitching: Ineffective early in the season, excellent later.

Best Game by a Starting Pitcher: Andy Benes against St. Louis, August 29 (9 2 0 0 1 10 Game Score: 92)

Indicators for 1991 were: Up 9.8

Number of regulars having good seasons by their own standards: One (Darrin Jackson)

1991 Over-Achiever: Jackson

1991 Under-Achiever: Craig Lefferts

Infield: Fair

The two guys acquired from Toronto, McGriff and Fernandez, are good players and had good years. The Padres never really had a regular second baseman or third baseman, and the production from third base was awful.

Outfield: Poor, but could have been worse.

The Padres went into the season with only one outfielder, Gwynn, but the development of Darrin Jackson provided significant help. Jerald Clark in left field is a joke.

Catching: Excellent.

Benito Santiago has his faults, but who's better?

Starting Pitching: Solid to strong.

The Padres had two Grade-A starting pitchers, Benes and Hurst. San Francisco had no one of the same quality, Houston had only one and Cincinnati had only one. After the big two they had Greg W. Harris, who was brilliant in twenty starts. The injury to Ed Whitson prevented the Padres from having starting pitching on a par with the best in the league.

Bullpen: Poor.

Craig Lefferts was so inconsistent that the closer's spot fell on the 38-year-old shoulders of Larry Andersen, who immediately popped the discs in his neck again.

Percentage of Offense Created by:

Young Players: 17%
Players in Their Prime: 58%
Past Their Prime: 25%

Team Age:

Age of Non-Pitchers: 28.5
Age of Pitching Staff: 29.0
Overall Team Age: 28.68

In retrospect, the critical decisions were: There is probably nothing the Padres could have "decided" within the last two years which would have made 1991 a championship season. The big gamble of a year ago, the exchange of two stars, worked out well enough in 1991.

THAT AND THE OTHER

Chris Berman, Have You Considered:

Oscar (Dressed up) Azocar
Tinkerbell Faries
Derek (Goodyear) Lilliquist
Mike Basso (Profundo)

Throwback: Craig Lefferts

Attendance Trend: Flat. Their attendance is where it was in 1986.

Players with a Chance for 3000 career hits:

Gwynn	32%
Fernandez	11%
McGriff	3%

Record Watch: Fred McGriff has a chance to be a 500-homer man, about a 27% chance. He could hit more home runs than any other player of our generation.

Best Interview: Larry Andersen

Best Fundamental Player: Tony Gwynn

Worst Fundamental Player: Benito Santiago

Best Defensive Player: Tony Gwynn

Worst Defensive Player: No one stands out. Darrin Jackson may be stretched to cover center field, but he's a good outfielder. The weak defensive *positions* are second and third.

Best Knowledge of the Strike Zone: Tony Gwynn

Least Command of the Strike Zone: Benito Santiago

Fastest Runner: It was Bip Roberts. After the trade it's probably Thomas Howard.

Slowest Runner: Fred McGriff

Best Baserunner: Tony Fernandez

Most Likely to Still be Here in 2000: Andy Benes

Best Fastball: Benes

Best Breaking Pitch: Bruce Hurst

Best Control: Greg W. Harris

Oddest Collection of Abilities: Darrin Jackson

The Most Knowledgeable Person About Local Baseball History Is: Frank Kern

Most-Similar Players:

to C Benito Santiago, B.J. Surhoff
to 1B Fred McGriff, Will Clark
to 2B Bip Roberts, Jeff Treadway
to 3B (Nobody Home)
to SS Tony Fernandez, Juan Samuel
to LF Jerald Clark, Mike Huff
to CF Darrin Jackson, Kevin Reimer
to RF Tony Gwynn, Willie McGee

Most Fun to Watch: Benito Santiago or Craig Lefferts

Least Fun to Watch: Jerald Clark

Managerial Type: Dann Bilardello

Among the All-Time Team Leaders: Tony Gwynn is the Padres' all-time best player, and holds the franchise records for career batting average (.328), runs scored, hits, doubles, triples and stolen bases. Garry Templeton was also among Padres' all-time leaders in several areas, and Bip Roberts was second in Padres' history in career batting average (.291). Benito Santiago will become prominent on the Padres' leader lists within two years.

Town Team:

C—Bob Boone
1B—Deron Johnson
2B—Solly Hemus
SS—Ray Boone
3B—Graig Nettles
LF—Ted Williams
CF—Gavy Cravath
RF—Kevin Mitchell
SP—Don Larsen

Post-Season Transactions:

December 8, Bip Roberts and Craig Pueschner traded to Reds in exchange for Randy Myers.

What Needs to Be Done For 1992:

The number one thing that needed attention was to improve the bullpen. This was done, we hope, with the Randy Myers trade. The second biggest need is to add power to the outfield, and I don't know how the Padres are going to do that. Oscar Azocar might help in a platoon role.

The third biggest need is to make good decisions at two infield spots, second base and third. The Padres have multiple candidates at each position—Faries and Shipley at second with maybe Teufel or somebody else, and Coolbaugh or Howell at third with Redington and Teufel among the longshots.

The Padres' "solution" to their infield problems last year was to patch things up with old guys (Jim Presley and Marty Barrett) and when that didn't work hope one of the young kids would get hot. Well, if they try that approach again in 1991 they're probably going to strike out again. What they need to do is either choose a second baseman from within the system—I'd say Paul Faries—or find some other young guy who has a little talent and is willing to bust his hump, and give him the job.

Outlook for 1992:

I think the battle for the NL West in 1991 should come down to two teams, San Diego and the Dodgers. The Dodgers are a formidable organization, and have many strengths to draw on that the Padres can't match.

The Padres' front-line talent is very good (see "Padre Present") but they need to get *something* from the other guys. Last year, the other guys were terrible. Clark, Coolbaugh, Presley, Abner, Lampkin, Faries, Howell, Vatcher . . . what an awful collection of players. Obviously, the top guys have to get better support than that if the Padres are going to contend.

There are some players here that I like. I think Paul Faries could be a decent second baseman, and Coolbaugh could be OK at third. Ricky Bones has a chance to be a good fourth starter.

Index of Leading Indicators for 1992: Down 7.9

Positive Indicators: 1. Strong Play at end of season

Negative Indicators:

1. Team appears to be not as good in 1991 as won-lost record suggests

Due for a better season: Dennis Rasmussen

Likely to have a worse season: Darrin Jackson

1992 Won-Lost Record will be: 85-77

PADRE PRESENT

The Padres' front-line talent is probably the best in this division. The Padres have four position players who are about as good as anybody in the league at their positions, those being Benito Santiago, Fred McGriff, Tony Fernandez and Tony Gwynn. While San Francisco last year had no Grade-A starting pitchers and Cincinnati and Houston had one apiece, the Padres had two, Benes and Hurst. I don't know that anybody else in the division has six players as good as the Padres' top six.

There isn't much behind it, so to a great extent the Padres' season depends on

a) how many of those six guys have good years, and

b) whether or not those guys are healthy.

I think the Padres can win this division. I doubt that they can win the division if one of those six players has a major injury.

While we're here, let's also deal with the Hall of Fame chances of those six gentlemen.

Tony Gwynn is a probable Hall of Famer, having compiled about 70% of a Hall of Fame career so far.

Bruce Hurst, two years older than Tony, has little chance of being a Hall of Famer, but has what one could call the background scenery of a Hall of Fame career, so that if he were to have, let us say, a three-year run in which he goes 58-28, those three years might make him a Hall of Famer because of the other things that he has already done, the four seasons of 15 to 18 wins.

I think **Fred McGriff** will be a Hall of Famer, just a personal opinion, but not based on what he has done so far. He's got 20% of a Hall of Fame career at this point; I just happen to believe he'll get the other 80%.

Tony Fernandez, in my opinion, is following the path of Garry Templeton, and will run to ground before his accomplishments acquire the magnitude that the Hall of Fame requires. He had a hell of a year last year, though, and got no credit for it.

It's too early to talk about **Andy Benes,** who has tremendous ability but no Hall of Fame type accomplishments at this point.

The toughest one to figure is **Benito Santiago.** Santiago is the top catcher of his generation, for better or worse, and that phrase would ordinarily describe a Hall of Famer. The precise Hall of Fame standards for a catcher are difficult to discern, and the voting appears somewhat arbitrary. Santiago isn't well liked or universally respected, but being well liked doesn't influence the voting significantly, and the respect would turn around quickly if the Padres won a couple of titles. If pushed to it, I would have to say that at this point his career is *not* in a Hall of Fame approach pattern.

When I say that I think the Padres could win this division, the number one thing I'm focusing on is the starting pitching. With Benes and Hurst the Padres have two rotation anchors. Greg Harris was very, very good the last three months of 1991, after missing almost the entire first half with tendinitis in the right elbow, so the Padres could have *three* Grade A starters in 1992, and that makes them a contender.

There is the possibility that Ed Whitson could come back, although I don't expect him to, and Ricky Bones is the kind of guy who may begin to pitch better about the third or fourth time he goes around the league. Dennis Rasmussen had a 3.74 ERA last year. If the Padres have four good starting pitchers and Tony Gwynn and Fred McGriff and Tony Fernandez and Benito Santiago and Randy Myers does the job in the bullpen . . . well, they're going to win unless the other guys are just awful. We know they've got Gwynn and McGriff and Fernandez and Santiago; those aren't question marks. The big question mark is whether they're going to have two good starting pitchers or three or four.

PADRE FUTURE

If the Padres have any good prospects in the minors, I didn't spot them. The best prospect in the system is **Ricky Bones,** but he's a major leaguer now. **Jim Lewis** is a 27-year-old relief pitcher who posted a 3.38 ERA at Las Vegas last year, where anything under 4.50 is good, but was wild and ineffective when called to the majors. **Matt Mieske** is a 24-year-old outfielder who spent last year in A-ball. He's old for a prospect, but this summer will be just his third as a pro, and he has won two minor league batting titles already. Mieske's On Base percentage last year, .456, was the highest in professional baseball, and he also had 39 stolen bases and good power. **Manuel Cora,** age seventeen, hit .359 in the Arizona rookie league last summer. He doesn't really have a position yet.

Frank Seminara, 24 years old, is a right-handed starting pitcher who was left unprotected by the Yankees and drafted by the Padres after going 16-8 with a 1.90 ERA at Prince William in 1990. The Padres moved him to Wichita (AA) and he pitched very well there (15-10, 3.38 ERA in a hitters' park. Wichita had a staff ERA of 4.57 and finished well over .500). **Jeremy Hernandez** is a gangly right-handed reliever, pitched fairly well at Las Vegas. **Tom Redington** is a 23-year-old third baseman who hit

.284 at Wichita and is thought to be a prospect, but he's slow and hit only five homers.

Robbie Beckett, the Padres' number one draft pick in 1990, went 2-14 with an 8.23 ERA for Charleston (South Carolina) last year. Their number one pick in 1991 was **Joey Hamilton,** a right-handed starting pitcher from Georgia Southern, who didn't sign until late September, and so didn't pitch last year. They also had a supplemental first-round pick as a result of the loss of Jack Clark, and picked **Greg Anthony,** who is supposed to have a Bob Gibson type body, and pitched well in seven starts in rookie ball.

THE SAN FRANCISCO GIANTS
• IN A BOX •

Won-Lost Record: 75-87 .453
Rank among 26 teams: 20th
Over Last Five Years: 425-385 .525
Rank over Five Years: Tied for 5th
In Last Ten Years: 793-827 .490
Rank over Ten Years: 17th

Best Player: Will Clark

Weak Spot: Starting Catcher

Best Pitcher: Trevor Wilson

Staff Weakness: Lack of reliable starters

Best Bench Player: Mike Felder

Best Young Player: Matt Williams

Best Looking Player: Kevin Bass

Ugliest Player: Willie McGee

This isn't a question of ugliness, but the Giants must lead the league in receding hairlines.

Most Pleasant Surprise, 1991: None

Biggest Disappointment, 1991: Steve Decker

Best Minor League Prospect: Royce Clayton

Who Is: A shortstop, the Giants' #1 draft pick in 1988. Clayton isn't a good hitter yet, but he's young, plays good defense, and the organization is high on him. If he plays well in spring training the Giants will be under pressure to hand him a job. Decker's failure to play well after jumping from Double-A last year may hurt the chances of Clayton, who spent 1991 in the Texas League. If Clayton does play my guess is he'll hit around .240 with no secondary offense, which wouldn't look too bad after a few years of Jose Uribe.

Other Prospects: **John Patterson,** Clayton's keystone partner at San Antonio last year, is a better hitter than Clayton right now. Patterson is two years older, which is one reason he ranks below Clayton as an all-around prospect. The Giants had a pitcher in A-ball last year, **Rich Huisman** (pronounced like Heisman), who struck out 216 men in 182 innings. A staffmate, **Kevin McGehee,** was almost as impressive.

Designated Malcontent: Kevin Mitchell. Mitchell, of course, has been traded, which is what happens to malcontents.

Park Characteristics: Because of the weather, Candlestick Park is not a good place to hit. The park is very weather-sensitive. If it's a cool summer, Candlestick will reduce batting averages and ERAs; if it's a warm summer in the Bay area, Candlestick may function as a hitter's park. 1991 was a cool summer, so extremely few runs were scored here. The Giants scored and allowed only 611 runs in Candlestick, as opposed to 735 on the road.

The Park Helps: No one, but Matt Williams has hit 40% more home runs at Candlestick than on the road. That will even out over time.

The Park Hurts: Attendance.

ORGANIZATIONAL REPORT CARD

Ownership:	C
Upper Management:	A−
Field Management:	C
Front-Line Talent:	B+
Second-Line Talent:	D
Minor League System:	C

Comment: Owner Bob Lurie gets a certain amount of press b[y] saying kind of stupid things, but he doesn't do the destructiv[e] things that some owners do that make it hard for the people unde[r] him to do their jobs. I figure he's about as good as the next guy.

Roger Craig did a fine job here in his first few years, 1986 t[o] 1989, and he may have good years ahead of him. On the othe[r] hand, he may have given San Francisco whatever he had to give and it might be time for the organization to move on.

TEAM LEADERS:

Batting Average: Willie McGee .312
Last Ten Years (Season): Will Clark, 1989, .333
Last Ten Years (Total): Will Clark, .302

Home Runs: Matt Williams, 34
Last Ten Years (Season): Kevin Mitchell, 1989, 47
Last Ten Years (Total): 1. Will Clark, 146
2. Kevin Mitchell, 143

RBI: Will Clark, 116
Last Ten Years (Season): Kevin Mitchell, 1989, 125
Last Ten Years (Total): Will Clark, 563

Wins: Trevor Wilson, 13
Last Ten Years (Season): Mike Krukow, 1986, 20
Last Ten Years (Total): Scott Garrelts, 69

Winning Percentage: Trevor Wilson, 13-11 .542

Strikeouts: Trevor Wilson, 139
Last Ten Years (Season): Mike Krukow, 178 in 1986
Last Ten Years (Total): Krukow, 802

ERA: Trevor Wilson 3.56

Saves: Dave Righetti, 24

Doubles: Will Clark, 32

Triples: Will Clark, 7

Extra Base Hits: Will Clark, 68

Walks: Robby Thompson, 63

Stolen Bases: Mike Felder, 21

Runs Created: Will Clark, 110

Runs Created Per Game: Will Clark, 7.3

Secondary Average: Robby Thompson, .341

League Leaders: Will Clark led the league with a .592 sluggin[g] percentage. Willie McGee was first in batting average on the road .345, and ground ball/fly ball ratio, 3.97.

Stat of the Year: I probably drive you crazy with this stuff, but I love looking for similar seasons. How's this for a match:

G	AB	R	H	2B	3B	HR	RBI	BAvg	SlPct.
156	571	69	152	23	3	34	94	.266	.496
157	589	72	158	24	5	34	98	.268	.499

One of those seasons is Matt Williams, 1991 Giants. The other is Frank Thomas, 1962 Mets. I'll leave you to figure out which one is which.

1991 SEASON

Background: Since Roger Craig came here in 1986 the Giants had posted five straight winning records, winning the division in 1987 and 1989. In 1990 they slumped to 85-77.

Outlook: The Giants absolutely expected to be back at or near the top of the division in 1991.

Getaway: It couldn't have been worse. The Giants lost their first two games of the season—and never got back in the race.

Low Point of the Season: The early part of the season went from bad to worse. By May 24 the Giants had dropped to 12-29.

Roger Craig remained optimistic. "Just wait," he told a reporter. "In a month or six weeks, you're going to be asking us how we did it. You're going to be asking us how we got back in the race." In reality, I doubt that any team in history ever overcame a 12-29 start to win anything, and the Giants were not destined to be an exception to the rule.

High Point of the Season: Remaining sixteen games under .500 until June 19 (25-41), the Giants played good ball the last part of June, all of July and early August to reach .500 at 55-55 on August 11. They were able to close the gap from 15 games behind in late June to six, a remarkable accomplishment in its own right.

Stretch Drive: The Giants spent only two nights at .500, 55-55 on August 11 and 57-57 on August 15. They had a second horrible slump then, losing 21 of 28 games to fall to 64-78. They finished with 75 wins, and their season wasn't that good.

Most Exciting Games of the Season: October 4 and 5, Black and Wilson throttled the Dodgers at the Stick to take the title from the Evil Blue Empire.

Major Injuries: Kevin Mitchell was out from May 22 until June 25 (except a few games) to have surgery to repair ligaments in his left knee. Willie McGee missed almost all of July with a pulled muscle in his rib cage, which was the only part of the year when the Giants played well. Kevin Bass also missed with a sore left knee.

Offense: See article

Defense: Fairly good. Three Giant infielders are good glove men, and even at shortstop the defense wasn't the worst in the league. The catching situation was unsettled, and the defense in the outfield was poor, but if you had to choose between defense in the infield and defense in the outfield, you'd always choose the infield.

Pitching: Atrocious. The Giants never could establish a rotation, and their bullpen was in and out. Away from Candlestick the Giants had a staff ERA of 4.69.

Best Game by a Starting Pitcher: Trevor Wilson's two-hitter to eliminate the Dodgers, October 5 (9 2 0 0 2 6 Game Score: 87)

Worst Game by a Starting Pitcher: Gee, there are so many to choose from.

Indicators for 1991 were: Down 8.1

Number of regulars having good seasons by their own standards: Four

1991 Over-Achiever: Robby Thompson

1991 Under-Achiever: Kevin Bass

Infield: The Giants' infield, even granting that the shortstop play was on the horrible side, is as good as any in baseball. The Giants have superb players at three infield positions, giving them as much power and as much defense in the infield as any major league team.

Outfield: Fair to poor. Two 1991 outfielders, Kevin Mitchell and Willie McGee, are former MVPs, but both are in their 30s, and both are injury prone. Darren Lewis could be very good.

Catching: Spotty. The Giants' catching wasn't as bad as some people wrote. Giant catchers hit .216 with 8 homers and 54 RBI, which is bad but not as bad as some other teams, plus they cut off the running game fairly well, even Terry Kennedy. The Giants were using inexperienced catchers for the most part and using them in unstable combinations, which probably contributed to the failures of the pitching staff. The Giants had an ERA of 3.77 with Decker catching, 3.99 with Manwaring but 4.50 with Kennedy.

Starting Pitching: Very Poor

Bullpen: Better than starting rotation, still not championship quality.

Percentage of Offense Contributed By:
- **Young Players:** 17%
- **Players in Their Prime:** 61%
- **Veterans:** 22%

Team Age:
- **Age of Non-Pitchers:** 28.7
- **Age of Pitchers:** 28.8
- **Overall Team Age:** 28.75

In retrospect, the critical decisions were: See article, "Nothing Works"

THAT AND THE OTHER

Lookalikes: Jeff Brantley and Jeff Montgomery

Chris Berman, Have You Considered: Billy (None Too) Swift

Hall of Fame Watch: Will Clark plays in the manner of a Hall of Famer, and has about one-third of a Hall of Fame career behind him. It is still a very open question whether his career will or will not reach that level; the next two or three years are critical for him. The late **Kevin Mitchell** played at a Hall of Fame level for a period of three years, but is slightly behind Clark in terms of Hall of Fame-type accomplishments, and being two years older than Clark is in a substantially weaker overall position. **Matt Williams** will have to have bigger years than his last two to make the Hall of Fame, but is beginning to build a resume. **Willie McGee** has two batting titles and an MVP Award and has played on several championship teams; if he was three years younger he might be a viable Hall of Fame candidate, but he's a longshot as it is.

Throwback: Will Clark

Attendance Trend: The 1991 attendance total was 1.7 million, the lowest since 1986. Attendance has grown in the Rosen/Craig era, but not dramatically.

Players with a Chance for 3000 career hits:

Will Clark	20%
Willie McGee	7%
Matt Williams	2%

Best Fundamental Player: Bud Black

Worst Fundamental Player: Willie McGee

Best Defensive Player: Robby Thompson

Worst Defensive Player: Mark Leonard

Best Knowledge of the Strike Zone: Darren Lewis

Least Command of the Strike Zone: Matt Williams

Fastest Runner: Mike Felder

Slowest Runner: Kevin Mitchell

Best Baserunner: Mike Felder

Most Likely to Still be Here in 2000: Will Clark

Best Fastball: Trevor Wilson

Best Breaking Pitch: Burkett has come up with a good curve. Nobody here throws a real breaking pitch. They all throw that wet-fingered fastball that Craig is famous for.

Best Control: Francisco Oliveras

Oddest Collection of Abilities: Robby Thompson

Never Going to be As Good as the Organization Thinks He Is: Royce Clayton

Manager's Pet Strategy: Willie McGee had more Sacrifice Bunts last year (8) than he had had in his entire career before coming to San Francisco.

Why is this man in the Major Leagues: Terry Kennedy

Most-Similar Players:

to C Steve Decker, Chris Hoiles
to 1B Will Clark, Fred McGriff
to 2B Robby Thompson, Greg Gagne
to 3B Matt Williams, Ron Gant
to SS Jose Uribe, Al Newman
to LF Kevin Mitchell, Ivan Calderon
to CF Darren Lewis, Bernie Williams
to RF Willie McGee, Tony Gwynn

Most Fun to Watch: Mike Kingery

Least Fun to Watch: Kevin Mitchell

Managerial Type: Mike Kingery

Among the All-Time Team Leaders: The Giants list their team records in two categories, one from 1883 and the other from 1958. No current Giant is anywhere in the hard part, but on the easy list Will Clark is already among the team leaders in most categories, and will continue to mount. He will shoot to third on the list in most areas before the competition becomes *really* stiff (Mays and McCovey).

A little bit of research: See article, "Willie Mays"

Town Team:

C—Joe Ferguson
1B—Frank Chance
2B—Tony Lazzeri
SS—Joe Cronin
3B—Bob Elliott
LF—Wally Berger
CF—Joe DiMaggio
RF—Harry Heilmann
SP—Lefty Gomez

Post-Season Transactions:

December 1, Kevin Mitchell booked for rape, battery and false imprisonment, being investigated for "rape with a foreign object"

December 9, charges dropped against Kevin Mitchell

December 11, Kevin Mitchell and Mike Remlinger exiled to Seattle in exchange for Billy Swift, Mike Jackson and Bob Melvin

Outlook for 1992:

The team which won this division in 1987 and 1989 was put together very quickly, relying heavily on used parts—Rick Reuschel, Mike LaCoss, Candy Maldonado. Brett Butler and Kevin Mitchell had been with two other teams before they came here. It would not have been easy to keep the old engine running with the best of decisions and, as I said earlier, I don't know that the Giants in the last two years have made consistently good decisions. Manager Roger Craig, a wonderful man, is old, not in perfect health, and at times poorly motivated. The Giants have serious talent, and serious problems.

Index of Leading Indicators for 1992: +5.0

Positive Indicators: None of note

Negative Indicators: Note of note

Due for a better season: Mark Leonard

Likely to have a worse season: Robby Thompson

1992 Won-Lost Record will be: 77-85

THE GIANT OFFENSE

The 1991 Giants scored 649 runs, a good number under the circumstances. The Giants scored more runs in road games than the Atlanta Braves did (343-331), but the cold Candlestick weather created pitcher's duels. The Giants played well at home (43-38, as opposed to 32-49 on the road) but without scoring many runs.

STATS Inc. lists batting records for each team by batting order position—what the leadoff men hit, the number two hitters, etc. These charts are often interesting, and I thought about including them in this book, but decided against it. The Giants, however, are especially interesting:

	AB	R	H	2B	3B	HR	RBI	SB	BB	Avg
1st	661	107	165	23	12	5	36	32	64	.250
2nd	668	89	183	38	5	10	64	17	46	.274
3rd	659	96	204	35	7	31	133	7	49	.310
4th	615	89	159	23	3	38	105	7	65	.259
5th	610	66	153	20	6	28	89	8	56	.251
6th	599	65	141	21	5	16	45	12	57	.235
7th	570	47	131	25	2	9	62	3	44	.230
8th	567	45	110	15	8	3	39	7	46	.194
9th	514	45	99	15	0	1	32	2	44	.193

The meat of the Giant order—spots two through five, where Clark, Mitchell, Williams, Thompson and McGee hit, in various combinations—was extremely good, probably the best in baseball when you remember what park they were playing in. But the rest of the offense was a bunch of 97-pound weaklings. The leadoff men scored 107 runs, which is a fair total for the leadoff spot, not because they were good but because the guys coming up after them were *so* good. Then the offense ended completely at the fifth spot. The sixth hitters drove in only 45 runs—some teams are up around a hundred there—and the Giants really had two "pitchers" in the batting order, the real pitcher and the shortstop. The Giant offense couldn't go around the corner, so they just didn't get the big innings they needed to come from behind.

NOTHING WORKS

When a traditional contender posts a season's record of 75 wins and 87 losses, the question of what the key decisions were does not invite a friendly response. Throughout their time in San Francisco Al Rosen and Roger Craig have maneuvered swiftly, decisively and, in 1987 and again in 1989, brilliantly. In 1991 they couldn't convert hamburger into meat loaf.

I think there were six key decisions which shaped the Giants' 1991 season. Those were:

1. Replacing Brett Butler in center field with Willie McGee
2. Failing to make Trevor Wilson a starting pitcher at the beginning of the season
3. Counting on Steve Decker to be the number one catcher
4. Signing Dave Righetti to be the relief ace
5. Signing Bud Black as a starting pitcher
6. Assigning playing time to Mike Felder

Of the six critical decisions, three seem to me to be somewhat strange. A year ago Brett Butler and Willie McGee were both available, McGee as a free agent and Butler by contract options. Both are center fielders and leadoff men. The Giants let Butler go, and signed McGee reportedly at a salary well beyond what they had been willing to do for Butler.

Why they did this is anybody's guess. You and I shouldn't overlook the possibility that Brett Butler may not be as much fun to have on your team as he is to watch, and also we shouldn't overlook the possibility that the Giants' decision-makers really are stupid enough to think that Willie McGee is a better hitter than Brett Butler just because he has a higher batting average.

That, of course, was Al Rosen's decision, presumably endorsed by Roger Craig. Craig's contributions to this mess were

a) starting the year with Trevor Wilson buried in the bullpen. A highly touted prospect for several years, Wilson made seventeen starts in 1990 and pitched brilliantly in two stretches, although his overall record was not brilliant (8-7, 4.00 ERA). For reasons he never bothered to explain to anybody, Craig decided to struggle along for a month and a half with some of the sorriest starting pitchers in the league before seeing whether Wilson could build on his successes of 1990.

b) deciding to make Mike Felder, picked up in spring training, a quasi-regular in the wake of injuries to Mitchell and McGee. Felder had been with Milwaukee since the mid-eighties, generally hitting around .250 with no power, and eventually playing himself out of a job. The Giants signed him, he played real well for a month, and Craig began to assign him duties which exceeded his capabilities.

These three decisions I hated at the time they were made, and said so. But two other decisions, which I endorsed heartily, didn't work out any better. Steve Decker was to be the starting catcher; I picked him as Rookie of the Year. It didn't work out.

The first free agent to sign a year ago was Bud Black. Black signed for $2.5 million per year, a reasonable salary for a pitcher of his quality, but he didn't pitch as well as he might have, posting a 12-16 record and an ERA over the league average.

The sixth decision, the signing of free agent reliever Dave Righetti, had no observable impact on the team, pro or con. Righetti was expensive and ordinary, but better than the man he had replaced (Steve Bedrosian). Bedrock was traded to Minnesota for a couple of minor-league pitchers.

The Giants no doubt had their share of bad luck in 1991—the injuries, the ineffectiveness of Mike LaCoss. It would be a copout to attribute their off year to injuries and bad luck. They fell out of contention because they made a long series of decisions that didn't work.

Will 1991 be any different? I don't know. Everything comes to an end. Rosen and Craig aren't young men. To this point—January 1—all the Giants have done this winter is get a few bad actors off the roster. That may well be a necessary first step. The Giants, who once led the majors in clubhouse Christians, now lead in rapists. OK, accused rapists; it ain't anything to be happy about. The Giants may *need* to scrape their gills a little before they worry about anything else.

By itself, getting rid of people isn't going to make the Giants a championship team. The Giants need pitching. Swift and Mike Jackson certainly will improve the Giants' bullpen, but the Giants can't use six short relievers (Brantley, Righetti, Swift, Jackson, Beck and Oliveras), so somebody will have to try to make it as a starter, somebody like Righetti or Swift. That's iffy, and doesn't figure to substantially improve the starting rotation. Craig, if he stays, will probably give up on the whole idea of a starting rotation, and revert to his habit of shuttling people between the bullpen and the starting job. They need to make some decisions, and they need to make some decisions that work.

TWO THOUSAND YEARS OF WILLIE MAYS

What is it *possible* for a great player to do in a great year? Suppose that a great player, a Willie Mays or a Joe DiMaggio, hits in good luck for an entire season. What kind of stats could he compile? Suppose that he hits in bad luck for an entire year, what then? Could Willie Mays hit .250 in a given season, just by sheer bad luck?

What if he played forever, what would Willie Mays do? Would he ever drive in 200 runs in a season? Would he ever break Joe DiMaggio's consecutive-game hit streak? What would be his best games? Would he ever get seven hits in a game? Would he ever drive in fifteen men in a game? What are the limits here?

I put Willie Mays' career batting record in a computer, and ordered the machine to simulate two thousand years of Willie Mays' at bats. Here's the process, in outline:

1) Determine whether Mays played in this particular game.

2) Determine a number of plate appearances for the game—normally 4 or 5, but on occasion anywhere from 1 to 8. It's set to reproduce Mays' actual plate appearance per game.

3) Randomly select conditions for the first at bat (that is, runner on second, two out, or whatever).

4) Randomly select an outcome, based on Mays' career production.

5) Go on to the next at bat.

At bat after at bat, for two thousand years; it takes about three days on my little home computer. If he got on base I'd check to see if he stole a base and/or scored a run. Of course everything is not random, so that's a limitation of the simulation. Also, I based everything on Mays' *career* stats, which may not have been a good idea; it might have been better to base the simulation on only his stats from 1954 to 1965, let us say. That might have given a fairer sense of what was *possible* for a player like Willie Mays in his *best* seasons. Anyway, I didn't. Here's the questions:

1. What were his best seasons?

Here are a few of his best:

Sim Year	G	AB	R	H	2B	3B	HR	RBI	BB	SO	SB	Avg.
29	156	583	145	201	44	3	50	127	83	77	16	.345
84	152	548	131	200	33	5	39	137	77	63	21	.365
148	157	597	129	202	30	10	46	155	60	70	16	.338
226	152	562	137	203	23	13	45	133	78	79	24	.361
694	153	567	139	185	34	10	49	150	78	71	18	.326
1411	159	605	131	174	25	6	54	137	65	92	17	.288
1744	159	545	123	184	23	10	44	137	99	69	23	.338
1800	160	580	132	198	29	4	50	149	64	68	12	.341
1842	156	571	117	207	32	8	32	116	70	68	13	.363

Because I used *career* stats rather than *prime* stats, the best seasons of the simulated Mays, in 2000 years don't look much different than the best seasons of the real Willie Mays.

2 What were his worst seasons?

Here are a few of the worst:

Sim Year	G	AB	R	H	2B	3B	HR	RBI	BB	SO	SB	Avg.
591	158	556	96	146	26	7	23	90	88	73	15	.263
826	152	559	88	132	20	5	21	89	89	85	18	.236
895	154	570	91	158	31	3	21	78	74	97	14	.277
1196	153	549	88	152	31	10	18	88	71	81	16	.277
1203	152	553	90	141	21	6	16	79	73	83	21	.255
1425	160	595	89	149	24	7	27	103	65	104	16	.250
1585	155	554	110	141	26	7	22	79	77	83	21	.255
1996	158	578	95	151	29	6	18	72	73	94	20	.261

So you see, it is *possible* for a player to hit .350 one year, .250 the next just by random chance. It is *possible* for a player to hit 50 home runs one year, 20 the next just by random chance.

One thing I wondered was whether the simulated Mays would

ever have a 50/50 season (50 homers, 50 stolen bases), but I eliminated that possibility by using the stats for Willie's full career. For his career as a whole Mays stole only 18 bases per season, so based on that information he would never be expected to steal more than about 30.

Even in 2000 years, the robot-Mays never threatened Maris' home run record or Hack Wilson's RBI total; his highs were 54 and 155. He never hit .400, and never came close.

Mays drove in 100 runs in a season, in the simulation, 71% of the time. He scored a hundred runs 88% of the time. He hit .300 about 60% of the time.

3 Best Games

Mays' best game line, in the 2000 years, was 5 5 5 7 (Five at bats, 5 runs scored, 5 hits, 7 RBI). He had that exact game line twice; other interesting game lines included

AB	R	H	BI
5	5	5	3
6	5	6	4
6	1	6	0
2	5	1	2
4	2	4	7
7	3	6	6

In the entire period the simulated Mays drove in seven runs in a game three times, but never eight, which is interesting because in real life he *did* drive in eight runs in a game, at least once. He never approached the single-game record of twelve RBI, by Jim Bottomley. He had six hits in a game many times (nine times), but never had seven hits in a game. He scored five runs in a game many, many times, but never six. He hit for the cycle 81 times, and hit four homers in a game three times, but never five.

4. Batting Streaks

Mays longest batting streak, in 2,000 simulated seasons, was 34 games. He never remotely approached DiMaggio's record.

Boggs and DiMaggio

Then I did the same thing with Wade Boggs and Joe DiMaggio, creating 1,000 simulated seasons for each player. Here are years six and seven of the simulation for DiMaggio:

Sim Year	G	AB	R	H	2B	3B	HR	RBI	BB	SO	SB	Avg.
6	154	592	135	200	41	12	38	150	79	39	3	.338
7	141	553	96	146	27	8	18	79	62	37	2	.264

Suppose that a *real* player did this; suppose that in real life a player drove in 150 runs one year, won the MVP Award if not the triple crown, and then the next year was an ordinary player. Every explanation under the sun would be offered for his decline, and ultimately one explanation would come to be the accepted one—he got fat and lazy after a winter of celebration, or he was affected by the absence of X, who hit behind him in his big year, or he had a minor injury that he was compensating for, or even that he began pressing after a slow start. Do you suppose that *anybody* would write that he was the same player, just hitting in tougher luck? That's my point: that when a player has an off year, even a terrible year, there may not be any reason for it. It may be just the breaks of the game.

DiMaggio in Game 36 of Year 165 posted a box score line of 5 4 5 9, nine RBI, and also hit for the cycle in that game. He drove in nine runs on five other occasions, and in game 19 of Year 593 drove in ten runs, his box score line 6 4 4 10. Like Mays, he had six hits in a game many times, but never seven. Unlike Mays, he did once score six runs in a game (5 6 5 2). The imitation DiMaggio hit as high as .392 for a season, but never .400. He never drove in twelve runs in a game, or 170 in a season. He had batting streaks as long as 48 games, but never 56. He hit as many as 49 home runs in a season, but never 50. Probably his best overall season was year 803:

Sim Year	G	AB	R	H	2B	3B	HR	RBI	BB	SO	SB	Avg.
803	145	561	139	220	47	15	39	148	65	32	7	.392

One of the basic things I was asking myself, which provoked me to undertake this silly exercise, is whether these guys, given enough time, could be expected to break all the records. Would Mays or DiMaggio, given enough time, hit 62 homers, drive in 200 runs, hit in 60 straight games and hit .400? Well, the answer is "no", at least given the assumptions I used here.

I have often noted that almost all major records are set when the conditions for setting them are ideal or nearly ideal. Almost all the big batting records (for a season) were set in the 1920–1937 era, when the conditions of the game most favored the hitter. What we learn here is that a great player, even when the luck is running with him, generally can't overpower that, and break those records under ordinary conditions. Obviously Joe DiMaggio, if he played under the conditions of the National League in 1930, would have a hell of a chance to drive in 190 runs in a year—but under the conditions that he *really* played under, he probably never would. Although he would periodically drive in 150 runs or 160 or more, he would never, no matter how long he played, mount a serious challenge at Wilson's record. Of course, I only simulated a thousand years; if you simulated 5,000 years and used DiMaggio's first five years as the basis of the simulation, you might get a different answer.

The simulated Wade Boggs, however, did break one big record. The Boggs model made repeated runs at .400. After hitting .356 in Year 1, he pushed his high to .365—three points off his real career high—in year 6. That stood as his career high for 24 simulated seasons, until he hit .377 in Year 30. In Year 49 he matched Rod Carew, hitting .388. Twenty-six years later, in Year 75, he pushed it to .394, with 232 hits. In Year 112 he pushed even closer, hitting .396 in a 156-game season.

Following that, almost 200 years passed before the Boggs' model made another run at .400. In year 293 he hit .381.

Finally, in year 358, the simulated Boggs broke through with the .400 season he had sought for so long—and it was a monster. This is the season's totals for the Boggs image in year 358:

Sim Year	G	AB	R	H	2B	3B	HR	RBI	BB	SO	SB	Avg.
358	146	579	106	246	45	5	12	97	81	41	4	.425

That season, which would break the major league record for batting average by one point (Hornsby hit .424) is a plain fluke, the greatest fluke season that occurs in the 4,000 simulated seasons that I created here. Think about it: after trying 357 times to hit .400 and failing all 357 times, the simulated Boggs not only hit .400, but cleared it with fourteen hits to spare. It's a Bob Beamon feat.

In the remaining 642 seasons, the simulated Boggs battled the .400 mark many times, and succeeded in breaking it four other times, five times total in the 1,000 seasons. His other .400 batting marks were .401, .405, .404 and .405.

What this suggests, to me, is that when Wade Boggs was in his

TRACERS

When he was with the New York Giants, outfielder Heinie Mueller was notorious for having tried to break up a double play by leaping into the air between first and second bases to catch the relay throw in his mouth. When he joined the Boston Braves a few years later, Mueller showed he had maintained his famous baserunning style.

With a teammate on third base during a game in 1929, Mueller laid down a suicide squeeze bunt along the first-base line. As Mueller scurried up the line, Giants first baseman Bill Terry charged to scoop up the bunt. As Terry flashed near him, Mueller dived to the ground. Terry threw home to catch the runner trying to score from third. When the dust cleared at the plate, Mueller was still face down in the base line, covering his head as if he were a doughboy under artillery fire. The New York catcher strolled over and gently applied the tag.

Back on the bench, Braves manager Judge Emil Fuchs asked Mueller why on earth he stayed sprawled in the dust. "I didn't think they'd notice me there," Mueller answered.

—David Cataneo, *Peanuts and Crackerjack.* 1991, Page 52.

Before we get into the procedure here, let me call your attention to one thing. Bill Terry throws home on a suicide squeeze? How often does that really happen?

Mueller was with the Braves in 1928 and '29, but didn't play a hell of a lot. In 1929, when this incident supposedly took place, he batted only 105 times. In checking this one out I decided to begin with 1929 because it is specifically named, and also because 1929 was the only season Judge Fuchs managed. But if I didn't find it there I would have to check 1928.

The first thing I did was consult a 1929 guide for that season's N.L. schedule, and then it was on to the library and *The New York Times* microfilm.

The Giants and Braves were first scheduled to meet on April 20 in Boston, but their entire three-game series was rained out. The teams first met on April 26 at the Polo Grounds. Mueller played in both games of the series. The game accounts in *The New York Times* are very detailed, and discussed any little odd incident that occurred in the match. They're religious about pointing out fielding and baserunning blunders. They don't mention anything like this.

The two teams got together again in mid-May for a five-gamer at Braves Field. On the 16th, the Braves won the first game of a doubleheader, 4-3, then lost the nightcap. Following the game accounts by *Times* writer William E. Brandt, this note appeared:

LINDSTROM COMPLETES PLAY.

Heinie Meuller [sic] added to his fame in the first game. He poked a fly straight up in the air. It looked foul until the wind carried it down in front of home plate. Hogan caught it on the first bounce and his throw to Lindstrom nailed Harper going to third. Meuller, all the while, was arguing with the umpire, so Lindstrom completed the double play by racing all the way across to first base.

In their broadest outlines, then, these two stories share certain qualities: Mueller is doubled up when he should easily have made first safely, in a game against the Giants in 1929. In both cases there is an unusual double play. But they differ in many specifics: a suicide squeeze vs. a pop fly; Bill Terry at first vs. Freddie Lindstrom at third; Mueller lying on the ground vs. Mueller arguing with the umpire. The remark which is the comic punch line of the anecdote wouldn't fit in this incident.

Still, it seems reasonable to guess that the 1991 anecdote may be a (very) twisted version of the May 16 incident. If you assume that is true, it is interesting to note that the *real* double play is much more remarkable than the anecdotal one. A 3-2-3 double play—I've seen that. I've never seen it on a suicide squeeze, but it could certainly happen on a safety squeeze. But a 2-5 double play with the third baseman making a tag at third *and* a play at first? I've never heard of that before—but that's what really happened.

Anyway, Mueller played in five more games against the Giants that season, with little fanfare and with no other incident of a similar nature. From what I can tell, he earned his release on or soon after July 2, sporting a .204 batting average and a reputation as a memorable baserunner.

prime it *was* possible for him to have hit .400; not likely, but possible. The odds against it each year were about 200-1, so the odds even in a ten-year period remained strongly against him, about 20-1. But it was possible.

The most home runs hit in a season by the simulated Boggs was 20—four less than his actual career high. This suggests that Boggs' 24-homer outburst in 1987, the year of the home run, could not probably have resulted from a simple performance aberration; it is extremely likely that there was something about the 1987 playing conditions which was truly different, and which made this event possible. I mention this because no one has ever really figured out *why* the home run totals exploded in 1987; we only know that they did. The Boggs' home run anomaly is further evidence that there *was* something peculiar about that season.

The Boggs' clone never broke or seriously threatened Joe DiMaggio's record 56-game streak, his longest being 42 games. He scored 100 runs consistently, and drove in as many as 98 runs. He hit as many as 60 doubles in a season. Boggs, of course, rarely had big, big games as did Mays and DiMaggio.

One final comment, before I let this go. In real life Wade Boggs' career batting average is .345, but in the thousand-year simulation it worked out to .344. When I saw that I thought I'd made some little mistake in the program, having to do with how sacrifice bunts are scored or something; surely, I thought, over a thousand years you could count on a .345 hitter to really hit .345?

Not so; even in a thousand years, a batting average does not become a precisely reliable statement of the player's true ability. Boggs career batting average is .3448; the imitation Boggs had 202,350 hits in 587,402 at bats, for an average of .34448. The discrepancy (.00031+) is only 185 hits, well within the range of chance in a sample this large. **Even if players played for a thousand years, not all the breaks would even out.** Ain't that somethin'?

THE CINCINNATI REDS
• IN A BOX •

1991 Won-Lost Record: 74-88 .457
Rank among 26 teams: 21st
Over Last Five Years: 411-398 .508
Rank Over Five Years: 11th
In Last Ten Years: 791-827 .489
Rank over Ten Years: 18th

Best Player: Barry Larkin

Weak Spot: Left Field

Best Pitcher: Jose Rijo

Staff Weakness: At the end of the 1991 season, the staff weakness was the shallowness of the starting pitching. The Reds had Browning, Rijo when he was healthy and then a grab bag. But they have fixed that weakness, at least on paper, by adding Greg Swindell and Tim Belcher to the rotation.

Best Bench Player: Dave Martinez

Best Baseball Name: Ted Power

Best Young Player: Hal Morris

Hal Morris turns 27 in June, so he is not really a young player. (He went to college before baseball, and then spent an extra year in the minor leagues.) But he's the closest thing they have to a good young player.

Best Looking Player: Barry Larkin

Ugliest Player: Joe Oliver

Most Pleasant Surprise, 1991: Jeff Reed

Biggest Disappointment, 1991: Randy Myers

Best Minor League Prospect: See article, "Red Alert"

Designated Malcontent: Randy Myers

Park Characteristics: A few years ago—I think before the 1988 season, although I may be off a year—the Reds cut the height of their outfield walls. At the time I didn't think anything much about it, but as the data has developed it is apparent that Riverfront Stadium has become a tremendous place to hit home runs. Here, I'll run some data; the chart below gives the home runs hit and allowed by the Reds in Cincinnati and on the road over the last four years:

Year	Home	Road
1988	146	97
1989	130	123
1990	143	106
1991	181	110

Riverfront Stadium as it now is inflates home run totals by about 38%, marking it as one of the best home run parks in the major leagues.

The author was very slow to pick up this change, and several of his evaluations of Cincinnati players have been misguided because of that. The author expresses his regrets.

The Park Helps: Paul O'Neill, Chris Sabo.

The Park Hurts: The young pitchers.

ORGANIZATIONAL REPORT CARD

Ownership:	D
Upper Management:	B+
Field Management:	B+
Front-Line Talent:	C
Second-Line Talent:	C
Minor League System:	C+

TEAM LEADERS:

Batting Average: Hal Morris, .318
Last Ten Years (Season): Morris, 1991, .318
Last Ten Years (Total): Kal Daniels, .301

Doubles: Paul O'Neill 36

Triples: two players with 4

Home Runs: Paul O'Neill, 28
Last Ten Years (Season): Eric Davis, 1987, 37
Last Ten Years (Total): Davis, 177

Extra Base Hits: Sabo and O'Neill, 64 each

RBI: Paul O'Neill, 91
Last Ten Years (Season): Dave Parker, 1985, 125
Last Ten Years (Total): Eric Davis, 532

Stolen Bases: Barry Larkin, 24

Runs Created: Chris Sabo, 103

Runs Created Per Game: Larkin, 7.3

Secondary Average: Paul O'Neill .368

Wins: Jose Rijo, 15
Last Ten Years (Season): Danny Jackson, 23 in 1988
Last Ten Years (Total): Tom Browning, 107

Winning Percentage: Jose Rijo, 15-6 .714

Strikeouts: Rijo, 172
Last Ten Years (Season): Mario Soto, 274 in 1982
Last Ten Years (Total): Tom Browning, 889

ERA: Jose Rijo, 2.51

Saves: Rob Dibble, 31

League Leaders: Tom Browning threw 32 gopher balls, easily the most in the league. Hal Morris led the NL in batting average vs. right-handed pitchers, at .336. Jose Rijo allowed fewer baserunners per nine innings than any NL pitcher.

Stat of the Year: See article, "Blind Chance"

1991 SEASON

Background: The Reds opened the 1991 season as the defending World Champions. The World Championship had been marred to a certain extent by a serious injury to Eric Davis, a franchise player, and then by Davis's unhappiness at the way he was treated after the injury.

Outlook: The Reds and Dodgers were co-favorites to win the division.

Getaway: The Reds opened the season pitching well, but not hitting. The team batting average was .230 in April, .242 in May. However, with a staff ERA of 2.95 in April, the Reds never dropped seriously under .500 or out of the race. They were 11-8 at the end of April. In May, cracks began to open in the pitching staff (Jack Armstrong), and the team was 23-23 at the end of May.

High Point of the Season: In June the Reds swaggered back into the pennant race. They hit .292 for the month, the bullpen had 13 saves in 14 chances. When Chris Hammond beat Pete Harnisch 1-0 in the Astrodome on July 5, the Reds were ten games over (44-34). The Reds at that point seemed as good a bet as anybody to win the NL West.

Low Point of the Season: And then everything fell apart. The Reds lost ten straight games, dropping to 44-44. Seven of the ten losses were in Cincinnati; the Reds dropped an entire seven-game homestand. The bullpen, for years the strongest element of the team, was unable to hold a lead.

Stretch Drive: That wasn't really the low point of the season. The Reds caught a life jacket, and stabilized around .500 for a month and a half. On August 30 the Reds were 64-64, the last time they would be at .500. September was a nightmare, and the Reds won only 10 of their last 34 games.

Major Injuries: Injuries contributed heavily to the 88 losses. **Barry Larkin** was out with an inflamed elbow from May 18 to June 3 (the Reds got hot without him) and missed some of September with an achin' achilles (the Reds were already dead.) **Jose Rijo** was out a month after he broke an ankle trying to steal second base (does that make it breaking and entering?) The Reds played OK in that period, too, but while the Reds held up OK without their best pitcher and hitter, they sagged when lesser players were out. **Eric Davis** missed more time with injuries than ever before, missing weeks with a strained thigh muscle and a month with the lingering effects of the kidney injury of the 1990 World Series. Davis who had batted 412 to 474 times every year in the previous five, dropped to 285 in 1991.

People have been saying for years that **Reggie Sanders** had an Eric Davis body, and when he got to play, he proved it. Sanders played a week and then separated his shoulder making a diving catch, and was out the rest of the year. **Scott Scudder, Glenn Braggs, Norm Charlton and Bill Doran** also suffered injuries during the season.

Offense: See article, "The Big Red Wreck"

Defense: Fair. The lack of a real second baseman kept it from being what you would call a good defense. Doran doesn't get around very well anymore, and Duncan's not really a second baseman. The Reds don't have any butchers in the field, though.

Pitching: Very disappointing.

Best Game by a Starting Pitcher: Jose Rijo against the Mets, August 24 (9 2 0 0 1 9 Game Score: 91).

Indicators for 1991 were: Down moderately (−3.9)

Number of regulars having good seasons by their own standards: Six

1991 Over-Achiever: Barry Larkin

1991 Under-Achiever: Eric Davis

Infield: Well above Average. The Reds have three hitters in the infield (Morris, Sabo and Larkin) and decent defense.

Outfield: Below average. Hatcher has no business being a regular anyway, and Glenn Braggs is marginal. Eric Davis wasn't a good player last year, which left Paul O'Neill as the Reds' only quality outfielder. Reds outfielders hit .246 with 20 homers, 74 RBI per position.

Catching: Fair. Reds catchers hit 14 homers and drove in 73 runs, among the best totals in the league, and were average in terms of stopping the running game.

Starting Pitching: Not good. Armstrong was terrible, Hammond and Charlton got hurt and Browning didn't have an especially good year.

Bullpen: Not good.

Percentage of Offense Created by:
Young Players: 17%
Players in Their Prime: 75%
Past Their Prime: 8%

Team Age:
Age of Non-Pitchers: 27.1
Age of Pitching Staff: 27.6
Overall Team Age: 27.28

In retrospect, the critical decisions were:

Following their World Championship in 1991, the Reds did what most championship teams do: nothing. They had two marginal second basemen and two marginal catchers and two relief aces, and they figured that was good enough.

THAT AND THE OTHER

Hall of Fame Watch: The Reds' best Hall of Fame candidate is **Barry Larkin,** but Larkin has no more than 15% of a Hall of Fame career to date, and is injury prone. However, many other Reds are of interest to the Hall of Fame's long-range screening committee. **Eric Davis** would have been an almost certain Hall of Famer had he been able to a) play 150 games a year, and b) cut his strikeouts by 20%. His chances of reaching Hall of Fame levels, as of right now, are bleak. He probably *won't* hit 400 home runs, and absolutely won't get anywhere near 3,000 hits.

Hal Morris is not likely to have a Hall of Fame career, but does have a career batting average of .320, which is certainly noteworthy. **Jose Rijo** will emerge as a Hall of Fame candidate if he can ever have a big year. **Tom Browning** is like Bruce Hurst—the background scenery of a Hall of Fame career, but missing the highlights. **Rob Dibble**—I don't know what to make of his career, but he doesn't have any *real* Hall of Fame accomplishments yet.

Chris Berman, Have You Considered: Scott (Iraqi) Scudder

Throwback: Chris Sabo

Attendance Trend: The Reds have drawn much better the last two years than they did in the mid-eighties, when they were down.

Players with a Chance for 3000 career hits: Barry Larkin 4%

Best Interview: Chris Sabo

Probably Could Play Regularly For Another Team: Mariano Duncan

Best Fundamental Player: Barry Larkin

Worst Fundamental Player: Mariano Duncan

Best Defensive Player: Barry Larkin

Worst Defensive Player: Glenn Braggs

Best Knowledge of the Strike Zone: Bill Doran

Least Command of the Strike Zone: Mariano Duncan

Fastest Runner: Barry Larkin

Slowest Runner: Joe Oliver

Best Baserunner: Larkin

Most Likely to Still be Here in 2000: Reggie Sanders

Best Fastball: Rob Dibble

Best Breaking Pitch: Tom Browning

Best Control: Tom Browning

Never Going to be As Good as the Organization Thinks He Is: Joe Oliver

Why is this man in the Major Leagues instead of therapy: Rob Dibble

Most-Similar Players:

to C Jeff Reed, Joel Skinner
to 1B Hal Morris, Carlos Quintana
to 2B Bill Doran, Dickie Thon (??)
to 3B Chris Sabo, Paul O'Neill
to SS Barry Larkin, Shawon Dunston
to LF Billy Hatcher, Joe Orsulak
to CF Eric Davis, no one
to RF Paul O'Neill, Ron Gant

Most Fun to Watch: Sabo

Least Fun to Watch: Billy Hatcher

Managerial Type: Herm Winningham

Among the All-Time Team Leaders: Despite their long history, the Reds' leader lists are dominated by the stars of the seventies, and to a lesser extent the fifties. The dominant names are Rose, Bench, Frank Robinson, Pinson, Concepcion, Edd Rousch. **Eric Davis** had climbed onto the top ten in career homers, the top five in stolen bases, before his departure.

Tom Browning is one of the Reds' ten best all-time pitchers. No other current Red figures to become prominent on the all-time leaders list for many years.

Town Team:

C—Buck Ewing
1B—Pete Rose
2B—Bill Doran
SS—Barry Larkin
3B—Buddy Bell
LF—Jim Wynn
CF—Garry Maddox
RF—Dave Parker
SP—Jim Bunning
MGR—Miller Huggins

Post-Season Transactions:

October 28, Fired Stan Williams as pitching coach, hired Larry Rothschild.

October 28, Released or otherwise disposed of Carmelo Martinez and Ted Power.

November 15, Traded Jack Armstrong, Scott Scudder and Joe Turek to Cleveland for Greg Swindell

November 27, Traded Eric Davis and Kip Gross to Los Angeles for Tim Belcher and John Wetteland

December 1, Claimed Bob Geren on Waivers

December 10, Mariano Duncan signed with Phillies

What Needs to Be Done For 1992:

The Reds have done the one thing they most needed to do, which is end the Eric Davis era and re-build the starting rotation. From now on it's mostly hope.

Outlook for 1992:

There was a two-day story in mid-winter about the resignation of the Reds' team physician, who ripped the front office on his departure for not providing the facilities needed to care for the Reds' players the way they should be cared for. I take this to signify turmoil in the Cincinnati offices. A well-run front office, even concluding that his opinions were baseless, would probably have found a way to mollify him.

One cannot mistake the fact that the Reds have had an unusual number of injuries in recent years. It isn't just Eric Davis. The other two most-talented players produced by the Reds' system in the eighties, Barry Larkin and Kal Daniels, have been almost as injury prone as Davis. Jose Rijo can't stay healthy for a full year. Reggie Sanders comes up, and he gets hurt. I have to think that there may be a problem here that needs attention.

On the other hand, the trades for Tim Belcher and Greg Swindell give the Reds, on paper, as good a four-man starting rotation as anyone in baseball (Rijo, Browning, Swindell and Belcher). The Reds' infield is good. The Reds have one good outfielder in O'Neill, and may have another good one in Sanders. The bullpen was great in '90, and could be again in '92. There is no reason to think that this team can't bounce back very strong.

Index of Leading Indicators for 1992: +16.4

Positive Indicators: The Reds are simply a better team than their 1991 won-lost record reflects.

Negative Indicators: 1. Played poorly late in the season
2. Poor AAA team

Due for a better season: Rob Dibble

Likely to have a worse season: Jeff Reed

1992 Won-Lost Record will be: 83-79

BLIND CHANCE NOT ONLY BLIND, BUT OCCASIONALLY STUPID

Reds ace Jose Rijo, who finished the season 15-6, pitched extremely well in all six of the games that he lost. On April 21 he gave Atlanta just 3 hits and 2 runs in six innings, but was charged with a 3-2 defeat. On May 6 he gave the same (two runs in six innings) to the other division champs, the Pirates, but was tagged with a 3-1 loss. After winning seven straight games and missing some time with an injury, Rijo pitched brilliantly against the Padres on August 10, but lost 1-0. In his next start in San Francisco five days later Rijo gave the Giants no earned runs in seven innings, but two runs scored on an error by Sabo, and Rijo again was charged with the defeat.

After ripping off six more wins, Rijo lost in Houston on September 20, again because of an un-earned run. And in his final start of the year on October 6, Rijo struck out ten Padres and gave up three runs, but lost to Andy Benes, 3-2. These are the game lines and game scores for his six losses:

	IP	H	R	ER	BB	SO	
L, 0-1	6	3	2	2	2	5	Score: 61
L, 1-2	6	6	2	2	3	5	Score: 54
L, 8-3	7	7	1	1	0	9	Score: 68
L, 8-4	7	4	2	0	2	7	Score: 70
L, 14-5	6	6	3	2	1	4	Score: 53
L, 15-6	8	7	3	3	2	10	Score: 64

In his six losses Rijo pitched 40 innings, gave up only 33 hits, struck out 40, walked ten and had a 2.25 ERA.

With STATS Inc. we figure something called "tough losses", which basically is anytime a pitcher pitches well but loses, that's a tough loss. All six of Rijo's losses were tough losses.

You might think now that I was about to conclude that Rijo was the unluckiest pitcher in the league if not the universe, that with any kind of luck he should have gone 21-0 or something. Well, the odd thing was that for the season as a whole, Rijo's offensive support was the *best* of any National League pitcher, 5.6 runs per nine innings.

Rijo didn't win a lot of games 9-7 or anything. Of his 15 wins, there were only two cheap wins, two games when he didn't pitch well but won. What happened was that the Reds, while subjecting Rijo to no support in six critical games, showered him with runs in other games when he pitched equally well. Rijo beat the Cubs 12-2 in Wrigley Field (May 11), beat the Giants 9-4 (May 22), beat Philadelphia 9-3 (June 10), beat Atlanta 8-2 (August 20), beat the Mets 7-0 (August 24), beat Los Angeles 6-0 (September 10), beat Houston 10-0 (September 15) and beat Atlanta 8-0 in Atlanta (September 26).

According to John Pardon, only one pitcher in professional history won twenty games without a loss. That was Tony Napoles, who went 18-0 for the Peekskill Highlanders of the North Atlantic League in 1946, then won four more games in the playoffs.

THE BIG RED WRECK

The Reds' offense in 1991 suffered from poor timing. The team batting average dropped seven points with men in scoring position, when batting averages normally go *up*, and the Reds hit almost two-thirds of their home runs with the bases empty. As a consequence of these things the Reds scored 32 runs fewer than predicted by the runs created formula, the largest discrepancy in the league. The Reds' offense *should* have been above average, but wasn't.

In one way, the Cincinnati offense was the opposite of San Francisco's. The Giants had a formidable "center" to the offense, the spots two through five, but were weak otherwise. The Reds' offense in the five-six-seven-eight spots was probably as good as anybody's. Here are the triple crown stats for those spots:

	HR	RBI	Avg.
Fifth	25	100	.265
Sixth	16	77	.267
Seventh	16	71	.241
Eighth	14	58	.240

That's far better production than the Giants got from that part of the order, and as good as the Braves. Their production from the second spot—Barry Larkin—was terrific. But the Reds didn't really have a leadoff man much of the year, got only 92 runs out of the leadoff spot, and with Eric Davis hitting .235 and Paul O'Neill forced into the cleanup spot, the Reds production from the middle of the order was nowhere near as good as that of the Braves or Giants or Cubs or Pirates. The Reds got 84 RBI out of the third spot, 98 out of the cleanup men.

RED ALERT

You probably know this, but in the 1950s paranoia about communism was so pervasive that the Cincinnati Reds, for a couple of years, chose to be called "Redlegs". It was a bad thing to be a "Red", you see. I was thinking about this, with the collapse of the Red empire in 1991, wondering if somehow the Reds got accidentally included under the red banner again.

Anyway, the Reds' best prospect is **Reggie Sanders,** who is the reason for the Eric Davis trade. He's a 24-year-old center fielder, great body, probably the number one candidate for NL Rookie of the Year in 1992. He's a .280 hitter with some speed and some power. **Scott Bryant** is also a 24-year-old outfielder, a little bigger than Sanders but without the same speed or power, but still could have enough to make a major league career. He'll hit for average, probably, and that's the first thing they look for.

Mo Sanford, who started five games for the Reds last year, is the organization's other top prospect. He's huge (6-foot-6), right-handed, throws hard and is beginning to find his control. I love the guy, as a prospect, but we all know he wasn't thrilled with the winter's news, the trades for Swindell and Belcher, so he'll be fighting Hammond and Charlton for the fifth spot in the rotation. Well, he'll probably start. My best guess is that the Reds aren't counting on Hammond, because of his injury, and have Charlton pencilled into Randy Myers' role in the bullpen, which makes Sanford the fifth starter. Since 1989 he's 35-14 in the minor leagues, and has averaged more than a strikeout an inning at every stop in professional ball, including the big club in '91.

Freddie Benavides is a shortstop who will never hit his weight. **Bennie Colvard** is a power/speed outfielder with a seven-to-one strikeout to walk ratio, still at AA at age 25. Well, not *real* speed, but he did steal 27 bases for Cedar Rapids one year. **Tim Costo** is a big first baseman who for some reason is talked about quite a bit although he can't play. **Dan Wilson** was the top draft pick in 1990, and is believed to be a hot prospect, don't ask me why. I guess I'd describe him as being "about like Jeff Reed, but young enough to get over it."

The most interesting "prospect", abusing the term, is **Terry Lee,** a 30-year-old behemoth first baseman. Lee was a prospect ages ago, never hit real well, got hurt and was out of baseball for a time. He started hitting the hell out of the ball in 1990, and continued to do so last year, hitting .304 at Nashville. He's probably never going to get a shot, but if he ever does get 300 at bats in a decent hitter's park, I'll guarantee you he'll hit.

THE HOUSTON ASTROS
• IN A BOX •

1991 Won-Lost Record: 65-97 .401
Rank among 26 teams: 25th
Over Last Five Years: 384-426 .474
Rank over Five Years: 21st
In Last Ten Years: 805-815 .497
Rank over Ten Years: 15th

Best Player: Jeff Bagwell

Weak Spot: Right Field

For the 1991 season as a whole, Astro right fielders hit .225 with six home runs, 57 RBI.

Best Pitcher: Pete Harnisch

Staff Weakness: Jim Deshaies

Best Bench Player: Casey Candaele

Best Young Players: 1. Jeff Bagwell
2. Luis Gonzalez
3. Andujar Cedeno
4. Craig Biggio
5. Steve Finley

Best Looking Player: Luis Gonzalez

Ugliest Player: Ken Oberkfell

Most Pleasant Surprise, 1991: Jeff Bagwell

Biggest Disappointment, 1991: Jim Deshaies

Best Minor League Prospect: The people considered the best prospects for the last year are Andujar Cedeno, now with the big team, and Kenny Lofton, now with Cleveland. That probably leaves **Jeff Juden** as the top prospect.

Who Is: Juden is an elephant (6 foot 7, 245 pounds) who split 1991 between AA and AAA. Right-handed starting pitcher, pitched extremely well at Tucson (3.18 ERA) although supposedly he was working on controlling his curve and changeup, and not throwing his 90+ fastball much. Tucson had a staff ERA of 4.34 and finished 79-61. Juden will probably replace Deshaies in the Astros rotation.

Other Prospects: **Scott Servais,** a 24-year-old catcher, will probably move into a major league backup job after jumping his batting average from .218 (1990) to .324 (1991) at Tucson.

Chris Hatcher (Burlington, A Ball, outfielder) is regarded as a prospect although he struck out 180 times and didn't do anything especially well at bat. **Tom Nevers,** the Astros number one pick in 1990, is a shortstop who had a good year at Asheville (A Ball), hitting 16 home runs. He may move to another position, but he'll move up.

The Astros had four first-round and supplemental picks last year as a result of the loss of free agents, but none of the four has yet done anything to distinguish himself as a pro.

Eric Anthony remains a prospect—in fact, I still like him, and still think he's going to be a good player. **Trent Hubbard** is a 28-year-old second baseman who might make a major league roster when expansion comes. He had a hell of a year at AA. His partner was **Frank Kellner,** a 25-year-old shortstop who also played well, and has a better chance of having a little career because he is three years younger. Andy Mota is a 26-year-old second baseman who hit .299 at Tucson; you can see how high the Astros are on him, in that they're planning to move Biggio to second base. **Howard Prager,** a 25-year-old first baseman, is also a prospect after hitting .305 at Jackson.

Designated Malcontent: Mark Portugal.

Park Characteristics: The toughest home run park in the National League, favors the pitcher in almost every way. The Astros hit 27 home runs in Houston, 52 on the road, and had an ERA of 3.55 in Houston, 4.49 on the road.

The Park Helps: Harnisch, Kile, Osuna.

The Park Hurts: Bagwell, Gonzalez, Caminiti.

ORGANIZATIONAL REPORT CARD

Ownership: D
Upper Management: B−
Field Management: Seems OK
Front-Line Talent: C−
Second-Line Talent: D
Minor League System: B

Comment: The 1991 season was the beginning of a building cycle for the Astros. The Astros, losing Nolan Ryan to free agency and Mike Scott to injury, decided that they were never going anywhere with the talent they had, so it was time to dump veterans and start over.

They've made a very solid beginning. The 1991 season was a bad one for the Astros in terms of wins and losses, but it was an outstanding season in terms of building the team. The Astros have about half a dozen good young players on the roster now who weren't there a year ago. Two trades worked out great, getting Bagwell for Andersen, and getting Harnisch plus Finley for Glenn Davis. The organization's own key prospects (Gonzalez, Osuna, Cedeno, Kile) played and weren't obviously overmatched. They've come a substantial distance in one year.

TEAM LEADERS:

Batting Average: Craig Biggio, .295
Last Ten Years (Season): Jose Cruz, 1983, .318
Last Ten Years (Total): Jose Cruz, .291

Home Runs: Jeff Bagwell, 15
Last Ten Years (Season): Glenn Davis, 34 in 1989
Last Ten Years (Total): Glenn Davis, 166

RBI: Jeff Bagwell, 82
Last Ten Years (Season): Glenn Davis, 101 in 1986
Last Ten Years (Total): Glenn Davis, 518

Wins: Pete Harnisch, 12
Last Ten Years (Season): Mike Scott, 20 in 1989
Last Ten Years (Total): Scott, 110

Winning Percentage: Harnisch, 12-9 .571

Strikeouts: Harnisch, 172
 Last Ten Years (Season): Mike Scott, 306 in 1986
 Last Ten Years (Total): Nolan Ryan, 1526

ERA: Harnisch, 2.70

Saves: Al Osuna, 12

Doubles: Ken Caminiti, 30

Triples: Steve Finley, 10

Extra Base Hits: Luis Gonzalez, 50

Stolen Bases: Steve Finley, 34

Runs Created: Jeff Bagwell, 98

Runs Created Per Game: Bagwell, 6.4

Walks: Bagwell, 75

Secondary Average: Bagwell, .291

League Leaders: Jeff Bagwell led the league in being hit with a pitch, 13 times. Craig Biggio led the catchers in putouts, total chances and passed balls. Pete Harnisch led the NL in fewest hits per nine innings, 7.02, and opposition batting average, .212.

1991 SEASON

Background: Following their division championship in 1986, the Astros struggled for two years. In this period the Astros accumulated a number of veteran pitchers in an attempt to bolster the staff to championship quality. This was moderately successful, and the Astros made a decent run at the Giants in 1989, falling six games short.

The Astros had a poor season in 1990, however (75-87), and made the decision to clear out the by-now-ancient pitching staff and re-set the clock.

Outlook: In the wake of the trade/departure by free agency/loss to injury of Glenn Davis and six key pitchers (Juan Agosto, Larry Andersen, Jim Clancy, Danny Darwin, Mike Scott, Dave Smith) it was apparent to everyone that the Astros could not compete in 1991.

Getaway: The Astros won four of their first seven games. A late rally over the Braves in Atlanta on April 15 pushed them over .500.

High Point of the Season: That *was* the high point of the season. The Astros were never over .500 again.

Stretch Drive: From then on the Astros lost consistently, but without the humiliating twelve-game losing streaks that sometimes break the spirit of a young team. The Astros were 8-11 in April, 10-18 in May, 11-17 in June, 12-13 in July, 12-17 in August, 10-18 in September and 2-3 in October.

Most Exciting Game of the Season: August second against the Dodgers at the Astrodome. The Astros took a 7-0 lead on a three-run homer by Andujar Cedeno and a big triple by Steve Finley. The Dodgers fought back with a homer and a double by Strawberry and a triple by Samuel, among other things, to make it 7-6 after eight. In the top of the ninth the Dodgers scored two to take the lead on a pinch-hit single by Chris Gwynn, a bunt by Sharperson and a single by Alfredo Griffin. In the bottom of the ninth Jay Howell walked Luis Gonzalez and Craig Biggio with one out. Lasorda brought in John Candelaria, his left-handed short man, to pitch to Steve Finley, so Howe pinch-hit with Rafael Ramirez. Ramirez ripped a two-run double to give the Astros a 9-8 win.

Major Injuries: The Astros weren't counting on anybody enough to be undermined by any injuries, and suffered nothing devastating. Among those who were out for a time with one thing or another were Xavier Hernandez, Jimmy Jones, Mark McLemore, Scott Servais and Mark Portugal.

Offense: Below average, but not terrible. The Astros scored 605 runs. In a normal park they would have been close to the league average.

Defense: Spotty and inexperienced. The addition of Steve Finley gave the Astros one good up-the-middle defender, but Biggio still doesn't throw well, the shortstops made 42 errors and the second basemen were just stop-gap type guys. The Astros were probably the weakest defensive team in the league.

Pitching: Very poor. Away from the Astrodome Houston pitchers allowed a slugging percentage of .411, which is unacceptable.

Best Game by a Starting Pitcher: Pete Harnisch against the Mets, June 9 (9 3 0 0 3 11 Game Score: 89).

Worst Game by a Starting Pitcher: Ryan Bowen at Cincinnati, September 13 (1⅔ 8 8 8 1 2 Game Score: 8).

Indicators for 1991 were: Up 9.1

Number of regulars having good seasons by their own standards: Three (Finley, Biggio, Candaele)

1991 Over-Achiever: Finley

1991 Under-Achiever: Ramirez

Infield: Fairly decent. Bagwell at first was among the best in the league, and Caminiti played well. Houston second basemen hit .231 with five home runs and little defense, while their shortstops hit better but made errors.

Outfield: Fair/poor. One of the three positions (right field) was the worst in the league. The other two (Gonzalez and Finley) were OK but not among the best in the league.

Catching: OK. Biggio can't throw, but you can live with that to get a hitter.

Starting Pitching: Awful. One guy was good (Harnisch), one guy was fair (Kile) and the rest were hammered.

Bullpen: Very poor. The Astros had 23 blown saves (second most in the majors, only Montreal had more), took 34 losses in the bullpen (most in the major leagues) and had a bullpen ERA of 3.86 (tenth in the National League.)

Percentage of offense created by:

Young Players: 73%
Players in Their Prime: 23%
Past Their Prime: 4%

Team Age:

Age of Non-Pitchers: 25.9
Age of Pitching Staff: 25.7
Overall Team Age: 25.81

The Astros of 1991 were by far the youngest team in the National League.

In retrospect, the critical decisions were: The critical decision was the mid-1990 decision to cash in their chips and start over. This decision made the 1991 season what it was, but will also make future seasons better.

THAT AND THE OTHER

Lookalikes: Al Osuna and Alfred E. Neuman

Hall of Fame Watch: The Astros most viable Hall of Fame candidate in recent years has been Mike Scott, who was forced into retirement by injuries before his accomplishments made him a serious Hall of Fame candidate.

Chris Berman, Have You Considered: Jeff (Have you been treating the old) Bagwell

Throwback: Bagwell

Attendance Trend: Downward. Houston attendance has never been great. In 1988, in the wake of the 1986 championship, the Astros drew almost two million (1,933,505). They slipped to 1.8 million in 1989, 1.3 million in 1990 and 1.196 million in 1991.

Players with a Chance for 3000 career hits: Craig Biggio 3%

Probably Could Play Regularly For Another Team: Eric Anthony would have a better shot in almost any other park.

Best Fundamental Player: Steve Finley

Worst Fundamental Player: Andujar Cedeno

Best Defensive Player: 1. Ken Caminiti
2. Steve Finley

Worst Defensive Player: Craig Biggio. I doubt that he'll be any better at second than he was at catcher.

Best Knowledge of the Strike Zone: Casey Candaele

Least Command of the Strike Zone: Andujar Cedeno

Fastest Runner: Steve Finley

Slowest Runner: Caminiti is probably the slowest regular

Best Baserunner: Biggio

Most Likely to Still be Here in 2000: Jeff Bagwell

Best Fastball: Jeff Juden

Best Breaking Pitch: Darryl Kile

Best Control: Jim Corsi

Oddest Collection of Abilities: Craig Biggio

Why is this man in the Major Leagues: Mark Davidson

Best Local Sportswriter: Ken Hand

Most-Similar Players:

to C Craig Biggio, B.J. Surhoff
to 1B Jeff Bagwell, Luis Gonzalez
to 2B Casey Candaele, Alvaro Espinoza
to 3B Ken Caminiti, Luis Rivera
to SS Andujar Cedeno, Mark Lewis
to LF Luis Gonzalez, Brian Hunter
to CF Steve Finley, Lance Johnson
to RF (Astros have no right fielder)

Most Fun to Watch: Jeff Bagwell

Least Fun to Watch: Eric Yelding

Managerial Type: Casey Candaele

Among the All-Time Team Leaders: Mike Scott reached third place on the list of Astros' career wins (110, behind Joe Niekro and Larry Dierker) and fourth in career strikeouts (1318, behind same two and Ryan). With his retirement no remaining Astro is among the team leaders.

Town Team:

C—Gus Mancuso
1B—Gus Zernial
2B—Grady Hatton
SS—Craig Reynolds
3B—Max Alvis
LF—Jo Jo Moore
CF—Jim Busby
RF—Carl Reynolds
SP—Nolan Ryan
SP—Roger Clemens
SP—Doug Drabek

Post-Season Transactions:

November 19, Asked waivers on Jim Corsi, Dwayne Henry, Jose Tolentino and Javier Ortiz

December 10, traded Dave Rohde and Kenny Lofton to Cleveland for Willie Blair and Ed Taubensee

Why does a team with a staff ERA of 4.00 release relievers with ERAs of 3.19 (Dwayne Henry) and 3.71 (Jim Corsi)? You understand this? Of course they're protecting prospects, but don't you usually protect the people who play well?

What Needs to Be Done For 1992: Nothing dramatic. They need to keep on course, keep adding talent.

Outlook for 1992: They should be quite a bit better. I don't think they're ready to win the division yet, but you never know.

Index of Leading Indicators for 1992: Up 28.1

The Astros Leading Indicators for 1992 are the most positive of those for any National League team.

Positive Indicators: 1. Team Age

Negative Indicators: 1. Poor play late in the season

Due for a better season: Darryl Kile

Likely to have a worse season: Craig Biggio

1992 Won-Lost Record will be: 82-80

THE BAGWELL BUNGLE

In conjunction with STATS, Inc., I produce a fall book called the *Major League Handbook*. In the 1991 edition of this book, released in November 1990, we projected the 1991 performance of all major league players. In that we had a side chart called "These Guys Can Play Too and Might Get a Shot", which listed the projected stats for some players that we did not expect to be in the major leagues but whom we regarded as being capable hitters if they happened to get a shot.

In that chart we listed Jeff Bagwell. We had Bagwell projected to hit about .318. We didn't think anything of this at the time, but Peter Gammons wrote a review of the book, a very nice review which helped us sell quite a few copies. Anyway, Gammons pointed out, in a questioning way, that while we had projected Bagwell to hit .318, we had projected Tony Gwynn to hit only .317 and everybody else in the National League to hit less. "Jeff Bagwell is going to win the National League batting title?" Gammons asked quizzically, implying that something was a little amiss here.

To be honest, none of us were aware until then that we had projected Bagwell to have a higher average than anyone else. If we *had* been aware of it, we would have intervened in the projection system somehow to make it come out differently—probably we would have given Tony Gwynn an extra hit, or taken one away from Bagwell. We wouldn't have let it go, because rookies very rarely win batting championships, so it makes no sense to project that a rookie is going to win the batting title. We weren't in the business of projecting who was going to win the batting title, so we didn't think through what the individual projections might have implied about that issue, anymore than we thought through what they might have implied about who was going to win the pennant or who was going to go into the Hall of Fame or any other side issue. It just wasn't what we were doing.

So when Gammons pointed out that we had "picked" Bagwell to win the batting title, I thought that this was eminently fair criticism. It is irrational to project a rookie to hit for a higher average than any veteran, and in retrospect we should have taken care to avoid it.

Let me explain why this would happen. Over a period of years a player's batting average goes up and down—a good year, a bad year. When we project what a player will do *next* year, we take the center, and adjust it for aging patterns. If a player has hit .300 and then .330, we'll project him to hit about .315—maybe .320 if he's young, or .310 if he's aging, but somewhere around .315. But for Bagwell—and for many minor league players—we don't have multi-year information to work with; we have one year, and that's it. We don't know whether it represents his good year or his off year, so we assume that it represents a typical year. What can happen is that the minor league player's *good* year will be contrasted with Tony Gwynn's *typical* year, and the minor league player, if he is an outstanding hitter, may come out ahead.

It isn't technically accurate to say that we projected that Jeff Bagwell would win the National League batting title, because in fact we hadn't even projected him to play; we thought he would spend the season in AAA. It certainly isn't accurate to say that I had *predicted* that Bagwell would win the batting title, because I never made any such prediction. I've never made any prediction at all about who was going to win the batting title in a particular season, and I don't intend to start. I don't know how you could do this.

Well, more people would read Gammons' review than would ever see the book. The book is a little self-published thing that we print about 7,000 copies of; the review ran in a paper with a circulation that's probably in the millions, and then too media people take what Peter Gammons says more seriously than they take what I say. So this comment began to echo, and it echoed, and it echoed. For some reason, the idea that I had predicted that Jeff Bagwell was going to win the 1991 National League batting title caught hold in the media's collective consciousness, and was repeated in print or on the air dozens of times that I became aware of, and probably hundreds of times that I missed.

From then on, almost every review of the *1991 Major League Handbook* repeated Gammons' comment in a different form. Gammons had buried the remark at the end of the review, after he had explained the context; other reviewers tended to headline it, and to state it without explaining that this was an inference from the data, and not our intention. In shorter pieces this "prediction" often became the sole basis of the reviewer's reaction to the book. Even some reviews of *this* book, *The Baseball Book 1991*, said that I had predicted that Jeff Bagwell would win the 1991 NL batting title, even though what I had *actually* said about the subject was that "If he had come up in Fenway (Park), in my opinion, he would have won some batting titles. Playing in the Astrodome, of course, he probably won't." Also, I picked Steve Decker as the number one candidate for NL Rookie of the Year. Obviously, if I thought Jeff Bagwell was going to win the batting title, I would also have picked him to be the Rookie of the Year.

Twice, I heard someone on *ESPN* say that I had predicted that Jeff Bagwell would win the NL batting title. One quote was "Stat analyst Bill James argues that Jeff Bagwell will win the National League batting title *this season*." Argues? *Baseball America* mentioned it—I don't know, two or three times in different contexts. Somehow, this obscure inference, buried in a mass of computer-generated statistics, had become more noteworthy as something I said than any of the thousands of things that I actually *did* say or write during the season.

If this became tiresome for me, it became positively irritating for Bagwell, since nearly every story written about *him* was saying the same thing, and a rookie really doesn't need that kind of pressure. Incidentally, none of the people who passed along this prediction ever called me up and asked "Did you really say this? Is this an accurate reflection of your comments?" Never happened.

In a perfect world, one would like to think that if I'm going to make a million-to-one prediction, it's up to me to make this decision. But I realized a long time ago that

a) I don't get to decide what other people are going to say about me, and

b) a very high percentage of what is written in the newspapers is not exactly accurate.

For example, dozens of newspaper stories about me ten years ago reported that I had started the *Baseball Abstract* out of my garage, although this was not true and I have no idea where it originally came from. You just have to roll with it; you'll drive yourself crazy if you start making frantic efforts to keep the record straight.

This particular misrepresentation, however, was very risky for me. For almost ten years, I've been trying to show people that you *can* predict major league performance from minor league performance, and we have made tremendous strides in that area. We've gone from one percent of the interested public believing this to probably 20%. We've reached the point at which many or most of the teams will take the time to *look* at our major league equivalencies, although the GM himself may still think we're just making a wild guess.

This situation had the potential to undermine everything we had accomplished.

Look, I have tremendous confidence in our ability to project how a player will hit in the major leagues, over time. But how a player will hit *in a season* is another matter. How he will hit in two months under great pressure, I haven't a clue. I had confidence that Jeff Bagwell would eventually be a good major league hitter—but you know and I know that it was quite possible for Bagwell to hit .186 for two months and get sent to Tucson. If that had happened my reputation for being able to project major league stats from minor league ones would have been destroyed. The argument over this process, which has been going on since 1983, would have been irretrievably lost. For the rest of my life, anytime I tried to project what a player would do in the major leagues, somebody would have said "what about Jeff Bagwell?" There had been so much publicity about that "prediction" that it had become the test by which the credibility of those methods was going to be tried.

So Jeff Bagwell became, for 1991, my favorite player. If three games were on TV and the Astros were one of them, I'd watch the Houston game to see how Bagwell did. When I saw the box scores, Houston's was the first one I checked.

And in the end, Jeff Bagwell saved my butt.

He didn't win the batting title, of course, and he didn't do *exactly* what we had projected for him. This chart compares the projected to the actual season:

	G	AB	R	H	2B	3B	HR	RBI	SB	Avg
Projected	140	500	65	159	34	6	3	62	3	.318
Actual	156	554	79	163	26	4	15	82	7	.294

That's not a particularly good projection for a first-year player. A particularly good projection for a first-year player would be this:

Juan Gonzalez

	G	AB	R	H	2B	3B	HR	RBI	SB	Avg
Projected	151	551	74	145	30	4	26	90	3	.263
Actual	142	545	78	144	34	1	27	102	4	.264

or this:

Brian McRae

	G	AB	R	H	2B	3B	HR	RBI	SB	Avg
Projected	149	565	76	146	29	8	8	68	18	.258
Actual	152	629	86	164	28	9	8	64	20	.261

or this:

Milt Cuyler

	G	AB	R	H	2B	3B	HR	RBI	SB	Avg
Projected	125	450	77	113	11	6	5	43	36	.251
Actual	154	475	77	122	15	7	3	33	41	.257

All of those projections appeared in the 1991 *Handbook*, along with the celebrated Jeff Bagwell projection, and obviously I would have been thrilled if any of those had received the same attention. But it could have been a lot worse. It could have been Steve Decker, who I had picked as the NL Rookie of the Year:

Steve Decker

	G	AB	R	H	2B	3B	HR	RBI	SB	Avg
Projected	135	485	56	140	17	1	16	75	5	.289
Actual	79	233	11	48	7	1	5	24	0	.206

or Jose Offerman:

Jose Offerman

	G	AB	R	H	2B	3B	HR	RBI	SB	Avg
Projected	155	600	91	162	9	3	2	51	53	.270
Actual	52	113	10	22	2	0	0	3	3	.195

Decker and Offerman will eventually have the seasons that we projected for them, but I would have hated like hell to be hanging day by day on their 1991 performance.

In the end, the Bagwell "prediction" did more to help the credibility of our predictions than it did to hurt. Late in the season, a Houston reporter and a TV sports guy were nice enough to write and say in public that before the season, nobody but Bill James thought that Jeff Bagwell was going to be this good. I thank them for remembering. We've got Jeff Bagwell projected to hit .315 this year, and we've changed our policy.

From now on we're going to check and see who we have "predicted" to win the batting title.

THE TORONTO BLUE JAYS
• IN A BOX •

1991 Won-Lost Record: 91-71 .562

Rank among 26 teams: 5th
Over Last Five Years: 449-361 .554
Rank over Five Years: 2nd
In Last Ten Years: 890-729 .550
Rank over Ten Years: 1st

Over the last ten years the Blue Jays' record is the best in baseball.

Best Player: Roberto Alomar

Weak Spot: Shortstop

Best Pitcher: Tom Henke

Staff Weakness: Long Relief (Jim Acker)

Best Bench Player: In 1991, Ed Sprague

Best Young Player: 1. Roberto Alomar
2. John Olerud

Best Looking Player: Pat Borders

Ugliest Player: Tom Henke

Most Pleasant Surprise, 1991: Devon White

Biggest Disappointment, 1991: Dave Stieb

Best Minor League Prospect: See article, "They Come in Waves"

Park Characteristics: See article, "The Blue Jay Offense"

The Park Helps: All the hitters. Joe Carter hit especially well in the Dome last year.

The Park Hurts: Jimmy Key has pitched quite a bit better on the road the last two years. Jose Guzman also had a 3.82 home ERA, 2.28 road ERA, but of course that's just one season.

The 1991 Blue Jays were only one game better in the SkyDome (46-35) than on the road (45-36). Over the last six years the Blue Jays' home field advantage is the *smallest* of any American League team.

ORGANIZATIONAL REPORT CARD

Ownership: B
Upper Management: A
Field Management: C
Front-Line Talent: A
Second-Line Talent: B+
Minor League System: A

Comment: I've always liked the Blue Jays because the Blue Jays make decisions for the long run more often than any other major league team. That's my inclination; I always want the teams that I am rooting for to make those decisions which build up the talent base, as opposed to those which exploit the talent base to maximize current production. The Blue Jays produce as many players as they can, and more than anybody else, and figure that in the long run that will make them a winning team.

TEAM LEADERS:

Batting Average: Roberto Alomar, .295

Last Ten Years (Season): Tony Fernandez, 1987, .322
Last Ten Years (Total): Fernandez, .289

Doubles: Roberto Alomar, 41

Triples: Roberto Alomar, 11

Home Runs: Joe Carter, 33

Last Ten Years (Season): George Bell, 1987, 47
Last Ten Years (Total): Bell, 197

Extra Base Hits: Devon White, 67

RBI: Joe Carter, 108

Last Ten Years (Season): George Bell, 1987, 134
Last Ten Years (Total): Bell, 728

Stolen Bases: Devon White, 53

Runs Created: Joe Carter and Roberto Alomar, 107 each

Runs Created Per Game: 1. Alomar, 5.94
2. Carter 5.91

Secondary Average: Joe Carter, .339

Wins: Jimmy Key, 16

Last Ten Years (Season): Dave Stieb, 1990, 18
Last Ten Years (Total): Stieb, 135

Winning Percentage: Todd Stottlemyre, 15-8, .652

Strikeouts: Duane Ward, 132

Last Ten Years (Season): Dave Stieb, 1984, 198
Last Ten Years (Total): Stieb, 1337

ERA: Jimmy Key, 3.05

Tom Candiotti, who split the year between Toronto and Cleveland, had more strikeouts than Ward and a better ERA than Key, but didn't qualify for either distinction based solely on his performance with the Blue Jays.

Saves: Tom Henke, 32

League Leaders: Joe Carter tied for the AL lead with 162 games played, and he led the league with 10 HBP. Olerud tied for the league lead with 10 sacrifice flies.

1991 SEASON

Background: The Blue Jays in the late eighties had a series of successful but still very frustrating seasons. In 1985 the Blue Jays won the division, but lost in the playoffs. In 1986 they won 86 games and were in contention, but finished fourth. In 1987 they blew the division title in the last week. In 1988 they missed the division title by two games. In 1989 they won the division title, but were annihilated in the playoffs. In 1990 they again missed the division title by two games.

Throughout this, Pat Gillick had acquired the reputation as "Stand Pat", largely because of his unwillingness to make petty little in-season maneuvers to help the team feel better about itself. In the winter of 1990–1991 Gillick blasted that reputation into oblivion by announcing the biggest trade in many years, the exchange of two stars (Tony Fernandez and Fred McGriff) for two other stars (Roberto Alomar and Joe Carter). The Blue Jays also allowed George Bell, their cleanup hitter for many years, to walk away without an offer, and traded Junior Felix for Devon White. The debates about these moves were the basic premise of the Blue Jay season on opening day, 1991.

Outlook: There are only two good teams in this division, Boston and Toronto. Almost everybody picked one team or the other.

Getaway: The Blue Jays won six of their first eight games.

Low Point of the Season: The Blue Jays played the 1991 season without either hot streaks or slumps, and thus avoided either great high points or low points. After 40% of the season (June 19) the Blue Jays were only three games over .500 (33-30), but the Red Sox were doing no better, and the Blue Jays were never in a bad position.

High Point of the Season: October 2, Blue Jays scored two in the bottom of the ninth to beat Bryan Harvey and clinch the divisional title.

Stretch Drive: Same as the rest of the season. Leaving out the five games in October, the Blue Jays' worst month was August, when they were 15-14 (.517). Their *best* month was July, when they were 15-11 (.577). They were just the same all year.

Most Exciting Game of the Season: September 24 in Anaheim. With the pennant race at its apex, the Blue Jays and Angels were scoreless going into the tenth, Jim Abbott having given up only two hits. Maldonado led off with a single, Olerud sacrificed him to second, Tabler walked, and Pat Borders hit one out of the park. With Boston rained out, Toronto moved to a two-game lead.

Major Injuries: **Dave Stieb,** 4-3 in the early season, went on the Disabled List June 1 with a herniated disc and didn't pitch again. His future is in doubt. **Tom Henke** was out from April 12 through May 17 with a pulled groin muscle, and he also missed the second half of September with a sore shoulder. **Kelly Gruber** missed more than a month with a "sprained ligament and chip fracture" of his right thumb. **Ken Dayley** suffered from dizzy spells and vertigo, and pitched only twice.

Offense: See article

Defense: Fairly good. The additions of Alomar and Devon White gave the Blue Jays two Gold-Glove types up the middle. The Blue Jays were left with an inexperienced shortstop, a weak arm in right field and a few other problems, but nothing that was going to cost them a lot of games.

Pitching: Excellent. Toronto's 3.50 ERA led the American League by a good margin, and that's a hell of an accomplishment in their park. On the road they had a staff ERA of 3.16, which is sensational, and is the basic difference between the Blue Jays and the Red Sox. The Red Sox had a staff ERA of 4.14 on the road. Turn those figures around and leave everything else the same, and Boston would win this race by more than ten games.

Most Valuable Player: Roberto Alomar

Best Game by a Starting Pitcher: Jimmy Key vs. Cleveland, June 13 (9 2 0 0 0 5 Game Score: 88)

Worst Game by a Starting Pitcher: Tom Candiotti against California, September 23 (⅔ 6 7 7 1 1 Game Score: 12)

Indicators for 1991 were: Up 8.1

Number of regulars having good seasons by their own standards: Four (Alomar, White, Carter and Myers)

1991 Over-Achiever: Devon White

1991 Under-Achiever: Manuel Lee

Infield: Fair. Alomar was an MVP candidate, Olerud and Gruber were average, and Lee was poor.

Outfield: Excellent. Both Carter and White were very good, and the production from an assortment of players in left field was surprisingly good (.269 average with 16 homers, 75 RBI from their left fielders. Blue Jay left fielders also hit 34 doubles and stole 20 bases.) Of course, Joe Carter did play a third of the season in left field.

Catching: Fairly good. Blue Jay catchers hit .255 with 13 homers and 38 doubles. They were average in terms of stopping the running game.

Starting Pitching: Very good, especially in the control department. Blue Jay starters walked only 340 men in more than a thousand innings.

Bullpen: The bullpen struggled occasionally, as everybody's does, but it's very good. While Henke was out Ward filled in as the stopper and was great. The Blue Jays led the majors in team saves, with 60.

Percentage of offense created by:

Young Players:	39%
Players in Their Prime:	36%
Past Their Prime:	25%

Team Age:

Age of Non-Pitchers:	28.2
Age of Pitching Staff:	28.1
Overall Team Age:	28.18

In retrospect, the critical decisions were: The two critical moves were the trade for Devon White and the mid-summer acquisition of Tom Candiotti, which stabilized the rotation in the absence of Dave Stieb. Because the Blue Jays won their division, there is a tendency to speak well of *all* of their trades, but the Blue Jays' 1991 team was not dramatically different than in recent years. They won 91 games and lost the playoffs; that's what this team does. The critical decision was the decision fifteen years ago to build such a good organization.

THAT AND THE OTHER

Hall of Fame Watch: **Joe Carter** has about 30% of a Hall of Fame career, which in view of his age (32) means that he won't make the Hall of Fame unless he has an MVP season or plays unusually well in his late thirties. New Blue Jay **Jack Morris** is a likely Hall of Famer, but not a lock. **Dave Stieb** has no chance of making the Hall of Fame unless he can come back and pitch well again. I believe **Roberto Alomar** should have a Hall of Fame career, but that's in the future. The Hall of Fame chances of **Tom Henke** are almost impossible to estimate because there are only two relievers in the Hall of Fame, but I would guess that Henke has little or no chance of being selected.

Chris Berman, Have You Considered:

John (I didn't mean to be) Olerud
Pat Borders (on the bizarre)

Throwback: Dave Stieb

Attendance Trend: Up and Up and Up

Players with a Chance for 3000 career hits:

Roberto Alomar,	28%
Dave Winfield,	27%
Joe Carter,	4%

At first glance it seems absurd to say that a 23-year-old player has established a 28% chance of getting 3,000 hits, but that's what the formula says, and I can't argue with it. Alomar leads all players born 1968 or later in career hits (685), and also has more hits than anyone born in 1967 or 1966. In other words, he has more career hits than anyone else in his age group. If he averages 170 hits a year for the next ten years—Steve Sax' pace—he'll be 33 years old and 615 hits away from 3,000.

Best Interview: Joe Carter

Probably Could Play Regularly For Another Team: Rob Ducey

Best Fundamental Player: Roberto Alomar

Worst Fundamental Player: Pat Borders

Best Defensive Player: Devon White

Worst Defensive Player: Ed Sprague

Best Knowledge of the Strike Zone: John Olerud

Least Command of the Strike Zone: Pat Borders

Fastest Runner: Devon White

Slowest Runner: Pat Borders

Best Baserunner: Devon White

Most Likely to Still be Here in 2000: John Olerud

Best Fastball: Tom Henke

Best Control: Jimmy Key

Most Overrated Player: Devon White, historically. White played great last year.

Most Underrated Player: Greg Myers

Oddest Collection of Abilities: Pat Borders

Why was this man in the Major Leagues: Mookie Wilson

Gets Ahead of the Hitters Most Often: Tom Henke

Gets Ahead of the Hitters Least Often: Tom Candiotti, now with LA, pitches exceptionally well when behind in the count.

Most-Similar Players:

to C Greg Myers, Chris Hoiles
to 1B John Olerud, Larry Walker
to 2B Roberto Alomar, Jody Reed
to 3B Kelly Gruber, Steve Buechele
to SS Manuel Lee, Felix Fermin
to LF Candy Maldonado, Sid Bream
to CF Devon White, no one
to RF Joe Carter, Howard Johnson

Most Fun to Watch: Jimmy Key

Least Fun to Watch: Manuel Lee

Managerial Type: Mookie Wilson

Among the All-Time Team Leaders: **Dave Stieb** is by far the best pitcher in Blue Jay "history", holding the franchise records for games, wins, strikeouts, etc. **Tom Henke** holds the record for saves, and **Jimmy Key** is second or third on the Toronto pitching lists, behind Stieb and sometimes Jim Clancy.

The Blue Jays' team records are impressive in view of their 15-year-history. The most prominent of the current Blue Jay hitters is **Rance Mulliniks,** who has been here ever since.

Town Team:

C—Jimmy Archer
1B—Tip O'Neill
2B—Chub Collins
SS—Arthur Irwin
3B—Frank O'Rourke
LF—Jeff Heath
CF—Goody Rosen
RF—George Selkirk
SP—Fergie Jenkins

Post-Season Transactions:

October 28, released Mookie Wilson, Dave Parker and Cory Snyder
December 3, Tom Candiotti signed with Dodgers as free agent
December 18, Jack Morris signed as a free agent
December 19, signed Dave Winfield to a one-year contract

What Needs to Be Done For 1992: There aren't any big problems that need to be solved. The key things are to improve the shortstop situation, see if John Olerud can step up his production a little bit and try to get Derek Bell's career off on the right foot.

Outlook for 1992: The Blue Jays are the most reliable product in baseball. They haven't had a true off season for many years, and there's no reason to think they will in 1992.

Unless something unexpected happens they only have to beat one team, the Red Sox. They might not do that, and then too somebody else might sneak in a good season, but if you're a betting man and not a Red Sox fan, you have to put your money on the Blue Jays.

Index of Leading Indicators for 1992: Down Slightly (4.1)

Positive Indicators: 1. The team in 1991 did not score nearly as many runs as would be expected from their other offensive stats. In all likelihood, that was due primarily to bad luck, and the team probably will score more runs this year.

2. The Blue Jays are a relatively young team.

Negative Indicators: 1. Natural tendency of good teams to decline.

Due for a better season: 1. Dave Stieb if healthy
2. Pat Borders
3. Kelly Gruber

Likely to have a worse season: Devon White

1992 Won-Lost Record will be: 89-73 (1st Place)

THEY COME IN WAVES

The Blue Jays' top prospect at the moment is **Derek Bell,** who was *Baseball America*'s Minor League Player of the Year in 1991. Bell is a 23-year-old outfielder, has some power and good speed. I think he was a pretty good pick for the award. Bell's MLEs from 1991 show him hitting .322 in the major leagues, with 11 homers and 19 stolen bases in 119 games.

Because Bell had never hit exceptionally well prior to 1991, we cannot state with confidence that that represents his real level of ability. For a 22-year-old player (he was 22 in 1991) to make a strong stride forward as a hitter is fairly common, and thus it is reasonable to think that Bell might prove to be an outstanding major league hitter, but we still have to consider his hitting record over a period of years, which is much less impressive.

Bell is a strong candidate for the American League Rookie of the Year in 1992. The Blue Jays released Mookie Wilson (about frigging *time*, don't you think?) and Dave Parker, clearing playing time in the outfield; still, in the past they have normally brought young players along slowly, and then they did sign Dave Winfield, although it is assumed Winfield will be the DH. I'm not saying Bell is going to hit .320, but I like him, and he *might*.

The Blue Jays produce so many prospects that they make you wonder what the other teams find so hard about the process. **Eddie Zosky,** 24 years old, has a chance to be the Blue Jays' starting shortstop. He's a .250-range hitter, which is better than Manuel Lee last year, and is said to be a fine defensive shortstop. **Nigel Wilson** is another of the Blue Jays' assembly-line outfielders. He hit .301 with power and speed in the Florida State League, a tough place to hit, but he's 22 years old. **Carlos Delgado** may well be the best of the bunch. Delgado hit .286 with 18 homers and was the best defensive catcher in the Sally League in 1991; he is 19 years old. He's huge for a 19-year-old catcher—six-foot-three, 206.

First baseman **Domingo Martinez,** only 24 years old despite spending three years at Knoxville, moved up to Syracuse in 1991 and had by far his best season (.313 with 17 homers, 83 RBI); he may wind up as a regular first baseman on an expansion team. He's a better player than Doug Ault was, I'll tell you that. Hard-throwing right-hander **Alex Sanchez** continues to have control troubles.

THE BLUE JAY OFFENSE

The early returns leave no doubt that the Sky Dome is one of the best hitter's parks in baseball. The Blue Jays hit 23 points better in the Dome than on the road (.269 to .246), and their pitchers allowed a batting average 21 points higher in Toronto (.248 to .227). There were 147 home runs hit in Toronto's home games, 107 in their road games. It also appears to be a very good doubles park. It's too early to know for sure, but this may now be the best park for a hitter in the American League.

What this points out is that Toronto's offense in 1991 was really not very good, and in fact was probably the weakest offense for a championship team in several years. The Blue Jays scored only 684 runs, well below the American League average, despite playing in a terrific hitter's park. They were eleventh in the league in runs scored. Their offense had 724 Runs Created, only 684 actual runs, so their offense is not quite as bad as the run total suggests, but

1) the offense was not *efficient*, and

2) even at 724 runs, that's not good.

The offense was probably relatively inefficient because the leadoff man (Devon White) was very good but not really a leadoff man, and the cleanup hitters (John Olerud and others) were OK but not really cleanup hitters.

Well, to digress for a minute. A year ago the Blue Jays traded Freddie McGriff, their first baseman and cleanup hitter, and asked John Olerud, then 22 years old, to replace him. At the All-Star break last year Olerud was hitting .230 and had driven in only 29 runs. A Toronto sportswriter wrote an article remarking on this—that the Blue Jays' cleanup hitter had only 29 RBI in half a season—but when I checked STATS data, I noticed that

a) Olerud actually had less than a hundred at bats in the cleanup spot at that time, but

b) He was hitting around .150 with men in scoring position.

So there was *something* to the remark, but it was not quite true that the Blue Jays' cleanup hitter had driven in only 29 runs at the All-Star break. Olerud hit better in the second half, finishing at .268 with 68 RBI, and also hit around .300 with men in scoring position over the second half of the season. I thought a year ago that Olerud should have a good future as a major league hitter, and that's still what I think.

Anyway, the Blue Jays' offense was strong in spots one to three (White, Alomar, Carter), and then was about done. Their cleanup hitters finished the year with a .425 slugging percentage and 88 RBI, both figures poor for the cleanup spot. While Toronto cleanup hitters drove in 88, those for Boston drove in 103. While Toronto number five hitters drove in 76 runs, Boston's drove in 94. While Toronto number six hitters drove in 80 runs, Boston's drove in 98. So from the cleanup spot on, Boston's offense, which wasn't great either, was still beating Toronto's.

The Blue Jay offense should be better this year. Blue Jay designated hitters were terrible in 1991, hitting only five home runs and driving in 56 runs, both totals by far the lowest in the league. The designated hitters for the other thirteen teams averaged 23 homers and 89 RBI. One assumes that Dave Winfield will do better than five homers and 56 RBI. John Olerud will be better this year, and it would be a great disappointment if Derek Bell didn't hit better than Mookie Wilson. Roberto Alomar might be able to step up another notch. Offsetting those gains are the likelihood of a poorer season from Devon White, and the possibility that Joe Carter could begin to show the signs of aging. Put it all together, and I'd bet on the Blue Jays to score 65 runs more in 1992 than they did in '91.

THE BOSTON RED SOX

• IN A BOX •

Won-Lost Record: 84-78 .519
Rank among 26 teams: Tied for 8th
Over Last Five Years: 422-388 .521
Rank over Five Years: 8th
In Last Ten Years: 851-768 .526
Rank over Ten Years: 4th

Best Position Player: Still Wade Boggs

Weak Spot: Right Field

Best Pitcher: Rocket

Staff weakness: Group of 35-year-old free agents and castoffs (Danny Darwin, Matt Young, Dan Petry)

Best Bench Player: Steve Lyons

Best Young Player: Phil Plantier

Best Looking Player: Ellis Burks

Ugliest Player: Danny Darwin

Most Pleasant Surprise, 1991: Joe Hesketh

Biggest Disappointment, 1991: Danny Darwin or Matt Young

Best Minor League Prospect: Probably Jeff McNeely

Who Is: An outfielder, won the Carolina League batting championship with a .322 mark and stole 38 bases. He was a fourth-round pick in 1989, and is 21 years old.

Other prospects: The Red Sox system has just coughed up two young hitters who are going to hit about 700 home runs between them (Plantier and Mo Vaughn), so expecting more right away would be greedy. If **Tim Naehring** has recovered from the back surgery, he could be one of the better-hitting middle infielders in baseball. **Scott Cooper** is a decent enough third baseman who's been stuck behind Boggs for two years now, and AA third baseman **Colin Dixon** also played very well last year.

The Red Sox have three catching prospects. **Eric Wedge,** third-round pick in 1989, has been bumped through the system quickly without doing anything much with the bat. **Todd Pratt** almost dropped off the prospect list by putting in three desultory seasons at New Britain, but took up weightlifting and had an excellent 1991 season, hitting much better than Wedge.

Scott Hatteberg, a catcher out of Washington State, was the Sox' top pick in the draft last June. He hit OK in half a season, and isn't ashamed to take a walk.

Outfielder **Greg Blosser,** a hot prospect a year ago, had a miserable season at New Britain but could come back to life. Center fielder **Wayne Housie** is too old to be considered a prospect, but could have a Dave Gallagher-type career.

Designated Malcontent: Jack Clark

Park Characteristics: Fenway Park is not as much of a hitter's park as it once was, although it still favors the hitter more than the pitcher. As always, the park favors *right-handed* pitchers and power hitters, but *left-handed* high-average hitters.

The Park Helps: Wade Boggs hit more than a hundred points better at home than on the road last year (.389 and .282). Lifetime, Boggs has hit .381 at Fenway, .310 on the road.

The Park Hurts: All of the pitchers except Clemens. Carlos Quintana isn't exactly *hurt* by Fenway, but he hits so many ground balls he isn't helped as much as other Sox hitters.

ORGANIZATIONAL REPORT CARD

Ownership: B
Upper Management: B
Field Management: Unknown
Front-Line Talent: B
Second-Line Talent: B+
Minor League System: A

TEAM LEADERS:

Batting Average: Wade Boggs, .332
Last Ten Years (Season): Wade Boggs, 1985, .368
Last Ten Years (Total): Boggs, .345

Doubles: Boggs and Reed, 42 each

Triples: Mike Greenwell, 6

Home Runs: Jack Clark, 28
Last Ten Years (Season): Tony Armas, 1984, 43
Last Ten Years (Total): Dwight Evans, 229

Extra Base Hits: Wade Boggs, 52

RBI: Jack Clark, 87
Last Ten Years (Season): Jim Rice, 1983, 126
Last Ten Years (Total): Rice, 720

Stolen Bases: Mike Greenwell, 15

Runs Created: Wade Boggs, 107

Runs Created Per Game: Boggs, 7.4

Secondary Average: Jack Clark, .416

Wins: Roger Clemens, 18
Last Ten Years (Season): Roger Clemens, 1986, 24
Last Ten Years (Total): Clemens, 134

Winning Percentage: Joe Hesketh, 12-4 .750

Strikeouts: Roger Clemens, 241
Last Ten Years (Season): Roger Clemens, 1988, 291
Last Ten Years (Total): Clemens, 1665

ERA: Clemens, 2.62

Saves: Jeff Reardon, 40

League Leaders:

1) Boggs led the American League with 25 intentional walks and a .389 batting average in his home park. This was the fifth consecutive year that Boggs had led the American League in intentional walks, which establishes a major league record.

2) Carlos Quintana had the highest ratio of ground balls to fly balls in the league, 2.79 to 1.

3) Roger Clemens led the league in a number of categories, like ERA (2.62), innings pitched (271), batters faced (1077), shutouts (4), and strikeouts (241).

4) Joe Hesketh's winning percentage (.750) was the best in the American League.

1991 SEASON

Background: The Red Sox won this division in 1988 and in 1990, not with great teams but teams good enough. The Sox fan's self-image, grounded in the 49-year period between 1918 and 1967 when the Sox won only one pennant, is that of the team which somehow can never win. As the Red Sox began to win periodic pennants—1967, 1975, 1986—this image became more difficult to sustain, and the self-pity of Red Sox fans has begun to focus more on the failure to win the World Series. The serious frustration of the fan whose team never wins has evolved into a more genteel frustration with the results of post-season play.

Outlook: Exactly like this year. The division boils down to the Red Sox, the Blue Jays and a miracle. In that scenario, the Red Sox have a heck of a chance.

Getaway: See article, "Stopped at the Line"

Low Point/High Point: See article

Stretch Drive: See article

Most Exciting Game of the Season: August 12 at Toronto.

Major Injuries: Danny Darwin and Matt Young both signed as free agents a year ago. Both had sore shoulders. Darwin spent four months on the DL, Young two months. When they did pitch, Darwin finished with a 5.16 ERA, Young 5.18.

Dana Kiecker missed June and most of July with a sore right elbow, and was nowhere near as effective as Darwin and Young.

Tim Naehring suffered through an 0-for-39 streak before calling it quits on May 18 with a bone spur in his back. It was removed in June, but he did not play again.

As he did in 1990, John Dopson missed almost the entire season due to elbow surgery.

At the end of July, Jeff Gray suffered a stroke caused by an enlarged blood vessel, and missed the rest of the season. He is said to be recovering well.

Offense: Fair to poor. The Red Sox scored 731 runs against a league average of 727, which with the help of Fenway isn't good. Two outfielders didn't hit much (Burks and Brunansky), and Peña doesn't hit at all. The first baseman (Quintana) doesn't hit for power. Boggs, Greenwell, Reed and Clark have to be *really* good to turn that into a quality offense, and in 1991, they weren't *that* good.

Defense: Fair. The Red Sox are an average defensive team—one Gold Glove type (Peña), one butcher (Greenwell) and a bunch of other guys.

Pitching: Roger Clemens is the best pitcher in baseball. Behind him, they're survivors.

Best Game by a Starting Pitcher: Roger Clemens against Cleveland on April 13 (9 3 0 0 0 11 Game Score: 92)

Worst Game by a Starting Pitcher: Clemens vs. Texas, May 18 (5 13 9 9 2 4 Game Score: 7)

Indicators for 1991 were: Down Significantly (−10.4)

Number of regulars having good seasons by their own standards: Two (Quintana and Rivers)

1991 Over-Achiever: Joe Hesketh

1991 Under-Achiever: Danny Darwin

Infield: Above average.

Outfield: Below average.

Catching: Don't buy it. Peña doesn't hit for average or walk or hit for power and is average in terms of throwing out runners (33%; league average 32%). It's hard to believe that his other defensive skills could justify his place in the lineup.

Starting Pitching: Fair. The addition of Viola makes the Red Sox starting pitching for 1992 above average. Harris remains an underrated pitcher; nobody knows whether Hesketh's arm will let him pitch 185 innings a year, but he knows how to pitch.

Bullpen: Pretty Good. The good years by Gray and Hesketh strengthened the Red Sox long relief enormously, and took the pressure off Jeff Reardon, who had his best season in three years.

Percentage of Offense Contributed By:

Young Players:	21%
Players in Their Prime:	42%
Veterans:	37%

Team Age:

Age of Non-Pitchers:	29.5
Age of Pitching Staff:	30.9
Overall Team Age:	30.1

The Red Sox were the second-oldest team in the American League, and the oldest in this division.

In retrospect, the critical decisions were: The critical decision of 1991 was the attempt to bolster the pitching staff with veteran pitchers of modest accomplishment. It didn't work, and by the time the Red Sox turned to the pitchers who *could* win, they were so far behind that they needed a miracle.

THAT AND THE OTHER

Hall of Fame Watch: **Wade Boggs** is a Hall of Famer. I wrote about Bruce Hurst that he had the background scenery of a Hall of Fame career, but not the highlights. Well, **Roger Clemens** has the highlights, and needs only to fill in the scenery. If Clemens pitches another eight years and goes 100-100, he'll go in the Hall of Fame.

Jack Clark, a Hall of Fame candidate for much of his career, has apparently fallen short, barring a remarkable late-in-life renaissance (see Willie Stargell). **Tony Peña** also fell short of the Hall of Fame, by a slightly wider margin, although he's had a fine career.

No one else here is in the middle of a Hall of Fame career. **Mike Greenwell** is a longshot.

Chris Berman, have you considered: Scott (The Man who Corrupted) Hatteberg

Attendance Trend: The Red Sox have established a franchise attendance record every year since 1988. Like the Blue Jay's they're pushed against the limits of their park capacity.

The park capacity is 34,142. Multiply that by 81 and you've got 2,765,502. Their 1991 attendance was 93% of that. This is a new phenomenon in baseball, for a team to lose the capacity to grow in attendance simply because the park won't hold any more people.

Players with a Chance for 3000 career hits:

Wade Boggs, 40%
Mike Greenwell, 14%

Best Interview: I don't know—probably a groundskeeper or somebody. Ticket taker.

Probably Could Play Regularly For Another Team: Scott Cooper

Best Defensive Player: Tony Peña

Worst Defensive Player: Mike Greenwell

Best Knowledge of the Strike Zone: Wade Boggs

Least Command of the Strike Zone: Luis Rivera

Fastest Runner: Ellis Burks

Mike Greenwell led the Red Sox in two of the basic speed-related categories, triples and stolen bases, and the system of speed scores picks Greenwell as the Red Sox' fastest player. Burks, on the other hand, has apparent speed but has yet to put it to much use in a baseball uniform.

Slowest Runner: Jack Clark

Best Baserunner: Greenwell

Most Likely to Still be Here in 2000: Phil Plantier

Best Fastball: Roger Clemens

Best Breaking Pitch: Roger Clemens

Best Control: Roger Clemens

Most Overrated Player: Tony Peña

Most Underrated Player: Greg Harris

Oddest Collection of Abilities: Carlos Quintana

Why is this man in the Major Leagues: Dan Petry

Gets Ahead of the Hitters Most Often: Clemens

Gets Ahead of the Hitters Least Often: Kevin Morton

Best Local Sportswriter: Peter Gammons

Most-Similar Players:

to C Tony Peña, Mike Heath
to 1B Carlos Quintana, Felix Jose
to 2B Jody Reed, Roberto Alomar
to 3B Wade Boggs, Tony Gwynn
to SS Luis Rivera, Kevin Elster
to LF Mike Greenwell, Ivan Calderon
to CF Ellis Burks, Ken Griffey, Jr.
to RF Tom Brunansky, Jesse Barfield

Most Fun to Watch: Phil Plantier

Least Fun to Watch: Jack Clark

Managerial Type: Steve Lyons

Among the All-Time Team Leaders: Wade Boggs still has the highest batting average in Red Sox history, but his margin over the Splinter is down to one point (.345 to .344), so that figures to get away from him within two years. He is moving up the lists in other areas—sixth in career hits, fourth in doubles. The competition is stiff.

The pitching competition, of course, is less rugged. Roger Clemens is Boston's all-time leader in strikeouts (1424) and winning percentage (.687). He is among the leaders in innings, starts, wins and shutouts. The guy at the top of those lists is Cy Young. If he stays with the Red Sox for the rest of his career Clemens will probably get all of their major pitching records.

Town Team:

C—Mickey Cochrane
1B—Candy LaChance
2B—Jerry Remy
SS—Rabbit Maranville
3B—Pie Traynor
LF—Joe Kelley
CF—Jimmy Ryan
RF—Tommy McCarthy
SP—John Clarkson
MGR—Leo Durocher

Post-Season Transactions:

October 8, hired Butch Hobson as manager
December 19, signed Frank Viola as a free agent

What Needs to Be Done For 1992: The Red Sox need to find a way to convert the unused potential into real ability in a meaningful way. They had Jeff Bagwell; they traded him away for a few hours of Larry Andersen's company. They had an extra first baseman (Mike Marshall), and rather than turning that into an asset they let it become a problem. They need to *decide* who they want to play—Plantier or Vaughn or Clark or Quintana or Brunansky—and get the other guys off the roster in exchange for something they can use.

Outlook for 1992: The situation is not obviously different than it was a year ago. The Red Sox have a pretty good team with some problems which they don't seem to take seriously, and the competition is thin. If Butch Hobson is good and Ellis Burks comes back strong and Viola is good, the Red Sox will win.

Index of Leading Indicators for 1992: Up 4.2

Positive Indicators/Negative Indicators: See Milwaukee comment

Due for a better season: Ellis Burks

Likely to have a worse season: Joe Hesketh

1992 Won-Lost Record will be: 86-76

ROGER CLEMENS AND FENWAY PARK

I think it was Jim Brosnan who once said that what sportswriters do mostly is sit in bars and argue about things, and then go home and write up all the clever bullshit they think they should have said at the time. I don't know about sportswriters in general, but it's always worked for me.

I had an argument last summer with a friend of mine who had focused on the fact that Roger Clemens' ERA over a period of several years is about the same in Fenway Park as it is on the road. We were talking about the effects of Fenway on Clemens and on pitchers in general, and he was saying that the effects of Fenway are overrated. His argument was that pitchers just shouldn't worry about the Wall, shouldn't let it intimidate them. Just go out and pitch the same in Fenway as you would somewhere else, like Clemens does, and don't let the park mess with your mind.

There are two flaws in this argument. First, the fact that Clemens' ERA is the same in Fenway as it is on the road *doesn't* show that Clemens is not disadvantaged by the park. The typical pitcher has an ERA thirty or forty points *better* in his home park than he does on the road. If Clemens' ERA is *the same*, then that shows that Fenway Park *is* working against him, not that it isn't.

That's the minor point. Suppose that we think about this in a one-dimensional sport, like high jumping. Suppose there is a high jumper, call him Robert Clemens, who is capable of high-jumping seven-foot-five. Suppose there is another jumper, call him Roger Ojeda, who is capable of high-jumping only six-foot-nine, maybe seven foot if he has the jump of his life.

Now, you could do a thousand high jumps and keep stats, and you might find that Clemens cleared the seven-foot bar exactly as often as he cleared the six-foot bar. You might find that he was 91% at six foot, and 91.3% at seven foot. In exactly the same way that my friend had concluded that it didn't really make much difference whether a pitcher is in Fenway Park or someplace else, you might conclude that it didn't really make any difference whether the high jump bar is set at six foot or seven. And, for Robert Clemens, you might be right; it *doesn't* make any difference whether the high jump bar is at six feet or seven.

But, of course, to apply this conclusion to an ordinary high-jumper would be silly. To take Clemens' stats, and then tell Ojeda not to worry about whether the high-jump bar was set at six feet or seven because it doesn't make any difference to Clemens, would create an obvious problem.

Fenway Park isn't a barrier to Roger Clemens because he throws so hard, has such good control and his fastball rides in on a right-hander, so it's all but impossible to pull. But it makes no sense to conclude that an ordinary pitcher shouldn't worry about the Wall because it doesn't matter (much) to Clemens.

STOPPED AT THE LINE

There was a bleak beginning, but it passed quickly. The Red Sox lost two out of three at Toronto to open the 1991 season, then came home to Cleveland and lost three out of four. Seventeen wins in twenty-one games put the Red Sox in first place. They were 18-9; Toronto was 18-13. They held first place until the last week of May, and then began to trade positions with the Blue Jays. Neither team was playing well. On June 6 the Red Sox were 26–25, but only a game and a half out. On June 19 they were 33-30, but in a virtual tie for first.

On June 20 the Blue Jays began to win with some consistency. The Red Sox didn't. By July 15 the Blue Jays were 53-35; the Red Sox were still only one game over .500 (43-42), and fading out of the race.

At that point the Red Sox appeared to panic, and fell into a serious slump. All three outfielders stopped hitting at the same time. By August 7—the low point of the season—the Red Sox were 50-57, 11 and a half games behind Toronto. In Kansas City, where the Red Sox have played badly for time out of memory, the Sox lost three straight and were shut out twice in a row. It was fourth and long; the Blue Jays were prepared to take the kick and run out the clock. The Red Sox began to play some new guys, Phil Plantier and Mo Vaughn, just to see what they could do. They decided to let Hesketh start a few times.

It will be forgotten, but it was one of the most impressive things that happened in the 1991 season. The Red Sox put on a run. From Kansas City the Red Sox went to Toronto on August 9 for what appeared to be a meaningless four-game series.

In the first game of the series the Red Sox pounded David Wells and relief help for 12 runs on 21 hits. On August 10 Greg Harris stopped the Blue Jays on four hits, another 7-1 win. On August 11 the Red Sox scored five in the first against Jimmy Key, and held on for a 9-6 win.

On August 12 Roger Clemens started against Jose Guzman, the Blue Jays' rookie right-hander who had been pitching brilliantly. The Red Sox scored two in the first, but Candy Maldonado hit a three-run homer in the bottom of the inning, and the Blue Jays added one in the second for a 4-2 lead. In the top of the third the Red Sox scored three to re-take the lead, 5-4, but the Blue Jays scored two immediately to take it back, and added one in the fourth to make it 7-5. Clemens was knocked out in the fifth and Guzman didn't come out for the sixth. This was perhaps a critical mistake, as Duane Ward, who pitched the sixth for Toronto, gave up four quick runs to give Boston a 9-7 lead. They traded runs then, and the Red Sox held on for an 11-8 win.

They had hit the Hail Mary. In the four games:

- Wade Boggs went 9-for-20 (.450) and scored seven runs.
- Carlos Quintana went 7-for-16 (.438), hit two homers and drove in five runs.

• Jack Clark went 7-for-15 (.467) with a double, triple and homer and drove in ten runs.

• Mike Greenwell went 12-for-21 (.571) and drove in six runs.

• Ellis Burks went 8-for-18 (.444) with two doubles and a homer.

• The Red Sox as a team hit .399 (67-for-168).

That cut the Blue Jay lead to seven games, and the Red Sox stayed hot, and the Blue Jays were sent reeling, which incidentally also put the Tigers back in the race.

The Red Sox won four of their next five games after leaving Toronto, bringing them up to .500 (58-58) and cutting their deficit to four and a half games. A ten-inning, 7-6 win over Cleveland on August 22 cut it to three and a half.

Toronto got hot, and pushed the lead to six and a half by September 1. In the first week of September both teams won almost every game, and the lead stayed at six and a half, but in the second and third weeks of September the Red Sox continued to win. Winning 15 of 19 games in the first three weeks of September, the Red Sox were only a half-game out on September 21.

They missed the tackle. It was ultimately unsuccessful, but the Red Sox put on a six-week charge which should not be entirely forgotten. Between August 8 and September 21 the Red Sox went 31-10, and wiped out eleven games of an eleven-and-a-half game deficit. What nobody could miss is that they were chasing a team that was better than they were—and yet they caught them, like a linebacker running down a wide receiver with an eleven-yard head start. The race was twice lost. They lost the race in July, and then they lost it again in late September. I don't know whether it was the killer instinct that was missing, or just the third starter. They missed the tackle, but hey, that was some chase.

THE KING OF DOUBLIN'

BY DANIEL GOLDEN

In 1931, Earl Webb hit 67 doubles.

Nobody has since.

Sixty years is a long time for a record to stand, but the sixtieth anniversary of the Red Sox outfielder's daily doubles passed with Webb resting in the comfortable obscurity which has long since enveloped his memory. In a year of milestones, no cannons were fired for the "King of Doublin'," as he was dubbed by Boston reporters catering to Irish locals. ESPN did not look up his old box scores, comparing the current leader to Webb's pace. No grainy films were hauled out, showing him sliding into second ahead of a tag. The commissioner paid no homage to his memory. No aging sportswriters recalled his two-baggers for obscure Sunday-morning cable shows.

Earl Webb would have preferred it that way. He didn't like the bright lights anyway—in fact, he almost missed his destiny by that aversion. In the traditional baseball fable (see Stan Musial *et al.*), the son rebels at following the father into the mines and, much to the old man's displeasure, runs off to hit .331 lifetime instead. Webb's story was the reverse. Born in 1898 in Bon Air, Tennessee, Webb grew up in another Tennessee town, Ravenscroft, where he quit school at the age of 11 to work in the mines with his dad. He labored 10 hours a day at five cents an hour, and loved every minute. "In those days, I could think of no work as thrilling as laboring in the coal mines," he would say.

Webb began to play baseball after the mine doctor advised him to exercise and fill his lungs with fresh air after breathing coal dust all day. Soon he was pitching for the town team on Sundays. In 1918 Webb received an offer to pitch for the Memphis team in the Southern Association. His father, who had been an amateur pitcher and outfielder, urged him to accept, but Webb refused. He had a sweetheart, he was scared of going to the city, and he liked mining. It was not until 1920, after Webb's marriage posed family responsibilities that a miner's salary could not easily afford, that his father could persuade him to report to Memphis.

Memphis sent Webb to Clarksdale, in the Mississippi State League, where he made his debut as a pitcher-outfielder in 1921. After returning to Memphis to pitch in 1922, he was sold to the New York Giants, but balked. If Memphis was too big for him, what was New York City? He finally ventured to Gotham the next spring, and the Giants farmed him out to Pittsfield in the Eastern League. Webb played the outfield between mound assignments, and hit better than he pitched. With a 37-47 record in 118 games as a minor league right-hander—"I had plenty of stuff for the major leagues, but no control," he would say—he decided to switch positions. "It came my turn to pitch and I looked the manager in the eye and said, 'Nothing doing. I'm an outfielder or nothing from now on, and if you don't like it I'll go home.' "

In 1924, his first year as an every-day player, Webb led the Eastern League with 42 doubles. He hit .329 for the Toledo Mud Hens in 1925, and late in the season the Giants called him up, shipping Hack Wilson down to make room on the roster. But Webb had only three major-league at bats before John McGraw gave him a ticket to Louisville in the American Association, where Webb batted .333 in 1926.

Brought up by the Cubs in 1927, Webb belted two homers on Opening Day, one against Grover Cleveland Alexander. He hit .301 that year, but slumped to .250 in 1928, and Manager Joe McCarthy dumped him. Back in the minors in 1929, he produced a monster season in the Pacific Coast League: .357 with 37 homers and 164 RBI in 188 games—not to mention 56 doubles.

Webb comes across in contemporary newspaper interviews as the ultimate Ring Lardner rube, relishing his successes and blaming managers for his failures. He had played for McGraw and McCarthy, but he never met a manager he liked until he was traded to the Red Sox in 1930. Manager John "Shono" Collins had been a light-hitting outfielder for the Red Sox and White Sox from 1910 to 1925, and batted .250 for the Black Sox in the 1919 World Series. (Although the Macmillan Encyclopedia lists Collins' nickname as "Shano," The *Boston Globe* referred to him during his tenure as "Shono" or, occasionally, "Shauno.") Collins, Webb said years later, "understood me, sympathized with me, and did his best to make me a better ballplayer. Other managers had little if any interest in me, and until I went to work for Collins I was never inspired to play."

In particular, Webb had never been inspired to field. If there had been a designated hitter rule in his era, Webb would have had a better shot at a full major league career. Instead, his lack of range had kept him on the trading block or the bench, or in the minors. But under Collins' tutelage, the self-described "All-America stumbler" learned to get a jump on batted balls. "I finally educated myself to start with the crack of the bat, and I no longer was baseball's worst outfielder," Webb said later.

Fly-catching well enough to stay in the lineup, he was the team's best hitter in 1930 with a .323 average, 16 homers and 30 doubles. In 1931, reporters covering the Red Sox wrote that Webb's fielding continued to improve, although he still led the league's right fielders in errors.

"Of course, my ability to hit has kept me in the game," Webb told the *Chattanooga Times* in 1931. "No manager would have had any patience with me if I had not been something of a batter. I came by my hitting ability naturally. Always did have a wonderful eye. If I do say it myself, I am not the worst shot in the world with any kind of a weapon. Yes, sir, I'm pretty fair with a 32-20 Colt, a Browning automatic shotgun or a Remington .22 rifle. But I can bring in a turkey or other game without a gun. Old Earl ain't so bad with a bow and arrow."

On March 3, 1931, Webb reported to the Red Sox spring quarters in Pensacola, Fla. Trim and fit after a winter of hiking and fishing in the Tennessee hills, Webb smashed a 550-foot homer in an exhibition game on March 22 against the semi-pro House of David. An old-timer named "Blackie" Rhodes, who had seen every game played on the Pensacola field since 1896, was quoted the next day as saying that Webb's clout was the longest ever hit there.

Webb "looks like a sweet hitter to me," Collins told *Globe* reporter Mel Webb Jr. (no relation). "See the way he steps into that ball, and he shifts his punch to left and center field as if he liked it." Coach Hugh Duffy observed that Webb was driving pitches that he would usually miss or pop up.

Late in the month the ballclub broke camp and barnstormed north. It was a time of mourning for the sports world: Notre Dame football coach Knute Rockne was killed in a plane crash, while two bitter enemies, American League founder Ban Johnson and current league president Ernest Barnard, died 16 hours apart. Asked about the prospects of the Red Sox, who had finished last six years in a row, Collins made two predictions, both phrased in the negative. The team would not finish last, and it would not lose 100 games. Mel Webb Jr. offered his own prediction: "As the Sox come North, there will be nothing more interesting to watch than the hitting of Earl Webb."

The Red Sox promptly dropped their first three games to the Yankees in the Bronx, even though Babe Ruth was sulking about a rules change that made a sacrifice fly count as an out on a player's batting average. (Hampered by the new rule, the Babe hit only .373 in 1931.) Hitless in the opener, Webb soon went on a tear. By late May, he had a remarkable 22 doubles in his first 34 games, as well as six homers, 33 RBI, and a .340 average. In a double-header against the Washington Senators he crashed four doubles and a triple. Already battling to escape the cellar, the Sox lost both games.

In June and July, Al Capone pleaded guilty to tax evasion, President Hoover gave a speech to the Indiana Republican Editorial Association criticizing pessimists who saw the hole rather than the doughnut, and Webb rocketed into the .370s. Even his outs were memorable: on July 23, he hit into a triple play against the White Sox, but homered in the same game. He was only stopped by injuries of the self-inflicted variety, missing one game when he cut two fingers with a pocket-knife, and another when

Earl WEBB

he mistakenly applied iodine instead of eye lotion to an inflamed eye. He "got the surprise of his life," according to the *Globe*, and howled in agony for several minutes.

By the end of July Webb's quest to break George Burns' 1926 record of 64 doubles in the season was the talk of Boston sports pages. The Red Sox were so pathetic in the early 1930's, mired in their own Great Depression post-Bambino and pre-Yawkey, that beat reporters had little worth writing about except Webb. This *Globe* lead on July 25, 1931, was typical: "Earl Webb made his 44th double yesterday, but it was one of only five hits the Red Sox were able to negotiate."

Batting from the left side with a split-handed grip, Webb drove most of his doubles to the opposite field. The Green Monster would not be built until 1934, but left field and left-center in Fenway were already prime doubles territory because of the park's spacious dimensions. The foul line distance was almost the same then (318) as it is now (315), but center field was 468 feet; it would be reduced to 390 in the 1934 renovations. Webb ripped many doubles off the lower fence then in place, or onto the slope leading up to it, known as Duffy's Cliff. Overall, he hit 37 doubles at Fenway and 30 on the road.

The Red Sox faithful followed Webb's quest avidly. "People would go down there to see him," recalls Ed McNulty, a longtime fan who attended a dozen games in 1931 as a 16-year-old. "No matter what the score was, they'd wait around until the ninth inning to see if he'd get another double."

Webb's teammates also rooted for him to crack Burns' record, but they had a more personal stake in his home runs. Whenever a Red Sox player hit a homer he would receive a watch from a local manufacturer as part of a promotional gimmick. Since Webb was the team's only slugger—he would finish with 14 homers, the only Red Sox in double figures—he distributed his timepieces to the other players. Pitcher Milt Gaston, now 96 and living in Florida, remembers that Webb, a "honey of a fellow," gave him one of the watches.

In September, as Mahatma Gandhi appealed to Americans for help in a radio address from a London settlement house, Webb began to slump. Fans rooted in vain for doubles, and teammates for watches. The pressure of chasing Burns dropped Webb's average to its eventual .333. When he slugged his 61st double on Sept. 15, the *Globe* reported that Webb "appears to be over-anxious, and the harder he tries for doubles, the harder they come."

Then he rallied, belting two doubles on Sept. 16. The next day he tied Burns's record in the first game of a double-header against Cleveland, and eclipsed it in the ninth inning of the second game with a drive onto Duffy's Cliff off Pete Jablonowski. *Globe* reporter James C. O'Leary crowed, "Webb is not through yet and before the end of the season ought to set a new mark that will stand for five years if not longer."

Webb added two more doubles in the final 11 games, and the season ended happily for his club as well. The Red Sox fulfilled Collins' predictions, finishing sixth with a 60-92 record. (They would revert to form in 1932 with a last-place, 43-111 record; Collins was fired during the 1932 season.)

The day after the 1931 season ended, at the suggestion of Mayor James Michael Curley, the Red Sox and Boston Braves played a benefit game for the unemployed in front of nearly 20,000 fans. Three autographed baseballs were auctioned off. Each was signed by Mayor Curley and two of Boston's favorite ballplayers: Babe Ruth and Earl Webb.

The disparaging of Webb's record began almost as soon as he had established it. Shono Collins explained the accomplishment not in terms of Webb's strength, but in terms of his weakness. "It's pretty simple," Collins explained. "He's too slow to reach third base." Nobody seemed quite willing to say that this was a rather remarkable accomplishment for a guy who didn't run well enough to catch a city bus.

Local writers chimed in, charging Webb—as they sometimes do Wade Boggs today—with deliberately running triples into doubles to pad his league-leading total. Webb had three triples in 1931. "There have been times," wrote Mel Webb Jr., "when, watching Webb start to run his hits, there has been a suggestion of viewing the situation, and, as had happened several times, not being in position to reach third base because of some poor bit of judgment in the field or some peculiar quirk taken by the ball." Of course, there was that total of 70 doubles and triples, which is more than any other major league player hit that year, and in fact is one of the highest totals of all time.

Webb faded badly in 1932, and was traded to Detroit in mid-season for Dale Alexander, who went on to win the batting title. Less than two years after setting the record Webb was back in the minors to stay. He had lasted seven years in the majors, with only three seasons of 400 at bats, and a career average of .306. The 67 doubles in 1931 represent almost half of his lifetime total of 155. Like Owen Wilson's 36 triples in 1912, Webb's record was an astonishing freak in an otherwise unremarkable career.

Released to Milwaukee in 1934, Webb led the American Association in hitting (.368). With Knoxville in 1936 he led the Southern Association in home runs (20) and hit .348. His playing days ended after the 1937 season, with a career minor league average of .333; he is listed in Volume II of the SABR's *Minor League Baseball Stars*. After retiring Webb became a foreman in the West Virginia coal mines, and died in 1965 in his native Tennessee.

His record endures. Nobody has hit 60 doubles since Joe "Ducky" Medwick belted 64 in 1936, and the post-World War II high is 56, accomplished by George Kell in 1950. In 1991, when there were more doubles hit in the majors than in any previous season ever, Rafael Palmeiro led both leagues with 49—still 18 short of the King of Doublin'.

THE DETROIT TIGERS
• IN A BOX •

1991 Won-Lost Record: 84-78 .519
Rank among 26 teams: Tied for 8th
Over Last Five Years: 408-402 .504
Rank over Five Years: 14th
In Last Ten Years: 858-761 .530
Rank over Ten Years: 3rd

Best Player: In my opinion, the Tigers' best player last year was Mickey Tettleton, hard pressed by Tony Phillips and Lou Whitaker. Tettleton has been up and down, and there is some logic to saying that, based on performance over the last two seasons, the Tigers' best player is Cecil Fielder.

Weak Spot: Left Field (Incaviglia)

Best Pitcher: Umm, Gullickson, I guess

Staff Weakness: Lack of anybody with a fastball

Best Bench Player: Tony Phillips is the best bench player in baseball. If you count him as a regular, their best bench player is Dave Bergman.

Best Baseball name: Cecil Fielder

Best Young Player: 1. Travis Fryman
2. Milt Cuyler

Best Looking Player: Travis Fryman

Ugliest Player: Paul Gibson

Most Pleasant Surprise, 1991: Bill Gullickson

Biggest Disappointment, 1991: Pete Incaviglia

Best Prospect: See article, "Tiger Cubs"

Other Prospects: See article

Designated Malcontent: Pete Incaviglia

Park Characteristics: A low-average, power park, better for a pitcher than a hitter and better for a left-hander than a right-hander.

The Park Helps: Cecil Fielder hit 27 of his 44 homers in Tiger Stadium last season.

The Park Hurts: Milt Cuyler hits the ball on the ground, and might have a better batting average in a turf park. His speed is of great value to the Tigers because the center field area in Tiger Stadium is so large.

ORGANIZATIONAL REPORT CARD

Ownership:	B−
Upper Management:	C+
Field Management:	A−
Front-Line Talent:	C
Second-Line Talent:	B
Minor League System:	B+

Comment: The Tigers are beginning to get it turned around. Two years ago the Tigers' talent base was so emaciated that they were forced to gamble on veteran players looking for a chance. Two of their gambles, Fielder and Gullickson, worked out extremely well, while some others didn't (Moseby, Incaviglia, Te[rrell]).

That period appears to be over for the Tigers. The Tigers no[w] have young players—two in the majors (Fryman and Cuyler) a[nd] more on the way. I don't think they're up to the level of the R[ed] Sox and Blue Jays yet, but they should be there in a year.

TEAM LEADERS:

Batting Average: Tony Phillips, .284
Last Ten Years (Season): Alan Trammel, 1987, .343
Last Ten Years (Total): Trammell, .290

Doubles: Travis Fryman, 36

Triples: Milt Cuyler, 7

Home Runs: Cecil Fielder, 44
Last Ten Years (Season): Fielder, 1990, 51
Last Ten Years (Total): Lou Whitaker, 178

Extra Base Hits: Cecil Fielder, 69

RBI: Cecil Fielder, 133
Last Ten Years (Season): Fielder, 1991, 133
Last Ten Years (Total): 1. Trammell, 685
2. Whitaker, 676

Stolen Bases: Milt Cuyler, 41

Runs Created: Cecil Fielder, 110

Runs Created Per Game: Lou Whitaker, 7.6

Secondary Average: Mickey Tettleton, .435

Wins: Bill Gullickson, 20
Last Ten Years (Season): Jack Morris, 1986, 21
Last Ten Years (Total): Morris, 147

Winning Percentage: Gullickson, 20-9 .690

Strikeouts: Frank Tanana, 107
Last Ten Years (Season): Jack Morris, 1983, 232
Last Ten Years (Total): Morris, 1582

ERA: Tanana, 3.77

Saves: Henneman, 21

League Leaders: Cecil Fielder led the major leagues with 13[3] RBI, and along with Canseco led with 44 home runs. Rob Dee[r] struck out 175 times to lead the majors, and was second in th[e] league behind Lou Whitaker in GIDP (grounded into doubl[e] play) frequency. Whitaker and Deer grounded into three doubl[e] plays apiece.

Bill Gullickson's 35 starts tied him for the AL lead (with fiv[e] others), as did his twenty wins (with Scott Erickson). He thre[w] fewer pitches per batter, 3.27, than any other AL pitcher. Wal[t] Terrell led the league in inducing ground ball double plays, wit[h] 1.4 per nine innings.

Stat of the Year: The Tigers last year got more home runs fro[m] their four and five spots in the batting order (80) than the Cleve-land Indians hit altogether (79).

991 SEASON

ackground: The Tigers, traditional contenders, collapsed in 1989, losing 103 games. In 1990 they began the process of crawling back, signing Cecil Fielder and riding him back to respectability.

utlook: The Tigers were generally picked third to fifth in the division. I picked them last, myself, but I was in a minority.

etaway: The Tigers opened the season in a win-one lose-one pattern, and for the most part stayed in that pattern until April 28, when they were 8-9. Their first streak was a hot streak, beginning on a road trip to Kansas City, which pushed their record to 16-10 on May 10.

ligh Point of the Season: The Tigers slipped quickly to .500, and stayed within a few games of .500 until July 30 (50-49).

The Tigers had been fighting their pitching staff all year. They played .500+ ball in July (14-12) despite a staff ERA of 5.87. In August the pitching suddenly improved, and the Tigers had a spurt of 19 wins in 27 games. On August 26 the Tigers opened a trip to the West Coast with a 5-1 win over the Angels, pushing their record to 69-57. The Tigers were tied for first place with less than six weeks to play.

tretch Drive: The Tigers treaded water on the trip to the coast, which was to be expected, but also failed to make any headway on the following homestand. The Blue Jays got hot, and were it not for the memories of 1987 the race would have been all but over by September 10.

ow Point of the Season: A 9-5 loss to Milwaukee on September 22, which capped a six-game losing streak and virtually eliminated the Tigers. The last three losses were a series sweep by Milwaukee in Detroit.

Most Exciting Game of the Season: August 25 at Tiger Stadium, see article.

Major Injuries: Trammell missed ten days in early July with a sore left wrist, then mid-July through mid-August with a sprained ankle and sore knee.

Pete Incaviglia was out for three weeks in June with a sore rib cage muscle, and three weeks later with a sprained right wrist.

The Tigers lost Mike Henneman for a month in the midst of the pennant race due to a sore right shoulder.

Jerry Don Gleaton was out for five weeks with an inflamed left rotator cuff.

Lloyd Moseby was troubled by a hamstring, among other things, and spent 48 days on the disabled list.

Al Leiter missed three weeks with a strained stomach muscle.

Offense: See article, "Swing Hard"

Defense: Good in Tiger Stadium, not so good on the road. The Tigers' double play combination is very quick on the double play, but they don't scurry around as well as they once did. This is fine in Tiger Stadium, where the grass is long, but not so good on artificial turf. In the outfield the Tigers have a brilliant center fielder and two sluggers or attempted sluggers, which is an OK combination in Tiger Stadium, but not good in a park with a large outfield area.

Pitching: Very Poor

Best Game by a Starting Pitcher: Frank Tanana against California, August 7 (9 4 0 0 0 3 Game Score: 86)

Worst Game by a Starting Pitcher: Bill Gullickson against KC, July 14 (2⅔ 7 7 7 0 2 Game Score: 18)

Indicators for 1991 were: Down Forcefully (21.3)

Number of regulars having good 1991 seasons by their own standards: Three (Phillips, Whitaker, Tettleton)

1991 Over-Achiever: Lou Whitaker

1991 Under-Achiever: Pete Incaviglia

Percentage of Offense Created by:

Young Players:	19%
Players in their Prime:	42%
Past their Prime:	39%

Team Age:

Age of Non-Pitchers:	28.6
Age of Pitching Staff:	31.2
Overall:	29.7

Infield: The Tigers' infield put a hell of a lot of runs on the board. Tiger infielders hit 102 home runs and drove in 389 runs—25 homers and 97 RBI per spot. While many teams have two infielders who don't hit much (shortstop and one other), the Tigers got production from everybody—102 RBI from their shortstops, 111 runs scored from their second basemen. Trammell and Whitaker. Man, there's never been anything like them.

Outfield: Very poor. The potent offense of the infield and Tettleton disguised the fact that the Tiger outfielders were pretty awful. As a group they hit .221 with an average of 16 homers, 63 RBI per slot. For three Gold Glove winners that might be OK, but for one Gold Glove type and two behemoth sluggers, it's terrible.

Catching: Outstanding.

Starting Pitching: Better than I expected, still below average.

Bullpen: Poor. The Tigers' bullpen ERA of 4.66 was the second-worst in the major leagues.

In retrospect, the critical decisions were: The things that made the 1991 season interesting were the free agent signings of Bill Gullickson (1991) and Cecil Fielder (1990).

THAT AND THE OTHER

Lookalikes: Did you ever notice that the guy who played the manager in the fifties musical *Damn Yankees* looks exactly like Sparky?

Hall of Fame Watch: If their careers ended today, **Trammell** and **Whitaker** probably would not get in the Hall of Fame. Trammell and Whitaker are the kind of players who have traditionally been selected to the Hall of Fame by the Veteran's Committee. With that door all but closed, they need to build their credentials with durability in order to have a good chance at selection by the BBWAA.

Fielder will make the Hall of Fame if he hits 500 home runs, won't if he doesn't. His chance of hitting 500 home runs is about 33%.

Chris Berman, Have You Considered:
Frank (Yes, we have no) Tanana
Skeeter (Were You Born in a) Barnes
Screwdriver Phillips

Throwback: Dan Gladden

Attendance Trend: Downward, although there was an uptick last year with a better team. The Tigers' attendance last year was only 100,000 better than it was in 1989, when they lost 103 games.

Players with a Chance for 3000 career hits:
Alan Trammell, 6%
Lou Whitaker, 4%

Record Watch: See article

Probably Could Play Regularly For Another Team: Rich Rowland

Best Fundamental Player: Alan Trammell

Worst Fundamental Player: Incaviglia

Best Defensive Player: Milt Cuyler

Worst Defensive Player: Incaviglia

Best Knowledge of the Strike Zone: Lou Whitaker

Least Command of the Strike Zone: Travis Fryman

Fastest Runner: Milt Cuyler

Slowest Runner: Cecil Fielder

Best Baserunner: Cuyler or Trammell

Most Likely to Still be Here in 2000: Travis Fryman

Best Fastball: Sparky Anderson

Best Breaking Pitch: Frank Tanana

Best Control: Bill Gullickson

Oddest Collection of Abilities: Rob Deer

Never Going to be As Good as the Organization Thinks He Is: Rico Brogna

Why is this man in the Major Leagues: Walt Terrell

Gets Ahead of the Hitters Most Often: Bill Gullickson

Gets Ahead of the Hitters Least Often: John Cerutti

Local Neanderthal Sportswriter: Joe Falls

Most-Similar Players:
to C Mickey Tettleton, Matt Nokes
to 1B Cecil Fielder, Fred McGriff
to 2B Lou Whitaker, Alan Trammell
to 3B Travis Fryman, Carlos Baerga
to SS Alan Trammell, Lou Whitaker
to LF Tony Phillips, Terry Pendleton
to CF Milt Cuyler, Brian McRae
to RF Rob Deer, Mark McGwire
to DH Pete Incaviglia, Carmelo Martinez

Most Fun to Watch: Milt Cuyler

Least Fun to Watch: Incaviglia

Managerial Type: Dave Bergman

Among the All-Time Team Leaders: The Tigers career batting records are probably the most impressive of any team. Trammell and Whitaker are among the top ten in most categories, but they're not going to reach the top in anything.

Town Team:
C—Ted Simmons
1B—John Mayberry
2B—Charlie Gehringer
SS—Doc Lavan
3B—Steve Boros
LF—Kirk Gibson
CF—Ron Leflore
RF—Kiki Cuyler
SP—Ed Reulbach
SP—Billy Pierce
SP—Ed Cicotte
SP—Milt Pappas
SP—Hal Newhouser
SP—Bob Welch

Post-Season Transactions:
December 8, signed Dave Bergman to a one-year contract
December 20, agreed to terms with Dan Gladden on a two-year contract.

What Needs to Be Done For 1992: The policy of plodding back into the race with veteran free agents has worked well for two years. If it is followed any further, it's going to become destructive. The Tigers have young arms—DeSilva, Gore, Aldred. They *don't* have a pitching staff that's going to help them win 90 games. They need to start trying to incorporate the young arms into the pitching staff.

Outlook for 1992: I'm not optimistic. I think the team overachieved in 1991.

Index of Leading Indicators for 1992: Down 6.5

Positive Indicators: None worth mentioning

Negative Indicators: Five of the seven indicators are down, but none by any significant margin.

Due for a better season: Incaviglia and Milt Cuyler

Likely to have a worse season: Phillips, Tettleton, Gullickson and Whitaker

1992 Won-Lost Record will be: 77-85

MV WHAT?

Cecil Fielder finished second in the voting for the American League Most Valuable Player Award, receiving nine first-place votes from the panel of 28 writers. He was angry about this. "They told me last year I had to play on a contender," Fielder told the Associated Press. "Now, Cal Ripken plays on a sixth-place team and they tell me he's an MVP. It's a shame the way things go down . . . It's a joke as far as I'm concerned the way things were done this year. I'm just done with it. If anybody put together two years like I did, they'd be MVP. So it's just a bunch of garbage."

Well, to begin with, who was the MVP? To me, it was obvious that Ripken deserved the award, but "it's obvious" is no better excuse for a logical argument than "It's a shame" or "It's a joke." I don't believe that any statistical analysis can tell one infallibly who the MVP was, but the fact is that statistics *are* used to guide the MVP voting—Candy Maldonado didn't get a single vote—and so I would argue that they should be used *carefully*, to *inform* the vote, rather than being interpreted on an intuitive level.

The best logical path that I can suggest to lead from raw statistics to a statement of value is to compare each player to a replacement-level player at the same position. How much better was Cecil Fielder than the man you could replace him with? In numbers, that leads to these questions:

1) How many runs did the player create?
2) How many runs would probably have been created by a replacement-level player given the same amount of playing time in the same park.
3) How many runs did the player save on defense?

That's "value"—doing something that an ordinary, garden-variety ballplayer wouldn't do.

Each of those things can be estimated from the statistics—how many runs the player created, etc. We'll leave out the third issue because it doesn't have any sensible impact on the discussion, unless you want to argue that Cecil Fielder deserved the MVP Award for his glovework.

I estimate that Cecil Fielder created about 110 runs for the Detroit Tigers in 1991.

I estimate that a replacement-level first baseman—a bad ballplayer, to be short—making the same number of outs for this team would probably have created about 80 runs.

Fielder was about 30 runs better than a replacement-level player.

Now, 30 runs is a lot. Thirty runs are a big deal in a pennant race; only a very good ballplayer is 30 runs better than the guy you could probably replace him with. But an MVP?

By using the same method, Cal Ripken was about 84 runs better than a replacement-level shortstop. He didn't lead the league, either; Frank Thomas did. These were the top ten in the American League, not counting pitchers:

1.	Frank Thomas	86
2.	Cal Ripken	84
3.	Ken Griffey, Jr.	69
4.	Danny Tartabull	69
5.	Paul Molitor	65
6.	Julio Franco	63
7.	Wade Boggs	61
8.	Roberto Alomar	57
9.	Edgar Martinez	54
10.	Lou Whitaker	53

Among the other players who rank well ahead of Fielder by this analysis are Jose Canseco, Rafael Palmeiro, Mickey Tettleton, Joe Carter, Chili Davis, Devon White and Tony Phillips—all mentioned as MVP candidates, and with good reason. Among those who rank only *a little bit* ahead of Cecil Fielder are Carlos Baerga and Steve Sax.

Now, I'm not saying that the method is absolutely correct—in fact, I'll say flat out that I think its selection of the number one man is wrong. Sabermetricians do the best they can to construct analytical methods which are objective and precise, but there are options in analysis. I estimate that Cecil Fielder created 110 runs for the Tigers, but then the runs created formula doesn't consider *everything*, so who knows; it might have been 115. I estimate that a replacement-level first baseman given the opportunity to make 482 outs for the Detroit Tigers would create about 80 runs, but you can't measure that *precisely*; it could have been 75. Seventy? Well, maybe.

Counting statistics are precise; Cecil Fielder hit *exactly* 44 home runs last year. Statements of value are imprecise, approximate, and so I'll believe that Cecil Fielder might have been a better player than, say, Carlos Baerga or Steve Sax. I don't *know* that he was better, of my own knowledge, but if you tell me he was better I won't argue with you.

But better than Ripken?

I'll tell you what I think: I think the whole idea that Cecil Fielder is an MVP candidate is weird. I think it's just one of those off-the-wall ideas which has somehow taken root in our culture and acquired credibility at a certain level, like Nehru jackets or junk bonds. I mean, I can see voting for Ripken or Thomas or Alomar or Carter or Canseco, but I really can't understand why *anyone* would think Cecil Fielder was the best player in the American League.

Cecil Fielder said that "if anybody put together two years like I did, they'd be MVP." But you know, there *are* other guys who have had years like this, and I don't remember that they all won MVP Awards. I asked a computer to search for the most-comparable season in baseball history to Cecil Fielder's 1991 year. The answer: Dick Stuart in 1963.

Both Fielder and Stuart hit .261.

Both led the league in runs batted in.

Both were first basemen.

Both played for teams which didn't win the pennant or even have especially good years.

Their numbers are below:

	G	AB	R	H	2B	3B	HR	RBI	Avg.	SlPct.
Fielder	162	624	102	163	25	0	44	133	.261	.513
Stuart	157	612	81	160	25	4	42	118	.261	.521

Now, they're not identical players—Stuart was an awful first baseman and didn't drive in *quite* as many runs as Fielder, although he did lead the league. On the other hand, while Stuart was slow, he wasn't *as* slow as Fielder, and his competition wasn't nearly as stiff as Fielder's. No one in the American League had an MVP year in 1963—and yet Stuart finished 13th in the voting for the award.

In fact, if you look at *all* of the players who have had years like Fielder had, you'll find that *none* of them received serious consideration for the MVP Award. I identified the ten most-similar seasons to Cecil Fielder's. Those were:

Ralph Kiner, 1948
Gil Hodges, 1951
Rocky Colavito, 1959
Rocky Colavito, 1962
Dick Stuart, 1963
Hank Aaron, 1966
Carl Yastrzemski, 1969
Jeff Burroughs, 1977
Gorman Thomas, 1979
Tony Armas, 1984

All of these players except Colavito in 1962 hit 40 or more homers. Many or most of them led the league in RBI, although none drove in quite as many runs as Fielder (they averaged 117 RBI, ranging from 103 to 127). Most were slow runners and made limited contributions on defense, like Fielder. All hit around .260, overall .264, and had all-around numbers comparable to Cecil. This chart compares Fielder to the group average:

TRACERS

> I relieved most of the time and there was a doubleheader, either in 1938 or 1939, and I pitched five innings in the first game and four innings in the second game as a reliever. Hank hit three home runs in the two games and everybody was happy. And I still remember Mickey Cochrane saying, "Fellas, lock yourselves in your rooms tonight because the Jews in Detroit are going crazy."
>
> —Harry Eisenstat in Ira Berkow and Hank Greenberg's *Hank Greenberg: The Story of My Life,* Page 104: 1989.

Harry Eisenstat came to Detroit in 1938, and was traded to Cleveland on June 14, 1939, so this event would have had to happen sometime between April Fool's Day, 1938, and Flag Day, 1939. The specific fact given which is easiest to trace is that the Tigers were playing a doubleheader.

The *1939 Reach Guide* and *1940 Spalding Guide* list the games played by each team in 1938 and 1939, so it's easy to compile from that a list of the doubleheaders played by the Tigers. I started with the ones played in Tiger Stadium, since Eisenstat specifies that this happened in Detroit, and started with the scheduled doubleheaders.

In the four scheduled Tiger Stadium doubleheaders in this period (three in 1938, one in 1939) Greenberg homered in only one, on May 30, 1938, and Eisenstat pitched in only one, on July 4 that season.

I checked the un-scheduled doubleheaders, created by rain-outs. The first was on June 17, 1938. Greenberg homered in the second game but Eisenstat pitched in neither.

The second was on June 21; nothing notable happened.

The third was on July 8; again Greenberg homered, this time in the first game, but again Eisenstat did not pitch.

On July 30, the Tigers and Athletics met for two at Tiger Stadium, and it was this doubleheader that Eisenstat remembered. In the opener, Eisenstat pitched in relief and pitched OK (2 3 1 1 0 1), and Greenberg did homer. The Tigers won, 10-7, and Eisenstat got the win.

Eisenstat pitched again in the nightcap, this time brilliantly (4 2 0 0 1 2), and, aided by another Greenberg home run, the Tigers came back from a 7-5 deficit with three in the bottom of the eighth. Eisenstat again was the winner.

So Eisenstat pitched two, not five innings in the first game, and Greenberg hit two, not three homers in the doubleheader. But hey, it's been fifty years, right? The basic events that Eisenstat recalled did happen on July 30, 1938.

By the way, I checked the Detroit paper of July 31.

No riots were reported in the Jewish Quarter.

—Rob Neyer

	G	AB	R	H	2B	3B	HR	RBI	Avg.	SlPct.
Fielder	162	624	102	163	25	0	44	133	.261	.513
Average	157	592	99	156	25	2	41	117	.264	.524

The comp players on average drew three more walks than Fielder, 81-78.

And none of them was taken seriously as an MVP candidate. In 1959 the Indians had a pretty good year and Colavito finished a distant fourth in the voting. Four of the other guys finished seventh or eighth in the MVP poll, and the other five finished between 13th and 19th—about where Fielder belonged. So where the hell does the idea come from that these are MVP numbers?

Wait a minute—I have a partial answer for you, and I'll get to that in a minute. Let me point out a couple of other things first: Harmon Killebrew and Henry Aaron. Harmon Killebrew used to do this every year, didn't he—.260 with 44 homers? None of Killebrew's years made the ten-most-comparable list, but several made the second ten, and he did that consistently from 1961 to 1970. He did win the MVP Award in 1969, when he drove in 140 runs and the Twins won their division, but then a lot of other years he didn't win it, either. What I'm saying is, what does Cecil Fielder do that makes him different than Harmon Killebrew?

Or Henry Aaron—Jeez, think of all the years that Aaron would match Fielder's power stats, hit for an average 60 points higher and throw in 15 or 20 stolen bases and *still* not win the MVP Award. For that matter, why would you vote for Cecil Fielder over Jose Canseco, another .260 hitter with 44 homers but a better baserunner and a better defensive player?

Well, the answer in part is "RBI Leader." Fielder did lead the major leagues in RBI, and the league RBI leader is always the first player considered for the MVP Award. In the last forty years RBI leaders have won 36 MVP Awards—almost three times as many awards as have been won by batting champions, and an actual *majority* of the awards won by position players in that period (36 of 71). Many hitters have won the MVP Award if they led the league in RBI even if they played for non-winning or even non-contending teams (Andre Dawson, Hank Sauer) or were players who really didn't do anything *except* drive in runs (Jeff Burroughs, George Foster).

Still, that something may have happened before is not. . . . George Bell, 1987, is a precedent, not a rationale. I guess I should celebrate the fact that, in the end, the right player *did* win the award in '91. That's progress, I guess.

I would not try to force Fielder himself to realize that other players contribute more, and it is perhaps too much to ask of journalists that they not prey on his expectations to get a story.

It's a silly story. For Cecil Fielder to complain about not getting the MVP Award is like Bill James complaining about the Nobel committee.

SWING HARD, YOU NEVER KNOW WHEN YOU MIGHT HIT SOMETHING

The 1991 Tigers had a power-hitting offense which led the majors in home runs, and also scored more runs than any other team except Texas.

The Tigers' batting average was low (.247), and a common theme of stories written throughout the season could be summarized as "How about those Tigers. They're last in the league in hitting, they're last in pitching, but somehow they're still in the race." The cover story in *Baseball Weekly* on August 23, as the Tigers drove toward a brief hold on first place is an example:

"In dealing with a quirky team that has the worst batting average and ERA—yet is contending—(Anderson) is in contention with a team that nobody thought had a chance."

"If you look at them," concedes Blue Jays manager Cito Gaston, "a lot of their stats really are strange."

The Tigers' offensive stats are not *terribly* strange, and generally make sense if you look at them to see if they make sense. The Tigers' batting average was low, but Offense can be stated statistically in two parts—batting average, and secondary average. Batting average states the regularity of hitting singles. Secondary average summarizes the essential parts of scoring runs *other* than the regularity of hitting singles.

The Tigers' .247 batting average was the lowest in the American League, but their secondary average of .315 was by far the highest in the majors, and was more than 50 points higher than any other team in the division. There are three parts of secondary average—power, walks, and stolen bases. The Tigers were a little above average in stolen bases, and led the majors in both walks and power.

So it's not *really* surprising that they could score runs. The Tigers did score a few more runs than would be projected by the runs created formula, but only a few more (800 Runs Created, 817 Runs Scored). It is not uncommon for a team that is last in the league in batting average to be near the top in runs scored, and the success of the Tigers only creates a puzzle if you use batting average to stand for team offense.

The other part of that story was the strikeouts; the Tigers over the winter of 1990–1991 added two strikeout lions to a lineup which had already struck out more than average, triggering speculation that the 1991 team would break the all-time record for strikeouts. Rob Deer was not only a new outfielder, but also the team's new mascot; from now on they will be known as the Detroit Deer. This was another element to the story: The Tigers are last in the league in hitting, last in pitching, *and first in strikeouts.* As if this was a separate part of an offense.

Of course, as most of you know, strikeouts by themselves are of virtually no significance as an offensive statistic. The common notion that a strikeout is worse than other outs because the strikeout freezes the runners is essentially unfounded, although there is a tiny loss in this way. The Tigers grounded into fewer double plays than any other American League team, in part because of the strikeouts. If you strike out, there's no double play, and GIDP are a *much* more important offensive stat than strikeouts, vastly more costly.

In the end, the Tigers did break the American League record for team strikeouts, but failed to break the major league mark, which remains in the hands of the 1968 Mets.

AUGUST 25

The Tigers had moved into a tie for first place the night before, and were playing Seattle. The Mariners scored two in the first off Terrell, but Lou Whitaker evened the score with a two-run homer off Erik Hanson in the bottom of the inning.

For seven innings after that, nobody scored. Terrell and Hanson traded zeroes. Each team regularly had men in scoring position, but couldn't get the RBI single.

Finally, in the top of the ninth, Dave Valle put the Mariners ahead with a solo home run. The score stood at 3-2 going into the bottom of the ninth.

Erik Hanson had thrown 130 pitches. That's a lot of pitches in today's baseball. A starting pitcher rarely goes that long, but the Mariners had been having trouble in the bullpen, and Lefebvre was trying to push Hanson as far as he could. Eight innings was as far as he could. With the left-handed Dave Bergman due to lead off the ninth, Lefebvre called Russ Swan in to get the left-hander.

Who, of course, didn't bat; Sparky sent Alan Trammell to the plate. Swan got Trammell for the first out.

Mike Schooler came in for the save. He needed two outs, and there was nobody on.

Travis Fryman singled.

Scott Livingstone singled.

Tony Phillips hit for Skeeter Barnes and singled, Fryman scoring. 3-3, still one out.

Schooler got Cuyler for the second out.

Another left-hander up, Whitaker. Rob Murphy came in to pitch to him.

Whitaker singled, Livingstone scored, and that was the bal game. It was the Tigers' sixth of seven straight wins, and kep them in a first-place tie.

The Tigers faded quickly after that. Every winter needs moment.

RECORD WATCH

1. Cecil Fielder has about a 4% chance to hit 700 career hom runs, which has been done by only two players. I see the negatives—late start, one-dimensional talent, obesity—but Fielder i part of a very small group, the guys who can hit 45 or 50 homer a year. Fielder has hit 95 home runs in the last two years. Th only other players to hit 95 home runs in two years were Bab Ruth (many times, career best of 114 in 1927–28), Jimmie Fox (106 in 1932–33), Ralph Kiner (101 in 1949–50), Roger Maris (10 in 1960–61), Willie Mays (99 in 1964–65), Hank Greenberg (98 ir 1937–38), Ted Kluszewski (96 in 1954–55), and Hack Wilson (9 in 1929–30). Fielder is the ninth.

2. Frank Tanana still has a chance to win 300 games in hi career, if he can ever have a couple of 17-win seasons. This char compares Tanana to the last six 300-game winners at the same age:

1.	Steve Carlton	285
2.	Tom Seaver	264
3.	Don Sutton	258
4.	Nolan Ryan	231
	Gaylord Perry	231
6.	**Frank Tanana**	**220**
7.	Phil Niekro	162

TIGER CUBS

We believe the Tigers' best pitching prospect at the moment is **John DeSilva,** a right-handed starting pitcher, 24 years old. He was an eighth-round draft pick in 1989 after playing at BYU, where he was the WAC player of the year. The Tigers have inched him through the system although he has pitched well everywhere (28-17 career, 2.92 ERA). He has struck out 403 men in 389 innings, plus he has outstanding control. At London (AA) in 1991 he struck out 80 men in 74 innings, walking 24, giving up only 51 hits and posting a 2.81 ERA. Promoted to Toledo, he had a 4.60 ERA but maintained the great strikeout/walk ratio (56-21 in 59 innings). His best pitch is a late-breaking slider, and he has an above-average major league fastball. I don't really understand why the Tigers brought up guys like Gakeler and Ritz ahead of DeSilva, but maybe there was a reason.

An article in the January 10 edition of *Baseball America*, however, discussed the Tigers' pitching prospects and didn't mention DeSilva at all. According to them, the Tigers' best pitching prospect is **Greg Gohr.** Gohr is another right-handed starting pitcher, a month younger than DeSilva. He was the Tigers' first-round draft pick in 1989, and jumped from A ball to AAA in 1991, pitching just fair (10-8, 4.61 ERA).

Other Tiger pitching prospects include **Steve Cummings** (27-year-old veteran of the Toronto system; don't see why he's a prospect), **Johnny Doherty** (24-year-old reliever, had a fairly good year at AA), **Buddy Groom** (26-year-old left-hander, was 7-1 at London but 2-5 at Toledo), **Dave Haas** (5.23 ERA at Toledo), and **Kurt Knudsen,** a right-handed reliever who has been consistently effective in the minor leagues. We will stick by the statement that DeSilva is the best pitching prospect in the system.

Catcher **Rich Rowland,** now 25 years old, is better than many teams' backup catchers and a few guys who are number one. He's got a little power, he draws some walks, and he's adequate defensively. He's kind of a poor man's Mickey Tettleton.

Shawn Hare, also 25, is a left-handed hitting outfielder who hit .310 with a .504 slugging percentage at Toledo last year (major league equivalent: .268 with a .439 slugging percentage). He may make the Tigers this year, and what a platoon combination that would be, Deer and Hare. **Rico Brogna** was considered the Tigers' #1 prospect a year ago. He's a 22-year-old first baseman who was unable to handle AAA pitching, and was unimpressive when returned to AA.

JIM VAN SCOYOC

BY JACK ETKIN

The interview with PMX Industries had sailed past the introductory stages and was going well for Jim Van Scoyoc. Big changes were looming in Norway, Iowa, where he had taught industrial arts and coached baseball, and being an educational coordinator for this new company in Cedar Rapids, Iowa, sounded appealing.

Van Scoyoc is an accomplished furniture maker and finds machinery fascinating. He could have pondered plenty of mechanical intricacies at PMX, a maker of brass and copper sheets and strips. There would have been travel to learn about machinery PMX was planning to introduce, and Van Scoyoc would either then pass the knowledge on directly to the workers or arrange for someone to come train them.

The salary was in the $40,000 range, far better than Van Scoyoc had ever made teaching. He was in his 26th year at Norway High School where his baseball teams had become legendary for winning a slew of state titles and regularly beating bigger schools. But in October 1990, Van Scoyoc was virtually certain Norway High was going to soon meet the fate common to schools in small Iowa towns and be amalgamated out of existence.

PMX, a subsidiary of Poong Son Corp., a Korean firm, was an intriguing alternative for Van Scoyoc. It began operating in Cedar Rapids in January 1990, and employs up to 700. Moreover, PMX has been hiring, not retrenching, so the 15-mile drive from Norway to Cedar Rapids brought with it something Van Scoyoc felt was ebbing away in education: a future.

Sally Miller, the administrative manager interviewing Van Scoyoc, described the nature of the work at PMX and then steered their discussion down an unusual avenue. She had read of Van Scoyoc's baseball accomplishments, knew of his long involvement in the game and felt something had to be cleared up.

"She said, 'I'd be willing to offer you a position right now if I knew you had baseball out of your system,'" Van Scoyoc recalled. "Then she asked me if I had it out of my system, and I told her I couldn't guarantee it. It turned out to be prophetic, didn't it. About two weeks later, the Tigers offered me the job at Niagara Falls. I had no idea it was coming."

Becoming the pitching coach in Niagara Falls, N.Y., where the Detroit Tigers have a farm team, the Niagara Falls Rapids, in the short-season Class A New York-Penn League, qualified as fantasy for Van Scoyoc. And why not? At 48, he thought his chances of ever working fulltime in baseball were remote. Hard experience told him thinking otherwise was folly.

Van Scoyoc had spent 16 seasons working as a bird dog, or recommending scout, for Bill Clark, who roamed the Midwest in search of players for Cincinnati for 18 years and Atlanta the last three before becoming the head of the Braves' international scouting operations after the 1991 season. There had been a few nibbles about something more permanent in baseball, but nothing had panned out for Van Scoyoc.

In the fall of 1988, he had talked with the Cleveland Indians about scouting five states in the Midwest. They were going to pay him $20,000, but matters ended when they wouldn't lease a car for him. Within weeks, the Braves approached Van Scoyoc about scouting Virginia and the Carolinas for $19,000. Less money would have brought the added inconvenience of being far from his family; Van Scoyoc wasn't upset when the Braves hired someone already living in that area.

A slight improvement from bird dog came Van Scoyoc's way in 1989, courtesy of Clark and the Braves. "We put him on as a paid part-timer," Clark said. "I think for $100 a month. And he had his expenses covered if I sent him to do something. He was quite happy with that. It was an involvement in baseball he really appreciated. It was his first contact as a paid person in professional baseball."

A part-time scout was better than nothing. And a concerted effort to find work in baseball had led Van Scoyoc to nothing. "I spent hours and hours writing letters and sending them to all the scouting directors and player personnel directors for every ball team," he said. "I've still got all the files back home. I kept duplicates of every letter I sent. I kept all the replies. There's 26 teams, so I sent two letters to every team and in some cases, three.

"Very seldom did I ever get a reply back. Out of all those letters, there was what you would call one positive reply from Baltimore saying they still hadn't hired one coach for their Bluefield team and they would keep me in mind for that. I never heard any more from them.

"Doug Melvin (then the Orioles' player personnel director) was the one who wrote. I guess for somebody who doesn't remember names it sticks in my mind because it was semi-positive, and I got my hopes up."

Van Scoyoc was understandably ecstatic after Tom Petroff offered him the job in Niagara Falls. Petroff became Detroit's director of field operations in August 1990, after years in college baseball. He had been the baseball coach at the University of Northern Colorado from 1970–85, but when that program was scaled back, Petroff moved to the University of Iowa as an assistant coach in July 1985.

Petroff had become acquainted with Van Scoyoc at national coaching conventions but got to know him better once he came to Iowa, since Norway is close to Iowa City. "He always had pretty good ballclubs," Petroff said. "They were well organized. They were sound fundamentally. He had good control of the players as well as the game, and he was very successful."

After being hired, Petroff made a tour of the Tigers' farm system in August 1990, and reported back to Tigers president Bo Schembechler and Joe McDonald, senior vice president for player procurement and development, the following month. "I think I realized how Bo Schembechler, being a person involved with success at Michigan, wanted people who could teach the game," Petroff said. "We had some openings (on the minor league staff). And I always had it in the back of my mind that there are a lot of good people who are in amateur baseball."

Van Scoyoc taught at Norway during the 1990–91 school year. However, since high school baseball in Iowa begins in late May, he did not coach what, indeed, proved to be Norway's final season. In January 1991, what was in the wind became official: Norway High was closing.

Enrollment had dropped to 97. Population in the town was 583 in the 1990 census, down from the 1980 figure of 633. Through the process known in Iowa as whole-grade sharing, Norway students in grades nine through 12 now go to Benton Community High School in Van Horne, Iowa, some 15 miles northwest of Norway.

When Norway won its final 1A state title in 1991, Van Scoyoc was with the players in spirit only. He was far away, working with raw professionals and riding buses around upstate New York and parts of Ontario. About six weeks before leaving for Niagara Falls, Van Scoyoc, sitting in his industrial arts classroom, said, "I couldn't imagine what it would be like if I didn't have a job coming up early in June in baseball. I couldn't imagine what I'd be like mentally. I never thought I'd ever see a day that baseball meant this much to me, if you want to know the truth."

To prepare himself for the uncertainties at Niagara Falls, Van Scoyoc took two weeks off and went to Lakeland, Fla., where the Tigers and their farmhands hold spring training. Norway High didn't pay him his salary, close to $1,200, while he was away. No one reimbursed Van Scoyoc for his travel and other expenses. And Detroit didn't pay him while he was in Florida and staggered by the uncertainty.

"You're used to be being in a program where you know everybody's name," Van Scoyoc said. "All of a sudden, you've got 156 players, and you don't know anybody. You don't know any names."

There were different misgivings upon arriving at Niagara Falls. "For several days it was a struggle, asking yourself if you should be here, if you're capable of it," Van Scoyoc recalled just past the halfway point of the season. "Making goddamn sure these guys don't take advantage of me because I hadn't been a professional coach. After a while, I learned most of those kids are just as scared as I was."

Few had to make the cultural adjustments Van Scoyoc did. Along with Gary Calhoun, the Niagara Falls manager, and Stan Luketich, another coach, Van Scoyoc lived at the Olde Niagara House, a bed and breakfast, that boasts of charm, comfort and convenience. There's probably all of that for tourists making the short walk down Buffalo Avenue to behold the water rushing over the American and Horseshoe Falls after making the sweep around Goat Island, the spit of land that separates those majestic cataracts.

Van Scoyoc didn't spend enough time at the Olde Niagara House to worry about charm or comfort. As for convenience, what mattered most was that the Olde Niagara was a short drive from Sal Maglie Stadium, home of the Rapids. Maglie, a Niagara Falls native, was 119-62 in a big-league career spent mostly with the New York Giants. Pitching inside with ruthless efficiency earned Maglie his nickname, "The Barber."

Just inside the gate leading to the Rapids' dugout, right up against the stands, is a fitting tribute to Maglie: a barber's chair. Van Scoyoc passed it every time he headed toward the Rapids' clubhouse and a small dressing room with overhead pipes he shared with Calhoun and Luketich. The barber's chair meant Van Scoyoc was in a familiar and peaceful world and had left behind the occasional surprises in a city of about 60,000, or a hundred times larger than Norway.

"I wasn't used to a bank being open during the noon hour," Van Scoyoc said. "That was cultural shock to me. We're trucking down Pine Avenue, and somebody says, 'Hey, we got to stop at the bank.' I looked at Gary and said, 'You can't stop at the bank. It's 12:15. They're out to dinner,' thinking like back home they close at 12 and come back at 1.

"In the big city, they don't do that. They do most of their business over the noon hour. I said, 'That's an eye-opener.' These guys are looking at me like, 'What log did he crawl out from under?' "

All the commerce in Norway is on Railroad Street. That includes the Benton County Savings Bank, two grain elevators, a library, fire department, post office, barber shop, the Petro and Provisions convenience store and JP's Railroad Street Connection, a tavern that is now something of a misnomer since the Chicago & North Western trains rumble through Norway but no longer stop there.

On the western edge of town, the trains hurtle into the rural expanse after passing the Norway diamond. The tracks themselves are part of the town's baseball lore. Lefthanded hitting Hal Trosky is said to have once driven a ball far over the right field fence and out onto the highway. The ball bounced, legend has it, and carried to the tracks.

Trosky was born in Norway in 1912. Even though he moved to Cedar Rapids and died there in 1979, Norway can claim him forever since Trosky is buried there. He was a slugging first baseman who had some huge seasons for Cleveland in the 1930s. His best year was 1936 when he led the American League with 162 runs batted in—10 more than runner-up Lou Gehrig—hit 42 home runs—second to Gehrig's 49—and averaged .343.

In a career that lasted 11 seasons and was interrupted by World War II, Trosky hit 228 home runs and batted .302. At the outset of his career, he would return to Norway for Trosky Day, a celebration that welcomed the town's favorite son back from the big leagues. Town teams from Norway, Watkins, Walford and Newhall played, with the two winners squaring off. Norway native Alec Schulte, 73, can reminisce about one such Trosky Day.

"He batted third in the lineup, and I batted fourth," Schulte said. "The pitcher from Walford was Wayne Bruce, who was playing professionally. He walked Hal on four pitches to pitch to me, and I hit the ball over the fence.

"When I came around to home plate, there stood a major leaguer to shake my hand. It was the biggest thrill I got in baseball."

Trosky lived at 100 Tuttle Street while in Norway. That has been the home of Van Scoyoc and his wife, Sheryl, since 1968. They have two sons and one daughter. Aaron, their middle child, is a 22-year-old infielder, whom the Yankees drafted in the 21st round in 1989. He began last season by hitting .310 in 17 games at Class A Greensboro, before moving up to Class A Fort Lauderdale where he hit .228.

Aaron's baseball bloodlines don't flow entirely from his father. One of Sheryl's brothers is pitcher Mike Boddicker, who will be in his 10th season in the majors this year. In the first-floor room that serves as Van Scoyoc's office, the pictures of Boddicker stand out from the plaques commemorating state titles, the team pictures and even the clock Van Scoyoc received in 1983 for being elected national coach of the year by the National Baseball Coaches Association.

There is Boddicker with the Baltimore Orioles, there he is with the Boston Red Sox and finally there he is with the Kansas City Royals. All the pictures are taken from the chest up. Two other photographs are more striking. In one, Boddicker is standing on the mound, shoulders slightly hunched. In the other, he has a bat in his hand and is poised to swing. Both pictures were taken in the summer of 1975 when Boddicker was wearing a uniform that said, "Norway."

"I feel lucky because I probably should never have made it with my physical abilities," Boddicker said. "But I could never imagine myself doing anything else. That's all we all wanted to be when we were growing up was major league ballplayers. To get a chance to play one day in the big leagues was all any of us ever dreamed about. Maybe I made up for everybody else who couldn't."

In addition to Boddicker and Trosky, a third big-leaguer came from Norway. Bruce Kimm, now the third base coach for the San Diego Padres, spent four seasons catching with the Tigers—brushing with fame in 1976 as Mark Fidrych's catcher—Cubs and White Sox. Those three are the tip of the Norway iceberg. Since 1968, seven players from Norway have been drafted, the last being Kimm's son, Tyson, a shortstop who was taken by Seattle in 1991 but opted for college at Creighton.

In 1968, Van Scoyoc became the assistant to Norway baseball coach Bernie Hutchinson and succeeded Hutchinson as head coach in the summer of 1971. Iowa high schools stopped playing a spring season in 1972 and a fall season in 1985. Under Van Scoyoc, Norway won seven state championships in the summer and five in the fall.

Victory processions were a way of life in Norway. The team would return from the 1A state tournament in Marshalltown, Iowa, and a fire truck, with townspeople in tow, would go out to the west edge of Norway to meet the bus carrying the latest state champions and usher them home with siren and horns blaring.

"I didn't have to do any selling on why it's good to be good," Van Scoyoc said. "It was already here. Some of these places, it's like pumping up a tire with a two-inch hole. You're never going to get anywhere; there are just no believers."

Just looking at Van Scoyoc can inspire belief. He has powerful arms, broad shoulders and a strong upper body. At 6-foot-4 and 230 pounds, Van Scoyoc is what the slender, severe farmer, pitchfork at his side, posing with his austere wife in "American Gothic," the celebrated painting by Grant Wood of Cedar Rapids, would look like if he had spent less time tilling the fields and taken to pumping iron.

Van Scoyoc was born March 13, 1943, in Ladora, Iowa. His father, Jim, and mother, Blanche, ran Van's Cafe, a 24-hour truck stop located on Highway 6. The Van Scoyocs could see how the interstate highway system was making the backroads commercially obsolete, and just after Van Scoyoc had graduated from HLV Community High School (Hartwick, Ladora and Victor) in Victor, Iowa, they bought a restaurant in nearby Marengo, Iowa, and moved there. By then, Van Scoyoc had learned life had a seamy side.

"I've seen just about everything," he said. "Seeing married women out with single guys and have their husbands catch 'em and take it out on the single guy by sticking a broken beer bottle in his face. Poor sucker takes about a hundred stitches. Then you got to clean up the mess after that.

"I'd prefer not to talk about the sexual exploits I'd seen by age 15. Lots of drinking. Lots of alcoholics. Lots of family fights. Wives coming in to drag their husband out.

"Saw a guy lay $26,000 on the counter in cash at 2 o'clock in the morning. Was drunk and just got paid for a contracting job he'd done. Was going through a divorce. Was so damned drunk he couldn't move. And he got killed about two weeks later. Run his car into a semi. Pinned him in. They couldn't get him out.

"I think that's one of the reasons I'm as quiet as I am, to be quite honest with you. You see every asshole there is to see. You try and not be like that. There were some good people though, too."

When he was 16, Van Scoyoc went to a St. Louis Cardinals tryout camp in Cedar Rapids that lasted three days. He made the cut after the first day and was asked to return to play in games the final two days. "The only thing I can remember about it was how huge the ballpark was," Van Scoyoc said. "And there was a young black fellow from Kentucky. I don't remember his name. He was the same age I was. He just hit the hell out of the ball off me, I'll never forget. Almost went out of that ballpark. Went off the top of the fence, I remember.

"We spent a lot of time together. Unfortunately I do not remember his name. That was the first contact I ever had with a black, too."

Van Scoyoc's last chance to play professional baseball was a mystifying offer that came in 1974, nine years after he had graduated from William Penn College in Oskaloosa, Iowa. A scout from the New York York Yankees approached Van Scoyoc after he had pitched his team to a victory in the American Amateur Baseball Congress tournament at Battle Creek, Mich., and asked if he had an interest in signing a contract.

"I was standing talking to three other guys," Van Scoyoc said. "I can remember looking at him and saying, 'What in the hell are you talking about?'

He said, 'Would you be interested in playing professional baseball?'

" 'Well of course I would. I'm no fool. But what makes you want to sign somebody my age?'

"He said, 'Well you are 21, aren't you?' I said, 'What makes you think I'm 21.' He handed me the program. It had my birthdate listed as '53 instead of '43. Had me listed as 21 instead of 31.

"He thanked me for pointing that out to him and saving him the embarrassment. We got to small-talking, and I told him I had a ballplayer at home who would probably play high professional baseball some day. He never even asked me who the kid was, but I told him anyhow. He was Mike Boddicker."

An injury forced Van Scoyoc to make the conversion from something other than a hard thrower. He was pitching for the Norway town team against Watkins on July 4, 1969, and in the eighth inning of the game at Watkins, Van Scoyoc threw "one curveball too many" and felt something pop in his right elbow. It was 18 months before he was again able to pitch, albeit with an altered approach. "If you can't throw hard, you've got to throw to a location," Van Scoyoc said. "Obviously I learned something because the guy (from the Yankees) offered me a contract."

Van Scoyoc had a more realistic chance to play professionally in 1965, the year the June amateur draft began. While every team bypassed Van Scoyoc in that process, the Cardinals later asked him to pitch at their farm club in Cedar Rapids in the Class A Midwest League.

Van Scoyoc had a dilemma. He had just graduated from Willima Penn. The Vietnam War was heating up. He had a teaching contract at Amana (Iowa) High School. But the Cardinals were calling, and he wanted to play.

"I knew I was going to get drafted if I signed that pro contract," Van Scoyoc said. "So I went to the president of the draft board in Iowa County and presented her with my dichotomy. She assured me if I signed the baseball contract, I would be drafted very shortly after that. She recommended I try the teaching route, which might be a little bit safer for me. I got drafted six months later, anyway."

Something inexplicable then occurred. Van Scoyoc went to Des Moines to take a physical. He came home and was told to return for another chest X-ray. He came home and never heard from the Army again. "You've about got to ask yourself what in the hell happened," Van Scoyoc said. "I have no idea. I went to take the physical in Des Moines with three guys. Not one of us went into the Army."

Unfortunately, the Cardinals' interest in Van Scoyoc had waned. They were stretching their signing timetable to its limits in 1965 when he had passed his 22nd birthday. By the time he had finished his bizarre encounter with the military, Van Scoyoc was 23, too old for the Cardinals or any other team. "So I had my first year of pro ball in 1991," he said, "and it was everything I thought it would be."

Niagara Falls rose from a 2-10 start to make history. The Rapids' pitchers strung together four successive shutouts from June 29–July 2, setting a New York-Penn League record with 36 straight scoreless innings. The old record of 26 consecutive shutout innings had been set by the Corning Red Sox in 1956.

Calls began coming from *USA Today* and ESPN. *How many innings is it now?* The Rapids were about one more shutout away from becoming a national story. The barber's chair would have made nice footage, a local touch to spice up the tale.

Any chance the Rapids had for any coast-to-coast publicity came to an abrupt halt in the fifth game; Corey Reincke gave up a three-run home run in the top of the first inning. "It was no mistake home run either," Van Scoyoc said. "I can still see the ball going over the left-center field fence.

"Every ballpark we were in this summer is just as clear in my mind as if we played there yesterday. I guess I ended up with a more heightened awareness of the whole situation. Got to looking forward to getting on the bus and seeing something you haven't seen before. The other guys are thinking I was crazy. 'What the hell do you want to get on a bus and ride three hours for?' It didn't bother me. It never bothered me."

This recollection came five months after that pitch of Reincke's soared into flight and three months after Van Scoyoc rode a bus from Welland, Ontario, to Niagara Falls following the final game of the season. The Rapids finished in third place in their division, and at 36-42, fell one victory short of making the playoffs. Van Scoyoc's staff had a 3.83 ERA, which was tied for ninth in the 14-team league. What bothered Van Scoyoc was the descent it took to reach that level and the feeling that, short of actually throwing strikes for his pitchers, he had done everything possible for them.

On July 30, the Rapids were 23-19, second in their division and their 3.40 ERA was fourth in the league. The next night, the visiting St. Catherines Blue Jays scored six runs in the eighth inning on two three-run homers off reliever Shawn Turri and beat the Rapids 10-9.

The slide had started, not that one miserable loss would make any trend clear to Van Scoyoc as he sat in Michael's Restaurant on Pine Avenue, a short drive from the ballpark. When the restaurant closed, it was after midnight. Van Scoyoc went outside and made the short walk to the corner of 29th Street and Pine, stopping beside a street lamp in front of Virtuoso Upholstering.

That same night in Detroit, the Tigers beat California 3-1. Cecil Fielder homered twice and Rob Deer, once. Walt Terrell pitched a complete game. Detroit is a seven-hour drive across Ontario. In baseball terms, the distance from Detroit to Niagara Falls is a voyage to the far reaches of the solar system, yet there is a link, one Van Scoyoc could see in his daily work with his pitchers.

"I feel like I'm an important part of 12 players lives, at least as far as baseball goes," Van Scoyoc said. "And that'll change because baseball is continually sorting. It's a sifting process. The only thing I can liken it to is how they used to sort shot for shotgun shells.

"They'd go up to the top of a tall shot tower and pour the molten lead and get a screen. As it mixes with the air it forms little blobs. As it would drop, it would cool in either big drops or small drops. The big ones would be caught at the top, and the smaller they got, they'd be caught at the bottom."

Across the street was Scipicone Bros. Meat Specialists, quiet at this hour. Next to it, the door was open at the Friendly Tavern. A woman pulled up and double parked. After a few minutes inside, she returned to her car and drove off. If her evening had been ruined, it wasn't because of two three-run home runs.

Silvery clouds floated past a moon that was almost full. Van Scoyoc was occasionally spitting tobacco juice. But for that sound, Van Scoyoc's street-corner baseball harmonizing would have been a cappella.

"I would like to have been doing this 20 years ago," he said. "I think I enjoyed doing what I was doing and never realized there would be this much enjoyment at doing a job in baseball.

"Before I was just a teacher, first, and a coach, second. Now I'm just a coach and it's a baseball job and I like it. I never thought I would enjoy it this much."

Anyone familiar with Van Scoyoc wouldn't have been surprised by his self-doubt earlier in the evening, his worries as he sat in Michael's Restaurant that he might be in over his head. Later, in the final weeks of the season, Van Scoyoc was tormented by his pitchers' inability to throw strikes and wondered just what else he could do short of taking the mound for them.

Van Scoyoc's pitching pedigree, or lack thereof, was of little consequence to his pitchers. They weren't fazed by his lack of professional playing experience. "If the organization didn't have confidence in him, they wouldn't have hired him," said Sean Bergman, the Tigers' fourth-round pick in 1991 out of Southern Illinois University. "So I feel he has the ability to do the job. I believe you can learn from everybody. Tom House has a great reputation as a pitching coach. If they said they were having a meeting with Tom House or a meeting with Jim Van Scoyoc, more people would show up to the meeting with Tom House because of his reputation. But I think Jim's a good pitching coach. He makes you think about what you're going to do."

Van Scoyoc's tendency to see the worst-case scenario looming doesn't spill over into his relationships with players. Still, it's a personality quirk, and Clark, the Braves scout who has known Van Scoyoc since the days when Max Elliott was playing shortstop at Norway High and on his way to becoming the sixth-round draft pick of the San Diego Padres in 1971, has repeatedly chided Van Scoyoc about his lack of self-confidence. "I sent Jim to St. Cloud, Minn., last year to scout an eight-state Legion tournament," Clark said. "I said, 'Go on up there. We're going to pick up your expenses. You take game cards, and anybody you see you think we need to follow, well, you get the information.'

"Jim questioned whether he could do it, and then when he brought it back, he questioned whether he'd done a good job or not. He had the squares filled out. He had the information we needed. He did an excellent job. From what I knew about the couple of teams I had in that tournament I thought he graded them like I might've graded them had I been there. But he was so insecure about what he was doing."

Clark believes this uncertainty stems from Van Scoyoc's insular existence. Van Scoyoc doesn't dispute that notion; he grew up, went to college and worked in a sliver of east-central Iowa and never really spent an extended period of time away from those roots until his summer in Niagara Falls.

His sojourn there changed Van Scoyoc. Calhoun, the Rapids' manager, and Luketich, their other coach, are more easygoing and extroverted than Van Scoyoc. Who would have expected Van Scoyoc, accompanied by Luketich, to ever step on stage at a Niagara Falls night spot and do a karioke rendition of Bachman Turner Overdrive's classic "Taking Care of Business?"

"If I'm back in Iowa," Van Scoyoc said, "there's no way in hell that happens. That's how they loosened me up a little bit. I'm grateful for that, too. That's how I've been my whole life."

Like Clark, Petroff, the Tigers' director of field operations, has talked to Van Scoyoc about being more self-assured. But this is a different relationship, since Petroff is Van Scoyoc's boss. "He'll be alright," Petroff said. "He's just got to believe in himself. And he does. Every once in a while he kind of shortchanges himself. He's going to be OK. If not, he'd have been gone."

This season, Van Scoyoc will be the pitching coach at Bristol, Va., in the short-season Appalachian League. That league carries the "Rookie" classification, a notch below Niagara Falls' Class A attachment. Petroff wants Van Scoyoc to experience both entry-level points in the Tigers' farm system. The difference is that most of Bristol's players are fresh from high school. At Niagara Falls, they are coming from college.

Unlike last year, the Tigers are bringing Van Scoyoc to minor league spring training. When that ends in early April, he will stay in Florida and work in their extended spring program before going to Bristol. In all, Van Scoyoc's tenure with the Tigers will be six months this year, twice as long as 1991.

Van Scoyoc will find himself in southwestern Virginia, right on the Tennessee border, in Bristol. From there, his travels this summer will take him into Tennessee for games at Elizabethton, Johnson City and Kingsport, and up into the mountains of Virginia and West Virginia. The young Bristol pitchers will hear Van Scoyoc tell them how to approach their craft: "You got to think like you're dismantling a bomb; if you become the least bit uncontrolled and violent about it, you're going to lose that precision."

Van Scoyoc's summer in Niagara Falls will recede but never fade entirely from view. Dennis Walsh will have his sense of humor and buckling breaking pitch. Anytime he wanted, Walsh, a lefthander who didn't throw hard, could unleash The Curveball From Hell, as it was known in Niagara Falls.

Jimmy Henry, another lefthander, will be thinking two or three pitches ahead about how to set up a hitter and do it despite rarely topping 84 miles an hour.

Bergman, with the best arm on the Rapids' staff, will be using the four-seam fastball Van Scoyoc taught him, a pitch he could more reliably throw for strikes than his erratic two-seamer.

Something else will cross Van Scoyoc's mind next summer. He will be out in the bullpen, overseeing someone's throwing session and maybe suggesting changes, or in a dugout in Martinsville, Va., or on a bus, say, from Bluefield, W. Va., to Princeton, W. Va., taking in the Appalachian countryside and happily headed to another ballpark when he'll remember winter in Norway.

The high school has closed. Norway won't have a baseball team this year. Outside of his former players, few in Norway know what to talk about anymore when they see Van Scoyoc or feel comfortable chatting with him.

Worse, he found no work, despite his furniture-making talents. Norway is home to Van Scoyoc's ailing mother-in-law, so he's not about to leave that familiar sliver of east-central Iowa. If he did eventually depart, Van Scoyoc could find somewhere warmer and busier, somewhere with opportunities. But what could Van Scoyoc find that would be as inherently satisfying if he turns his back on the game it took so long to wedge his way into?

"I'll be 49 years old in March. I don't feel like it, mentally or physically," Van Scoyoc said. "But you know because of past experience in your whole life, people look at you from a different point of view and say, 'Hey, this guy's old. Do we want to employ him?'

"Now you're in a position where you're doing something where you're happy, but you're not making an awful lot of money and you're wondering whether for the rest of your family, for your wife in particular, this is a good deal. Should you just throw the pride thing away and say, 'Oh hell, let's just get on with life?' Go get a job in a factory, 7 till 4 or 7 til 3:30, what the hell ever.

"Fly me to Cleveland or some place in Georgia or North Carolina, looking at some manufacturer's machinery or some product and making your $40,000 a year and getting your health insurance paid for. Maybe getting retirement benefits. Should you just say, 'The hell with baseball?'

"I asked my wife that question. You know what she said to me? 'Do you really think you've given it enough time?' That was pretty sobering."

The laugh Jim Van Scoyoc tossed off was that of a grateful man.

THE MILWAUKEE BREWERS

• IN A BOX •

1991 Won-Lost Record: 83-79 .512
Rank among 26 teams: 13th
Over Last Five Years: 416-394 .514
Rank over Five Years: 10th
In Last Ten Years: 813-804 .503
Rank over Ten Years: 14th

Best Player: Paul Molitor

Weak Spot: Right field, First Base when Molitor wasn't there

Best Pitcher: Chris Bosio

Staff Weakness: Bullpen

Best Young Player: Bill Spiers

Best Looking Player: Jaime Navarro

Ugliest Player: Dave Nilsson

Most Pleasant Surprise, 1991: Bill Wegman

Biggest Disappointment, 1991: Franklin Stubbs

Best Minor League Prospect: See article

Other Prospects: See article

Designated Malcontent: Gary Sheffield

Park Characteristics: The dimensions are fairly short (315 down the lines), so people always think this is a hitter's park. In mid-summer, when the ball travels, it is a hitter's park; the Brewers will score more runs at home than on the road in mid-summer. But cold weather favors the pitcher, and because so many games here are played in cold weather, on balance the park does not favor a hitter. If you sort parks into hitter's, pitcher's and neutral, it's in the neutral category.

The Park Helps: Jaime Navarro has pitched much better in Milwaukee than on the road the last two seasons.

The Park Hurts: No one especially.

ORGANIZATIONAL REPORT CARD

Ownership:	B
Upper Management:	New
Field Management:	New
Front-Line Talent:	C
Second-Line Talent:	D−
Minor League System:	C

Comment: In recent years I have been extremely critical of the Brewers' management. I've never felt that Selig and associates didn't know what they were doing. What I've thought is that they were not really paying attention. Like George Bush, they were distracted by global issues while things went to hell on the home-front.

TEAM LEADERS:

Batting Average: Willie Randolph, .327
Last Ten Years (Season): Paul Molitor, 1987, .353
Last Ten Years (Total): Molitor, .304

Doubles: Paul Molitor, 32

Triples: Molitor, 13

Home Runs: Greg Vaughn, 27
Last Ten Years (Season): Rob Deer, 1986, 33
Last Ten Years (Total): Robin Yount, 168

Extra Base Hits: Paul Molitor, 62

RBI: Greg Vaughn, 98
Last Ten Years (Season): Cecil Cooper, 1983, 126
Last Ten Years (Total): Robin Yount, 839

Stolen Bases: Molitor, 19

Runs Created: Molitor, 137

Runs Created Per Game: Molitor, 8.1

Secondary Average: Greg Vaughn, .330

Wins: Bill Wegman and Jaime Navarro, 15 each
Last Ten Years (Season): Ted Higuera, 1986, 20
Last Ten Years (Total): Higuera, 92

Winning Percentage: Bill Wegman, 15-7 .682

Strikeouts: Chris Bosio, 117
Last Ten Years (Season): Higuera, 1987, 240
Last Ten Years (Total): Higuera, 1019

ERA: Wegman, 2.84

Saves: Doug Henry, 15

League Leaders:

1. Paul Molitor led the majors in runs (133), hits (216), at bats (665), and plate appearances (752), and tied for the AL lead with 13 triples.

2. Greg Vaughn went 7 for 11 with the bases loaded, a .636 average. I'm not sure why we figure this, but that was the best mark in the major leagues. The Brewers as a team hit .352 with the bases loaded.

Stat of the Year: I think Greg Vaughn may have hit the Oakland A's better than any other hitter hit one team. Vaughn hit .415 against the A's with five doubles, six homers and 20 RBI in 12 games. His slugging percentage against Oakland was .976.

1991 SEASON

Background: See article, "A Page is Turned"

Outlook: For several years expectations had been high. By the spring of 1990 more people were beginning to catch on that this team might not come together.

Getaway: .500 ball. The Brewers were 2-2, 3-3, 4-4, 5-5, 6-6, 8-8 and 9-9 before a four-game streak pushed them to 13-9.

Low Point of the Season: After that there was no good news for a long time. The Brewers lost eight straight, dropping to 13-17. By June 9 they were 23-31. They hung around that level, winning some and losing some. On July 14 they were 38-46, which was bad enough, but then they went into a slump. Between July 15 and August 3 they lost 14 of 19 games. On August second the Rangers beat them 15-1. On August third they beat them again, 14-5. By early August—the nadir of the season—the fate of Dalton and Trebelhorn had been sealed.

Stretch Drive: The Brewers played extremely well the rest of the season. From August 4 to the end of the season the Brewers were 40-19.

Had the Brewers played even remotely as well in the middle part of the year, Tom Trebelhorn's entire biography would have been different. The Brewers would have won this race, Trebelhorn and Dalton would have kept their jobs, and the Brewers might have been in contention for several years.

Most Exciting Game of the Season: May 1 vs. the White Sox. The Sox took a five-run lead into the fifth, but the Brewers scored six. The Sox tied it in the seventh, and it remained 6-6 going to the 15th inning. Chicago put three on the board in the top of the inning, but Milwaukee matched them in the bottom of the inning. The Brewers finally won the game, 10-9, with a run in the 19th inning.

Major Injuries: Ted Higuera started only six games, and underwent surgery to repair a torn rotator cuff in July.

Gary Sheffield missed two-thirds of the season with a sore shoulder and wrist.

Ron Robinson pitched only one game before surgery to remove a bone spur in his right elbow ended his season.

Reliever Edwin Nunez lost three months to back surgery.

Candy Maldonado spent several weeks on the disabled list with a broken bone in his left foot.

Dan Plesac was troubled by tendinitis the first half of the season. He didn't go on the disabled list, but gave up 14 hits in nine and a third innings in his first few appearances, then didn't pitch for a couple of weeks.

Offense: The Brewer offense last year was tremendously efficient, scoring 799 runs with offensive stats which would normally have yielded only 746. This was the largest discrepancy between runs created and runs scored in the major leagues, being about three times the normal runs created error.

Defense: Average. They could use more speed in the outfield.

Pitching: Poor.

Best Game by a Starting Pitcher: Jaime Navarro vs. Cleveland, May 24 (9 4 0 0 0 6 Game Score: 85)

Worst Game by a Starting Pitcher: April 14, Don August against Toronto (1 6 6 6 0 2 Game Score: 19)

Indicators for 1991 were: Up a Tiny Bit (+4.1)

Number of regulars having good seasons by their own standards: Six (Randolph, Molitor, Vaughn, Gantner, Spiers, Hamilton)

1991 Over-Achiever: Willie Randolph

1991 Under-Achiever: Franklin Stubbs

Infield: Lacking in power and perhaps defensive range, but pretty good otherwise. Brewer infielders hit only 35 home runs, or nine per position.

Outfield: Mediocre. Brewer outfielders hit .259 with 18 homers, 12 stolen bases per slot. Bichette in right field is a drain on the team offensively. Yount was having a good year until September 1, but ruined his season's stats with a terrible slump late in the year.

Catching: Among the best in the league.

Starting Pitching: Thin. Three guys were alright (Wegman, Bosio and Navarro) but the rest were poor even for a supporting cast.

Bullpen: Bad. The Brewers bullpen had 27 losses (league average: 21), blew 21 save opportunities (league average: 18) and had an ERA of 4.18 (league average: 3.77).

Although Dan Plesac was terrible in 1990 and wasn't 100% physically, the Brewers continued to count on him to be their closer. They went through several candidates for the closer role until it was finally claimed by Doug Henry. Henry's performance over the last couple of months was one of the keys to the Brewers' strong finish.

Percentage of offense created by:

Young Players: 36%
Players in Their Prime: 16%
Past Their Prime: 48%

Team Age:

Age of Non-Pitchers: 30.2
Age of Pitching Staff: 27.0
Overall Team Age: 28.90

The Brewers of 1991 had the oldest offense in the division.

In retrospect, the critical decisions were:

1. Failing to support the bullpen before the season started.
2. Misjudging the abilities of Franklin Stubbs and Dante Bichette.

THAT AND THE OTHER

Lookalikes: Ted Higuera and Fernando Valenzuela

Hall of Fame Watch: Robin Yount is a certain Hall of Famer. The other major Hall of Fame candidate is Paul Molitor, who is still playing great and has more than 2,000 hits behind him.

Willie Randolph, now with the Mets, is also a Hall of Fame candidate, albeit a longshot. Randolph will be hurt by the new rules concerning the Veteran's Committee, but could help his cause if he can get the Mets back to the World Series.

Chris Berman, Have You Considered:

Jaime (the Guns of) Navarro
Chuck (Just when things look) Crim

Throwback: Jim Gantner

Attendance Trend: Down. The Brewers 1991 attendance was down 500,000 from 1989, and was the lowest since 1986.

Players with a Chance for 3000 career hits:

Robin Yount, 97%
Paul Molitor, 39%
Willie Randolph, 3%

Best Fundamental Player: Paul Molitor

Worst Fundamental Player: Gary Sheffield

Best Defensive Player: I'm not sure. Probably Dante Bichette.

Worst Defensive Player: Don't know.

Best Knowledge of the Strike Zone: Willie Randolph

Least Command of the Strike Zone: Dante Bichette

Fastest Runner: The Brewers do not have anyone in the lineup who is especially fast. I believe the three fastest Brewer regulars are Molitor, Spiers and Bichette, and all three of those run about the same.

Slowest Runner: The Brewers also don't have anyone who is especially *slow* in their lineup. The "slow positions", at which the slow players are concentrated on almost all teams, are catcher, first base and (in the American League) Designated Hitter. The Brewers catcher (Surhoff) runs fairly well, their first baseman (Stubbs) runs deceptively well and their DH (Molitor) is still a fast runner.

Best Baserunner: Molitor or Spiers

Most Likely to Still be Here in 2000: I doubt that anybody on the 1991 team will still be here in 1995, let alone 2000. Well, Molitor will last until 1995.

Best Fastball: Julio Machado

Best Breaking Pitch: Don August

Most Likely to Shoot You After a Traffic Accident: Uh, no . . .

Best Control: Bill Wegman

Oddest Collection of Abilities: B.J. Surhoff

Why is this man in the Major Leagues: Dale Sveum

Gets Ahead of the Hitters Most Often: Bill Wegman

Gets Ahead of the Hitters Least Often: Mark Lee

Most-Similar Players:

to C BJ Surhoff, Craig Biggio
to 1B Franklin Stubbs, Sid Bream
to 2B Willie Randolph, Ozzie Smith
to 3B Jim Gantner, Tom Herr
to SS Bill Spiers, Jeff Blauser
to LF Greg Vaughn, Jay Buhner
to CF Robin Yount, George Brett
to RF Dante Bichette, Darrin Jackson

Most Fun to Watch: Paul Molitor

Least Fun to Watch: Franklin Stubbs

Among the All-Time Team Leaders:

Robin Yount is at the top of the Brewer records in every offensive category except career batting average, where he trails Molitor and Cecil Cooper, stolen bases (trails Molitor) and slugging percentage. Molitor and Gantner both figure prominently on most of the lists.

Ted Higuera is the Brewers' all-time strikeout leader with 1019.

Town Team:

C—Red Wilson
1B—Joe Hauser
2B—Lave Cross
SS—Tony Kubek
3B—Ken Keltner
LF—Harvey Keunn
CF—Ginger Beaumont
RF—Al Simmons
SP—Addie Joss
SP—Burleigh Grimes
SP—Kid Nichols

Post-Season Transactions:

October 30, Phil Garner hired as manager

December 10, traded Chuck Crim to the Angels for Mike Fetters and minor league pitcher Glenn Carter.

December 11, traded Dale Sveum to Phillies for Bruce Ruffin.

December 11, Julio Machado named as a murder suspect in Venezuela.

What Needs to Be Done For 1992: At this writing, it isn't clear whether the Brewers intend to regard 1992 as a building year, or whether Bando and Garner intend to make an immediate push for the pennant. My feeling is that there is *so* little young talent here that the Brewers have nothing to lose by gambling on a 1992 push. They probably won't win, but hell, they finished only eight games out in 1991; if enough things break right they could salvage a second championship out of the Molitor/Yount years before they have to replace those guys.

Outlook for 1992: I'm not optimistic. Molitor, Yount and Gantner, still key players on this team, are very old. Willie Randolph, who had a super year in 1991, is gone by free agency. Bill Wegman was the Brewers' best starting pitcher last year, but I doubt that he can pitch at the same level again. Doug Henry, the new relief ace, has no history of consistent success. You never know who can win, but that's too many question marks to make the Brewers a favorite.

Index of Leading Indicators for 1992: Down 2.9

Positive Indicators: 1. Strong Play Late in the Season

Negative Indicators: 1. Team Age

The Brewers indicators for 1992 are about the same as the Red Sox, except stronger. In both cases the strongest positive indicator is that the team played well late in the season. The Red Sox, however, didn't *really* play well late in the season; they just played a little better than they had earlier. In both cases the strongest negative indicator is the age of the offense. The Red Sox, however, aren't *really* an old team; they're just old enough for it to be a negative indicator. The Brewers of 1991 really did have an old lineup, and this will be a problem for them as they begin their rebuilding cycle. In both cases, the indicators as a whole are mixed, and don't strongly suggest that the team will be better or worse in 1992.

Due for a better season: Gary Sheffield

Likely to have a worse season: Molitor

1992 Won-Lost Record will be: 82-80

PICKY, PICKY

B.J. Surhoff was credited with five stolen bases last year, but it was really six. In the game of August 1, 1991, the Brewers trailed by one run in the eleventh inning, but had runners on first and third. The man on first, representing the winning run, was Surhoff.

Surhoff took second base, and the Royals did not throw. The Milwaukee scorer ruled defensive indifference, no stolen base. This is an application (or mis-application) of rule 10.08 (g), which reads "No stolen base shall be scored when a runner advances solely because of the defensive team's indifference to his advance. Score as a fielder's choice."

Many times in a lopsided game, a blowout, the first baseman will not hold the runner on first on the bag. It may not have to be a blowout; it may be, let's say, a 4-1 game, losing team at bat, runner on first and two out. Particularly with a left-handed hitter at the plate, the defensive manager may figure that he doesn't want to hold the runner on first, give up a hit through the hole and set up a three-run homer. He may elect not to hold the guy on first, and the runner may take second without a throw. The intent of rule 10.08 (g) is that a stolen base is not to be credited in that situation, since it is more of a gift than a theft.

But you simply cannot rule that the defense is *indifferent* to the winning run moving into scoring position in the eleventh inning. It was a clear mis-application of the rule, and if Surhoff (or the Brewers) had appealed the ruling to the league office, it unquestionably would have been reversed.

What the official scorer thought happened was that the Royals did not want to risk throwing to second with another runner on third. He thought, therefore, that the Royals had conceded Surhoff second base rather than risk the throw, and he thought that was defensive indifference.

Well, he was wrong on both points. First, the Royals had *not* conceded the play. The Royals *were* holding Surhoff on first, and Hal McRae said after the game that the pitcher simply fell asleep, and let Surhoff get too big a jump on him. Second, it *doesn't matter* if they had conceded the play, because that is not what the rule covers. "Conceding" the base is not the same as being "indifferent" to the base. I have seen other cases like this where the official scorer blew it and the team appealed, and in every case the ruling was reversed.

A PAGE HAS TURNED

Following their championship year in 1982 the Brewers dropped quickly to the basement, finishing last in 1984. Not to worry; young talent was on the way.

In the mid-1980s the Brewers were widely reported to have the best farm system in baseball. I've never been exactly sure how this got started, but *Baseball America* decided that the Brewers had the best organization in baseball, and everybody figured they're the experts so they must be right. People would rave about the Brewers' prospects, and you couldn't talk them out of it. I could never understand what the hell they were talking about. People were all excited about a group of prospects (B.J. Surhoff, Billy Joe Robidoux, Joey Meyer, Dale Sveum, Glenn Braggs, Juan Nieves, Lavelle Freeman) who, taken as a group, were not only not exciting, but not really even very interesting.

And on the seventh day the Lord rested. The unfortunate consequence of this hype was that the Brewers' front office thought they had everything under control. And, in a period in which the Brewer organization wasn't *really* producing much of anything, the Brewers were inert. They didn't trade, they didn't sign free agents, they didn't take any actions to rebuild the system. As time passed and the team couldn't get into the pennant race, frustration inevitably set in. And Harry Dalton was very slow to pick up on the fact that his team simply wasn't going anywhere.

I've never felt that Harry Dalton was stupid. Well, one time. When he came up with that pay-for-performance scale I thought he was stupid, but I never really thought that he wasn't capable of running a major league organization. I think he just mis-allocated his time and energy, and the victim of that was Tom Trebelhorn.

Trebelhorn was a pretty good manager. I could never understand his fascination with stolen bases. The Brewers used to lead the league in stolen bases every year. Trebelhorn was a one-time high school teacher, and reporters always regarded him as pretty much of a gentleman and something of a scholar. This puts him in the general class of managers with Steve Boros, who was a gentleman and a scholar, and who liked to steal bases, and who didn't win, either. It has always puzzled me that smart, educated, new-wave type managers seem incapable of understanding something which by and large old-line school-of-hard-knocks type managers understand instinctively: that the math on the stolen base doesn't work out. The stolen base is an occasional play; when the occasion come up and you can take the base, it helps. But if you start doing a lot of it you'll lose as many runs by the guys caught stealing as you gain from the stolen bases.

But that's just one thing. It wasn't that Trebelhorn couldn't manage. The real problem was that Glenn Braggs couldn't play. Trebelhorn became a victim of the unjustified expectations for a group of young Brewers who couldn't play.

BREWERS BREWING

The Brewers best prospect at the moment is probably **Cal Eldred,** who is a 24-year-old right-hander. A University of Iowa product, Eldred was the Brewers' top pick in the '89 June draft (17th overall). He pitched last year at Denver (AAA), a hitter's park, and finished with a 3.75 ERA and 168 strikeouts in 185 innings. He did walk 84 batters. He has a nice curve and a fastball in the high eighties, and pitched well in a September trial with the Brewers. He's an excellent candidate for the American League Rookie of the Year Award.

A year ago, catcher **Dave Nilsson** wasn't even listed among the organization's top ten prospects. But after hitting .418—that's four-eighteen—in 65 games with El Paso last summer, the Australian native was listed as the #4 prospect in the Texas League. He is only 22.

El Paso is probably the best place in baseball to compile showy hitting stats, which have to be taken with a grain of salt. El Paso first baseman **John Jaha** ended up with awesome triple crown stats (.344, 30, 134), but he is 25 years old. His MLEs show him as a major league hitter, and the Brewers do need a first baseman.

Duane Singleton, an outfielder and Milwaukee's fifth-round pick in 1990, has speed (42 SB) and will draw an occasional walk. He'll be 20 years old this summer.

Milwaukee's #1 pick in last year's draft, a high school pitcher named Kenny Anderson, had not signed as of October.

A sandwich pick to compensate for the loss of Rob Deer was used to select another high school pitcher, left-hander **Tyrone Hill.** At Beloit (Midwestern League), Hill struck out 76 men in 60 innings.

Jim Olander, who was the MVP in the American Association, is a 29-year-old center fielder. His last good year was 1986.

THE NEW YORK YANKEES
• IN A BOX •

1991 Won-Lost Record: 71-91 .438

Rank among 26 teams: 23rd
Over Last Five Years: 386-422 .478
Rank over Five Years: 20th
In Last Ten Years: 830-787 .513
Rank over Ten Years: 9th

Best Player: 1. Steve Sax
2. Roberto Kelly

Weak Spot: Third Base

Best Pitcher: Scott Sanderson

Staff Weakness: Numerous holdovers from Steinbrenner regime

Best Baseball Name: Bam Bam Meulens

Best Young Player: Roberto Kelly

Best Looking Player: Steve Sax

Ugliest Player: Eric Plunk

Most Pleasant Surprise, 1991: Mel Hall or Matt Nokes

Biggest Disappointment, 1991: Hensley Meulens

Best Minor League Prospect: Brien Taylor

Who Is: The first player taken in the June draft, a left-handed pitcher. Due to his highly publicized and acrimonious contract negotiations, Taylor did not sign in time to pitch in the minors in 1991. He did go to the instructional league, where his fastball was, as advertised, very impressive.

Other Prospects: **Ed Martel** is a right-handed starting pitcher, spent all of last season at Albany in the Eastern League. In 163 innings, he struck out 141 and walked only 55, finishing with a 2.81 ERA. He'll be 23 this season.

John Ramos is a 26-year-old catcher, comparable to Rich Rowland of the Tigers. He has a little power, will take a walk, and is no threat to the major league starter, in this case Nokes. He could play for a lot of teams.

Brad Ausmus is another catcher, spent half of last season in A ball, half in AA. Ausmus was a 48th round pick in 1987, so he's got some long odds to beat, but he can hit a little, stole 31 bases last year, and according to *Baseball America* "drew rave reviews for his defensive ability."

Outfielder **Carl Everett** was the Yankees' top pick in 1990. Listed as the #4 prospect in the Sally League, Everett hit .271, slugged .335, and struck out 122 times last season.

Third baseman **Elston Hansen** was impressive in the rookie Gulf Coast League, hitting .327 with an on base percentage of .441. He may move to second.

Designated Malcontent: Too numerous to mention.

Park Characteristics: You probably know this stuff. With the left field area being reduced in several stages the park is now neutral in terms of favoring the hitter or the pitcher. It still favors a left-hander.

The Park Helps: Mel Hall

The Park Hurts: Scott Sanderson had a 4.66 ERA in Yankee Stadium, 3.12 on the road.

ORGANIZATIONAL REPORT CARD

Ownership:	F
Upper Management:	D
Field Management:	Unknown
Front-Line Talent:	D
Second-Line Talent:	D+
Minor League System:	D

TEAM LEADERS:

Batting Average: Steve Sax, .304

Last Ten Years (Season): Don Mattingly, 1986, .352
Last Ten Years (Total): Mattingly, .314

Doubles: Steve Sax, 38

Triples: A couple of guys had 4

Home Runs: Matt Nokes, 24

Last Ten Years (Season): Dave Winfield, 1982, 37
Last Ten Years (Total): Winfield, 192

Extra Base Hits: Sax, 50

RBI: Mel Hall, 80

Last Ten Years (Season): Don Mattingly, 1985, 145
Last Ten Years (Total): Mattingly, 827

Stolen Bases: Roberto Kelly, 32

Runs Created: Steve Sax, 92

Runs Created Per 27 Outs: Mel Hall, 5.3

Secondary Average:
Jesse Barfield, .352 as part-time player.
Kevin Maas, .346 as a regular.

Wins: Scott Sanderson, 16

Last Ten Years (Season): Ron Guidry, 1985, 22
Last Ten Years (Total): Guidry, 83

Winning Percentage: Scott Sanderson, 16-10 .615

Strikeouts: Sanderson, 130

Last Ten Years (Season): Dave Righetti, 1983, 169
Last Ten Years (Total): 1. Guidry, 856
2. Righetti, 838

ERA: Sanderson, 3.81

Saves: Steve Farr, 23

League Leaders: Can't find any. Sanderson was second in the league with a 4.48 to one strikeout to walk ratio, and John Habyan was second with 20 Holds. The Yankees as a team did lead the league in stolen base percentage (75.2%).

1991 SEASON

Background: I've written this several times, but the signing of free agents is a treadmill strategy. Any group of players over the age of 28 will decline. If you build your team around veteran players, your team will fight constant declines. Throughout the 1980s the Yankees fought a losing battle with the treadmill.

Outlook: There was no reason to think anything would be different in 1991.

Getaway: The Yankees were 7-16 by May 7.

High Point of the Season: The Yankees played well for a long period of time following the 7-16 start. On July 13, Johnson and Farr shut out the Angels to push the Yanks' record to 41-40, the first and only time all season they were above five hundred.

Low Point of the Season: Then reality set in, and the Yankees lost two-thirds of their games over the next two months.

Stretch Drive: And the Yankees continued to play badly all the way to the wire.

Most Exciting Game of the Season: September 23, Yankees used a Grand Slam homer from Matt Nokes and four RBIs from Roberto Kelly to battle back from a 7-1 deficit to beat Milwaukee.

Major Injuries: Roberto Kelly was out from July 6 through August 12 with a sprained right wrist. Jesse Barfield missed a month with a stress fracture in his right ankle.

Mike Witt (almost) missed the entire season due to a sore elbow. Pascual Perez missed the first half of the season with a stiff right shoulder.

Offense: Poor. The Yankees were average in terms of power and speed, but below average in both batting average and walks, and thus didn't have many big innings.

Defense: Poor. Nokes doesn't throw well, they still don't have a third baseman and nobody is a Gold Glove candidate.

Pitching: Poor.

Best Game by a Starting Pitcher: Scott Sanderson vs. the Mariners on May 3 (9 3 0 0 0 9 Game Score: 90)

Worst Game by a Starting Pitcher: There were two Game Scores of Six—Sanderson on July 31 against the Twins (1⅔ 3 8 8 8 1 0), and Dave Eiland on August 7 in Chicago (3 10 8 8 1 0)

Indicators for 1991 were: Significantly up (+12.2)

Number of regulars having good seasons by their own standards: Four (Sax, Nokes, Hall and Espinoza)

1991 Over-Achiever: Sax

1991 Under-Achiever: Mattingly

Infield: Poor. The Yankees got only 34 home runs out of their four infield slots, or 8.5 per slot, with an average of 54 RBI and a .264 average.

Outfield: Better than the infield. Yankee left fielders (Mel Hall, Roberto Kelly) hit 28 homers and drove in 98. Their center fielders (Kelly and Bernie Williams) hit only .246 but had some power and some speed. Their right fielders hit only .231 but did hit 22 home runs. The outfield defense also wasn't bad until they signed Tartabull.

Catching: Good. Nokes hit enough to justify his arm.

Starting Pitching: Horrible. Yankee starting pitchers had a 5.07 ERA for the season, and threw only three complete games, a major league record low.

Bullpen: Good, the strongest element of the team. Steve Farr, John Habyan and Steve Howe all pitched quite well, and Cadaret, Guetterman and Monteleone were all fairly good.

Percentage of offense created by:

Young Players: 38%
Players in Their Prime: 41%
Past Their Prime: 21%

Team Age:

Age of Non-Pitchers: 27.6
Age of Pitchers: 30.2
Overall Team Age: 28.71

In retrospect, the critical decisions were: The only real decisions of the summer were who to grab with the number one pick in the draft and when to fire Stump Merrill. There isn't anything you can "decide" which is going to make any difference when you don't have any talent to work with.

THAT AND THE OTHER

Hall of Fame Watch: Two current Yankees are viable Hall of Fame candidates, those being **Don Mattingly** and **Steve Sax. Mattingly** appeared two years ago to be a sure thing, but began to suffer back trouble in 1990, and played regularly last year but was pretty bad. I still suspect that he will wind up in Cooperstown. The Hall of Fame has historically been kind to three types of players which include Mattingly:

a) those who had brilliant phases within a longer career,
b) high-average hitters, and
c) those who play in New York.

Mattingly has had a career not unlike that of Jim Bottomley. Bottomley was a left-handed high-average hitter with some power, a great RBI man. Bottomley was a very good player from 1924 to 1929, and hung on from 1930 to 1937 as a so-so player. This chart compares Mattingly's record to this point to Bottomley's career totals:

	G	AB	Runs	Hits	2B	3B	HR	RBI	SB	Avg
Mattingly	1269	5003	719	1570	323	15	178	827	11	.314
Bottomley	1991	7471	1177	2313	465	151	219	1422	58	.310

There's a sidebar on Steve Sax's new contract; I'll talk about him then.

Chris Berman, Have You Considered:

Kevin (Critical) Maas
Jesse (Doesn't this pitching staff make you want to) Barfield
Steve Howe (many chances does he *get*, for Chrissakes)

Throwback: Mattingly

Trivia Time: Most managers have a favorite coach who serves as their right-hand man, who goes with them from job to job. Billy Martin had Art Fowler, Leo Durocher had Frank Shellenback, etc. Who was Joe McCarthy's right-hand man?

Attendance Trend: Sharply Downward. 1991 was the third straight year of decline, taking the Yankees from 2.63 million in 1988 to 1.86 million in 1991.

Players with a Chance for 3000 career hits:

Steve Sax, 42%

Best Fundamental Player: Don Mattingly

Worst Fundamental Player: Mel Hall

Best Defensive Player: Bernie Williams? Alvaro Espinoza? I'm not sure.

Worst Defensive Player: Danny Tartabull

Best Knowledge of the Strike Zone: Don Mattingly

Least Command of the Strike Zone: Hensley Meulens

Fastest Runner: Probably Bernie Williams

Slowest Runner: Probably Jesse Barfield. Barfield at 32 has become one of the slowest outfielders in the majors.

Best Baserunner: Pat Kelly

Most Likely to Still be Here in 2000: Hensley Meulens

Best Fastball: Tom Seaver

Best Breaking Pitch: Scott Sanderson

Best Control: Scott Sanderson

Oddest Collection of Abilities: Kevin Maas

Never Going to be As Good as the Organization Thinks He Is: Pat Kelly

Why is this man in the Major Leagues: Torey Lovullo

Gets Ahead of the Hitters Most Often: Steve Farr

Gets Ahead of the Hitters Least Often: Tim Leary

Best Local Sportswriter: Moss Klein or Allen Barra

Trivia Answer: Jimmy Burke, an old third baseman who had managed the two St. Louis teams years earlier. He was McCarthy's lieutenant from 1926 (in Chicago) until 1933, when his health forced him to retire. After that McCarthy's top aide was Art Fletcher.

The Most Knowledgeable Person About Local Baseball History Is: Gee, there's so many candidates. Ray Gonzalez, maybe.

Most-Similar Players:

to C Matt Nokes, Terry Steinbach
to 1B Don Mattingly, No one very similar
to 2B Steve Sax, Julio Franco
to 3B Pat Kelly, Geronimo Peña
to SS Alvaro Espinoza, Casey Candaele
to LF Mel Hall, Ivan Calderon
to CF Roberto Kelly, Mike Devereaux
to RF Jesse Barfield, Tom Brunansky
to DH Kevin Maas, Greg Vaughn

Most Fun to Watch: Jesse Barfield

Least Fun to Watch: Tim Leary

Managerial Type: Torey Lovullo

Among the All-Time Team Leaders: Don Mattingly is the only current Yankee who shows up on the all-time lists. He is eighth with 323 doubles, eleventh in home runs (178), and tenth with 827 RBI. His .314 batting average has him in fifth place, behind Ruth, Gehrig, Combs and DiMaggio.

Town Team:

C—Blimp Hayes
1B—Lou Gehrig
2B—Frankie Frisch
SS—Phil Rizzuto
3B—Joe Torre
LF—Hank Greenberg
CF—Sliding Billy Hamilton
RF—Joe Medwick
SP—Whitey Ford
SP—Sandy Koufax

Post-Season Transactions:

October 28, released Chuck Cary
October 29, hired Buck Showalter as manager
November 15, released Eric Plunk and Bob Geren
December 19, Steve Howe arrested in Wyoming for possession of cocaine
January 6, signed Danny Tartabull

I don't really understand why the Yankees released Eric Plunk. Plunk is 28, has always been erratic and was hit even harder last year than his 4.76 ERA would suggest, but on the other hand he had ERAs the three previous years of 3.00, 3.28 and 2.72, and even last year he struck out 103 men in 112 innings.

What Needs to Be Done For 1992: The Yankees need to start acquiring and developing *young* ballplayers. They're never going to win anything with a bunch of 32-year-old hitters unless those guys are supported by a core of young athletes.

Outlook for 1992: The Yankees are making some progress; they are *beginning* to get their world put back together. Bernie Williams and Pat Kelly didn't play particularly well last year, but they'll be better. Bam Bam was awful last year, but I think he'll have years when he isn't awful.

For the present, the Yankees are a dreadful team, a collection of 28- and 30-year-old guys who were supposed to be good and didn't quite make it. In any season, some players in that class will have good years—last year Sanderson, Nokes, Mel Hall and Steve Farr—but they won't do it consistently. Probably three of those four guys will be off significantly in 1992.

Danny Tartabull is a perfect Yankee signing; he'll fit right in with Pascual Perez and Tim Leary. This team's motto is "Take the Money and Run". Tartabull is an amazing hitter, but he's as bad in the outfield as he is good at bat, plus he's surly, a bad baserunner and gets hurt a lot. At $5 million a year, he's a perfect Yankee signee. Until they get at least two or three pitchers that they can count on to give them good years, it's almost unimaginable that they could win the division.

Index of Leading Indicators for 1992: Up very slightly (+3.3)

Positive Indicators: 1. Normal tendency of bad teams to improve.
2. Outstanding AAA team.

Negative Indicators: 1. Poor play late in season.

Due for a better season: Mattingly

Likely to have a worse season: Mel Hall

1992 Won-Lost Record will be: 74-88

STEVE SAX AND THE NEW CONTRACT

Steve Sax has an estimated 42% chance to get 3000 hits in his career. On a certain level this is a shocking claim. My friend Barry Rubinowitz, in discussing some similar player who appeared to be pulling within view of the summit, propounded a simple rule: nobody gets 3000 hits unless he's a great player. I couldn't come up with an exception, and the player, whoever he was, saw his chance fade from 40 to 0 within a couple of years.

Steve Sax is not the kind of player that we think of as being of historical magnitude. If he gets 3000 hits he will of course make the Hall of Fame, but if he doesn't get 3000 he'll draw little support. Less than twenty players in history have 3000 hits. Can Steve Sax crack company *that* stiff?

Maybe not, but he is certainly giving it a run. Sax has more hits than any other major league player of his age. By the age of 31 (he turned 32 in January) Sax had amassed 1,781 hits—almost 60% of the 3,000. He has 170 hits more than Lou Brock had at the same age, 160 less than Pete Rose.

Sax signed a new contract early last season, a four-year contract for a good salary. The contract was widely ripped by the press, which saw a flaw in giving a four-year contract to a 31-year-old player whose speed was a central skill.

I don't know how the contract will work out, of course, but I think there's a misleading inference or assumption here. Players who have speed as a central skill age exceptionally *well*, not poorly. The foundation logic, I think, is this:

1) as players age they lose their speed,
2) older players therefore have to depend on their *other* skills, their non-speed related skills, therefore
3) players who have speed as a central skill will not age well.

That may make sense, but it's not true. Let me give you a few names: Lou Brock, Bill Bruton, Luis Aparicio, Dave Lopes, Maury Wills, Joe Morgan, Willie Mays. Well, I don't want to imply a comparison between Steve Sax and Willie Mays. Mays lasted a long time for many reasons, not just because of his speed.

Look at players who run well as a group, and you'll see that they age very well. Think about speed on a ten-point scale, five average. Each position *requires* a certain degree of speed; you can't play center field unless your speed is at least a "6", let us say. You can play first base if you run "2", third base if you run "4", but a second baseman needs to run at least average, at least "5".

Now, if a guy runs a "7" to begin with, like Sax, then the loss in speed isn't fatal; at the age of 35 he'll still run a "5". But if a second baseman *doesn't* have speed as a central skill, what happens? Let's say he runs a "5" to begin with; by age 32 he'll run a "4", and then he's too slow to play the position, like Marty Barrett or Johnny Ray. Dave Cash. The only way he can stay in the game is to move to a position which doesn't require as much mobility, like first base or DH. A four-year contract to a 31-year-old player is a questionable risk for anyone except a superstar, and Sax isn't a superstar. But I *don't* believe that it's an especially bad risk for a player with speed.

Just as we went to press Steve Sax was traded to the White Sox for minor players, which in itself will hurt him if he's ever up for the Hall of Fame. The Yankees reportedly "felt that they had to get Steve Sax out of the infield to win."

I've written many times about the tendency of teams to blame their best players for their generalized shortcomings, and this is certainly a classic example of that syndrome. Sax *does* have his faults. I've never believed that Sax was as bad an infielder as the press believed, but the Yankees have been watching him for three years, and if *they* think he can't play second, I'll take their word for it.

So how about left field? Look at the team leaders last year. Sax led the league in hits, and extra base hits. The guys the Yankees need to get rid of are the guys who didn't.

THE BALTIMORE ORIOLES
• IN A BOX •

Won-Lost Record: 67-95 .414
Rank among 26 teams: 24th
Over Last Five Years: 351-457 .434
Rank over Five Years: 24th
In Last Ten Years: 784-833 .485
Rank over Ten Years: 21st

Best Player: Cal Ripken

Weak Spot: 1. Second Base
2. Lack of power in the outfield

Best Pitcher: Gregg Olson

Staff Weakness: No starting pitcher

The Orioles' biggest problem is the weakness of their starting rotation.

Best Bench Player: None really

Best Baseball Name: RIP kin

Best Young Player: Leo Gomez

Best Looking Player: Gomez

Ugliest Player: Paul Kilgus

Best Looking Player's Wife: Amy Worthington

Most Pleasant Surprise, 1991: Todd Frohwirth

Biggest Disappointment, 1991: Ben McDonald

Best Minor League Prospect: Arthur Rhodes

Who Is: Regarded as a young Vida Blue. For those of you who are too young to remember Vida Blue, Vida was a tremendous athlete when he was young, with a body like a front-rank NL quarterback, Elway or Kelly or Boomer or one of those. He was a black guy, left-handed, quick, strong, and could throw a high fastball by anybody. Rhodes pitched eight games in the majors last year after pitching very well at Hagerstown (AA).

Other Prospects: Probably the number two prospect is Ricky Gutierrez, a 21-year-old shortstop. Gutierrez was regarded as brilliant defensively but not too likely to hit until he got to Rochester (AAA), where he hit .306 in 49 games. He is a good percentage player—good strikeout to walk ratio (81 walks in 133 games last year), good stolen base percentage (15 for 16 last year.)

Park Characteristics:

The Orioles have a new park, Camden Yards. The park appears to favor a left-handed hitter, and of course if it favors a left-handed hitter then it will also favor a left-handed pitcher. It's 319 feet to left, 334 to right, and the deepest part of the fence is 410 feet, which is slightly to the left of center.

Our guess is that the Yards will favor a *hitter*, as opposed to a pitcher, but that's just a guess and nobody really knows. The foul territory is *very* small, smaller than any park built in many years, and that's an important factor in favor of the hitter. It has all kinds of quirks and spaces into which a ball can roll, so the number of doubles and triples hit may be high, and is almost certain to be higher than it was at Memorial Stadium, where the ball almost always bounces toward center.

The Park Will Help: A guess is that it might help Sam Horn. It doesn't seem likely that it will help the *team* right away, since the Oriole offense is essentially based around right-handed power hitters (Ripken, Milligan, Glenn Davis, Leo Gomez).

The Park Might Hurt: The right-handed power hitters, and the right-handed pitchers.

ORGANIZATIONAL REPORT CARD

Ownership:	B−
Upper Management:	B−
Field Management:	C+
Front-Line Talent:	D
Second-Line Talent:	B
Minor League System:	B−

TEAM LEADERS:

Batting Average: Cal Ripken, .323
Last Ten Years (Season): Ripken, 1991, .323
Last Ten Years (Total): Eddie Murray, .298

Doubles: Cal Ripken, 46

Triples: Mike Devereaux, 10

Home Runs: Cal Ripken, 34
Last Ten Years (Season): Ripken, 1991, 34
Last Ten Years (Total): Ripken, 259

Extra Base Hits: Cal Ripken, 85

RBI: Cal Ripken, 114
Last Ten Years (Season): Eddie Murray, 1985, 124
Last Ten Years (Total): Ripken, 942

Stolen Bases: Mike Devereaux, 16

Walks: Randy Milligan, 84

Runs Created: Cal Ripken, 134

Runs Created Per Game: Cal Ripken, 7.7

Secondary Average: Randy Milligan, .334

Milligan's .334 secondary average was way down from his 1990 figure of .486. Sam Horn had a secondary average of .397 as a part-time player.

Wins: Bob Milacki, 10
Last Ten Years (Season): Mike Boddicker, 1984, 20
Last Ten Years (Total): Boddicker, 79

Winning Percentage: Milacki, 10-9 .526

Strikeouts: Milacki, 108
Last Ten Years (Season): Mike Boddicker, 1986, 175
Last Ten Years (Total): Boddicker, 830

ERA: Milacki, 4.01

Saves: Gregg Olson, 31

League Leaders:
Ripken led the major leagues in extra base hits, with 85 (46 doubles, 5 triples, 34 homers). Ripken also led in total bases (368) and fielding percentage at shortstop (.986).

1991 SEASON

Background: From 1983 to 1988 the Orioles slipped away from the pennant race. From 98 wins and a World Championship in 1983, the Orioles slipped to 85 wins in 1984, then to 83, then to 73, to 67 and finally to 54. The overall strengths of the organization, on every level, were eroding.

In 1989 the Orioles won 87 games, and almost pulled out a pennant. In 1990 they relapsed, and so the Orioles opened 1991 hoping to find that the 1989 season wasn't a pure fluke, that they really were on the way back.

Outlook: On January 10, 1991, the Orioles acquired Glenn Davis in a trade. Davis, who had hit 30 homers a year regularly in the Astrodome, was looked upon as the cleanup hitter the Orioles had needed, and generated a degree of optimism about the 1991 season. Still, few experts picked the Orioles to win the division. They were generally picked third to fifth in the division. I picked them third.

Getaway: It quickly became apparent that these predictions were optimistic. Glenn Davis opened the season on the disabled list. The Orioles lost their first two, won two to get even and then began to lose in Texas, in Milwaukee, in Chicago, in California and in earnest.

Low Point of the Season: By May 27 they were 13-28, and any thoughts of having a competitive team in 1991 were quickly forgotten.

High Point of the Season: The Orioles played .500 ball for about two months from late May to late July. The high point of the season was a doubleheader sweep in Kansas City on June 23, 11-8 and 9-8, which gave them a record of 26-41.

Most Exciting Games of the Season: See article, "June 23"

Stretch Drive: The Orioles stayed about fifteen games under .500 until July 25, and then started losing again, although not as badly as they had early in the year.

Major Injuries: Glenn Davis missed the better part of the season with a "stretched spinal accessory nerve" in his neck. Davis' absence was devastating to the team in the early part of the year.

Dave Johnson was out for most of May and June with a strained groin.

Dwight Evans missed a month with a strained Achilles tendon in his left foot.

Ben McDonald spent 49 days on the disabled list due to a sore flexor muscle in his right elbow, and was never completely healthy.

Craig Worthington went on the disabled list with a hamstring, and lost his job to Leo Gomez.

Bill Ripken missed a month with a strained rib cage.

Offense: Offensive. The Oriole offense was one-dimensional, consisting almost entirely of right-handed power hitters. Their average was low and they were very slow.

Defense: Good. Mike Devereaux was a very pleasant surprise in center field. Ripken played dramatically better in the field than he had in recent years, as he did at bat. Leo Gomez at third was better than anybody thought. Chris Hoiles was better than the reputation that preceded him. The Orioles played well defensively.

Pitching: Indefensible. The Orioles' pitching staff was the worst in the major leagues.

Best Game by a Starting Pitcher: Bob Milacki had the top two, both 81 Game Scores, in Kansas City on June 22 (8 3 0 0 0 5), and against the Yankees on September 9 (9 5 0 0 1 5).

Worst Game by a Starting Pitcher: Jeff Ballard's start in Cleveland on June 26 was the worst effort by a starting pitcher in the major leagues in 1991. The line was 3 10 10 10 3 0, a game score of −4.

Indicators for 1991 were: Strongly Positive (+15.5)

Number of regulars having good seasons by their own standards: Three (Cal Ripken, Devereaux and Sam Horn)

1991 Over-Achiever: Chito Martinez

1991 Under-Achiever: Ben McDonald

Infield: Average or above average, even with a big gap at second base. The Orioles had an MVP shortstop, got 24 homers and good defense out of their third basemen (mostly Gomez) and are knee-deep in first basemen (Glenn Davis, Randy Milligan, David Segui, Sam Horn. Horn DHs because he's the worst defensive first baseman of the group.)

Outfield: Very weak. Devereaux was excellent in center, but they got neither power nor average nor defense out of the wings.

Catching: Fair.

Starting Pitching: Horrible, the worst in the major leagues. Early in the season, with Ben McDonald and Dave Johnson both hurt and Jeff Ballard being battered, the Orioles literally had *no* starting pitchers that they could feel good about. Bob Milacki, 10-9 with a 4.01 ERA, was their stop starter for the season, and their starting pitchers had an aggregate ERA of 5.29.

The starting pitching did improve late in the year. Mike Mussina, called up in August, was brilliant in twelve starts.

Bullpen: Good. Gregg Olson wasn't as good last year as he had been the previous two, but he wasn't bad, either, and he received strong support from Frohwirth, Jim Poole and Mike Flanagan.

Percentage of Offense Created by:

Young Players:	18%
Players in Their Prime:	74%
Veterans:	8%

Team Age

Age of Offense:	28.5
Age of Pitching Staff:	27.0
Overall Age:	27.87

In retrospect, the critical decisions were:

The critical decision of 1991 was the trade of Steve Finley and Pete Harnisch for Glenn Davis, a move which at this time can only be described as ill-fated.

THAT AND THE OTHER THING

Hall of Fame Watch: **Cal Ripken** is almost a certain Hall of Famer based on what he has already accomplished. No one else on the team will even be allowed to attend his induction ceremony.

Chris Berman, Have You Considered: Todd (Who Never Could) Frohwirth a damn

Throwback: Cal Ripken

Attendance Trend: Showing solid, even stunning growth in a down cycle for the team. In 1987, when the Orioles had exactly the same record as 1991 (67-95) they drew 1.84 million fans. Last year they drew 2.55 million, a franchise record. And that figure will go through the roof in 1992.

Players with a Chance for 3000 career hits:

Cal Ripken, 46%

Ripken has an estimated 3% chance to get 4000 hits in his career, as well as an estimated 24% chance to hit 500 home runs.

Record Watch: See article, "Smoke and Computers"

Probably Could Play Regularly For Another Team: Tito Bell

Best Fundamental Player: Cal Ripken

Worst Fundamental Player: Ben McDonald

Best Defensive Player: Second Base, Billy Ripken

Worst Defensive Player: Sam Horn

Best Knowledge of the Strike Zone: Randy Milligan

Least Command of the Strike Zone: Chito Martinez

Fastest Runner: Brady Anderson

Slowest Runner: Craig Worthington and Sam Horn

Horn may be the slowest player in the major leagues. Craig Worthington is almost as slow.

Best Baserunner: Brady Anderson

Most Likely to Still be Here in 2000: Cal Ripken

Best Fastball: Ben McDonald

Best Breaking Pitch: Gregg Olson

Best Control: Dave Johnson

Oddest Collection of Abilities: David Segui

Why is this man in the Major Leagues?: Jose Mesa

Gets Ahead of the Hitters Most Often: Mike Mussina

Gets Ahead of the Hitters Least Often: Mark Williamson

Best Local Sportswriter: Boswell, of course

The Most Knowledgeable People About Local Baseball History Are: Ted Patterson, John Steadman, Vince Bagli

Local Neanderthal Sportswriter: John Steadman

Most-Similar Players:

to C Chris Hoiles, Greg Myers
to 1B Randy Milligan, Dan Pasqua
to 2B Billy Ripken, Manuel Lee
to 3B Leo Gomez, Dean Palmer
to SS Cal Ripken, Ryne Sandberg
to LF Joe Orsulak, Billy Hatcher
to CF Mike Devereaux, Steve Finley
to RF Dwight Evans, Dave Parker

Most Fun to Watch: Ben McDonald

Least Fun to Watch: Craig Worthington

Managerial Type: Billy Ripken

Among the All-Time Team Leaders:

Cal Ripken is probably the second-greatest player (non-pitcher) in the history of the Orioles, behind Brooks Robinson. On the team leader lists he is behind Robinson and Eddie Murray in most things, but will pass Murray in most categories in two or three years.

Town Team:

C—Wilbert Robinson
1B—Jimmie Foxx
2B—Cupid Childs
SS—Cal Ripken
3B—Judy Johnson
LF—Harold Baines
CF—Al Kaline
RF—Babe Ruth
LHP—Lefty Grove
RHP—Eddie Rommell

Post-Season Transactions:

November 9, re-signed Glenn Davis for two years

December 7, re-signed Dwight Evans for one year

December 11, traded Bob Melvin to Kansas City in exchange for Storm Davis

December 19, signed Rick Sutcliffe to a one-year contract

What Needs to Be Done For 1992: The re-building of the pitching staff is the major job yet to be accomplished. The only pitchers sure to be in the rotation are Mussina, McDonald and Milacki, and those three were a combined 20-22 in 1991.

Outlook for 1992: There is a substantial distance to go before the Orioles are back in the race. They should be *better* because they're not as bad a team as their 67-95 record would indicate.

Index of Leading Indicators for 1992: Up 17.4

Positive Indicators: Six of the seven indicators for the Orioles are positive, all by small amounts but there is a significance in their consistency.

Negative Indicators: The one indicator which is down is that the Orioles of 1991 were not a young team.

Due for a better season: Glenn Davis

Likely to have a worse season: Cal Ripken

1992 Won-Lost Record will be: 79-83

SMOKE AND COMPUTERS

It was reported in *USA Today* on October 1 that "Research by the Orioles shows [Cal Ripken] can be the ninth player in history to hit 35 home runs and strike out less than 50 times in a season. That puts him in the company of Ted Williams." This is a masterpiece of creative bullshit, a simple two-sentence statement which manages to shave the truth six different ways (I will enumerate them in a minute) to reach a bogus conclusion. Let me point out to you what is wrong with this:

1) It begins by arbitrarily selecting two categories in which the player happens to have excelled, and putting them together as if they represented a test of excellence.

Of course there is a logic which puts home runs and strikeouts together—but then, there is a logic which puts home runs and *anything* together. Home runs and stolen bases? That's a category. Home runs and doubles? I've seen that one—Willie Stargell is the only player since World War II to have 40 doubles and 40 homers in a season. Home runs and RBI? Of course. Home runs and Batting Average? If you ignore logic and purpose, any two categories can be put together into a unique test of excellence.

2) It then treats Ripken as having *done* something which in reality he *hasn't* done; he merely had a chance to do it. Ripken had a *chance* to do this, but then he *didn't*. He hit 34 home runs, not 35.

3) When you read that Ripken would be the ninth person to do this, how many times do you think it's been done? You think it's been done eight times, right?

Wrong. It's been done fourteen times, but only by eight different players. Ted Williams did it four times, Gehrig three times, etc. Saying that Ripken would be the ninth *player* to do it is literally true but deceptive.

4) Then somebody made a mistake. The research found that this had been done fourteen times (by eight different players) *in the American League*, and I'm certain that is what was originally reported by the Orioles' media office. But somebody failed to report the critical words, "in the American League", and thus made a true statement into a false one. It's actually been done by *nineteen* different players, not eight, but it happens that eleven of the nineteen have been in the National League. It's been done a total of 34 times by the 19 players.

5) Having shaved the truth three times and nicked it once, the reporter then reaches the incredible conclusion that this puts Ripken in a class with Ted Williams! At it's best, this merely puts Ripken in a class with Williams in this one limited respect, ignoring all of Williams' other accomplishments.

What the reporter has done here is

a) ignore the fact that Ted Williams did this not once, but *four times*, and

b) assume that Ted Williams is representative of the class.

If Cal Ripken had hit 35 home runs with less than 50 strikeouts, that would put him in a class with Andy Pafko. That would put him in a class with Willard Marshall. That would put him in a class with the other guys who did this *once*—not with Ted Williams.

6) What is *most* wrong with this statistical cut-and-paste, however, is that the category is precisely defined so that Ripken appears to be *in the company of* a group of players who in reality have done as well as he has **or better.**

Look, if a player has hit 35 home runs and struck out 45 times, how do you find a list of comparable players? If you're doing it *honestly*, you look for guys who have 30-40 home runs with 40-50 strikeouts; then the player will be in the middle of both lists, and you'll have a group of hitters who have done something which is truly comparable.

But if you have *no* maximum, no upper boundary, and bottom boundaries which are right underneath Ripken, then everybody on both lists is *better* than he is *in both respects*. A player who might have hit 50 home runs and struck out 11 times would be included in the group—but a player who had 34 home runs or 51 strikeouts is not good enough, even though in reality his accomplishment is much more comparable to Ripken's. Anybody who is just a little bit worse than he is in either respect is eliminated, so that all of the players "in his group" are actually his superiors.

You can do this with any player, and find a way to group him "with" a group of players who in reality are all better than he is. Take the most ordinary player in the league—let's say Dante Bichette. Bichette isn't an ordinary player, he's a bad player, but you get the point. What you need to do is:

a) pick out his strengths, his *best* numbers, and ignore his weaknesses. Bichette had 15 home runs, 14 stolen bases and 12 outfield assists, which are his best numbers so we'll take those.

b) Set those as minimums or near-minimums—let's say, all players who are in double figures in home runs, stolen bases and outfield assists.

c) Identify all the players who have this peculiar combination of accomplishments, and

d) Treat the best players in that group as if they were typical of it.

The group you wind up with in this case is Dante Bichette, Kirby Puckett, Ruben Sierra, Mike Devereaux, Ken Griffey Jr., Joe Carter, Paul O'Neill, Darryl Strawberry, Rickey Henderson and Barry Bonds—in other words, Dante Bichette and a bunch of guys who are a hell of a lot better than he is.

I realize I'm ranting about this, but let me tell you why. I work in arbitration cases, on behalf of ballplayers. On every arbitration team there's always somebody who wants to do this kind of stuff. If you're doing an arbitration case for Dante Bichette, there's always somebody on your side who wants to draw up an exhibit showing all of the major league players who are in double figures in home runs, stolen bases and outfield assists, thereby putting Dante Bichette in a class with Kirby Puckett, Ruben Sierra, Ken Griffey Jr., Joe Carter, Darryl Strawberry and Barry Bonds. They figure this will impress an arbitrator, which it will if the arbitrator is a complete idiot. If the arbitrator has two brain cells firing, all you're going to accomplish is to blow your own credibility. If the team argues that Dante Bichette is in a class with Sammy Sosa and Mark Whiten and you argue that he's in a class with Barry Bonds and Kirby Puckett, who do you think is going to win?

You want me to put Pete O'Brien in a group of the best players in baseball? That's easy. Ken Caminiti? I'll guarantee you I can do it. Look, Cal Ripken is a great ballplayer—in fact, I might even argue that Cal Ripken is a better *all-around* player than Ted Williams was, although he's not in Williams' zip code as a hitter.

It is now obvious that Cal Ripken *will* break Lou Gehrig's consecutive-game streak unless he suffers a very serious injury. His superb 1991 season eliminates almost entirely the chance that he could be benched before reaching that level.

For several years I have thought that the public and media generally underestimated Ripken's chance of breaking the record. No more; if anything, the media now has decided that the record is a foregone conclusion, when in my opinion it is still somewhat more likely than not that Ripken will suffer the injury that will make it impossible for him to continue. I estimate that his chance of completing the drive now is between 40 and 45%.

Ripken may play as many games in his career and go to bat as many times as anyone ever has. The record for career games played is 3,562, by Pete Rose. Ripken has played about 200 more games than Rose had at the same age (both celebrate birthdays in-season.) Comparing age-for-age, it is difficult for Rose to gain ground on Ripken, whom he is "behind", unless he plays more than 162 games in a season.

So it becomes a question of how long Ripken will play. Rose played until age 45, which will be very difficult for Ripken to approach, much less match. On the other hand, one should not forget this:

a) that the most important factor in staying in the game to an advanced age is the quality of play, and

b) Ripken is a better player than Rose was.

So he's got a chance to play more games than anybody ever has—and by so doing, to break any number of records.

But Ripken's 1991 ratio of home runs to strikeouts is not historically remarkable. His ratio of home runs to strikeouts is not among the 150 best of all time. Even among players with 30 or more home runs, it ranks only 74th on the all-time list. Don Mattingly has done better three times (35 homers, 41 strikeouts in 1985, 31/35 in 1986 and 30/38 in 1987).

Cal Ripken is a great ballplayer, but *it doesn't help* to make these kinds of arguments. People instinctively know that it's bullshit, and that perpetuates suspicion about statistical argument. You know the things people say—there are lies, damn lies and statistics, etc. Our options are to strip the numbers down into TV-screen blurbs, or to build them up into logical arguments. When we make these kinds of arguments, intentionally deceptive, we put up barriers which make it harder to involve the statistics in a logical evaluation of the player's contribution to his team.

BASEBALL FROM THE INSIDE AND OUTSIDE

Eddie Epstein
Director of Research and Statistics
Baltimore Orioles

I almost went back to the outside. As hard as it may be for some of you to imagine, I almost left baseball during the summer of 1991. I decided to stay, but sometimes I am still not sure which perspective I hold, outside or inside.

I want to make it clear that I did not play professional baseball or college baseball or whatever, which is why I usually consider myself (and am considered by most people) an outsider. My background is in economics; I have a Master's Degree in Economics. My academic experience involved a lot of training in statistical modeling (formulating statistical models to explain/predict various phenomena), apart from the pizza and Strat-O-Matic baseball.

Let me explain my job. I am not a statistician in the strictest sense in that I do not really compile statistics, except for maintaining day-by-day performance logs for every player in the Orioles' organization. (Actually, that task requires a hell of a lot of compilation, but you get my point. I do not compile a player's basic stat line or how each player hits with runners in scoring position.) I generate statistical analyses that are used in two primary contexts. They are the evaluation of professional talent and the negotiation of major league player contracts. (I also help our manager in preparing for upcoming series, but that does not comprise a large part of my workload.)

Evaluating talent sort of makes me a scout, but I "scout" with the numbers instead of with my eyes. This often puts me in conflict with traditional baseball people and conventional baseball wisdom. (I have become convinced that the latter phrase is a contradiction in terms.) Many people in baseball and even some in our organization do not believe that systematic analysis of baseball statistics has any real place in the evaluation of talent. Actually, some of them don't believe that the analysis of baseball statistics has any real place in baseball, period, but that's another story. For thousands of years people thought that the earth was flat and they were wrong, too.

In any event, I evaluate performance of professional players in a manner probably similar to how a stock analyst evaluates stocks. I attempt to measure player performance in a more thorough way than the "traditional" statistics and, using certain "indicator" numbers, attempt to predict how players will perform in the future. For example, at the end of each minor league season I create databases with every position player and pitcher who played in a full-season minor league. I then calculate statistics for each player, including some I have invented like the "Epstein Average." I adjust these statistics for league and ballpark. I will then print various rankings of players, for example, the best offensive performances at Class AA for that season. In 1990, Jeff Bagwell had the 2nd best season at Class AA (behind some guy named Frank Thomas) and his exceptional production indicated that he had the ability to be an outstanding offensive player at the big league level. However, when I begin to rate prospects I do not rely solely on performance. The context of a player's performance, even apart from the contexts of league and ballpark, must be considered in this type of evaluation. For example, a player's age and experience relative to his classification (e.g. Class AA) are important indicators of a player's ability. Getting back to Jeff Bagwell, 1990 was his first full professional season and he played that year at the age of 22, certainly not "too experienced" or "too old" to be at AA. These factors, combined with his outstanding season when adjusted for league and ballpark, gave strong indication that he would likely be an offensive force in the major leagues. All of these factors applied to Frank Thomas, of course. By the way, the "Epstein Average" is a thorough evaluation of a player's rate of offensive production, including batting average, power, walks, stolen bases, etc., which is expressed along the same scale as a batting average so it can be understood by more people. In 1991, the American League had a batting average of .260. The league Epstein Average (or EPS) was .257. Frank Thomas led the majors in 1991, as he led the minors in 1990, in EPS at .355.

You might be asking how this information is used by the Orioles. Not enough, I would say. Just kidding. (Well, maybe half-kidding.) If we are talking about a trade with a team, someone (usually Roland Hemond) will probably ask me who my "best" prospects are in that organization. I will go back to my lists of the last two or three seasons, see which players have done well in my rankings and then produce my prospect list. How have "my players" done? I can say that I have been right about players more often than I have been wrong.

I am also asked to evaluate specific trades or specific players. It is hardly unusual for my analysis to run contrary to what "traditionalists" say. Once again, I'll stack my track record against anyone else's. I am evaluating ***performance,*** not **ability.** The two are related, but not perfectly. When I first started working for the Orioles, I sometimes had the impression that I was working for a mechanic in a hardware shop because I heard the word "tools" used so often. The word "tools" is usually a baseball person's favorite word. It means the collection of a player's physical talents. What I measure is how a player performs on the field during games, because performance is what professional sports are about. Great "tools" and lousy performance is a lousy player.

Let me digress. One would think that major league clubs would evaluate their evaluators. That is, that clubs would keep track of which scouts, coaches, etc. have a good record in evaluating talent. Unfortunately, that is not so. Very often, a person's input is based strictly on reputation and perception and not on his actual track record. **That usually happens because no one is keeping tabs on his record in evaluation.** It seems obvious to me that one would want to use a person's track record, even if it is a compilation of subjective judgments, in assessing a person's performance. It is amazing how that is not really done too often in baseball, **EVEN WHEN ASSESSING PLAYERS.**

Anyway, I can say that I am consulted on virtually every major league player transaction. A lot of people would like to be in that position so I suppose I shouldn't make it sound like I am complaining too much. Actually, the evaluation of professional talent is a lot of fun. I have great freedom to spend time looking at and analyzing data. I can suggest trades and player moves and suggest them to the top baseball people in the organization.

The other major part of the job is not usually as enjoyable. Negotiating major league player contracts can be very frustrating. As of now, I do very little of the actual negotiation. That is handled by Roland Hemond and Lon Babby (our general counsel) for the arbitration players and by Doug Melvin, Frank Robinson, and Lon for the players not yet eligible for arbitration. My task is to provide statistical support for the negotiations. If it looks like an arbitration hearing is possible, then I prepare virtually all of the club exhibits for the arbitration.

In baseball, salaries are determined on the basis of comparability. An agent will argue that a player is comparable to players A, B, and C while the club may argue that the player is comparable to C, but not to A and B, and is also comparable to players D and

E, who have lower salaries than players A and B. A player's salary is normally a fairly predictable function of his service time and his statistics. Unfortunately for me, the club cannot use my original statistics ("those guns" as Bill once described them in a piece about salary negotiation and arbitration). That is one reason why the salary negotiation process can be frustrating for me. The statistics that are still in the mainstream (like batting average, home runs, and RBI—I call those three "The Unholy Trinity") are often inadequate in describing a player's contribution to his team.

The contract negotiation season seems to get longer every year. While some work is done during the season in keeping track of our players relative to other players in their service class, the main work begins during the World Series. I am responsible for preliminary analyses and salary projections for our players. As negotiations begin, I have to keep Roland, Doug, Frank, and Lon "armed" with information to use during actual negotiations. This information consists of many things, but at the core is the performance of a given player to others in his service class and to the class one year ahead. The 1991 salary of a player one year ahead of our player has relevance to the 1992 salary of our player. Obviously, I will not spend time comparing an outfielder to a pitcher, but all salaries in a given service class are relevant in that they establish "a market" of salaries.

How would I summarize the differences between the "inside" and "outside" of baseball? On the inside, what typically counts are opinions. A lot of baseball people don't believe that any right or wrong exists about the game. They think it's all opinion.

From the outside, it is obvious that some things just "are." (Facts do not cease to exist because they are ignored."—Huxley) Bill once wrote a piece *(1984 Baseball Abstract)* about an outsider's view of baseball in which he compared baseball people (players, executives, etc.) to men in a forest. For me, the best passage went like this: "But perspective can be gained only when details are lost. A sense of the size of everything and the relationships between everything—this can never be put together from details. For the most essential fact of a forest is this: The forest itself is immensely larger than anything inside of it. That is why, of course, you can't see the forest for the trees; each detail, in proportion to its size and your proximity to it, obscures a thousand or a million other details." This is not a knock at Sparky Anderson, for example, but just because he's been in the game for almost forty years doesn't mean he knows what the correlation coefficient is between runs scored and on-base percentage, or how many teams which led their league in offense (runs scored) have won division titles or pennants compared to the number which have won titles leading in defense (runs allowed). Yet, these facts have great relevance in formulating policies for major league teams. You probably don't ask a pilot to fix a jetliner.

I hope you've enjoyed this. I have enjoyed writing it. Thanks, Bill.

JUNE 23

Friday night's game was rained out, and so a doubleheader was scheduled for Sunday. In the first game Kansas City took a 5-0 lead. When Baltimore cut it to 5-4, Kansas City put it back to 8-4. Chris Hoiles hit a grand slam home run in the ninth to tie it, and the Orioles added three in the tenth for a win. The Orioles had eight hits and seven runs off of KC relief ace Jeff Montgomery, who threw 63 pitches in the game.

In the second game Baltimore took a 1-0 lead; KC tied it at one in the bottom of the inning. Baltimore took a 3-1 lead, but Kansas City tied it up again in the bottom of the inning, the sixth. Baltimore scored two in the seventh and three in the eighth to mount an 8-3 lead, but Kansas City scored five in the bottom of the ninth to send it back to extra innings. Baltimore scored a run in the tenth to win it.

The doubleheader took more than eight hours of playing time. It was a shaping moment in the careers of at least two men. Chris Hoiles opened the day hitting below .200 and not playing much. He entered the first game in the eighth inning as a pinch runner for Sam Horn, hit the grand slam home run in the ninth and got to catch the second game, in which he added two singles and a double. His playing time increased sharply after that, and he opens the 1992 season as the Orioles' number one catcher.

On the other hand, Royals' pitching coach Pat Dobson was at this time running the pitching staff. Hal McRae was new in his job, and didn't claim to know much about pitching, so he was letting Dobson run the staff. McRae lost confidence in Dobson after this devastating doubleheader, and Dobson resigned before the season was over.

MIKE FLANAGAN

JACK ETKIN

A delayed flight, a drowsy arrival at a hotel near dawn, a bus bogged down in traffic on the way to the ballpark or any scheduling mishap could trigger the remark that became a standing joke among the Baltimore Orioles. Mike Flanagan, listening to the inevitable complaining, would chime in: "Six or seven more years of this shit, and I'm out of here."

His derisive tone wasn't serious, not after the gratitude Flanagan felt last season when at 39 he savored baseball's equivalent of the afterlife. Flanagan's return to Baltimore came after a spring training when he arrived as a non-roster player with no promises. In his 15th season in the big leagues, Flanagan made a smooth transition from starting to a relief role. "I've had a lot of dreams answered this year," he said.

That was six weeks before another wish came true for Flanagan on the last day of the season. He is the Orioles' lone link to their past glory and added a fitting nostalgic tug to their final game at Memorial Stadium. With one out in the top of the ninth inning, Flanagan came on and struck out the two Detroit batters he faced just before the climax to the Orioles' weekend of turn-back-the-clock festivities.

In his 62 previous relief appearances, Flanagan ran from the bullpen to the mound. On this Sunday afternoon, he walked slowly through the opening in the left-field fence and kept that same pace, trying to keep his composure while summoning up memories. "I felt like I was coming in for the generations that went before," Flanagan said. "I so much wanted to do well for them, even more so than myself. I wanted to make that last walk for all the other starters and I guess all the warriors of the past, and it was going to be the last walk in from there. I'd done it so many times as a starter. Plus it was more of a relaxing thing for me, I guess, too because I was feeling a tremendous weight on me going in."

With good reason. The Tigers scored four runs in the top of the first and were ahead 7-1 after five innings. The only suspense for 50,700, the Orioles' largest crowd of the season, was when Flanagan would appear. Their "We Want Mike" chant arose in the eighth inning. "It just kept getting louder," Flanagan said, "and I found myself almost wanting to hide in the security of the bullpen."

There are diamond narcissists who strut and posture and can play to their audience with, say, a home run trot that would have to be timed with a sundial or a torrent of fist-pumping after a vital strikeout. Not Flanagan. Finding himself "so much more than the game, that's never been my way."

Flanagan knows what there is to know about pitching in big games. He can remember Detroit in the twilight of the 1987 season when he was pitching for Toronto. After 11 shutout innings against Jack Morris, Flanagan left a scoreless game, the 161st of the season. A victory would have clinched a tie for the division title. Toronto fell 3-2 in 12 innings and lost the final game and the division crown to the Tigers the following day.

Flanagan can recall the ballyhoo surrounding three World Series starts, even the live-wire anticipation of opening the 1979 Series for the Orioles; Flanagan pitched a complete game and beat Pittsburgh 5-4. Now here he was closing out the Orioles' dreary 1991 campaign, one they had mistakenly bannered "A Season to Remember" in their promotions, taking the mound with a feeling of magnitude that approached and in some ways surpassed anything he had ever experienced.

"Even in a World Series, you felt like a unit when you walked out there as a starter," Flanagan said. "This was one of the few times I've ever really felt that the focus was on me and what I was going to do. That was unsettling, nerve-wracking."

The multitudes' adulation warmed to "Flan-eee, Flan-eee," as Flanagan finally made his way across the field where he had first appeared in 1975. Thirteen pitches later, Flanagan walked past the third base line and entered the Orioles' dugout after striking out Dave Bergman and Travis Fryman. Flanagan is not given to curtain calls, but this time he responded to the fans' urging. As he emerged from the dugout, his black and orange Orioles jacket was draped over his pitching arm, more out of habit than necessity. "I don't know why I had it on my left shoulder," Flanagan said, "because I was obviously not going to go back out again unless we scored six runs." What followed was a scene from central casting, and the Orioles captured it on a video they made of the weekend's events. Flanagan waved his Orioles cap, starting with a nod toward the screen behind home plate and working his way to all four corners of the stadium where the Orioles will never again play.

The final gesture was to left field where Orioles bullpen coach Elrod Hendricks was standing at the opening of the fence. "I felt he helped me so much this year and all through the years," Flanagan said. "He was standing at the fence waving his hat. That's kind of where I ended. It was kind of like a last salute. Again, I didn't feel that was for me but a final salute to the stadium."

Nearly eight months earlier, spring training was approaching, and Flanagan wasn't thinking about curtain calls. Not after being yanked off stage in 1990 and seeing his career come to an apparent end. Flanagan rose from those depths to stir memories at the start of last season.

On Opening Day, he came on in the top of the ninth and pitched a scoreless inning in the Orioles' 9-1 loss to Chicago. The remnants of a Memorial Stadium crowd of 50,213 gave Flanagan a standing ovation when he was introduced, another when he entered the game in the ninth and yet another when he finished the inning.

After the game, Flanagan quipped, "I got a bigger ovation than Dick Cheney, and he had a better spring than I did." Secretary of Defense Cheney, basking in the afterglow of victory following the Persian Gulf War, was at Memorial Stadium that afternoon.

The following day, Flanagan talked about his return with Mike Boddicker, a former Orioles teammate pitching for Kansas City, and told Boddicker: "I could quit tomorrow, and it would all have been worth it."

Flanagan has known the exhilaration of playing with a pennant winner in 1979 and the bigger thrill of being on a World Series champion in 1983. He won the American League Cy Young Award in 1979 and as of Opening Day had 139 victories as an Oriole, fourth in club history behind Jim Palmer, 268; Doug McNally, 181, and Mike Cuellar, 143. These heights and this Orioles longevity notwithstanding, Flanagan didn't think his cameo appearance in a blowout would command such a response, and the three standing ovations stunned him.

"I didn't expect it, and I didn't know what the reaction would be," Flanagan said. "I thought I'd just slide out there. It was to a point where I didn't know how to describe it."

Hendricks, the Orioles' bullpen coach since 1978, had a theory about this emotional outpouring. For all but a trace of Flanagan's stay in Baltimore, Hendricks has been with the Orioles. He left when they traded him to the New York Yankees on June 15, 1976, in the nine-player trade that brought Baltimore pitcher Scott McGregor and catcher Rick Dempsey, and returned after the 1977 season. For nearly all of Flanagan's 328 starts with the Orioles, it was Hendricks who warmed him up.

On August 31, 1987, hours before the deadline when post-season rosters had to be finalized, the Orioles, seeking youth, traded Flanagan, then 35, to Toronto, a team that needed a left-hander for the stretch drive. In return for Flanagan, the Orioles received pitchers Jose Mesa and Oswald Peraza, unknowns in Baltimore except to those with an intimate working of the Blue Jays' farm system or devotees of winter ball in the Dominican Republic and Venezuela. Flanagan was in his Orioles uniform when the trade was completed. He changed and left quickly on a private jet the Blue Jays chartered to bring him from Baltimore to Toronto before the midnight deadline. Since Oriole fans never bid Flanagan farewell, they relished his rather unexpected return on Opening Day.

"Elrod said, 'This was kind of their way of thanking you for all that time. They never had a chance to thank you,' " Flanagan said. "I looked at it in those terms, and I felt so lucky in that I played with a lot of good players who may be retired and never came back or never came back and got to play. To come back and be in an Oriole uniform and to get that [reception], that was just special."

Flanagan's triumphant return to Baltimore had its beginnings in labor strife. The owners' lockout shortened spring training in 1990 and handicapped Flanagan. "I never really got going," he said. "I don't think it hurt the 20-year-olds, but it hurt me." He won his first two starts but then was battered in his next three, going 0-2 with an 8.71 ERA.

Jimmy Key and John Cerutti, two lefthanders younger than Flanagan, were also struggling. But when the Blue Jays decided to add righthander Steve Cummings to balance their staff, Flanagan was the logical choice to leave. Toronto released him May 8, 1990. "Initially I was in shock," Flanagan said. "I don't thin[k] anybody's ever prepared for it. It was such a bizarre beginnin[g] with the lockout. I had about five innings in spring training. [I] could tell I wasn't throwing the ball like I could or had. You don['t] know if you've lost it and that's that. So I was a little confuse[d] at times too because nothing hurt, but yet I didn't feel like I wa[s] throwing the ball good."

Flanagan returned to his Timonium, Md., home and afte[r] clearing waivers, calls began coming in from other clubs. Other[s] perhaps thought he could still pitch. Flanagan wasn't sure. H[e] decided to visit Arthur Pappas, the team physician of the Bosto[n] Red Sox whose surgical deeds "saved my career on a couple o[f] occasions." Flanagan expected Pappas to explain that the finit[e] number of pitches in his arm had been used up, and that, indeed[,] the end had arrived.

Pappas diagnosed a weakness—but no tears—in a shoulde[r] muscle in the rotator cuff group and had a different message. "H[e] said, 'I don't know what you want me to tell you,' " Flanaga[n] said. " 'Your arm is no worse than it was 10 years ago.' I said[,] 'How bad was it 10 years ago?'

"He said, 'With a reasonable amount of therapy I don't se[e] why you can't go back and throw like you threw years ago. Yo[u] really haven't done any more damage.' "

Flanagan had endured rehabilitation after injuries to a knee[,] Achilles tendon and shoulder. Having heard Pappas' assessment[,] Flanagan had to decide if he had "the fire in the belly" to tak[e] another slow journey down the comeback trail. "You have to sa[y] this is a long process, progress is minuscule at first," Flanaga[n] said. "It took me a long time to get in that mode."

Throughout May, June and July, Flanagan became an avid fl[y] fisherman and wasn't pondering a comeback. That sport require[s] a motion similar to pitching, and after a few hours, Flanaga[n] found his arm would tire and he wasn't able to hold it as high[.] "So the thing was if I'm going to be a fly fisherman then I hav[e] to start the rehabilitation," he said. "That was the spark to get m[e] back into therapy, not so much to be a pitcher again but to hav[e] two equal arms."

In mid-August, Flanagan began a therapy program at Chil[-]dren's Hospital in Baltimore. Throwing was part of the program[,] along with filming and biomechanical analysis. "You start gettin[g] involved in it again," Flanagan said, not referring to proper fl[y] fishing technique.

A January ritual at Memorial Stadium drew Flanagan in a littl[e] deeper. On the first Monday after New Year's Day, pitchers, no[t] all of whom are in the Orioles' organization, begin working ou[t] there beneath the stands. Hendricks invited Flanagan to join th[e] group, just as he had for the 15 previous winters, telling him tha[t] was the only way Flanagan would really find out how his arm felt

Flanagan accepted, albeit with misgivings about just what he was doing. No team had expressed an interest in him, so Flanagan knew any invitation to spring training would carry no guarantees. Furthermore, he had auditioned for ESPN "and thought that maybe it was time to start another career."

The winter throwing takes place beneath the right field stands. Since the Orioles clubhouse is on the third-base side of Memorial Stadium, Flanagan would dress, walk down the runway to the dugout he inhabited for so many years and step onto the familiar field. "You cut across from that dugout, across the field to the other side," Flanagan said. "It's kind of like going out towards the mound, and the feelings come back of going out there for one more battle."

In the winter stillness, freeze frames from the past came to mind as Flanagan glanced around the empty stadium. Along with the images came familiar but faint sounds. The wind and cold of January toned down Earl Weaver's shrieking and muffled the cheering from the crowd. "Just cutting across was like you could hear the voices of the past there or look into the corner and remember a play," Flanagan said. "There's not too many areas of that park where something doesn't flash, and cutting across, they all kind of come back in a rush."

Flanagan kept throwing throughout January and waiting for the phone call that would direct his future. "My arm feels terrific. No pain," he said. "Elrod, who had seen me throw for years, changed my mechanics. He said, 'Your arm's lower than it was when you were here.' All of a sudden the ball started to be alive again. They call it 'easy hard' where you're not trying to throw the ball hard, but it jumps."

There were other definite signs of progress. In the inevitable comparison with pitchers from the Orioles and other organizations, Flanagan, whose fastball is below major league average, saw he was throwing as hard as some. A more favorable gauge: his control was better than most. But the question of where all this was leading began to weigh on Flanagan.

"I remember one Friday I came in, and there were a lot of guys in front of me to throw," he said, "which meant I had to wait maybe an hour. I was going, 'Geez, what am I doing this for?' I was thinking about not getting changed and just going back home. Elrod came down and said, 'How come you're not going to throw?'

"I said, 'I don't know why I'm doing it. I don't have any offers. I don't know if I want to go. If ESPN calls tomorrow or something, I'm going to take it.' He said, 'Keep throwing. Something good's going to happen.' I kept throwing. Now we're past the first of February. It's about a week to go before camp opens."

ESPN ended up hiring Jerry Reuss to fill a position on its West Coast announcing team. And the Orioles offered Flanagan a spring training tryout that he accepted. "There's nothing going on anywhere else," Flanagan reasoned. "Six weeks in Florida can't be so bad. When I get back, it's opening of trout season. I thought when I left, if I make it, then I'm in my bed half the time. And if I don't, I'm in my bed the whole time. So how bad can this be?"

When the Orioles' pitchers gathered in Sarasota, Fla., a comeback more celebrated than Flanagan's officially began. Jim Palmer, 45 and enshrined in the Hall of Fame, had ended his career with the Orioles in 1984. He had designs on returning. Hitters made him think otherwise soon after the exhibition games began. Palmer's quest, however fanciful, aided Flanagan when he showed up in Florida.

"What it helped was the pre-exhibition schedule, that two weeks leading up to the games," Flanagan said. "It stopped me from having to predict what I was going to do. It got me through that period where I could just go out and throw and do my running and I didn't have to say, 'Well, I hope I win 10 games,' or 'I hope I'm a starter,' or 'I hope I'm a reliever.'

"It just got me through that period to when the games came, the results answered those questions."

Besides being analytical, Flanagan has one of the drier clubhouse wits. When he joined the Blue Jays, he took Phil Niekro's spot on the roster. Tim Kurkjian, who covered the Orioles for the *Baltimore Sun* but now works for *Sports Illustrated*, was walking along a Toronto street when Flanagan, accompanied by Boddicker, pulled up and offered him a ride in the rental car provided by the Blue Jays. "This was Phil Niekro's car," Flanagan said. "I found his teeth in the glove compartment."

Last season, Kurkjian called Flanagan after the Orioles' Sam Horn became the first non-pitcher to strike out six straight times in one game. Horn's ignominy came July 17 in a 15-inning game at Kansas City and gave him a share of the one-game record for consecutive strikeouts with Carl Wellman, a pitcher for the St. Louis Browns in 1913. "Three strikeouts is a hat trick," Flanagan said, "four is a sombrero, five is a golden sombrero and six is now called a Horn. Seven would have been a Horn of Plenty. When you make history, you've got to put your name on it."

Flanagan's history had been as a starter until last season. He had made just 17 relief appearances. One of those came in 1975, when he made his big-league debut with the Orioles on September 5, ten came in 1976 and three were in 1977, his first full season with the Orioles.

Last year, Flanagan appeared in 64 games, 63 of them in relief. While his record was 2-7—on a sixth place team that finished 67-95—his ERA was 2.38. Of his 98⅓ innings, 94⅓ came in relief, the fourth highest total in the American League behind Duane Ward of Toronto, 107⅓; teammate Todd Frohwirth, 96⅓; and Detroit's Paul Gibson, 96.

Flanagan and Frohwirth, a righthander, were the set-up tandem the Orioles used to get to closer Gregg Olson. Flanagan allowed just 84 hits and held lefthanders to an average of .181 (23 for 127), the lowest in the league for pitchers who had faced at least 125 lefthanded batters. He stranded 35 of the 47 runners he inherited.

"The biggest adjustment is facing maybe a Harold Baines three nights in a row whereas as a starter, I'd face him three at bats one night and not see him for three months," Flanagan said. "You face him three different days with the game relatively on the line, 'Do I change? Do I pitch the same pattern?' That part of the game has been an adjustment to getting guys out on three different days with the tying run on base.

"[As a starter] two of those at-bats could come with no one on base or him leading off an inning. If you're up a few runs, you say, 'I'll pitch him away, and if he gets a single to left, big deal.' "

Nothing crucial was hanging in the balance when Flanagan made his slow walk from the bullpen on the final day of the season. A news bulletin accompanied Flanagan; the Orioles used their DiamondVision screen to announce that Flanagan had agreed to a contract for 1992 that gives the Orioles an option for 1993.

"When the game had started, I hadn't agreed to terms yet," Flanagan said. He had given Bob Teaff, his agent, the authority to finalize the deal during the game. Flanagan is guaranteed $600,000 this season with a chance to earn more through incentives. Every game he starts is worth two points; every relief appearance, one. Thirty points will bring Flanagan $50,000, and he'll receive that same amount when he piles up 36 points, 42, 47, 54 and 60, meaning he can earn $300,000 in incentives.

If they wish, the Orioles can enter into the same deal in 1993. Flanagan didn't turn around to glance at the DiamondVision and didn't learn he was signed until after the game. He was thinking of the past and more concerned with the moment, namely getting Bergman and Fryman out, than anything in the future. "With Bergman there was a 2-2 pitch that I thought was a strike," Flanagan said. Home plate umpire Tim Welke called it a ball. "I thought to myself, 'God, if you don't get one today, you'll never get one,' " Flanagan said. "So I'll never ever complain for a pitch."

Flanagan came back with a curveball that Bergman missed. "The place kind of erupted again," Flanagan said, "and I had to actually step back off the mound for a while to regroup." He fell behind Fryman 2-0 but threw another full-count curveball that Fryman missed by so wide a margin he could have been swinging a cricket bat and not have made contact.

After his emotional curtain call, Flanagan went up the runway to the Orioles' clubhouse. Lined up were Brooks Robinson, Frank Robinson, Jim Palmer, Lee May, Rich Dauer, Bobby Grich, Doug DeCinces, Tippy Martinez, Dennis Martinez—in all 78 participants in the post-game ceremony. "These people hadn't even seen what happened," Flanagan said. "They said, 'How'd it go?' I was under the impression they had seen it, but they'd just heard the crowd. I said, 'I got through it.' "

Other than Flanagan, Cal Ripken Jr., is the only current Oriole to play on Baltimore's 1983 world champions, managed by Joe Altobelli. Earl Weaver again took the Baltimore reins in June 1986 and kept them through 1987, retiring for good after the Orioles tumbled to last. By current standards, the 73 games they won that year represent progress.

By Weaver's lofty norm, enough was enough. He managed the Orioles from the midpoint of the 1968 season through 1982. Under Weaver, the Orioles won six division titles, four pennants and one World Series. The only time they finished as low as fourth, they still won 90 games in 1978.

The Orioles have had one winning season since 1985. In the intervening six years, they have plummeted to 424-546 (.437) and set a major league record by starting the 1988 season with 21 consecutive losses on their way to a club record with 107 defeats.

To younger Orioles, the days of Weaver, the days when the Orioles were always in contention and frequent participants in the post-season are relics uncovered on an archaeological dig. "When they talk about '83 or '79, there're not many people in the clubhouse that were here," Flanagan said. "So instead of asking people or having the stories embellished, I was there. I only embellish them a little bit."

There are plenty of stories about Weaver. He smoked Raleigh cigarettes, which came with a coupon that could be saved and exchanged for merchandise. Eyeing his pack of Raleighs on his desk one day, Weaver pointed to the coupon and said, "That's how I got Al Bumbry."

Weaver's style wasn't to saunter about the clubhouse, making small talk with his players just to ensure a rapport existed. He wasn't one to praise his players. The games were supposed to be won, not lost. Every night was a battle. Under Weaver, the Orioles won a lot of battles. When the defeats were particularly difficult, Weaver had to be approached like a mine field.

After a bitter loss in Kansas City when Amos Otis lined the winning hit off Don Stanhouse in the ninth inning, Weaver sat behind his desk, white hair tousled, and attacked an ear of corn with maniacal zeal. Every few bites, he looked up and said, "Fuckin' Otis." Nothing more. He did this several times before launching into a tirade on Stanhouse's misplaced pitch.

On the final weekend of last season, Flanagan recalled, Weaver was "about as happy as I'd ever seen him." Weaver kidded Flanagan, telling him he was an old goat but still succeeding. And Flanagan, like most of the Orioles who played for Weaver and 'at times didn't understand him at all," thanked him for what he managed to put together and sustain.

"As years go on," Flanagan said, "and you play in other places and see the new era of players and how much of a business it's become, it was kind of a last, I don't know, unselfish, I don't exactly the word I'm looking for, but the last real teams. There was a oneness with that club, and maybe it was a common unity against Earl at that point, but certainly we did not have a problem with different personalities and all different people and everybody got along and had fun."

For the final homage to their stay in Memorial Stadium, the Orioles used a cinematic effect. With the theme from "Field of Dreams" filling the stadium, former players trotted from the dugout, initially one at a time. Brooks Robinson to third. Frank Robinson to right. Jim Palmer to the mound. Flanagan returned to the mound and was reunited with the likes of Palmer, Dave McNally, Pat Dobson, Mike Cuellar, McGregor and ultimately a host of pitchers who were once Orioles. "I remember going out and seeing the marks I had just made, thinking of them as being kind of the last marks on it," Flanagan said. "I saw the hole where I'd landed, and knew it was mine. It was just overwhelming."

Almost 50 pitchers were staring toward 10 catchers, one of whom was Dempsey, an Oriole from 1976–1986. By simply hinting at a catcher's action, Dempsey did enough to put all these pitchers on the same wave length. "He didn't really crouch down," Flanagan said. "He just started giving signals to the mound, and all of a sudden, it caught everyone's eye and everyone kind of shook their head. And I said, 'This is amazing.' He did it smiling, kidding around, and everybody shook their head. It was a classic moment."

After 38 seasons at Memorial Stadium, the Orioles have left their 33rd Street roost and moved to a new downtown home: Oriole Park at Camden Yards. Opening Day is April 6 against Cleveland. Outside of setting a club attendance record of 2,552,753 and having Ripken win the Most Valuable Player Award in the American League, the Orioles pulled up stakes without a winning month and were never higher than tied for fifth after the sixth game of the season, April 15. Their 1991 season, forgettable to most, was something Flanagan will cherish.

"We lost 95, the most I've ever been on a team and lost, and yet it was the most self-gratifying season for me ever," he said. "I never thought I'd make the team. I'd always gone to spring training knowing I had a job since 15–16 years ago. It was very different. Everyone seemed so young, but the coaching staff still was kind of believing in me, which gave me an opportunity to make the club."

He entered games at times he used to depart, inheriting predicaments he once left to others. He adapted to a role that brings little renown in the daily game stories and learned about the resilience of his pitching arm in 1991. If this is his final season, Mike Flanagan can accept that in ways he couldn't before because "I guess I just kind of showed myself an inner strength that maybe I didn't think I had."

THE CLEVELAND INDIANS

• IN A BOX •

1991 Won-Lost Record: 57-105 .352

Rank among 26 teams: Last
Over Last Five Years: 346-464 .427
Rank over Five Years: Last
In Last Ten Years: 713-907 .440
Rank over Ten Years: Last

Best Player: Carlos Baerga

Weak Spot: First Base

Best Pitcher: In 1991, Swindell. After the trade of Swindell their best remaining pitcher is Steve Olin.

Staff Weakness: Yes

Best Bench Player: Mike Aldrete

Best Baseball Name: Alomar

Best Young Player: Carlos Baerga

Best Looking Player: Sandy Alomar Jr.

Ugliest Player: Doug Jones

Most Pleasant Surprise, 1991: Albert Belle, sort of

Biggest Disappointment, 1991: Doug Jones

Best Minor League Prospect: Jim Thome

Who Is: A third baseman, 21 years old. Thome started 1991 in the Eastern League, moved to the PCL and spent September in Cleveland. His MLEs show him hitting around .300, with little power but some walks. *Baseball America* listed Thome as the #1 prospect in the Eastern League.

Thome was a September callup and played fairly well, so he probably will be the Indians' third baseman this year. Our MLEs show him hitting only four major league home runs, but that could be very misleading for four reasons. First, we have projected him into the Cleveland Park with the current dimensions, which are very long. Second, the MLE is based on his 1991 season, when he hit only eight homers in 543 at bats (combining three levels of play). In 1990 he hit 16 homers in 235 at bats. Third, the power totals of young players are often deceptive; many times a player's power won't emerge until age 23 or 24. Fourth, Thome is a big guy, 6'3" and 200 pounds. He may eventually be a major league power hitter. He looks like a young, left-handed hitting Carney Lansford. If they get real lucky he's a young George Brett, but that's a longshot.

Other Prospects: **Manny Ramirez,** a high school outfielder ou of New York, was the Indians' top pick in the '91 June draf Assigned to Burlington of the Appalachian League, Ramirez hi .326 with 19 homers, 63 RBI in 215 at bats.

Tracy Sanders was a 58th-round pick in 1990, but establishe himself as a prospect last summer by hitting 18 homers and drawing 83 walks in the Carolina League (A). He is reportedly a poo outfielder.

Jeff Mutis was over his head in three major league starts, bu the 25-year-old lefty posted a 1.80 ERA with Canton-Akron (Eastern League) last year. In four minor league seasons he has struc out 273 and walked only 124.

Designated Malcontent: Albert Belle

Park Characteristics: Subject to change at a moment's notice The stadium will accommodate very long dimensions if the Indians choose to leave the fences a long way away, and in 1991 the did, making Cleveland Stadium (as they now call it) the poores home run park in baseball.

The Park Helps: Charles Nagy, all pitchers.

The Park Hurts: All hitters except guys like Alex Cole and Feli Fermin with *no* power. Albert Belle hit only eight of his 28 homer last year in Cleveland, which is about the same percentage as th entire team. The Indians hit only 22 home runs in Cleveland (5 on the road) and allowed 41 at home (69 on the road).

ORGANIZATIONAL REPORT CARD

Ownership: F
Upper Management: C−
Field Management: Who knows
Front-Line Talent: D−
Second-Line Talent: B
Minor League System: C+

Comment: See article, "Perpetual Progress"

TEAM LEADERS:

Batting Average: Carlos Baerga, .288

Last Ten Years (Season): Pat Tabler, 1986, .326
Last Ten Years (Total): Julio Franco, .295

Doubles: Albert Belle, 31

Triples: Mark Whiten, 7

ome Runs: Albert Belle, 28

Last Ten Years (Season): Joe Carter, 1989, 35
Last Ten Years (Total): Carter, 151

xtra Base Hits: Belle, 61

BI: Albert Belle, 95

Last Ten Years (Season): Joe Carter, 1986, 121
Last Ten Years (Total): Carter, 530

tolen Bases: Alex Cole, 27

uns Created: Carlos Baerga, 82

uns Created Per Game: Albert Belle, 5.3

econdary Average: Belle, .319

Vins: Mike Nagy, 10

Last Ten Years (Season): Greg Swindell, 1988, 18
Last Ten Years (Total): Tom Candiotti, 72

Vinning Percentage: Nagy, 10-15 .400

trikeouts: Greg Swindell, 169

Last Ten Years (Season): Len Barker, 1982, 187
Last Ten Years (Total): 1. Swindell, 756
2. Candiotti, 753

RA: Greg Swindell, 3.48

aves: Steve Olin, 17

eague Leaders:

1) Alex Cole had the worst ratio of RBI to total bases of any major league player.

2) Denis Boucher tied for the league lead with four balks.

3) Swindell had the best strikeout to walk ratio of any major league pitcher, 5.45 to 1.

991 SEASON

Background: Since the trade of Rocky Colavito for Harvey Kuenn on April 17, 1960, the Indians have been trapped in a tunnel which seems only to grow increasingly dark. Through generations of players and owners and managers for a length of time which seems to defy logic, the Cleveland Indians have remained essentially the same—a bad club made up of young guys who are going to be good sometime.

In 1990 there was a bond/tax issue in Cleveland to decide on a new stadium, which passed. By early 1991 it was apparent that Hank Peters, the Indians General Manager, was on the way out and a new man would be on the way in. These events generated a certain amount of low-level, long-range optimism.

Outlook: I thought the Indians would have a decent year. For the Indians, 60 wins is a bad year and 85 is a great year. I thought it would be a pretty good year, some other people didn't, and the nation as a whole had zero interest in the subject.

Getaway: The Indians played competitive baseball for the first month of the season.

High Point of the Season: Two games in Oakland, May 4 and 5. On May 4 the Indians battered the A's for a 20-6 win, in which Chris James drove in nine runs (22% of his season's total). They followed that up by pounding Bob Welch and relievers for 15 more runs on May 5, raising their record at that point to 10-11.

Low Point of the Season: The Indians flew to Seattle on May 7, and fell into a slump which lasted the rest of the season. By July 3 the Indians were 24-51. They had lost 40 of 54 games.

Most Exciting Game of the Season: The Indians again victimized the Athletics, this time in Cleveland on July 25. Trailing 7-4 going to the bottom of the eighth, the Indians put men on second and third with two out. Eckersley was summoned to quell the uprising, but pinch hitter Mike Aldrete singled to drive in two runs, making it 7-6. Jerry Browne pinch hit for Chris James, and hit a two-run home run into the right field bleachers. Cleveland 8, Oakland 7.

Stretch Drive: By September 8 the Indians were 44-93, figuring to lose about 110 games. With the help of their September callups (Jim Thome and Eric Bell) and taking advantage of other team's callups, the Indians won 13 of their last 25 games to avoid posting one of the worst records in history.

Major Injuries: **John Farrell** underwent extensive elbow surgery in October 1990 and missed the entire '91 season. After yet another elbow surgery he is expected to miss all of this season as well.

Keith Hernandez missed the season after surgery to repair a herniated disc in his back.

Eric King missed six and a half weeks with a strained right shoulder.

Sandy Alomar Jr. suffered a series of nagging injuries before going on the disabled list for good on July 29 with a strained flexor muscle in his right hip. He is expected to be at full strength this season.

Pitcher **Mike York** spent 51 days on the disabled list with tendinitis in his elbow, and **Rudy Seanez** was out with a groin pull for about as long.

Offense: The Indians scored only 576 runs in 1991, the fewest of any major league team.

As I'm certain you know, the Indians a year ago mailed their fences halfway to Canada, making it very difficult to hit a home run in their home park. Their team batting average was .254, only six points below average, but their secondary average was .193—no power, speed or walks. The Indians, having moved the fences back in order to concentrate on speed and defense, stole only 84 bases. This was the third lowest total in the major leagues.

Defense: The Indians led the league in errors, by a wide margin.

Pitching: Because of the unnatural dimensions the Indians' staff ERA was only 4.23, not far from the league average of 4.09. In reality their pitching staff was as bad as the rest of the team.

Best Game by a Starting Pitcher: Eric King threw a two-hitter at the Rangers on August 5, Game Score 89 (9 2 0 0 1 7).

Worst Game by a Starting Pitcher: Also Eric King, September 8 against Toronto (2⅓ 8 7 6 2 1 Game Score: 13)

Indicators for 1991 were: Up very slightly (4.4)

Number of regulars having good seasons by their own standards: Three (Baerga, Belle, Fermin)

1991 Over-Achiever: Albert Belle

1991 Under-Achiever: Chris James

Infield: Below average, but not far below. One infielder, Baerga, is actually a good player, and the only glaring weakness in the infield was the lack of a first baseman who could hit in the middle of the order.

Outfield: Below average, but with talent.

Catching: The injuries to Sandy Alomar Jr. were one of the two key factors in the Indians' bleak season.

Starting Pitching: The weakest element of the team. After Greg Swindell the Indians starting pitching was a crapshoot.

Bullpen: The ineffectiveness of Doug Jones, more than any other one thing, pitched the Indians' season into chaos. Steve Olin emerged as the closer late in the year and was OK, but the supporting cast in the bullpen was equally ineffective. The Indians had only ten "Holds" in the entire season, ten situations in which a save opportunity was passed from one reliever to another. Every other major league team had at least twice as many. The Indians had a bullpen ERA of 4.31 (12th in the league), took 26 relief losses (Milwaukee led the league with 27) and blew more than a third of their save opportunities.

Percentage of offense created by:

Young Players:	78%
Players in Their Prime:	22%
Past Their Prime:	0%

Team Age Analysis:

Age of Offense:	24.9
Age of Pitching Staff:	27.3
Overall Team Age:	25.91

In retrospect, the critical decisions were: The much ridiculed decision to move the fences, while it certainly didn't *help* probably didn't hurt the team, either. They're hopeless.

THAT AND THE OTHER

Lookalikes: Glenallen Hill and Hal McRae

Hall of Fame Watch: Sure. Watch closely.

Chris Berman, Have You Considered: Mike (Alright) Aldret

Attendance Trend: Slipping back to the levels of the early 1980s. From 1980 to 1985 the Indians drew 650,000 to 1,000,000 a year. In 1986, with the arrival of the Jacobs brothers, there was a surge of optimism that pushed attendance close to 1.5 million. In 1991 after three straight years of decline, the Indians drew 1.05 million.

Players with a Chance for 3000 career hits: None

Best Fundamental Player: Sandy Alomar Jr.

Worst Fundamental Player: Alex Cole

Best Defensive Player: Sandy Alomar Jr.

Worst Defensive Player: Jerry Browne or Albert Belle

Best Knowledge of the Strike Zone: Jerry Browne

Least Command of the Strike Zone: Carlos Martinez

Fastest Runner: Alex Cole

Slowest Runner: Joel Skinner

Best Baserunner: Jose Gonzalez

Most Likely to Still be Here in 2000: Sandy Alomar Jr.

Best Control: Rod Nichols

Oddest Collection of Abilities: Alex Cole

Gets Ahead of the Hitters Most Often: Rod Nichols

Gets Ahead of the Hitters Least Often: Dave Otto
The departed Greg Swindell probably gets ahead of the hitters as consistently as any pitcher in the major leagues.

The Most Knowledgeable People About Local Baseball History Are:

1. Morris Eckhouse
2. Fred Schuld

Most-Similar Players:

to C Sandy Alomar, Brent Mayne
to 1B Carlos Martinez, Greg Briley
to 2B Mark Lewis, Mickey Morandini
to 3B Carlos Baerga, Robin Ventura
to SS Felix Fermin, Alvaro Espinoza
to LF Albert Belle, Dave Justice
to CF Alex Cole, Darryl Hamilton
to RF Mark Whiten, Wes Chamberlain

Among the All-Time Team Leaders: Doug Jones is the all-time saves leader with 128. No other current Indian appears on any of the top ten lists.

Town Team:

C—Ed McFarland
1B—Joe Kuhel
2B—Jim Delahanty
SS—Ed McKean
3B—Sal Bando
LF—Joe Vosmik
CF—Tommy Leach
RF—Ed Delahanty
SP—Urban Shocker
SP—Rube Marquard
SP—George Uhle

Post-Season Transactions:

November 15, traded Greg Swindell for Jack Armstrong, Scott Scudder and Joe Turek

December 6, traded Jesse Orosco to Milwaukee for a player to be named later

December 10, traded Rudy Seanez to Los Angeles for Dennis Cook and Mike Christopher

December 10, traded Willie Blair and Ed Taubensee to Houston for Dave Rohde and Kenny Lofton

December 16, signed Junior Ortiz to minor league contract

What Needs to Be Done For 1992: Just keep your head down and keep marchin'

Outlook for 1992: See article, "Clear the Mine"

Index of Leading Indicators for 1992: Up 44.2

The Cleveland Indians indicators for 1992 are by far the most positive in the majors, and in fact I believe are the most positive that I have ever seen. All seven indicators are positive. In declining order of importance:

1. The Indians of 1991 were the youngest team in the American League.
2. A team which loses 100 games in a season almost always does at least a little better the next year.
3. A team which slips by 20 games one year usually will recover to some extent the following year.
4. The Indians played better late in the season.
5. Both tests of team quality as contrasted to won-lost record show that the Indians of 1991, while legitimately a bad team, were not quite as bad as their won-lost record shows.
6. Their AAA team (Colorado Springs) was over .500.

This collection of indicators suggests that it is almost certain that the 1992 Indians will be better than the 1991 Indians. That's not saying they're going to be *good*; the Indians could improve by 15 games and still finish last. But they *will* be much better.

Due for a better season: Jerry Browne, Chris James

Likely to have a worse season: No one

1992 Won-Lost Record will be: 73-89

INDIAN NAMES

(See "Dances With Wolves")

Mark Whiten	Hunts Bear With Rock
Carlos Martinez	Buffalo Run Between Legs
Alex Cole	Fencemover
Albert Belle	Throws Ball At Fan
Carlos Baerga	One Who Can Play
Steve Olin	Swinging Gate
Greg Swindell	Lucky Dog
Tom Candiotti	Ball Floats Like Feather

ANOTHER ONE BITES THE DUST

It is an accepted fact by many fans that the Designated Hitter Rule has made the American League into an old man's league, keeping veterans around who can no longer run or play the field. I decided to check the average age of a player in each league. These averages are weighted by plate appearances—that is, if a player batted 600 times, his age counted 600 times as much toward the league average as that of a player who went to the plate only once.

The average age of an American League hitter in 1991 was 28.54 years.

The average age of a National League hitter was 28.57.

I also figured pitchers' ages, by weighted innings, wins and saves. The average National League pitcher *was* a little bit younger than his American League counterpart, so the overall National League average age is a tiny bit lower, but not enough that you could draw any conclusion. The notion that the American League is an old man's league turns out, like so much of our media wisdom, to be unfounded.

The Cleveland Indians had the youngest *lineup* in baseball last year, with the average plate appearance coming from a player 24.9 years of age. Their pitching staff was somewhat older (Candiotti, Orosco, Doug Jones), so the overall "Team Age" of the Indians (25.91) was slightly higher than that of the Houston Astros (25.81). Not coincidentally, the two youngest teams in baseball last year were also the two *worst* teams in baseball. Third- and fourth-youngest were the White Sox (27.25) and the Cincinnati Reds (27.28).

The *oldest* teams in baseball were:

1. Oakland	30.7
2. Los Angeles	30.6
3. Boston	30.1
4. Detroit	29.7
5. The Cubs	29.4

CLEAR THE MINE

At the beginning of the free agent era there was a widespread fear that free agency would lead to competitive imbalance. The argument was that if the players were free to go wherever they wanted, all of the best players would gravitate to the teams in the big markets—New York, Los Angeles, Chicago. Those teams would get better and better, and the teams in the small towns would drift away, unable to compete. The Yankees would go back to winning the pennant every year, and Kansas City would go back to losing a hundred games a year. Or, as I once wrote in a magazine article, "free agency will mean that the rich will grow richer and the poor will grow livestock for the rich."

This was the owners' argument, why free agency could not be allowed to exist: it would destroy competitive balance, and thus destroy baseball. This was so widely believed by sportswriters in the 1974–1977 era that it was virtually a truism, and the discussion proceeded from there to the question of how we could *prevent* this from happening.

Within a very few years it had become apparent that this was not happening at all. The best players were *not* being drawn to the best teams, and the teams which were able to attract free agents did not become dominant teams—in fact, by and large they didn't improve. In about 1982 George Foster said that there would never be another great team like the 1976 Reds, because salaries had gotten so high that no one could afford to keep a team of outstanding players together. This, in its turn, became the truism of the mid-1980s, and few sportswriters, in stating this, even noticed that it was diametrically opposed to the common wisdom of the previous decade. Originally free agency was supposed to *destroy* competitive balance; by the 1980s it was supposed to *enforce* competitive balance.

And, in fact, it did, or seemed to. Throughout baseball history competitive balance has implacably increased. There are eight or ten obvious ways to measure competitive balance in baseball, which include:

1) The standard deviation of winning percentage,
2) The average distance between the first-place team and the last-place team,
3) The number of teams finishing the season within ten games of first place,
4) The number of different teams winning the pennant in a ten-year period,
5) The number of pennants won by teams in New York and

Los Angeles, as contrasted with the number won by teams in small markets, and

6) The aggregate winning percentage of teams in New York and Los Angeles, as contrasted with the aggregate winning percentage of the teams in the smallest markets.

I assume most of these are self-explanatory. If the standard deviation of winning percentage is high, then competitive balance is low. If the distance between the first-place and last-place teams is great, competitive balance is low.

If you take any of these measures over time, you'll find that competitive balance has constantly increased. If you made up an "Index of Competitive Balance", then no matter how you constructed the formula you would find that competitive balance in baseball has increased absolutely without exception since the 1870s—that is, that competitive balance was greater in the 1880s than it was in the 1870s, was greater in the 1890s than it was in the 1880s, was greater in the 1900s than it was in the 1890s, etc. This continues to be true to this day; competitive balance was unquestionably greater in the 1980s than it had been in the 1970s. What happened in 1991, when two teams jumped from last place to first place, is a reflection of this fact: that the distance between last place and first place has shrunk to a fraction of what it once was.

The St. Louis Browns, who finished last in the American League in 1910, finished 57 games out of first place.

The Boston Red Sox, who finished last in the American League in 1930, finished 50 games out of first.

The Philadelphia A's, who finished last in the American League in 1950, finished 46 games out.

The Chicago White Sox, who finished last in the American League West in 1970, finished 42 games out.

The Minnesota Twins, who finished last in the American League West in 1990, finished only 29 games out.

As the gap between the best teams and the worst has narrowed, the dominance of baseball by teams in the large cities has declined. In the last ten years teams in New York and Los Angeles have won only seven of 40 division titles, an extraordinarily low percentage by historical standards, while teams from the smaller markets like Pittsburgh and Cincinnati have done well.

And I am now going to make a prediction.

In the 1990s, for the first time in baseball history, competitive balance will decline. For the first time in history, the distance between the best teams and the worst teams is going to increase over the next several years.

Why? Because what was widely predicted in 1975 is now beginning to happen: some of the teams are losing the ability to pay the salaries. Look at what has happened here. The Cleveland Indians had two good starting pitchers, Tom Candiotti and Greg Swindell. They're gone, and why are they gone? Because the Indians wanted to trade them for prospects?

The error of the 1970s was that we thought that the anti-competitive aspects of free agency would arrive *immediately*. The error of the 1980s was that we thought that since the anti-competitive aspects of free agency had not arrived immediately, they were not going to arrive at all.

As sportswriters, we have a very limited understanding of baseball economics, and an even more limited understanding of economics on a larger scale. Because of that, we dramatically underestimated *the distance between the teams' current salaries and the earnings potential of a baseball franchise.*

This came in two parts. First, we underestimated the distance between the amount of money teams took in and the amount they paid to their players. That distance was much greater than the teams had always told us it was, and to the extent that we had believed what we were told, we were wrong.

Second, we vastly underestimated—or totally ignored—the distance between the *actual* and the *potential* income of a major league franchise.

Putting those two together, what we didn't realize is that major leagues teams in 1975 had the *potential* to earn so much money that the salaries they paid to players at that time were relatively trivial. We thought—I wasn't even a sportswriter then, but I'll speak for the group—we thought that teams in small markets would lose their best players because they couldn't afford to double their salaries, when in fact they could. They could afford to double them, and triple them, and quadruple them and keep going.

The distinction between the Indians' trade of Swindell and moves which were made four or five years ago is subtle enough that it has evaded the attention of sportswriters, at least that I have noticed. Two years ago the Seattle Mariners traded Mark Langston because they couldn't afford to keep him as a free agent, which is similar to what has happened here. A year before that the Twins traded Frank Viola for the same reason, and yet the Twins are still competitive. Years and years ago, the Twins traded Bert Blyleven in part because they didn't know if they could retain him as a free agent.

Yes, but. I'm not saying that this situation is *completely* different, or that it doesn't have a common element with those other trades. I am saying that there is something new here. It's naked. It's absolute. **The Cleveland Indians have become the first team to abandon the hope of paying a competitive salary to a quality player.** In the Viola case in 1989 the Twins decided that they would be unable to reach an agreement *with Frank Viola*. They couldn't retain Viola—but they could retain Kirby Puckett and Kent Hrbek, and they could sign Jack Morris. They simply felt that Viola was over-reaching, and that they would be better off to cash him in for younger players with lower salaries.

This isn't an individual case in Cleveland. This is a blanket policy. The Cleveland Indians have decided, or seem to have decided, that they can't pay a competitive salary to *anybody*. Within a year, the Seattle Mariners are probably going to make the same decision.

Now, that's very different. If you lose an individual player who is good, you can deal with that. But if you are going to be forced to give up *everybody* who is good as soon as his salary matures, that's a different matter. The Indians were forced by circumstances to trade a pitcher who *is* good for three pitchers that they *hope* will be good. That's tough enough to do, but if you're smart and you're lucky, you can pull it off. But if you can't pay *anybody* who is good, if you can't pay the going rate, it isn't tough. It's impossible.

There's something else new this winter. This winter, for the first time in the fifteen-year history of free agency, the top free agents *did* go almost exclusively to the big cities. Toronto, which has now emerged as the third great and powerful city, got Jack Morris. Los Angeles got Candiotti. New York got Bonilla, Eddie Murray and Tartabull. At this moment, three of the five highest-paid players in baseball play in New York (Bonilla, Tartabull and Gooden).

So what's going to happen? This is not a jeremiad; I don't write that kind of shit. I've never written an article about how the world is going to hell in a handbasket, and I'm not going to start now.

A young fan may not understand this, particularly if he doesn't spend 37% of his life with a Baseball Encyclopedia under his arm, but throughout baseball history there have normally been teams which never won, never hoped to win and never came close to winning. I'm not talking about teams being bad like the Cleveland Indians of the 1980s, but about teams being twenty games a year worse than that. The Philadelphia A's from the mid-1930s to the mid-1950s would regularly finish forty to sixty games out of first place. A hundred losses for them was just another season. It wasn't always the Philadelphia A's, but it was always somebody.

What's going to happen is, that's going to come back. Since the institution of the amateur draft in 1965 we haven't had teams like that. We're going to have them again.

Obviously, that isn't going to be good for baseball—but neither is it going to be fatal. Baseball survived that way for seventy years; it can survive another ten.

To this point, free agency has been a wonderful thing for baseball. It has generated a lot of interest, a lot of talk, and that by itself is a benefit. Free agency pushed the teams to market themselves more aggressively, to work harder at selling themselves to the public, and that's been great for baseball.

Free agency also helped to increase competitive balance, and that was good for baseball.

There isn't any doubt that competitive balance is good for the game, but I also believe that there is such a thing as *too much* competitive balance.

Baseball needs great teams.

Great teams need somebody to beat up on.

If all the teams are about the same, if every team becomes as good as the next one, a sport becomes formless and indistinct, a shapeless lump of games. The games become random and therefore seem pointless. It is *defying* the odds that we love to see, watching things happen that can't happen or at least shouldn't happen. Parity is boring.

Also, as more teams become unwilling or unable to pay the salaries of quality players, the upward pressure on salaries is balanced by a downward pressure. If four teams, one in each division, would adopt a policy of not paying *anyone* more than a million dollars a season, those four teams would lose 100 games a year, but that would very significantly impact on the salary expectations of all the players throughout the league. What I cannot calculate—what I don't believe that *anybody* can calculate—is how rapidly the downward pressure on salaries will operate in relationship to the pulling apart of the league.

We underestimated baseball's earnings potential before, and perhaps we're underestimating it now. I see no reason to believe that major league teams, at this time, have a significant untapped economic potential. If a team cannot remain competitive, then it *loses* the ability to sell itself. Those teams in the thirties and fifties that lost a hundred games a year—they also drew 200,000 fans a season. You cannot draw two million fans a year to a team that is out of the race in May, no matter how cleverly you market them.

Major league baseball is entering a very rough period. The Cleveland Indians are the canary in baseball's coal mine, and the canary just dropped off his perch.

PERPETUAL PROGRESS

The Cleveland Indians are not without talent. You can make a list of the stages a player goes through from unknown to established major league player, like this:

1. Unknown Athlete
2. Exciting Amateur
3. Unproven Professional
4. Minor League Hot Shot
5. Unproven major leaguer with minor league credentials
6. Major league player of unproven quality
7. Good young player
8. Good player, period

One might generalize that a player, if he is destined to be a star, should move through one stage per season, and that if a player *fails* to move from one stage to the next in the course of two years, he endangers his chance of ever emerging as a quality player. If he's at stage one at age 19, he should be at stage two by age 20, at step three by age 21, etc. Of course, there are occasional players who reach the seventh level at the age of twenty and occasional players who don't reach the fourth level until age 27, but that's one of the fundamental things we use to evaluate a prospect, where he is in this chart in relation to his age. John Jaha isn't regarded as a potential superstar because he's just reached level four at the age of 25.

Anyway, the Cleveland Indians have *nothing* at level eight, but they have as much talent at levels four through seven as any major league team. They are not *long* in minor league hot shots, like the Braves are, but they have a few of them—Thome, Ramirez, Lofton. They are not *long* in good young players, but they have three, in Baerga, Belle and Alomar. There are organizations which have nothing in either category.

But what the Indians have is more guys in categories five and six than any other major league team. Whiten, Hill, Lewis, Rohde, Scudder, Armstrong, Allred, Jefferson—they've got a bunch of them. If the Indians could keep these players together as they matured, and if they could train them and support them properly, they would eventually emerge as a good ballclub.

They won't, of course. This is what the Indians have had for many years. In 1985 they had a group of guys at levels four through seven which included Julio Franco, Brett Butler and Joe Carter, but they finished last. In that sense, the Indians are exactly where they were in 1985, or 1978, or 1971 or 1964. Because of the economics of the game, the outlook for the Indians is dimmer now than it was then. It's frustrating, but don't start saying that none of these guys can play, because some of them sure as hell can.

THE PITTSBURGH PIRATES
• IN A BOX •

1991 Won-Lost Record: 98-64 .605

Rank among 26 teams: 1st
Over Last Five Years: 432-376 .535
Rank over Five Years: 4th
In Last Ten Years: 796-821 .492
Rank over Ten Years: 16th

Best Player: Barry Bonds

Weak Spot: As of now, right field.

Best Pitcher: Doug Drabek

Staff Weakness: None

Best Bench Player: Gary Redus

Best Baseball Name: Scott Bullett

Worst Baseball Name: Bob Walk

Best Young Player: Orlando Merced

Best Looking Player: Jay Bell

Ugliest Player: Mike LaValliere

Most Pleasant Surprise, 1991: Orlando Merced

Biggest Disappointment, 1991: Championship Series vs. Atlanta

Best Minor League Prospect: Kevin Young

Who Is: A third baseman, 22 years old. Young, a Southern Mississippi product, was the Pirates' seventh-round pick in 1990. He started 1991 in the Carolina League (A), and after half the season moved up to the Eastern League (AA) when John Wehner was promoted to Pittsburgh. His combined batting average for the two stops was .330, with a .496 slugging percentage. With Buechele signed for the next three seasons, Young may have to find another position.

Other Prospects: See article

Designated Malcontent: Barry Bonds

Park Characteristics: Reduces batting averages very slightly, good for doubles because of the turf, no left/right bias and neutral in terms of favoring hitter or pitcher.

The Park Helps or Hurts: No one significantly

ORGANIZATIONAL REPORT CARD

Ownership: D
Upper Management: B+ (For Doughty)
Field Management: A
Front-Line Talent: A
Second-Line Talent: B+
Minor League System: B

Comment: The Pirates over the next decade can be seen as engaged in a war between the field level management, which is superb, and the ownership, which is out to lunch. The shortcomings of the Pirate ownership group in time are certain to manifest themselves in the performance of the front office, and will ultimately undermine the ballclub. So it's kind of an interesting study, to see how long good talent management can stave off the effects of incompetent financial management.

Larry Doughty, the General Manager fired in January, was a good man. Is a good man.

TEAM LEADERS:

Batting Average: Bobby Bonilla, .302

Last Ten Years (Season): Bill Madlock, 1983, .323
Last Ten Years (Total): Bill Madlock, .291

Doubles: Bobby Bonilla, 44

Triples: Andy Van Slyke, 7

Home Runs: Barry Bonds, 25

Last Ten Years (Season): Barry Bonds, 1990, 33
Last Ten Years (Total): Bonds, 142

Extra Base Hits: Bonilla, 68

RBI: Barry Bonds, 116

Last Ten Years (Season): Bonilla, 1990, 120
Last Ten Years (Total): Bonilla, 500

Stolen Bases: Bobby Bonds, 43

Runs Created: 1. Barry Bonds, 118
2. Bobby Bonilla, 114

Runs Created Per 27 Outs: Barry Bonds, 8.1

Secondary Average: Barry Bonds, .516

Wins: John Smiley, 20

Last Ten Years (Season): Doug Drabek, 1990, 22
Last Ten Years (Total): Drabek, 77

Winning Percentage: Smiley, 20-8 .714

Strikeouts: Doug Drabek, 142

Last Ten Years (Season): Rick Rhoden, 1986, 159
Last Ten Years (Total): Drabek, 719

ERA: Randy Tomlin, 2.98

Saves: Bill Landrum, 17

League Leaders: See article

Stat of the Year: The hidden strength of the 1991 Pirates was the MVP-type performance by their platoon combination at first base/leadoff man. The Pirates a year ago lost Sid Bream to free agency, and there were people who wrote that this would drag the Pirates down in '91. The platoon combination of Merced and Redus played first base and led off, which is unusual. This chart gives the 162-game totals for the Pirates' first basemen and their leadoff men:

	AB	R	H	2B	3B	HR	RBI	SB	BB	Avg
Leadoff men:	663	125	174	31	4	16	71	25	86	.262
First Base:	646	129	176	31	4	15	69	17	90	.272

That gives you speed, batting average, power and walks in that spot. It's not Barry Bonds, but it was hardly a weak spot.

1991 SEASON

Background: The Pirates, building for several years despite organizational upheaval, won the division in 1990, but lost to Cincinnati in the playoffs.

Outlook: About half of the members of the media, not including me, were smart enough to pick the Pirates to repeat in 1991. Certainly most people realized that the Pirates were an outstanding team; what we didn't know was whether the Mets or Cubs would *also* be an outstanding team.

The Pirates' two best players and best pitcher went to salary arbitration a year ago, all seeking salaries in the three-million-plus range. Drabek won his case (I was on his team, which is *not* why he won), but Bonds and Bonilla lost. At the outset of spring training Bonds was unhappy about his contract/arbitration loss, and spoke freely about the subject. Manager Jim Leyland challenged him about it during a workout, telling him to quit bitching and get with the program, and he did, but many people wondered whether the salary bitterness would detract from the quality of the Pirates' performance.

Getaway: By April 28 the Pirates were 13-6, putting that question to rest.

Most Exciting Game of the Season: April 21 against the Cubs. The Pirates trailed 7-2 in the bottom of the eighth, but scored four that inning and one in the ninth to tie the game. In the top of the eleventh Andre Dawson hit a grand slam, and the Cubs tacked on an extra run for a 12-7 lead in the eleventh. The Pirates came back with *six* in the bottom of the inning off Heathcliff Slocumb and Mike Bielecki to win, 13-12. This may have been the most exciting game in the major leagues last year.

High Point of the Season: The Chicago and New York teams failed to jell, and the Pirates' only challenge came from an upstart St. Louis Cardinal team. After losing the first game of a four-game series with St. Louis in early August, Pittsburgh's lead over the Cards stood at just four games. The Pirates came back to win the next two, August 10 and 11.

In the finale, August 12, Pittsburgh trailed 3-2 in the bottom of the eleventh, but Bonds hit a two-run homer off Lee Smith to win the game, extend the Pirates' lead to seven games, and all but put an end to the pennant race.

Stretch Drive: Virtually exhibition games, and the Pirates continued to win.

Low Point of the Season: The only low point was the playoff against the Braves.

Major Injuries: Jeff King had back trouble, and was able to play only 33 games. He had surgery in December to remove a ruptured disc. King's replacement, John Wehner, played very well for five weeks before he, too, went out with a back problem. *His* ruptured disc was removed in September.

Bob Walk spent two months on the disabled list with a pulled hamstring.

Vicente Palacios missed a few weeks in August due to a strained right rotator cuff.

Offense: The Pirates led the National League last year in both batting average (.263) and secondary average (.272). Atlanta was second in both areas, at .258 and .269, for which reason those two teams scored far more runs than anyone else in the league. The Pirates led the league in runs scored, with 768, 19 more than Atlanta and 73 more than third-place Chicago.

Defense: Outstanding. All of the Pirates' up-the-middle defensive players (LaValliere/Slaught, Lind, Bell and Van Slyke) are good.

Pitching: The best in the league. The Pirates were second in ERA (3.44), behind a team that plays in a fluke park.

Best Game by a Starting Pitcher: John Smiley and Zane Smith both pitched one-hitters, Smiley on April 17 against the

Mets (9 1 0 0 0 4), and Smith on May 29 against the Cardinals (9 1 0 0 1 5).

Worst Game by a Starting Pitcher: Because Leyland goes to the bullpen so quickly (see "League Leaders"), the Pirates didn't have any truly horrible starts. The worst was Bob Walk's in New York on September 24 (4 5 7 7 3 2 Game Score: 21), and the Pirates won the game anyway. Leyland won't let a pitcher stay in to give up eight or nine runs, as some managers do.

Indicators for 1991 were: Strongly negative (−15.5)

Number of regulars having good seasons by their own standards: Five (Bonds, Bonilla, Slaught, Bell, Lind)

1991 Over-Achiever: Orlando Merced

1991 Under-Achiever: Bob Kipper

Infield: Excellent. The surprising thing is that although third base was perceived as a trouble spot for the Pirates all year, Pirate third basemen for the season hit .286 with 16 homers and 85 RBI. Bonilla played 67 games there.

Outfield: It was one of the better outfields in the history of baseball.

Catching: Very good. Pirate catchers hit .301 and drove in 70 runs, plus LaValliere is a Gold Glove candidate and Slaught throws well.

Starting Pitching: Excellent.

Bullpen: The weakest element of the team. Also because Leyland goes to the bullpen so quickly, the Pirates get a lot of wins from their relievers. The Pirates were pretty average in terms of blown saves (16), bullpen ERA (3.83) and relief losses (20).

Percentage of offense created by:

Young Players:	45%
Players in Their Prime:	49%
Past Their Prime:	6%

Team Age Analysis:

Age of Non-Pitchers:	27.5
Age of Pitching Staff:	28.2
Overall Team Age:	27.78

The Pirates of 1991 were the *youngest* team in the division, edging the Expos because the Expos have some older pitchers. The Pirates were much younger than the Cardinals, who were perceived as the young team in the division.

In retrospect, the critical decisions were: The critical event of the season was Leyland's decision to challenge Barry Bonds when Bonds was whining about his contract in spring training. Leyland put Bonds in the position of having to *prove* that he wasn't sulking. Had he not done that, the Pirate season could have been very different.

The other critical decisions were the successful solution to the first base problem, and Leyland's skillful managing of the third base time bomb.

THAT AND THE OTHER

Lookalikes: Stan Belinda and Ron Howard
Mike LaValliere and Bluto
Zane Smith and Darryl

Hall of Fame Watch: See article

Chris Berman, Have You Considered: John (Oh, I wish I was an Oscar Mayer) Wehner

Throwback: Jay Bell

Attendance Trend: Strongly upward. The Pirates' attendance has doubled since 1986, and established a franchise record in 1991.

Players with a Chance for 3000 career hits:

Bobby Bonilla	19%
Barry Bonds	9%

Record Watch:

Barry Bonds has 142 career home runs and 212 career stolen bases, for a power/speed number of 170.1. He is the age-group leader for his own group (born 1964) and also ahead of anybody two years his senior. Thus, Bonds is reasonably well positioned to make a run at the record his father once seemed likely to break, which is the career power/speed combination, 447.1, by Willie Mays.

Best Interview: Andy Van Slyke

Probably Could Play Regularly For Another Team: Gary Varsho

Best Fundamental Player: Andy Van Slyke

Best Defensive Player: Jose Lind

Worst Defensive Player: Gary Redus

Best Knowledge of the Strike Zone: Barry Bonds

Least Command of the Strike Zone: Jose Lind

Fastest Runner: Barry Bonds

Slowest Runner: Mike LaValliere

Best Baserunner: Andy Van Slyke

Most Likely to Still be Here in 2000: Three Rivers Stadium

Best Fastball: Vicente Palacios

Best Breaking Pitch: Randy Tomlin

Best Control: Zane Smith

Oddest Collection of Abilities: Gary Redus

Manager's Pet Strategy:

Leyland's most noted strategic quirk is the persistent bunting with Jay Bell, even in the first inning. He stopped doing that in mid-season 1991, however, probably because of increased confidence in Bell as a hitter.

Leyland is a fanatic about keeping people in their roles. He'll do a lot of stuff that seems weird to most of us to avoid getting a player out of his assigned role.

Gets Ahead of the Hitters Most Often: Zane Smith

Gets Ahead of the Hitters Least Often: Neal Heaton

Most-Similar Players:

to C Mike LaValliere, Mike Scioscia
to 1B Orlando Merced, Wes Chamberlain
to 2B Jose Lind, Jose Oquendo
to 3B Steve Buechele, Kelly Gruber
to SS Jay Bell, Jeff Blauser
to LF Barry Bonds, Will Clark
to CF Andy Van Slyke, Dave Henderson
to RF Bobby Bonilla, Ruben Sierra

Most Fun to Watch: Jose Lind

Least Fun to Watch: Barry Bonds

Managerial Type: Curtis Wilkerson

Among the All-Time Team Leaders:

Bonds is sixth on the Pirates' career home run list with 142, and sixth on the stolen base list with 212.

Bill Landrum's 58 saves rank him third on the Pirates' all-time list, far behind Kent Tekulve and Dave Giusti.

Although the Pirates have had many great position players in their history they have had few great pitchers. Doug Drabek will begin appearing on their all-time leader lists in 1992 if he has a good year.

Town Team:

C—Charley Bennett
1B—Rube Bressler
2B—Bill Hallman
SS—Bobby Wallace
3B—Charlie Deal
LF—Hank Sauer
CF—Honus Wagner
RF—Frank Thomas
LHP—Sam McDowell
RHP—Bill Doak

Post-Season Transactions:

December 2, Bobby Bonilla signed with Mets
December 12, signed Steve Buechele to a three-year contract
January 6, fired General Manager Larry Doughty

What Needs to Be Done For 1992: The Pirates' challenge in 1992 is to avoid being undermined by the loss of Bobby Bonilla. Bonilla is a fine player, but not so great that his loss need be devastating to a team of this quality.

Outlook for 1992: The Pirates still have more good players than anyone else in the division, and I would still pick them to win the division.

Index of Leading Indicators for 1992: Down 6.2

Positive Indicators: Nothing major

Negative Indicators: Nothing major

Due for a better season: Drabek will have a better won-lost record.

Likely to have a worse season: Orlando Merced

1992 Won-Lost Record will be: 91-71

LEAGUE LEADERS

Barry Bonds led the National League in many if not most analytical value categories. He created the most runs of any NL player, and created the most runs per out. He led in on base percentage, .410. He had the highest offensive winning percentage in the National League, .795, and the highest secondary average in the majors, .516. There is no question that Barry Bonds was the best hitter in the National League in 1991.

Bobby Bonilla led the league with 44 doubles.

Jay Bell led the National League in the number of outs made in 1991, as he had in 1990. He made 498 outs last year, second in the majors behind Harold Reynolds, which includes 30 sacrifice hits, a total which also led the league.

Mike LaValliere had a .998 fielding percentage, best in the National League for a catcher.

John Smiley's 20 wins tied him for the league lead with Glavine, and his .714 winning percentage tied him with Rijo. However, Smiley also had five "Cheap Wins", wins in games in which he didn't pitch well, which led the National League, while Doug Drabek tied for the NL lead in the opposite category, "Tough Losses", with seven.

Zane Smith had the best strikeout to walk ratio in the National League, 4.14 to 1. He also led in the two ground ball pitcher categories—ground ball to fly ball ratio (2.69 to 1), and grounded into double plays (1.1 per nine innings).

Jim Leyland led the National League in quick hooks, with 29.

The Pirates as a team led the league in batting average (.263), runs scored (768), doubles (259), sacrifice hits (99), sacrifice flies (66), walks received (620), intentional walks received (62) and on base percentage (.338). Their pitchers tied for the league lead in both complete games (18) and saves (51).

HALL OF FAME WATCH

In the last two years **Barry Bonds** has compiled about 30% of the star-type accomplishments which would make a Hall of Fame career. However, prior to that he had done really nothing which would be considered Cooperstown calibre, so it's an open question whether he will last long enough and have enough superstar seasons to earn a slot.

Bobby Bonilla, in my opinion, has comparatively little chance of making the Hall of Fame. An RBI man, a slugger without defensive value, doesn't make the Hall of Fame unless he drives in *at least* 1400 runs, and I don't believe Bonilla can last long enough to do that. He shows a 19% chance to get 3,000 hits, but because of his size and lack of speed I don't think that's realistic.

Doug Drabek would have to show unusual durability as a starting pitcher to make the Hall of Fame. Drabek strikes out just over five men per game, and a pitcher like that will ordinarily lose his consistency in his early thirties. He does have exceptional work habits.

Van Slyke will not make the Hall of Fame. He's a fine player, but he's a fine player like Carl Furillo was for the Dodgers of the fifties, like Hank Bauer was for the Yankees, like Curt Flood was for the Cardinals of the sixties. Good, but not good enough.

APPRENTICE PIRATES

Carlos Garcia is a major league shortstop, stuck behind Jay Bell. Garcia has spent the last three seasons in the minors proving that he is as good a player as Felix Fermin or Alvaro Espinoza, but faster and a little more erratic defensively. He's still only 24, and will eventually get a chance somewhere.

Jon Farrell was the Pirates' #1 pick last June. Drafted as a catcher, Farrell spent more time in center field last summer, with Welland in the rookie New York-Penn League. He showed good power, 20 doubles and 8 homers, but struck out 71 times in 241 at bats.

Joe Calder, a 19-year-old power-hitting outfielder, played in the Gulf Coast League last season. White Sox manager Jaime Garcia said of Calder, who slugged .480 in a pitchers' league, that "He reminds me a lot of a young Orlando Cepeda."

The Pirates have traded many of their top prospects in the last couple years—Willie Greene, Kurt Miller, Wes Chamberlain, Moises Alou—for veteran players.

STRIKEOUT THEORY REVISITED

In *The Baseball Book 1991* I discussed the question of how one could spot a group of pitchers whose record was likely to improve dramatically in the next season, and how one could spot a group of pitchers who were likely to decline. In that context, I put forward the theory that, for several reasons, these movements should be predicted by the ratio of strikeouts to wins. A pitcher who has a **high ratio of strikeouts to wins** should be a good bet to **improve** his won-lost record and his overall performance in the following season, while a pitcher who has a **low ratio of strikeouts to wins** should be likely to **decline** in the following season. This should work because this relationship embodies several biases.

I thought I would take a minute this year to see how the theory worked. I don't normally review in one book the predictions of the year before, for this reason. If I'm right about things or I'm wrong, this is trivial; what matters is what happened and why. If I start saying, "See, I was right about this" then I am obligated to say "But I was wrong about that", and the next thing you know I'm explaining *why* I said this and why it was wrong, and then I'm writing about myself, rather than writing about baseball. This book isn't about Bill James; it's about baseball.

But here we are dealing with a fixed, objective method, and thus in reviewing that method we are reviewing something separate from myself. We are evaluating a method that you could use for your own purposes—a trivial method, perhaps, but a potentially useful one. Anyway, here is the concluding section of the article from *The Baseball Book 1991*, amended to include 1992 review comments. The article was written as the Steve Searcy comment in the book, which was bad judgment, but that's life.

The 1990 pitchers with very high ratios of strikeouts to wins were:

Pitcher	W-L	SO	Ratio
Greg Mathews	0-5	18	inf
Marty Clary	1-10	44	44 -1
Steve Searcy	2-7	66	33 -1
Jamie Moyer	2-6	58	29 -1
Steve Avery	3-11	75	25 -1
Jeff Ballard	2-11	50	25 -1
Steve Wilson	4-9	95	23.8-1
Jose DeLeon	7-19	164	23.4-1
Chuck Cary	6-12	134	22.3-1
Matt Young	8-18	176	22 -1
Jim Clancy	2-8	44	22 -1
Sid Fernandez	9-14	181	20.1-1
Mark Langston	10-17	195	19.5-1
Chris Bosio	4-9	76	19.5-1
Mark Gardner	7-9	135	19.3-1
Mark Gubicza	4-7	71	17.8-1
Nolan Ryan	13-9	232	17.8-1
Saberhagen	5-9	87	17.4-1
Roy Smith	5-10	87	17.4-1
Jim Deshaies	7-12	119	17 -1
Mike Walker	2-6	34	17 -1
David Cone	14-8	232	16.6-1
Rick Reuschel	3-6	49	16.3-1

Notes:

1. There are 23 pitchers on this list, with a 1990 aggregate record of 120-232, .341. History suggests that their 1991 aggregate record will be about 213-174.

1992 Review—Cone's 1991 record was actually 14-10, so the group totals given above are in error by two games. The 23 pitchers did, as a group, improve substantially in 1991, but not as much as I had projected them to improve. As a group, these 23 pitchers won 20 more games than in 1990 (120 up to 140) and lost 86 fewer games (234 down to 146). They improved their aggregate winning percentage from .339 to .490.

2. On this particular list there are a large number of veteran pitchers who were having off years, like Langston, DeLeon and Sid Fernandez. That's not really the normal pattern; it's just what happened in this case.

3. These 23 pitchers can be sorted into four general groups, which are

the guys who probably won't even have jobs (4),
the guys who probably will be better but who cares (1),
the ones who were hurt and may still be (4), and
the guys we are really interested in (14).

Four guys on this list probably won't even be in the majors in 1991, those four being Mathews, Clary, Clancy and Walker. *1992 Review—that's a fairly accurate comment. Mathews and Clary were out of the majors in 1991, and Walker pitched only four innings at the end of the year. Clancy did pitch in 1991, and pitched much better than he had in 1990.*

Jeff Ballard will certainly be better in 1991 than he was in 1990, but after all, 3-7 is better than 2-11. I'm not sure that Ballard is a good draft pick. *1992 Review—that's a precisely accurate comment. Ballard did have a better won-lost record last year (6-12), but was really no more effective.*

Four guys on this list are established quality pitchers who were hurt—Bosio, Saberhagen, Gubicza and Reuschel. You will want to listen to the reports on them in March, and see if they're throwing OK, but even if they are they won't go real cheap. *1992 Review—again, that stands up alright. Two of the four guys on the list mounted strong comebacks in 1991, and two of them didn't.*

That leaves the fourteen guys we are really interested in, who are Steve Searcy, Jamie Moyer, Steve Avery, Steve Wilson, Jose DeLeon, Chuck Cary, Matt Young, Sid Fernandez, Mark Langston, Mark Gardner, Nolan Ryan, Roy Smith, Jim Deshaies and David Cone. If you can pick up four or five of those guys—say, Steve Avery, Steve Wilson, Chuck Cary, Mark Gardner and Jim Deshaies—you will probably have at least one pitcher who takes the league by storm in 1991.

*1992 Review—on a literal level the statement is certainly accurate: one of the five pitchers listed **did** take the league by storm in 1991. On another level it may not be as perceptive as we might hope. I did point you to Steve Avery as a possible cheap pickup in a rotisserie league, but in the same breath I also pointed you to Jim Deshaies and Chuck Cary, who were terrible.*

The other end of this was written as the Ron Robinson comment. In the Ron Robinson comment, I tried to spot pitchers who had very *low* ratios of wins to strikeouts in 1990. Here is the comment, edited in the same way:

Who are the pitchers that we should stay away from for 1991?

I used a cutoff here of 7.5 to 1. There were twenty-six major league pitchers in 1990 who had ratios of less than 7.5 strikeouts per win. In all likelihood, at least twenty of these pitchers will be *less* effective in 1991 than they were in 1990: *1992 Review—This was an accurate statement. Of the twenty-six pitchers given below, twenty-two or twenty-three were less effective in 1991 than they had been in 1990.*

Pitcher	W-L	SO	Ratio
Kevin Brown	12-10	88	7.3-1
Dan Petry	10-9	73	7.3-1
Gullickson	10-14	73	7.3-1
John Mitchell	6-6	43	7.2-1
Dennis Cook	9-4	64	7.1-1
Dave Stieb	18-6	125	6.9-1
Jimmy Key	13-7	88	6.8-1
Scott Garrelts	12-11	80	6.7-1
Scott Erickson	8-4	53	6.6-1
Tom Browning	15-9	99	6.6-1
Greg Hibbard	14-9	92	6.6-1
Kirk McCaskill	12-11	78	6.5-1
Tom Bolton	10-5	65	6.5-1
Mike LaCoss	6-4	39	6.5-1
Curt Young	9-6	56	6.2-1
Doug Drabek	22-6	131	6.0-1
Eric King	12-4	70	5.8-1
Neal Heaton	12-9	68	5.7-1
Mark Knudson	10-9	56	5.6-1
Mike Moore	13-15	73	5.5-1
John Cerutti	9-9	49	5.4-1
John Tudor	12-4	63	5.3-1
Dave Johnson	13-9	68	5.2-1
Ron Robinson	14-7	71	5.1-1
Bob Tewksbury	10-9	50	5.0-1
Bob Welch	27-6	127	4.7-1

1992 Comment—The first thing I am struck by on this list is that there were only two American League pitchers in 1991 who won twenty games, and both of them made the list of pitchers that we should stay away from (Scott Erickson and Bill Gullickson). However, looking more carefully, it quickly becomes apparent that Erickson and Gullickson are very much the exception to the rule. Mike Moore had a very good year in 1991, and two others guys (Jimmy Key and Bob Tewksbury) were about the same as in 1990. With those exceptions, everybody on the list was less effective in 1991 than he had been in 1990, and generally they were much less effective. Resuming now the original comment:

I listed this comment with Ron Robinson, because that's where it seemed most germane. Bob Welch has a ratio of 4.7 to 1, but then, nobody in his right mind expects Welch to go 27-6 again, anyway. Tewksbury is at 5 to 1, but probably not that much is expected of him, either, and you never know, he might fool us.

But Robinson—he went 14-7 last year, 12-5 after coming over to the American League, and a lot of people are going to look at that and figure with 35 starts, he could have a big year. I don't think it's likely. I think he's a lot more likely to go 12-14.

1992 Review—Robinson didn't go 12-14, he went 0-1, but apart from that this comment is precisely accurate. Welch did decline enormously, but Tewksbury did hold his own, so I was right to exclude him from the list. Back to the comment:

There are quite a few people on this list that I *wouldn't* encourage you to avoid. Dave Stieb is on the list, but he's high on the list, where the declines are moderate. He was 18-6 last year; if he declines to 16-10, that's no big deal. Same with Browning, Hibbard, Drabek and Jimmy Key; they can *decline*, and still help you. They probably will. *1992 Review—Stieb, of course, was hurt early in the year after going 4-3, so it would have been better not to single him out as the exception. Other than that, the comment could not possibly be more accurate. I cited Browning, Hibbard, Drabek and Jimmy Key, who were an aggregate 64-31 in 1990. They did decline in 1991, all of them except arguably Key, but still won 56 games among the four of them (51 losses), so they still helped the teams they were playing for.*

But the guys between Drabek and Tewksbury—I'd be very leery of drafting any of those. As a group, they went 95-66 last year. They'll be 55-68 next year. If you knew the stock market was going to go down that much next year, would you buy stocks?

1992 Comment—there were eight pitchers between Drabek and Tewksbury, the eight pitchers who went 95-66 in 1990. One of those (John Tudor) retired, and six of the other seven suffered serious performance declines in 1991.

I had predicted that these pitchers would decline from 95-66 to 55-68. In fact, they declined to 34-40, which breaks down as 17-8 by Mike Moore, 17-32 by the other six guys. The 1991 ERAs of the pitchers in this group included 7.97 (Mark Knudson), 7.07 (Dave Johnson) 6.23 (Robinson), 4.60 (Eric King) and 4.57 (Cerutti).

It is my honest reaction, in reviewing the results of the first year, that the method obviously merits further attention. This tool is intended to help a rotisserie league player do two things:

a) spot a pitcher who might be good, and cheap, in the upcoming season, and

b) make a list of pitchers to avoid because of a high risk of performance declines.

What we did here is to use this ratio to draw up a list of candidates, and then, by sorting through the list of candidates with common sense, narrow it down.

In the first category, spotting phenoms, we were not spectacularly successful—but neither were we utterly unsuccessful. We had a list of five pitchers who might turn out to be tremendous rotisserie bargains. One of those five, in fact, was almost certainly the most-improved pitcher in the major leagues in 1991. That, in my opinion, is enough to justify the effort.

In the second effort, we *were* spectacularly successful. The method pointed to a list of pitchers who, as a group, suffered extraordinary setbacks in 1991.

What is a little difficult to understand intuitively is how a simple two-element ratio like this could so consistently point to pitchers who were going to get hurt—and yet it does. What the ratio tells us is whether the pitcher is working at the limits of his ability. A pitcher who is working at the limits of his ability—as Robinson was a year ago—has a high risk of injury.

Looking ahead to 1992, then, who does this method say are the pitchers to watch, and the pitchers to avoid.

First, the guys to avoid. I would say, based on their 1991 ratios of strikeouts to wins, there are five pitchers in the major leagues that you should avoid at all costs in the 1992 rotisserie draft. Those five are Bill Gullickson, Scott Erickson, Mike Bielecki, Bill Wegman and Greg Hibbard.

In 1991 those five had an aggregate won-lost record of 79 wins, 46 losses. It says here that in 1992, as a group, they will lose half of their wins, and will lose more games than they win. Their won-lost record will drop from 79-46 to somewhere around 42-47.

On the "dramatically up" side, I'll list six pitchers in the "A" Group: Brian Barnes of Montreal, Alex Fernandez of the White Sox, David Cone of the Mets, Greg Swindell of Cincinnati, Rod Nichols of Cleveland and Erik Hanson of Seattle.

Those six pitchers had a 1991 won-lost record of 47 wins, 70 losses—an average of 8-12. In 1992 they will, as a group, win 70 or more games, and have a winning percentage of .550 or better.

That's the "A" group, the guys that I have no reservations about recommending. There's a "B" group, too—guys that I would be more reluctant to recommend for one reason or another, but who also have very high ratios of strikeouts to wins. That group includes Xavier Hernandez of Houston, Tom Gordon of Kansas City, Ron Darling of Oakland, Melido Perez of the White Sox, Bobby Witt of Texas, Rob Dibble and Norm Charlton of Cincinnati, Jose DeLeon of St. Louis and Randy Johnson of Seattle.

You could probably figure out what the question marks were yourself—will Tom Gordon be a starter or in the bullpen, will Bobby Witt be healthy, will Xavier Hernandez even get a look. I've had Jose DeLeon on my teams for two years, and I have zero confidence that he is ever going to start winning again, even though all of my logical analysis tells me that he will. Nonetheless, I am absolutely sure that this group of pitchers will, *as a group*, pitch much better in 1992 than they did in 1991.

There's a "C" group, too, which is "guys who also have extremely high ratios of strikeouts to wins, but who I can't recommend at all. The four pitchers in this group are Chris Haney of Montreal, Bruce Ruffin of Milwaukee, Jim Deshaies of Houston and Tim Leary of New York. I can't recommend Haney because I don't know anything about him. Ruffin did have a rather striking improvement in his strikeout/walk ratio last year, which means that he is throwing a new pitch and learning to handle it, so something may happen in his career. But after posting won-lost records of 6-10, 6-10, 6-13 and 4-7 over the last four years, I can't recommend him. Deshaies and Leary have pitched well at times in their careers and may do so again, but I basically regard Tim Leary as the Lincoln Savings and Loan of major league baseball.

Pitchers who have very low ratios of wins to strikeouts decline so much and so consistently in following seasons that I *would* recommend that you absolutely avoid any pitcher with a ratio of less than six strikeouts per win, and be very careful of anybody with less than seven K per win. But on the other side you can't be so indiscriminate—you can't draft a whole bunch of guys like Tim Leary and Jim Deshaies just because they have high ratios of wins to strikeouts, or your staff is going to be one gem and a bunch of losers. There is room for one gamble like that on a pitching staff, maybe two.

Information works best for you when you can combine it with other information to reach a conclusion. If you take a list of pitchers who have very high ratios of strikeouts to wins, and you combine that with some other information, that's how you'll pick the Steve Averys and miss the Chuck Carys. If you take the pitchers with high ratios of strikeouts to wins and also look at the indicators for their teams, then you can have two things working for you, rather than one.

The magic number here is about 15 to 1; if you take the pitchers who have 15 times as many strikeouts as wins in 1991 they will, *as a group*, have a dramatically better record in 1992 than they did in 1991. But if you just take that list and pick a pitcher off of it at random, God knows what you may get. Pick a pitcher off that list that you like for some other reason. Knowledge is built of combinations of information.

THE ST. LOUIS CARDINALS

• IN A BOX •

1991 Won-Lost Record: 84-78 .519

Rank among 26 teams: 8th (Tie)
Over Last Five Years: 411-399 .507
Rank over Five Years: 12th
In Last Ten Years: 846-773 .523
Rank over Ten Years: 6th

Best Player: See "Note 1"

Weak Spot: Left field

Best Pitcher: Lee Smith

Staff Weakness: Willie Fraser

Best Bench Player: Geronimo Peña

Best Name for a Cardinal: Rod Brewer

Best Young Player: Ray Lankford (See "Note 2")

Best Looking Player: Todd Zeile

Ugliest Player: Bryn Smith

Most Pleasant Surprise, 1991: Felix Jose

Biggest Disappointment, 1991: Bernard Gilkey

Best Minor League Prospect: Donovan Osborne

Who Is: A left-handed pitcher, the Cardinals' first-round pick in the 1990 June draft. At Arkansas in 1991 he was 8-12, but had a good 3.63 ERA (it's a hitter's league) and struck out 130 men with only 43 walks in 166 innings.

Other Prospects: See "Note 3"

Designated Malcontent: Lee Smith

Park Characteristics: See "Note 4"

ORGANIZATIONAL REPORT CARD

Ownership:	A
Upper Management:	C
Field Management:	B
Front-Line Talent:	D
Second-Line Talent:	B+
Minor League System:	D

Comment: The Cardinals' ownership, the Busch family, does what ownership is supposed to do: provide the money and expect results, without micro-managing the organization. 1991 was a good year, but the people in the front office have yet to really prove that they know what they're doing. In 1990 they made two excellent trades (see "critical decisions").

TEAM LEADERS:

Batting Average: Felix Jose, .305

Last Ten Years (Season): Willie McGee, 1985, .353
Last Ten Years (Total): McGee, .297

Doubles: Felix Jose, 40

Triples: Ray Lankford, 15

Home Runs: Todd Zeile, 11

Last Ten Years (Season): Jack Clark, 1987, 35
Last Ten Years (Total): Clark, 66

Extra Base Hits: Jose, 54

RBI: Todd Zeile, 81

Last Ten Years (Season): Pedro Guerrero, 1989, 117
Last Ten Years (Total): Willie McGee, 545

Stolen Bases: Lankford, 44

Runs Created: Felix Jose, 88

Runs Created Per Game: Milt Thompson, 5.9

Secondary Average: Ozzie Smith, .296
Geronimo Peña had a secondary average of .335 as a part-time player.

Wins: Ken Hill and Bob Tewksbury, 11

Last Ten Years (Season): Andujar and Tudor, 1985, 21 each
Last Ten Years (Total): Bob Forsch, 70

Winning Percentage: Chris Carpenter, 10-4 .714

Strikeouts: Ken Hill, 121

Last Ten Years (Season): Jose DeLeon, 1988, 208
Last Ten Years (Total): DeLeon, 691

ERA: DeLeon, 2.71

Saves: Lee Smith, 47

League Leaders: See "Note 5"

1991 SEASON

Background: The glory years of the Cardinals, 1980–1987, turned ordinary in 1988, and the era came to an end when Whitey Herzog resigned in mid-season, 1990.

Outlook: The Cardinals were starting over. The Cardinals had half of a young lineup, half of a veteran lineup and an unsettled pitching staff, so nobody knew what to make of them. Expectations were not high.

Getaway: The Cardinals opened the season with a nine-game road trip, but survived that with a 4-5 record, then got hot on a thirteen-game homestand. By the end of April they were 13-8.

High Point of the Season: The Cardinals continued to play well throughout the middle of the summer, and by June had established themselves as the Pirates' only challenge from within the division. On August third the Cardinals beat the Pirates, 6-5 in ten innings, to close within 4½ games of first place. Todd Zeile won the game with a homer in the bottom of the tenth.

Low Point of the Season: The Cardinals then lost five of their next seven, and the Pirates quickly re-established their lead.

Stretch Drive: As September opened, the Cardinals stood at 69-59, eight games in arrears to the Pirates. They had no realistic shot at the pennant, but stranger things have happened. The Cards went 15-19 after September 1, and finished fourteen games behind.

Most Exciting Game of the Season: See article, "Busch Blather"

Major Injuries: The Cardinals lost three quality pitchers for the entire 1991 season. Todd Worrell and Joe Magrane both underwent nerve transplant surgeries on their elbows, and the Cards have hopes of both of them pitching this season. Frank DiPino also underwent elbow surgery last year; he is not expected to be ready at the start of the season.

On July 7, Pedro Guerrero suffered a hairline fracture in his leg after colliding with Tom Pagnozzi in pursuit of a foul bunt. He was on the disabled list for 39 days.

Ken Hill was out for the last three weeks of July with a sore right elbow.

Bernard Gilkey missed a month with a chipped bone in his right thumb.

Offense: As they have had for ten years, the Cardinals had a low-power, high-average offense with good speed. They were last in the league in home runs (68), but second in stolen bases (202).

The Cardinals didn't really have a leadoff man. Lankford hit there because he's fast, but St. Louis leadoff men hit .247 and scored only 89 runs on the season, very low figures. They didn't have a number three hitter or number four hitter, getting only 23 homers out of those two spots combined with a .262 batting average. However, they got wonderful production out of the number two spot (92 walks, .288 average, 107 runs scored and 39 stolen bases, mostly Ozzie Smith) and stronger-than-average output from spots five through eight. (Ozzie Smith is also a key to that. Most teams use their shortstop as the number eight hitter, and get nothing from the spot. Being able to put the shortstop in a key offensive role means that the guy who would be hitting seventh (often the catcher) hits eighth instead, and there's an extra player from an "offensive" spot like right field or third base to be placed in the sixth or seventh slot of the batting order. Adding it all up, the offense was about average, neither good nor bad.

Defense: The Cardinals were an extremely good defensive team, with a fast outfield, sure-handed infielders and a top-flight defensive catcher. Todd Zeile led the league in errors at third base, but actually his defense there was a pleasant surprise in view of his lack of experience.

Pitching: Average.

Best Game by a Starting Pitcher: Bryn Smith's three-hitter against Montreal, September 23 (9 3 1 1 1 6). The Cardinals did not have a shutout by a starting pitcher during the season, although they had five combined shutouts.

Worst Game by a Starting Pitcher: Omar Olivares against the Reds on July 27 (3⅔ 8 8 7 2 1 Game Score: 13)

Indicators for 1991 were: Up Moderately (+8)

Number of regulars having good seasons by their own standards: Five (Jose, Ozzie Smith, Zeile, Pagnozzi and Milt Thompson)

1991 Over-Achiever: Felix Jose

1991 Under-Achiever: Jose Oquendo

Infield: Good to excellent.

Outfield: Poor; not enough offense in left and center.

Catching: Offense weak, but defense compensates.

Starting Pitching: The biggest reason the Cardinals couldn't compete with the Pirates is that they really don't have a number one starting pitcher. They don't have anybody like Drabek or Smiley or Glavine or Dennis Martinez who can pitch 250 innings and win fifteen to twenty games. Jose DeLeon, who was supposed to be their ace, has been plagued by two seasons of amazing bad luck and sporadic control troubles, during which he has posted a won-lost record of 12-28 although he hasn't pitched anything like that badly.

What they had was five guys who were all pretty decent. None of the five (DeLeon, Tewksbury, Hill, Olivares and Bryn Smith) was *good*, but none of them was *bad*, either. They could get the game to the bullpen most of the time.

Bullpen: And the bullpen was fairly good. Lee Smith, although he may well be as vile a person as his teammates in Boston and Chicago would say he was, is nonetheless one of the greatest relief pitchers of all time, and still barrelling along in his mid-thirties. Two of his setup men were ineffective, but the other three were good.

Percentage of Offense Created By:

Young Players:	47%
Players in Their Prime:	22%
Veterans:	31%

Team Age:

Age of Non-Pitchers:	28.5
Age of Pitching Staff:	29.4
Overall Team Age:	28.89

In retrospect, the critical decisions were: Four things. There was a lot of talk a year ago about the Cardinals trading Ozzie Smith, but they decided to hang onto him, and he delivered a stellar season. That's one, the decision *not* to trade Ozzie. Second, the decision to move Todd Zeile from catcher to third base, one of the most hotly debated issues of the winter of 1990–1991, worked out better than I would have dreamed, as Zeile was OK defensively and excellent with the bat.

Third, the Cardinals in 1991 derived benefits from two in-season trades of 1990, the trade of Tom Brunansky for Lee Smith and that of Willie McGee for Felix Jose. The trades are . . . well, I don't want to hype them, but it's hard to imagine how they could have worked out any better.

Fourth, the Cardinals a year ago let Vince Coleman leave as a free agent, and put rookie outfielders in left and center to replace Coleman and McGee. Although Gilkey in left was a disappointment, Lankford last year was as good as Coleman normally is, and with any luck will be better next year.

THAT AND THE OTHER

Lookalikes: Joe Torre and Rich Little
Jose DeLeon and Orlando Cepeda

Hall of Fame Watch: If Ozzie Smith doesn't get a plaque I'm writing my congressman. Lee Smith is still a longshot.

Chris Berman, Have You Considered: Mark (Potato) Grater

Throwback: Tom Pagnozzi

Attendance Trend: Strongly downward in recent years. The Cardinals' 1991 attendance of 2.45 million was their lowest since 1984.

Players with a Chance for 3000 career hits: None

Record Watch: The record for career saves is 341, by new Hall of Famer Rollie Fingers. Jeff Reardon has 327 saves and had 40 last year, and Lee Smith has 312 career and 47 last year, so that record will be shattered within the next two years, probably this year. Reardon will break the record first, but the real questions are

1) When these two are through, which one will have the record, and

2) How long will he be able to hold it?

My money is on Lee Smith. Smith is two years younger than Reardon—no big deal—but he is also more of a power-type pitcher, and in my opinion is simply a better pitcher than Reardon. Reardon over the last two years has pitched only 111 innings, recording 61 saves; Smith has pitched 156 innings, recording 78 saves. I think he'll get the record, and I think he'll hold it for at least ten years.

Best Interview: Joe Magrane

Probably Could Play Regularly For Another Team: Geronimo Peña

Best Fundamental Player: Ozzie Smith

Worst Fundamental Player: Gerald Perry

Best Defensive Player: Ozzie

Worst Defensive Player: Pedro Guerrero

The Cardinals unexpectedly re-signed Pedro, and are talking about playing him in left field. That'll be fun.

Best Knowledge of the Strike Zone: Ozzie

Least Command of the Strike Zone: Ray Lankford

Fastest Runner: Ray Lankford or Geronimo Peña

A few years ago, in one of the *Abstracts*, I introduced a method called "Speed Scores", which was a method of looking at *all* of the things in a player's record which reflect speed, and attempting to boil the raw speed out of the other events. The method considers six things as indicative of speed: Stolen Base Attempts, Stolen Base Percentage, Triples, GIDP Frequency, Runs Scored, and Defensive Position and Range.

Despite a relatively poor stolen base percentage, Ray Lankford had the highest speed score of any player in 1991 (8.5). Geronimo Peña is also very fast.

Slowest Runner: Pedro Guerrero

Best Baserunner: Ozzie Smith

Most Likely to Still be Here in 2000: Todd Zeile

Best Fastball: Lee Smith or DeLeon

Best Breaking Pitch: I don't know

Best Control: Bob Tewksbury

Oddest Collection of Abilities: Jose Oquendo

Why is this man in the Major Leagues: Willie Fraser

Gets Ahead of the Hitters Most Often: Bryn Smith

Gets Ahead of the Hitters Least Often: Juan Agosto

Best Local Sportswriter: Bernie Micklausz

The Most Knowledgeable People About Local Baseball History Are: Bob Broeg and Bill Borst

Most-Comparable Players:

to C Tom Pagnozzi, Jeff Reed
to 1B Andres Galarraga, Candy Maldonado
to 2B Jose Oquendo, Jose Lind
to 3B Todd Zeile, Robin Ventura
to SS Ozzie Smith, Willie Randolph
to LF Milt Thompson, Jim Eisenreich
to CF Ray Lankford, Brian McRae
to RF Felix Jose, Steve Finley

Most Fun to Watch: Ozzie Smith

Least Fun to Watch: Bernard Gilkey

Managerial Type: Rex Hudler

Among the All-Time Team Leaders: See "Note 6"

A little bit of research: See article, "Ozzie's Glove"

Town Team:

C—Yogi Berra
1B—Charlie Grimm
2B—Red Schoendienst
SS—Art Fletcher
3B—Harry Steinfeldt
LF—Cool Papa Bell
CF—George Van Haltren
RF—Roy Sievers
SP—Pud Galvin
MGR—Earl Weaver

Post-Season Transactions:

November 21, re-signed Rich Gedman for one year
November 25, traded Ken Hill (p) to Montreal for Andres Galarraga (1b)
December 19, Pedro Guerrero agreed to salary arbitration
See article, "Hill/Galarraga"

What Needs to Be Done For 1992: The key thing for the Cardinals in the next few years is whether the good young players (Lankford, Jose, Zeile) develop into *better* players, and whether the other young guys (Gilkey, Peña, Alicea) develop into players at all. That being the case, what the Cardinals need to do now is make sure that those players are properly supported, that they are surrounded by people who can help them set goals and reach them, rather than letting their careers drift.

Outlook for 1992: See article, "A Basis for Pessimism"

Index of Leading Indicators for 1992: Down 19.4

Positive Indicators: None

Negative Indicators: All Seven

Due for a better season: Jose DeLeon

Likely to have a worse season: Felix Jose

1992 Won-Lost Record will be: 76-86

BUSCH BLATHER

Rob Neyer

I was in St. Louis visiting family on April 21, and since I had never seen a Cardinals' game and the Phillies were in town, I decided to spend an afternoon at the ballpark. As it turned out, I lucked into the most exciting game of the Cardinals' season.

Ken Hill started for St. Louis, but he didn't have it, and after 2½ innings the score was five-zip Phillies. After six, it was 6-1, but then the Cards came up with four in the seventh to make it a ballgame.

After 8½ the score still stood at 6-5, Phils. Lefty Mitch Williams was brought in to record the save, but Felix Jose greeted him with a line single to left. Gerald Perry was due next. Perry doesn't handle left-handers very well, and I was sure that Torre would pinch-hit with Guerrero, who had been given the day off. When Perry came to the plate, I couldn't believe it—figured Torre was either asleep or planning to bunt.

Williams' first pitch was a fastball (what else?), and Perry killed it, a triple to deep right center to tie the game.

So now the Cards had Perry on third, nobody out. Leyva ordered intentional walks to Craig Wilson and Tom Pagnozzi, loading the bases. Game over, right? With Oquendo due up, *now* Torre went to the bench for Guerrero. Pedro popped to the second baseman—one out. Next was the pitcher's spot, and Rex Hudler stepped out of the dugout. He popped to the shortstop—two out. Bernard Gilkey lifted a fly to short right center. Three out, Williams was out of it, and we settled back into our seats.

In the top of the tenth Lee Smith blew away the Phils on a fly ball and two swinging strikeouts.

Ozzie Smith led off the bottom of the inning. Williams struck him out with three pitches, but Ray Lankford worked his way on with a walk. Everybody in the park, including the Wild Thing, knew Lankford was going down to second. Williams threw over four straight times to no avail, and with the count 1-0 on Jose, Lankford took off. Safe. With the count now 2-0, they went ahead and intentionally walked Jose.

That brought up Gerald Perry again. He slapped a hard grounder to Kruk, who hitched but threw to second in time to force Jose. That left Lankford at third and . . . but wait a minute! Lankford never stopped running! Thon threw a strike to the plate, just as Lankford was arriving. Daulton had the ball secured for a split second, but that was all. Lankford ran him over like Christian Okoye stepping through a high school cornerback. The ball ended up on the ground (along with Daulton), and that was the game. In one of the toughest scoring decisions I've ever seen, Daulton drew an error on the play.

. . .

Random Notes on the Game and Busch Stadium:

• Prior to the game and for the first five innings, the aisles were overrun with beer vendors: Bud, Bud Light, Busch. In retrospect, this should not have been a surprise.

• The scores of other games were constantly flashing on two auxiliary scoreboards, which is a nice change from Royals Stadium, where you're lucky if you see other scores every two or three innings. I was able to follow the wild Cubs-Pirates game (see Pirates "Most Exciting Game"), and I thought maybe the scoreboard guy was hanging out with the off-duty beer guys until I watched Sportscenter that night.

• Have you ever watched a Busch Stadium game on TV, and thought, "Wow, look at how many of the fans are wearing red." Well, a lot of people *do* wear red to the game (the official team jackets are very popular), but all of the seats are red, too, so from a distance the empty red seats look like red-clad fans.

• Around the top of the stadium, there is a flag flown for every National League team, and each of the Cardinals' minor league affiliates. I noticed that the San Diego flag was still brown, though they had already changed their colors to blue and red.

• Craig Wilson twice grounded out to Charlie Hayes at third base. The first time, Hayes bounced the ball to first, and I thought, "What a lousy throw." But when he did it the second time too, I realized that he was doing it on purpose, apparently to eliminate any chance of a high throw. I didn't see Hayes play on TV very often, so I don't know if this was his SOP on artificial turf.

• During the seventh-inning stretch, they play the Budweiser song. "Take Me Out to the Ball Game" isn't heard until after the eighth inning.

• Beyond the fence in deep, deep left center there is a big Anheuser-Busch eagle made of lights. I gather that when a Cardinal hits a home run (a rare event last year, and there were none this day) the eagle lights up and flaps its wings. What I can't figure out is why there is a net covering the eagle. It would take a Roy Hobbs drive to get near the thing, and if someone *does* hit a ball that far, he deserves to break some lights.

• In addition to witnessing the most exciting game of the year, I probably saw Ray Lankford at his best. Besides winning the game almost single-handedly in the tenth, Lankford singled, doubled, tripled, and played brilliant defense in center field. He made a believer out of me.

• After the season, while working on this comment and some other stuff for St. Louis In A Box, I called the Cardinals' office. While I was on hold they played highlights of this game.

—Rob Neyer

OZZIE'S GLOVE

One of the stats that I use to measure defense is called "range factor". Range Factor is very simple: it's just the number of defensive plays per game that a player has made. It doesn't include errors; just plays actually made (putouts and assists) per game played at a position. These are Ozzie Smith's range factors since he came into the league:

Year	Defensive Games	Range Factor
1978	159	5.11
1979	155	5.23
1980	158	5.75
1981	110	5.84
1982	139	5.86
1983	158	5.21
1984	124	5.40
1985	158	5.15
1986	144	4.74
1987	158	4.82
1988	150	5.02
1989	153	4.52
1990	140	4.21
1991	150	4.21

I have about a dozen comments here, which I'll struggle to organize:

1) The *pattern* of Ozzie's range factors is the prototypical pattern which would be displayed by almost all players if they were fortunate enough to come to the majors in their early twenties and play a couple of thousand games at a position. After coming into the league his range factors increased significantly for two or three years as he learned to play the hitters. Then they stabilized, then in his late twenties they began to decline, as the gains in knowledge no longer compensated for the loss in quickness. Virtually all players' range factors decline after they pass thirty.

2) The *raw numbers* in Ozzie's prime are amazing. In the early eighties Ozzie was making nearly six plays per game, which is almost unheard of. The major league leader last year was Barry Larkin, who made 5.19 plays per nine innings.

3) One of the problems with range factors in the past has been that we didn't have defensive innings played, leaving open one avenue for possible distortion in the category. A player who played many partial games would have a misleading range factor.

4) With modern stats this is no longer a problem, since STATS INC. and a couple of other organizations keep and publish counts of defensive innings at a position.

5) Ozzie's range factors based on plays *per nine innings* over the last two years would be 4.41 and 4.53, rather than 4.21 each year. His per-inning range factors for earlier years, if we had the data, could not be lower than the ones above, and would normally be higher. So the basic conclusion—that Ozzie's range is nowhere near what it once was—would not be altered.

Range factors per-game are always lower than per-nine innings. Barry Larkin's range factor in 1991, per game, would be 4.96.

6) (Finally reaching a conclusion) Ozzie's Gold Glove in 1991 is kind of a joke. Ozzie isn't the best defensive shortstop in the league anymore; Barry Larkin is.

I've always thought I was Ozzie Smith's biggest fan. I argued in 1985 that he should have won the MVP Award, and was shocked and disappointed when he finished far down the list in the voting. I think he's a no-questions-asked Hall of Famer. But I don't believe he's still the best defensive shortstop in the league, and I was surprised that he won the award. I thought the realization that he had lost a step at short, not from the stats but just from watching him play, was widespread.

7) Ozzie did lead the league in fielding percentage (.987), as he often has, and established a record for fewest errors by a shortstop playing 150 games. That's good, but what does it amount to? The *lowest* fielding percentage of any regular shortstop in the league was .960, so based on 639 total chances (Ozzie's number) that's a difference of 18 plays. The difference between Ozzie and Larkin in range is more like a hundred plays.

8) Having said that, I would be lying if I told you that there was a reliable way to move from defensive statistics to an estimate of how many runs the player has saved with his glove.

Ozzie Smith is not only an outstanding *defensive* player, but also has become one of the best *offensive* shortstops of his era, which is not widely recognized. We can state with reasonable accuracy what Ozzie's offensive value is: offensively, as I mention in Note 1, he was about 52 runs better than a replacement-level shortstop.

Now, that's not precise; it might be 50, it might be 54. It might be 42 or 62, but it's somewhere in there. But we can't really do that defensively; we can try, but we have to make assumptions which are so vague that they call the entire process into question.

9) Even assuming that he is *not* a legitimate Gold Glove winner, Ozzie remains an MVP candidate. If you replaced Ozzie with a good AAA shortstop you'd lose 52 runs, and that's one of the largest figures in the league. Barry Bonds was +71, Terry Pendleton +63.

HILL/GALARRAGA

The development of Rheal Cormier gave the Cardinals six starting pitchers, and they decided that Ken Hill was the one they wanted to move. The trade of Ken Hill for Galarraga combines several formulaic elements of a smart trade. First, the Cardinals are trading a player coming off his best season ever (Hill) for a player whose value is lower now than it has ever been. Look at it this way: would the Expos have given up Galarraga for Ken Hill a year ago, or two years or three years ago? They certainly would not have. The Cardinals took advantage of a good year by Ken Hill to trade him for a man who has always been a better player.

Second, the Cardinals moved in their fences this winter, which will probably make all of their pitchers look worse (and their hitters look better) in the 1992 final statistics.

Third, the Cardinals traded for a power hitter coming out of a poor hitter's park, and thus acquired a player who may be a better hitter than his stat record, over a period of years, would show.

Those are three things that I have always preached: trade for a player when his stock is down, not for a player coming off his best year. Adjust your talent to suit your park. Trade for hitters coming out of pitcher's parks and pitchers coming out of hitter's parks.

Having said that, I have to say that instinctively I don't especially like the trade. I liked Ken Hill a year ago, as you may remember, and had expected him to have his best year in 1991, as he did. For that reason, I don't see his 1991 year as representing his upper limit, but simply a case of his finally doing what he was capable of. Galarraga is the opposite; when he had his monster season in 1988 I knew he was over his head and said so, so naturally I don't see his 1991 debacle as being as much of an anomaly as many people would see it.

I ask two questions: which player has a better chance of being a quality contributor for the next five seasons, and which player has a better chance of having star-quality seasons? To me, the answers are both Ken Hill. I don't think *either* of them will have star seasons, but I think Ken Hill has a 10% chance of surprising us, and Galarraga maybe 8%. I think Galarraga is about 50-50 to be a quality player for several years, and Hill a little better than 50-50.

But I don't *hate* the trade, either. I see the logic of it; I see the possibility that the Cardinals have picked up a cleanup hitter cheap. Hey, a good many players have had MVP seasons immediately after being given up on for lost—Maris, Frank Robinson, Dick Allen. I like Galarraga more now than I liked Terry Pendleton a year ago.

A BASIS FOR PESSIMISM

The seven factors of a team's performance which have been shown to predict the team's up or down movement in the following season are:

1) The Plexiglas Principle. Teams which improve this year will tend to relapse next year, and vice versa.

2) The AAA Team. A team with a strong AAA affiliate will tend to do better in the following year than an equal major league team with a weak AAA affiliate.

3) The Ratio of Wins to Runs Scored and Allowed. A team which wins *more* games than predicted by the Pythagorean theory will tend to decline in the following season by the amount of over-production.

4) The ratio of runs scored to runs created. A team which scores more runs than predicted by the runs created formula in one season will tend to decline in the next season.

5) The won-lost record itself. Everybody is drawn toward the center. Winning teams tend to decline; losing teams tend to improve.

6) Late-season performance. A team which plays poorly late in the season tends to carry over the poor performance to the following season.

7) Team age. Old teams tend to decline; young teams tend to improve.

All seven of these factors are working *against* the Cardinals in 1992; all seven indicate that decline in 1992 is more likely than improvement. I arranged them above in order of impact; the largest negative indicator is number one, and the smallest is number seven (although the Cardinals were thought of as a young team, in fact they were very slightly *older* than an average major league team.)

The Cardinals got very good years from some veteran players last year—Ozzie, Lee Smith, Thompson. Bryn Smith, Bob Tewksbury and Pedro Guerrero contributed. I'm not sure that those players will still be at the same level in 1992, and I'm not sure that the improvements of the younger guys will offset the declines of the older ones. I think that the expectations for the 1992 Cardinals may be too high, but there's really no way of knowing other than to run the race and see who wins.

Since I've written this, and since I'm going to pick the Cardinals to finish with a record of 74-88, people are going to write that I'm down on the Cardinals this year. I'm not, really; it's mostly just the data. The indicators say they'll be off this year and I'll go with that because riding with the indicators more or less guarantees that I'll be right more times than wrong in each book. I need those guarantees because I'm not smart enough to figure out anything at all about who is going to win without them. Obviously, the Cardinals have come a long way in one year.

TRACERS

A modest and well-liked person, [Ernie] Nevers, surprisingly, had a baseball incident stand out in his mind over some of his football achievements. He told about it in a recent letter to Stanley Grosshandler, a staunch fan who lives in Hales Corners, Wis.

"I was sent in to pinch-hit against the Senators—it was my first time at bat in the majors—leading by a big score," Nevers recalled. "Walter Johnson was the pitcher and he blew a couple of strikes past me. I couldn't even get the bat off my shoulder.

"Well, he walked up to the catcher to take the ball from him and as he started back to the mound he told me, 'The next one will be right down the middle, kid.' It was, and I got a double. Johnson was just trying to make me look good."

—Ernie Nevers' obituary in *The Sporting News*, 5/22/76.

Nevers, as most of you know, was one of the greatest football players of all time. He also pitched for the St. Louis Browns in parts of three seasons, with a lifetime 4.64 ERA.

Total Baseball has the date of every player's major league debut. According to *Total Baseball*, Nevers first appeared in a major league game on April 26, 1926. I checked the newspaper for the account of that game. Nevers did debut as a pinch-hitter, batting for Win Ballou, and the Browns did have a big lead at the time. He did not hit a double, however; he made out. And he was not facing Walter Johnson, or any other Senator, but Joe Shaute of the Indians.

Nevers would hit only two doubles in his major league career. The 1969 edition of *The Baseball Encyclopedia* has career batting records for pitchers, so I checked there to see how many times Nevers was used as a pinch hitter. According to Macmillan, the game in 1926, his debut, was Nevers' only major league pinch hitting appearance, and he never had a pinch hit at all.

So Nevers' story of a pinch-hit double off of Walter Johnson in his first major league at bat is at odds with the reference books on a very basic level; Nevers says he had a pinch hit *then*, and Macmillan says he never had one at all. But Nevers could very possibly have batted against Johnson at some later point and simply confused the incident in his mind. It was necessary to check every Browns-Senators contest in 1926 and 1927 (the latter was Johnson's final season) to see whether something like this could have happened.

I found every Browns-Senators game in 1926; Nevers appeared in only two of them. On July 31, Walter Johnson and Milt Gaston squared off as starting pitchers in Sportsman's Park. Gaston was hammered in the top of the first, and Nevers came in to relieve with two outs and four runs in. He got the next man out, and eventually pitched the rest of the game, eight and a third innings. In the meantime, Johnson was throwing a six-hitter, one of the last shutouts of his career.

Nevers faced The Big Train three times, but he did not hit a double. He *did* get a single, in the top of the fourth with one out. At that point, the score was five-nothing. It seems a little early to be giving gifts. Nevers was pitching well at that point, although he later threw gopher balls to Goslin, Judge and Rice.

If the memory has any foundation in fact, however, this has to be it, because that was the only hit that Nevers would ever get off Walter. On August 24, Nevers started (and lost, 6-0) against Washington, and he did hit a double, but his opponent was not Johnson but rather General Crowder. That was his only double of the season.

I checked all 23 games between the Browns and the Nats in 1927, and here is what I found:

Johnson appeared four times against St. Louis, all starts, going 0-2.

Nevers pitched only one-third of an inning against Washington all season.

Not only did Nevers not bat against Johnson, he did not bat against *any* Washington pitcher.

So what are we to make of all this? I suppose we haven't eliminated the possibility that Nevers doubled against Johnson in a spring training game or exhibition of some kind. He may have remembered the 1926 single off the greatest pitcher in the world so many times that it grew an extra base in his memory. The story has elements of truth in it. Nevers did once get a meaningless hit off Walter Johnson, he did once hit a double off a Washington pitcher, and he did make his major league debut as a pinch hitter for a team that had a big lead. As often happens, his memory combined three or four different events that actually happened into one. And who it was that told him the next one would be right down the middle and when this happened, we're just never going to know.

—Rob Neyer

NOTE 1

Best Player: Ozzie Smith, who has been the Cardinals' best player over the last ten years, is pushed for that position now by Felix Jose. I would still consider Ozzie the best of 1991, but probably Jose or Zeile (or Lankford) will be the best in 1992.

To expand on that just a little bit, Ozzie was an estimated 52 runs better *as an offensive player* than a replacement level shortstop. This marks him as the Cardinals' most irreplaceable *offensive* player; Jose was +43, and Zeile +40. So if you add in the Gold Glove defense, it is apparent that Ozzie remains an extremely valuable player.

NOTE 2

Best Young Player: The three obvious candidates to be described as the Cardinals' best young player are Lankford, Zeile and Jose. Felix Jose had the best year of the three, but he is a year older than Zeile and two years older than Lankford, which is a significant difference at this age, and he had never played particularly well before 1991. Between Zeile and Lankford I would point out two things:

1) that Lankford had a better year as a 24-year-old rookie in 1991 than Zeile did as a 24-year-old rookie in 1990, and

2) that Lankford has *more* skills than Zeile, more diverse skills.

So I choose Lankford, but it's very close. You can make a good argument for any of the three.

NOTE 3

Other Prospects: St. Louis had three first-round picks in the draft last June, including two as compensation for the loss of free agents Ken Dayley and Vince Coleman. **Dmitri Young** was the first chosen, fourth overall. A third baseman for now, Young is a switch-hitter who supposedly looks a lot like Kevin Mitchell. Young hit just .256 last summer, but he was only 17 and *Baseball America* listed him as the #2 prospect in the Appalachian League.

The Ken Dayley pick (21st overall), from Toronto, was used on left-handed pitcher **Allen Watson,** who went to A ball and pitched OK. The Vince Coleman pick was used to select right-hander **Brian Barber.** Also at A ball, Barber was hammered in his first nine starts (0-6, 7.69), but rebounded to strike out 84 men in 73 innings.

The Cardinals have nothing at AA or AAA. Their AAA team, Louisville, went 51-92; the AA team was 49-87. Donovan Osborne and Rheal Cormier would appear to be the only prospects on either team.

NOTE 4

Park Characteristics: Busch Stadium for many years has been the second-poorest home run park in the National League. The Cardinals in 1992 are moving in their fences, which will cause substantial increases in the home run totals for all of their regulars. Until it happens, there's no way of knowing how substantial the increases will be. The Cardinals played very well in their home park in 1991 (52-32 at home, 32-46 on the road). That was the largest home-field advantage in the major leagues, but over a period of years their home field advantage has *not* been particularly large. It's been smaller than average.

The Park Helps: Moving the fences in will probably help Todd Zeile more than anyone else. Zeile, Galarraga, Lankford, Guerrero.

The Park Hurts: My guess is that the pitcher most negatively affected by the fence move will be Omar Olivares, but that's a guess.

NOTE 5

League Leaders: Two Cardinals established significant league records in 1991, Lee Smith the league record for saves (47) and Ozzie the record for fewest errors by a shortstop (8).

Ozzie Smith has laid down 173 Sacrifice Bunts in his career, quite a few more than any other active player. Alfredo Griffin is second with 129. Ozzie also established little league records of one sort or another all the time, most years leading the league in this or that at shortstop.

NOTE 6

Among the All-Time Team Leaders: The Cardinals' team batting records are so awesome that Ozzie Smith, after ten years of All-Star performance, is just beginning to appear on the bottom of the lists in most areas. Ozzie is third on the stolen bases list, with 352. He has a ways to go catch the top two, Vince Coleman (549) and Lou Brock (888).

With 126 saves, Todd Worrell trails all-time Cardinal leader Bruce Sutter by just one. He may never get there, and then on the other hand maybe that record will be broken by Worrell and Lee Smith in the same year. Smith needs 53 to tie.

THE PHILADELPHIA PHILLIES

• IN A BOX •

1991 Won-Lost Record: 78-84 .481

Rank among 26 teams: 17th
Over Last Five Years: 367-442 .454
Rank over Five Years: 23rd
In Last Ten Years: 788-830 .487
Rank over Ten Years: 20th

Best Player: John Kruk

Weak Spot: Third Base

Best Pitcher: Terry Mulholland

Staff Weakness: Peculiar fondness for Jason Grimsley

Best Bench Player: Randy Ready

Best Baseball Name: Randy Ready

Best Young Player: Mickey Morandini or Wes Chamberlain
Both Morandini and Chamberlain will be 26 years old in April, and while I *like* both of them, neither is firmly established as a regular, so it is a reach to describe either as a good young player.

Best Looking Player: Jose DeJesus

Ugliest Player: John Kruk

Best Looking Player's Wife: Lynne Daulton

Most Pleasant Surprise, 1991: Tommy Greene

Biggest Disappointment, 1991: Darren Daulton

Best Minor League Prospect: Andy Ashby

Who Is: A right-handed starting pitcher who will receive every opportunity to break into the Phillies' rotation. Ashby is big, 6'5", 24 years old, right handed. Ashby pitched last year for Scranton/Wilkes-Barre in the International League, where one manager remarked, "Probably as good a stuff as anybody in the league, but he gets himself in trouble with walks." He finished 11-11, 3.46 ERA.

Other Prospects: See article, "Phillie Prospects"

Park Characteristics: Veterans Stadium is a hitter's park. It's a real good park for doubles and triples, helps batting averages a little bit and is fair for home runs.

ORGANIZATIONAL REPORT CARD

Ownership: C−
Upper Management: B
Field Management: B
Front-Line Talent: D−
Second-Line Talent: D
Minor League System: D

Comment: Lee Thomas has been here since June, 1988, and th Phillie farm system is still basically inert. If the Phillies don't begi to make *real* progress this season, progress in terms of rebuildin the talent base rather than simply getting good years out of guy like Mitch Williams, Thomas' ability to direct the system wi come into question.

What the Phillies have done so far is snarf up young ballplayer left lying around by other systems—Wes Chamberlain from Pitts burgh, Jose DeJesus from Kansas City, Braulio Castillo from th Dodgers, Dave Hollins from San Diego, Tommy Greene fron Atlanta, Len Dykstra from the Mets. You can add Kyle Abbot from the Angels; I think he's just as good. The Phillies needed t do that, because they didn't have young ballplayers of their own and they've done it brilliantly.

TEAM LEADERS:

Batting Average: John Kruk, .294

Last Ten Years (Season): Len Dykstra, 1990, .325
Last Ten Years (Total): John Kruk, .301

Doubles: Dale Murphy, 33

Triples: John Kruk, 6

Home Runs: John Kruk, 21

Last Ten Years (Season): Mike Schmidt, 1983, 40
Last Ten Years (Total): Mike Schmidt, 234

Extra Base Hits: John Kruk, 54

RBI: John Kruk, 92

Last Ten Years (Season): Mike Schmidt, 1986, 119
Last Ten Years (Total): Mike Schmidt, 717

Walks: John Kruk, 67

Stolen Bases: Lenny Dykstra, 24

uns Created: John Kruk, 99

uns Created Per Game: Kruk, 6.7

econdary Average: John Kruk, .327

Darren Daulton had a secondary average of .330, but he wasn't quite a regular.

Vins: Terry Mulholland, 16

Last Ten Years (Season): Steve Carlton, 1982, 23
Last Ten Years (Total): Kevin Gross, 60

Vinning Percentage: Mitch Williams, 12-5 .706

trikeouts: Tommy Greene, 154

Last Ten Years (Season): Steve Carlton, 1982, 286
Last Ten Years (Total): Carlton, 984

RA: Tommy Greene, 3.38

aves: Mitch Williams, 30

eague Leaders: Jose DeJesus led the National League in walks allowed, 128, but he at least partially offset that by allowing only .35 home runs per nine innings, percentage points more than major league leader Jose Rijo.

991 SEASON

ackground: Following their last championship season in 1983 the Phillies fell quickly to the bottom of the league, finishing fifth in 1985. They opened 1991 with a string of four straight losing seasons, and pressure was building on the Phillies to give their fans something to cheer for.

utlook: No one looked upon the Phillies as likely division winners. The hopes were that they could play .500 or better ball.

etaway: After winning three of their first five games the Phillies lost nine out of ten, which cost Nick Leyva his job.

irst High Point of the Season: The team spurted forward, under Jim Fregosi, and reached .500 (18-18) on May 18.

On the morning of May 6 Len Dykstra and Darren Daulton had a high-speed collision with a tree, and left the lineup for the hospital. The drive to .500 was completed without these two in the lineup.

Most Exciting Game of the Season: Depends on whether you like pitching duels or slugfests.

On May 17 in Philadelphia the Phillies and Cubs played scoreless baseball through fifteen innings. Thon drove in Dale Murphy with the winning run in the bottom of the sixteenth. This game was a pivotal point in the career of Tommy Greene. Greene got the win with four innings of brilliant relief work, which earned him a start, in which he threw a no-hitter, which put him in the starting rotation.

On June 5 in Atlanta it was tied up after nine, 8-8. The Phillies came up with two in the top of the tenth, but the Braves matched that in the bottom of the inning. The visitors scored two more in the top of the eleventh. With the Phillie bullpen empty, Jose DeJesus came in to finish up. He gave up one run and left two on base to escape with the first save of his career. Final score, Phils 12, Braves 11.

Low Point of the Season: The Phillies fell into another slump in late May. This slump lasted for two months. On July 28, the Phillies lost their seventh in a row, dropping their record to 40-58. At that point, they occupied last place, 21½ games out of first, and there were no obvious signs that the Phillies would improve.

High Point of the Season: And then, inexplicably, they won thirteen straight games. Relief ace Mitch Williams picked up four wins in five games, all four of them in extra-inning games, and notched up a fifth win two days later. The Phillies allowed only 33 runs in the thirteen wins, raising their record to 53-58 on August 12.

Stretch Drive: Although out of the race, the Phillies continued to play fairly well through the rest of August and September. They couldn't catch .500, but they stayed close to it.

Major Injuries: See article

Offense: Awful. The Phillies had both the lowest batting average and the lowest secondary average in the division, so it must be said that they were fortunate to score as many runs as they did (629, fifth in the division.) Their leadoff hitter was hurt and they have only one middle-of-the-order type hitter (Kruk).

Defense: Poor. Daulton had an awful year throwing out runners, and they didn't really have a regular second baseman. While Dykstra was out they didn't have a real center fielder. Murphy is slow and Chamberlain is awkward, so the outfield defense was pretty ugly. The Phillies *allowed* 261 doubles, which is more than were hit by any National League team.

Pitching: Greatly improved; see "Re-Armament"

Best Game by a Starting Pitcher:

A two-hitter by Terry Mulholland against Montreal, September 18, has the highest game score. Mulholland pitched a shutout, walked *no one* and struck out ten for a Game Score of 93. Right behind is Tommy Greene's no-hitter, in which he also struck out ten but walked seven.

Worst Game by a Starting Pitcher: August 16, Bruce Ruffin at Wrigley Field (1/3 6 6 6 1 0 Game Score: 14)

Indicators for 1991 were: Down 8.1

Number of regulars having good seasons by their own standards: Two, and they were both first basemen (Kruk and Jordan)

1991 Over-Achiever: John Kruk

1991 Under-Achiever: Von Hayes

Infield: Fair to poor. The Phillies split playing time at three infield spots—Kruk and Jordan at first, Morandini and Backman at second, Hayes and Hollins at third. The combinations provided neither notable offensive punch nor exceptional defensive consistency.

Outfield: No better in terms of how they performed last year, but the talent is better. An outfield of Chamberlain, Dykstra and Kruk might put 300 runs on the scoreboard, which is what you want from your outfield.

Catching: Disappointing.

Starting Pitching: Much improved.

Bullpen: Much improved.

Percentage of offense created by:

Young Players:	36%
Players in Their Prime:	21%
Past Their Prime:	34%

Team Age:

Age of Non-Pitchers:	29.5
Age of Pitching Staff:	28.1
Overall Team Age:	28.90

In retrospect, the critical decisions were: The free agent signing of Darren Daulton, which was big news a year ago, did nothing to help the Phillies rebuild. What has counted for the Phillies is Thomas' exceptional judgment in trades.

THAT AND THE OTHER

Lookalikes: Len Dykstra and Howdy Doody

Hall of Fame Watch: See "Cooperstown Cubs"; **Dale Murphy** is only candidate.

Chris Berman, Have You Considered: Bruce Ruffin the Kicker

Throwback: John Kruk

Attendance Trend: Flat. Philadelphia's attendance has held u well while the team hasn't been winning, as they've continued t draw almost two million a year, and edged back over two millio last year.

Players with a Chance for 3000 career hits: Dale Murph 3%

Record Watch:

Dale Murphy leads all active players in career strikeouts, wit 1,720, and would break the record if he were to play long enoug He probably won't; the record is 2,597, by Reggie.

Best Interview: John Morris

Probably Could Play Regularly For Another Team: Mora dini can play, if they'll let him.

Best Fundamental Player: Dale Murphy

Worst Fundamental Player: Wes Chamberlain

Best Defensive Player: Charlie Hayes

Worst Defensive Player: Mariano Duncan

Trivia Time: Who won the most games in a Phillies' unifor Robin Roberts, Steve Carlton or Grover Cleveland Alexa der?

Best Knowledge of the Strike Zone: John Kruk

Least Command of the Strike Zone: Charlie Hayes

Fastest Runner: Len Dykstra

Slowest Runner: Dale Murphy

Murphy is the slowest outfielder in the majors who is playin regularly on artificial turf, or at least was until McReynolds wa traded to Kansas City.

Best Baserunner: Dykstra or Morandini

Most Likely to Still be Here in 2000: Tommy Greene

Best Fastball: Jose DeJesus

Best Control: Terry Mulholland

Oddest Collection of Abilities: John Kruk

Never Going to be As Good as the Organization Thinks H Is: Andy Ashby

Why is this man in the Major Leagues: Jim Lindeman

Most Likely to Wipe Out 25% of the Starting Lineup: Len Dykstra

Gets Ahead of the Hitters Most Often: Mulholland

Has Never Been Known to Get Ahead of a Hitter: DeJesus

Trivia Answer: Steve Carlton, 241. Roberts won 234 for the Phillies, Alexander 190.

Local Neanderthal Sportswriter: Peter Pascarelli

Most-Similar Players:

to C Darren Daulton, Dave Valle
to 1B Ricky Jordan, Greg Briley
to 2B Mickey Morandini, Luis Sojo
to 3B Charlie Hayes, Ken Reitz
to SS Dickie Thon, Spike Owen
to LF Wes Chamberlain, Mark Whiten
to CF Len Dykstra, Ellis Burks
to RF Dale Murphy, Eddie Murray

Most Fun to Watch: Kruk

Least Fun to Watch: Dale Murphy

Managerial Type: Wally Backman

Among the All-Time Team Leaders:

Von Hayes, traded to California, was among the Phillies' all-time leaders in several categories—fourth in stolen bases (202), ninth in home runs (124). With his trade no current Phillie is among the team leaders in anything worth mentioning.

Town Team:

C—Roy Campanella
1B—Harry Davis
2B—Danny Murphy
SS—Monte Cross
3B—Jimmie Dykes
LF—Del Ennis
CF—Reggie Jackson
RF—Vic Wertz
SP—Bucky Walters
MGR—Joe McCarthy

Post-Season Transactions:

December 8, acquired Kyle Abbott and Ruben Amaro Jr. from California for Von Hayes.
December 9, traded catcher Darrin Fletcher to Montreal in exchange for Barry Jones
December 10, signed Mariano Duncan as free agent
December 11, traded Bruce Ruffin for Dale Sveum
December 13, Dickie Thon signed with the Texas Rangers as a free agent
December 18, re-signed Mitch Williams
December 19, announced they would not offer Joe Boever a contract, making him a free agent

What Needs to Be Done For 1992:

The number one thing is that they need to sort out their infield. The Phillies need to decide whether John Kruk is their first baseman, or whether Kruk is an outfielder and Jordan is the first baseman. They need to decide whether their second baseman is Mickey Morandini or Ruben Amaro or Wally Backman or Mariano Duncan or who. They need to decide whether Dave Hollins is their third baseman or not. They need to stop piddling around, hoping somebody will impress them, and decide who they want to rest their fate with.

The second key thing is to develop a *hitter* who can bat in the middle of the order. Wes Chamberlain is the obvious candidate.

Outlook for 1992: In one sentence, my view of the Philadelphia Phillies is that they played well enough last year that many people have failed to notice that they're really not a very good ballclub. One can see the possibility of the Phillies *developing* into a better team as the season progresses. They have young players. No one, including me, expects the Phillies to win, but it could be their best season in several years.

Index of Leading Indicators for 1992: Down 1.6

Positive Indicators: Played well late in the season.

Negative Indicators: Team Age

Due for a better season: Wes Chamberlain

Likely to have a worse season: Ricky Jordan

1992 Won-Lost Record will be: 78-84

PHILLIE PROSPECTS

Baseball America thinks he's a prospect and the Phillies are going to give him a job so I'll list **Andy Ashby** as the top prospect, although frankly I'm not enthusiastic about him. I'm not sure that anybody the Phillies have *is* a prospect. As of right now, **Kim Batiste** is the Phillies' starting shortstop in 1992. Shawon Dunston without the power. He's played 529 minor league games so far (a lot), never drawing more than 17 walks in a season, but he's supposed to have a good arm, great range and his MLEs show him hitting around .250.

In the Roger McDowell trade the Phillies picked up **Braulio Castillo,** a 23-year-old center fielder with a history of alcohol abuse. He had an extremely good year at San Antonio, hitting .300 with a little power and twenty-plus steals.

Baseball America compiles lists of the top ten prospects in all the minor leagues. Aside from Ashby (#9 in the International League) and Castillo (#9 in the Texas League), the only other Philadelphia farmhand to appear on those lists is outfielder **Tony Longmire,** the #7 prospect in the Eastern League. Longmire came to the Phillies, with Wes Chamberlain, from the Pirates in the Carmelo Martinez "deal". Longmire started out last season with triple-A Scranton/Wilkes-Barre but struggled, and was demoted to Reading in the Eastern League, where he played better. Longmire's MLEs look like Pat Sheridan or somebody.

He doesn't show up on any prospect lists, but a right-handed pitcher named **Donnie Elliott** may be worth watching. In A ball last year he struck out 184 men in 158 innings. Elliott will be 23 this summer. Elliott was selected by Seattle in the Rule 5 draft, which means they have to keep him on the major league roster all season or offer him back to Philadelphia.

The Phillies' #1 pick in the June draft (tenth overall) was **Tyler Green,** a right-hander out of Wichita State. Green pitched only 28 innings after signing, but was 3-0 with a 1.29 ERA. In the 28 innings he struck out 39 men and gave up only ten hits.

THE VON HAYES TRADE

From the Phillies' standpoint, I love the Von Hayes' trade. From the Angels' standpoint, I don't understand why they made it.

The Phillies got two players, Ruben Amaro Jr. and Kyle Abbott, in exchange for Von Hayes. Amaro is 27 years old, a second baseman and a pretty good *offensive* player for a second baseman (unlike his father, who was a weak-hitting glove wizard). He'd probably hit .270-.280, walk occasionally and could steal some bases, although his stolen base percentage may not be good. He's probably a little better hitter than Morandini. The Angels edge him through the farm system at a snail's pace, so one suppose that his defense is not going to push him toward more playin time. He was an outfielder-infielder for several years, apparentl has become a full-time infielder. I like him, but you have t understand that for a player who stays in the minors until age 2 to become a real player would be extremely rare.

But the other guy, Abbott—well, I'm sure Whitey knows wha he's doing, but apart from the fact that they already have thre outstanding left-handed starters, I don't know why the Angel gave up on him. I see *no* reason why Abbott should not be pitcher. Abbott is 6′4″, 195, a lefty, throws hard and throw strikes. He was the Angels' first-round draft pick in 1989, pitche poorly in 1990 but very well at Edmonton last year. He was 14-10 3.99 ERA. A 3.99 ERA at Edmonton is good. Their staff ERA las year was 4.72, and they had a winning record. His strikeout/wall data was 120-46, which is super. He's a Grade A prospect, and really don't understand why you trade a Grade A prospect fo Von Hayes.

INJURY LIST

Lenny Dykstra and Darren Daulton spent 111 and 66 days, respectively, on the disabled list.

On June 14, Tom Browning broke Von Hayes' right wrist wit a pitched ball. Hayes didn't return until mid-September.

Jason Grimsley missed half the season with a bum elbow. Pa Combs had a bone spur and chips removed from his elbow i August and missed the remainder of the schedule. He is expecte to open 1992 in the minors.

Randy Ready missed parts of June and July with a straine back muscle.

Ken Howell had a bone spur removed from his shoulder i spring training and was expected back sometime in June. Instead he spent the whole season on the disabled list, and is not bein counted on for 1992.

RE-ARMAMENT

In 1990 the Phillies appeared to have none of the elements of a championship pitching staff. Their top four starting pitchers were Pat Combs (10-10, 4.07 ERA), Terry Mulholland (9-10, 3.34), Bruce Ruffin (6-13, 5.38) and Jose DeJesus (7-8, 3.74). Their relie ace was Roger McDowell, who had 22 saves and a 3.86 ERA.

Although their team stats were not dramatically improved i

1991, you have to say that their starting rotation has come a great distance in one year. Before last season the Phillies obtained Mitch Williams in a trade with the Cubs, and Williams was much better in the closer role.

Mulholland emerged in 1991 as a legitimate Grade A pitcher, going 16-13 in 232 innings with a strikeout/walk ratio almost three to one.

Tommy Greene moved into the rotation in May, and pitched better than Mulholland.

Jose DeJesus continues to battle his control, but battled it to a tie last year (10-9, 3.42 ERA).

The addition of Kyle Abbott gives the Phillies a chance at a solid four-man rotation, with Andy Ashby as the fifth starter.

I don't mean to entirely ignore Cliff Brantley, who pitched well late last year (2-2, 3.41 ERA). Since they've gotten rid of Bruce Ruffin, you can see why they'd need Brantley. Brantley has never had a winning record in the minor leagues. By seasons beginning in 1986, he's gone 3-5, 3-10, 9-11, 3-9, 5-13 and 6-7.

THE CHICAGO CUBS
• IN A BOX •

1991 Won-Lost Record: 77-83 .481
Rank among 26 teams: 18th
Over Last Five Years: 400-407 .496
Rank over Five Years: 16th
In Last Ten Years: 787-826 .488
Rank over Ten Years: 19th

Best Player: Ryne Sandberg

Weak Spot: Center Field

Best Pitcher: Greg Maddux

Staff Weakness: The signing of Mike Morgan gives them two proven starting pitchers.

Best Bench Player: Hector Villanueva or Doug Dascenzo

Best Baseball Name: Mark Grace

Best Young Player: The Cubs have *no* position players who are both good and young. The best answer is Mark Grace, but at 28 (in June) Grace is not young for a ballplayer.

Best Looking Player: Sandberg

Ugliest Player: Hector Villanueva

Most Pleasant Surprise, 1991: Chuck McElroy

Biggest Disappointment, 1991: Dave Smith and Danny Jackson

Best Minor League Prospect: Lance Dickson

Who Is: A right-handed pitcher, the Cubs' top pick in the 1990 draft. With an awesome curve and a better-than-average fastball, Dickson dominated three levels of minor league competition in 1990 (0.94 ERA) before struggling in three starts with the Cubs. Determined not to rush Dickson, last spring the Cubs decided to start him out in AAA no matter how well he pitched in spring training. He started out in Iowa where he had left off in 1990. In early June he broke his foot covering first base, and was lost for most of the rest of the season. He had made 15 starts with a 2.86 ERA and 92 strikeouts in 91 innings. Dickson came back in late August and pitched well, and again pitched well in the Puerto Rican winter league, so he seems to be recovered from the injury.

Other Prospects: After Dickson, the Cubs took right-hander **Ryan Hawblitzel** in the '90 draft. Hawblitzel went 12-2 last year with Winston-Salem in the Carolina League (A), where managers named him the #6 prospect in *Baseball America*'s poll.

Peoria right-hander **Jason Doss** struck out 154 batters in 143 innings. He'll be 21 this season, which is about all I know about him. **Earl Cunningham** was the Cubs' top pick in the 1989 draft. He hit 19 home runs with Peoria last year, but hit .239, drew 10 walks and struck out 145 times. *Baseball America* lists shortstop **Rey Sanchez** as the #5 prospect in the American Association, but he doesn't figure to push Shawon into early retirement. I wouldn't be surprised if he wound up as the starting shortstop for one of the expansion teams, though.

The Cubs used their first draft pick (12th overall) last June to select outfielder **Doug Glanville,** a burner. He hit .303 and stole 17 bases in 36 games at Geneva (A ball).

The Cubs picked up three young pitchers in September trades: **Turk Wendell, Yorkis Perez** and **Chuck Hartsock.** Wendell was 11-3 last summer with a 2.56 ERA, but he's more famous for his superstitions than his pitching. Wendell doesn't wear socks under his baseball stirrups, brushes his teeth between each inning and asks the umpire to roll the ball to him on the mound.

Park Characteristics: Despite the occasional denials of hitters who talk about the wind only blowing out fifteen games a year, Wrigley Field is one of the three best hitter's parks in baseball. If the wind blew in 81 games a year, it would still be a hitter's park. It's got short power alleys, great visibility and little foul territory.

The Park Helps: Andre Dawson

The Park Hurts: The pitching staff

ORGANIZATIONAL REPORT CARD

Ownership:	B
Upper Management:	
Jim Frey Group	D−
Larry Himes	B
Field Management:	B
Front-Line Talent:	B+
Second-Line Talent:	D−
Minor League System:	C−

TEAM LEADERS:

Batting Average: Ryne Sandberg, .291
Last Ten Years (Season): Ryne Sandberg, 1984, and Mark Grace, 1989, .314
Last Ten Years (Total): Mark Grace, .297

Doubles: Ryne Sandberg, 32

Triples: Shawon Dunston, 7

Home Runs: Andre Dawson, 31
Last Ten Years (Season): Dawson, 1987, 49
Last Ten Years (Total): Ryne Sandberg, 205

RBI: Andre Dawson, 104
Last Ten Years (Season): Dawson, 1987, 137
Last Ten Years (Total): Ryne Sandberg, 749

Extra Base Hits: Sandberg, 60

Stolen Bases: Cedric Landrum, 27

Runs Created: Ryne Sandberg, 114

Runs Created Per Game: Sandberg, 7.0

Secondary Average: Sandberg, .381

Wins: Greg Maddux, 15
Last Ten Years (Season): Maddux, 1989, 19
Last Ten Years (Total): Rick Sutcliffe, 82

Winning Percentage: Maddux, 15-11 .577

Strikeouts: Maddux, 198
Last Ten Years (Season): Maddux, 1991, 198
Last Ten Years (Total): Sutcliffe, 909

ERA: Maddux, 3.35

Saves: Dave Smith, 17

League Leaders: Greg Maddux led the majors with 37 starts, and led the NL with 263 innings and 1070 batters faced.

Stat of the Year: Doug Dascenzo established a National League record by playing 242 consecutive errorless games in the outfield.

1991 SEASON

Background: The Cubs' history over the last ten years has been erratic—good years and bad years in random combinations. 1989 was a good year, 1990 a bad one (77-85).

Outlook: After the 1990 season the Cubs signed three name free agents, Danny Jackson, George Bell and Dave Smith. This generated a surge of optimism about the upcoming season.

Getaway: The Cubs opened with nine games at home, and won six. Travelling to Pittsburgh, the Cubs beat Doug Drabek for the second time in the opening days of the season, raising their record to 7-3. That was the **High Point of the Season.**

Then What? Then they hit the road. Following the nine-game homestand was an eleven-game road trip, two days at home and another six games on the road. By the end of that they were back to .500, and when they slipped *below* .500 on the subsequent homestand Don Zimmer was fired.

Low Point of the Season: June 28 at Wrigley Field. Bob Scanlan got hammered as the Cubs lost to the Cardinals, 6-14. It was their twelfth loss in thirteen, six losses by one run.

The Cubs had rallied briefly after Jim Essian's arrival, pushing their record back over .500. In two weeks the Cubs went from 31-29 to 32-41, and from 6½ to 12½ games out of first place.

Stretch Drive: The Cubs fought back gamely through July, getting back to .500 on August 5 (52-52). They stayed around .500 until September 10 (69-69), then looked at the calendar and their uniforms and decided they knew what had to be done.

Most Exciting Game of the Season: July 25 against Cincinnati. The Cubs scored three in the first, and held the 3-0 lead until the seventh, when the Reds answered with three of their own. The game went extra innings, ten, twelve, fourteen. The Reds scored in the top of the fourteenth, but the Cubs jumped Tim Layana for two in the bottom of the inning, pulling out a 5-4 win.

Major Injuries: See "Injury Box"

Offense: Poor. The Cubs scored 386 runs in Wrigley Field, but only 309 on the road.

The Cubs scored 695 runs as opposed to a league average of 663. Since the Cubs' margin over the league (five percent) is *less than* the amount by which Wrigley Field inflates their offensive stats (eight and a half percent), that means that their offense is actually below average when adjusted for context. But because they don't adjust for the raw totals, the Cubs always *think* they have a good offense, so they don't do anything to correct its problems.

Defense: Fairly good. The weak spots were catcher, center field and left, but there were also strong points.

Pitching: Below average. The Cubs' pitchers are better than they look in the stats, but this isn't a *good* staff.

Best Game by a Starting Pitcher: Greg Maddux' 1-0 three-hitter against the Phillies on October 2 (9 3 0 0 0 6 Game Score: 87)

Worst Game by a Starting Pitcher: Shawn Boskie against Pittsburgh, July 2 (3 11 8 8 1 1 Game Score: 5)

Indicators for 1991 were: Up 13.7

Number of regulars having good seasons by their own standards: Two (Sandberg and Chico Walker)

1991 Over-Achiever: Chico Walker

1991 Under-Achiever: 1. Jerome Walton
2. Mark Grace

Infield: The Cubs hoped to have the best infield in the majors. It didn't happen. Mark Grace, a singles-hitting first baseman, didn't hit as he has. The third base play was unsteady. Sandberg was unbelievable.

Outfield: A hole in center field, but good output from the wings.

Catching: Very poor. Cub catchers hit .230 on the season, with 23 homers and 69 RBI. Much of the power came from Hector Villaneuva, who isn't really a catcher.

Starting Pitching: Weak.

Bullpen: The ERA of the Cubs' bullpen was dramatically better than that of their starters (3.46 to 4.35). No other National League team had a comparable split.

Paul Assenmacher has been a quality pitcher for years, and McElroy was as good as a left-handed setup man can be. Offsetting these things was the very poor performance of Dave Smith in the closer role early in the season. The Cubs blew 28 save chances, tying Montreal for most in the league.

Percentage of Offense Created by:
Young Players: 4%
Players in Their Prime: 31%
Veterans: 65%

Team Age:
Age of Non-Pitchers: 30.6
Age of Pitching Staff: 27.9
Overall Team Age: 29.43

The Cubs' 1991 starting lineup was the oldest in the division. The percentage of their offense accounted for by young players (4%) was the lowest of any major league team. The percentage accounted for by players 31 or older (65%) was the highest of any major league team. All three of the Cubs' best hitters—Sandberg, Dawson, Bell—and several members of the supporting cast are at an age when a player's performance normally declines.

In retrospect, the critical decisions were: See article, "1991 Cubs"

THAT AND THE OTHER

Lookalikes: Ryne Sandberg and Scott Sanderson

Hall of Fame Watch: See article, "Cooperstown Cubs"

Chris Berman, Have You Considered: Laddie Renfro (Valley)

Attendance Trend: Good. The Cubs drew 2.3 million last year, less than they drew with the 1989 championship team, but well ahead of what they were drawing in the mid-eighties.

Players with a Chance for 3000 career hits:

Ryne Sandberg	35%
Andre Dawson	19%
George Bell	12%
Mark Grace	3%

Record Watch: See article, "Cooperstown Cubs"

Probably Could Play Regularly For Another Team: Jose Vizcaino

Best Fundamental Player: Sandberg

Worst Fundamental Player: Luis Salazar

Best Defensive Player: Sandberg

Worst Defensive Player: George Bell

Best Knowledge of the Strike Zone: Mark Grace

Least Command of the Strike Zone: Shawon Dunston

Fastest Runner: Cedric Landrum

Dunston is the fastest regular.

Slowest Runner: Hector Villaneuva

George Bell is the slowest regular, since Berryhill has been traded.

Best Baserunner: Dunston

Most Likely to Still be Here in 2000: Sandberg. He'll be 40.

Best Fastball: Chuck McElroy

Best Breaking Pitch: Lance Dickson

Best Control: Greg Maddux

Most Overrated Player: Mark Grace

Most Underrated Player: Paul Assenmacher

Oddest Collection of Abilities: Dwight Smith

Never Going to be As Good as the Organization Thinks He Is: Rick Wilkins

Gets Ahead of the Hitters Most Often: Frank Castillo

Gets Ahead of the Hitters Least Often: Danny Jackson

The Most Knowledgeable Person About Chicago Cub History Is: Eddie Gold

Most-Similar Players:

to	C	Rick Wilkins, Gilberto Reyes
to	1B	Mark Grace, Dave Magadan
to	2B	Ryne Sandberg, Cal Ripken
to	3B	Luis Salazar, Dickie Thon
to	SS	Shawon Dunston, Greg Gagne
to	LF	George Bell, Chili Davis
to	CF	Jerome Walton, Gerald Young
to	RF	Andre Dawson, Dale Murphy

Most Fun to Watch: Ryne Sandberg

Least Fun to Watch: Dave Smith

Managerial Type: Doug Dascenzo

Among the All-Time Team Leaders: Cub batting records go back 116 years, although for some reason they only list their career pitching records from 1900. The greatest players in Cub history include Cap Anson, Ernie Banks, Ron Santo, Billy Williams, Gabby Hartnett. Ryne Sandberg, of course, is moving steadily up the Cubs' all-time batting lists. His 205 homers tie him with Bill Nicholson for fifth. His 297 stolen bases have him third behind Tinker and Chance (Evers is fourth). His 976 runs place him sixth. Sandberg appears on most of the other lists, but further down.

Andre Dawson has 152 homers as a Cub, which is ninth.

No current pitchers are among the all-time leaders except Assenmacher, who is near the bottom of the save list.

Town Team:

C—Bob O'Farrell
1B—Phil Cavaretta
2B—Germany Schaefer
SS—Herman Long
3B—Fred Lindstrom
LF—Wally Berger
CF—Fred Lynn
RF—Jack Smith
SP—Chick Fraser

Post-Season Transactions:

November 22, named Jim Lefebvre manager

December 3, signed free agent Mike Moore for four years

December 19, Rick Sutcliffe signed a one-year deal with Baltimore

What Needs to Be Done For 1992:

1. Sort out the starting pitching. After Maddux and Moore, the Cubs have got to find two or three starters out of a group including Lance Dickson, Frank Castillo, Danny Jackson, Shawn Boskie, Mike Harkey, and Bob Scanlan.

2. Find a center fielder, or at least settle on a platoon combination.

Outlook for 1992: Mixed. The Cubs have only two starting pitchers, but Castillo and Dickson have a chance to be *really* good, so with Moore there could be a dramatic improvement in the rotation. The Cubs *may* have a better handle on the needs of their team now than they did a year ago, but they have so many hitters in their mid-thirties that the offense will probably continue to be mediocre.

Index of Leading Indicators for 1992: Down 10.2

Positive Indicators: None Significant

Negative Indicators: 1. Team Age

Due for a better season: Danny Jackson

Likely to have a worse season: Andre Dawson

Overdue for a better season, but I'm about to give up: Jerome Walton

1992 Won-Lost Record will be: 73-89

THE 1991 CUBS

I would cite three decisions as critical to the 1991 Chicago Cubs:

1) The decision to replace Mitch Williams as relief ace with free agent Dave Smith.
2) The decision to sign Danny Jackson as a free agent.
3) The decision to haul Gary Scott out of A ball to play third base.

All three worked out poorly. The first decision—to sign Smith and actually expect the fat old fart to pitch—is inexcusable, the sort of hopeless decision that Victorian bozos like Jim Frey are going to make sometimes as long as people let them run baseball teams. Smith, 36 years old on opening day, had been pitching 60 innings a year in Houston with consistently good ERAs, so Frey and frumpany decided well, hey, a pitcher's a pitcher, what's all this stuff about Wrigley Field being different from the Astrodome? They traded the powerful but erratic Mitch Williams to Philadelphia, and counted on Smith to save the games, which of course he couldn't.

The decision to sign Danny Jackson wasn't necessarily a bad gamble, but it didn't work out any better; Danny got hurt and had a worse ERA than Smith.

The decision to put Gary Scott at third base with only 35 games of AA ball under his belt can obviously be second-guessed, but I wouldn't. I saw the Cubs play a few times in spring training, and Scott was playing *so* well down there that really, there wasn't any decision to be made. The Cubs did need help at third base, and knew they did. Scott looked like a superstar. Maybe there's an argument to be made for having an organizational policy that you simply don't jump a kid three levels based on three weeks of spring training games; you call the kid in on February 22 and tell him that no matter *what* he does the first two weeks of spring training, he's still going out. But such a policy, if it were in force, might at other times prevent *good* decisions—Chuck Knoblauch and Jeff Bagwell, for example, although those guys did have a year of AA. I think that absent such a policy, *anybody* watching Scott play in spring training would have made him the opening day third baseman. We just have to hope that it doesn't break him.

A couple of other decisions which seemed big at the time turned out to be more or less irrelevant to the season. The signing of George Bell is first. In last year's book I wrote (p. 389–390) that "to win in Wrigley Field you almost have to lead the league in runs scored. To lead the league in runs scored, you have to be among the top two or three in on-base percentage, which just means that you have to have people on base to score runs, which would be common sense if it were not empirically demonstrable. The Cubs last year were tenth in the league in on-base percentage, and they've done absolutely nothing over the winter to change that. They'll finish third or fourth."

Well, that's exactly what happened. George Bell is a fine hitter, but he doesn't do what the Cubs needed somebody to do, which is get on base. The Cubs were second in the league in home runs, but their offense, hamstrung by a .309 on-base percentage, scored 73 runs less than Pittsburgh, and the Cubs finished in a tie for fourth. See, what the Cubs *thought* they needed was somebody "to hit behind Andre Dawson and make the pitchers pitch to him", which is the kind of malarkey that passes for business acumen among too many major league organizations. Having George Bell hit behind Andre Dawson cut Dawson's intentional walks from 21 to 3—and had no effect whatsoever on Dawson's other stats, which is what you would find 97% of the time if you studied the issue, rather than basing your decisions on intuition and bullshit. What the Cubs *really* needed—and still need—wasn't George Bell, it was Brett Butler or Tim Raines, both of whom were available at the same time. The Cubs needed (and still need) somebody to get on base *in front of* Dawson and Sandberg, because that's how runs are scored in the real world.

Anyway, the decision to sign George Bell had no impact on the team even though Bell had a solid enough year. The other thing the Cubs were wrong about a year ago was that they tremendously overestimated the quality of their catching. They thought they had two quality catchers (Girardi and Berryhill) when in reality they had two catchers who were both pretty bad. But there was no meaningful decision to be made there; there was nothing they could have "decided" that would have transformed either Girardi or Berryhill into a quality player. Catching turned out to be a major weakness, but there was probably nothing that could have been done about it without opening a hole somewhere else.

FORTY-TWO SEPTEMBERS

In September last year the Cubs went 8-18. It didn't matter much; they were out of the race anyway.

The aggregate won-lost record for all teams is, of course, always .500, in each month and in each decade.

Up until 1950, the Cubs played about as well at one time of the year as at another. Since 1950 they have followed a consistent pattern of playing well early in the year, and poorly late in the year. I looked at it over time:

In the 1950s (1950–1959) the Cubs had a .465 winning percentage in May, but .439 in September. That's only a .026 difference, but still, over the course of ten years it is a difference.

In the 1960s their winning percentage was .474 in May, but .424 in September.

In the 1970s their winning percentage was .532 in May, .436 in September.

In the 1980s their winning percentage was .502 in May, .450 in September.

We're now two years into the 1990s, and so far in the 1990s the Cubs have played .500 ball in May, but .382 in September.

These patterns are not, of course, confined to May and September; I just used those for simple illustration. For more than 40 years the Cubs have played as well as the next team early in the season, but poorly late in the year.

Three points. First, this can't be a fluke; the Cubs have sustained a pattern for more than 40 years. Since 1950 the Cubs have played more than 1100 games in May and more than 1100 in September, with a winning percentage 58 points higher in May than September.

Second, there must be a cause for it which is intrinsic to the organization, rather than the creation of the individuals who play the games and the men who pull the strings. We're talking about many generations of players and management here.

Third, the simplest explanation—that the Cubs are just not as good as their opposition—doesn't explain the data. If the Cubs were simply not as good as their opponents, they would be worse than their opponents in May *and* September.

For many years, the Cubs have allowed an argument about the *causes* of their late-season collapse—is it the ballpark or isn't it—to distract them from addressing the *solution*. It doesn't **matter** why the Cubs have played so poorly in September for 42 years; what matters is that they stop doing so.

And the obvious solutions are

1) Improve the bench, and

2) *Use* the bench.

I'm not saying that will work, but that seems like the first thing you'd try if your team was collapsing late in the year: get the regulars more rest. It's been 40 years, and the Cubs have yet to try the obvious solution.

COOPERSTOWN CUBS

The Hall of Fame credentials of **Dale Murphy** are very similar to those of **Andre Dawson,** so I thought I would discuss the two of them together. It is my view of these two players that:

a) both are overwhelmingly qualified when judged by the standards historically applied by the Veteran's Committee, which now is all but officially closed to players of the post-war era, but

b) neither is overwhelmingly qualified when judged by the standards of the Baseball Writers Association of America.

I'm speaking here of what these players have accomplished *so far;* I'm not talking about what their credentials might be when they hang up on their agents. I compared these two players to the last fifteen outfielders selected to the Hall of Fame by the BBWAA, who are Carl Yastrzemski, Willie Stargell, Billy Williams, Lou Brock, Hank Aaron, Frank Robinson, Al Kaline, Duke Snider, Willie Mays, Ralph Kiner, Mickey Mantle, Roberto Clemente, Stan Musial, Joe Medwick, and Ted Williams.

All of those fifteen players have higher career batting averages than Dale Murphy, whose career average is .267. Dawson's average is a little higher, .282, but Dawson still beats only one of the fifteen players in batting average, that being Ralph Kiner, whose career average was .279. Willie Stargell's average was .282, the same as Dawson's.

Eleven of the fifteen players hit more homers than Dale Murphy, and all of those eleven also hit more homers than Dawson, who is just behind Murphy.

Twelve of the fifteen drove in more runs than Dawson, and fourteen drove in more runs than Murphy.

All fifteen of the Hall of Fame outfielders had significantly higher on base percentages than Dawson. Murphy's on base percentage is higher than Lou Brock's, but lower than the other fourteen outfielders. On base percentage is the most important offensive statistic, but has comparatively little impact on Hall of Fame voting, which tends to be shaped by triple crown stats and specialty accomplishments.

This chart compares Dawson and Murphy to the group averages of the last fifteen Hall of Fame outfielders:

	AB	Runs	Hits	2B	3B	HR	RBI	BB	SB	Avg	Slug
Dawson	8348	1199	2354	417	92	377	1335	522	304	.282	.489
Murphy	7856	1191	2095	348	39	396	1252	980	161	.267	.472
Average	9280	1599	2808	487	97	444	1579	1236	176	.303	.519

All of the fifteen had more runs created than Dawson or Murphy except Ralph Kiner, who had a short career. All of the fifteen had more runs created per out than Dawson or Murphy except Lou Brock.

So in general, the typical Hall of Fame outfielder is still some distance ahead of Dawson and Murphy, who obviously aren't going to catch up in things like batting average and runs created per game, but might in the "counting" stats like home runs and RBI.

I also had a couple of "Record Watch" notes about Andre, which I will throw in here although they don't exactly fit.

1) Andre Dawson leads all active players in career power/speed number, with 336.6 (377 home runs, 304 stolen bases). Although seasonal norms in power/speed number have been pushed up and up and up since Willie Mays retired, Mays' totals of 660 home runs and 338 stolen bases (Power/Speed number of 447.1) has remained as the most impressive career combination, and Dawson has almost no chance of being the man who breaks it. Rickey Henderson, on the other hand, does have a chance.

2) Dawson has a better chance of breaking the National League record for career sacrifice flies. The career records for Sac Flies are:

Major Leagues	Henry Aaron,	121
American League	Brooks Robinson,	114
National League	Henry Aaron,	113

With records in the low 100s, there are three active players over 100: Brett with 106, Yount with 105 and Dawson with 101. Obviously, *some* of these records are going to be broken. Either Brett or Yount could break the American League record this season, and Dawson has a clear shot at the NL record or even the major league record. Sacrifice Fly records have only been maintained since 1954.

Ryne Sandberg I think will go into the Hall of Fame. He's about where Dawson is in terms of Hall of Fame type accomplishments so far, but years younger. **George Bell** is a longshot, but has a chance because he could compile numbers—3000 hits, 500 home runs—that demand entry despite his negatives.

INJURY BOX

Mike Harkey started four games in April before going on the disabled list for the rest of the season. He underwent surgery to repair a cartilage tear in his right shoulder. Harkey pitched in the fall instructional league with mixed results, and the Cubs are not counting on him being ready in April.

Joe Girardi spent 111 days on the disabled list because of a bulging disc in his back.

Danny Jackson was on the disabled list for three months and won only one game when he did pitch. His physical problems included a lower abdominal strain and a pulled groin muscle. According to Jim Lefebvre, Jackson "feels the best he has felt in the offseason in eight years."

Rick Sutcliffe made only 18 starts because of a "tired right shoulder", and Dave Smith suffered from knee problems all season, spending 40 days on the disabled list.

THE NEW YORK METS
• IN A BOX •

1991 Won-Lost Record: 77-84 .478

Rank among 26 teams: 19th
Over Last Five Years: 447-360 .554
Rank over Five Years: 3rd among 26 teams
In Last Ten Years: 876-741 .542
Rank over Ten Years: 2nd

Best Player: Howard Johnson

Weak Spot: Catcher

Best Pitcher: Bret Saberhagen

Staff Weakness: Bullpen support

The staff was weakened in 1991 by being forced to carry Doug Simons, a kid pitcher claimed under Rule 5. This made the staff one man short, which no one would have noticed if the big four had pitched 250 innings apiece.

Best Bench Player: Darryl Boston

Best Young Player: It was Gregg Jefferies; now, no one

Best Looking Player: Dwight Gooden

Ugliest Player: Sid Fernandez

Most Pleasant Surprise, 1991: Keith Miller

Biggest Disappointment, 1991: Dave Magadan

Best Minor League Prospect: See article, "Met Prospects"

Park Characteristics: It's a pitcher's park. Poor visibility increases strikeouts; long grass reduces extra base hits.

The Park Helps: Power pitchers

The Park Hurts: Line drive hitters

ORGANIZATIONAL REPORT CARD

Ownership:	D
Upper Management:	Too soon to tell
Field Management:	B+
Front-Line Talent:	D
Second-Line Talent:	A
Minor League System:	D

TEAM LEADERS:

Batting Average: Gregg Jefferies, .272

Last Ten Years (Season): Dave Magadan, 1990, .328
Last Ten Years (Total): Keith Hernandez, .297

Doubles: Howard Johnson, 34

Triples: Vince Coleman, 5

Home Runs: Howard Johnson, 38

Last Ten Years (Season): Darryl Strawberry, 39 in 1987 and '88
Last Ten Years (Total): Strawberry, 252

Extra Base Hits: Hojo, 76

RBI: Howard Johnson, 117

Last Ten Years (Season): Hojo, 1991, 117
Last Ten Years (Total): Strawberry, 733

Stolen Bases: Coleman, 37

Runs Created: Hojo, 107

Runs Created Per Game: Howard Johnson, 6.4

Secondary Average: Howard Johnson, .468

Wins: David Cone, 14

Last Ten Years (Season): Dwight Gooden, 1985, 24
Last Ten Years (Total): Gooden, 132

Winning Percentage: Gooden, 13-7 .650

Strikeouts: David Cone, 241

Last Ten Years (Season): Gooden, 1984, 276
Last Ten Years (Total): Gooden, 1541

ERA: Cone, 3.29

Saves: John Franco, 30

League Leaders:

1. Howard Johnson had more extra base hits than any other National League player (34 doubles, 4 triples and 38 homers). That's 76 total; add in 30 stolen bases and Johnson reached scor-

ing position under his own power more than a hundred times. His 38 home runs, 117 RBI and 15 sacrifice flies all led the National League, and the fifteen sac flies tied a National League record for a switch-hitter.

2. David Cone tied Roger Clemens for the major league lead in strikeouts with 241.

3. Frank Viola allowed more hits, 259, than any major league pitcher.

4. Dave Magadan led the league in percentage of pitches taken, with 63.6%.

1991 SEASON

Background: The talk of the winter was the loss of Darryl Strawberry. The Mets of 1986–1989 were the best team in the National League, although they didn't always play like it. In 1989 they finished second, behind the Cubs. In 1990 they won 91 games and again finished second, behind the Pirates.

The Cubs were a fluke. The Pirates were legitimately better than the Mets.

Outlook: With the loss of Strawberry and uncertainty about Gooden's arm, perennial expectations that the Mets would take on all comers began to fade. Some people thought they were still the best team in the division; some didn't. Some people thought Vince Coleman would add a dimension to the Mets' offense; some didn't.

Getaway: As of April 26, the Mets stood at 11-6, tied for first with the Pirates. Articles were written saying that Hubie Brooks would make the Mets forget Strawberry.

High Point of the Season: The Pirates quickly pulled in front, but the Mets stayed over .500, usually six to eight games over .500, throughout the first half. Three days after the All Star break the Mets were riding high. They had just beaten the Padres for their ninth win in a row, and had closed to within 2½ of the Pirates. They were 49-34.

Low Point of the Season: Then the Mets began to lose more than they won, and then they began to lose them all. In August the Mets lost eleven straight games, giving them 23 losses in 28 games. In that span they fell from four back of Pittsburgh to 12½ back, and cost Buddy Harrelson his job.

Most Exciting Game of the Season: On August 8 Frank Viola beat Doug Drabek, 4-3. That was the last time there seemed to be any hope.

Stretch Drive: The Mets stumbled through September in a daze, trying to figure out what they had and where they were going with it. There was a sense of shock that the outstanding team of the late eighties had suddenly gone, and they sat like a man whose wife has left him for the plumber, staring awkwardly at a door which is never going to open.

Major Injuries: Sid Fernandez fractured a wrist in March, and didn't get into a game until July. After eight starts he went out with knee problems, and underwent surgery in September. He has reportedly lost 35 pounds, and is expected to be ready for spring training. He pitched very well in his eight starts.

Vince Coleman missed the entire second half of the season with a torn hamstring.

Hubie Brooks missed the last seven weeks due to a herniated disc in his upper back and a pinched nerve in his shoulder.

Dwight Gooden spent 44 days on the disabled list with a sore shoulder, and underwent arthroscopic shoulder surgery in September. Supposedly the procedure was similar to Mark Gubicza's August, 1990, operation. Gubicza's 1991 ERA was 5.68.

Offense: Mediocre. With the loss of Strawberry and the decay of McReynolds the Mets had only one middle-of-the-order hitter, Howard Johnson. With the injury to Vince Coleman they didn't have a leadoff man the second half.

Defense: As always, pitiful. The Mets had a third baseman playing shortstop (Johnson), a who-knows-what-he-is playing second and third, no true center fielder, in and out catching and old guys in left and right. They turned only 112 double plays (11th in the league), made 143 errors (same), and allowed an above-average number of stolen bases.

Pitching: Unable to meet expectations, but still above average.

Pitching stats can be sorted into a few categories for which the pitcher is almost entirely responsible (strikeouts, walks, home runs allowed, hit batsmen, wild pitches, balks), and the categories which really reflect the performance of the team, but which are charged to the pitcher, which is everything else. The Mets had a 3.56 team ERA, which is not good for a team in this park, but if you ignore the defensive stuff for which the pitcher gets blamed and focus on the three key pitcher-only stats, you get a different picture. The Mets were second in the league in strikeouts. They were second in the league in (fewest) walks. They were second in the league in (fewest) home runs allowed. They were following Houston in strikeouts, Pittsburgh in walks and the Dodgers in home runs, so their combination of those three stats was the best in the league.

Best Game by a Starting Pitcher: In the closing days of the 1991 season David Cone pitched two spectacular games, a one-hitter against the Cardinals on September 20 (9 1 0 0 1 11) and a three-hitter against the Phillies on the last day of the season in which he struck out 19 (9 3 0 0 1 19). The game scores, 95 and 99 respectively, were the highest in the National League in 1991.

Worst Game by a Starting Pitcher: June 5, Dwight Gooden in Cincinnati (4 11 7 7 4 5 Game Score: 13)

Indicators for 1991 were: Basically Neutral (Up 1.1)

Number of regulars having good seasons by their own standards: One (Howard Johnson)

1991 Over-Achiever: Keith Miller

1991 Under-Achiever: Dave Magadan

Infield: Weak offensively, weak defensively.

Outfield: Not as bad as the infield. The combined stats of the Mets' 1991 right fielders don't look *terribly* different from a Strawberry season—.245 with 26 homers, 88 RBI. Their center fielders hit .267 and stole 50 bases, and McReynolds wasn't the worst left fielder in the league.

Catching: Met catchers in 1991 hit .226 with 5 homers.

Starting Pitching: Above average

Bullpen: Above average, I guess. The closer (Franco) allowed a batting average of .271, too high for that role. Harrelson probably should have gone to his bullpen sooner than he did. The Mets had only 21 holds, fewest in the league, although they had two pitchers pitching well in a setup role (Innis and Peña). Harrelson tended to wait until the Mets were behind after seven, pinch hit for the pitcher and bring in Innis to finish the loss, rather than letting him participate in the wins.

Percentage of Offense Created by:

Young Players:	19%
Players in their Prime:	55%
Veterans:	26%

Team Age:

Age of Non-Pitchers:	28.9
Age of Pitching Staff:	28.4
Overall Team Age:	28.68

In retrospect, the critical decisions were:

1) Failing to make a better offer to Strawberry early in the negotiating process.

2) Failing to take decisive action to resolve the position quandaries in the infield. The Mets entered the 1991 season not knowing who their second baseman was, who their shortstop was, who their third baseman was. They left the same way.

THAT AND THE OTHER

Hall of Fame Watch: See article

Chris Berman, Have You Considered: Mackey (Don't Give Me Any) Sasser

Throwback: Hubie Brooks

Attendance Trend: Dropping like a stone. The Mets drew 3.06 million in 1988; it's dropped to 2.92, 2.73 and 2.28.

Players with a Chance for 3000 career hits:

Eddie Murray,	63%
Bobby Bonilla,	19%
Gregg Jefferies,	4%

Record Watch:

1. Vince Coleman has 586 Stolen Bases by age 29, which puts him years ahead of Lou Brock's pace. Brock still holds the NL record for stolen bases (938). Although I've never liked Coleman as a player and still don't, he obviously has a chance to last long enough to break the NL record.

It is also, I suppose, not inconceivable that he could wrest the major league record from Rickey Henderson. I doubt it. Coleman is *behind* Henderson's total at the same age (always has been, since he started later), and, since Henderson is a better player than Coleman, it is likely that Henderson will last longer and consequently steal more bases in his thirties.

2. Eddie Murray has 1469 career RBI, and an outside chance to be among the top ten RBI men of all time. The number ten man is Ted Williams, with 1839. At 93 RBI per year, Murray is four years away from Williams.

Best Interview: David Cone

Probably Could Play Regularly For Another Team:

The 1991 Mets had a good bench for such a bad team. The Mets four top hitters and five of their top six hitters all batted 227 to 275 times, those being Keith Miller, Darryl Boston, Rick Cerone, Mackey Sasser and Mark Carreon.

Best Fundamental Player: Kevin McReynolds last year, Bill Pecota now

Worst Fundamental Player: Mackey Sasser

Best Defensive Player: Todd Hundley

Worst Defensive Player: Mackey Sasser

Best Knowledge of the Strike Zone: Dave Magadan

Least Command of the Strike Zone: Garry Templeton

Fastest Runner: Vince Coleman

Slowest Runner: was Kevin McReynolds, now probably Dave Magadan

Best Baserunner: Vince Coleman

Most Likely to Still be Here in 2000: Todd Hundley

Best Fastball: Saberhagen or Cone

Best Breaking Pitch: Saberhagen or Cone

Best Control: Saberhagen

Oddest Collection of Abilities: Dave Magadan

Never Going to be As Good as the Organization Thinks He Is: Kevin Elster

Manager's Pet Strategy: Torborg, in contrast to Harrelson, loves to get into his bullpen. In Chicago he'd let Jack McDowell stay in, but anybody else was gone at the first sign of trouble.

Why is this man in the Major Leagues: Charlie O'Brien

Gets Ahead of the Hitters Most Often: Saberhagen

Most-Similar Players:

to C Mackey Sasser, Greg Myers
to 1B Dave Magadan, Todd Benzinger
to 2B Gregg Jefferies, Jeff Blauser
to 3B Howard Johnson, Joe Carter
to SS Kevin Elster, Bill Spiers
to LF Kevin McReynolds, Pete O'Brien
to CF Vince Coleman, Gary Pettis
to RF Hubie Brooks, Kirk Gibson

Most Fun to Watch: Howard Johnson

Least Fun to Watch: Kevin McReynolds

Managerial Type: Hubie Brooks

Among the All-Time Team Leaders:

Howard Johnson is the only current Met on any of the batting lists. He is second with 178 homers, third with 560 RBI, tied for second with 191 stolen bases, fourth with 547 runs, etc. Kevin McReynolds was also on most of the batting lists, which by the way are extremely unimpressive even if you make allowances for the fact that the Mets are an adolescent franchise. *Ed Kranepool,* for Chrissakes, holds the Mets' record for career hits. And nobody's pushing him.

Dwight and Sid appear on most of the career pitching lists. Gooden sits third in wins (132), innings pitched (1714), and strikeouts (1541), behind Seaver and Koosman.

Post-Season Transactions:

October 29, declined to offer arbitration to Garry Templeton
November 1, named Jeff Torborg as manager
November 27, signed Free Agent Eddie Murray
December 2, signed Free Agent Bobby Bonilla
December 9, traded Blaine Beatty to Montreal for minor league outfielder Jeff Barry
December 10, traded Hubie Brooks to California for Dave Gallagher
December 11, sent Keith Miller, Kevin McReynolds and Gregg Jefferies to the Royals for Bret Saberhagen and Bill Pecota
December 19, agreed to arbitration with Darryl Boston
December 20, signed free agent Willie Randolph

What Needs to Be Done For 1992: Despite the debacle of 1991, the Mets are not starting over. The Mets have made wholesale changes, none of which is intended to pay off more than four months from now. For the first time in years, they have a real lineup—a catcher (Hundley), a second baseman (Randolph). What needs to be done now is to convert the team on paper into a team on the field—and that job is in the hands of a man with good credentials (Torborg).

Outlook for 1992: The Mets expect to be back in the race.

Index of Leading Indicators for 1992: Up 1.6

Positive Indicators: In baseball, when a team declines sharply in one season they tend to recover the next season. This is called the Plexiglas Principle.

Negative Indicators: Poor play late in the season.

Due for a better season: Dave Magadan, if he plays

Likely to have a worse season: John Franco

1992 Won-Lost Record will be: 85-77

HALL OF FAME WATCH

It is a measure of how far the Mets have fallen that nobody in the Mets' 1991 lineup could reasonably be considered a Hall of Fame candidate. All of the Mets' Hall of Fame candidates except Dwight Gooden were among the comings and goings of the winter. Six players have enough of a chance to be worth talking about. Those are:

1) **Eddie Murray.** Murray probably will go in the Hall of Fame. He probably will get 3,000 hits, although that's not certain. Murray has 2,502 career hits. The last eight 3,000-hit men had an average of 2,606 at the same age. Two of them, Brock and Yastrzemski, had less than Murray at the same age, and Carew had only a few more. His chance of getting 3,000 hits, which I now estimate at 63%, will go dramatically up or dramatically down this year. If he can hold his job he could get there by 1995, when he'd be 39.

Even if he doesn't get 3,000 hits, he's got a good shot at election. The Hall of Fame standards for a first baseman probably aren't that much different than the standards for an outfielder, and Eddie's totals are very comparable to those of Dale Murphy and Andre Dawson, who I discussed a few pages ago. Comparable, but slightly better.

2) **Bobby Bonilla** I talked about in the Pittsburgh comment. Basically I don't think he can do it.

3) **Gregg Jefferies** hasn't done anything Hall of Famish yet, but he's too young for it to be said that he won't.

Vince Coleman, I suppose, could make the Hall of Fame if he steals a thousand bases. I can't see Vince Coleman as a Hall of Famer. Howard Johnson could still emerge as a candidate.

I'm going to discuss the three starting pitchers in a slightly different form. I drew up a chart comparing the leading winners in each year of birth with the career pattern of a typical 300-game winner, based on the last six pitchers to clear that Mark (Nolan Ryan, Don Sutton, Phil Niekro, Tom Seaver, Steve Carlton and Gaylord Perry).

Many young pitchers are ahead of the "schedule" of a 300-game winner, which happens in part because 300-game winners are often pitchers who don't pitch a lot of innings when they're young. **Dwight Gooden** has 132 career wins. A typical 300-game winner had 58 wins at the same age, so Gooden, despite his recent struggles, is still 84 wins ahead of schedule for a 300-win career. This is the largest head start in the major leagues; many guys are ahead of schedule, but nobody else is that much ahead of schedule. And none of the six 300-game winners had won more than 95 games by age 26, that being Tom Seaver's total.

Bret Saberhagen, seven months older than Gooden, has 110 career wins, which still leaves him way ahead of schedule, and in fact ahead of any recent 300-game winner except Tom Seaver.

Frank Viola, four years older than Saberhagen, joins the Red Sox with a career total of 150 wins. He is still ahead of the pace of a typical 300-win career. Viola has 150 wins by age 31; the schedule calls for 144. Understand the premise: there are *many* pitchers ahead of schedule, but almost all of them can be expected to drop off the pace at some point. Where Viola is now is very similar to being the pace-setter at the midway point of a marathon.

All things taken in, Dwight Gooden is the best Hall of Fame candidate of the three. Gooden has a career record of 132 wins, 53 losses. If he piles on bulk numbers over the rest of his career—100 wins, 100 losses—he'll have a record 232-153, which is a Hall of Fame record by the standards which have historically been applied.

But both Saberhagen and Viola are solid Hall of Fame candidates in their own right. Viola has had two losing seasons in three years (13-17 in 1989, 13-15 in 1991), but he's still a top quality pitcher. Steve Carlton was 10-19 in 1970, 13-20 in 1973. Many pitchers have to make adjustments in their early thirties. Warren Spahn at age 31 (1952) was 14-19. Tom Seaver in the three-year stretch which parallels Viola's by age posted records of 11-11, 22-9 and 14-11. Nolan Ryan at age 31 went 10-13 with a 3.71 ERA. The next year he went 16-14, and Buzzie Bavasi said he could replace him with two 8-7 pitchers. A pitcher of that quality can make adjustments.

I know more about Saberhagen, of course, than I do the other two. When Saberhagen is feeling 100%, he's as good a pitcher as God ever made. He can do anything. He throws 90+, changes speeds without tipping it, has super control, throws a sharp curve and a knee-buckling slider, fields his position brilliantly. He was born knowing how to pitch, how to set up the hitter, how to move the ball in and out and up and down, vary the pitches and the location.

Saberhagen never forgets to notify the opposition that the inside corner is his, once every game. He puts a batter on his ass, one batter, every start, usually in the first two innings, usually a good hitter, usually a right-hander. He never hits him, and there's never an argument that follows, although there might be a flare-up or two until the National Leaguers get used to him. Who else can do all that?

The thing is that he's not a hundred percent, for one reason or another, about 30% of the time. When he gets to be thirty years old, will that percentage go to fifty—or will it go to seventy? That's the key to Bret Saberhagen's Hall of Fame chances: how many starts will he get before injuries drag him down? When he's 40 years old and throws 80, he'll still be able to win, the way John

Tudor was able to win at the end. The question is, will he be there?

MET PROSPECTS

Best Minor League Prospect: Todd Hundley

Who Is: A switch-hitting catcher, and Randy Hundley's son. Hundley had always been regarded as a defensive catcher who wouldn't hit, but put on fifteen pounds and hit 14 home runs for Tidewater. He'll open 1992 as the Mets' starting catcher.

Other Prospects: Anthony Young, the Mets' top prospect a year ago, was called up, made eight starts for the Mets and pitched well (3.10 ERA), so I don't know whether to consider him a prospect or a pitcher.

Outfielder **Jeromy Burnitz** was the Mets' top pick in the 1990 June draft. In 1991 he played in the AA Eastern League with Williamsport, where he hit 31 home runs, but struck out 127 times and hit .225.

Pat Howell played for St. Lucie (A) and Williamsport (AA) last summer, and in addition to being listed the #7 prospect in the Florida State League by *Baseball America*, he was named the league's fastest baserunner, best defensive outfielder and most exciting player. Howell, 23, hit a combined .252 with one home run, but stole 64 bases.

Third baseman **Butch Huskey** spent all of last season at Columbia in the South Atlantic League. He led the league with 26 home runs, slugged .520, and stole 22 bases at age 19.

Huskey's teammate, right-hander **Jose Martinez,** went 20-4 with a 1.49 ERA and a strikeout-to-walk ratio better than five to one. He was the only twenty-game winner in the minor leagues last year. Martinez, 21 and skinny (6'2", 155), throws a good curve and a great change, along with a fastball in the low eighties. According to *Baseball America*, the Mets don't believe he will pitch in the majors unless he can add six or seven MPH to his fastball. He was listed as the #10 Sally League prospect. Managers are more impressed with fastballs than with stats, and so are higher on perennial prospect **Sidd Finch,** who continues to impress the radar gun but has lost the strike zone.

Chris Donnels is a first/third baseman, played half the season in Tidewater before being called up. His MLEs show him as a .260–.275 hitter who could draw a hundred walks.

Terry Bross is a six-foot-nine relief pitcher, said to be the Mets' closer of the future. He started 1991 in Tidewater and struggled, walking 32 men in 33 innings. Bross found his control after a demotion to the Eastern League, and spent September with the Mets.

VETERAN STATUS AND CLUTCH PERFORMANCE: A MATCHED-SET STUDY

Do veteran players hit better in the clutch? It is universally accepted by baseball announcers and emphasized by retired players that situational hitting is a skill acquired over time. "He's the type of veteran player who knows how to adjust to a situation like this," Tim McCarver will tell you if, let us say, Alan Trammell should come to the plate with a man in scoring position after the sixth inning.

With the explosion of information about situational batting performance, it has become possible to evaluate this assumption. I decided on a matched-set study. You know what a matched-set study is; it proceeds from the conditional clause "other things being equal", and tries to figure out how to hold everything else equal. Other things being equal, a veteran will hit better in a clutch situation than a rookie or an inexperienced player.

To get an answer to that question, I searched the 1989 and 1990 seasons, looking for *sets of two players with extremely comparable batting stats, one of whom was a veteran and the other of whom was a young, inexperienced player.*

I had 41 sets of players, 82 players in the study. For example, Craig Worthington, 1989, was matched with Dave Henderson, 1989. This chart compares their batting stats:

Player	AB	H	2B	3B	HR	BB	SO	BAvg	OBP	SlPct
Worthington	497	123	23	0	15	61	114	.247	.334	.384
Henderson	579	145	24	3	15	54	131	.250	.315	.380

Worthington and Henderson had almost the same batting average (.247, .250) and slugging percentage (.380, .384). Their doubles, triples and home runs were very much the same. Their strikeout to walk ratios, though not as close as the other data, are vaguely similar. This coincidence focuses our attention on the key difference between them: Worthington in 1989 was a rookie, 24 years old. Henderson was a veteran, 31 years old in midsummer; he had played 926 major league games before that season.

Incidentally, Henderson is also considered, among baseball fans, to be a well-established "clutch" hitter, which no one would say about Craig Worthington. This will often happen in this study, simply because, as time passes, some veterans will come to be known as "clutch" players. Among the veterans in this study are Paul Molitor, Dale Murphy, George Brett, Ozzie Smith, Eddie Murray, Gary Gaetti, Pedro Guerrero, Dave Parker, Tom Brunansky, Kent Hrbek, Dave Winfield, Andre Dawson and

Alan Trammel, all of whom have been described countless times as clutch hitters, proven clutch hitters. To say that they're *not* proven clutch hitters would be regarded by many in the media as libelous. They're veterans; they've been in big games, they've won big awards, they've driven in big runs, and they have acquired that image—but I didn't select them for that reason. *The inclusion of known "clutch" hitters in the "veteran" group of the study was not by design; it was merely an inevitable accident.*

I controlled for similarity in ten categories, the ten listed in the Worthington/Henderson chart (At Bats, Hits, Doubles, Triples, Home Runs, Walks, Strikeouts, Batting Average, On-Base Percentage, Slugging Percentage). I did *not* control for runs scored or RBI as elements of similarity, because this would obviously bias the study *against* a finding of superior clutch performance for either group. Let us take, for example, Bip Roberts and Alan Trammell, 1990 season:

Player	G	AB	R	H	2B	3B	HR	RBI	BB	SO	Avg.
Roberts	149	556	104	172	36	3	9	44	55	65	.309
Trammell	146	559	71	170	37	1	14	89	68	55	.304

Roberts was 26 years old at that time, with 579 major league at bats prior to the season; Trammell was 32 years old, with more than 6,000 prior at bats.

Although Roberts and Trammell had quite similar overall batting records, Trammell drove in twice as many runs as Roberts. This *may* have happened because Trammell hit better in key RBI situations than did Roberts, or it may have happened for some other reason. If I had not allowed this to happen in matched sets, then I would have been banning from the study any match in which one player hit dramatically better in key situations than the other. I wanted to *find* those cases, not *ban* them.

I also didn't control for stolen bases, because baserunning doesn't have anything to do with the study, so Roberts, who stole 46 bases, is matched with Trammell, who stole only 12.

Most of the matched sets will have one fairly significant difference in the players. In the Worthington/Henderson match, there was a fairly significant difference in at bats (579/497). In the Roberts/Trammell match, there was a fairly significant difference in home runs (14/9). The multiple controls prevent these things from becoming inappropriately large. If the home run edge for Trammell created a significant difference in slugging percentage, then that might have been enough to prevent Trammell and Roberts from coming out as a matched set. But Trammell's slugging percentage is .449, Roberts' .433—no real difference, so the match goes through.

While there are differences in the players in *individual* cases, these differences all but disappear in the larger picture of 41 players in each group. Bip Roberts, a young players with 9 homers, is matched with a veteran with 14 homers—but then, Dave Justice, a young player with 28 homers in 1990, is paired with Kent Hrbek, a veteran with 22 homers:

Player	AB	H	2B	3B	HR	BB	SO	BAvg	OBP	SlPct
Justice	439	124	23	2	28	64	92	.282	.373	.535
Hrbek	492	141	26	0	22	69	45	.287	.377	.474

Justice was then a 24-year-old rookie, the Rookie of the Year; Hrbek was a 30-year-old veteran with more than a thousand major league games before the season.

If you put Justice and Roberts together, you have 37 home runs; if you put Hrbek and Trammell together, you have 36. The individual differences tend to disappear—but since *all* of the players in one group are veterans and *all* of the players in the other group are young players, that one difference, rather than washing out, becomes larger and larger the more players are included.

Of the "inexperienced" players, none had played more than 500 major league games by the *end* of the season being compared. In every comparison, the "veteran" player was *at least* five years older than the younger player. In every case, the "veteran" player had played *at least* 500 more major league games than the young player. Those were *minimums*.

The following chart gives the average performance of a player in each group:

Player	AB	R	H	2B	3B	HR	RBI	BB	SO	Avg.
Young	526	70	145	26	3	12	62	54	78	.275
Veterans	539	68	149	26	4	12	65	53	74	.276

A few of the other comparisons: Jack Howell and Dale Murphy (1989), Kevin Seitzer and Brett Butler (1989), Mark Grace and Julio Franco (1989), Todd Benzinger and Eddie Murray (1989), Ken Caminiti and Brook Jacoby (1989), Jose Oquendo and Tommie Herr (1989), Sammie Sosa and Gary Gaetti (1990), Ken Griffey Jr. and Tim Wallach (1990), Kal Daniels and Andre Dawson (1990), Roberto Alomar and Julio Franco (1990). Let's look at Benzinger and Murray, because if I don't you'll never believe that Todd Benzinger had a year in which he hit as well as Eddie Murray:

Player	G	AB	R	H	2B	3B	HR	RBI	BB	SO	Avg.
Benzinger	161	628	79	154	28	3	17	76	44	120	.245
Murray	160	594	66	147	29	1	20	88	87	85	.247

Benzinger was 26 years old at that time, and had played less than 200 major league games before the 1989 season.

After forming the two matched groups of players, I checked the performance of all the individuals (and therefore, the groups) in seven situations, each related in some way to clutch performance. I got this data by using a computer modem and the information of *STATS Online*; this information is also available to you if you're interested, call 1-708-676-3322. The seven situations I chose to compare were:

Batting with no one on base,
Batting with runners on base,
Batting with no one on and none out (leading off),
Batting with runners in scoring position,
Batting after September 1,
Batting in the late innings of close games, and
Batting with two strikes.

Both groups of players, the young players and the veterans, made noticeable adjustments to the game situation. In other words, situational hitting clearly does exist; offensive events are non-random in unmistakable ways. Of course, the changes described here may well represent the "adjustments" of pitchers and defenses, rather than the adjustments of hitters, but at the moment we really don't care. We're studying the effects, not the causes.

With no one on base the 82 players hit .269 overall, with a .329 on-base percentage and a .398 slugging percentage.

With men on base the 82 players hit .286 overall, with a .355 on-base percentage and a .413 slugging percentage.

Leading off an inning the two groups of players hit .268.

With men in scoring position they hit .275.

The next three statements I'm going to make here are the essential summary of the conclusions, so I'm going to put them in bold face. The three statements work at cross-purposes, so don't take them all as one.

1) The adjustments of the two groups of players are extremely similar, and only different to a very small extent.

2) There are many apparent differences between the groups of players, attributable mostly to the ways they are used by their managers.

3) To the tiny extent that one might conclude that one group of players was better than the other in clutch situations, one *would* have to conclude that the veterans had performed better. One would be much more likely to reach that conclusion, rather than the opposite conclusion. **No difference in clutch performance between the two groups is statistically significant on its own,** but there may be a pattern of data sufficient to reasonably conclude that the veterans did perform a tiny bit better in key situations.

1) The adjustments of the two groups of players are extremely similar, and only different to a very small extent.

Let's look at the situations one by one:

With No One On

The overall batting averages of the two groups is .276—.275 in the one group, .276 the other. With no one on base, the average of each group falls by seven points.

The young players, who hit .275 overall, fell off to .268.

The veteran players, who hit .276 overall, fell of to .269.

Both groups fell off by 7 points in batting average.

The "young" group had an overall slugging percentage of .406, the veterans of .404. This also fell with no one on base—to .399 for the young players, .398 for the veterans.

There are no significant differences in the adjustments of the two groups of players to this situation.

With runners on base

Both groups of players hit better with men on base.

The batting average of the young players increased to .286.

The batting average of the veterans increased to .286.

Both groups also increased their on-base and slugging percentages with men on base.

The young players increased their slugging percentage to .415. The veterans increased their slugging percentage to .411.

Again, there is no significant difference in the adjustments made to this situation.

Leading off an inning

Leading off an inning, a hitter's fundamental goal is to get on base. In this situation, the pitchers appear to get more of what they want: the on-base percentage of both groups drops.

However, the on-base percentage of the young players drops considerably more than the on-base percentage of the veterans. The on-base percentage of the young players, which is .343 overall, drops to .322. The on-base percentage of the veterans, which is .333 overall, drops to .328. One group drops 21 points in on-base percentage; the other group drops five.

There are more than 6,000 plate appearances in each half of the data for this sub-group—that is, both the young players and the veterans had over 6,000 plate appearances leading off an inning.

It does appear in this group that the veterans adjust slightly better to the situation than do the young players.

The difference, incidentally, is in batting average, not walks. The young players actually walk *more* often than the veterans do in leadoff situations—7.8% of plate appearances for the young players, 7.1% for the veterans. But their batting average drops more—.275 to .264 for the young players, .276 to .269 for the veterans.

What appears to happen is that the young players make an inappropriate adjustment to the situation, concentrating on taking pitches rather than taking what the pitchers give them. But the data which shows this would not pass a test of significance.

Batting with runners in scoring position

This, of course, is a standard and fundamental test of clutch performance. If I had decided to choose only one game situation to compare the groups of players, this would have been it.

There is no significant difference in the batting performance of the two players with runners in scoring position. Both groups of players hit .275, as a group, with runners in scoring posi-

tions. Veteran players, as a group, do *not* hit significantly better with runners in scoring position than do young and inexperienced players.

Sometimes the veterans did do well with men in scoring position. Julio Franco, a veteran in 1989, did hit .407 with men in scoring position. Mark Grace, a young player having a similar season with the bat, hit well with runners in scoring position, but not nearly *that* well.

Alan Trammell, whose RBI total was cited earlier, hit .379 with runners in scoring position. Bip Roberts was OK in those situations (.280), but he was a hundred points behind his partner.

But then, sometimes they didn't, either. Tom Brunansky, a veteran, hit only .213 with men in scoring position in 1990. Sometimes the young players hit well with runners in scoring position. Gary Sheffield in 1990 hit .336 with runners in scoring position. Dave Justice as a rookie hit .319 with ducks on the pond. Roberto Alomar in 1990 hit .338 in that situation.

Late innings of a close game

The veteran players, in the study, did hit better in the late innings of a close game than did the young and inexperienced players.

In the late innings of close games, the young players studied batted 3,432 times, hitting .255 with 72 home runs, a .369 slugging percentage.

The veteran players batted 3,477 times, hitting .270 with 77 home runs, a .389 slugging percentage.

Although the difference is comparatively slight and *could* result from chance, this would not be likely. The difference in late & close production—15 points in 3400 at bats—is slightly more than 50 hits, or slightly more than one hit per player studied.

Batting with two strikes

There is no apparent difference in the batting of the two groups of players after they have two strikes on them.

The aggregate batting average of the young players, with two strikes on them, fell to .205.

The aggregate batting average of the veterans also fell to .205.

The slugging percentage of the young players fell to .290.

The slugging percentage of the veterans also fell to .290.

September/October batting performance

The batting performance of players late in the season is different from the other situational performance areas studied for two reasons:

1) There are many other things, other than situational adaptation, which could cause one group or the other to do better late in the season, and

2) As a "clutch" category, it is too broadly defined. While it is true that the most important games of the season are played in September and October, it is also true that the *least* important games of the season are played in September and October. It is unclear to me whether this has any meaning as a clutch category.

In any case, the veterans *did* play somewhat better in September than did the younger players. The veterans, who hit .276 overall, also hit .276 in September/October. The home run rate of the veteran players *increased* in September from 22 home runs per 1000 at bats to 25 home runs.

The young players, who hit .275 overall, dropped to .265 after September 1. Their home run rate remained constant, at 22 home runs per 1000 at bats.

Minor league teams, of course, don't play in September. Tracy Ringolsby has told me that he has observed that young players tend to start dragging a little late in the season, rookies in particular, because this is new to them. They're used to the season being over. There may be some validity to that observation.

2) There are many apparent differences between the groups of players, attributable mostly to the ways they are used by their managers.

Let me note a few of those:

a) The young players scored slightly more runs and drove in slightly fewer. The young players, as a group, scored 2,869 runs and drove in 2,538. The veteran players, having essentially identical seasons, scored 2,788 and drove in 2,651.

b) This occurred because their managers were much more likely to position the veterans in the 3, 4 or 5 spots in the batting order. The young players, as a group, had 35% of their at bats from the 3, 4 or 5 spot in the batting order. The veteran players had 44% of their at bats in the middle spots.

Craig Worthington, a rookie, had only 14 at bats in the middle of the order. Dave Henderson, a veteran having the same season, had 276 at bats in the middle of the order—for a team with a much better offense.

Jack Howell, a relatively young player hitting .228 with 20 homers in 1989, had *no* at bats in the middle of the order. Dale Murphy, a veteran star hitting .228 with 20 homers for another team, batted 534 times in the middle of the order.

c) The young players were asked to bunt far more often than veterans hitting at the same level. The young players laid down 169 sacrifice bunts as a group. The veterans bunted only 103 times.

d) The veteran players were intentionally walked much more often than the young players. The young players were intentionally walked 205 times; the veterans, 264 times.

These things are not surprising, of course, but think about what this means. The managers *treat* the players as if the veterans were more dangerous—even though we know that they are not. The young players are asked to bunt more and are intentionally walked less—even though they are performing just as well.

e) The veteran players grounded into 12% more double plays, 502 to 448. To some degree, this is probably a consequence of the bunting, as one reason managers bunt is to avoid the double play. If you bunt less you're going to get more double plays.

It also may have to do with speed. However:

f) The stolen base percentage of the veterans, which was not controlled in the selection, was significantly better than the stolen base percentage of the younger players. The veterans, as a group, stole 24 *more* bases than the youngsters (594-570), while being caught 30 *less* times (258-288).

g) The veterans also hit 11% more triples (145-131), the largest percentage difference in any of the controlled categories. Of course, the numbers are small.

One thing that strikes me here is how little effect there is to the managerial strategies described. Managers, we have noted, give the veteran players many more at bats in the middle of the batting order, about twenty percent. They asked their veterans to bunt less often. No doubt they also pinch hit *for* their veterans less often, and pinch hit *with* their veterans more often, although I didn't specifically study these things.

In spite of this, the increase in the number of at bats with runners in scoring position is extremely small. The "young" players had 24.2% of their at bats with runners in scoring position. The veterans had 24.4%.

The veterans have, in a typical season, two more RBI—at a cost of two less runs scored.

The concentration of at bats in the middle of the order, the bunting, etc.—they have almost no effect on the player's production. In the end, the young players bat just about as often in key situations, and drive in and score just about as many runs.

3) To the tiny extent that one might conclude that one group of players was better than the other in clutch situations, one *would* have to conclude that the veterans had performed better.

I have cited two reasons why one might reach this conclusion already:

1) The on-base percentage of veteran hitters drops less dramatically in leadoff situations than the on-base percentage of young players.

2) The veteran players did hit better in the late innings of close games than did the young players.

I won't cite the superior September performance of the veterans in this area, since I don't really know that it represents "situational" performance. However, there are several other little markers of clutch performance which turn up in the study which I haven't mentioned yet, either because I just haven't gotten to them, or because I dismissed them earlier as insignificant.

3) The veteran players in the study delivered 33% more sacrifice flies than did the young players. Veteran players in the study delivered 247 sacrifice flies. Young players delivered 186.

Let us think about why this might have happened. The veteran players, because they batted more times in the middle of the season, could have had more sacrifice fly *opportunities* than the young players—but they didn't. The number of at bats with runners in scoring position, as I pointed out a moment ago, is only a fraction higher for veterans than for young players.

It could have happened, in part, because of the bunts. Sacrifice bunts and sacrifice flies do compete, at a certain level; if a player is asked to bunt with a runner on third, that eliminates a sac fly opportunity.

This doesn't wash, however, because the increase in sacrifice flies for older players (61) is nearly as large as the decrease in sacrifice bunts (66). Since only a small percentage of sac bunts are used with runners on third, that seems very unlikely. It might *contribute* to the difference, but it certainly wouldn't *explain* it. I mentioned earlier that the batting average of the two groups of players with runners in scoring position is the same, .275. What I didn't mention, however, is that *the veteran players strike out slightly less often with runners in scoring position than do the young players.* With runners in scoring position the young players struck out 163 times per 1000 at bats. The veteran players struck out only 147 times per 1000 at bats. The overall strikeout rate for the veteran players was lower, but the advantage grew slightly with men in scoring position.

4) The young players homered more often with the bases empty. The veteran players homered more often with men on base.

The young players hit 22.8 home runs per 1000 at bats with the bases empty. With men on base, their home run rate dropped to 21.6.

The veterans homered 21.5 times per 1000 at bats with the bases empty. With men on base, their home run rate *increased* to 23.1.

This is a relatively small difference—a shift of about 20 home runs in 9,000+ at bats—and overall the slugging percentage of the veterans with men on base did *not* outpace that of the young players.

5) With men in scoring position, the veteran players not only struck out less, but homered more. With men in scoring position the veteran players homered 126 times, the young players 93 times in three percent fewer at bats.

With men in scoring position the veterans had a slightly higher slugging percentage (.400-.393).

With men in scoring position the veterans delivered .382 RBI per at bat. The young players delivered .373 RBI per at bat.

What appears to have happened, again, is that the young players may have made an inappropriate adjustment to the situation. Some of the young players, it would appear, may shorten their strokes with men in scoring position, trying to deliver a base hit. They maintain their averages by so doing, but sacrifice power.

The power of the veteran players actually *increased* when there were runners in scoring position. The power of the young players decreased.

6) The young players hit distinctly more home runs (142-129) when leading off an inning. The two things that happened in leadoff situations were

a) the young players hit more home runs, and

b) the veterans got on base more.

In other words, the veterans made the appropriate adjustment to the situation more successfully.

7) The young players were 68 for 108 stealing bases in the late innings of a close game. The veterans were 88 for 121. Although the veterans were better base stealers overall, the difference was magnified in the late innings of close games.

Probably none of this data is significant on its own. It's all little tiny stuff, undetectable unless you look carefully at the data. However, looking carefully at all the data, I see seven reasons to believe that the veteran players *may* adjust more successfully to game situations. I see *no* reason to believe that the young players perform better in these situations.

Before I get into the proper summary here, there are two quick points that I wanted to make.

First, it is now apparent that the Strat-O-Matic assumption of random occurrence needs to be modified. I use models to analyze offense sometimes; I'm sure some of those studies are reported in these pages somewhere. Those models, like table games, assume that offensive events occur at random.

Well, we knew anyway that offensive events do *not* occur completely at random, but this study emphasizes that point. We're dealing here with two groups of .275 hitters. With no one on base, both groups drop to the .260s. With men on base, both go up to .286. What's that tell us? *It ain't random.* It's not a big deal, but it certainly *is* significant enough that it has *got* to be dealt with before any model, simulation or game can be considered realistic. I know it's a pain in the butt to re-design the games, but we've got to do it to keep step with what we know.

As it is now, many games or most games include "clutch" factors for hitters and pitchers—although in truth there is no *real* evidence that anyone has a measurable ability to hit in the clutch. Those factors, in essence, immortalize flukes. They take a random chance event—that someone may, in a particular year, have hit .219 with runners in scoring position, or may have had a low RBI rate—and pretend that it is a real function of his skill, when it simply isn't.

What *I* recommend is, get rid of that junk, and replace it with uniform codes for situational adjustments. Take something *out* of the game which is phony and artificial, and replace it with something which is real and verifiable. That's got to make a better game, doesn't it? In any event, five years from now any table game which doesn't adjust for situational changes in offense is going to be outdated.

Second, the decrease in batting averages and slugging percentages after two strikes is merely a natural consequence of the increase in strikeouts.

The media has always told us how important it was for a pitcher to get ahead of the hitter, make the hitter defend the plate, etc. I've never done any research on this before. The only research I know of is Peter Palmer's, and Pete has confirmed that players do, in fact, hit much better when ahead in the count than when behind in the count.

Batters don't hit well with two strikes on them because, after all, they strike out a lot. All strikeouts pass through the two-strike path.

If you take out the strikeouts, however, the batting averages and slugging percentages of both groups of players change only a little bit. The players do "protect the plate" and lose power with two strikes, but only a little. Overall, the players in the study hit .319 and slugged .459 when not striking out. After two strikes, they hit .310 and slugged .451 when not striking out.

The essential conclusion here is that the adjustments to situations made by young hitters and veteran hitters are virtually identical. I would be very happy if I could stop with that conclusion. Almost all studies of clutch performance, to this point, have tended to find that it really doesn't exist; it muddies the waters to complicate that essential argument by reporting the tiny footprints of a mythical beast.

I know very well that what I have written here may be misreported. I know that some people will use what I have found to reinforce the assumption that veterans have a superior ability to hit in the clutch. I'm sorry, but I have to tell the truth. I cannot report that there is *no* evidence that veterans adjust better to key situations when in fact there *is* such evidence, however slight.

I'll tell you what I think has happened. You must remember that baseball is often reported to us by ex-ballplayers, who before they were ex-players were *veteran* players.

I think that some ballplayers, smart ballplayers like Tim McCarver, *do* learn through experience to adjust to game situations. I think, however, that these players have no real concept of the *size* or significance of those adjustments, and, factoring them into the game through intuition and memory, grossly misinterpret their impact. I suspect, further, that many players, perhaps most players, never learn to make any such adjustments at all, further reducing the statistical magnitude of these effects.

I think, in short, that a roach is being reported to be the size of an elephant—but that there really *is* such a roach.

THE MONTREAL EXPOS
• IN A BOX •

1991 Won-Lost Record: 71-90 .441

Rank among 26 teams: 22nd
Over Last Five Years: 409-400 .506
Rank over Five Years: 13th
In Last Ten Years: 817-799 .506
Rank over Ten Years: 11th

Best Player: Ivan Calderon

Weak Spot: First Base
Or left field if Calderon moves to first.

Best Pitcher: Dennis Martinez

Staff Weakness: Inexperience

Best Bench Player: Was Dave Martinez

Best Young Player: 1. Delino DeShields
2. Larry Walker
3. Marquis Grissom

Best Looking Player: Junior Noboa

Ugliest Player: Ivan Calderon

Best Looking Player's Wife: Toni Darling

Most Pleasant Surprise, 1991: Bret Barberie

Biggest Disappointment, 1991: Tim Wallach

Best Minor League Prospect: Wilfredo Cordero

Who Is: See article, "Ear to the Ground"

Park Characteristics: Tends to crumble.

The Park Helps: Since the latest re-modeling three years ago, Olympic Stadium has become one of the best pitcher's parks in baseball. The Expos had a staff ERA of 2.86 at home last year, 4.27 on the road.

The Park Hurts: Wallach, Calderon, all hitters.

Bureaucrats often ask us for phenomenal acts of faith. "Don't worry, the bridge is safe now", "Exposure levels are far too low to pose a human health risk" and "We have drawn up careful plans for that contingency" are a part of our everyday lexicon.

However, even for the government, "A 55-ton chunk of concrete fell off the stadium today and crashed to the ground, but it's nothing to worry about" is a bit of a stretch. Don't you think you'd *worry* about that, just a little bit? Did you guys *know* this 55-ton chunk of the stadium was going to fall off? Did you know it wasn't going to be 56 tons, or 200? Did you know it wasn't going to fall when there were people around? How do you know there's not going to be another one tomorrow? What happens if there's an earthquake during a game? Don't these seem to you to be fair questions?

ORGANIZATIONAL REPORT CARD

Ownership: D
Upper Management: Too soon to tell
Field Management: Ditto
Front-Line Talent: D
Second-Line Talent: B−
Minor League System: A

TEAM LEADERS:

Batting Average: Ivan Calderon, .300

Last Ten Years (Season): Tim Raines, 1986, .334
Last Ten Years (Total): Tim Raines, .302

Doubles: Larry Walker, 30

Triples: Marquis Grissom, 9

Home Runs: Ivan Calderon, 19

Last Ten Years (Season): Andre Dawson, 1983, 32
Last Ten Years (Total): Tim Wallach, 190

Extra Base Hits: Larry Walker, 48

Stolen Bases: Grissom, 9

Runs Created: Ivan Calderon, 85
Calderon's 85 runs created were the lowest team-leading total in the major leagues. Every other team had at least one player creating more than 85 runs.

Runs Created Per Game: Calderon, 6.3

Secondary Average: 1. Delino DeShields .361
2. Ivan Calderon .360

RBI: Calderon, 75

Last Ten Years (Season): Tim Wallach, 1987, 123
Last Ten Years (Total): Wallach, 831

Wins: Dennis Martinez, 14

Last Ten Years (Season): Bryn Smith, 1985, 18
Last Ten Years (Total): Bryn Smith, 80

Winning Percentage: Dennis Martinez, 14-11 .560

Strikeouts: Martinez, 123

Last Ten Years (Season): Floyd Youmans, 1986, 202
Last Ten Years (Total): Bryn Smith, 829

ERA: Dennis Martinez, 2.39

Saves: Barry Jones, 13

League Leaders: Dennis Martinez' 2.39 ERA led the majors, as did his five shutouts. Also, he tied for the NL lead with nine complete games. With 177 career wins, Martinez ranks seventh among active pitchers.

Marquis Grissom stole 76 bases, a major league high.

Delino DeShields saw more pitches per plate appearance, 4.23, than any other National Leaguer. Not coincidentally, he also led the league with 151 strikeouts.

Ivan Calderon had a .627 slugging percentage against left-handed pitchers, the best in the league.

Gilberto Reyes threw out 53.1% of would-be basestealers, easily the best percentage in baseball.

Stat of the Year: Montreal *cleanup* hitters in 1991 hit .229, with just 17 home runs and no triples.

1991 SEASON

Background: As the decade turned—not this one, but the last one—the Expos were cited as the "Team of the Eighties". For various reasons the "Team of the Eighties" never quite arrived, but the Expos were a good, competitive ballclub through most of the decade.

In the late 1980s the Expos farm system dried up, and simultaneously they began losing their best players to age, injury and free agent defection. The front office fell into disarray. One General Manager ran off with the wife of one of the owners or something, and another was cashiered for no apparent reason. Still, under the astute direction of Buck Rodgers, the Expos remained a competitive team, winning 85 games in 1990.

Outlook: No one expected *less* in 1991. After the 1990 season the Expos had traded Tim Raines, one of their two best players of the 1980s, to the Chicago White Sox in exchange for Ivan Calderon and Barry Jones.

Getaway: The Expos opened the season on the road, losing five out of seven. They came home and continued to lose. By April 27 they were 5-13, already a substantial distance behind the Mets and Pirates.

Mike Fitzgerald missed the first two months of the season due to a hairline fracture of his right wrist. Starters Mark Gardner and Brian Barnes both missed the first month of the season, Gardner after off-season shoulder surgery and Barnes with a pulled muscle in his shoulder.

On June 3, with the Expos holding a record of 20 wins and 29 losses, Buck Rodgers was fired, and replaced by coach Tom Runnells.

High Point of the Season: June 22 at Cincinnati. The Expos gained ground on the .500 mark through most of June. When they beat Jack Armstrong on that date they were 33-35, the closest to .500 they would ever get.

Most Exciting Game of the Season: June 17 against Houston. The Astros scored in the first off Oil Can Boyd before the Can settled down and pitched seven scoreless innings. Jim Deshaies, in his best outing of the season, was mowing the Expos down. Montreal finally broke through in the bottom of the ninth, scoring one to tie, and it went into extra innings.

Tim Burke gave the Astros one in the eleventh, but the Expos came back with a run off Al Osuna. It stayed at 2-2 until the bottom of the sixteenth, when Dave Martinez won the game with a sacrifice fly.

The next night, Montreal again beat the Astros 3-2, this time in only twelve innings.

Low Point of the Season: For a month after that the Expos lost more games than they won; on July 15 they were 40-47. The Expos didn't play badly in that period, but the offense was in a collective slump and they lost a lot of close games.

What often happens in baseball is that a minor slump triggers a major slump, and so it was with Montreal. After July 15 the Expos lost 19 of 23 games, dropping their record to 44-66, by far the worst in the division. In this stretch Mark Gardner threw a nine-inning no-hitter at Los Angeles, but lost, and GM Dave Dombrowski traded away veteran pitchers Tim Burke, Oil Can Boyd and Ron Darling. Pitching coach Larry Bearnarth left the team to be with his family.

Stretch Drive: Finally Olympic Stadium itself began falling apart, and the Expos embarked on a historic 26-game road trip to complete the season (two homestands were converted to road games to allow the stadium to be secured). They played .500 ball from their hotel rooms, and finished the year with 21 wins in their last 35 games.

Major Injuries: See article, "Injury Box"

Offense: Very poor. The Expos traded their leadoff man (Tim Raines), and got no production from their traditional three-four hitters, Galarraga and Wallach.

Lacking punch, the Expos attempted to compensate by stealing a billion bases, and this worked as well as it usually does. The Expos led the league in stolen bases, and finished last in the league in runs scored.

Defense: Below average. Longtime manager Buck Rodgers was a defense-first manager, and left the Expos a solid defensive base—shortstop Spike Owen, catchers Fitzgerald and Reyes, third baseman Tim Wallach.

To a substantial degree this defense collapsed in 1991. Wallach is getting old; Andres Galarraga, a fine defensive first baseman, was fat and injured. Left fielder Ivan Calderon can't play the field; second baseman Delino DeShields, a quick and talented player, didn't develop defensively as well as hoped.

Pitching: Below average.

Best Game by a Starting Pitcher: Dennis Martinez threw a perfect game at Dodger Stadium on July 28 (9 0 0 0 0 5).

Worst Game by a Starting Pitcher: Chris Haney in St. Louis on September 30 (3⅔ 7 7 7 3 2 Game Score: 16)

Indicators for 1991 were: Down 2.1

Number of regulars having good seasons by their own standards: Three (Calderon, Owen and Walker)

1991 Over-Achiever: Calderon

1991 Under-Achiever: Galarraga

Infield: Very poor. Second base (DeShields) was strong offensively, but not defensively. Spike Owen played well and was the best of the four, but he's not an All Star. The play at first base and third base was last-place calibre.

Outfield: By far the strongest element of the team. Expo left fielders (mostly Calderon) hit .283 with 20 homers, 35 stolen bases (which had no value, since they were offset by 16 caught stealing) and 90 RBI. Their center fielders hit .267 and stole 77 bases (Grissom). Their right fielders (Larry Walker) hit .295 with 41 doubles, 14 homers and 17 more steals. Those are excellent totals in a pitcher's park. Fourth outfielder Dave Martinez filled in at all three spots and played as well as the starters.

Catching: Offense so weak the defense couldn't possibly compensate. Expo catchers hit .218 for the year and scored only 34 runs.

Starting Pitching: A little below average. Dennis Martinez is as good a pitcher as there is in the league, but none of the other seven starting pitchers used during the year distinguished himself.

Bullpen: Awful, the weakest element of a last-place team. The Expos bullpen lost 31 games, the most of any major league team, and blew 28 save opportunities, tying for the National League lead.

Percentage of offense created by:

Young Players:	56%
Players in Their Prime:	33%
Past Their Prime:	11%

Team Age:

Age of Non-Pitchers:	27.1
Age of Pitching Staff:	28.9
Overall Team Age:	27.84

The Expos of 1991 had the youngest starting lineup in the division, but a veteran pitching staff (Martinez, Darling, Boyd, Burke. Even Mark Gardner is now 30.)

In retrospect, the critical decisions were: See article, "How Did this Happen"

THAT AND THE OTHER

Hall of Fame Watch: Anyone on the Expos would have to be considered a Hall of Fame longshot.

Throwback: Tim Wallach

Attendance Trend: Buffalo

Players with a Chance for 3000 career hits: None

Record Watch: Delino DeShields has 98 Stolen Bases by the age of 22, making him his age group leader and ahead of almost anybody's pace. At that age you can't take it seriously.

Best Defensive Player: Spike Owen or Gilberto Reyes

Worst Defensive Player: Ivan Calderon

Best Knowledge of the Strike Zone: Ivan Calderon

Least Command of the Strike Zone: Marquis Grissom

Fastest Runner: Marquis Grissom

Slowest Runner: Tim Wallach

Best Baserunner: Dave Martinez

Umm, don't you usually do this sort of thing *before* you get the job? The September 9 issue of *The Sporting News* reported that Tom Runnels "recently huddled with veteran catcher Ron Hassey. 'I asked how Tony LaRussa would do things,' Runnels said. 'Mainly we talked about the ways he uses computers and some of the little things he does to get an edge.' "

Most Likely to Still be Here in 2000: Matt Stairs

Best Fastball: John Wetteland

Best Breaking Pitch: Brian Barnes and Mark Gardner

Best Control: Dennis Martinez

Oddest Collection of Abilities: Delino DeShields

Why was this man in the Major Leagues: Ron Hassey

Gets Ahead of the Hitters Most Often: Dennis Martinez

Gets Ahead of the Hitters Least Often: Brian Barnes

Most-Similar Players:

to C Gilberto Reyes, Rick Wilkins
to 1B Andres Galarraga, Candy Maldonado
to 2B Delino DeShields, Chuck Knoblauch
to 3B Tim Wallach, Gary Gaetti
to SS Spike Owen, Greg Gagne
to LF Ivan Calderon, John Kruk
to CF Marquis Grissom, Ray Lankford
to RF Larry Walker, John Olerud

Most Fun to Watch: Gilberto Reyes

Least Fun to Watch: Tim Wallach

Managerial Type: Ron Hassey

Among the All-Time Team Leaders: Tim Wallach has played more games for the Expos than anyone else, and consequently holds many of their team records.

A little bit of research: See article, "Wallach's Case"

Town Team:

C—Ed Wingo
1B—Tim Harkness
2B—Sherry Robertson
SS—Sam LaRoque
3B—Pete Ward
LF—Roland Gladu
CF—Pete LePine
RF—Paul Hodgson
SP—Joe Krakauskas

Post-Season Transactions:

November 15, picked up Gary Carter off the waiver wire
November 25, traded Andres Galarraga for Ken Hill
December 9, traded Barry Jones to the Phillies for Darrin Fletcher and cash
December 9, waived Nelson Santovenia
December 11, traded Dave Martinez, Scott Ruskin and minor league infielder Willie Greene to Cincinnati for John Wetteland and minor league pitcher Bill Risley

What Needs to Be Done For 1992:

1. Break in the young infielders.
2. Sort out the pitching staff.

Outlook for 1992: The Expos lost 90 games last year, and they probably aren't that bad a team. The fact that two teams have vaulted from last to first in one year doesn't mean that I'm going to start predicting it as a regular thing.

In a sense, Expo fans should hope for a bad year now. If the Expos are determined to do it, they can probably get back in the race this year. But if they do that, they won't be able to examine what they have in the way of young infielders (Barberie, Stairs, Cordero), and they may push their long-awaited championship further away, rather than drawing it closer.

Index of Leading Indicators for 1992: Up 23.3

Positive Indicators: 1. Team Age
2. Plexiglas Principle

Negative Indicators: None Significant

Due for a better season: Delino DeShields

Likely to have a worse season: Ivan Calderon

1992 Won-Lost Record will be: 78-84

WALLACH'S CASE

I did a computer run to see which active player had lost the most home runs to the park or parks he had played in. The answer: Tim Wallach. Wallach has hit 76 home runs in his career in Montreal, as opposed to 119 on the road. Assuming that a player in a neutral park will usually hit as many home runs at home as on the road (which he will), Wallach has probably lost about 43 home runs in his career by playing in Montreal, more than any other major league player. Wallach has hit 61% of his career home runs on the road, which is also the highest percentage for any active player with a hundred or more home runs.

Did you ever think about Tim Wallach as compared to Brooks Robinson? Think about it. Robinson's team won many championships, so he had many chances to put his defensive skills on display, which he did magnificently. This gave Robinson an aura of greatness unsupportable by logical analysis. Robby had an MVP year early in his career, and with playing for great teams and being a nice guy he became a famous clutch hitter and a legendary glove wizard. I'm not pushing any of that aside and I'm certainly not putting down Robinson, but if you look at what's in the book, there isn't a lot of difference between Wallach and Robinson. Both are .260–.270 hitters with medium-range power. Both are slow and walk 50–60 times a year. Both are outstanding defensive third basemen, although Robinson was famous for it and Wallach isn't.

Three things have worked against Wallach—his park, the fact that his teams have never been able to get over the hump, and the fact that he was behind Mike Schmidt in his best years. I'm not trying to put him in the Hall of Fame. I'm just saying that I think if you put him in the right park, where he might average 25 homers a season rather than 20, where he might get a chance to show the world what *he* could do with the glove . . . well, he might be thought of as one of the better players of the generation.

INJURY BOX

Ivan Calderon missed the final month with a shoulder injury and had arthroscopic surgery in September. The Expos played better without him, but he is expected to be healthy for spring training.

Outfielders Darren Reed and Moises Alou both spent the entire season on the disabled list. Alou was out after shoulder surgery, and Reed's wrist was broken by a pitched ball during spring training. Alou has recovered fully, but Reed is not expected to be ready by April.

Chris Nabholz missed the second half of June and all of July with tendinitis in his left shoulder.

Andres Galarraga went on the disabled list May 26 with a pulled hamstring, then had arthroscopic knee surgery on June 8. He didn't return to the lineup until July 4. The Expos played better without him, too.

Larry Walker spent two weeks on the disabled list with a hamstring problem.

Injuries to Mike Fitzgerald, Mark Gardner and Brian Barnes were mentioned earlier.

EAR TO THE GROUND

Wilfredo Cordero is a tall, rangy 20-year-old shortstop. He hit .261 with 11 homers, 52 RBI at Indianapolis before his season was ended July 31 by a broken hand.

There was an article by Bill Koenig in the November 8–14 edition of *USA Today Baseball Weekly* choosing Nine "Stars of the Nineties". Cordero was the first player listed. Koenig said that Cordero "had the best glove and best arm in the Class AAA American Association."

Other Prospects: Matt (the People Under the) **Stairs** is another young infielder who hit .333 last year at Harrisburg, the highest average of any second baseman in pro ball. His MLEs look terrific—.309 with some speed, a good strikeout/walk ratio and line-drive power. A member of the Canadian Olympic team, Stairs was a free agent (I guess we don't draft Canadians) and signed with the Expos in 1988. He's built like a second baseman (5-9, 178), hits like a third baseman. With DeShields on hand and Wallach fading, his future may be at third. His future may also be present.

The same may be true for **John VanderWal,** a left-handed, line-drive hitting outfielder who could lead the league in doubles within a couple of years. The trades of Dave Martinez and Andres Galarraga, sending Calderon to first, open up playing time for somebody, and VanderWal appears to be the man. He *can* hit, enough to hold the job.

Rondell White is a 20-year-old with an Andre Dawson body, has hit well in his first two minor league stops but can't throw. At Sumter last year he hit .260 with 12 homers, 51 stolen bases, 57 walks.

We could spend a page on this. The Expos have got *prospects.*

HOW DID THIS HAPPEN?

In retrospect, the critical decisions of the 1991 Expos were:

1. The trade of Tim Raines for Ivan Calderon and Barry Jones. Despite the very positive reviews it has received for a year, this exchange hurt the team. Calderon isn't as good a player as Tim Raines, offensively or defensively, and the addition of Barry Jones to the bullpen was about like mailing yourself a letter bomb.

2. Although first base is the easiest spot to find backup players—old outfielders who can still hit a little—the Expos failed to have the position backed up. When Galarraga didn't produce, they had nothing.

3. The firing of Buck Rodgers in early June was premature, and led to the subsequent unravelling of the team. The Expos fired one of the best managers in baseball because he had a slow start. By that standard, Earl Weaver could have been fired anytime.

RBI RATES AND CLUTCH PERFORMANCE

Does a player's RBI rate reflect how he has hit with runners in scoring position to *any* extent? In the old world, when situational data did not exist and assumptions could not be challenged with hard facts, many people took RBI rates to be a pure test of clutch performance. When a player had a good RBI rate for his other stats—let's say, Eddie Murray, 1991, hitting just .260 with 19 homers and 23 doubles, but driving in 96 runs—many people would take this to be proof that he had hit exceptionally well in clutch situations or at least RBI situations, overlooking the fact that he hits in the middle of the order for a team with an outstanding leadoff man.

We know now, of course, that this is greatly overdone, that RBI rates are essentially defined by opportunities and abilities, and also now we have actual data on what players have hit with runners in scoring position. The question here is, *do RBI rates provide ANY evidence about batting performance with runners in scoring position?* Take an old-time player for whom we have no actual data—let's say, Mickey Mantle in 1958, when Mantle had a very poor RBI rate (.304 with 42 homers, but only 97 RBI). Is it a reasonable inference that Mantle probably did not hit well with runners in scoring position in that particular season?

I play a table game sometimes with players from a long time ago. The people who make the cards for that game use RBI rates to influence the cards; there's a "clutch factor", which is really a way of giving credit for extra RBI. Here's the question I'm really asking: is there a justification for that?

I'll give you the answer first, and then explain the study. The answer is that it is a *reasonable* assumption in an *extreme* case. It is *likely* that Mantle did hit poorly in 1958 with runners in scoring position, but it is not a *safe* assumption; it could be wrong even when the data is extreme.

The assumption would have about an 80% chance to be correct if you could check the data—but a 20% chance to be wrong. The less extreme the RBI "discrepancy", the greater chance that your assumption would be wrong.

Here's what I did. First I generated four lists of players with poor RBI rates. Those were

1) The 1991 players with the lowest ratios of RBI to total bases.
2) Same thing, but limited to players with 15 or more homers.
3 and 4) Same things again, but for the 1990 season.

Then I compiled the same lists for the players with the *best* RBI rates. This gave me eight lists of players, four of whom had extremely good RBI rates, and four of whom had extremely poor RBI rates.

Then I called STATS Online, and checked

1) how those players had hit with runners in scoring position, and
2) their home run and extra-base hit frequencies with men on base and with the bases empty.

The players with extremely good RBI rates had, in fact, hit somewhat better with runners in scoring position than the players with extremely poor RBI rates. They didn't hit a *lot* better, nor did they hit *consistently* better. The differences in RBI rates were primarily created by opportunities, and only to a lesser extent by performance, but there was a performance variable.

The players with extremely poor RBI rates, as a group, hit .283 overall—but slipped to .258 with men in scoring position.

The players with extremely good RBI rates, oddly enough, had exactly the opposite data. They hit .258 overall, but .283 with runners in scoring position.

The players with poor RBI rates also had slightly fewer extra base hits with men on base than they did overall, while the players with good RBI rates had very slightly higher rates of extra base hits with men on base. This, however, was a very minor factor in the RBI differential.

In a typical 600-at bat season, the players with **good** RBI rates batted 170 times with runners in scoring position, and had 48 hits for a .283 average.

In a typical 600-at bat season, the players with **poor** RBI rates batted only 128 times with runners in scoring position, and had 33 hits for a .258 average.

The difference in *opportunity* is 33%.

The difference in *performance* is 9%.

Of the players with poor RBI rates, 78% hit worse with runners in scoring position than overall—but some didn't.

Of the players with good RBI rates, 80% hit better with runners in scoring position than overall—but some didn't.

An instructive comparison here is Tony Phillips, 1991, with Eddie Murray, whom we mentioned earlier. This chart compares their 1991 stats:

Player	G	AB	R	H	2B	3B	HR	RBI	Avg.
Phillips	146	564	87	160	28	4	17	72	.284
Murray	153	576	69	150	23	1	19	96	.260

They had comparable seasons, but Phillips was clearly better, except in RBI. Phillips had more hits, more doubles, more triples, only two less homers, and more total bases. In spite of this, he had 25% fewer RBI. Murray made the "good RBI" list; Phillips made the "poor RBI" list. (This was not a "matched set" study, like the one comparing young players and veterans in clutch situations.)

You might think, then, that it would be safe to assume that Murray was a proven RBI man, that he had hit better in RBI situations than had Phillips—but he didn't. In fact, Murray hit only .258 with runners in scoring position, two points less than his overall average. Phillips hit .322 with runners in scoring positions, almost forty points better than his overall average, and more than sixty points better than Murray did.

You know that expression, "close enough for government work"? I wind up this study about where I started it. I think it is better not to try to use RBI rates to infer anything about clutch performance. You can do it, and if you're careful you might be right more often than you're wrong. If you want to do government work, maybe that's close enough.

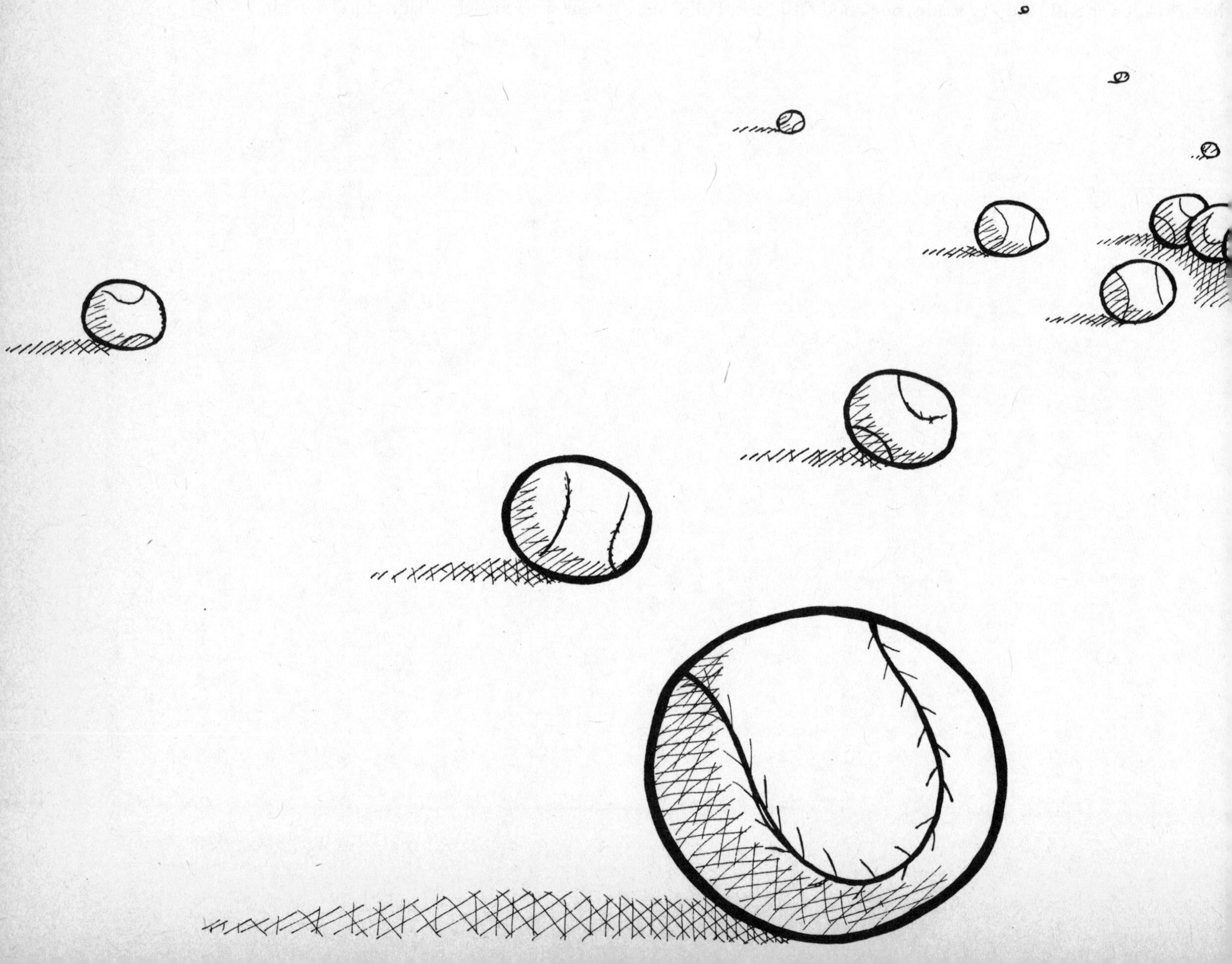

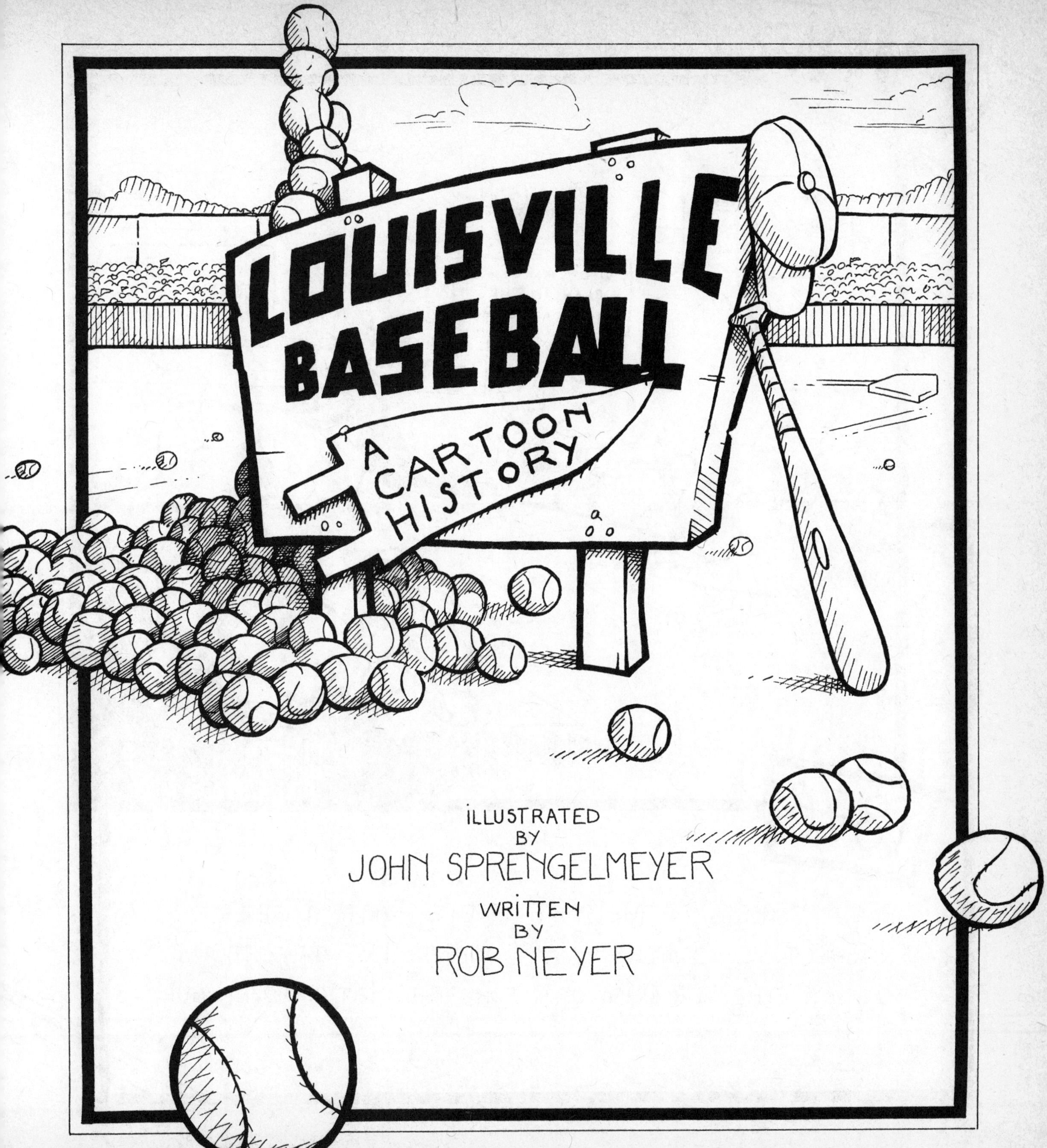
LOUISVILLE
BASEBALL
A CARTOON HISTORY
ILLUSTRATED
BY
JOHN SPRENGELMEYER
WRITTEN
BY
ROB NEYER

EVENTS

1876

WILLIAM HULBERT MEETS WITH THREE PROSPECTIVE OWNERS AT LOUISVILLE'S GALT HOUSE TO LAY THE GROUNDWORK FOR THE NATIONAL LEAGUE.

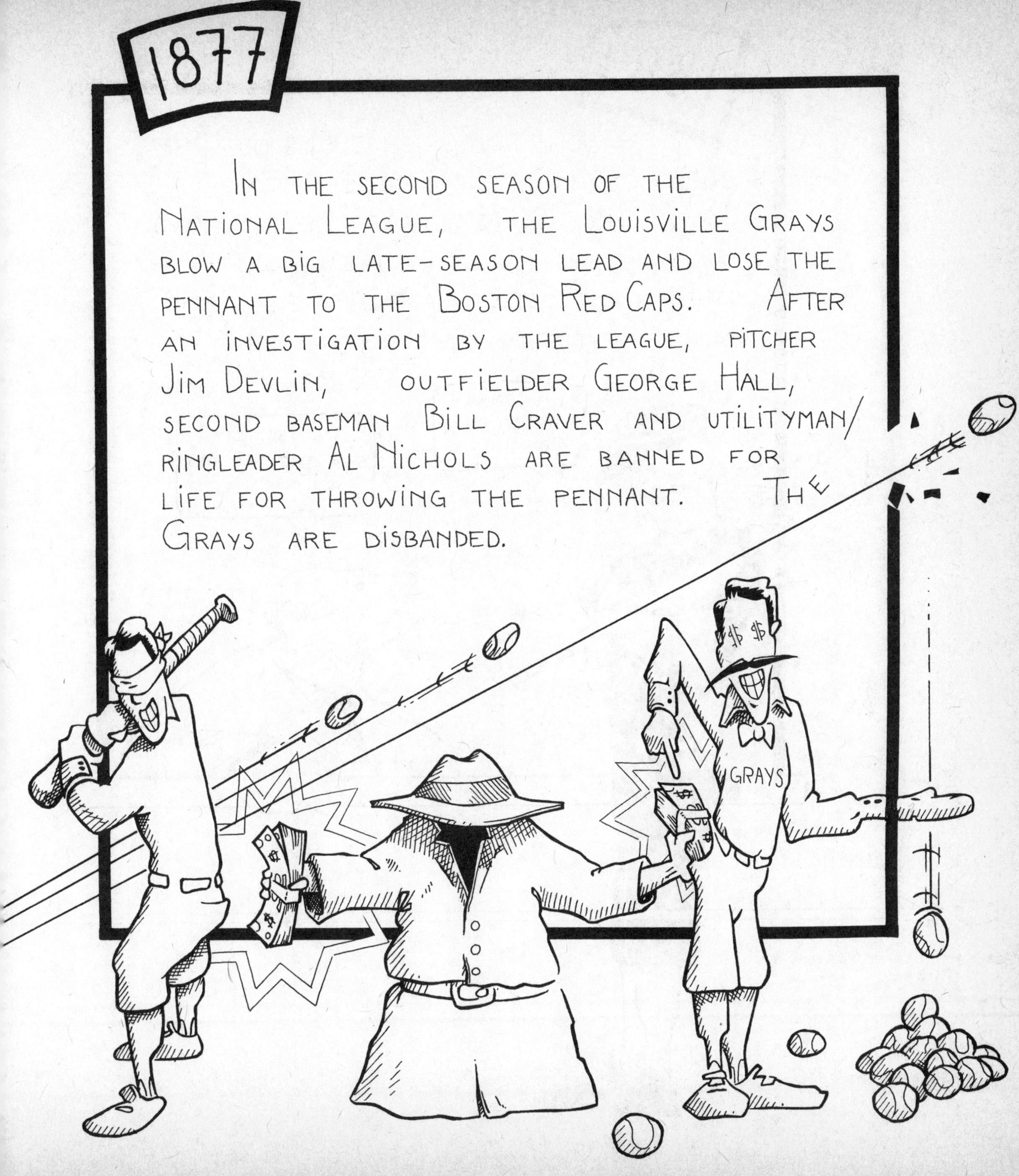
1877
In the second season of the National League, the Louisville Grays blow a big late-season lead and lose the pennant to the Boston Red Caps. After an investigation by the league, pitcher Jim Devlin, outfielder George Hall, second baseman Bill Craver and utilityman/ringleader Al Nichols are banned for life for throwing the pennant. The Grays are disbanded.
GRAYS

1884
JOHN HILLERICH TURNS OUT THE FIRST LOUISVILLE SLUGGER TO PETE BROWNING'S EXACT SPECIFICATIONS. SOON, EVERY PLAYER IN THE LEAGUE WANTS THEIR OWN CUSTOM-MADE LUMBER, AND AN INSTITUTION IS BORN.
I'M GONNA MAKE YOU RICH, HILLY.
I'D SETTLE FOR THE TWO BITS YOU OWE ME.

Louisville pitcher Guy Hecker bats .341 to earn the American Association batting title. "Blond Guy", who also plays first base and the outfield, is the only pitcher ever to win a major league batting title.

THE LOUISVILLE COLONELS OF THE AMERICAN ASSOCIATION WIN ONLY 27 GAMES WHILE LOSING 111, THE SECOND WORST RECORD IN MAJOR LEAGUE HISTORY.

A DEVASTATING TORNADO HITS LOUISVILLE IN LATE MARCH, KILLING SEVENTY-SIX PEOPLE. THE COLONELS BECOME TEMPORARILY KNOWN AS THE CYCLONES, AND WIN THE AA PENNANT WITH AN 88-44 MARK. THEY TOP THE SEASON OFF BY BEATING THE NATIONAL LEAGUE BROOKLYN BRIDEGROOMS IN AN EARLY VERSION OF THE WORLD SERIES.

JOE McCARTHY TAKES OVER AS MANAGER OF COLONELS. IT IS IN LOUISVILLE THAT McCARTHY FORMULATES HIS TEN COMMANDMENTS OF BASEBALL.

1921

JAY KIRKE, WELL-KNOWN BASEBALL "CHARACTER", COLLECTS 282 HITS FOR LOUISVILLE, THE ALL-TIME AMERICAN ASSOCIATION RECORD.

1921

McCARTHY'S COLONELS WIN THE AMERICAN ASSOCIATION AND FACE THE POWERHOUSE BALTIMORE ORIOLES IN THE JUNIOR WORLD SERIES. DOWN THREE GAMES TO TWO IN A NINE-GAME FORMAT, LOUISVILLE WINS THREE IN A ROW IN BALTIMORE TO TAKE THE CHAMPIONSHIP. THE COLONELS BEAT LEFTY GROVE THREE TIMES IN THE SERIES.

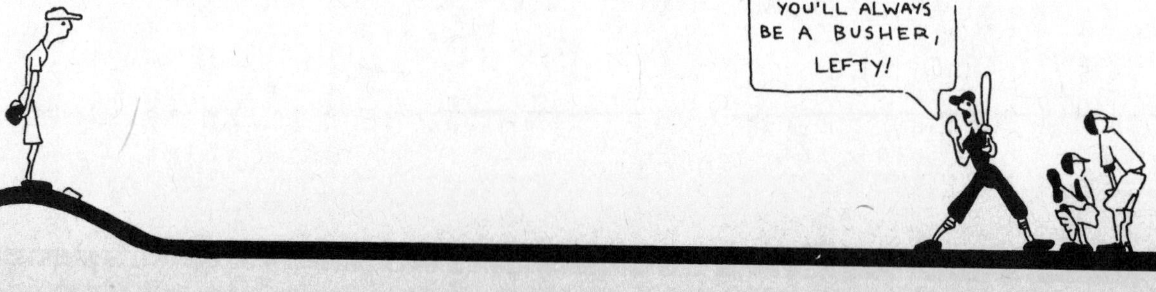
YOU'LL ALWAYS BE A BUSHER, LEFTY!

1925

BOY, I SURE HOPE I'M DOING THE RIGHT THING.

McCARTHY AGAIN LEADS THE COLONELS TO THE AMERICAN ASSOCIATION FLAG BEFORE LOSING THE JUNIOR WORLD SERIES TO BALTIMORE IN A REVERSAL OF 1921, FIVE GAMES TO THREE. SOON AFTER, "MARSE JOE" LEAVES FOR THE BIG LEAGUES, WHERE HE WINS NINE PENNANTS AND SEVEN WORLD SERIES. HE IS ELECTED TO THE HALL OF FAME IN 1957.

LOUISVILLE 1
CHICAGO 296
NEW YORK 765

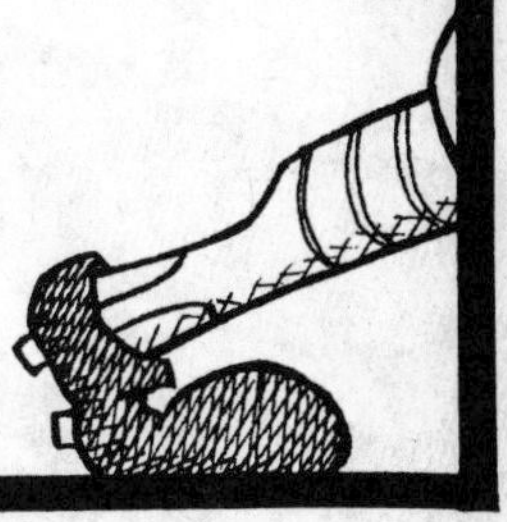

1932

A 13-YEAR-OLD NAMED HAROLD REESE WINS THE LOUISVILLE AREA MARBLES CHAMPIONSHIP. THE MARBLES ARE CALLED "PEE-WEES".

HAROLD ALWAYS WINS.

PLAYERS

- Born in Ekron, Ky., 1918
- 1938 and 1939, starred for Louisville Colonels
- Captained famous Brooklyn Dodger teams of '40s and '50s
- Spent three years in Navy in WWII
- Helped ease Jackie Robinson's entry into major leagues
- Elected to Hall [illegible] Fame in 1984

- Born in Louisville, 1861
- As Louisville rookie in 1882, hit .378 to capture first of three batting titles
- 1884, took possession of first Louisville Slugger
- Nicknamed "The Gladiator" because of often fruitless battles with fly balls
- Illiterate, alcoholic, and nearly deaf

- Born David Bell in Louisville, 1928
- Nicknamed by parents after Cards' catcher Gus Mancuso
- Drove in 100+ runs four times with Cincinnati
- Collected first New York Met hit
- Father of third baseman Buddy Bell

- Born just across the Ohio River from Louisville, 1909
- Batted better than .300 eight times
- Considered consummate number two hitter
- Played in four World Series, for Cubs and Dodgers
- Elected to Hall of Fame, 1975

- Born in Louisville, 1860
- Hit 25 homers in 1884 for Chicago White Stockings, due to extremely short dimensions
- Best known for defensive brilliance
- Managed Louisville Colonels in 1892

1944
NICK POLLY, COLONELS' THIRD BASEMAN, SETS AN AMERICAN ASSOCIATION RECORD WITH 147 WALKS.
1ST BASE

1949
MAY 24, MAURICE "MICKEY" McDERMOTT STRIKES OUT 20 ST. PAUL SAINTS IN NINE INNINGS. LOUISVILLE WINS 3-1. McDERMOTT SOON CALLED UP TO PITCH FOR THE RED SOX.

1959
JUNE 16, COLONELS' PITCHER JUAN PIZARRO THROWS A NO-HITTER AT THE CHARLESTON SENATORS. STARTING AGAINST CHARLESTON FOUR DAYS LATER, PIZARRO DOESN'T ALLOW A HIT UNTIL TWO ARE OUT IN THE EIGHTH INNING.
base hit /bās hĭt/ n. A hit by which the batter reaches base safely without an error or force play being made.
OH YEAH.
Senators

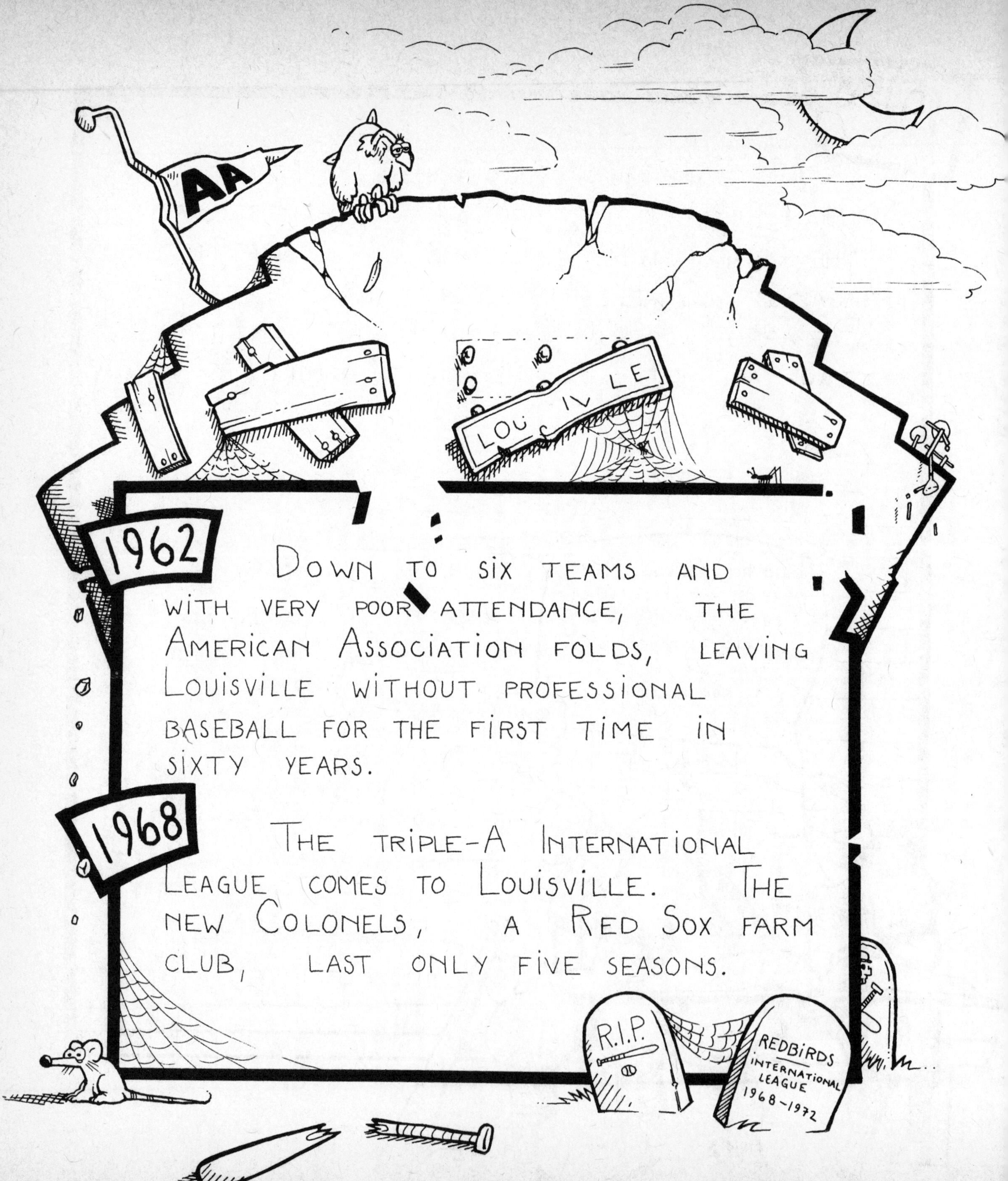
AA
LOUISVILLE
1962
DOWN TO SIX TEAMS AND WITH VERY POOR ATTENDANCE, THE AMERICAN ASSOCIATION FOLDS, LEAVING LOUISVILLE WITHOUT PROFESSIONAL BASEBALL FOR THE FIRST TIME IN SIXTY YEARS.
1968
THE TRIPLE-A INTERNATIONAL LEAGUE COMES TO LOUISVILLE. THE NEW COLONELS, A RED SOX FARM CLUB, LAST ONLY FIVE SEASONS.
R.I.P.
REDBIRDS
INTERNATIONAL LEAGUE
1968–1972

1982

THE AMERICAN ASSOCIATION MAKES A TRIUMPHANT RETURN TO LOUISVILLE WHEN ST. LOUIS' TRIPLE-A FARM CLUB MOVES FROM SPRINGFIELD. LOUISVILLE BASEBALL FANS, WITHOUT A PRO TEAM FOR NINE YEARS, RESPOND WITH A RECORD-SETTING ATTENDANCE OF 868, 418, SHATTERING THE MINOR LEAGUE RECORD!

1983

LOUISVILLE BECOMES FIRST MINOR LEAGUE TEAM IN HISTORY TO DRAW OVER A MILLION FANS IN ONE SEASON — OUTDRAWING THREE MAJOR LEAGUE CLUBS!!

TEAMS

GRAYS N.L. 1876–77

- 1876, Charter member of the National League
- Best player was pitcher Jim Devlin
- Team disbanded after three players conspired to throw 1877 pennant

ECLIPSE A.A. 1882–84

- Joined the American Association, then a "major" league, in 1882
- Best players were Pete Browning and Guy Hecker
- Highest finish was third, in 1884

COLONELS A.A. 1885–91

- 1885, Eclipse changed name to Colonels
- Generally mediocre aside from 1890 pennant
- Best players included Browning and outfielder Chicken Wolf, who was with the Eclipse/Colonels all ten years the franchise existed
- The American Association folded after 1891 season

COLONELS N.L. 1892–99

- Colonels, with a greatly altered roster, joined the National League in 1892
- 1895, Fred Clarke takes over in left field. Two years later, he was named player-manager
- Colonels dropped from league in 1899. Hall of Famers Clarke, Honus Wagner and Rube Waddell, plus Tommy Leach and Deacon Phillippe, sent to Pittsburgh, forming nucleus of Pirate power plant

COLONELS A.A. 1902–62

- Charter member of the new American Association, which began play in 1902
- Captured 15 A.A. pennants between 1902 and 1962 (1909, '16, '21, '25, '26, '30, '39, '40, '44, '45, '46, '54, '60, '61, '62), easily more than any other club, and won four Junior World Series
- Longtime Louisville stars included outfielder Butch Simons (.331 over nine seasons) and pitcher Austin Ben Tincup (179–133 in twelve seasons)
- When Association folded after 1962, Colonels had won last three pennants

- BOSTON'S INTERNATIONAL LEAGUE FARM TEAM MOVES TO LOUISVILLE IN 1968
- BEST PLAYERS WERE CARLTON FISK, DWIGHT EVANS, AND CECIL COOPER
- 1972, COLONELS FINISHED WITH BEST RECORD IN LEAGUE BUT LOST PLAYOFFS TO TIDEWATER
- CLUB MOVED TO PAWTUCKET IN 1973

COLONELS
I.L.
1968–72

- 1982, ST. LOUIS CARDINALS TRIPLE-A FARM TEAM MOVED TO LOUISVILLE
- BEST PLAYERS INCLUDED ANDY VAN SLYKE AND TODD ZEILE
- REDBIRDS A.A. CHAMPIONS IN 1984 AND 1985

REDBIRDS
A.A.
1982–PRESENT

THE END

PART TWO

PLAYER RATINGS

AMERICAN LEAGUE CATCHERS

1. Mickey Tettleton, Detroit

Has been an MVP candidate in two of the last three seasons. In 1989 he helped the Orioles from 95 losses to within two games of the division title, and was the top MVP candidate the first half the season before fading in the second half. In 1990 he didn't have as good a year, but last year he was by far the best hitting catcher in the majors, driving in 89 runs and scoring 85, and the Tigers also had a surprise season. Tettleton also threw out 38% of opposing base stealers, well over the major league average of 32%.

---

2. Brian Harper, Minnesota

Although the American League catchers are a solid group, behind Tettleton there is no obvious number two. Any of the players I have rated 2 through 8 are really about the same. Harper, who I have rated second, isn't outstanding, and Surhoff, who I have rated eighth, certainly isn't bad. Harper is a lifetime .292 hitter with many doubles, but can't throw. He threw out only 22% of opposition baserunners last year, lowest percentage in the American League, but that is the most overrated facet of the game.

3. Carlton Fisk and Ron Karkovice, Chicago

Having caught more games than any other catcher in history, Fisk remains a power threat and one of the best throwing catchers in the league. Karkovice is the best backup in baseball, and would be a quality regular if his production held up.

4. Terry Steinbach, Oakland

His hitting stats are hurt by playing in Oakland, but he still hits as well as any catcher in the league except Tettleton, Nokes and Harper. Works well with pitchers, defense above average, has a good record of remaining healthy.

5. Ivan Rodriguez, Texas

Wonderful defensive catcher, threw out 49% of opposition base stealers for a team whose pitching staff is notorious for failing to hold the runner. Despite his .264 batting average last year he may be overmatched, as a hitter, for the next year or two, but a .264 batting average is terrific for a 19-year-old catcher.

Rodriguez played 271 minor league games, which is more than most outstanding prospects historically have played, at catcher or any other position. Johnny Bench played 265 minor league games, Yogi Berra played 188, Bill Dickey 249, Mickey Cochrane 164. Fisk and Gary Carter played a few more, 346 (Fisk) and 311 (Carter). People will write that Rodriguez was rushed to the major leagues, but actually, when you have a player with this kind of ability it is *ab*normal to keep him in the minors longer than two years, as San Diego did with Santiago and then Alomar. Abnormal, and probably counterproductive.

6. Matt Nokes, New York

What Nokes did last year was simply to meet his career norms while playing regularly. This was a first for him; from his 32-homer season as a rookie through 1990 he was either up or down every year, and couldn't stay in the lineup through injuries and slumps. His arm is below average and he doesn't have the reputation for being good with pitchers, but you have to say something good about a catcher who can hit 24 homers.

7. Mike Macfarlane, Kansas City

Macfarlane (or McFarling, as Joe Morgan calls him) hit .277 last year with a .506 slugging percentage, essentially Johnny Bench's career norms (.267 and .476). He also played exceptionally well on defense, but it was his first good year and it ended early due to a broken collarbone. We'll need to see him do it for more than two months to know if he's for real.

Brent Mayne, who took over after Macfarlane was hurt, is too good to warm the bench, and will probably be traded.

8. B.J. Surhoff, Milwaukee

A pretty good player, not demonstrably worse than Brian Harper, who I ranked second. His .289 batting average last year offsets some of his weaknesses. He never walks, has no power and steals bases in a manner that makes you wish he really wouldn't, adding up to a secondary average of .145 last year. Dave Nilsson, who hit .418 in 65 games at El Paso, will force the trade of Surhoff if he has a good year at Denver.

---

9. Sandy Alomar, Cleveland

Expected to move into the front rank, he didn't last year because of injuries. I doubt that he has superstar potential. His career batting and slugging percentages are comparable to Surhoff, Macfarlane and Steinbach, below the other guys. His defense will add to that, but he's got to stay healthy.

10. Pat Borders (RH) and Greg Myers (LH), Toronto

Borders started slowly with the bat last year, but played better defensively than he has. Myers played up to his ability for the first time. Despite the number ten ranking this is *not* a weakness. These guys are both pretty good.

11. Lance Parrish, California

Still has power and a throwing arm, but has hit below .240 three of the last four years. Strikes out a lot and rivals Sam Horn and a couple of others as the slowest major league players. Backup John Orton is a good Texas League player.

12. Chris Hoiles, Baltimore

Despite the ranking, I like this guy, too. He hit eleven homers as a half-time player last year, so he could hit twenty or more. He came up with a bad defensive rep but threw out 35% of opposition runners, and the Oriole staff had a 4.19 ERA with him behind the plate, as opposed to 4.87 with Bob Melvin. Melvin's gone; Jeff Tackett is penciled in as the backup. He's a catch-and-throw guy, a .210 hitter who is supposed to have an arm.

13. Dave Valle and Scott Bradley, Seattle

Valle is a Gold Glove candidate but a lifetime .228 hitter without much power. Bradley is a .257 hitter with no power, and isn't a Gold Glove candidate, either.

14. Tony Pena, Boston

Probably will be out of a job by season's end, replaced by Eric Wedge, Todd Pratt or Scott Hatteberg. Pena's defense is still good, but he grounded into 23 double plays last year while driving in only 48 runs, an unacceptable ratio. In his prime (1983–84) he would have more homers than double plays in a season, but over the last three seasons his ratio is four GIDP for each homer.

Despite continuing stories about the shortage of good catchers, you'll note that no one in the American League is really desperate for a catcher right now. The four guys we have rated at the bottom—Parrish, Hoiles, Valle and Pena—really aren't bad players. It's just that everybody else is a little bit better.

NATIONAL LEAGUE CATCHERS

1. Mike LaValliere and Don Slaught, Pittsburgh

Both hit around .290 last year with secondary offensive skills as good as those of the other catchers. LaValliere won a Gold Glove a few years ago, Slaught didn't and won't but doesn't embarrass himself in the field. Third catcher Lloyd McClendon is a valuable pinch hitter/spare outfielder, a nice player to have around.

2. Benito Santiago, San Diego

His 1991 season (.267 with 17 homers, 87 RBI) was taken to be just doing his job, but nobody else in the league gets 87 RBI from their catchers. His defense has come under attack after years of glowing reviews, and I'm really not in a position to evaluate that in any depth, but it's hard to sustain a good reputation for several years when you're one of the best players on a bad team. If the team keeps losing, sooner or later the stars are going to take the rap for it.

3. Mike Scioscia, Los Angeles

He lost some playing time last year to Gary Carter, and with Carter gone may have trouble getting it back from Carlos Hernandez. Hernandez, who I thought was a major league player a year ago, hit .345 at Albuquerque, which didn't do anything to dissuade me. Scioscia is a consistent .260 hitter in a tough park with a great strikeout/walk ratio and some power, plus he blocks the plate well, handles the staff well and throws adequately. That's a good package.

4. Tom Pagnozzi, St. Louis

Threw out 70 runners stealing last year, 13 more than anybody else in baseball, and was rewarded with a Gold Glove. His .264 batting average is pretty much the sum of his offensive accomplishments, but he could show some power this year with the fences in St. Louis being brought in a few feet.

5. Jeff Reed (LH) and Joe Oliver (RH), Cincinnati

They played better than expected last year, and may continue to do so this year, because they're a natural platoon combination. Reed can hit right-handers for consistent singles, but can't do anything with a left-hander, and Oliver has some power against a left-hander, but can't pull a right-hander who has any kind of fastball. Defense is average, Reed probably a little bit the better.

6. Steve Decker, San Francisco

He flopped last year, but he's still going to be a good one. Even last year, although he hit .216, his secondary offensive skills and his defense were as good as those of most catchers or a little better. The Giants had a 3.77 ERA with Decker catching, as opposed to 4.50 with Terry Kennedy and 3.99 with Kurt Manwaring. Manwaring is a good backup.

Here's a philosophical question for you: was it a mistake for San Francisco to in essence announce that Decker was the regular catcher *before* the winter of 1990–1991? Did that put extra pressure on Decker, so that after a winter of waiting he was thinking "I've got to do this *now*. This is what I've been waiting all winter for." Would a shorter fuse have been better for him?

We'll never know. It's just something to think about.

7. Greg Olson, Atlanta

Olson made the All-Star team in 1990, and was out of a job at the start of 1991. He's nothing special—a .250 hitter with a few doubles, a below-average arm—but he kept his head in the game and out-lasted the people who were supposed to replace him. The dramatic improvement of the

Braves' pitching staff is certainly a point in his favor.

The Braves have two backup catchers, Jerry Willard and Francisco Cabrera, that I would love to get my hands on if I was dealing for another team. Willard is 32 years old and not a glove man, but a better hitter than Olson. Cabrera isn't a catcher, but could help somebody as a first baseman or designated hitter.

8. Darren Daulton, Philadelphia

Daulton has exceptional secondary offensive skills for a catcher. Catchers normally have secondary averages in the .150 to .200 range (Mike LaValliere, .176, Benito Santiago, .190, Tom Pagnozzi, .185, Jeff Reed, .189, Brian Harper, .170, Terry Steinbach, .164, B.J. Surhoff, .145, etc.). There are a few guys who get into the mid-.200s, but then there are two catchers today who walk a lot and have power, so their secondary averages get way up there. Those are Mickey Tettleton (.435 last year, .367 career) and Darren Daulton (.330 last year, .306 career).

That *helps* Darren Daulton, but by itself it doesn't make him a ballplayer. That's why he deserves a good contract if he hits .270 and throws well, as he did in 1990. Last year he threw out only 18% of base stealers, the lowest percentage in the majors for a regular. If you hit .196, throw out 18% of base stealers and get hurt, as Daulton did last year, somebody's going to take your job away, no matter what your other offensive skills may be.

The Phillies over the winter let Steve Lake go as a free agent *and* traded Darrin Fletcher, which means either

a) they know something we don't, or
b) they're trying to make a big show of confidence in Daulton despite his horsebleep season.

9. Todd Hundley, New York

I expect him to hit around .250 with 10 or 12 home runs, 20 to 25 doubles, strikeout to walk ratio poor but normal, not the worst in the league. Combined with the good defense which is expected of him this gives him a chance to be the Rookie of the Year if he has a year near the top of his range, and a chance to be the best catcher the Mets have had since Gary Carter grew old five years ago.

10. Hector Villaneuva, Rick Wilkins, Joe Girardi and others, Chicago

Nobody is sure what the Cubs will do for a catcher. Villanueva, who seems to be emerging as the number one candidate because he has hit so well, is overweight and isn't much of a catcher. Wilkins throws well and hits better than Gilberto Reyes, but has miscellaneous defensive problems as well as being a .220 hitter. Girardi was hurt last year, and has to hit .280 to play. If it was up to me I'd probably let Villanueva play, accept the fact that the opposition is going to steal 150 bases and hope he drives in a hundred runs to compensate. He has real power (20 homers in 305 major league at bats), but there is a limit to how many runs you can drive in batting behind Andre Dawson and George Bell.

11. Gilberto Reyes and Darrin Fletcher, Montreal

Reyes and Fletcher are both Dodger rejects, and are in the tradition of Dodger rejects since Joe Pignatano. Reyes cuts off the running game but is a .202 hitter. Fletcher will hit a little but if a guy is traded twice before he gets a chance to establish himself it's a good bet something is missing.

12. Scott Servais (RH) and Eddie Taubensee (LH), Houston

At this writing the plan is that Craig Biggio will go to second base or someplace else, and Servais and Taubensee will platoon behind the plate. Both hit .300 in AAA last year, Servais (says) hitting .324 for Tucson, Taubensee hitting .310 for Colorado Springs (Indians).

The odds are that one of them will take the whole job within a couple of years. Servais should hit around .270 but with no power, and he's slow even for a catcher, so he'll have to play defense to keep his part of the job. Taubensee will hit a few points lower but with a little bit of power.

AMERICAN LEAGUE FIRST BASEMEN

1. Frank Thomas, Chicago

He is simply the best hitter in baseball. He's one of half a dozen players in history who could hit .320 with great power *and* a huge number of walks—Thomas, Ted Williams, Mantle, Jimmie Foxx, Gehrig, Babe Ruth. Ralph Kiner was close, had more power. Only two things could keep Thomas from being one of the greats of the game—an injury, and a swelled head.

2. Rafael Palmeiro, Texas

An awesome hitter, too, Al Oliver-type hitter. Hard line drives three times a game. It seems odd now to reflect that the Cubs dumped Palmeiro, in part, because he didn't hit for power. Palmeiro, who hit 14 homers for the Cubs in half a season when he was 22 years old (1987) dropped to 8 homers (with a .307 average) at age 23, earning a ticket to Texas. While the Cubs use Mark Grace at first base (9 homers a year), Palmeiro had 26 homers last year and 49 doubles.

3. Cecil Fielder, Detroit

The notion that he's some sort of MVP candidate is silly, but he's a scary hitter. There's a long article about him in the Tiger comment, so I won't repeat that here.

---

4. Kent Hrbek, Minnesota

The only thing sillier than the idea that Fielder should be MVP is the idea that Kent Hrbek is a Gold Glove candidate. Tom Kelly sells this pap because

a) he wants Hrbek to take pride in his fielding,

b) it's a standard part of a manager's job to show loyalty to his horses, and

c) he figures the media is too ignorant to know any better.

The media passes this on to the public because

a) we all tend to believe what we're told,

b) it's a standard part of the media's job to pass along the wisdom of the manager, and

c) they don't know any better.

It's a joke. Hrbek has soft hands and does a good job of scooping up low throws, plus he has a pretty good arm and he's alert, which counts a lot. On the other hand, he can't get out of his own way, so he can't chase down a loose ball, in the air or on the ground, and more important than that he's so heavy that anytime he has to put his glove up in the air his center of balance is automatically off. There were at least ten plays in the seven-game series that Hrbek either couldn't make or couldn't make *right*, but Jack Buck just kept blabbering about what a great defensive first baseman he was because Tom Kelly had told him so. Hrbek's a terrific hitter, but he's a B-minus first baseman, and Tom Kelly knows it. Kelly's just bullshitting us. Watch the game with your own eyes, and you'll see what I mean.

5. Wally Joyner, Kansas City

His medium-range power will disappear on the move to Kansas City, so what kind of a season he has will depend on the accommodation he makes to the park—turf, long power alleys. If he shortens his stroke and is happy to make contact he can hit .320 with 12 homers and 40 doubles, and still get his hundred RBI. If he tries to pull the ball to keep his 20 homers he'll hit .260 with 12 homers and 60 RBI. Glove is always good, runs the bases well although he's not fast.

6. John Olerud, Toronto

A young Rusty Staub. More than 40% of his hits were for extra bases last year (48 of 116), a higher percentage than Frank Thomas or even Rafael Palmeiro. He did a good job as an RBI man over the second half of the season, and he has an excellent chance to be one of the half-dozen best hitters in the league during the 1990s.

7. Mark McGwire, Oakland

His struggles became serious last year. Because of his walks his secondary average is still good and his defense is still good, but he seems to lose ten percent every year with the bat, and a .201 batting average/.383 slugging percentage just isn't going to cut it no matter how much you walk. This is his free agent year, so he might be ready to take back some of what he's lost.

---

8. Randy Milligan/ Glenn Davis, Baltimore

The Orioles have four first basemen in their lineup, the other two being Sam Horn and David Segui. Milligan is a good hitter but now 30 and yet to have a full, healthy season. Davis is a power hitter, but coming off two straight injury seasons it is hard to know where his skills are now, either.

9. Carlos Quintana Mo Vaughn, Boston

Quintana is a lifetime .285 hitter and a good defensive first baseman, but pounds the ball into the ground. Vaughn could be good but has yet to get playing time, much less prove that he's good.

10. Don Mattingly, New York

Played almost every day last year, driving in 68 runs and scoring 64. He had a secondary average of .187, little more than half the norm for a first baseman. He has been a great player, but what he did last year, despite the .288 batting average, isn't enough to keep him in the lineup.

11. Tino Martinez, Seattle

Has hit .320 and .326 the last two years at Calgary. As a major leaguer I see him as a .265 hitter with a slugging percentage in the low .400s.

---

12. Reggie Jefferson/ Carlos Martinez, Cleveland

Jefferson is a 6'4", 210 pound first baseman, acquired from the Reds system. He'll probably start the year as the Indians' first baseman, and is 50/50 to keep the job, at best. He hasn't done anything that suggests to me that he'll be a good player. Martinez hit .284 last year and .300 in '89, but he's a singles-hitting first baseman with no walks and poor defense.

13. Von Hayes/ Lee Stevens, California

Hayes is looking for a comeback at age 33. His batting averages since 1986:

1986 .305
1987 .277
1988 .272
1989 .259
1990 .261
1991 .225

If Hayes fails to become young again the job will pass to Lee Stevens, who could hit .270 with some power, but his strikeout/walk ratio and defense won't help him and his power will be limited enough that you might not see it for a month or so, in which case the job would pass to Don Barbara.

14. Franklin Stubbs, Milwaukee

Typical year would be .232 with 19 homers, 59 RBI. The Brewers may move Paul Molitor to first and pick up a veteran to DH. It's hard to see how it could hurt.

NATIONAL LEAGUE FIRST BASEMEN

1. Will Clark, San Francisco

Has driven in 522 runs in the last five years, 104 per season. His walks have dropped steadily since 1988 (100, 74, 62, 51), but may go back up with the trade of Kevin Mitchell. Great offense, great defense.

2. Fred McGriff, San Diego

The only real question about McGriff is whether he should rank just below Will Clark, or just ahead of him. Clark in his career has created 110 runs per season, McGriff 107.

3. Jeff Bagwell, Houston

.300 hitter, surprising power, making a good defensive adjustment to first base. After his long, long home run against Pittsburgh last year he started over-swinging, and struck out more often in a month than he ought to in a year. He struck out 116 times last year, but will cut that by 30% this year. He's going to be an All Star.

4. Hal Morris, Cincinnati

Possibly the number one candidate to win the batting title. He's a lifetime .320 hitter, 27 years old, a left-hander and plays in a decent hitter's park. That's everything you look for in picking a batting champion.

5. John Kruk, Philadelphia

Typical season is .291 with 14 homers, 77 RBI, 78 walks. He's a good, mid-line first baseman, somewhat miscast as a star on a team that doesn't have any stars. He'd be well placed as a number six hitter for the Pirates or Braves.

6. Mark Grace, Chicago

Had a poor season in 1991 but remains a career .297 hitter, excellent defense, excellent hit and run man, good strikeout/walk ratio and the best baserunner among National League first basemen other than the Pirate platoon. No power.

7. Ivan Calderon, Montreal

Said to be moving to first base after the trade of Galarraga (major league teams will tell you that playing first base is tougher than sportswriters say, but deep down they believe anybody can do it with a winter's practice.) Calderon will be a butcher at first, but that's alright, he was a butcher in left, too. As a hitter he's even with Galarraga. A typical season for Galarraga would be .259 with 20 homers, 83 RBI, while Calderon's typical season would be .278 with 20 homers, 81 RBI.

Tim Wallach may also play some first base for the Expos if he isn't traded to the Yankees.

8. Eddie Murray, New York

Putting together the .330 mark in 1990 and the .260 last year he's hit .295 over the two-year span, so I would conclude that the balance of evidence is that he can still hit some although his power is down. Hasn't driven in a hundred runs since 1985.

9. Andres Galarraga, St. Louis

Galarraga will definitely bounce back from 1991 to some extent. He's going to a better hitter's park, with new fences in St. Louis, and he will be challenged by 1991's disappointment to lose some weight. He won't have 1988 again (.302 with 42 doubles and 29 homers) because that's not his real level of ability, but he'll be better than 1991.

10. Gary Redus/ John Wehner/ Jeff King, Pittsburgh

As I pointed out in the Pittsburgh comment, the Redus/Merced platoon last year was terrific. Merced apparently is headed to right field, to cover the hole left by the departure of Bonilla. Redus is a year older (35), Wehner is essentially an unknown and they're two right-handed hitters, so there's no platoon. King's a career .227 hitter with a slugging percentage below .400. Leyland will probably come up with something in spring training.

11. Sid Bream/ Brian Hunter, Atlanta

Bream is a backup player who has improbably stumbled into regular status for several years. Hunter was a pleasant surprise in '91 but would be marginal if you were counting on him for a whole season—a .250 hitter with limited power.

12. Los Angeles (Unknown)

The Dodgers may play Eric Karros or Kal Daniels at first base, and they have Todd Benzinger if they want to play him. Karros is a *good* hitter, would hit around .285 with a slugging percentage around .450, so he'll be on my Rookie of the Year list. Daniels' defense would be an adventure.

AMERICAN LEAGUE SECOND BASEMEN

1. Roberto Alomar, Toronto

24 years old, great offense, great defense. Speed, 53 stolen bases. What else is there?

2. Julio Franco, Texas

Despite his 1991 batting championship, I am told the value of his baseball cards has hardly risen at all, and on that basis he remains the most underrated player in baseball. He's just average defensively, but in a class of his own as a hitter . . . 1991 season parallels that of another second baseman/batting champ, Bobby Avila in 1954:

	G	AB	R	H	2B	3B	HR	RBI	BB	Avg	OBP	SPct
Franco	146	589	108	201	27	3	15	78	65	.341	.408	.474
Avila	143	555	112	189	27	2	15	67	59	.341	.405	.477

3. Chuck Knoblauch, Minnesota

What he did last year is his real level of ability, and not a fluke in any way. A lot of second basemen win Rookie of the Year Awards or come close, but often those players don't develop from that point because of injuries. Look just at the second basemen who have had good rookie years for the Twins—Bernie Allen (1962), Rod Carew (1967), Bob Randall (1976), Tim Teufel (1984). Only Carew was able to get better than he was when he came up, and he had to struggle through several serious injuries to show progress.

4. Lou Whitaker, Detroit

Had a super year last year, drawing 90 walks and hitting 23 homers to give him an on base percentage of .391 and a secondary average of .411. Offensively, he was one of the keys to the Tiger offense, which was able to score runs despite a low batting average. Defensively, he committed only four errors, leading the league in fielding percentage (.994). His typical season—.274 with 16 homers, 71 RBI, 93 runs scored—would be pretty good if he was an outfielder.

5. Jody Reed, Boston

The best second baseman the Red Sox have had since Marty Barrett. Seriously, is he the best they've had since Bobby Doerr? It may be premature to say that, but he's getting there, in large part because he *has* been able to remain healthy while adapting to the job. Reed has hit more doubles per at bat than any other active player, the top five being Reed, Boggs, Sabo, Brett and Mattingly.

6. Harold Reynolds, Seattle

His value is more defensive than offensive. He's a Gold Glove second baseman, led the major leagues in double plays turned. He's durable, a base stealer and good for 34 doubles a year. A good player; could be rated higher.

7. Steve Sax, White Sox

Similar player to Reed, with more speed. Unusually durable for a second baseman, good singles and doubles hitter. There's an article about him with the Yankee comment.

8. Carlos Baerga, Cleveland

Who knows how good he really is or might be, playing for a real team? I'm sure we'll find out in four years. For 1992, the Indians may play him at second or third or somewhere else; they need to get Mark Lewis and Jim Thome both in the lineup, and seem reluctant to do the obvious thing, which is get rid of Fermin, put Lewis at short and Thome at third. Anyway, I don't claim to know how good Carlos Baerga really is, but on the basis of what I know I like him a lot.

Dave Rohde, a 28-year-old second baseman acquired from Houston, is becoming the Jack Perconte of the 1990s. He's one of the better-hitting second basemen in the game, but nobody will give him a job.

9. Pat Kelly/ Mike Gallego, New York

Kelly is said to be a defensive wiz at second, plus he'll steal 30 bases and probably hit as well as the next second baseman. Gallego played very well last year for the A's, and sold the year to the Yankees, the Yankees being the only organization around which takes one-year accomplishments on blind faith. He's 31 years old and has never done anything noteworthy before last season, so I wouldn't expect a lot of him in '92.

I doubt that Pat Kelly will ever be as good a ballplayer as Steve Sax is.

10. Keith Miller, Kansas City

A mid-westerner, and probably damned glad to be back in the midwest. It's unclear to me, and as far as I know unclear to everybody, whether Miller failed to make it as the Met's second baseman because he just couldn't do it, or because the Mets couldn't leave him alone long enough to find out. I'm sure I'll catch hell for saying this, but the Mets were as bad as a woman. Every 28 days they had to put Gregg Jefferies back at second base and see if he'd figured out how to play second while he was watching from third. Among the unanswered questions about Miller is whether he has the quickness to play second base on artificial turf.

11. Billy Ripken, Baltimore

Basically a slow Harold Reynolds who is less durable and less consistent with the bat. His secondary average last year was .098.

12. Luis Sojo, California

It says something about the position that Luis Sojo manages to rate *ahead* of two other American League second basemen. Sojo hit .258, which is alright, with OK defense but only 14 walks and no power. Sojo led the American League in sacrifice bunts (19), despite which he somehow managed to ground into 12 double plays. His ratio of double play balls to RBI (20) was the worst of any major league regular last year.

13. Oakland (Mike Bordick, Lance Blankenship and Randy Ready, or you pick one.)

If Weiss is healthy Bordick may get the first shot at second base. The A's may patch the position with a trade before opening day.

14. Milwaukee (Unknown)

The top candidates here are Jim Gantner, returning after a free agent fling, and William Suero, acquired from the Toronto system last summer. Ganter at 38 is astonishingly close to being the same player he was ten years ago. Suero has been up and down like a yo-yo, at times (1990) looking like a pretty good prospect, at other times (1991) looking disinterested on defense and making you wonder whether he would hit his weight.

NATIONAL LEAGUE SECOND BASEMEN

1. Ryne Sandberg, Chicago

One of the ten best of all time.

2. Robbie Thompson, San Francisco

It's difficult to find the right offensive role for him in a power-laden offense, but Thompson has some power (47 homers in the last three years), some speed (40 stolen bases in the same period), a few walks (63 last year) and good defense. Thompson, Sandberg and Lind are the only good, veteran second basemen in the league right now.

3. Jose Lind, Pittsburgh

The best defensive second baseman in baseball, with a 5.68 range factor and a .989 fielding percentage. Both figures are close to the best in baseball. Hits around .260, which is his only offensive asset. Well, he's a good baserunner for a guy who doesn't steal bases.

4. Delino DeShields, Montreal

If I could have one piece of information to evaluate the defense of an infielder, what I'd want to know is the ratio of his double plays to his errors. A good second baseman should have a ratio of 6-1 or 7-1, like Lind (80-9), Thompson (98-11) or Sandberg (68-4). DeShields' 1991 ratio (73-27) was the worst of any major league second baseman playing 600 innings except Jefferies (15-6) or Treadway (35-15).

Offensively, DeShields would help you if he hit .230. With 90 walks, some power and 50 stolen bases a year, he'll always be able to score runs.

5. Willie Randolph and Bill Pecota, New York

Everybody below that line (↑) has real weaknesses. Randolph even at age 37 has more things to point to with pride than any of the others—a .327 batting average, a .424 on base percentage, a super strikeout/walk ratio, lightning hands on the double play. If .327 doesn't represent his real ability, he's still a good hitter, a .280 hitter, and he's well backed up. Pecota is a good second baseman, better placed there than at third base or short.

6. Juan Samuel, Dodgers

Played at an MVP level for half a season. I'm not impressed. He hit .271 in 1991 with 12 homers and 23 stolen bases, but this is offset by:

1) Poor defense,
2) Poor strikeout/walk ratio,
3) Poor second half of season,
4) Poor seasons at bat in previous three years.

7. Mickey Morandini (LH) and Mariano Duncan (RH), Philadelphia

Could be a successful platoon arrangement. Duncan, formerly a switch hitter, is a cleanup hitter against a left-handed pitcher, but can't hit right-handers at all. In 1990 he hit .410 against left-handers, best in the majors, but .226 against right-handers. Last year he hit .314 with a .492 slugging percentage against left-handers, but hit .218 against right-handers.

Morandini, on the other hand, hit .265 as a rookie against right-handed pitching, but .185 against left-handers. So putting them together, they should be a pretty fair platoon combination.

8. Jose Oquendo and Geronimo Peña, St. Louis

Oquendo had been a quality second baseman for several years until 1991, when he did not play well. He may be a terrific second baseman for Miami in 1993, because Peña played awfully well last year, with 15 stolen bases, 16 extra base hits and 38 runs scored in 185 at bats.

9. Jeff Treadway and Mark Lemke, Atlanta

Treadway is one of the better hitting second basemen in the league, but not a good glove. Lemke is a good glove, but hadn't hit until the World Series. To be among the stronger combinations in the league Lemke will have to hit more, because Treadway isn't going to become a glove man.

10. Bill Doran/ Bip Roberts, Cincinnati

Doran is still a fine offensive player, but back and knee troubles have ruined his defense. With the loss of Duncan it appears Roberts may back up Doran at second and play left field, or Roberts could win the second base job entirely. Roberts is a fine hitter for a second baseman, and you'll get different reviews of his defense from different people. His ratio of double plays to errors was fair (36 to 7), but his range factor and fielding percentage were a little below average.

11. Paul Faries or Craig Shipley, San Diego

Faries apparently inherits the job with the trade of Roberts, although he played only four games at second base in 1991. A year ago I thought Faries could hit .260 in the majors, but he hit .177, which raises a question. I still think he has a *chance* to be good, though. If Faries doesn't look like he can do the job defensively or winds up at third base, the job will slip to Craig Shipley, a 29-year-old Dodger reject who won't hit enough to hold the job.

12. Craig Biggio, Houston

At least, that's what they say in January. Biggio hits like a second baseman, but I can't be optimistic about his defense there for the next three years. The job could fall back to Casey Candaele or Andy Mota.

AMERICAN LEAGUE THIRD BASEMEN

1. Wade Boggs, Boston

Career .345 hitters are still in short supply. Add in 40-plus doubles for seven straight years and 90 walks a year, add in improved defense at third base . . . well, you've got your basic Hall of Famer.

STATS, Inc. maintains zone ratings, which evaluate a player's coverage of his defensive area. Boggs had the best zone rating of any major league third baseman, getting 306 outs on 321 balls in his area (95.3%). I don't say that's the God's truth; it's just a piece of information which counts in his favor.

2. Robin Ventura, Chicago

Probably the most improved player in the major leagues last year, driving in 100 runs with 23 homers, 80 walks. A .264 batting average won't get your attention, and he's not fast. He hit only 25 doubles.

3. Kelly Gruber, Toronto

His slugging percentages over the last four years are .438, .448, .512 and .443. With that record you just have to throw out the .512 and say that his career figure, .445, is his norm. That's still good. If you project his 1991 figures to fulltime play you get .252 with 29 homers, 93 RBI, but he missed 49 games with a thumb problem.

4. Edgar Martinez, Seattle

A better hitter than Ventura or Gruber, but defense keeps him from rating higher. With a .307 batting average and 84 walks he's on base constantly, and that is the most important offensive statistic in baseball. He had 50 extra base hits last year, so you can't ignore his power.

He does have a poor record of hitting with men in scoring position, hitting .244

n 1990 and .219 last year—overall seventy points below his average.

5. Travis Fryman and Tony Phillips, Detroit

Phillips is 33 years old (in April), and cannot be expected to repeat his wonderful season of 1991, which was by far the best of his career. (On the other hand, if you're looking for players who could be managers, Phillips is one to keep in mind. He's a bright, articulate man and a smart ballplayer.)

Fryman may play short when Trammell isn't able to play. To rate as a top-flight third baseman he will need to hit more than the 21 homers he hit last year, as his .259 batting average and poor strikeout/walk ratio don't help his case. Fryman's ratio of double plays to errors (12 to 11) was the poorest of any major league third baseman (600 or more innings) except for Carlos Baerga, Luis Salazar and Howard Johnson.

6. Mike Pagliarulo/ Scott Leius, Minnesota

One of the best platoon combinations in baseball last year, hitting .282 between them. If Pagliarulo can get away from trying to repeat what he did in 1987 he could have still better years, although I'm not sure Leius can stay in the .280s. I'd compare them to Mulliniks and Garth Iorg in Toronto, where Mulliniks (the left-handed hitter) was consistently good, and Iorg stayed there and kept his job for several years although he wasn't really very productive. Pagliareilus is a better defensive player than Mullinorg, though.

---

7. Gregg Jefferies, Kansas City

The next four guys are the unprovens, the guys who haven't proven that they're good, but haven't proven that they aren't, either. Jefferies will hit .290–.310 for Kansas City, with enough doubles, walks and stolen bases to be the best-hitting third baseman in the league other than Boggs. It's very much an open question whether he can play third base, but my guess is he can if he's given two years to work at it.

On the other hand, I thought for three years that Kevin Seitzer was bound to snap out of it sooner or later. He never did, and opens 1992 fighting for an at bat here or there.

8. Leo Gomez, Baltimore

.260-range hitter (despite .233 average last year), but will walk a hundred times a year and hit 25 to 30 homers a year. Aggressive defensive third baseman, made only seven errors in more than a hundred games. He's where Robin Ventura was a year ago, where Matt Williams was the year before that.

9. Dean Palmer, Texas

If he stays in the lineup he will threaten the record for strikeouts in a season, 189, which doesn't mean that he can't play. He has more power than Gomez, which is saying something because Gomez has power, and is two years younger than Gomez, so he may ultimately be a better hitter than Leo. Gomez is ahead of him at this point.

10. Jim Thome, Cleveland

I could have him rated way too low. He's the opposite of Gomez and Palmer, a George Brett, Carney Lansford type hitter as opposed to a Mike Schmidt type. Has an outstanding chance to be 1992 Rookie of the Year. I project him to hit around .290, with only five home runs but a chance to surprise on the power.

---

11. Gary Gaetti, California

It has been three years since you could say he has played well. I'm not sure that any third baseman can help a team win with a .290 on base percentage no matter how good his defense is, and I'm not sure Gaetti's defense is all that good anymore. His range factor was very high and he led the majors in double plays at third base, but on a staff with three left-handed starting pitchers there are a lot of ground balls to third base. At 33, I'm not expecting a big comeback.

---

12. Gary Sheffield or Jim Gantner, Milwaukee

As each year passes it seems more unlikely that Sheffield will ever play up to his ability. Gantner may play second or third, so Sheffield, in a sense, is competing for a job with William Suero, the other (known) candidate for the second base position. Maybe they'll platoon them, based on which one feels like playing today.

13. Charlie Hayes and Mike Gallego, New York

Hayes is a terrific defensive third baseman, but neither Hayes nor Gallego will hit enough to be an everyday third baseman, and both are right-handed hitters so you can't platoon them. The Yankees had four guys just like this last year—Velarde, Leyritz, Lovullo and Blowers. The only difference is that now they have six of them, rather than four. OK, OK, I'm sure the Yankees have released a couple of the group, and I know that none of them last year was as good a defensive player as Hayes, but you get my point. If you don't have a whole ballplayer or a platoon combination, then what exactly do you have?

14. God Only Knows, Oakland

The A's say that Carney Lansford is coming back. He was lousy two years ago, when he was 33, but the A's won so a lot of people think he must have been good.

The A's have also signed Randy Ready. They could put him in the lineup, like the Rangers did with Toby Harrah a few years ago, and tell him to lead the league in walks, and he'd do it. They wouldn't get much else out of him, but with Henderson and Ready hitting 1-2 Canseco would drive in 140 runs.

NATIONAL LEAGUE THIRD BASEMEN

1. Howard Johnson, New York

He ranks first if he plays third base. The talk is that he may not, that the Mets may put Pecota or Magadan or Chris Donnels on third, and Johnson in the outfield.

As I said in the comment about Keith Miller, it's impossible for me to judge whether he has played badly on defense for the last several years because he really can't play third base, or merely because of the stuttering, inconsistent way in which he was used. If it was my team, I'd announce in spring training that Johnson was my third baseman and Magadan could back up Eddie Murray and pinch hit, and if he could show me that he could play the outfield I'd get him a few at bats out there. I think by letting Magadan or Pecota force Johnson off his natural position, you're risking a continuation of the Who's-On-First routine of the last three years. Despite the additions of Murray and Bonilla, Johnson will remain the Mets' best hitter, and one of the outstanding power/speed combinations in baseball. A man like that deserves a little respect.

2. Chris Sabo, Cincinnati

In a typical 162-game season he has 65 extra base hits—42 doubles, 2 triples, 21 homers. Add in 32 stolen bases per season, and he's in scoring position almost a hundred times.

3. Matt Williams, San Francisco

He's slow and strikes out four times for every walk, but Williams is one of the best RBI men in the National League, and one of the best defensive third basemen. He has played more major league games in his career than Sabo (536-520) although he is four years younger, so obviously at the end of the day he will have had a better career than Spuds. For now, Sabo still rates an edge.

4. Terry Pendleton, Atlanta

The ranking is pretty low for an MVP, but then, he's a pretty unusual MVP. In fact, I wonder if Pendleton may be the most improbable MVP of all time—improbable, based on how likely an MVP candidate he would have seemed to be at the start of the season. Here's a player who has been around for years and has never been an All-Star or a .300 hitter or a power hitter, signing a free agent contract with a last-place team. He's among the most improbable *batting champions* of all time (Debs Garms, Joe Torre, Phil Cavaretta), and among the most improbable MVPs (Steve Garvey, Bob Elliott, Hank Sauer, Willie Hernandez).

Pendleton had the highest range factor in the majors again last year, as he often did with St. Louis. It's also interesting to note that Pendleton is the third player to have an MVP season immediately *after* signing as a free agent, although as of yet no player has had an MVP season immediately *before* leaving his team as a free agent. The other two free agents who won MVP awards were Andre Dawson and Kirk Gibson. I mention that because we often talk about players like Buechele and Tartabull having career seasons in their option year, and then not playing at the same level after signing, but there are now three MVPs to argue that there's another side to it.

---

5. Steve Buechele, Pittsburgh

His combined totals with Pittsburgh and Texas: .262 with 22 homers, 85 RBI. He is now believed to be the best defensive third baseman in the major leagues, and had the best ratio of double plays to errors (24 to 7) of any major league third baseman except Bill Pecota (15 to 4). I wouldn't expect him to have the same numbers again this year, but Leyland does instill good work habits in his team, and that could pay off over a period of years.

6. Todd Zeile, St. Louis

Played surprisingly well at third base and he's a good hitter (.280 with 11 homers, 81 RBI). With the Cardinals moving in their fences, I wouldn't be surprised if he hit 30 homers this year. He's only 26, and a young player who hits doubles (he hit 36 last year) will often turn them into homers as he ages. The fence adjustment might accelerate the process.

7. Lenny Harris/ Mike Sharperson, Los Angeles

Platoon of two .280 to .300 hitters both run well, both walk more than they strike out, both do adequate job defensively. Dave Hansen, a 23-year-old left handed hitter, is chomping at the bit, but Harris and Sharperson don't *need* to be replaced. Hansen could take over from Sharperson as the left-handed part of the platoon combination.

---

8. Bret Barberie/ Tim Wallach/ Matt Stairs, Montreal

Wallach is probably finished at 34, but you have to respect the fact that he did have an excellent season just one year ago. Barberie didn't seem to have a lot going for him until last year, when he played brilliantly both at Indianapolis (.312, secondary average of .537) and for Montreal (.353, secondary average of .309). He was 23 years old last year, so it is reasonably likely that his improvement is real, and he has become a quality player. Let's put it this way: if you don't want him, I'd like to have him.

In last year's book I didn't put either Jeff Bagwell or Chuck Knoblauch on the list of top Rookie of the Year candidates because, while I was very high on both players, I didn't think either would be in the majors before June, since they were coming out of AA. Well, I don't want to repeat that mistake with Matt Stairs. Stairs played at AA last year, and doesn't have an obvious job opening behind Barberie

Wallach at third base, behind DeShields at second and with Wilfredo Cordero also trying to wedge his way into the lineup, but I wanted to say this anyway: that if he comes out of spring training with a job, Matt Stairs is capable of winning the 1992 NL Rookie of the Year Award. The success of Bagwell and Knoblauch, both skipping AAA to win the Rookie Awards, may also make people less reluctant to try that for a couple of years.

9. Ken Caminiti, Houston

.250 hitter, not a lot of power, not a Gold Glove, no speed. He might hit better in another park, but up to now has hit more career homers in Houston (16) than on the road (15). He's 29, so he's probably not getting any better. He's not *bad*, but he's marginal.

10. Dave Hollins, Philadelphia

Appears to have won the job by hitting .298 with power in 56 games after returning from Scranton. He's not *that* good; he's a better player than Charlie Hayes, but not a .300 hitter or a real power hitter. Real good athlete, very strong, switch hitter.

11. Scott Coolbaugh or Paul Faries, San Diego

Neither of these guys has any star potential, and neither of them hit well enough last year to stay in the lineup when the chance was given. This is a critical position for the Padres, because they have enough star players—Santiago, McGriff, Fernandez, Gwynn, Benes, Hurst—to have a good year, but they can't do it if their third basemen are hitting .220 and making 40 errors.

The Padres have never had a good third baseman in their 23-year-history, yet they let Dave Hollins (above) go to Philadelphia by not protecting him on the 40-man roster after he had a solid year for Wichita in 1989.

The Padres desperately need punch in the outfield, yet they virtually gave away Warren Newson after he posted secondary averages of .562 (Riverside, 1988, 130 games), .489 (Wichita, 1989, 128 games) and .399 (Las Vegas, 1990, 123 games).

12. Luis Salazar and Chico Walker, Chicago

Negatives for Salazar include age (36), speed, batting average, strikeout/walk ratio and defense at third base. One of the problems with playing in Wrigley Field is that it adds twenty points to everybody's average, which disguises weaknesses. A .230 hitter hits .250, so he stays in the lineup. Walker's a fun player, and should have had a major league career but just never caught a break. He's almost as old as Salazar. Gary Scott hit .208 at Iowa, so may be back to AA this year.

AMERICAN LEAGUE SHORTSTOPS

1. Cal Ripken, Baltimore

Ratio of double plays to errors (114 to 11) was the best among major league shortstops. Just a note: had his MVP year with nobody hitting behind him. The Orioles got Glenn Davis, and the people who do that kind of thing all wrote how good this would be for Cal Ripken, to have somebody hitting behind him. Ripken started out hot, and the same people all said, "See, he's having a big year because Glenn Davis is hitting behind him, to protect him." Then Davis got hurt and missed the year, and nobody said a word about it, but then this year they're writing exactly the same shit about Kevin Mitchell and Ken Griffey Jr.

2. Ozzie Guillen, Chicago

He may be the worst percentage player in baseball. His secondary average is nothing (.128 last year, .134 career), and even that is padded by stolen bases which are worse than useless because they're generated by poor percentage base stealing (58% last year, 63% career. Anything below 65% will result in a net loss of runs scored by the team.) Still, he's Ozzie—durable, consistent, smart, cheerful, a .270 hitter and occasionally brilliant on defense. His APBA card may be useless, but he's better than his card for a lot of reasons. The White Sox got him for LaMarr Hoyt, and they ain't ever giving him back.

3. Alan Trammell, Detroit

In view of his age (34), injury history (101 games played last year) and up-and-down batting record (.248 in 1989, .243 last year) he probably shouldn't rate third in the league, but there's nobody else to put there. Trammell doesn't throw as well as he used to, but he's a smart player, and makes a better offensive contribution than your typical shortstop even if he hits .240.

4. Bill Spiers, Milwaukee

Played well last year, and will rate second in the league if he can do it for more than one year and for more than 401 at bats. At worst, he's a hell of an improvement over Dale Sveum.

---

5. Greg Gagne, Minnesota

Most organizations would have dumped him sometime between 1987 and 1991. It is to Tom Kelly's credit that he stayed with him until he could find somebody *better*, rather than reacting to Gagne's negatives. Gagne is a low-average hitter, terrible strikeout/walk ratio (100 to 28 in his career), poor stolen base percentage (60% in his career) and because of injuries and other things he has never batted 500 times in a season. He's basically the same player as Kurt Stillwell, but whereas Hal McRae dumped Stillwell, *then* looked around and discovered that he didn't have anybody better, Kelly has been able to focus on Gagne's assets and live with his liabilities until somebody better comes along. Sure, the Royals were in last place when McRae dumped Stillwell, but then, the Twins hit last place, too.

6. Dick Schofield, California

A year ago I thought Schofield was going to have his best year. After he came back from the minors in '90 he had adjusted his game to a remarkable extent. Rather than swinging at everything and trying to hit the ball hard, he was laying back on the pitch, letting the bad ones go by and slapping the ball to the opposite field. His average was up, his walks were up, his strikeouts were down, and the only thing he was giving up was his piddly eight homers a year. I thought sure that if he could continue to do this he would have his best major league season.

Well, you know what happened. He started the season playing the way he had ended 1990, hitting .275 in April, .254 in May and .264 in June. Then, as the season went on, he forgot all about it, went back to lunging at pitches and trying to drive them past the force of gravity. He hit .233 in July, .176 in August and .157 in September, with 15 strikeouts and four walks. For a full year, All-Star Game to All-Star Game, he had hit .290—yet he gave it away to go back to his roots.

What I don't understand is this: why doesn't somebody *remind* him, in a direct, forceful way, of what he's supposed to be doing? Why doesn't the manager simply make a "deal" with him: you want to play, stop swinging from the heels. Why don't you call him in on April 6 and say, "OK, Dick, here's the deal. As long as you concentrate on meeting the bat with the ball, you're going to play. As soon as you *stop* doing that, as soon as you start over-swinging, you're going to take three days off. I see you trying to drive the ball on Monday, you don't play again until Friday. Work hard in batting practice, and we'll start clean on Friday." What is wrong with this plan?

---

7. Felix Fermin/ Mark Lewis, Cleveland

Fermin has served the Indians well as a stopgap, filling in at shortstop for three years without being appreciably worse than a bunch of other guys. Lewis as a hitter is exactly where Fermin is, but being several years younger has time to become a good hitter. (Last year Fermin hit .262, Lewis .264. Fermin had a secondary average of .113, Lewis of .108.) Fermin's a pretty bad player, but at least he *does* what he is capable of doing; he doesn't hit .280 one year and .225 the next. Lewis didn't impress defensively last year, but is still believed to be the Indians' shortstop for the future, which in this case means until he starts to make some real money.

8. Omar Vizquel, Seattle

Best major league player in ten years named "Omar". He walks more than most shortstops who hit like he does (45 times last year), is a pretty good percentage player and had a ratio last year of 105 double plays to 13 errors (8 to 1; major league norm is 4.6 to 1).

9. Luis Rivera, Boston

Played well last year, but still struck out so much (86 times in 414 at bats) that it might be hard for him to sustain his .258 batting average. The Red Sox know that Rivera isn't a championship quality shortstop, but with Naehring out their options were limited. It would be an upset if Naehring were able to play short this year, and the third option (Mike Brumley) is not really an option.

10. Alvaro Espinoza and Mike Gallego, New York

I have no idea where Gallego is going to play, so I'll list him everywhere. Espinoza is basically the same player as Fermin, a guy who makes most of the routine plays in the field and hits enough singles to disguise the fact that he's putting almost no runs on the scoreboard.

11. Dickie Thon, Texas

His signing was taken to be a sign that the Rangers are serious about trying to win this year. On that level, I think he's irrelevant to the Rangers' drive for the title. He's a so-so defensive player with a secondary average of .165 last year, and I don't really see him as being any better player than Jeff Huson, maybe worse.

It's all irrelevant to the Rangers' pennant chances. If they walk 675 men they're not going to win if Honus Wagner comes back to earth and inhabits Thon's body.

12. Eddie Zosky, Toronto

Looks like any other shortstop, a .240 hitter with no other offensive skills. He'll have to shine in the field to hold his job. No obvious star potential.

13. Walt Weiss, Oakland

At his best he was a middle-of-the-pack shortstop, not as good as Bill Spiers, but probably about even with Gagne or Schofield. Because of the A's success he was terribly overrated. There's really no way to know how much of his ability he still retains.

14. David Howard, Kansas City

Doesn't do anything well. Doesn't hit, doesn't have a shortstop's arm, makes mistakes. He won't hold the job long enough to develop.

NATIONAL LEAGUE SHORTSTOPS

1. Barry Larkin, Cincinnati

Only his injury record keeps him from being considered with Sandberg, Ripken, Canseco, Bonds—the best players in baseball. There isn't anything he can't do except stay healthy.

2. Ozzie Smith, St. Louis

Article about him in the St. Louis comment. He's still one of the best in baseball.

3. Tony Fernandez, San Diego

Had a fine season in San Diego, not that anybody noticed. He's no longer a .300 hitter, but at least he's become consistent in the .270 range. When he had 213 hits in 1986 he never walked, so his on-base percentage wasn't any better then (.338) than it was last year (.337), since he'll take a walk now. Defensively, he's still one of the best.

4. Jay Bell, Pittsburgh

A better hitter than Fernandez, but doesn't go in the hole as well as a shortstop might (you know you're not getting to quite everything when your manager argues in defense of you that a shortstop's range is overrated). Still, 56 extra-base hits are a lot for a shortstop (32 doubles, 8 triples, 16 homers). I also wonder if there's ever been a player before who had 56 extra base hits and 30 sacrifice bunts in the same season. I'd bet there hasn't.

5. Shawon Dunston, Chicago

He has four positives—the famous throwing arm, his speed, a little power and he can keep his batting average above .250, which many shortstops can't. His offense isn't really much, with a career on-base percentage of .287. Overall defense is a little above average.

6. Rafael Belliard/ Jeff Blauser, Atlanta

Belliard is an awfully weak hitter, even for a shortstop, but an above average defensive shortstop. Blauser hits well for a shortstop but has been unable to hold the job because of shoulder injuries and inconsistency.

7. Kevin Elster/ Bill Pecota, New York

Elster's a career .224 hitter, but his secondary offensive skills are *good* for a shortstop (career secondary average is .218), plus his defense, whatever his flaws, is vastly better than any other option the Mets have had. Pecota doesn't have the powerful arm or quick feet which make you think he can play shortstop, but he can play short the way he does everything else, by reliably doing what he is capable of doing. He doesn't throw *hard*, but throws quickly and accurately.

There are five National League teams which are depending on young shortstops to one degree or another. I'm going to rate those five on the basis of what I see as their ultimate potential, rather than their 1992 performance. I don't know that there's any way to know whether a young player is going to have a smooth transition to the majors. Here's how I see them:

8. Wilfredo Cordero, Montreal

Anyone who can play *well* in the American Association at the age of 19 has got a chance to be a big star. In 1992 he may not hit a lot—in fact, he may not even play; they may continue to play Spike Owen. If Cordero plays, my guess is that he will hit below .250 with 10-12 homers, but that in time he's going to be a good hitter.

9. Andujar Cedeno, Houston

The only one of the group already in possession of a job. He's not a bad hitter, but I'm skeptical of him, for reasons which can be summarized in two words: Sammy Sosa. It's hard for a hitter to set a foundation of success and build on it if he has *no* control of the strike zone. Cedeno will strike out so much—possibly 150 to 170 times a year, with almost no walks—that I expect it to inhibit his growth as a hitter, plus any power he has will be partially negated by the Astrodome. He probably won't steal more than fifteen bases a year.

Still, you have to be impressed by what he was able to accomplish in 1991. When not striking out he hit .345, with 13 doubles and 9 homers in less than half a season. Just about the same as Sammy Sosa in 1989.

10. Jose Offerman, Los Angeles

Alfredo Griffin was terrible last year (double play/error ratio barely two to one), so Offerman's time has got to come. He can hit .270, .280, with no power but enough walks and stolen bases to be one of the better offensive shortstops in the league. He will have to cut his error rate significantly in order to hold a job.

11. Royce Clayton, San Francisco

A .250 hitter with no appreciable power, but could walk 50–60 times and steal 30–40 bases. He hasn't played AAA ball yet, and the 1991 frustrations of Steve Decker, who tried unsuccessfully to jump from AA, may discourage the Giants from putting him in the lineup despite their need for a shortstop.

In many ways, I still like Andres Santana better than I do Clayton. Santana is two years older than Clayton (born 1968 as opposed to 1970) and was the top prospect in the system until he fractured his leg in 1989. He's been moved to second base, and is hardly ever talked about as a prospect anymore although he hit .316 with 45 stolen bases at Phoenix last year.

12. Kim Batiste, Philadelphia

He is older than Cordero, Offerman, Cedeno or Clayton (born 1968), and his offensive skills are limited. He'll hit around .250, strike out eight times for every walk and hit less than five homers a year. He's not a base stealer, although he could steal 15. Still, if his defense is good and he hits .260, as opposed to .240, he could keep the job. Dale Sveum, who doesn't do anything well, is the backup.

AMERICAN LEAGUE LEFT FIELDERS

1. Rickey Henderson, Oakland

There's an article about him in the Oakland comment. Sure, he gets hurt, but I'd rather have 120 games a year of Rickey Henderson than 162 games of any other left fielder in the league.

2. Roberto Kelly, New York

A center fielder moved to left by Bernie Williams, Kelly brings the position better defense than most of the guys who will follow—Albert Belle, Kevin Mitchell, Greenwell, Polonia. He's a .282 hitter with power and speed, improved command of the strike zone. He's capable of having an MVP season.

3. Albert Belle, Cleveland

Kevin Mitchell's typical season is .275 with 33 homers, 97 RBI. Albert Belle's career record in seasonal notation (per 162 games) shows .261 with 30 homers, 113 RBI. Of course, Belle hasn't had that season yet; he's had partial seasons interrupted by injuries and infantile behavior—but if you're going to put Mitchell ahead of Belle, how do you justify that? Good citizenship? Good health record? Good defense? They're comparable hitters and outfielders, and Belle is five years younger and has accomplished what he has accomplished in a tougher hitter's park.

Whether Belle is actually as good a hitter . . . as *great* a hitter as he appeared to be in 1991 is unclear. To hit 28 homers in 461 at bats in a park where home runs are as scarce as three-piece suits in a bowling alley . . . hell, Babe Ruth couldn't do that. I thought Belle was a good hitter, but I never thought he was that good. Because of injuries and suspensions and unexplained absences, he doesn't have a multi-year batting record for us to evaluate.

4. Kevin Mitchell, Seattle

He's only 30, and the bad news about im has tended for the last year to obscure he good stuff, which is:

a) he can hit, and

b) he does a good job of staying in the lineup. Until last year he had batted 500 times a year for three straight years.

In a better hitter's park than he's had efore, he should be able to drive in a undred runs for Seattle.

5. Greg Vaughn, Milwaukee

Decent outfielder, also could drive in a undred runs. He was overrated when he ame up, people talked about him as a otential superstar when he wasn't. At 26 e should be moving into his prime, which don't think is going to involve any MVP easons, but he could be an All Star.

6. Tim Raines, Chicago

He's been a disappointment for several ears, but still stole 51 bases and scored 02 runs last year. He's not an especially ood outfielder, but he's fast and doesn't rop balls or throw them away. He doesn't ave a good arm, but he's thrown out almost a hundred runners in his career by etting the ball where it is supposed to be when it is supposed to be there.

7. Mike Greenwell, Boston

He's regressed. A typical year for him is 311 with 17 homers, 34 doubles, 98 RBI—but in what should be his prime, he asn't had that season since 1988. Good aserunner, and a constant source of musement in left field.

---

8. Derek Bell, Toronto

Number one candidate for 1992 Rookie of the Year, but Candy Maldonado is still around (played well after joining Toronto) and Dave Winfield, too, so the Blue Jays won't stay with Bell if he hits .225 through the end of May. Should hit around .300 with power, speed. He made 16 errors last year, most of any minor league outfielder.

9. Pedro Munoz, Minnesota

Should have been a regular last year. Munoz is quite a bit better hitter than Dan Gladden, the regular last year. He should hit .280 or better with 20 homers, 20 stolen bases—a Gary Matthews type player, maybe like Kevin McReynolds a couple of years ago. He'll be under pressure because the Twins are defending a championship and Gladden was very popular in Minnesota, but Munoz is a good player.

10. Luis Polonia, California

A .300 hitter, above average leadoff man, 70% base stealer. He draws more walks than he used to, resulting in a slightly better on base percentage. No arm, poor outfielder. I guess that's repetitious; if any of these guys had Mark Whiten's arm he wouldn't be playing left field, he'd be in right or center.

11. Kevin Reimer (Reason), Texas

Hit 20 homers last year, which is more than I would have expected of him. He's a brutal outfielder, worse than Polonia and Greenwell, and if he bats 550 times he'll strike out 130 with 45 walks, but if he keeps hitting the Rangers could have three outfielders with 30 homers apiece.

Last year Valentine used a platoon system with Reimer rarely playing against left-handers. He shared playing time at DH with Downing and Stanley, in left field with Daugherty and also with Gary Pettis (Pettis in center with Gonzalez shifting to left). Reimer being younger than the others and a better hitter, he may move up to regular status, or may not. He could be a career DH, but they don't do that for some reason.

12. Luis Mercedes, Baltimore

Another Rookie of the Year candidate, should hit around .300 if he gets 400 at bats. He's comparable to Luis Polonia—a singles hitter with some speed but not Rickey Henderson/Vince Coleman speed, some walks but not Rickey Henderson/Brett Butler walks. Not regarded as a good defensive outfielder.

Another Orioles' youngster, David Segui, is also a singles hitter who is capable of hitting .300, but is more of a first baseman than an outfielder. He is regarded as a young Keith Hernandez type, but is lost behind Milligan, Davis and Sam Horn.

13. Kirk Gibson/ Chris Gwynn, Kansas City

When the Royals acquired Chris Gwynn, Chuck Woodling observed that at least he was a better hitter than Ozzie Canseco. The Royals are talking about Gwynn as a regular, bringing up the question of when and where Gwynn got to be a better player than Kirk Gibson. They were teammates for several years in Los Angeles, and I don't think Lasorda was ever tempted to bench Gibson and play Gwynn, or for that matter was ever tempted to play Gwynn even when Gibson was hurt. I've been very skeptical of Gwynn over the years, but he has developed to the point at which I don't think he'd be a complete washout as a regular. He's got the potential to be the new Candy Maldonado—a .270 hitter with 12–15 homers. Kirk Gibson is a great player for about three days at a time.

14. Dan Gladden, Detroit

Won't hold the job. Part of his value to the Twins was that the left field area in the Metrodome is enormous, so you need two center fielders. In Tiger Stadium, where the outfield is small, Gladden will be your basic 34-year-old .245 hitter with no power.

NATIONAL LEAGUE LEFT FIELDERS

1. Barry Bonds, Pittsburgh

Despite Pendleton's MVP Award, Bonds was clearly the best player in the league again last year. It isn't unusual for a player to follow up an MVP season with another year equally good, and yet not win the MVP Award. A few reporters will figure that he's had his chance, so let's honor somebody else, and if you get a close vote those few reporters will push the consensus to the other contender. Sandy Koufax, for example, won the MVP Award in 1963 in his first great year (25-5, 1.88 ERA), but then didn't win it in 1965 or 1966, when he was even better, although he did carry the Dodgers to the pennant both years. Roberto Clemente, after winning the MVP in 1966, had a better year in 1967, but slipped to third in the voting. Steve Garvey, who won the MVP Award his first year as a regular in 1974, had the same season every year for the next six years and some a trifle better, but never won the award again.

2. Eric Davis, Los Angeles

Eric Davis the hitter will lose a lot more, in moving to Dodger Stadium, than Darryl Strawberry did. Davis is coming from Riverfront Stadium, a good hitter's park (although Davis himself didn't hit his home runs there).

Davis, as you know, has never been healthy. The artificial turf in Cincinnati may have contributed to that—or it may not have. If Davis is able to stay healthy in Los Angeles and play 150 games a year, a few points off his slugging percentage will be a small price to pay.

The talk about Davis' injuries and his strikeouts have tended to blind some people to the fact that, injuries and all, strikeouts and all, he has been tremendously productive when in the lineup. Per 162 games played in his career, Davis has averaged 33 homers, 47 stolen bases with the best stolen base percentage in baseball history, 80 walks, 105 runs scored and 101 RBI. He doesn't *have* to do that to help the Dodgers; if he can play 152 games and drive in 91 runs and score 95, that's fine. How valuable he will be, in his particular case, is more a function of how often he plays than of how well he plays.

3. George Bell, Chicago

I don't know if you've noticed this, but the ranks of left fielders in the National League have been decimated in the off-season. Kevin McReynolds and Kevin Mitchell, left fielders for two of the league's premiere franchises, have been traded to the American League. Ivan Calderon of Montreal, who had a good year last year, has been moved to first base (probably). Kal Daniels of the Dodgers has seen his career put in limbo by the Dodgers' acquisition of Eric Davis. Pedro Guerrero, a first baseman for several years, may be back in left field. Lonnie Smith, playing left for the Braves in the World Series, may not be on a roster this year.

So George Bell rates third, mostly by virtue of being a known quantity, an RBI guy. His 1991 season (.285, 25 homers, 86 RBI) is basically his typical season (.286, 28 homers, 101 RBI), and isn't impressive for Wrigley Field, but there are a lot of guys worse. He's not a good outfielder, but then left fielders are not normally good outfielders. Wes Chamberlain and Mark Leonard aren't good outfielders, either, and you can't count on them to drive in 90 runs.

4. Bip Roberts, Cincinnati

A good leadoff man, a lifetime .291 hitter who should steal 40 bases and score a hundred runs for the Reds if he stays in the lineup. As a leadoff man/outfielder, a great improvement over Billy Hatcher.

5. Darryl Boston/ Mark Carreon, New York

The Mets are talking about movin Howard Johnson to the outfield to get Bi Pecota and Dave Magadan in the lineu but another reason this would be a mi take is that it would leave Boston an Carreon without a place to play. Boston i the two years since coming to the Mets ha hit .273 and .275, totalling 16 homers, 3 stolen bases and 37 doubles in 631 at bat Carreon in his major league career has ba ted 596 times with a .272 average, 21 hom ers, 65 RBI. What's wrong with that? Wh do you want to put those guys on th bench and play Dave Magadan?

Bobby Bonilla may play left field. If sc he rates second.

6. Luis Gonzalez, Houston

He hit .254 last year, and I'm not reall sure that he's ever going to hit a lot bette than that—maybe .270, .275. On the othe hand his power output—28 doubles, 9 tr ples, 13 homers—is solid for 473 at bats i the Astrodome, and, figuring that he wa 23 years old and will add 100 at bats *and* little more power as he ages, he should h enough doubles and homers to keep him self in the league for several million do lars. If he gets in the right park or th Astros move in their fences, I wouldn't b surprised if he would turn into a 30-home man.

7. John VanderWal, Montreal

The Expos have traded Dave Martine and are expected to move Ivan Caldero to first base, leaving left field apparentl open for VanderWal. He's a line-drive hit ter, hits the ball down the lines and int the gaps. I don't expect him to hit mor than .270 (understanding that a .270 hitte can hit .300 for one year by sheer luck) but I expect him to hit enough doubles (3 a year) and draw enough walks (50 or mor a year) to make himself a valuable part o an offense. If Larry Walker is Reggie Jack son, he's Joe Rudi, so to speak.

8. Wes Chamberlain, Philadelphia

A poor man's George Bell. A bad outelder, good right-handed hitter with ower. He's got to hit 20 homers a year to ave a career, and I expect he will, but the eal question is, will he hit enough to scare eople? Will he hit 28 homers a year, or 5? Probably not.

9. Mark Leonard, San Francisco

As a hitter, he looks more like George Brett than anybody I've ever seen. I don't nean that he's going to hit .390 or get ,000 hits (he's not), but just the elenents—the stance, the swing, the followhrough. I think he's a little taller than Brett, but put him in a Royals' uniform nd do a little Hollywood makeup, and ou could fool people.

I've been selling Leonard for three years ow, ever since he hit .345 with 50 doules, 15 homers, 118 walks and 118 RBI at San Jose. The dream season for Leonard as a major leaguer is that he might hit .290, draw a hundred walks, hit 35 doubles and 20 homers and create as many runs as Kevin Mitchell. I definitely believe that he is capable of having that season, but then in any year not that many players have the best seasons that they're capable of having.

Leonard isn't a good outfielder, and the Giants' outfield is a mess. I think the Giants are following the Yankee third base theory of building an outfield, figuring if two bad ballplayers aren't equal to one good one then maybe they should have four or five. The Giants have Darren Lewis, who is good, and then they have Willie McGee, Kevin Bass, Mike Felder, Cory Snyder, Chris James and Leonard. I'm not sure whether they still have Mike Kingery or not. They need to release about two-thirds of this Chinese fire drill, but they're making a bad mistake if they wind up giving 250 at bats to James and 150 to Snyder and 220 to Kevin Bass without giving Leonard a real chance to show what he can do.

10. Otis Nixon, Atlanta

Was having a super year, the 1991 overachiever of the year, until stopped by drug abuse. A career .246 hitter, he hit .297 and was on target to score a hundred runs. He hit .329 in Atlanta, .246 on the road, primarily because of the long grass on the Atlanta infield, which enabled him to kill bunts in front of the third baseman. He won't stay where he was last year. He's just not a .300 hitter.

11. Pedro Guerrero/ Bernard Gilkey/ Milt Thompson, St. Louis

The Cardinals say Guerrero will be back in left field after four years as a first baseman. Guerrero's 1991 hitting stats—8 homers, 70 RBI, .272—certainly don't represent the kind of year he is capable of having, even at 36, if he stays healthy and the Cardinals do move their fences in. He's still capable of hitting .315 with 25 homers, 90 RBI. On the other hand, "healthy" is far from a given here, and Guerrero is so slow that we can't be optimistic about his ability to play the outfield. He wasn't a very good outfielder five years ago.

Bernard Gilkey, given the job as a rookie in 1991, hit just .216 but with a surprising secondary average of .295—five homers (in half-time play), 39 walks and 14 stolen bases. I wouldn't give up on Gilkey's chance of being a good player.

The odd man out, as usual, is Milt Thompson, who hit .307. The odd thing was that in 1990 *Thompson* was given a job in the outfield, and *he* hit .218, playing himself into obscurity, but then last year he picked up the pieces from Gilkey, who had done the same thing.

12. Jerald Clark, San Diego

Shouldn't be a regular. Shouldn't be a platoon player. I would rather have any of the three Cardinals (Guerrero, Gilkey or Thompson) as my left fielder than Clark.

AMERICAN LEAGUE CENTER FIELDERS

1. Ken Griffey Jr., Seattle

As a superstar, he's still more potential than production, but the production is impressive in itself—.327, 22 homers, 100 RBI. This should be the year when his power explodes, when Griffey hits 35 or more homers if he is going to do it.

2. Kirby Puckett, Minnesota

There has been some talk about Kirby moving out of center field, as he doesn't quite have a center fielder's speed anymore. The natural time to do this would be when Gladden leaves, which he has, but the obvious candidate to replace Gladden is Munoz, who isn't a center fielder, so it apparently isn't going to happen.

On a certain hard-headed level, Kirby isn't as good a player as people think he is. Although he hit .319 last year his secondary average was .209, which leaves him, as an offensive player, a distance behind Griffey, who hit .327 with a secondary average of .363. Kirby walked only 31 times, and he grounded into 27 double plays, more than any other major league player. In terms of runs created per out, he ranks below Dave Henderson and Devon White, ranks even with Juan Gonzalez and isn't within a mile of Griffey. He isn't a great offensive player, and neither is he a great defensive player.

Taking the complete package, any manager would kill to have him.

If he ever has injuries, he doesn't mention it. If he ever has conflicts with his manager or his teammates, we never hear of it. If Kirby knows how much he gets paid to play baseball, he's never mentioned it. He gives the impression of being totally immersed in the *game* that he is playing, the game on the field. It's hard to overstate how much it means to an organization to have a guy like that, because he sells to his teammates the attitude that Tom Kelly would sell them if he could.

3. Devon White, Toronto

The best defensive outfielder in baseball, he was never much of an offensive player until last year, when he had

- 40 doubles
- 10 triples
- 17 homers
- 33 stolen bases
- 55 walks
- 110 runs scored

Here's a question for you: why would *anyone* think that Cecil Fielder had had a better year than Devon White? How would you justify that? Comparing the two of them, Fielder starts out 27 home runs ahead (44-17), which certainly is a big item, but offset by the facts that White had 15 more doubles, 10 more triples, 33 more stolen bases and a batting average 21 points higher. I'm not interested in what the math *exactly* totals up to or how you compute it, but it seems pretty obvious that if you trade off all of White's *hitting* advantages against the 27 homers, White had about as good a year on offense as Fielder did. Then if you look at *defense*—the best center fielder in the game against a fat, slow first baseman—it's a mismatch. There's no way in hell Fielder could be as valuable as White, is there? Then if you add in the fact that White's play led Toronto to a division title . . . well, why would you vote for Fielder?

4. Juan Gonzalez, Texas

His future may not be in center field, but that's about the only thing we can say it isn't. Only a dozen or so hitters in history have shown his kind of power at age 21—Frank Robinson, Mel Ott, Eddie Mathews, Tony Conigliaro. If his power increased by ten percent per year until he was 27, it would mature at about 48 homers a year. The upside potential is scary.

5. Ellis Burks, Boston

Had a poor season in 1991, but his typical year (.283 with 21 homers, 88 RBI) is a good one, plus he's an above average center fielder. Excellent secondary average, rarely grounds into a double play; bad knees may trouble him the rest of his career.

6. Mike Devereaux, Baltimore

In a way, the opposite of Burks—he had a fine season in 1991, but his typical year (15 homers, 61 RBI, .251) is less impressive. He also played brilliantly in center field, much better than we had been led to expect by the scouts. But he's a year and a half older than Burks, and Burks had been a better player for several years, so it's likely that in 1992 the natural order of the universe will re-assert itself.

7. Milt Cuyler, Detroit

Spectacular outfielder, got on base enough as a rookie (.335 on base percentage) to give him significant offensive value as well. He could steal 70 bases, maybe more. Maybe a hundred. If he develops just a little he should be one of the best in the league.

8. Dave Henderson, Oakland

A good player, but an up and down hitter and shouldn't be a center fielder at age 33. He's another guy, like Stewart and Eckersley, that the A's took on when his career was going nowhere, and turned him back into a star. Now a lot of people think that he's always been a star, and forget that he does have his weaknesses as well as his strengths. He's a career .263 hitter, and too slow to play center.

9. Brian McRae, Kansas City

Very comparable to Milt Cuyler; Cuyler started out the year behind him but wound up ahead of him. McRae's a switch hitter, hits left-handers well but not right-handers. Most guys like that never do learn to hit on their weak side, but maybe he'll be the exception.

Early last year, from April to Jun McRae played center field better than an one I'd ever seen. The Royals have ha Amos Otis and Willie Wilson in cent field for the last twenty years, so our sta dards as Royals' fans are high. It wasn spectacular plays that I'm talking abou although he also made a large number those. McRae read the ball off the b flawlessly, glided naturally to the ball an caught everything in stride. I developed rule of thumb: if you think the ball *mig* be caught, it's an out. I've never seen an body like that, who could just routine pocket balls in the gap that looked lik they might be doubles.

But the second half of the year h wasn't the same outfielder. He seemed t lose confidence in his instincts. Sever times the second half the year he turne the wrong way on the ball, which he ha never done earlier. Balls you thought h might catch began to hit the ground. H doesn't have much of an arm.

10. Robin Yount, Milwaukee

Was having a fine comeback seaso until a September slump ruined his num bers. He's talking about retiring now an the Brewers aren't taking him seriousl which is a bad combination because som times a man will do something he could b talked out of just to prove he's seriou about it. But he's one season short o 3,000 hits, and it's been a long time sinc anybody walked away from 3,000 hits.

11. Lance Johnson, Chicago

Extremely comparable *player* to Bria McRae and Milt Cuyler, but several year older and so lacking the potential growth Fine defensive center fielder—in fact, th defense in center in the American Leagu is better than I've ever seen it. McRae Johnson, Cuyler, White and Devereaux a deserved Gold Gloves last year. I don' know about Bernie Williams, but I neve thought Roberto Kelly was over-matche in center, and Williams was good enoug to move Kelly.

12. Bernie Williams, New York

Hit only .237 as a rookie, but walks and stolen bases are a deadly combination if you can hit .260. There's a line between McRae and Williams because McRae (and Cuyler) have proven they are good enough to stay in the lineup, while Williams hasn't. Apart from that, he's in the same class of player. He just needs to add twenty points to his average and steal enough bases to solidify his position.

13. Glenallen Hill/ Alex Cole, Cleveland

Cole had one of the weirdest seasons of any major league player in 1991, in which he apparently played himself out of a job despite hitting far better than anyone could reasonably have expected.

Cole came out of nowhere the second half of 1990 to steal 40 bases in 63 games, so when the Indians moved their fences way back after the 1990 season and announced they were building for speed and defense, it was assumed that they were making Alex Cole a key figure on their team. We all made fun of them for this, and so the Indians said that wasn't it, at all; they were rebuilding for speed anyway, and Cole just happened to be there. Then he started slowly and got hurt, spent some time at the bottom of the batting lists, so the idea was established that he was having a miserable year.

In the end, he hit .295 and drew 58 walks in 122 games, giving him an on base percentage way up there, .386. He completely lost the touch as a base stealer, dropping from 40/49 in 63 games to 27/44 in 122 games, and he isn't a good center fielder. If he loses the job in center field the Indians might consider making him a DH. Guys who can get on base 270 times a year and run are tough to find.

Glenallen Hill is the very epitome of the term "perennial prospect", a 27-year-old who has been two years away from greatness since he was 19. He hit .258 last year, and if he hits .258 he's not much different from Dave Henderson. He could hit 25, 30 homers a year and also steal some bases, but may have trouble keeping his average over .230.

14. Junior Felix or somebody, California

It's unclear who will be playing center for the new Angels; Felix is still the best bet.

I suppose I should say also that I was completely wrong in my analysis of the Felix/White trade a year ago (apart from anticipating that White would have a good year for Toronto) because I was missing a key piece of information. It has been learned that Felix is several years older than the age he has been claiming, which makes a tremendous difference in the way that we evaluate his future. Although a lot of people resist believing this, if you take a 22-year-old player and a 25-year-old player of the same ability, the 22-year-old player can be expected to get more than twice as many hits in his career, and to hit three times as many home runs. You can demonstrate this if you study the issue; it's not just scout's bullshit, although the scouts know the same thing. Felix, apparently with the complicity of Epy Guerrero, had been listed at 22 (in 1990) when he really was 25 or even older, so I had him tagged as a coming star when he probably isn't.

Felix played only 66 games last year due to a discombobulated calf muscle. If he's healthy, he's a decent player, and doesn't deserve to rank last in the league, but we don't know if he's healthy.

NATIONAL LEAGUE CENTER FIELDERS

1. Ron Gant, Atlanta

Has had two straight fine seasons. As is often the case, his stolen bases are just window dressing; they don't have any real value, since he is caught stealing enough to negate the value. That's true of Brett Butler, too. Gant, in a sense, is the player that Eric Davis was supposed to be, a guy who can play center field, get seventy extra base hits and drive in and score 100 runs a year. As a young player is supposed to, Gant has gained control of the strike zone as he has developed.

2. Brett Butler, Los Angeles

A leadoff man with a .401 on base percentage is hard to replace, as the Giants found when they tried to replace him with Willie McGee. There's a lot of attention paid to Butler's caught stealing, but he had 28 caught stealing last year, so if you just use those to cancel 28 walks, what do you have? You've still got a .296 hitter with 80 walks—a .377 on base percentage—and now you have to evaluate him as a base stealer who is 38 for 38. He doesn't score a hundred runs every year on blind luck.

3. Andy Van Slyke, Pittsburgh

He still can't hit left-handers (.195 against them last year), and you can't *prove* with any objective information that he's a good center fielder. He used to steal 30 bases a year, but those days are gone; it's more like ten a year now. Still, he's a smart player, a good percentage player with a secondary average of .350 (career, .346 last year). He's a 79% base stealer, which is super, hardly ever makes an error and has a fine arm. The Pirates win.

4. Len Dykstra, Philadelphia

Played almost as well last year as he had in 1990, but missed most of the year due to drinking and driving. If you take Brett

Butler and remove *durability* and *consistency*, you've got Len Dykstra. He does have a few other markers—a better arm than Butler, a little power—but basically, he's what Brett Butler would be if Butler didn't know how to stay in the lineup.

5. Vince Coleman, New York

Here's the difference between Brett Butler and Vince Coleman in a nutshell:

In the last four years Brett Butler has had on base percentages of .393, .349, .397 and .401. Vince Coleman has had on base percentages of .313 to .347.

Brett Butler has scored 100 runs each year.

Vince Coleman has not scored 100 runs in any of the four years.

Coleman is one of the best base stealers of all time, but stealing bases is a poor substitute for getting on base. The number of runs you generate by stealing 100 bases depends on how many times you are caught stealing as well as other variables, but is normally no more than you would generate by 35 walks.

Coleman in recent years has begun to get on base more, his on base percentages increasing from .313 (1988) to .316 to .340 to .347. But just as his offense is beginning to get interesting, his durability has declined. He's not a true star, he's never been a true star, and at 30 years old he's not likely ever to become one.

6. Steve Finley, Houston

Had his first good year last year, hitting .285 with 34 stolen bases. A fairly good year, anyway. He had Vince Coleman's on base percentage (.331) and Brett Butler's stolen base totals (34 of 52). He's a good defensive center fielder.

7. Ray Lankford, St. Louis

More star potential than Finley—two years younger and a better athlete. He hit nine homers as a rookie, but that will probably double with a year's experience and closer fences. His batting average, strikeouts and walks as a rookie are comparable to Ron Gant's:

	AB	Hits	BB	SO	Avg.
Gant	563	146	46	118	.259
Lankford	566	142	41	114	.251

Gant went back to the minors in his second year, but grew from this platform to hit for a better average and with a better K/W ratio. There is no guarantee that Lankford will follow.

8. Reggie Sanders, Cincinnati

Biggest questions about him will be his durability and defense. He should hit around .270 as a rookie, double-figure home runs, 25 or 30 steals and a slugging percentage in the low .400s. Has a chance to be a star. He's being compared to Eric Davis because he plays in Cincinnati, but may actually play more like Reggie Smith.

9. Darren Lewis, San Francisco

He doesn't have power and doesn't have Vince Coleman speed, so he'll have to get on base like Butler to be among the better hitting center fielders. He is a disciplined hitter, and I like his chances. His defense has received good reviews.

Willie McGee may also play here. He'd rank about the same.

10. Darrin Jackson, San Diego

Players often have fluke years at age 27. Jackson was 27 last year, when he hit 21 home runs, which is about 18 more than anybody expected. He's stretched to play center, and nobody expects him to continue to hit for power, but he has earned a chance to be a regular.

11. Marquis Grissom, Montreal

Like Jackson, except that his season is less impressive. A leadoff hitter with a .310 on base percentage is about as useful as a cleanup hitter with seven home runs.

12. Chicago (Unknown)

I've been a believer in Jerome Walton, but obviously *something* isn't working for him. Doug Dascenzo is a good backup/25 at bat guy, but can't hold the job. Cedri Landrum could steal 75 bases but he' have to get 60 of them as a pinch runner Chico Walker is a career minor league forced into center by desperation. If it wa my team I'd send Walton back to Iow and tell him we hope you have a good yea because we need you, and then I'd platoo Landrum with Dascenzo, using Dascenzo a switch hitter, as a right-handed hitter.

AMERICAN LEAGUE RIGHT FIELDERS

1. Jose Canseco, Oakland

The best power hitter in baseball, a fact disguised to a large extent by the Oakland Coliseum. It isn't a *question* whether he could hit 50 homers a year in a good hitter's park; the question is whether he could hit 60. In his two 40-homer seasons (1988 and 1991) he has hit a total of only 32 home runs in Oakland, with 54 on the road. He's also a base stealer, an above-average outfielder and draws enough walks to have a fairly good on base percentage.

2. Ruben Sierra, Texas

My friend Raymond Riley believes that Sierra is the best player in baseball, so in rating him second at his own position I probably should explain why he isn't.

1. Sierra's *package* of offensive stats in a typical year—35 doubles, 25 homers, 15 stolen bases, almost 200 hits, etc.—is certainly stunning, but the one most important offensive statistic is on base percentage. Canseco's career on base percentage is .348; Sierra's is .325.

2. The most important variable in offense *other* than on base percentage is power. Canseco has more power than any other player in the world.

3. Canseco plays in a park that hurts him; Sierra plays in a park that helps him. In the same park, Canseco's stats would be so much better than Sierra's that there would be no question. Canseco has hit 50% more home runs in his career than Sierra has (209 to 139), but in neutral parks he has hit 102% more (117 to 58).

Sierra's a great player. Canseco is better.

3. Joe Carter, Toronto

The third MVP candidate among AL Right Fielders is Carter. Carter as a hitter is very comparable to George Bell, whose place he took in the batting order. Let's compare their records in seasonal notation:

	AB	R	H	2B	3B	HR	RBI	BB	SO	SB	Avg.
Carter	625	86	165	32	4	28	103	36	101	23	.263
Bell	619	86	177	32	4	28	101	35	76	7	.286

Bell strikes out a little less and has a better batting average, but otherwise they're dead even as hitters, but Carter is a better outfielder and better baserunner.

4. Shane Mack, Minnesota

Two years ago (1990) he hit .326 with 8 homers as a half-time player. I thought *that* was a fluke. Last year he hit .310 with 27 doubles, 8 triples and 18 homers in 442 at bats. Obviously, he's made a believer out of me. He'll move up another hundred at bats this year. It'll be interesting to see whether he carries his batting average with him.

5. Phil Plantier, Boston

Muddy situation here—the Red Sox have Quintana, Vaughn, Plantier and Brunansky to play first base and right field, and haven't been able to make a deal. Brunansky can't play anymore; he'd rank about twelfth if I considered him the regular.

Plantier, assuming he stays in the lineup, figures to hit about .280 with a slugging percentage over .500, 25 to 40 home runs. He's an awesome hitter, in other words. His ability to play the outfield is suspect, plus the last player who came up and hit like Plantier did for two months (Willie McCovey, 1959) fell into a tremendous slump the next year and lost his job, even though he would in time prove to be a great hitter.

A year ago the scouts were trying to tell us that Plantier had a big swing, and wouldn't hit major league pitching. What we need is some *accountability* here: who were the idiots that were feeding *Baseball America* this pap, and what are they telling us now? What we saw when he came up is that Plantier hits funny, hits out of a squat. That's about all it takes to make a lot of scouts suspicious.

6. Danny Tartabull, New York

Tartabull's an amazing hitter. If all the power hitters in baseball were in identical parks and they were all healthy and batting 600 times in the year, Jose Canseco and Frank Thomas would have the best hitting stats, but Danny Tartabull would have the third best. He's a better hitter than Sierra or Fielder or Bonds or Bonilla or anybody, anybody except Canseco or Thomas.

Having said that, there's no way I would have signed him as a free agent. He's

a) an awful outfielder,
b) a bad baserunner,
c) injury prone, and
d) impossible to get along with.

He was also *reported* to be greedy, money-driven, and he did have a big year in his option year, tending to confirm this suspicion.

You remember the movie "Twins", where Arnold Schwarzenegger and Danny DeVito were supposed to be twins as a result of a genetic experiment, but Arnold got all the good traits and DeVito got all the bad stuff? Danny Tartabull is Kirby Puckett's evil twin—he got all the bad stuff that Kirby doesn't have. Who needs him.

7. Jay Buhner, Seattle

For several years injuries had prohibited him from emerging as a regular, but he finally was healthy last year and didn't disappoint, hitting 27 homers. With Kevin Mitchell's acquisition the Mariners should have an 80-homer outfield.

8. Rob Deer, Detroit

The best .179 hitter in baseball history. His batting average accounts for only 32% of his offensive value, so it is unfair to evaluate him as a career .218 hitter, but it is an irresistible habit to look. His secondary average was .408 last year, .382 in his career. His typical season is .218 with 31 homers, 86 RBI a year, and what do you say about a guy who drives in 86 runs a year?

There's a hell of a lot of people who don't.

9. Mark Whiten, Cleveland

Everybody tells me that he has the best throwing arm in baseball. Not "everybody", of course; I mean everybody I talk to about stuff like this. Personally, I haven't seen him put this arm on display in a game situation, and until I do I'm sticking with Jesse Barfield.

Whiten wasn't bad last year, not bad for a rookie power hitter in a park that doesn't allow home runs. He hit .243 with a .388 slugging percentage, not good enough numbers to keep him in the lineup, but if he can hit .260 his power and throwing arm will make him a rich man.

10. Dwight Evans and Joe Orsulak, Baltimore

Evans turned 40 in December; he's still an effective offensive player. Orsulak is 30, and will be out of the majors in two years.

11. Kevin McReynolds, Kansas City

There's an article about him in the Kansas City comment. I think he's too slow to play right field in Kansas City, but he may be challenged by the trade and have a better year than I think he can.

12. Sammy Sosa/ Dan Pasqua, Chicago White Sox

Sosa had such a miserable year that many people have written him off. That's premature. He's 23 years old, he's an athlete and he hit well in 1989, fairly well in '90. There's no guarantee that his career will pull out of its freefall, but there's no guarantee that it won't, either.

Pasqua is a marginal defensive right fielder, a productive hitter with a .251 lifetime average, but walks and power. If you could graft Pasqua's plate discipline onto Sosa's body you'd have a heck of a player.

13. Dante Bichette, Milwaukee

Doesn't do anything well enough to stay employed. He's got a little speed, a little power, a good throwing arm. If he could hit .270 he'd stay around, but he won't.

14. Hubie Brooks, California

Obviously is on his last option. As Joey Amalfitano once said to Bobby Bonds, "Bobby, you know where you are. If you've got any bullets left in the gun, you'd better fire 'em." May platoon with Von Hayes.

NATIONAL LEAGUE RIGHT FIELDERS

1. Darryl Strawberry, Los Angeles

Darryl turned 30 in March, so his career enters a new phase. His speed has disappeared, dropping from 36 stolen bases in 1987 to 10 last year. He's driven in 90 or more runs in six of the last eight years, and has yet to ground into as many as ten double plays in a year.

2. Bobby Bonilla, New York

Will lose 20–25 points off his batting average in moving from Pittsburgh to Shea Stadium, but pick up a few homers. This should leave him, at a guess, hitting .260–.280 with 25 to 35 homers in a season. He's not Strawberry—he's tougher but slower—but he gives the Mets back essentially what they lost in Strawberry.

Jim Leyland, urging people to stop thinking of Bonds and Bonilla as one, said last summer that "They're really different players. One has speed, the other one doesn't. One of them's a power hitter, the other one really isn't."

Here's the question:

Which one isn't a power hitter?

3. Tony Gwynn, San Diego

Now 32 years old and hasn't won a batting title in two years, but his 1991 batting average (.317) and slugging percentage (.432) were near his career norms.

4. Dave Justice, Atlanta

His career record in seasonal notation is much like Albert Belle's: it shows him doing things he hasn't done yet. Per 162 games played Justice has hit 33 doubles and 32 homers, driving in 108 runs. Obviously, he's going to be an MVP candidate if he can play 155 games, but hasn't yet.

Justice is awkward, and as a consequence of that isn't a good outfielder or baserunner. He hurt himself last year by simple awkwardness, and he'll do it again. But he's a young power hitter in a power hitter's park, and that's a nice combination.

5. Larry Walker, Montreal

Man, there are some *good* right fielders in this league. The difference between the number one man (Strawberry) and the number eight man (Dawson) is not large.

Walker has power and speed, and hit .290 last year. He's a year younger than Justice, and probably as good a hitter if the two were in the same park. In the two years they have been in the league Walker has hit more home runs in road games than Justice has (21-19), but has been out-homered 31-14 in his home park, creating the impression that Justice has much more power.

6. Paul O'Neill, Cincinnati

A good grunt ballplayer, a perfect contrast to Eric Davis. Davis looks sensational but doesn't play half the time, and his skills are slowly slipping away. O'Neill looks ordinary but just keeps playing a little better and a little better, working his way up to 28 homers and 91 RBI last year. He also steals a few bases (14 per season) and has a pretty good strikeout to walk ratio (107 to 73 last year). Above average outfielder, good arm.

7. Felix Jose, St. Louis

Adjusted his stroke to become a line-drive hitter last year, now must re-adjust it for the new dimensions in Busch. When he came up the A's regarded him as a young Don Baylor type, but that didn't work in St. Louis, so he switched his style and hit .305 with 40 doubles, 8 homers.

8. Andre Dawson, Chicago

I don't mean to put him down by ranking him eighth. He's been a great player, and with 31 homers and 104 RBI last year he obviously hasn't placed an order for a wheel chair yet. With only 22 walks and four stolen bases, he can't be considered a potent offensive player at this point in his career. He played full time and scored only 69 runs. I originally had him ranked much higher, but had to keep adjusting him downward when I compared his runs created per game to those of the other guys. Dawson created 5.0 runs per game last year, Felix Jose 5.6. With Jose being ten years younger it is hard to argue that Dawson is going to *gain* on him in 1992.

---

9. Orlando Merced, Pittsburgh

The plan at the moment is to move Orlando Merced to the outfield, abandoning first base to some combination of players to be announced.

Merced hit significantly better than I expected last year, and is young enough (turned 25 in November) that we should assume that his better-than-expected performance may represent his development as a hitter, rather than a fluke year. I don't foresee a brilliant future for him. He entered pro ball as a shortstop, as many players do, and has been tried at all eight positions. What I suspect is going to happen is that he's going to fall into a second-year slump and be pushed back into a platoon role, either in the outfield or at first base.

10. Dale Murphy, Philadelphia

Just another player now, a cleanup hitter who should hit about seventh. Joe Dimaggio retired when he reached this stage of his career, but we can't expect everybody else to be Joe DiMaggio.

---

11. Kevin Bass, San Francisco

It's unclear who is going to play here—Bass or McGee or Cory Snyder or Mike Felder or Chris James or Mark Leonard. It does seem fairly certain that Bass can't play everyday anymore. My recommendation: put Mark Leonard in left and Darren Lewis in center, in right field make a platoon combination with Kevin Bass as the right-handed hitter. He's a switch hitter, but he has power right-handed, none left-handed. I think if you platooned him he'd stay healthy and the power would come out.

12. Eric Anthony/ Mike Simms, Houston

Bill Wood and I may be the only people left in the world who still believe in Eric Anthony, but I'm not giving up. I still like the guy. He went to Tucson last year and hit for average rather than power, but still struck out too much. I think he may be so confused now his ability won't come through until he gets traded to another team.

Mike Simms, on the other hand, probably doesn't have the ability to be more than a bit player in the majors. They'll start out the year platooning.

AMERICAN LEAGUE DESIGNATED HITTERS

1. Paul Molitor, Milwaukee

Scored 133 runs last year, 88 as a DH. If the Brewers had played better Molitor would have been an MVP candidate. Also can go to the field if need be, unlike the next three guys on the list.

2. Chili Davis, Minnesota

Was an MVP candidate, although he didn't hit as much as Molitor. Minnesota DHs hit .283 with 30 homers, 101 RBI.

3. Harold Baines, Oakland

Oakland DHs last year hit .280 with 27 homers, 112 RBI. That's mostly Baines, of course; he's been a DH now for five years, one of the few men ever to do the job for that long.

4. Jack Clark, Boston

Constant walks and power give him a secondary average over .400 (.416 last year, .408 career). In his prime he was one of the two or three best power hitters in baseball. He's lost something—thirty, forty points in batting average—but he's still a valuable man.

5. Dave Winfield, Toronto

His signing *should* make the Blue Jays tough to beat this year. Their Designated Hitters last year were just awful. I gave the stats with the team comment so won't repeat them, but if Winfield creates 90 runs as a DH that will improve the team by 30 or 40 runs, which will make them three or four games tougher to beat.

---

6. Sam Horn and one of the first basemen, Baltimore

Horn is the Orioles' only left-handed power threat, and a potent one at that. In the last two years he's batted 563 times, hitting 37 homers and driving in 106 runs. He's as slow as anyone in the majors and can't play the field, even first base, and the Orioles abound in right-handed designated hitters (Randy Milligan, Glenn Davis, Dwight Evans), so Horn probably won't increase his playing time despite his impressive power record.

7. Kevin Maas, New York

Has a career secondary average of .383, so he shouldn't have to hit .250 to keep his job. With an outfield of Roberto Kelly, Bernie Williams and Danny Tartabull, Maas will have to share DH time with Mel Hall, another left-handed hitter. Actually, Tartabull should be a fulltime DH, but doesn't want to do it.

8. Brian Downing, Texas

I assume that he may share the DH job with Rob Maurer, who I discussed in the Texas comment. Downing is 41 years old, but he still drives in runs and he still scores runs. The Angels were fools to release him.

9. George Brett, Kansas City

He missed most of April and May with injuries, and had only three RBI by early June. Trying to make up for lost time, he moved to DH and played every game the rest of the year, which was a mistake; at 39 (in May) he needs a day off now and then to stay sharp. He wasn't good last year, but he still hit 40 doubles, and he is just one year away from his last batting title. His average will go back up in '92.

10. Pete O'Brien, Seattle

O'Brien gave the Mariners good defense and 88 RBI last year. His defense was at first base, which he apparently has handed over to Tino Martinez. O'Brien isn't on base a lot, and his 1991 season—.248 with 17 homers—was his best year in the last three. He's now 34 years old.

---

11. Bo Jackson, Chicago

My own opinion of Bo is that he has limited *ability* as a baseball player, because hitting a baseball requires an extremely high level of hand/eye co-ordination. I mean, I'm sure that Bo has *good* hand/eye co-ordination in the ordinary sense, meaning that it's better than mine or my neighbors', but the guys who are really good hitters, Frank Thomas and Jack Clark and George Brett, are all at the 99th percentile of the population in hand/eye co-ordination. Bo isn't; he's at the 80th percentile. He can compensate for that to some extent by his other great assets, his strength, his concentration, his speed before the injury. Those things make him a decent hitter, but in my opinion he was just never destined to be an outstanding major league player, and wouldn't have been if he had played nothing but baseball from the age of 18. He just didn't have the ability.

The White Sox' DH production last year was the best in the league, with Frank Thomas being primarily a DH. The most interesting question is whether the presence of Thomas on the team will have a salutary effect on Bo as a hitter. Bo has never been a disciplined hitter, but in this case he can see so clearly how Thomas, his onetime junior teammate at Auburn, has moved far ahead of him as a hitter by learning to control the strike zone. It will be interesting to see whether he tries to follow Frank's lead and stop chasing bad pitches, or whether he continues to chase everything because

a) he's stubborn, or

b) it simply isn't possible to flip that switch at his age and level of experience.

It is unclear who will DH for the remaining three teams. Midwinter rosters for the Detroit Tigers may list **Tony Phillips** as the DH, but that's kind of a joke; Phillips plays everywhere, and Sparky has not normally used one regular DH. The Designated Hitter for the California Angels may be rotated among **Von Hayes, Hubie Brooks, Lee Stevens and Luis Po-**

lonia, or Buck Rodgers may choose one of them to be a regular DH and stabilize the defense.

Cleveland's DH . . . well, gosh, that could be anybody. If there is a regular DH it would most likely be **Carlos Martinez** or **Alex Cole**, but more likely than not they'll use the DH to share at bats among a group of players.

AMERICAN LEAGUE STARTING PITCHERS

1. Roger Clemens, Boston

He's by far the best—in fact, he's the best starting pitcher in baseball since Tom Seaver was in his prime. And Seaver wasn't any better.

2. Chuck Finley, California

His ERA was up last year because he wasn't 100% physically, but he still won 18 games to complete his third straight outstanding season. Over the three years total he is 52-27 with a 2.93 ERA, a record that stands up against anybody except Clemens (56-27, 2.58)

3. Jack Morris, Toronto

Gives the Blue Jays back what they lost in Dave Stieb—a tough, smart veteran right-hander . . . still very easy to run on. Won 13 of his 18 games last year in the Metrodome.

4. Mark Langston, California

His record over a period of years is a lot better than his reputation. He's pitched 220 innings every year of his career except one, and he's won 17 games (Seattle, 1984), 19 games (Seattle, 1987), 15 games (Seattle, 1988), 16 games (Seattle-Montreal, 1989) and 19 games (California, 1991). He's 115-101 lifetime, pitching almost entirely for bad teams . . . shuts off the running game exceptionally well for a power pitcher.

5. Nolan Ryan, Texas

The only mark against him now is that he can no longer pitch as many innings as some of the other guys. He's had winning records four straight years (41-25 over the last three), with good ERAs and eye-popping ERA components. Also, he has re-emerged as an authentic gate attraction, something which has been said about him throughout his career although it was usually not true. He started 20 times last year in Texas, only 7 times on the road, presumably because the Rangers wanted to take maximum advantage of his appeal.

6. Jimmy Key, Toronto

He doesn't have the equipment that the other top starters listed here have, but he gets more done with a batting practice fastball than anybody else in baseball today. He eliminates the running game and never walks anybody, which gives him two of Tommy John's advantages, but he isn't like Tommy because he works up in the strike zone, doesn't throw many ground balls.

7. Jack McDowell, Chicago

Still emerging as a top flight pitcher, and probably hasn't pitched as well wire to wire as the six guys listed ahead of him. When he's on his game he's as tough as anybody except Ryan or Clemens.

8. Frank Viola, Boston

Has had a cyst removed from his finger, one thing which kept him from pitching his best last year. Here's a question for you: did the Mets make a logical decision to sign Gooden rather than Viola, or an emotional decision? Gooden is younger and is perceived as essential to the Mets' integrity, but Viola is healthier and a better pitcher right now.

Viola is a left hander in Fenway Park. I don't see that as a *positive*, certainly, but dealing with a pitcher with this much savvy I don't see it as a big negative, either . . . Viola had the best record against base stealers of any National League pitcher last year. Base stealers were 6 for 22 when Viola was on the mound.

9. Jim Abbott, California

Abbott *does* throw ground balls, and consequently has been hurt by the fact that the Angels don't have a quality second baseman to turn the double play. He's improving his control, holding his walks constant (74, 72, 73) while his innings pitched have increased. He still doesn't have *great* control, but works ahead of the hitters and eliminates the running game. Base stealers last year were 12 for 26 against him, which means they would have been far better off just to stay on first.

Although a left-handed pitcher, Abbott has had trouble getting out *left*-handed hitters. This is going to become important if it persists, because the other teams are going to realize it after awhile and start stacking the lineups with left-handed hitters. In 1989 Abbott allowed left-handers a batting average of .325, as opposed to .263 against right-handers. In 1990 the figures were .318 and .292, and last year .303 and .233. To this point this hasn't affected the lineup selection (84% of the at bats against him were by right-handed hitters in 1991), but in time it will.

---

10. Kevin Tapani, Minnesota

Often compared to Catfish Hunter on the mound, he's 28-17 over the last two years. I have to rate him ahead of Scott Erickson because he pitched more innings with a better ERA, plus he had more strikeouts and fewer walks.

11. Erik Hanson, Seattle

Troubled last year by tightness in his elbow, didn't pitch as well as he had the previous two years. Still, he's 35-22 over the last three years, struck out 143 men in 175 innings last year and pitched some good games late in the year, so I doubt that there is anything seriously wrong with his arm.

12. Dave Stewart, Oakland

Didn't throw strikes last year, and paid for it in home runs (24) and walks (105). It's hard to know how much to take away from him for the one bad year, but quality pitchers have off years, and it doesn't necessarily mean they're finished.

13. Mike Moore, Oakland

Pitched brilliantly in 1989 (19-11, 2.61 ERA), poorly in 1990, pitched well again last year. He walked a hundred men last year for the first time in his career, but held opponents to a .229 batting average with only 11 homers. Had more than twice as many strikeouts last year as in 1990, when he obviously had some kind of unannounced injury.

14. Chris Bosio, Milwaukee

Like Moore, pitched well in 1989, poorly in 1990, well again last year. He has never been able to put together a big year, but was 15-10, 2.95 ERA in '89 and 14-10, 3.25 last year. Has excellent control, changes speeds very well which makes his fastball look faster than it is.

15. Scott Sanderson, New York

Winning 16 games for the Yankees (1991) was a more impressive accomplishment than winning 17 for the A's (1990). Over the last three years he's 44-30—with three different teams . . . pitched poorly in Yankee Stadium, but went 9-4 on the road. Jumps ahead of the hitters.

16. Scott Erickson, Minnesota

Would have ranked much higher if the season had ended August 1, but was pitching through an injury the last two months. I know I'm slow to come around here, but I have trouble seeing a guy who strikes out 108 men in 204 innings as a top rank pitcher . . . Base stealers were 4 for 14 against Erickson, this on a staff that had trouble stopping the run with almost any other pitcher. Left-handed hitters hit .295 against him, but right-handers only .191.

17. Randy Johnson, Seattle

Still has no concept of the strike zone, walking 152 men last year, but striking out 228 to finish with a 13-10 record (27-21 over a two-year period.) One consequence of the walks is that they limit the number of innings he can pitch. In modern baseball everybody comes out of the game after about 110 pitches, and Johnson has little chance to finish a game in less than 110 pitches, so he loses quite a few innings.

18. Bob Welch, Oakland

Finished 12-13 with a 4.58 ERA. Although Welch had a better year than Dave Stewart, I'd be more concerned about Welch possibly having lost it than I would Stewart. Welch, who struck out 7.01 men per nine innings in 1987, dropped to 5.88 in 1989, to 4.80 in his Cy Young season and to 4.13 last year. There just aren't many pitchers around who can win games with four strikeouts a game, but of course he has been a quality pitcher for a long time, so he may be able to make an adjustment and send that back up for a few years.

I'll mention this here because I forgot to mention it anywhere else: that Ron Darling is *exactly* the kind of pitcher that Duncan/LaRussa have worked wonders with in the past. Darling is a 31-year-old pitcher with a good arm whose career has stalled, meaning that he is exactly what Dave Stewart was, what Scott Sanderson was and Mike Moore and Dennis Eckersley and Rick Honeycutt. I'll bet you Darling wins 16-18 games this year.

19. Kevin Appier, Kansas City

Will have to fill the role of staff ace with Saberhagen gone. He's been streaky; he'll pitch three or four brilliant games, and then two or three bad ones.

The Deaf Frenchman's motion is not a thing of beauty. He flaps around, seems to be about to pop a stitch with every pitch, but he does get his fastball into the nineties and he does get the slider into the catcher's mitt.

20. David Wells, Toronto

He was 15-10, 3.72 ERA last year—and he'll do better this year. An efficient worker, throws strikes, throws hard. He reminds me some of John Smiley of the

Pirates—cocky, cagey—except he's a lot heavier.

Could also rate among top twenty: Frank Tanana, Bill Gullickson, Mike Boddicker, Bill Wegman, Jaime Navarro, Ron Darling, Juan Guzman, Jose Guzman.

NATIONAL LEAGUE STARTING PITCHERS

1. Doug Drabek, Pittsburgh

I evaluate pitchers primarily by what they have accomplished over a period of years, rather than on who has had the best year. Drabek certainly did not pitch as well as Glavine last year—but neither was he a lot worse. He pitched 12 innings fewer than Glavine (247-235) with an ERA a half-run higher (2.55-3.07). That's not a big deal; random luck can account for those differences. Drabek has four straight seasons with winning records and ERAs under 3.08; Glavine has had two winning records in those years, two losing records, and had never had an ERA better than 3.68 before last year.

2. Greg Maddux, Chicago

The best starting pitcher the Cubs have had since Ferguson Jenkins, his four-year record is almost as impressive as Drabek's. He's won fifteen or more games every year (total 67-46) with ERAs no higher than 3.46. In Wrigley Field for a team that *isn't* consistently good, that's a terrific record.

3. Tom Glavine, Atlanta

The Cy Young vote was a good one. Glavine's a relatively rare combination of a ground-ball pitcher who also strikes out (192) batters. Most power pitchers, like Ryan, Clemens, Cone, Gooden, throw up in the strike zone, where the batter either misses the ball or pops it up. Glavine, as Gubicza did in his big years and Jim Abbott does, gets strikeouts *and* ground balls, which makes him especially tough . . . has a career ERA of 4.12 in Atlanta, 3.54 on the road.

4. Dennis Martinez, Montreal

Led the National League in ERA (2.39), which was his fifth straight quality season (aggregate record 66-46, 2.88 ERA). Is he the best pitcher in baseball now who has never won twenty games? The best career, I mean . . . he's had 177 wins, never 20, and Frank Tanana has won 220 without ever winning 20. Martinez may have an improved chance to win 20 with a different manager.

5. Zane Smith, Pittsburgh

He led the National League in both ground ball/fly ball ratio (2.72 to 1) and strikeout to walk ratio (4.14 to 1). If you have only one statistic to evaluate a pitcher, strikeout to walk ratio is the one thing you want—better than won-lost record over a period of years, better than ERA, better than anything. ERA and won-lost record are very dependent on context and luck; strikeout to walk ratio isn't.

Tommy John-type pitchers, like Smith, normally have their best years in their thirties. Smith turned thirty in December, 1990 . . . his walks have dropped from 105 (1986) to 29.

6. Jose Rijo, Cincinnati

Rijo is the best pitcher in the National League when healthy. He's had ERAs the last four years of 2.39, 2.84, 2.70 and 2.51—in a home run park. Nobody else is that good—but he pitches only 180 innings a year.

7. Ramon Martinez, Los Angeles

Would have rated higher a year ago, but everything was down last year except his ERA. A 17-13 record with a contending team, 3.27 ERA in Dodger Stadium . . . it isn't what was expected of him, and he lost a third of his strikeouts in one year. Will have to prove he is healthy.

8. Greg Swindell, Cincinnati

Had the best strikeout/walk ratio in the majors last year (169 strikeouts, 31 walks). His career ratio is also outstanding (756/226), and he's been able to post a winning record (60-56) with the worst team in baseball over the last six years.

Although a lot of people suspect that he isn't 100% physically, he hasn't missed a start in two years.

9. Bret Saberhagen, New York

Credentials are discussed in Mets' Hall of Fame watch.

10. David Cone, New York

He's won 14 games three straight years, and there's been criticism of him directed at that, as in, "He's not a top-flight pitcher, he's just a 14-game winner." I think this is misguided, for several reasons.

First, so he wins 14 games a year; there's a hell of a lot of guys who don't. I'm listing the *best* pitchers in the league here, and of the seven guys listed above him not one has won 14 games in each of the last three years.

Second, the comment is edited against Cone by focusing on his last three years and ignoring his lucky year, which was 1988. Over the last four seasons he's 62–35, which is a damn good record.

Third, it implies that if a player wins 14 games for three straight years he couldn't have been consistently unlucky, when in fact he very easily could have. For a pitcher to have relatively poor luck in the won-lost categories for three years would be utterly unremarkable, like a coin coming up heads three times in a row.

I still expect him to have better years, 18- and 20-win years. But if he wins 14 every year, that's not bad.

11. Andy Benes, San Diego

With any luck, he'll be a Cy Young candidate. He may not be quite as overpowering as Cone or Saberhagen when Cone or Saberhagen is at the top of his game, but he's so strong and his motion is so easy that if they're both at 90% on a particular night he'll beat Saberhagen. That gives him a chance to rip off ten straight wins, and if he can do that and avoid a long slump, he's a Cy Young candidate.

12. Steve Avery, Atlanta

I know a lot of people would rate him among the top three in the league because he was so tremendous late last year, but we're talking about a 22-year-old kid who has pitched well for a few months. There's just no way of knowing whether, the next time he starts to struggle, he'll make a quick adjustment and save his season, or whether he'll lose eight or ten games before he figures out what the problem is. Until we find out, I'm not rating him at the top of the list.

13. Tom Browning, Cincinnati

I still believe, as I did a year ago, that he is not the pitcher he was a few years ago. He was 14-14 last year, 4.18 ERA, by which standard he is rated too high here. I don't believe that year was a fluke; I think that's about where he is right now. On the other hand, he's got a fine record over a period of years (62-40 over the last four), and that deserves respect.

•

14. Tom Candiotti, Los Angeles

Here's a question: when was the last time there was a knuckleball pitcher with a good team? I guess it would have been Phil Niekro in 1982–83 with Atlanta; he was 28-14 over the two years, after which Joe Torre released him.

See, baseball people don't *like* knuckleball pitchers. They like hard throwers. There's a strong prejudice against trick pitches and the pitchers who throw them. On a good team, where there are options, the manager is often afraid that the knuckleball will get away in a game situation and cost the team a win. But on a bad team, where there are fewer good options, a knuckleball pitcher gets more of a shot—so most knuckleball pitchers wind up starting for teams which are out of contention, where they pitch .500 ball, which reinforces the prejudice against them.

Candiotti's an outstanding pitcher, able to win consistently with Cleveland over a period of years. He didn't have any luck with Toronto, but he was one of the best pitchers in the American League last year. And as a 34-year-old knuckleballer, he's got ten years left.

15. John Smiley, Pittsburgh

He's a simple pitcher—throw hard, throw strikes, get ahead of the hitters, change speeds a little, move the ball in and out a little, let the hitters get themselves out. He's got a nasty slider that he doesn't use a lot early in the count. It's worked for a hundred years, and when the split-fingered fastball and the circle change are consigned to history, it'll still be workin'.

16. Bruce Hurst, San Diego

Has a record of six straight winning seasons, three straight ERAs of 3.29 or better. He probably should rate higher, in fact, but there's a lot of good starting pitchers in this league, more than in the American League. Incidentally, eight of the sixteen National League pitchers that I have rated so far are ex-American Leaguers, and a similar number of top American League pitchers are ex-National Leaguers.

17. John Smoltz, Atlanta

Tremendous stuff, also has three straight winning records, but has been prone to slumps.

Does it seem curious to you that baseball teams have been reluctant to try the personal coach approach? If a player makes a million dollars a year, and who doesn't these days, it doesn't seem to be an unreasonable investment to spend $30,000 to hire a coach to do whatever can be done to keep that player, specifically, on his game. A personal coach could know the mechanics and equipment of his player with a comprehensiveness that nobody could master in dealing with a changing list of eight or ten players. The personal coach could be a valuable resource for the organization in other ways:

1) he could get work done—film review, chart analysis, concept instruction—that a coach could not do for eight players, and thus could help in-

sure good work habits throughout the organization.

2) he could supervise the player's *diet* and *training habits* in more detail than can be done in any other way.
3) he could work to keep the player on an even emotional keel, and thus help to keep the dynamics of the team from becoming volatile.
4) he could give the manager *control of* and *information about* his resources that he couldn't get in any other way.

The manager could outline what he wants the personal coaches to do and not do—*don't* try to change his pitch selection, *don't* mess with his mechanics or delivery, *do* make him watch the film of every start and chart it for this and that and that, *do* make him study the charts and plan out how he is going to pitch to each hitter in his next start.

I'm not advocating this; I'm just saying it's a little surprising that it hasn't happened. Personal coaches are not rare in other fields. Tennis players, gymnasts, weight lifters and track and field stars have had personal coaches for dogs' years. Movie stars and TV actors may have *several* personal coaches. Political candidates will hire people to coach them in specific aspects of their performance. Generally speaking, anybody who makes a million dollars a year from his talent is going to hire people to keep that talent sharp.

It *hasn't* happened in baseball, I suspect, because of simple organizational things like the size and shape of the clubhouse. You suggest 25 personal coaches to a manager, and the first thing he's going to think about is 25 extra people in the clubhouse, 25 extra people on the airplane and 25 extra people milling around in spring training. That's natural; I'm not saying he's wrong to worry about that. But if he ever gets past that point and starts thinking about the things he could do with a staff of 25 assistants, he might wind up with a different position on it.

18. Terry Mulholland, Philadelphia

One more pitcher that Roger Craig failed to develop into a quality starter. A 16-13 record with a losing team, a 3.61 ERA in a hitter's park, a strikeout/walk ratio of 142/49. He's good.

19. Dwight Gooden, New York

Excellent offensive support for the last two years has disguised to a certain extent how much he has lost, but his strikeout/walk data is still strong, and he still has the basic assets of a quality pitcher—a fastball, good control, knowledge of how to pitch. I wouldn't be surprised if he was top three again next year.

20. Trevor Wilson, San Francisco

> "I watched the World Series and you can't help but compare," manager Roger Craig said. "I feel our players are just as good except for pitching, and that's an area we're trying to strengthen."
>
> Craig especially is high on Wilson, who should emerge as the No. 1 starter.
>
> "He has a chance to be a horse," Craig said. "it might not happen this year, but he's a strong kid."
>
> —*USA Today Baseball Weekly*, December 20–January 2

Uh, Roger, I don't mean to be presumptuous, but you realize you really are the last person in the English speaking world to figure this out. I mean, talk about being behind the curve, he has *been* your best pitcher for a year and a half now, and you're still talking about maybe next year.

Could also rate among top twenty: Charlie Leibrandt, Mike Morgan, Bob Ojeda, Tommy Greene, Randy Tomlin, Pete Harnisch, Tim Belcher.

AMERICAN LEAGUE RELIEF ACES

1. Bryan Harvey, California

Let's see . . . he held opponents to a batting average of .178, walked only 17 men while striking out 11.6 per nine innings, had a 1.60 ERA, saved 46 games and held batters to a .144 batting average with runners in scoring position. Anything else?

2. Dennis Eckersley, Oakland

The results weren't quite as impressive last year as the previous three years and he is 37 years old, but I'm guessing he'll still be in top form in '92. He saved 43 games last year. His strikeout/walk ratio was 87 to 6, not counting intentional walks. His ERA was up, but ERAs aren't a reliable reflection of ability in a span of 75 innings. If they were, he wouldn't have had a 0.61 ERA the year before.

3. Tom Henke and Duane Ward, Toronto

Henke missed time early and late with injuries, but it didn't hurt the team because:

a) he pitched brilliantly while he was available, and

b) Duane Ward pitched brilliantly when he wasn't.

Henke had almost as many saves (32) as hits allowed (33). He didn't blow a save opportunity until August.

4. Rick Aguilera, Minnesota

Doesn't have the sensational strikeout/walk ratio that characterizes the other top relievers, but holds batters to a batting average in the ones, saved 42 games in 51 chances. Held opponents to a .144 batting average after the All-Star game.

5. Jeff Montgomery, Kansas City

He pitched *more* than most of the other late-inning closers, facing 376 batters as opposed to 309 for Harvey, 299 for Eckersley, 190 for Henke and 275 for Aguilera. This caught up with him in mid-summer, when he pitched four innings in a game against Texas (the 18-inning game), then gave up twelve earned runs in his next seven outings. Take those out and his ERA was in the ones; after the All-Star break it was 1.06, and he saved 18 of 20.

---

6. Mike Henneman, Detroit

Whereas the other closers now are used only to finish a win, Sparky still brings in Henneman sometimes when the score is tied, which was the 1970s strategy. As a result of that Henneman picks up wins as well as saves, giving him a 49-21 career won-lost record. I am not suggesting that this is wrong; merely pointing out that it's different. Henneman pitched extremely well until stopped by an injury in August, came back to save a couple of games in September.

7. Gregg Olson, Baltimore

His curve was not as sharp as the previous two years, and the Orioles have to be concerned about him. The batting average against him was .262, too high for a closer. He was shelled in day games (0-5, 7.08 ERA, only seven saves in 20 games). He's still young.

8. Jeff Reardon, Boston

Pitched better than he had in recent years, saving 40 games in 49 chances. Good control, but vulnerable to the home run. As bad as Olson in day games (0-3, 6.88 ERA).

9. Bobby Thigpen, Chicago

He blew 9 save chances, which is quite a few, and had an unimpressive ERA (3.49), strikeout/walk ratio (47/38) and opposition batting average (.245). My opinion is that the White Sox would be better off to make Radinsky the closer.

10. Steve Farr, New York

The Yankees, after signing him as a free agent, didn't seem to know quite what to do with him early in the year. I suppose I shouldn't be surprised by this; the Yankees are not famous for knowing what to do with anybody. Anyway, Farr saved only two games early last year (April and May), then saved 14 games with a 0.00 ERA (23 scoreless innings) through June and July.

11. Steve Olin, Cleveland

Quisenberry or Tekulve-type, will emerge as the Indians' closer if they'll stop fighting it and let him. He saved 17 games in 22 chances last year including 7-for-7 in September, but the Indians are talking like they still don't know who their relief ace will be. Had a 2.19 ERA after the All-Star game.

12. Jeff Russell, Texas

Coming back from an injury, he pitched fairly well but blew ten save chances, most in the American League. The batting average of the first batter to face him was .390 (23 for 59), which probably accounted for most of the blown saves. Another power pitcher who gets ground balls, so he got ten double plays last year in 79 innings, but he gave up 11 home runs, which is too many for a relief ace.

13. Mike Schooler, Seattle

The Mariners are determined that he's going to be their relief ace whether he does the job or not, and so far he hasn't. He has a career won-lost record of 10-22, which you don't judge a relief ace by his won-lost record but I don't notice that any of the other guys are 10-22. His 1991 ERA (3.67) isn't that of a relief ace, but the Mariners have traded the other two candidates for the job (Swift and Mike Jackson), so he's got to do it.

14. Doug Henry, Milwaukee

A 28-year-old right-hander, he pitched spectacularly well over the last two months of 1991, and will open the season as the relief ace. His stats—1.00 ERA, .133 opposition batting average, 15 saves in 16 chances—couldn't possibly be any better, but percentages only become meaningful after hundreds of chances, so we don't really know what his level of ability is. When he's had a chance to step forward in the past he's tended to get hurt.

NATIONAL LEAGUE RELIEF ACES

1. Lee Smith, St. Louis

He's not as overpowering as the top guys in the American League (Harvey, Henke and Eckersley), but he's awfully good. He struck out 67 men, walked only 8 (not counting intentional), but the batting average against him was .249, whereas you'd like that to be in the ones. Saved 47 games in 53 chances, an excellent percentage as well as total.

2. Rob Dibble, Cincinnati

He was off his game the second half of 1991, but still has the best stuff in the National League, and struck out 13.6 men per nine innings to prove it. I think he'll get his temper under control a little this year, and get his ERA and his opposition batting average both back in the ones. It was a tough year for all the Reds.

3. Stan Belinda, Pittsburgh

I had him pegged as the Pirates' closer a couple of years ago, which I realize now was obviously premature. It made more sense to use him in a support role for a couple of years before increasing his responsibilities. He didn't have eye-popping numbers last year, but I like him because

a) he saved 16 games in 20 chances, an 80% success rate, and

b) he held opponents to a .184 batting average, the only NL "closer" except Wild Thing to hold batters under .200.

The Pirates have other pitchers that they also use in the closer role—Landrum, sometimes Mason, Palacios, Kipper and Patterson. Leyland has essentially rejected the idea that one of his relievers should be deified as a "closer", and the others considered not good enough to pitch with the game on the line. Power to him. If you can pitch in the sixth inning, you can pitch in the ninth.

4. Mitch Williams, Philadelphia

He had nine blown saves last year (he was 30 for 39), but this is a misleading stat because he stayed in the game and converted most of those blown saves into wins. He had a lot of games where he came in in the top of the ninth, let the tying run score but stayed in to win the game in 10 or 11 innings.

The batting average against him last year was .182, the best of any National League closer, and he held both left-handers and right-handers below .200. With runners in scoring position the batting average against him was .108, and for the first batter he faced it was .145. He is wild as hell, of course, walking 62 men and hitting eight more. Eight hit batsmen is a lot for a pitcher pitching 250 innings; for a reliever, it's amazing. John Burkett was the only National Leaguer to hit more, ten, and he pitched 207 innings. Williams also can't hold a baserunner, which is a common problem for a power pitcher.

5. Alejandro Pena, Atlanta

Did a tremendous job for the Braves the last six weeks, as I'm sure you know. To be honest, I never did understand why he wasn't a closer for the Dodgers, who had Jay Howell when he was there, or the Mets, who had John Franco. I've always thought he was a better pitcher than Howell or Franco, but they had that magic designation, "closer", and he didn't.

6. John Franco, New York

The batting average against him last year was .271, way too high for a closer, but he did get the first batter out 80% of the time, and so had 30 saves with only 5 blown saves, a good ratio. He's always pitched poorly late in the season, and did it again last year, posting a 5.40 ERA after September 1.

7. Dave Righetti/ Jeff Brantley/ Billy Swift, San Francisco

Of the three, Swift has by far the best credentials to be a closer. Actually, if three closers were better than one of the same ability, the Giants would be in great shape, because all three of these guys are reasonably well qualified to do the job. Righetti was 24 for 29 in save chances (83%), Brantley 15 for 19 (79%) and Swift 17 for 18 (94%). Swift also had the best ERA of the group (1.99) and the lowest opposition batting average (.224), pitched more games and innings than the other two and also pitched well in 1990.

In fact, my opinion is that Bill Swift at this point of his career is a more valuable property than Kevin Mitchell, for whom he was traded. The problem is that three relief aces *aren't* better than one, and one of these guys is going to have to try to patch a two-legged starting rotation.

8. Paul Assenmacher, Chicago

The Cubs don't know for sure who their relief ace is, not because Assenmacher can't do the job but because they have their head up their ass, and persist in thinking that Dave Smith maybe will make a comeback. Assenmacher's credentials are quite good. Last year he had the terrific strikeout/walk ratio (117 to 25 in 103 innings) and good opposition batting average (.223) that normally marks a closer.

He compiled these averages despite

a) pitching in Wrigley Field, and

b) pitching far *more* than a modern reliever is normally required to pitch.

Modern relievers have super per-inning ratios in large part because they're only asked to pitch three innings a week, and so can put everything they have into the effort. Assenmacher pitched 75 times, 103 innings, but had similar ratios.

9. Roger McDowell, Los Angeles

Failed to hold the closer job for the Mets or Phillies, but apparently will get a third chance with the Dodgers. He's a ground ball pitcher, so he needs his infield defense to be effective. The Dodgers' double play combination is Juan Samuel and Jose Offerman.

10. Randy Myers, San Diego

Returns to the closer role which he shared with McDowell in New York, later with Dibble in Cincinnati. He was an effective closer at one time. I don't see any reason he won't be again.

11. Al Osuna or Curt Schilling, Houston

Neither Osuna nor Schilling has credentials to be a closer, but then, neither does anybody else before he gets the chance. Osuna had a poor control record but did limit hitters to a .201 batting average. He saved only 12 games in 21 chances (57%), and the percentage *dropped* as the season went on.

12. Jeff Fassero, Mel Rojas or John Wetteland, Montreal

Fassero pitched well last year but is a 29-year-old minor league veteran with an 88-MPH fastball, so he isn't regarded as regular closer material. Rojas is younger and has a 94-MPH fastball, but has been a starter in the minors, and didn't seize the job last year when he had the chance. Wetteland has a good fastball and split-fingered fastball, and was once regarded as a coming star in Los Angeles, but has been struggling for three years. Let's face it; we have no idea who is going to be the closer in Montreal. They have several other candidates.

PART THREE

THE STATS

JIM ABBOTT

CALIFORNIA STARTING PITCHER 24 Years Old
18-11 2.89 ERA

Opponents Batting Average: .244
Offensive Support: 4.70 Runs Per Nine Innings
Double Play Support: .78 GDP Per Nine Innings

First Pitch is Hit: 16%
Gets Ahead of the Hitter: 53%
Gets Behind the Hitter: 47%
Gets Leadoff Man Out: 71%

1991 On Base Pct Allowed: .302
Slugging Percentage: .336
Stolen Bases Allowed: 12 Caught Stealing: 14

Pitches Left	AB	H	2B	3B	HR	RBI	BB	SO	AVG
Vs. RHB	767	179	26	3	11	57	64	133	.233
Vs. LHB	142	43	9	0	3	18	9	25	.303

	G	IP	W-L	Pct	H	SO	BB	ERA
At Home	17	129	8-7		109	78	35	2.57
On the Road	17	114	10-4		113	80	38	3.25
1991 Season	34	243	18-11	.621	222	158	73	2.89
Life 2.6 Years	37	245	15-14	.519	254	146	84	3.72

ROBERTO ALOMAR

TORONTO SECOND BASE 24 Years Old

Runs Created: 107
Offensive Winning Percentage: .687
Batting Average: .295 Secondary Average: .314

Most Often Bats: 2nd
Swings at First Pitch: 28%
Gets Ahead of the Pitcher: 52%
Hits Behind the Pitcher: 48%

1991 On Base Percentage: .354 Career: .343
1991 Slugging Percentage: .436 Career: .394
Batting Avg with Men in Scoring Position: .280

Switch Hitter		AB	R	H	2B	3B	HR	RBI	BB	SO	SB	AVG
Vs. RHP		446	60	141	29	8	4	42	46	51	42	.316
Vs. LHP		191	28	47	12	3	5	27	11	35	11	.246
At Home	80	313	47	93	23	8	6	40	35	36	28	.297
On the Road	81	324	41	95	18	3	3	29	22	50	25	.293
1991 Season	161	637	88	188	41	11	9	69	57	86	53	.295
Life 3.8 Years		636	89	182	32	6	8	60	55	84	38	.286

LUIS AQUINO

KANSAS CITY RELIEF PITCHER 27 Years Old
8-4 3.44 ERA 3 SAVES

Save Opportunities: 4 Blown Saves: 1 Holds: 1
Inherited Runners who Scored: 44%
Opponents Batting Average: .253
Double Play Support: .52 GDP Per Nine Innings

First Pitch is Hit: 13%
Gets Ahead of the Hitter: 49%
Gets Behind the Hitter: 51%
Gets First Batter Out: 70%

1991 On Base Pct Allowed: .308
Slugging Percentage: .374
Stolen Bases Allowed: 10 Caught Stealing: 6

Pitches Right	AB	H	2B	3B	HR	RBI	BB	SO	AVG
Vs. RHB	312	76	17	1	8	35	21	38	.244
Vs. LHB	289	76	16	4	2	32	26	42	.263

	G	IP	W-L	Pct	SO	BB	ERA	Sv
1991 Season	38	157	8-4	.667	80	47	3.44	3
Life 2.0 Years	53	204	10-7	.588	96	65	3.45	2

RICK AGUILERA

MINNESOTA RELIEF PITCHER 30 Years Old
4-5 2.35 ERA 42 SAVES

Save Opportunities: 51 Blown Saves: 9 Holds: 0
Inherited Runners who Scored: 24%
Opponents Batting Average: .183
Double Play Support: .78 GDP Per Nine Innings

First Pitch is Hit: 13%
Gets Ahead of the Hitter: 54%
Gets Behind the Hitter: 46%
Gets First Batter Out: 76%

1991 On Base Pct Allowed: .274
Slugging Percentage: .275
Stolen Bases Allowed: 7 Caught Stealing: 0

Pitches Right	AB	H	2B	3B	HR	RBI	BB	SO	AVG
Vs. RHB	104	19	5	1	1	13	11	25	.183
Vs. LHB	136	25	4	1	2	14	19	36	.184

	G	IP	W-L	Pct	SO	BB	ERA	Sv
1991 Season	63	69	4-5	.444	61	30	2.35	42
Life 4.2 Years	58	161	12-9	.551	125	48	3.33	19

KEVIN APPIER

KANSAS CITY STARTING PITCHER 24 Years Old
13-10 3.42 ERA

Opponents Batting Average: .255
Offensive Support: 4.72 Runs Per Nine Innings
Double Play Support: .52 GDP Per Nine Innings

First Pitch is Hit: 12%
Gets Ahead of the Hitter: 51%
Gets Behind the Hitter: 49%
Gets Leadoff Man Out: 73%

1991 On Base Pct Allowed: .307
Slugging Percentage: .357
Stolen Bases Allowed: 10 Caught Stealing: 8

Pitches Right	AB	H	2B	3B	HR	RBI	BB	SO	AVG
Vs. RHB	400	97	16	0	5	38	24	97	.243
Vs. LHB	403	108	25	1	8	41	37	61	.268

	G	IP	W-L	Pct	H	SO	BB	ERA
At Home	15	97	5-5		83	74	28	2.79
On the Road	19	111	8-5		122	84	33	3.97
1991 Season	34	208	13-10	.565	205	158	61	3.42
Life 1.8 Years	40	233	15-12	.542	234	165	71	3.43

JACK ARMSTRONG

CINCINNATI STARTING PITCHER 27 Years Old
7-13 5.48 ERA

Opponents Batting Average: .293
Offensive Support: 4.83 Runs Per Nine Innings
Double Play Support: .45 GDP Per Nine Innings

First Pitch is Hit: 16%
Gets Ahead of the Hitter: 49%
Gets Behind the Hitter: 51%
Gets Leadoff Man Out: 68%

1991 On Base Pct Allowed: .354
Slugging Percentage: .491
Stolen Bases Allowed: 12 Caught Stealing: 8

Pitches Right	AB	H	2B	3B	HR	RBI	BB	SO	AVG
Vs. RHB	243	75	11	0	12	36	19	58	.309
Vs. LHB	297	83	13	4	13	48	35	35	.279

	G	IP	W-L	Pct	H	SO	BB	ERA
At Home	12	66	4-8		74	44	30	6.38
On the Road	15	73	3-5		84	49	24	4.66
1991 Season	27	140	7-13	.350	158	93	54	5.48
Life 2.0 Years	39	203	12-16	.439	202	133	84	4.61

PAUL ASSENMACHER

CHICAGO RELIEF PITCHER 31 Years Old

7-8 3.24 ERA 15 SAVES

Save Opportunities: 24 Blown Saves: 9 Holds: 14
Inherited Runners who Scored: 41%
Opponents Batting Average: .223
Double Play Support: .26 GDP Per Nine Innings

First Pitch is Hit: 13%
Gets Ahead of the Hitter: 55%
Gets Behind the Hitter: 45%
Gets First Batter Out: 71%

1991 On Base Pct Allowed: .284
Slugging Percentage: .357
Stolen Bases Allowed: 8 Caught Stealing: 5

Pitches Left	AB	H	2B	3B	HR	RBI	BB	SO	AVG
Vs. RHB	247	61	7	3	9	33	21	68	.247
Vs. LHB	134	24	6	1	1	14	10	49	.179

	G	IP	W-L	Pct	SO	BB	ERA	Sv
1991 Season	75	103	7-8	.467	117	31	3.24	15
Life 5.3 Years	74	92	6-5	.569	87	34	3.34	7

STEVE AVERY

ATLANTA STARTING PITCHER 22 Years Old

18-8 3.38 ERA

Opponents Batting Average: .240
Offensive Support: 5.39 Runs Per Nine Innings
Double Play Support: .68 GDP Per Nine Innings

First Pitch is Hit: 15%
Gets Ahead of the Hitter: 52%
Gets Behind the Hitter: 48%
Gets Leadoff Man Out: 70%

1991 On Base Pct Allowed: .299
Slugging Percentage: .372
Stolen Bases Allowed: 21 Caught Stealing: 11

Pitches Left	AB	H	2B	3B	HR	RBI	BB	SO	AVG
Vs. RHB	624	159	29	2	18	70	53	104	.255
Vs. LHB	164	30	4	2	3	10	12	33	.183

	G	IP	W-L	Pct	H	SO	BB	ERA
At Home	18	106	9-5		100	66	33	3.75
On the Road	17	105	9-3		89	71	32	3.01
1991 Season	35	210	18-8	.692	189	137	65	3.38
Life 1.5 Years	37	206	14-13	.525	207	141	73	4.10

JEFF BAGWELL

HOUSTON FIRST BASE 24 Years Old

Runs Created: 98
Offensive Winning Percentage: .710
Batting Average: .294 Secondary Average: .291

Most Often Bats: 3rd
Swings at First Pitch: 32%
Gets Ahead of the Pitcher: 47%
Hits Behind the Pitcher: 53%

1991 On Base Percentage: .387 Career: .387
1991 Slugging Percentage: .437 Career: .437
Batting Avg with Men in Scoring Position: .301

Bats Right-Handed		AB	R	H	2B	3B	HR	RBI	BB	SO	SB	AVG
Vs. RHP		348	48	97	16	4	8	45	42	79	1	.279
Vs. LHP		206	31	66	10	0	7	37	33	37	6	.320
At Home	77	274	44	81	15	2	6	35	36	52	4	.296
On the Road	79	280	35	82	11	2	9	47	39	64	3	.293
1991 Season	156	554	79	163	26	4	15	82	75	116	7	.294
Life 1.0 Years		575	82	169	27	4	16	85	78	120	7	.294

DON AUGUST

MILWAUKEE STARTING PITCHER 28 Years Old

9-8 5.47 ERA

Opponents Batting Average: .301
Offensive Support: 6.64 Runs Per Nine Innings
Double Play Support: 1.04 GDP Per Nine Innings

First Pitch is Hit: 14%
Gets Ahead of the Hitter: 47%
Gets Behind the Hitter: 53%
Gets Leadoff Man Out: 63%

1991 On Base Pct Allowed: .358
Slugging Percentage: .450
Stolen Bases Allowed: 18 Caught Stealing: 4

Pitches Right	AB	H	2B	3B	HR	RBI	BB	SO	AVG
Vs. RHB	249	70	10	0	8	29	20	42	.281
Vs. LHB	302	96	12	3	10	50	27	20	.318

	G	IP	W-L	Pct	H	SO	BB	ERA
At Home	14	81	8-5		78	30	20	4.13
On the Road	14	58	1-3		88	32	27	7.34
1991 Season	28	138	9-8	.529	166	62	47	5.47
Life 2.1 Years	41	206	16-14	.531	230	85	74	4.64

CARLOS BAERGA

CLEVELAND THIRD BASE 23 Years Old

Runs Created: 82
Offensive Winning Percentage: .595
Batting Average: .288 Secondary Average: .196

Most Often Bats: 3rd
Swings at First Pitch: 20%
Gets Ahead of the Pitcher: 54%
Hits Behind the Pitcher: 46%

1991 On Base Percentage: .346 Career: .330
1991 Slugging Percentage: .398 Career: .397
Batting Avg with Men in Scoring Position: .280

Switch Hitter		AB	R	H	2B	3B	HR	RBI	BB	SO	SB	AVG
Vs. RHP		432	53	118	20	2	9	49	40	60	3	.273
Vs. LHP		161	27	53	8	0	2	20	8	14	0	.329
At Home	81	299	33	87	13	2	2	32	20	31	1	.291
On the Road	77	294	47	84	15	0	9	37	28	43	2	.286
1991 Season	158	593	80	171	28	2	11	69	48	74	3	.288
Life 1.6 Years		551	77	153	27	2	11	71	39	80	2	.278

HAROLD BAINES

OAKLAND DESIGNATED HITTER 33 Years Old

Runs Created: 89
Offensive Winning Percentage: .662
Batting Average: .295 Secondary Average: .326

Most Often Bats: 4th
Swings at First Pitch: 37%
Gets Ahead of the Pitcher: 50%
Hits Behind the Pitcher: 50%

1991 On Base Percentage: .383 Career: .347
1991 Slugging Percentage: .473 Career: .462
Batting Avg with Men in Scoring Position: .278

Bats Left-Handed		AB	R	H	2B	3B	HR	RBI	BB	SO	SB	AVG
Vs. RHP		405	67	119	20	1	16	72	67	53	0	.294
Vs. LHP		83	9	25	5	0	4	18	5	14	0	.301
At Home	69	227	34	60	11	0	11	52	36	38	0	.264
On the Road	72	261	42	84	14	1	9	38	36	29	0	.322
1991 Season	141	488	76	144	25	1	20	90	72	67	0	.295
Life 10.5 Years		596	77	172	30	4	21	94	56	91	3	.289

JESSE BARFIELD

NEW YORK RIGHT FIELD 32 Years Old

Runs Created: 38
Offensive Winning Percentage: .489
Batting Average: .225 Secondary Average: .352

Most Often Bats: 6th
Swings at First Pitch: 31%
Gets Ahead of the Pitcher: 47%
Hits Behind the Pitcher: 53%

1991 On Base Percentage: .312 Career: .338
1991 Slugging Percentage: .447 Career: .471
Batting Avg with Men in Scoring Position: .253

Bats Right-Handed		AB	R	H	2B	3B	HR	RBI	BB	SO	SB	AVG
Vs. RHP		176	17	30	8	0	8	24	19	58	0	.170
Vs. LHP		108	20	34	4	0	9	24	17	22	1	.315
At Home	42	130	21	30	7	0	11	30	20	31	1	.231
On the Road	42	154	16	34	5	0	6	18	16	49	0	.221
1991 Season	84	284	37	64	12	0	17	48	36	80	1	.225
Life 8.6 Years		540	82	140	25	3	28	82	63	140	8	.259

KEVIN BASS

SAN FRANCISCO RIGHT FIELD 33 Years Old

Runs Created: 39
Offensive Winning Percentage: .420
Batting Average: .233 Secondary Average: .252

Most Often Bats: 6th
Swings at First Pitch: 23%
Gets Ahead of the Pitcher: 52%
Hits Behind the Pitcher: 48%

1991 On Base Percentage: .307 Career: .320
1991 Slugging Percentage: .366 Career: .413
Batting Avg with Men in Scoring Position: .198

Switch Hitter		AB	R	H	2B	3B	HR	RBI	BB	SO	SB	AVG
Vs. RHP		248	24	57	5	4	4	25	31	41	5	.230
Vs. LHP		113	19	27	5	0	6	15	5	15	2	.239
At Home	63	167	21	35	2	2	5	17	21	35	4	.210
On the Road	61	194	22	49	8	2	5	23	15	21	3	.253
1991 Season	124	361	43	84	10	4	10	40	36	56	7	.233
Life 7.0 Years		531	67	143	26	5	14	67	37	71	17	.270

STAN BELINDA

PITTSBURGH RELIEF PITCHER 25 Years Old
7-5 3.45 ERA 16 SAVES

Save Opportunities: 20 Blown Saves: 4 Holds: 6
Inherited Runners who Scored: 34%
Opponents Batting Average: .184
Double Play Support: .23 GDP Per Nine Innings

First Pitch is Hit: 10%
Gets Ahead of the Hitter: 50%
Gets Behind the Hitter: 50%
Gets First Batter Out: 73%

1991 On Base Pct Allowed: .283
Slugging Percentage: .327
Stolen Bases Allowed: 13 Caught Stealing: 3

Pitches Right	AB	H	2B	3B	HR	RBI	BB	SO	AVG
Vs. RHB	149	25	2	2	6	26	21	46	.168
Vs. LHB	123	25	3	0	4	12	14	25	.203

	G	IP	W-L	Pct	SO	BB	ERA	Sv
1991 Season	60	78	7-5	.583	71	35	3.45	16
Life 1.7 Years	74	88	6-6	.500	82	40	3.67	14

BRIAN BARNES

MONTREAL STARTING PITCHER 25 Years Old
5-8 4.22 ERA

Opponents Batting Average: .233
Offensive Support: 3.71 Runs Per Nine Innings
Double Play Support: .56 GDP Per Nine Innings

First Pitch is Hit: 11%
Gets Ahead of the Hitter: 40%
Gets Behind the Hitter: 60%
Gets Leadoff Man Out: 67%

1991 On Base Pct Allowed: .333
Slugging Percentage: .371
Stolen Bases Allowed: 20 Caught Stealing: 8

Pitches Left	AB	H	2B	3B	HR	RBI	BB	SO	AVG
Vs. RHB	476	110	19	2	13	57	62	98	.231
Vs. LHB	104	25	5	2	3	13	22	19	.240

	G	IP	W-L	Pct	H	SO	BB	ERA
At Home	12	68	1-5		57	59	32	4.24
On the Road	16	92	4-3		78	58	52	4.21
1991 Season	28	160	5-8	.385	135	117	84	4.22
Life 0.9 Years	38	221	7-11	.400	188	164	107	4.02

TIM BELCHER

LOS ANGELES STARTING PITCHER 30 Years Old
10-9 2.62 ERA

Opponents Batting Average: .240
Offensive Support: 3.44 Runs Per Nine Innings
Double Play Support: .64 GDP Per Nine Innings

First Pitch is Hit: 13%
Gets Ahead of the Hitter: 52%
Gets Behind the Hitter: 48%
Gets Leadoff Man Out: 69%

1991 On Base Pct Allowed: .306
Slugging Percentage: .318
Stolen Bases Allowed: 17 Caught Stealing: 10

Pitches Right	AB	H	2B	3B	HR	RBI	BB	SO	AVG
Vs. RHB	344	67	10	2	6	33	29	74	.195
Vs. LHB	445	122	16	1	4	33	46	82	.274

	G	IP	W-L	Pct	H	SO	BB	ERA
At Home	17	121	7-4		111	102	34	2.67
On the Road	16	88	3-5		78	54	41	2.56
1991 Season	33	209	10-9	.526	189	156	75	2.62
Life 3.5 Years	40	232	14-11	.568	196	182	75	2.99

GEORGE BELL

CHICAGO LEFT FIELD 32 Years Old

Runs Created: 81
Offensive Winning Percentage: .571
Batting Average: .285 Secondary Average: .244

Most Often Bats: 5th
Swings at First Pitch: 22%
Gets Ahead of the Pitcher: 51%
Hits Behind the Pitcher: 49%

1991 On Base Percentage: .323 Career: .325
1991 Slugging Percentage: .468 Career: .484
Batting Avg with Men in Scoring Position: .235

Bats Right-Handed		AB	R	H	2B	3B	HR	RBI	BB	SO	SB	AVG
Vs. RHP		350	30	99	19	0	10	52	15	43	2	.283
Vs. LHP		208	33	60	8	0	15	34	17	19	0	.288
At Home	78	288	29	77	15	0	9	45	11	30	1	.267
On the Road	71	270	34	82	12	0	16	41	21	32	1	.304
1991 Season	149	558	63	159	27	0	25	86	32	62	2	.285
Life 8.2 Years		619	86	177	32	4	28	101	35	76	7	.286

JAY BELL

PITTSBURGH SHORTSTOP 26 Years Old

Runs Created: 85
Offensive Winning Percentage: .530
Batting Average: .270 Secondary Average: .260

Most Often Bats: 2nd
Swings at First Pitch: 29%
Gets Ahead of the Pitcher: 49%
Hits Behind the Pitcher: 51%

1991 On Base Percentage: .330 Career: .318
1991 Slugging Percentage: .428 Career: .375
Batting Avg with Men in Scoring Position: .286

Bats Right-Handed		AB	R	H	2B	3B	HR	RBI	BB	SO	SB	AVG
Vs. RHP		414	57	108	19	3	10	39	26	81	9	.261
Vs. LHP		194	39	56	13	5	6	28	26	18	1	.289
At Home	81	303	51	85	19	5	7	33	23	49	4	.281
On the Road	76	305	45	79	13	3	9	34	29	50	6	.259
1991 Season	157	608	96	164	32	8	16	67	52	99	10	.270
Life 3.1 Years		576	83	146	28	6	10	58	53	109	10	.254

RAFAEL BELLIARD

ATLANTA SHORTSTOP 30 Years Old

Runs Created: 31
Offensive Winning Percentage: .330
Batting Average: .249 Secondary Average: .108

Most Often Bats: 8th
Swings at First Pitch: 43%
Gets Ahead of the Pitcher: 44%
Hits Behind the Pitcher: 56%

1991 On Base Percentage: .296 Career: .286
1991 Slugging Percentage: .286 Career: .261
Batting Avg with Men in Scoring Position: .269

Bats Right-Handed		AB	R	H	2B	3B	HR	RBI	BB	SO	SB	AVG
Vs. RHP		258	19	65	7	2	0	23	16	49	1	.252
Vs. LHP		95	17	23	2	0	0	4	6	14	2	.242
At Home	77	173	20	44	6	2	0	15	10	26	0	.254
On the Road	72	180	16	44	3	0	0	12	12	37	3	.244
1991 Season	149	353	36	88	9	2	0	27	22	63	3	.249
Life 3.9 Years		359	39	81	6	3	0	25	27	59	10	.226

TODD BENZINGER

KANSAS CITY FIRST BASE 29 Years Old

Runs Created: 44
Offensive Winning Percentage: .400
Batting Average: .262 Secondary Average: .163

Most Often Bats: 5th
Swings at First Pitch: 34%
Gets Ahead of the Pitcher: 52%
Hits Behind the Pitcher: 48%

1991 On Base Percentage: .310 Career: .302
1991 Slugging Percentage: .351 Career: .383
Batting Avg with Men in Scoring Position: .267

Switch Hitter		AB	R	H	2B	3B	HR	RBI	BB	SO	SB	AVG
Vs. RHP		273	26	73	12	5	2	35	21	53	4	.267
Vs. LHP		143	10	36	6	0	1	16	6	13	0	.252
At Home	66	216	21	58	13	3	2	30	10	26	3	.269
On the Road	63	200	15	51	5	2	1	21	17	40	1	.255
1991 Season	129	416	36	109	18	5	3	51	27	66	4	.262
Life 3.7 Years		552	63	141	27	3	12	77	36	101	5	.255

ALBERT BELLE

CLEVELAND LEFT FIELD 25 Years Old

Runs Created: 71
Offensive Winning Percentage: .623
Batting Average: .282 Secondary Average: .319

Most Often Bats: 4th
Swings at First Pitch: 40%
Gets Ahead of the Pitcher: 48%
Hits Behind the Pitcher: 52%

1991 On Base Percentage: .323 Career: .302
1991 Slugging Percentage: .540 Career: .487
Batting Avg with Men in Scoring Position: .310

Bats Right-Handed		AB	R	H	2B	3B	HR	RBI	BB	SO	SB	AVG
Vs. RHP		329	43	92	20	1	20	61	20	72	1	.280
Vs. LHP		132	17	38	11	1	8	34	5	27	2	.288
At Home	63	236	23	60	15	0	8	35	11	49	2	.254
On the Road	60	225	37	70	16	2	20	60	14	50	1	.311
1991 Season	123	461	60	130	31	2	28	95	25	99	3	.282
Life 1.2 Years		586	69	153	33	5	30	113	32	134	4	.261

ANDY BENES

SAN DIEGO STARTING PITCHER 24 Years Old
15-11 3.03 ERA

Opponents Batting Average: .232
Offensive Support: 3.31 Runs Per Nine Innings
Double Play Support: .44 GDP Per Nine Innings

First Pitch is Hit: 13%
Gets Ahead of the Hitter: 53%
Gets Behind the Hitter: 47%
Gets Leadoff Man Out: 72%

1991 On Base Pct Allowed: .285
Slugging Percentage: .358
Stolen Bases Allowed: 10 Caught Stealing: 11

Pitches Right	AB	H	2B	3B	HR	RBI	BB	SO	AVG
Vs. RHB	370	87	13	2	10	32	27	74	.235
Vs. LHB	466	107	11	4	13	38	32	93	.230

	G	IP	W-L	Pct	H	SO	BB	ERA
At Home	17	111	6-5		117	94	35	3.73
On the Road	16	112	9-6		77	73	24	2.33
1991 Season	33	223	15-11	.577	194	167	59	3.03
Life 2.0 Years	37	239	15-12	.554	210	185	79	3.32

JUAN BERENGUER

ATLANTA RELIEF PITCHER 37 Years Old
0-3 2.24 ERA 17 SAVES

Save Opportunities: 18 Blown Saves: 1 Holds: 4
Inherited Runners who Scored: 4%
Opponents Batting Average: .189
Double Play Support: .42 GDP Per Nine Innings

First Pitch is Hit: 14%
Gets Ahead of the Hitter: 45%
Gets Behind the Hitter: 55%
Gets First Batter Out: 80%

1991 On Base Pct Allowed: .261
Slugging Percentage: .303
Stolen Bases Allowed: 3 Caught Stealing: 1

Pitches Right	AB	H	2B	3B	HR	RBI	BB	SO	AVG
Vs. RHB	122	22	4	2	4	14	5	31	.180
Vs. LHB	106	21	3	0	1	2	15	22	.198

	G	IP	W-L	Pct	SO	BB	ERA	Sv
1991 Season	49	64	0-3	.000	53	20	2.24	17
Life 7.2 Years	61	156	9-8	.525	128	78	3.79	4

DANTE BICHETTE

MILWAUKEE RIGHT FIELD 28 Years Old

Runs Created: 45
Offensive Winning Percentage: .331
Batting Average: .238 Secondary Average: .236

Most Often Bats: 6th
Swings at First Pitch: 33%
Gets Ahead of the Pitcher: 46%
Hits Behind the Pitcher: 54%

1991 On Base Percentage: .272 Career: .273
1991 Slugging Percentage: .393 Career: .394
Batting Avg with Men in Scoring Position: .218

Bats Right-Handed		AB	R	H	2B	3B	HR	RBI	BB	SO	SB	AVG
Vs. RHP		291	33	67	13	1	9	41	11	70	9	.230
Vs. LHP		154	20	39	5	2	6	18	11	37	5	.253
At Home	66	213	26	53	10	2	6	30	16	46	8	.249
On the Road	68	232	27	53	8	1	9	29	6	61	6	.228
1991 Season	134	445	53	106	18	3	15	59	22	107	14	.238
Life 1.9 Years		508	56	123	22	2	17	70	23	113	11	.241

CRAIG BIGGIO

HOUSTON CATCHER 26 Years Old

Runs Created: 79
Offensive Winning Percentage: .630
Batting Average: .295 Secondary Average: .211

Most Often Bats: 2nd
Swings at First Pitch: 32%
Gets Ahead of the Pitcher: 46%
Hits Behind the Pitcher: 54%

1991 On Base Percentage: .358 Career: .339
1991 Slugging Percentage: .374 Career: .371
Batting Avg with Men in Scoring Position: .280

Bats Right-Handed		AB	R	H	2B	3B	HR	RBI	BB	SO	SB	AVG
Vs. RHP		360	48	110	13	2	3	35	32	52	7	.306
Vs. LHP		186	31	51	10	2	1	11	21	19	12	.274
At Home	73	277	39	95	20	3	0	24	27	39	14	.343
On the Road	76	269	40	66	3	1	4	22	26	32	5	.245
1991 Season	149	546	79	161	23	4	4	46	53	71	19	.295
Life 3.0 Years		559	70	152	25	3	8	51	54	82	24	.272

JEFF BLAUSER

ATLANTA SHORTSTOP 26 Years Old

Runs Created: 54
Offensive Winning Percentage: .596
Batting Average: .259 Secondary Average: .318

Most Often Bats: 6th
Swings at First Pitch: 24%
Gets Ahead of the Pitcher: 54%
Hits Behind the Pitcher: 46%

1991 On Base Percentage: .358 Career: .335
1991 Slugging Percentage: .409 Career: .403
Batting Avg with Men in Scoring Position: .316

Bats Right-Handed		AB	R	H	2B	3B	HR	RBI	BB	SO	SB	AVG
Vs. RHP		224	30	52	9	0	7	28	29	39	4	.232
Vs. LHP		128	19	39	5	3	4	26	25	20	1	.305
At Home	64	174	32	47	6	0	7	32	31	25	2	.270
On the Road	65	178	17	44	8	3	4	22	23	34	3	.247
1991 Season	129	352	49	91	14	3	11	54	54	59	5	.259
Life 2.8 Years		508	63	133	25	4	12	57	52	98	7	.262

MIKE BIELECKI

ATLANTA STARTING PITCHER 32 Years Old
13-11 4.46 ERA

Opponents Batting Average: .262
Offensive Support: 5.03 Runs Per Nine Innings
Double Play Support: .78 GDP Per Nine Innings

First Pitch is Hit: 13%
Gets Ahead of the Hitter: 43%
Gets Behind the Hitter: 57%
Gets Leadoff Man Out: 64%

1991 On Base Pct Allowed: .319
Slugging Percentage: .420
Stolen Bases Allowed: 17 Caught Stealing: 9

Pitches Right	AB	H	2B	3B	HR	RBI	BB	SO	AVG
Vs. RHB	308	76	15	6	8	41	20	38	.247
Vs. LHB	345	95	16	3	10	42	36	37	.275

	G	IP	W-L	Pct	H	SO	BB	ERA
At Home	19	95	8-7		101	35	21	4.74
On the Road	22	79	5-4		70	40	35	4.12
1991 Season	41	174	13-11	.542	171	75	56	4.46
Life 4.3 Years	43	197	12-11	.515	196	114	81	4.19

BUD BLACK

SAN FRANCISCO STARTING PITCHER 35 Years Old
12-16 3.99 ERA

Opponents Batting Average: .251
Offensive Support: 4.03 Runs Per Nine Innings
Double Play Support: .84 GDP Per Nine Innings

First Pitch is Hit: 17%
Gets Ahead of the Hitter: 51%
Gets Behind the Hitter: 49%
Gets Leadoff Man Out: 71%

1991 On Base Pct Allowed: .313
Slugging Percentage: .396
Stolen Bases Allowed: 14 Caught Stealing: 11

Pitches Left	AB	H	2B	3B	HR	RBI	BB	SO	AVG
Vs. RHB	625	153	26	5	19	65	56	84	.245
Vs. LHB	175	48	5	0	6	27	15	20	.274

	G	IP	W-L	Pct	H	SO	BB	ERA
At Home	16	112	8-7		92	48	31	2.81
On the Road	18	102	4-9		109	56	40	5.28
1991 Season	34	214	12-16	.429	201	104	71	3.99
Life 7.6 Years	44	220	12-13	.492	209	111	65	3.74

MIKE BODDICKER

KANSAS CITY STARTING PITCHER 34 Years Old
12-12 4.08 ERA

Opponents Batting Average: .272
Offensive Support: 4.48 Runs Per Nine Innings
Double Play Support: .90 GDP Per Nine Innings

First Pitch is Hit: 15%
Gets Ahead of the Hitter: 49%
Gets Behind the Hitter: 51%
Gets Leadoff Man Out: 62%

1991 On Base Pct Allowed: .340
Slugging Percentage: .408
Stolen Bases Allowed: 17 Caught Stealing: 10

Pitches Right	AB	H	2B	3B	HR	RBI	BB	SO	AVG
Vs. RHB	337	81	12	2	6	37	30	57	.240
Vs. LHB	355	107	29	5	7	43	29	22	.301

	G	IP	W-L	Pct	H	SO	BB	ERA
At Home	17	111	7-8		111	50	29	4.07
On the Road	13	70	5-4		77	29	30	4.11
1991 Season	30	181	12-12	.500	188	79	59	4.08
Life 8.0 Years	38	247	16-13	.549	238	157	83	3.70

WADE BOGGS

BOSTON THIRD BASE 34 Years Old

Runs Created: 107
Offensive Winning Percentage: .734
Batting Average: .332 Secondary Average: .293

Most Often Bats: 1st
Swings at First Pitch: 7%
Gets Ahead of the Pitcher: 51%
Hits Behind the Pitcher: 49%

1991 On Base Percentage: .421 Career: .435
1991 Slugging Percentage: .460 Career: .471
Batting Avg with Men in Scoring Position: .310

Bats Left-Handed	G	AB	R	H	2B	3B	HR	RBI	BB	SO	SB	AVG
Vs. RHP		380	66	137	36	0	6	38	72	22	1	.361
Vs. LHP		166	27	44	6	2	2	13	17	10	0	.265
At Home	69	252	50	98	28	2	6	32	47	12	0	.389
On the Road	75	294	43	83	14	0	2	19	42	20	1	.282
1991 Season	144	546	93	181	42	2	8	51	89	32	1	.332
Life 9.1 Years		623	110	215	44	5	9	70	102	48	2	.345

BOBBY BONILLA

PITTSBURGH RIGHT FIELD 29 Years Old

Runs Created: 114
Offensive Winning Percentage: .731
Batting Average: .302 Secondary Average: .350

Most Often Bats: 4th
Swings at First Pitch: 37%
Gets Ahead of the Pitcher: 55%
Hits Behind the Pitcher: 45%

1991 On Base Percentage: .391 Career: .357
1991 Slugging Percentage: .492 Career: .472
Batting Avg with Men in Scoring Position: .308

Switch Hitter	G	AB	R	H	2B	3B	HR	RBI	BB	SO	SB	AVG
Vs. RHP		345	64	108	31	5	4	53	65	44	0	.313
Vs. LHP		232	38	66	13	1	14	47	25	23	2	.284
At Home	82	285	52	88	25	3	9	51	49	29	1	.309
On the Road	75	292	50	86	19	3	9	49	41	38	1	.295
1991 Season	157	577	102	174	44	6	18	100	90	67	2	.302
Life 5.7 Years		581	90	164	35	7	20	93	70	88	5	.283

SHAWN BOSKIE

CHICAGO STARTING PITCHER 25 Years Old
4-9 5.23 ERA

Opponents Batting Average: .294
Offensive Support: 3.98 Runs Per Nine Innings
Double Play Support: .63 GDP Per Nine Innings

First Pitch is Hit: 14%
Gets Ahead of the Hitter: 50%
Gets Behind the Hitter: 50%
Gets Leadoff Man Out: 56%

1991 On Base Pct Allowed: .361
Slugging Percentage: .456
Stolen Bases Allowed: 4 Caught Stealing: 2

Pitches Right	AB	H	2B	3B	HR	RBI	BB	SO	AVG
Vs. RHB	220	57	11	0	4	22	16	35	.259
Vs. LHB	291	93	18	6	10	43	36	27	.320

	G	IP	W-L	Pct	H	SO	BB	ERA
At Home	17	65	3-5		85	27	34	5.43
On the Road	11	64	1-4		65	35	18	5.04
1991 Season	28	129	4-9	.308	150	62	52	5.23
Life 1.1 Years	41	215	9-14	.375	236	105	79	4.57

BARRY BONDS

PITTSBURGH LEFT FIELD 27 Years Old

Runs Created: 118
Offensive Winning Percentage: .778
Batting Average: .292 Secondary Average: .516

Most Often Bats: 5th
Swings at First Pitch: 27%
Gets Ahead of the Pitcher: 57%
Hits Behind the Pitcher: 43%

1991 On Base Percentage: .410 Career: .367
1991 Slugging Percentage: .514 Career: .485
Batting Avg with Men in Scoring Position: .345

Bats Left-Handed	G	AB	R	H	2B	3B	HR	RBI	BB	SO	SB	AVG
Vs. RHP		309	65	92	15	3	18	77	75	43	29	.298
Vs. LHP		201	30	57	13	2	7	39	32	30	14	.284
At Home	79	261	47	71	8	1	12	51	49	42	16	.272
On the Road	74	249	48	78	20	4	13	65	58	31	27	.313
1991 Season	153	510	95	149	28	5	25	116	107	73	43	.292
Life 5.4 Years		579	105	156	34	6	26	84	90	97	39	.269

CHRIS BOSIO

MILWAUKEE STARTING PITCHER 29 Years Old
14-10 3.25 ERA

Opponents Batting Average: .244
Offensive Support: 4.62 Runs Per Nine Innings
Double Play Support: .97 GDP Per Nine Innings

First Pitch is Hit: 16%
Gets Ahead of the Hitter: 48%
Gets Behind the Hitter: 52%
Gets Leadoff Man Out: 71%

1991 On Base Pct Allowed: .302
Slugging Percentage: .350
Stolen Bases Allowed: 9 Caught Stealing: 4

Pitches Right	AB	H	2B	3B	HR	RBI	BB	SO	AVG
Vs. RHB	348	82	12	1	9	33	28	64	.236
Vs. LHB	418	105	16	3	6	39	30	53	.251

	G	IP	W-L	Pct	H	SO	BB	ERA
At Home	16	96	5-6		105	58	26	3.83
On the Road	16	108	9-4		82	59	32	2.74
1991 Season	32	205	14-10	.583	187	117	58	3.25
Life 4.2 Years	43	230	12-13	.477	230	151	59	3.79

DARYL BOSTON

NEW YORK CENTER FIELD 29 Years Old

Runs Created: 38
Offensive Winning Percentage: .637
Batting Average: .275 Secondary Average: .318

Most Often Bats: 1st
Swings at First Pitch: 26%
Gets Ahead of the Pitcher: 55%
Hits Behind the Pitcher: 45%

1991 On Base Percentage: .350 Career: .308
1991 Slugging Percentage: .416 Career: .402
Batting Avg with Men in Scoring Position: .288

Bats Left-Handed	G	AB	R	H	2B	3B	HR	RBI	BB	SO	SB	AVG
Vs. RHP		224	30	64	13	4	3	20	30	31	13	.286
Vs. LHP		31	10	6	3	0	1	1	0	11	2	.194
At Home	69	135	20	33	11	2	2	13	19	26	10	.244
On the Road	68	120	20	37	5	2	2	8	11	16	5	.308
1991 Season	137	255	40	70	16	4	4	21	30	42	15	.275
Life 4.6 Years		425	61	106	22	4	12	41	36	72	18	.250

OIL CAN BOYD

TEXAS STARTING PITCHER 32 Years Old

8-15 4.59 ERA

Opponents Batting Average: .277
Offensive Support: 3.85 Runs Per Nine Innings
Double Play Support: .49 GDP Per Nine Innings

First Pitch is Hit: 15%
Gets Ahead of the Hitter: 51%
Gets Behind the Hitter: 49%
Gets Leadoff Man Out: 71%

1991 On Base Pct Allowed: .329
Slugging Percentage: .448
Stolen Bases Allowed: 14 Caught Stealing: 12

Pitches Right	AB	H	2B	3B	HR	RBI	BB	SO	AVG
Vs. RHB	341	99	19	3	16	52	25	59	.290
Vs. LHB	367	97	25	4	5	30	32	56	.264

	G	IP	W-L	Pct	H	SO	BB	ERA
At Home	16	100	5-5		92	69	27	3.23
On the Road	15	82	3-10		104	46	30	6.26
1991 Season	31	182	8-15	.348	196	115	57	4.59
Life 5.7 Years	38	244	14-14	.503	251	140	65	4.04

JEFF BRANTLEY

SAN FRANCISCO RELIEF PITCHER 28 Years Old

5-2 2.45 ERA 15 SAVES

Save Opportunities: 19 Blown Saves: 4 Holds: 12
Inherited Runners who Scored: 28%
Opponents Batting Average: .225
Double Play Support: .57 GDP Per Nine Innings

First Pitch is Hit: 11%
Gets Ahead of the Hitter: 50%
Gets Behind the Hitter: 50%
Gets First Batter Out: 73%

1991 On Base Pct Allowed: .332
Slugging Percentage: .338
Stolen Bases Allowed: 17 Caught Stealing: 2

Pitches Right	AB	H	2B	3B	HR	RBI	BB	SO	AVG
Vs. RHB	161	40	7	1	5	20	16	39	.248
Vs. LHB	185	38	6	0	3	16	36	42	.205

	G	IP	W-L	Pct	SO	BB	ERA	Sv
1991 Season	67	95	5-2	.714	81	52	2.45	15
Life 2.6 Years	73	116	7-3	.708	86	49	2.94	13

SID BREAM

ATLANTA FIRST BASE 31 Years Old

Runs Created: 33
Offensive Winning Percentage: .474
Batting Average: .253 Secondary Average: .264

Most Often Bats: 5th
Swings at First Pitch: 29%
Gets Ahead of the Pitcher: 54%
Hits Behind the Pitcher: 46%

1991 On Base Percentage: .313 Career: .333
1991 Slugging Percentage: .423 Career: .421
Batting Avg with Men in Scoring Position: .256

Bats Left-Handed		AB	R	H	2B	3B	HR	RBI	BB	SO	SB	AVG
Vs. RHP		225	29	61	12	0	10	38	25	22	0	.271
Vs. LHP		40	3	6	0	0	1	7	0	9	0	.150
At Home	42	115	11	31	5	0	3	21	8	15	0	.270
On the Road	49	150	21	36	7	0	8	24	17	16	0	.240
1991 Season	91	265	32	67	12	0	11	45	25	31	0	.253
Life 4.9 Years		486	57	127	30	2	14	71	54	70	8	.262

GEORGE BRETT

KANSAS CITY DESIGNATED HITTER 39 Years Old

Runs Created: 65
Offensive Winning Percentage: .481
Batting Average: .255 Secondary Average: .265

Most Often Bats: 3rd
Swings at First Pitch: 36%
Gets Ahead of the Pitcher: 54%
Hits Behind the Pitcher: 46%

1991 On Base Percentage: .327 Career: .375
1991 Slugging Percentage: .402 Career: .496
Batting Avg with Men in Scoring Position: .236

Bats Left-Handed		AB	R	H	2B	3B	HR	RBI	BB	SO	SB	AVG
Vs. RHP		338	61	90	28	1	8	43	38	47	1	.266
Vs. LHP		167	16	39	12	1	2	18	20	28	1	.234
At Home	62	243	32	60	19	2	3	27	30	33	2	.247
On the Road	69	262	45	69	21	0	7	34	28	42	0	.263
1991 Season	131	505	77	129	40	2	10	61	58	75	2	.255
Life 14.9 Years		618	98	191	40	9	20	98	69	52	13	.308

GREG BRILEY

SEATTLE LEFT FIELD 27 Years Old

Runs Created: 39
Offensive Winning Percentage: .400
Batting Average: .260 Secondary Average: .207

Most Often Bats: 7th
Swings at First Pitch: 23%
Gets Ahead of the Pitcher: 54%
Hits Behind the Pitcher: 46%

1991 On Base Percentage: .307 Career: .322
1991 Slugging Percentage: .336 Career: .380
Batting Avg with Men in Scoring Position: .243

Bats Left-Handed		AB	R	H	2B	3B	HR	RBI	BB	SO	SB	AVG
Vs. RHP		342	33	90	15	2	2	17	26	41	22	.263
Vs. LHP		39	6	9	2	1	0	9	1	10	1	.231
At Home	68	185	19	46	4	1	2	12	17	19	11	.249
On the Road	71	196	20	53	13	2	0	14	10	32	12	.270
1991 Season	139	381	39	99	17	3	2	26	27	51	23	.260
Life 2.4 Years		473	56	122	24	4	9	46	45	77	21	.258

HUBIE BROOKS

NEW YORK RIGHT FIELD 35 Years Old

Runs Created: 49
Offensive Winning Percentage: .573
Batting Average: .238 Secondary Average: .303

Most Often Bats: 6th
Swings at First Pitch: 20%
Gets Ahead of the Pitcher: 50%
Hits Behind the Pitcher: 50%

1991 On Base Percentage: .324 Career: .319
1991 Slugging Percentage: .409 Career: .409
Batting Avg with Men in Scoring Position: .210

Bats Right-Handed		AB	R	H	2B	3B	HR	RBI	BB	SO	SB	AVG
Vs. RHP		236	32	55	6	1	11	33	26	49	1	.233
Vs. LHP		121	16	30	5	0	5	17	18	13	2	.248
At Home	49	172	25	41	6	1	4	22	27	28	2	.238
On the Road	54	185	23	44	5	0	12	28	17	34	1	.238
1991 Season	103	357	48	85	11	1	16	50	44	62	3	.238
Life 9.0 Years		606	68	165	29	3	15	84	40	103	7	.272

KEVIN BROWN

TEXAS STARTING PITCHER 27 Years Old

9-12 4.40 ERA

Opponents Batting Average: .284
Offensive Support: 4.57 Runs Per Nine Innings
Double Play Support: 1.28 GDP Per Nine Innings

First Pitch is Hit: 15%
Gets Ahead of the Hitter: 49%
Gets Behind the Hitter: 51%
Gets Leadoff Man Out: 67%

1991 On Base Pct Allowed: .362
Slugging Percentage: .404
Stolen Bases Allowed: 5 Caught Stealing: 11

Pitches Right	AB	H	2B	3B	HR	RBI	BB	SO	AVG
Vs. RHB	411	121	18	2	9	48	43	45	.294
Vs. LHB	410	112	22	2	8	52	47	51	.273

	G	IP	W-L	Pct	H	SO	BB	ERA
At Home	17	111	4-5		124	45	45	4.14
On the Road	16	100	5-7		109	51	45	4.70
1991 Season	33	211	9-12	.429	233	96	90	4.40
Life 2.5 Years	37	245	14-13	.522	247	122	92	3.82

TOM BROWNING

CINCINNATI STARTING PITCHER 32 Years Old

14-14 4.18 ERA

Opponents Batting Average: .266
Offensive Support: 4.77 Runs Per Nine Innings
Double Play Support: .51 GDP Per Nine Innings

First Pitch is Hit: 16%
Gets Ahead of the Hitter: 53%
Gets Behind the Hitter: 47%
Gets Leadoff Man Out: 70%

1991 On Base Pct Allowed: .309
Slugging Percentage: .427
Stolen Bases Allowed: 21 Caught Stealing: 6

Pitches Left	AB	H	2B	3B	HR	RBI	BB	SO	AVG
Vs. RHB	694	198	26	3	28	92	37	74	.285
Vs. LHB	212	43	14	2	4	22	19	41	.203

	G	IP	W-L	Pct	H	SO	BB	ERA
At Home	18	121	10-4		104	57	33	3.50
On the Road	18	109	4-10		137	58	23	4.94
1991 Season	36	230	14-14	.500	241	115	56	4.18
Life 6.9 Years	37	242	15-11	.588	234	129	64	3.80

TOM BRUNANSKY

BOSTON RIGHT FIELD 31 Years Old

Runs Created: 56
Offensive Winning Percentage: .452
Batting Average: .229 Secondary Average: .270

Most Often Bats: 6th
Swings at First Pitch: 28%
Gets Ahead of the Pitcher: 55%
Hits Behind the Pitcher: 45%

1991 On Base Percentage: .303 Career: .328
1991 Slugging Percentage: .390 Career: .437
Batting Avg with Men in Scoring Position: .232

Bats Right-Handed	G	AB	R	H	2B	3B	HR	RBI	BB	SO	SB	AVG
Vs. RHP		317	35	69	17	0	11	48	33	60	1	.218
Vs. LHP		142	19	36	7	1	5	22	16	12	0	.254
At Home	73	234	32	60	16	0	10	39	27	32	1	.256
On the Road	69	225	22	45	8	1	6	31	22	40	0	.200
1991 Season	142	459	54	105	24	1	16	70	49	72	1	.229
Life 9.4 Years		576	76	142	27	3	26	83	70	104	7	.247

STEVE BUECHELE

PITTSBURGH THIRD BASE 30 Years Old

Runs Created: 74
Offensive Winning Percentage: .546
Batting Average: .262 Secondary Average: .270

Most Often Bats: 7th
Swings at First Pitch: 26%
Gets Ahead of the Pitcher: 48%
Hits Behind the Pitcher: 52%

1991 On Base Percentage: .331 Career: .309
1991 Slugging Percentage: .440 Career: .399
Batting Avg with Men in Scoring Position: .302

Bats Right-Handed	G	AB	R	H	2B	3B	HR	RBI	BB	SO	SB	AVG
Vs. RHP		399	53	100	15	2	13	59	27	74	0	.251
Vs. LHP		131	21	39	7	1	9	26	22	23	0	.298
At Home	74	251	33	69	14	1	9	32	24	42	0	.275
On the Road	78	279	41	70	8	2	13	53	25	55	0	.251
1991 Season	152	530	74	139	22	3	22	85	49	97	0	.262
Life 5.6 Years		500	63	121	21	2	17	63	45	97	2	.241

JAY BUHNER

SEATTLE RIGHT FIELD 27 Years Old

Runs Created: 68
Offensive Winning Percentage: .643
Batting Average: .244 Secondary Average: .384

Most Often Bats: 6th
Swings at First Pitch: 28%
Gets Ahead of the Pitcher: 53%
Hits Behind the Pitcher: 47%

1991 On Base Percentage: .337 Career: .331
1991 Slugging Percentage: .498 Career: .471
Batting Avg with Men in Scoring Position: .213

Bats Right-Handed	G	AB	R	H	2B	3B	HR	RBI	BB	SO	SB	AVG
Vs. RHP		260	44	64	9	2	18	51	25	89	0	.246
Vs. LHP		146	20	35	5	2	9	26	28	28	0	.240
At Home	72	212	33	45	9	2	14	41	31	71	0	.212
On the Road	65	194	31	54	5	2	13	36	22	46	0	.278
1991 Season	137	406	64	99	14	4	27	77	53	117	0	.244
Life 2.1 Years		506	69	125	27	3	27	87	57	154	2	.247

JOHN BURKETT

SAN FRANCISCO STARTING PITCHER 27 Years Old

12-11 4.18 ERA

Opponents Batting Average: .277
Offensive Support: 4.22 Runs Per Nine Innings
Double Play Support: .61 GDP Per Nine Innings

First Pitch is Hit: 18%
Gets Ahead of the Hitter: 51%
Gets Behind the Hitter: 49%
Gets Leadoff Man Out: 64%

1991 On Base Pct Allowed: .332
Slugging Percentage: .392
Stolen Bases Allowed: 17 Caught Stealing: 16

Pitches Right	AB	H	2B	3B	HR	RBI	BB	SO	AVG
Vs. RHB	337	86	6	1	5	39	21	59	.255
Vs. LHB	467	137	25	1	14	62	39	72	.293

	G	IP	W-L	Pct	H	SO	BB	ERA
At Home	17	109	6-6		102	72	25	3.54
On the Road	19	97	6-5		121	59	35	4.90
1991 Season	36	207	12-11	.522	223	131	60	4.18
Life 1.9 Years	39	223	14-10	.591	231	136	66	4.00

ELLIS BURKS

BOSTON — CENTER FIELD — 27 Years Old

Runs Created: 60
Offensive Winning Percentage: .484
Batting Average: .251 Secondary Average: .266

Most Often Bats: 6th
Swings at First Pitch: 21%
Gets Ahead of the Pitcher: 51%
Hits Behind the Pitcher: 49%

1991 On Base Percentage: .314 Career: .344
1991 Slugging Percentage: .422 Career: .461
Batting Avg with Men in Scoring Position: .227

Bats Right-Handed		AB	R	H	2B	3B	HR	RBI	BB	SO	SB	AVG
Vs. RHP		339	39	84	21	1	9	33	28	60	6	.248
Vs. LHP		135	17	35	12	2	5	23	11	21	0	.259
At Home	63	232	25	62	18	2	8	25	20	36	2	.267
On the Road	67	242	31	57	15	1	6	31	19	45	4	.236
1991 Season	130	474	56	119	33	3	14	56	39	81	6	.251
Life 4.0 Years		632	100	179	38	6	21	88	56	99	22	.283

GREG CADARET

NEW YORK — RELIEF PITCHER — 30 Years Old

8-6 3.62 ERA 3 SAVES

Save Opportunities: 7 Blown Saves: 4 Holds: 11
Inherited Runners who Scored: 32%
Opponents Batting Average: .246
Double Play Support: 1.04 GDP Per Nine Innings

First Pitch is Hit: 10%
Gets Ahead of the Hitter: 44%
Gets Behind the Hitter: 56%
Gets First Batter Out: 68%

1991 On Base Pct Allowed: .335
Slugging Percentage: .365
Stolen Bases Allowed: 11 Caught Stealing: 8

Pitches Left	AB	H	2B	3B	HR	RBI	BB	SO	AVG
Vs. RHB	329	81	14	4	8	43	47	80	.246
Vs. LHB	118	29	7	0	0	11	12	25	.246

	G	IP	W-L	Pct	SO	BB	ERA	Sv
1991 Season	68	122	8-6	.571	105	59	3.62	3
Life 3.8 Years	68	126	8-5	.604	95	64	3.83	2

KEN CAMINITI

HOUSTON — THIRD BASE — 29 Years Old

Runs Created: 65
Offensive Winning Percentage: .467
Batting Average: .253 Secondary Average: .218

Most Often Bats: 4th
Swings at First Pitch: 36%
Gets Ahead of the Pitcher: 50%
Hits Behind the Pitcher: 50%

1991 On Base Percentage: .312 Career: .304
1991 Slugging Percentage: .383 Career: .348
Batting Avg with Men in Scoring Position: .287

Switch Hitter		AB	R	H	2B	3B	HR	RBI	BB	SO	SB	AVG
Vs. RHP		342	38	73	16	1	4	36	34	58	3	.213
Vs. LHP		232	27	72	14	2	9	44	12	27	1	.310
At Home	79	289	39	73	18	2	9	48	22	52	3	.253
On the Road	73	285	26	72	12	1	4	32	24	33	1	.253
1991 Season	152	574	65	145	30	3	13	80	46	85	4	.253
Life 3.5 Years		576	59	142	26	3	9	68	47	98	5	.247

BRETT BUTLER

LOS ANGELES — CENTER FIELD — 35 Years Old

Runs Created: 93
Offensive Winning Percentage: .665
Batting Average: .296 Secondary Average: .285

Most Often Bats: 1st
Swings at First Pitch: 21%
Gets Ahead of the Pitcher: 51%
Hits Behind the Pitcher: 49%

1991 On Base Percentage: .401 Career: .372
1991 Slugging Percentage: .343 Career: .375
Batting Avg with Men in Scoring Position: .309

Bats Left-Handed		AB	R	H	2B	3B	HR	RBI	BB	SO	SB	AVG
Vs. RHP		359	64	110	11	2	2	24	59	38	25	.306
Vs. LHP		256	48	72	2	3	0	14	49	41	13	.281
At Home	80	295	59	92	7	2	2	22	59	29	17	.312
On the Road	81	320	53	90	6	3	0	16	49	50	21	.281
1991 Season	161	615	112	182	13	5	2	38	108	79	38	.296
Life 9.4 Years		598	102	171	22	9	4	43	81	65	42	.286

IVAN CALDERON

MONTREAL — LEFT FIELD — 30 Years Old

Runs Created: 85
Offensive Winning Percentage: .730
Batting Average: .300 Secondary Average: .360

Most Often Bats: 3rd
Swings at First Pitch: 43%
Gets Ahead of the Pitcher: 45%
Hits Behind the Pitcher: 55%

1991 On Base Percentage: .368 Career: .338
1991 Slugging Percentage: .481 Career: .456
Batting Avg with Men in Scoring Position: .306

Bats Right-Handed		AB	R	H	2B	3B	HR	RBI	BB	SO	SB	AVG
Vs. RHP		309	46	84	13	2	8	44	33	42	23	.272
Vs. LHP		161	23	57	9	1	11	31	20	22	8	.354
At Home	62	224	30	69	8	2	7	29	26	35	17	.308
On the Road	72	246	39	72	14	1	12	46	27	29	14	.293
1991 Season	134	470	69	141	22	3	19	75	53	64	31	.300
Life 4.9 Years		592	87	164	36	4	20	81	55	102	19	.278

CASEY CANDAELE

HOUSTON — SECOND BASE — 31 Years Old

Runs Created: 55
Offensive Winning Percentage: .519
Batting Average: .262 Secondary Average: .206

Most Often Bats: 8th
Swings at First Pitch: 30%
Gets Ahead of the Pitcher: 51%
Hits Behind the Pitcher: 49%

1991 On Base Percentage: .319 Career: .318
1991 Slugging Percentage: .362 Career: .346
Batting Avg with Men in Scoring Position: .304

Switch Hitter		AB	R	H	2B	3B	HR	RBI	BB	SO	SB	AVG
Vs. RHP		303	29	76	13	6	3	37	25	34	3	.251
Vs. LHP		158	15	45	7	1	1	13	15	15	6	.285
At Home	77	235	22	69	11	5	1	33	26	27	6	.294
On the Road	74	226	22	52	9	2	3	17	14	22	3	.230
1991 Season	151	461	44	121	20	7	4	50	40	49	9	.262
Life 3.1 Years		456	50	117	20	6	3	34	40	48	9	.258

TOM CANDIOTTI

TORONTO STARTING PITCHER 34 Years Old

13-13 2.65 ERA

Opponents Batting Average: .228
Offensive Support: 3.52 Runs Per Nine Innings
Double Play Support: .34 GDP Per Nine Innings

First Pitch is Hit: 9%
Gets Ahead of the Hitter: 43%
Gets Behind the Hitter: 57%
Gets Leadoff Man Out: 73%

1991 On Base Pct Allowed: .288
Slugging Percentage: .337
Stolen Bases Allowed: 26 Caught Stealing: 8

Pitches Right	AB	H	2B	3B	HR	RBI	BB	SO	AVG
Vs. RHB	438	93	25	2	6	27	38	104	.212
Vs. LHB	449	109	16	8	6	40	35	63	.243

	G	IP	W-L	Pct	H	SO	BB	ERA
At Home	16	110	6-6		103	84	35	3.11
On the Road	18	128	7-7		99	83	38	2.25
1991 Season	34	238	13-13	.500	202	167	73	2.65
Life 5.6 Years	38	249	15-14	.519	239	155	82	3.51

JOSE CANSECO

OAKLAND RIGHT FIELD 27 Years Old

Runs Created: 116
Offensive Winning Percentage: .685
Batting Average: .266 Secondary Average: .472

Most Often Bats: 3rd
Swings at First Pitch: 27%
Gets Ahead of the Pitcher: 48%
Hits Behind the Pitcher: 52%

1991 On Base Percentage: .359 Career: .348
1991 Slugging Percentage: .556 Career: .518
Batting Avg with Men in Scoring Position: .266

Bats Right-Handed	G	AB	R	H	2B	3B	HR	RBI	BB	SO	SB	AVG
Vs. RHP		436	88	118	23	1	36	101	54	111	15	.271
Vs. LHP		136	27	34	9	0	8	21	24	41	11	.250
At Home	76	267	56	72	15	0	16	46	39	80	18	.270
On the Road	78	305	59	80	17	1	28	76	39	72	8	.262
1991 Season	154	572	115	152	32	1	44	122	78	152	26	.266
Life 5.3 Years		611	103	165	30	2	40	123	70	165	23	.270

JOE CARTER

TORONTO RIGHT FIELD 32 Years Old

Runs Created: 107
Offensive Winning Percentage: .683
Batting Average: .273 Secondary Average: .339

Most Often Bats: 3rd
Swings at First Pitch: 34%
Gets Ahead of the Pitcher: 47%
Hits Behind the Pitcher: 53%

1991 On Base Percentage: .330 Career: .308
1991 Slugging Percentage: .503 Career: .463
Batting Avg with Men in Scoring Position: .268

Bats Right-Handed	G	AB	R	H	2B	3B	HR	RBI	BB	SO	SB	AVG
Vs. RHP		450	62	111	30	2	23	76	38	84	11	.247
Vs. LHP		188	27	63	12	1	10	32	11	28	9	.335
At Home	81	321	49	93	23	1	23	64	23	65	9	.290
On the Road	81	317	40	81	19	2	10	44	26	47	11	.256
1991 Season	162	638	89	174	42	3	33	108	49	112	20	.273
Life 7.3 Years		625	86	165	32	4	28	103	36	101	23	.263

FRANK CASTILLO

CHICAGO STARTING PITCHER 23 Years Old

6-7 4.35 ERA

Opponents Batting Average: .252
Offensive Support: 4.03 Runs Per Nine Innings
Double Play Support: .40 GDP Per Nine Innings

First Pitch is Hit: 13%
Gets Ahead of the Hitter: 54%
Gets Behind the Hitter: 46%
Gets Leadoff Man Out: 74%

1991 On Base Pct Allowed: .304
Slugging Percentage: .351
Stolen Bases Allowed: 7 Caught Stealing: 4

Pitches Right	AB	H	2B	3B	HR	RBI	BB	SO	AVG
Vs. RHB	152	30	12	0	0	16	6	24	.197
Vs. LHB	273	77	11	2	5	28	27	49	.282

	G	IP	W-L	Pct	H	SO	BB	ERA
At Home	8	51	3-3		42	43	12	3.73
On the Road	10	61	3-4		65	30	21	4.87
1991 Season	18	112	6-7	.462	107	73	33	4.35
Life 0.5 Years	37	230	12-14	.462	220	150	68	4.35

ANDUJAR CEDENO

HOUSTON SHORTSTOP 22 Years Old

Runs Created: 27
Offensive Winning Percentage: .452
Batting Average: .243 Secondary Average: .227

Most Often Bats: 7th
Swings at First Pitch: 42%
Gets Ahead of the Pitcher: 39%
Hits Behind the Pitcher: 61%

1991 On Base Percentage: .270 Career: .262
1991 Slugging Percentage: .418 Career: .405
Batting Avg with Men in Scoring Position: .254

Bats Right-Handed	G	AB	R	H	2B	3B	HR	RBI	BB	SO	SB	AVG
Vs. RHP		171	22	44	9	2	9	26	8	50	4	.257
Vs. LHP		80	5	17	4	0	0	10	1	24	0	.213
At Home	36	134	14	30	7	2	4	21	5	41	1	.224
On the Road	31	117	13	31	6	0	5	15	4	33	3	.265
1991 Season	67	251	27	61	13	2	9	36	9	74	4	.243
Life 0.5 Years		567	59	134	28	4	20	79	20	173	9	.236

WES CHAMBERLAIN

PHILADELPHIA LEFT FIELD 26 Years Old

Runs Created: 45
Offensive Winning Percentage: .497
Batting Average: .240 Secondary Average: .264

Most Often Bats: 3rd
Swings at First Pitch: 41%
Gets Ahead of the Pitcher: 46%
Hits Behind the Pitcher: 54%

1991 On Base Percentage: .300 Career: .300
1991 Slugging Percentage: .399 Career: .408
Batting Avg with Men in Scoring Position: .250

Bats Right-Handed	G	AB	R	H	2B	3B	HR	RBI	BB	SO	SB	AVG
Vs. RHP		243	27	54	8	2	6	24	15	55	5	.222
Vs. LHP		140	24	38	8	1	7	26	16	18	4	.271
At Home	54	211	27	56	9	1	9	32	15	37	2	.265
On the Road	47	172	24	36	7	2	4	18	16	36	7	.209
1991 Season	101	383	51	92	16	3	13	50	31	73	9	.240
Life 0.7 Years		584	82	143	26	4	20	74	44	112	18	.245

NORM CHARLTON

CINCINNATI RELIEF PITCHER 29 Years Old

3-5 2.91 ERA 1 SAVE

Save Opportunities: 4 Blown Saves: 3 Holds: 3
Inherited Runners who Scored: 75%
Opponents Batting Average: .236
Double Play Support: .83 GDP Per Nine Innings

First Pitch is Hit: 15%
Gets Ahead of the Hitter: 50%
Gets Behind the Hitter: 50%
Gets First Batter Out: 63%

1991 On Base Pct Allowed: .306
Slugging Percentage: .336
Stolen Bases Allowed: 10 Caught Stealing: 7

Pitches Left	AB	H	2B	3B	HR	RBI	BB	SO	AVG
Vs. RHB	303	70	9	4	6	30	23	58	.231
Vs. LHB	87	22	4	0	0	16	11	19	.253

	G	IP	W-L	Pct	SO	BB	ERA	Sv
1991 Season	39	108	3-5	.375	77	34	2.91	1
Life 2.9 Years	61	147	9-8	.551	116	58	3.00	1

JERALD CLARK

SAN DIEGO LEFT FIELD 28 Years Old

Runs Created: 38
Offensive Winning Percentage: .429
Batting Average: .228 Secondary Average: .214

Most Often Bats: 5th
Swings at First Pitch: 39%
Gets Ahead of the Pitcher: 46%
Hits Behind the Pitcher: 54%

1991 On Base Percentage: .295 Career: .290
1991 Slugging Percentage: .352 Career: .371
Batting Avg with Men in Scoring Position: .239

Bats Right-Handed		AB	R	H	2B	3B	HR	RBI	BB	SO	SB	AVG
Vs. RHP		243	19	62	13	0	6	34	21	59	2	.255
Vs. LHP		126	7	22	3	0	4	13	10	31	0	.175
At Home	62	195	17	41	9	0	8	29	14	43	1	.210
On the Road	56	174	9	43	7	0	2	18	17	47	1	.247
1991 Season	118	369	26	84	16	0	10	47	31	90	2	.228
Life 1.2 Years		442	36	102	19	1	13	57	33	107	2	.232

ROGER CLEMENS

BOSTON STARTING PITCHER 29 Years Old

18-10 2.62 ERA

Opponents Batting Average: .221
Offensive Support: 4.44 Runs Per Nine Innings
Double Play Support: .60 GDP Per Nine Innings

First Pitch is Hit: 12%
Gets Ahead of the Hitter: 55%
Gets Behind the Hitter: 45%
Gets Leadoff Man Out: 74%

1991 On Base Pct Allowed: .270
Slugging Percentage: .328
Stolen Bases Allowed: 23 Caught Stealing: 16

Pitches Right	AB	H	2B	3B	HR	RBI	BB	SO	AVG
Vs. RHB	430	96	20	2	12	37	18	120	.223
Vs. LHB	563	123	26	6	3	45	47	121	.218

	G	IP	W-L	Pct	H	SO	BB	ERA
At Home	18	143	8-5		120	132	35	2.59
On the Road	17	129	10-5		99	109	30	2.66
1991 Season	35	271	18-10	.643	219	241	65	2.62
Life 6.5 Years	37	275	21-9	.687	231	256	75	2.85

JACK CLARK

BOSTON DESIGNATED HITTER 36 Years Old

Runs Created: 86
Offensive Winning Percentage: .647
Batting Average: .249 Secondary Average: .416

Most Often Bats: 4th
Swings at First Pitch: 35%
Gets Ahead of the Pitcher: 49%
Hits Behind the Pitcher: 51%

1991 On Base Percentage: .374 Career: .380
1991 Slugging Percentage: .466 Career: .482
Batting Avg with Men in Scoring Position: .242

Bats Right-Handed		AB	R	H	2B	3B	HR	RBI	BB	SO	SB	AVG
Vs. RHP		364	52	82	12	1	22	67	62	111	0	.225
Vs. LHP		117	23	38	6	0	6	20	34	22	0	.325
At Home	73	253	44	71	12	0	18	47	40	68	0	.281
On the Road	67	228	31	49	6	1	10	40	56	65	0	.215
1991 Season	140	481	75	120	18	1	28	87	96	133	0	.249
Life 11.8 Years		558	92	150	27	3	28	97	102	115	6	.269

WILL CLARK

SAN FRANCISCO FIRST BASE 28 Years Old

Runs Created: 110
Offensive Winning Percentage: .757
Batting Average: .301 Secondary Average: .333

Most Often Bats: 3rd
Swings at First Pitch: 36%
Gets Ahead of the Pitcher: 51%
Hits Behind the Pitcher: 49%

1991 On Base Percentage: .359 Career: .372
1991 Slugging Percentage: .536 Career: .512
Batting Avg with Men in Scoring Position: .336

Bats Left-Handed		AB	R	H	2B	3B	HR	RBI	BB	SO	SB	AVG
Vs. RHP		368	65	123	21	5	20	76	37	56	3	.334
Vs. LHP		197	19	47	11	2	9	40	14	35	1	.239
At Home	74	283	43	80	20	4	17	47	25	51	1	.283
On the Road	74	282	41	90	12	3	12	69	26	40	3	.319
1991 Season	148	565	84	170	32	7	29	116	51	91	4	.301
Life 5.5 Years		598	98	181	33	6	27	103	68	109	7	.302

ALEX COLE

CLEVELAND CENTER FIELD 26 Years Old

Runs Created: 55
Offensive Winning Percentage: .587
Batting Average: .295 Secondary Average: .279

Most Often Bats: 1st
Swings at First Pitch: 25%
Gets Ahead of the Pitcher: 51%
Hits Behind the Pitcher: 49%

1991 On Base Percentage: .386 Career: .384
1991 Slugging Percentage: .354 Career: .355
Batting Avg with Men in Scoring Position: .258

Bats Left-Handed		AB	R	H	2B	3B	HR	RBI	BB	SO	SB	AVG
Vs. RHP		325	45	90	12	2	0	13	44	40	21	.277
Vs. LHP		62	13	24	5	1	0	8	14	7	6	.387
At Home	56	182	28	53	9	0	0	14	33	27	11	.291
On the Road	66	205	30	61	8	3	0	7	25	20	16	.298
1991 Season	122	387	58	114	17	3	0	21	58	47	27	.295
Life 1.1 Years		538	88	159	19	6	0	30	75	74	59	.296

DAVID CONE

NEW YORK STARTING PITCHER 29 Years Old

14-14 3.29 ERA

Opponents Batting Average: .235
Offensive Support: 4.18 Runs Per Nine Innings
Double Play Support: .31 GDP Per Nine Innings

First Pitch is Hit: 12%
Gets Ahead of the Hitter: 49%
Gets Behind the Hitter: 51%
Gets Leadoff Man Out: 69%

1991 On Base Pct Allowed: .296
Slugging Percentage: .329
Stolen Bases Allowed: 27 Caught Stealing: 13

Pitches Right	AB	H	2B	3B	HR	RBI	BB	SO	AVG
Vs. RHB	323	69	9	1	6	31	23	118	.214
Vs. LHB	545	135	20	6	7	47	50	123	.248

	G	IP	W-L	Pct	H	SO	BB	ERA
At Home	17	115	6-7		112	118	36	3.91
On the Road	17	118	8-7		92	123	37	2.68
1991 Season	34	233	14-14	.500	204	241	73	3.29
Life 4.1 Years	40	248	16-10	.620	209	235	85	3.18

CHUCK CRIM

MILWAUKEE RELIEF PITCHER 30 Years Old

8-5 4.63 ERA 3 SAVES

Save Opportunities: 5 Blown Saves: 2 Holds: 13
Inherited Runners who Scored: 33%
Opponents Batting Average: .305
Double Play Support: .69 GDP Per Nine Innings

First Pitch is Hit: 19%
Gets Ahead of the Hitter: 48%
Gets Behind the Hitter: 52%
Gets First Batter Out: 65%

1991 On Base Pct Allowed: .351
Slugging Percentage: .416
Stolen Bases Allowed: 12 Caught Stealing: 1

Pitches Right	AB	H	2B	3B	HR	RBI	BB	SO	AVG
Vs. RHB	193	61	8	0	2	25	9	20	.316
Vs. LHB	184	54	7	0	7	30	16	19	.293

	G	IP	W-L	Pct	SO	BB	ERA	Sv
1991 Season	66	91	8-5	.615	39	25	4.63	3
Life 4.6 Years	73	116	7-7	.516	55	33	3.47	9

MILT CUYLER

DETROIT CENTER FIELD 23 Years Old

Runs Created: 61
Offensive Winning Percentage: .434
Batting Average: .257 Secondary Average: .276

Most Often Bats: 9th
Swings at First Pitch: 33%
Gets Ahead of the Pitcher: 53%
Hits Behind the Pitcher: 47%

1991 On Base Percentage: .335 Career: .333
1991 Slugging Percentage: .337 Career: .338
Batting Avg with Men in Scoring Position: .186

Switch Hitter	G	AB	R	H	2B	3B	HR	RBI	BB	SO	SB	AVG
Vs. RHP		353	55	89	9	6	3	25	39	73	33	.252
Vs. LHP		122	22	33	6	1	0	8	13	19	8	.270
At Home	76	221	45	54	6	2	1	15	35	31	26	.244
On the Road	78	254	32	68	9	5	2	18	17	61	15	.268
1991 Season	154	475	77	122	15	7	3	33	52	92	41	.257
Life 1.1 Years		493	80	126	17	7	3	38	53	96	39	.257

KAL DANIELS

LOS ANGELES LEFT FIELD 28 Years Old

Runs Created: 65
Offensive Winning Percentage: .621
Batting Average: .249 Secondary Average: .297

Most Often Bats: 5th
Swings at First Pitch: 30%
Gets Ahead of the Pitcher: 52%
Hits Behind the Pitcher: 48%

1991 On Base Percentage: .337 Career: .388
1991 Slugging Percentage: .397 Career: .489
Batting Avg with Men in Scoring Position: .291

Bats Left-Handed	G	AB	R	H	2B	3B	HR	RBI	BB	SO	SB	AVG
Vs. RHP		255	33	63	7	1	11	37	44	64	6	.247
Vs. LHP		206	21	52	8	0	6	36	19	52	0	.252
At Home	73	242	35	60	7	0	12	48	31	63	4	.248
On the Road	64	219	19	55	8	1	5	25	32	53	2	.251
1991 Season	137	461	54	115	15	1	17	73	63	116	6	.249
Life 4.0 Years		535	93	155	29	2	25	84	86	110	22	.289

RON DARLING

OAKLAND STARTING PITCHER 31 Years Ol

8-15 4.26 ERA

Opponents Batting Average: .254
Offensive Support: 3.61 Runs Per Nine Innings
Double Play Support: .46 GDP Per Nine Innings

First Pitch is Hit: 13%
Gets Ahead of the Hitter: 47%
Gets Behind the Hitter: 53%
Gets Leadoff Man Out: 68%

1991 On Base Pct Allowed: .325
Slugging Percentage: .414
Stolen Bases Allowed: 24 Caught Stealing:

Pitches Right	AB	H	2B	3B	HR	RBI	BB	SO	AVG
Vs. RHB	336	92	15	6	14	47	34	53	.274
Vs. LHB	391	93	15	4	8	42	37	76	.238

	G	IP	W-L	Pct	H	SO	BB	ERA
At Home	16	90	3-9		100	59	39	5.40
On the Road	16	104	5-6		85	70	32	3.28
1991 Season	32	194	8-15	.348	185	129	71	4.26
Life 7.1 Years	38	240	14-11	.564	219	171	92	3.56

DOUG DASCENZO

CHICAGO CENTER FIELD 28 Years Ol

Runs Created: 26
Offensive Winning Percentage: .393
Batting Average: .255 Secondary Average: .218

Most Often Bats: 1st
Swings at First Pitch: 35%
Gets Ahead of the Pitcher: 51%
Hits Behind the Pitcher: 49%

1991 On Base Percentage: .327 Career: .300
1991 Slugging Percentage: .314 Career: .294
Batting Avg with Men in Scoring Position: .167

Switch Hitter	G	AB	R	H	2B	3B	HR	RBI	BB	SO	SB	AVG
Vs. RHP		152	30	35	7	0	1	10	19	19	12	.230
Vs. LHP		87	10	26	4	0	0	8	5	7	2	.299
At Home	64	125	22	29	5	0	0	8	13	12	9	.232
On the Road	54	114	18	32	6	0	1	10	11	14	5	.281
1991 Season	118	239	40	61	11	0	1	18	24	26	14	.255
Life 1.9 Years		370	51	86	13	3	2	32	36	33	22	.232

DARREN DAULTON

PHILADELPHIA CATCHER 30 Years Old

Runs Created: 34
Offensive Winning Percentage: .475
Batting Average: .196 Secondary Average: .330

Most Often Bats: 6th
Swings at First Pitch: 15%
Gets Ahead of the Pitcher: 54%
Hits Behind the Pitcher: 46%

1991 On Base Percentage: .297 Career: .326
1991 Slugging Percentage: .365 Career: .360
Batting Avg with Men in Scoring Position: .290

Bats Left-Handed	G	AB	R	H	2B	3B	HR	RBI	BB	SO	SB	AVG
Vs. RHP		189	29	42	8	0	10	33	32	35	4	.222
Vs. LHP		96	7	14	4	0	2	9	9	31	1	.146
At Home	49	152	25	32	9	0	8	23	24	38	3	.211
On the Road	40	133	11	24	3	0	4	19	17	28	2	.180
1991 Season	89	285	36	56	12	0	12	42	41	66	5	.196
Life 3.5 Years		470	53	104	21	1	14	58	73	98	6	.222

CHILI DAVIS

MINNESOTA DESIGNATED HITTER 32 Years Old

Runs Created: 107
Offensive Winning Percentage: .725
Batting Average: .277 Secondary Average: .418

Most Often Bats: 5th
Swings at First Pitch: 35%
Gets Ahead of the Pitcher: 53%
Hits Behind the Pitcher: 47%

1991 On Base Percentage: .385 Career: .345
1991 Slugging Percentage: .507 Career: .431
Batting Avg with Men in Scoring Position: .283

Switch Hitter	G	AB	R	H	2B	3B	HR	RBI	BB	SO	SB	AVG
Vs. RHP		360	60	101	25	1	18	61	70	81	4	.281
Vs. LHP		174	24	47	9	0	11	32	25	36	1	.270
At Home	79	267	44	81	19	1	14	45	54	51	2	.303
On the Road	74	267	40	67	15	0	15	48	41	66	3	.251
1991 Season	153	534	84	148	34	1	29	93	95	117	5	.277
Life 9.0 Years		586	82	157	28	3	21	84	71	113	13	.268

STORM DAVIS

KANSAS CITY RELIEF PITCHER 30 Years Old
3-9 4.96 ERA 2 SAVES

Save Opportunities: 3 Blown Saves: 1 Holds: 4
Inherited Runners who Scored: 35%
Opponents Batting Average: .306
Double Play Support: 1.26 GDP Per Nine Innings

First Pitch is Hit: 16%
Gets Ahead of the Hitter: 45%
Gets Behind the Hitter: 55%
Gets First Batter Out: 61%

1991 On Base Pct Allowed: .367
Slugging Percentage: .437
Stolen Bases Allowed: 2 Caught Stealing: 2

Pitches Right	AB	H	2B	3B	HR	RBI	BB	SO	AVG
Vs. RHB	231	64	8	0	5	28	20	23	.277
Vs. LHB	227	76	13	3	6	45	26	30	.335

	G	IP	W-L	Pct	SO	BB	ERA	Sv
1991 Season	51	114	3-9	.250	53	46	4.96	2
Life 7.4 Years	43	210	14-11	.557	120	77	4.01	0

ALVIN DAVIS

SEATTLE DESIGNATED HITTER 31 Years Old

Runs Created: 48
Offensive Winning Percentage: .391
Batting Average: .221 Secondary Average: .236

Most Often Bats: 5th
Swings at First Pitch: 13%
Gets Ahead of the Pitcher: 54%
Hits Behind the Pitcher: 46%

1991 On Base Percentage: .299 Career: .381
1991 Slugging Percentage: .335 Career: .453
Batting Avg with Men in Scoring Position: .259

Bats Left-Handed	G	AB	R	H	2B	3B	HR	RBI	BB	SO	SB	AVG
Vs. RHP		361	26	78	13	1	8	55	40	59	0	.216
Vs. LHP		101	13	24	2	0	4	14	16	19	0	.238
At Home	72	226	23	52	10	0	6	35	29	44	0	.230
On the Road	73	236	16	50	5	1	6	34	27	34	0	.212
1991 Season	145	462	39	102	15	1	12	69	56	78	0	.221
Life 7.2 Years		575	78	162	29	1	22	93	93	76	1	.281

ERIC DAVIS

CINCINNATI CENTER FIELD 30 Years Old

Runs Created: 44
Offensive Winning Percentage: .602
Batting Average: .235 Secondary Average: .368

Most Often Bats: 4th
Swings at First Pitch: 25%
Gets Ahead of the Pitcher: 52%
Hits Behind the Pitcher: 48%

1991 On Base Percentage: .353 Career: .363
1991 Slugging Percentage: .386 Career: .509
Batting Avg with Men in Scoring Position: .217

Bats Right-Handed	G	AB	R	H	2B	3B	HR	RBI	BB	SO	SB	AVG
Vs. RHP		180	22	43	5	0	8	22	28	61	8	.239
Vs. LHP		105	17	24	5	0	3	11	20	31	6	.229
At Home	46	140	16	34	6	0	5	18	30	47	10	.243
On the Road	43	145	23	33	4	0	6	15	18	45	4	.228
1991 Season	89	285	39	67	10	0	11	33	48	92	14	.235
Life 5.3 Years		541	105	145	23	3	33	101	80	143	47	.268

ANDRE DAWSON

CHICAGO RIGHT FIELD 37 Years Old

Runs Created: 79
Offensive Winning Percentage: .550
Batting Average: .272 Secondary Average: .263

Most Often Bats: 4th
Swings at First Pitch: 30%
Gets Ahead of the Pitcher: 48%
Hits Behind the Pitcher: 52%

1991 On Base Percentage: .302 Career: .327
1991 Slugging Percentage: .488 Career: .489
Batting Avg with Men in Scoring Position: .297

Bats Right-Handed	G	AB	R	H	2B	3B	HR	RBI	BB	SO	SB	AVG
Vs. RHP		340	37	87	13	3	15	57	15	53	1	.256
Vs. LHP		223	32	66	8	1	16	47	7	27	3	.296
At Home	76	280	46	82	11	1	22	59	11	38	2	.293
On the Road	73	283	23	71	10	3	9	45	11	42	2	.251
1991 Season	149	563	69	153	21	4	31	104	22	80	4	.272
Life 13.4 Years		624	90	176	31	7	28	100	39	96	23	.282

ROB DEER

DETROIT RIGHT FIELD 31 Years Old

Runs Created: 60
Offensive Winning Percentage: .426
Batting Average: .179 Secondary Average: .408

Most Often Bats: 6th
Swings at First Pitch: 30%
Gets Ahead of the Pitcher: 52%
Hits Behind the Pitcher: 48%

1991 On Base Percentage: .314 Career: .325
1991 Slugging Percentage: .386 Career: .437
Batting Avg with Men in Scoring Position: .168

Bats Right-Handed	G	AB	R	H	2B	3B	HR	RBI	BB	SO	SB	AVG
Vs. RHP		310	46	53	8	1	16	46	62	129	1	.171
Vs. LHP		138	18	27	6	1	9	18	27	46	0	.196
At Home	66	218	35	42	5	2	12	31	46	87	0	.193
On the Road	68	230	29	38	9	0	13	33	43	88	1	.165
1991 Season	134	448	64	80	14	2	25	64	89	175	1	.179
Life 5.5 Years		540	79	118	20	2	31	86	82	196	6	.218

JOSE DeLEON

ST. LOUIS STARTING PITCHER 31 Years Old
5-9 2.71 ERA

Opponents Batting Average: .239
Offensive Support: 3.15 Runs Per Nine Innings
Double Play Support: .44 GDP Per Nine Innings

First Pitch is Hit: 11%
Gets Ahead of the Hitter: 48%
Gets Behind the Hitter: 52%
Gets Leadoff Man Out: 70%

1991 On Base Pct Allowed: .313
Slugging Percentage: .378
Stolen Bases Allowed: 12 Caught Stealing: 12

Pitches Right	AB	H	2B	3B	HR	RBI	BB	SO	AVG
Vs. RHB	277	62	11	2	6	21	18	74	.224
Vs. LHB	326	82	18	3	9	25	43	44	.252

	G	IP	W-L	Pct	H	SO	BB	ERA
At Home	16	89	3-4		78	65	33	2.42
On the Road	12	73	2-5		66	53	28	3.07
1991 Season	28	163	5-9	.357	144	118	61	2.71
Life 6.8 Years	38	232	11-15	.410	189	197	102	3.68

JIM DESHAIES

HOUSTON STARTING PITCHER 32 Years Old
5-12 4.98 ERA

Opponents Batting Average: .259
Offensive Support: 3.35 Runs Per Nine Innings
Double Play Support: .67 GDP Per Nine Innings

First Pitch is Hit: 14%
Gets Ahead of the Hitter: 44%
Gets Behind the Hitter: 56%
Gets Leadoff Man Out: 67%

1991 On Base Pct Allowed: .336
Slugging Percentage: .430
Stolen Bases Allowed: 21 Caught Stealing: 14

Pitches Left	AB	H	2B	3B	HR	RBI	BB	SO	AVG
Vs. RHB	498	127	30	4	15	59	53	80	.255
Vs. LHB	104	29	6	1	4	19	19	18	.279

	G	IP	W-L	Pct	H	SO	BB	ERA
At Home	10	65	2-3		50	37	27	3.72
On the Road	18	96	3-9		106	61	45	5.83
1991 Season	28	161	5-12	.294	156	98	72	4.98
Life 4.9 Years	37	226	12-12	.504	199	150	88	3.72

JOSE DeJESUS

PHILADELPHIA STARTING PITCHER 27 Years Old
10-9 3.42 ERA

Opponents Batting Average: .224
Offensive Support: 4.01 Runs Per Nine Innings
Double Play Support: .79 GDP Per Nine Innings

First Pitch is Hit: 12%
Gets Ahead of the Hitter: 42%
Gets Behind the Hitter: 58%
Gets Leadoff Man Out: 66%

1991 On Base Pct Allowed: .353
Slugging Percentage: .318
Stolen Bases Allowed: 19 Caught Stealing: 11

Pitches Right	AB	H	2B	3B	HR	RBI	BB	SO	AVG
Vs. RHB	279	60	12	1	6	23	39	53	.215
Vs. LHB	376	87	20	3	1	41	89	65	.231

	G	IP	W-L	Pct	H	SO	BB	ERA
At Home	12	77	4-5		67	52	54	3.39
On the Road	19	105	6-4		80	66	74	3.44
1991 Season	31	182	10-9	.526	147	118	128	3.42
Life 1.5 Years	39	215	11-12	.486	171	139	143	3.77

RICH DELUCIA

SEATTLE STARTING PITCHER 27 Years Old
12-13 5.09 ERA

Opponents Batting Average: .260
Offensive Support: 5.49 Runs Per Nine Innings
Double Play Support: .64 GDP Per Nine Innings

First Pitch is Hit: 12%
Gets Ahead of the Hitter: 48%
Gets Behind the Hitter: 52%
Gets Leadoff Man Out: 68%

1991 On Base Pct Allowed: .333
Slugging Percentage: .457
Stolen Bases Allowed: 4 Caught Stealing: 9

Pitches Right	AB	H	2B	3B	HR	RBI	BB	SO	AVG
Vs. RHB	358	84	21	0	20	54	24	64	.235
Vs. LHB	320	92	14	3	11	42	54	34	.287

	G	IP	W-L	Pct	H	SO	BB	ERA
At Home	15	90	7-4		80	48	31	4.72
On the Road	17	92	5-9		96	50	47	5.46
1991 Season	32	182	12-13	.480	176	98	78	5.09
Life 1.0 Years	38	221	13-15	.464	209	120	88	4.58

DELINO DeSHIELDS

MONTREAL SECOND BASE 23 Years Old

Runs Created: 74
Offensive Winning Percentage: .553
Batting Average: .238 Secondary Average: .362

Most Often Bats: 1st
Swings at First Pitch: 22%
Gets Ahead of the Pitcher: 54%
Hits Behind the Pitcher: 46%

1991 On Base Percentage: .347 Career: .360
1991 Slugging Percentage: .332 Career: .361
Batting Avg with Men in Scoring Position: .250

Bats Left-Handed	G	AB	R	H	2B	3B	HR	RBI	BB	SO	SB	AVG
Vs. RHP		374	58	93	13	4	7	37	62	93	36	.249
Vs. LHP		189	25	41	2	0	3	14	33	58	20	.217
At Home	65	238	41	63	9	1	3	15	44	64	24	.265
On the Road	86	325	42	71	6	3	7	36	51	87	32	.218
1991 Season	151	563	83	134	15	4	10	51	95	151	56	.238
Life 1.7 Years		614	88	161	25	6	8	56	93	143	57	.262

MIKE DEVEREAUX

BALTIMORE — CENTER FIELD — 29 Years Old

Runs Created: 80
Offensive Winning Percentage: .488
Batting Average: .260 Secondary Average: .275

Most Often Bats: 1st
Swings at First Pitch: 14%
Gets Ahead of the Pitcher: 50%
Hits Behind the Pitcher: 50%

1991 On Base Percentage: .313 Career: .306
1991 Slugging Percentage: .431 Career: .393
Batting Avg with Men in Scoring Position: .255

Bats Right-Handed		AB	R	H	2B	3B	HR	RBI	BB	SO	SB	AVG
Vs. RHP		441	62	109	20	4	13	43	33	85	15	.247
Vs. LHP		167	20	49	7	6	6	16	14	30	1	.293
At Home	75	305	39	77	13	4	10	35	22	58	8	.252
On the Road	74	303	43	81	14	6	9	24	25	57	8	.267
1991 Season	149	608	82	158	27	10	19	59	47	115	16	.260
Life 2.6 Years		554	74	139	24	5	15	61	44	92	20	.251

BILLY DORAN

CINCINNATI — SECOND BASE — 34 Years Old

Runs Created: 51
Offensive Winning Percentage: .589
Batting Average: .280 Secondary Average: .235

Most Often Bats: 1st
Swings at First Pitch: 25%
Gets Ahead of the Pitcher: 59%
Hits Behind the Pitcher: 41%

1991 On Base Percentage: .359 Career: .356
1991 Slugging Percentage: .374 Career: .377
Batting Avg with Men in Scoring Position: .268

Switch Hitter		AB	R	H	2B	3B	HR	RBI	BB	SO	SB	AVG
Vs. RHP		281	41	80	8	1	4	27	33	31	5	.285
Vs. LHP		80	10	21	4	1	2	8	13	8	0	.262
At Home	53	169	30	50	8	1	3	18	26	14	2	.296
On the Road	58	192	21	51	4	1	3	17	20	25	3	.266
1991 Season	111	361	51	101	12	2	6	35	46	39	5	.280
Life 8.0 Years		587	84	158	25	5	10	56	80	70	25	.269

KELLY DOWNS

SAN FRANCISCO — RELIEF PITCHER — 31 Years Old
10-4 4.19 ERA 0 SAVES

Save Opportunities: 2 Blown Saves: 2 Holds: 1
Inherited Runners who Scored: 31%
Opponents Batting Average: .239
Double Play Support: .81 GDP Per Nine Innings

First Pitch is Hit: 14%
Gets Ahead of the Hitter: 46%
Gets Behind the Hitter: 54%
Gets First Batter Out: 76%

1991 On Base Pct Allowed: .326
Slugging Percentage: .373
Stolen Bases Allowed: 15 Caught Stealing: 4

Pitches Right	AB	H	2B	3B	HR	RBI	BB	SO	AVG
Vs. RHB	195	41	7	0	6	26	27	42	.210
Vs. LHB	220	58	9	2	6	31	26	20	.264

	G	IP	W-L	Pct	SO	BB	ERA	Sv
1991 Season	45	112	10-4	.714	62	53	4.19	0
Life 3.5 Years	45	198	13-10	.561	131	69	3.65	0

ROB DIBBLE

CINCINNATI — RELIEF PITCHER — 28 Years Old
3-5 3.17 ERA 31 SAVES

Save Opportunities: 36 Blown Saves: 5 Holds: 0
Inherited Runners who Scored: 19%
Opponents Batting Average: .223
Double Play Support: .11 GDP Per Nine Innings

First Pitch is Hit: 12%
Gets Ahead of the Hitter: 54%
Gets Behind the Hitter: 46%
Gets First Batter Out: 66%

1991 On Base Pct Allowed: .280
Slugging Percentage: .322
Stolen Bases Allowed: 16 Caught Stealing: 5

Pitches Right	AB	H	2B	3B	HR	RBI	BB	SO	AVG
Vs. RHB	128	33	4	2	3	20	11	49	.258
Vs. LHB	173	34	5	1	2	14	14	75	.197

	G	IP	W-L	Pct	SO	BB	ERA	Sv
1991 Season	67	82	3-5	.375	124	25	3.17	31
Life 3.3 Years	74	102	7-4	.611	138	36	2.21	13

BRIAN DOWNING

TEXAS — DESIGNATED HITTER — 41 Years Old

Runs Created: 73
Offensive Winning Percentage: .617
Batting Average: .278 Secondary Average: .322

Most Often Bats: 1st
Swings at First Pitch: 10%
Gets Ahead of the Pitcher: 54%
Hits Behind the Pitcher: 46%

1991 On Base Percentage: .377 Career: .369
1991 Slugging Percentage: .455 Career: .425
Batting Avg with Men in Scoring Position: .258

Bats Right-Handed		AB	R	H	2B	3B	HR	RBI	BB	SO	SB	AVG
Vs. RHP		268	44	74	12	2	8	32	33	46	0	.276
Vs. LHP		139	32	39	5	0	9	17	25	24	1	.281
At Home	63	204	45	52	8	2	8	23	32	39	0	.255
On the Road	60	203	31	61	9	0	9	26	26	31	1	.300
1991 Season	123	407	76	113	17	2	17	49	58	70	1	.278
Life 13.8 Years		546	82	146	25	2	19	75	82	77	4	.267

DOUG DRABEK

PITTSBURGH — STARTING PITCHER — 29 Years Old
15-14 3.07 ERA

Opponents Batting Average: .274
Offensive Support: 4.83 Runs Per Nine Innings
Double Play Support: .58 GDP Per Nine Innings

First Pitch is Hit: 14%
Gets Ahead of the Hitter: 53%
Gets Behind the Hitter: 47%
Gets Leadoff Man Out: 65%

1991 On Base Pct Allowed: .321
Slugging Percentage: .385
Stolen Bases Allowed: 29 Caught Stealing: 15

Pitches Right	AB	H	2B	3B	HR	RBI	BB	SO	AVG
Vs. RHB	364	93	12	4	8	30	21	83	.255
Vs. LHB	530	152	29	1	8	49	41	59	.287

	G	IP	W-L	Pct	H	SO	BB	ERA
At Home	19	131	9-8		131	87	30	2.40
On the Road	16	104	6-6		114	55	32	3.91
1991 Season	35	235	15-14	.517	245	142	62	3.07
Life 5.1 Years	38	244	17-12	.587	224	142	66	3.19

SHAWON DUNSTON

CHICAGO SHORTSTOP 29 Years Old

Runs Created: 59
Offensive Winning Percentage: .446
Batting Average: .260 Secondary Average: .236

Most Often Bats: 7th
Swings at First Pitch: 30%
Gets Ahead of the Pitcher: 45%
Hits Behind the Pitcher: 55%

1991 On Base Percentage: .292 Career: .287
1991 Slugging Percentage: .407 Career: .395
Batting Avg with Men in Scoring Position: .271

Bats Right-Handed	G	AB	R	H	2B	3B	HR	RBI	BB	SO	SB	AVG
Vs. RHP		298	33	83	15	5	7	31	13	41	13	.279
Vs. LHP		194	26	45	7	2	5	19	10	23	8	.232
At Home	73	237	32	70	10	3	7	26	10	30	10	.295
On the Road	69	255	27	58	12	4	5	24	13	34	11	.227
1991 Season	142	492	59	128	22	7	12	50	23	64	21	.260
Life 5.6 Years		587	72	151	28	7	13	61	24	102	24	.258

LENNY DYKSTRA

PHILADELPHIA CENTER FIELD 29 Years Old

Runs Created: 47
Offensive Winning Percentage: .760
Batting Average: .297 Secondary Average: .378

Most Often Bats: 1st
Swings at First Pitch: 22%
Gets Ahead of the Pitcher: 52%
Hits Behind the Pitcher: 48%

1991 On Base Percentage: .391 Career: .361
1991 Slugging Percentage: .427 Career: .410
Batting Avg with Men in Scoring Position: .250

Bats Left-Handed	G	AB	R	H	2B	3B	HR	RBI	BB	SO	SB	AVG
Vs. RHP		152	28	44	7	2	1	6	21	7	15	.289
Vs. LHP		94	20	29	6	3	2	6	16	13	9	.309
At Home	30	118	29	38	7	2	3	6	20	10	14	.322
On the Road	33	128	19	35	6	3	0	6	17	10	10	.273
1991 Season	63	246	48	73	13	5	3	12	37	20	24	.297
Life 5.2 Years		550	92	155	33	5	9	47	66	59	36	.283

DENNIS ECKERSLEY

OAKLAND RELIEF PITCHER 37 Years Old
5-4 2.96 ERA 43 SAVES

Save Opportunities: 51 Blown Saves: 8 Holds: 0
Inherited Runners who Scored: 29%
Opponents Batting Average: .208
Double Play Support: 0.00 GDP Per Nine Innings

First Pitch is Hit: 12%
Gets Ahead of the Hitter: 65%
Gets Behind the Hitter: 35%
Gets First Batter Out: 78%

1991 On Base Pct Allowed: .235
Slugging Percentage: .365
Stolen Bases Allowed: 8 Caught Stealing: 1

Pitches Right	AB	H	2B	3B	HR	RBI	BB	SO	AVG
Vs. RHB	138	26	4	2	6	15	3	53	.188
Vs. LHB	150	34	4	0	5	18	6	34	.227

	G	IP	W-L	Pct	SO	BB	ERA	Sv
1991 Season	67	76	5-4	.556	87	9	2.96	43
Life 13.9 Years	48	207	12-10	.547	145	48	3.47	13

MARK EICHHORN

CALIFORNIA RELIEF PITCHER 31 Years Old
3-3 1.98 ERA 1 SAVE

Save Opportunities: 4 Blown Saves: 3 Holds: 25
Inherited Runners who Scored: 28%
Opponents Batting Average: .219
Double Play Support: 1.21 GDP Per Nine Innings

First Pitch is Hit: 15%
Gets Ahead of the Hitter: 56%
Gets Behind the Hitter: 44%
Gets First Batter Out: 76%

1991 On Base Pct Allowed: .255
Slugging Percentage: .309
Stolen Bases Allowed: 3 Caught Stealing: 3

Pitches Right	AB	H	2B	3B	HR	RBI	BB	SO	AVG
Vs. RHB	162	30	8	1	0	14	9	34	.185
Vs. LHB	126	33	8	1	2	13	4	15	.262

	G	IP	W-L	Pct	SO	BB	ERA	Sv
1991 Season	70	82	3-3	.500	49	13	1.98	1
Life 5.2 Years	73	120	7-6	.523	91	37	3.01	6

JIM EISENREICH

KANSAS CITY LEFT FIELD 33 Years Ol

Runs Created: 47
Offensive Winning Percentage: .500
Batting Average: .301 Secondary Average: .157

Most Often Bats: 5th
Swings at First Pitch: 32%
Gets Ahead of the Pitcher: 53%
Hits Behind the Pitcher: 47%

1991 On Base Percentage: .333 Career: .323
1991 Slugging Percentage: .392 Career: .400
Batting Avg with Men in Scoring Position: .324

Bats Left-Handed	G	AB	R	H	2B	3B	HR	RBI	BB	SO	SB	AVG
Vs. RHP		288	34	85	20	2	1	31	16	23	4	.295
Vs. LHP		87	13	28	2	1	1	16	4	12	1	.322
At Home	69	193	25	60	9	2	2	25	9	14	3	.311
On the Road	66	182	22	53	13	1	0	22	11	21	2	.291
1991 Season	135	375	47	113	22	3	2	47	20	35	5	.301
Life 3.6 Years		496	61	138	30	6	6	58	35	53	16	.279

SCOTT ERICKSON

MINNESOTA STARTING PITCHER 24 Years Old
20-8 3.18 ERA

Opponents Batting Average: .248
Offensive Support: 5.74 Runs Per Nine Innings
Double Play Support: .97 GDP Per Nine Innings

First Pitch is Hit: 15%
Gets Ahead of the Hitter: 50%
Gets Behind the Hitter: 50%
Gets Leadoff Man Out: 69%

1991 On Base Pct Allowed: .314
Slugging Percentage: .364
Stolen Bases Allowed: 4 Caught Stealing: 10

Pitches Right	AB	H	2B	3B	HR	RBI	BB	SO	AVG
Vs. RHB	345	66	13	3	5	34	26	68	.191
Vs. LHB	417	123	26	2	8	38	45	40	.295

	G	IP	W-L	Pct	H	SO	BB	ERA
At Home	15	97	10-3		97	51	29	3.53
On the Road	17	107	10-5		92	57	42	2.86
1991 Season	32	204	20-8	.714	189	108	71	3.18
Life 1.4 Years	38	235	21-9	.700	220	119	90	3.07

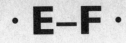

ALVARO ESPINOZA

NEW YORK SHORTSTOP 30 Years Old

Runs Created: 45
Offensive Winning Percentage: .342
Batting Average: .256 Secondary Average: .129

Most Often Bats: 8th
Swings at First Pitch: 45%
Gets Ahead of the Pitcher: 44%
Hits Behind the Pitcher: 56%

1991 On Base Percentage: .282 Career: .280
1991 Slugging Percentage: .344 Career: .315
Batting Avg with Men in Scoring Position: .250

Bats Right-Handed	G	AB	R	H	2B	3B	HR	RBI	BB	SO	SB	AVG
Vs. RHP		319	35	81	13	2	4	18	9	46	3	.254
Vs. LHP		161	16	42	10	0	1	15	7	11	1	.261
At Home	78	254	25	63	12	1	2	14	8	30	3	.248
On the Road	70	226	26	60	11	1	3	19	8	27	1	.265
1991 Season	148	480	51	123	23	2	5	33	16	57	4	.256
Life 3.2 Years		477	44	121	19	2	2	33	15	60	3	.254

FELIX FERMIN

CLEVELAND SHORTSTOP 28 Years Old

Runs Created: 37
Offensive Winning Percentage: .331
Batting Average: .262 Secondary Average: .113

Most Often Bats: 9th
Swings at First Pitch: 34%
Gets Ahead of the Pitcher: 46%
Hits Behind the Pitcher: 54%

1991 On Base Percentage: .307 Career: .305
1991 Slugging Percentage: .302 Career: .288
Batting Avg with Men in Scoring Position: .278

Bats Right-Handed	G	AB	R	H	2B	3B	HR	RBI	BB	SO	SB	AVG
Vs. RHP		303	20	77	9	2	0	23	16	21	4	.254
Vs. LHP		121	10	34	4	0	0	8	10	6	1	.281
At Home	68	210	20	61	8	2	0	20	16	11	4	.290
On the Road	61	214	10	50	5	0	0	11	10	16	1	.234
1991 Season	129	424	30	111	13	2	0	31	26	27	5	.262
Life 3.1 Years		480	46	121	11	2	0	32	34	31	6	.253

TONY FERNANDEZ

SAN DIEGO SHORTSTOP 30 Years Old

Runs Created: 70
Offensive Winning Percentage: .546
Batting Average: .272 Secondary Average: .228

Most Often Bats: 2nd
Swings at First Pitch: 37%
Gets Ahead of the Pitcher: 49%
Hits Behind the Pitcher: 51%

1991 On Base Percentage: .337 Career: .338
1991 Slugging Percentage: .360 Career: .394
Batting Avg with Men in Scoring Position: .308

Switch Hitter	G	AB	R	H	2B	3B	HR	RBI	BB	SO	SB	AVG
Vs. RHP		374	55	104	20	4	2	25	38	52	17	.278
Vs. LHP		184	26	48	7	1	2	13	17	22	6	.261
At Home	73	271	37	79	13	2	1	17	30	38	12	.292
On the Road	72	287	44	73	14	3	3	21	25	36	11	.254
1991 Season	145	558	81	152	27	5	4	38	55	74	23	.272
Life 7.2 Years		623	82	179	30	9	6	61	47	58	22	.287

STEVE FARR

NEW YORK RELIEF PITCHER 35 Years Old
5-5 2.19 ERA 23 SAVES

Save Opportunities: 29 Blown Saves: 6 Holds: 3
Inherited Runners who Scored: 26%
Opponents Batting Average: .219
Double Play Support: 1.03 GDP Per Nine Innings

First Pitch is Hit: 9%
Gets Ahead of the Hitter: 60%
Gets Behind the Hitter: 40%
Gets First Batter Out: 72%

1991 On Base Pct Allowed: .288
Slugging Percentage: .312
Stolen Bases Allowed: 2 Caught Stealing: 2

Pitches Right	AB	H	2B	3B	HR	RBI	BB	SO	AVG
Vs. RHB	144	29	6	0	2	15	9	37	.201
Vs. LHB	116	28	6	0	2	10	11	23	.241

	G	IP	W-L	Pct	SO	BB	ERA	Sv
1991 Season	60	70	5-5	.500	60	20	2.19	23
Life 5.5 Years	69	126	8-7	.512	104	49	3.22	13

ALEX FERNANDEZ

CHICAGO STARTING PITCHER 22 Years Old
9-13 4.51 ERA

Opponents Batting Average: .259
Offensive Support: 3.38 Runs Per Nine Innings
Double Play Support: .61 GDP Per Nine Innings

First Pitch is Hit: 13%
Gets Ahead of the Hitter: 52%
Gets Behind the Hitter: 48%
Gets Leadoff Man Out: 64%

1991 On Base Pct Allowed: .337
Slugging Percentage: .388
Stolen Bases Allowed: 15 Caught Stealing: 11

Pitches Right	AB	H	2B	3B	HR	RBI	BB	SO	AVG
Vs. RHB	389	103	13	5	12	54	46	81	.265
Vs. LHB	330	83	20	1	4	32	42	64	.252

	G	IP	W-L	Pct	H	SO	BB	ERA
At Home	17	96	5-7		80	70	36	4.48
On the Road	17	95	4-6		106	75	52	4.53
1991 Season	34	192	9-13	.409	186	145	88	4.51
Life 1.2 Years	38	225	11-14	.438	221	166	98	4.29

CECIL FIELDER

DETROIT FIRST BASE 28 Years Old

Runs Created: 110
Offensive Winning Percentage: .606
Batting Average: .261 Secondary Average: .377

Most Often Bats: 4th
Swings at First Pitch: 37%
Gets Ahead of the Pitcher: 50%
Hits Behind the Pitcher: 50%

1991 On Base Percentage: .347 Career: .346
1991 Slugging Percentage: .513 Career: .527
Batting Avg with Men in Scoring Position: .286

Bats Right-Handed	G	AB	R	H	2B	3B	HR	RBI	BB	SO	SB	AVG
Vs. RHP		465	76	116	16	0	31	102	53	122	0	.249
Vs. LHP		159	26	47	9	0	13	31	25	29	0	.296
At Home	81	305	56	78	12	0	27	75	41	72	0	.256
On the Road	81	319	46	85	13	0	17	58	37	79	0	.266
1991 Season	162	624	102	163	25	0	44	133	78	151	0	.261
Life 3.3 Years		510	82	133	21	1	38	105	64	143	0	.261

CHUCK FINLEY

CALIFORNIA STARTING PITCHER 29 Years Old

18-9 3.80 ERA

Opponents Batting Average: .244
Offensive Support: 5.38 Runs Per Nine Innings
Double Play Support: .83 GDP Per Nine Innings

First Pitch is Hit: 10%
Gets Ahead of the Hitter: 45%
Gets Behind the Hitter: 55%
Gets Leadoff Man Out: 70%

1991 On Base Pct Allowed: .330
Slugging Percentage: .385
Stolen Bases Allowed: 15 Caught Stealing: 14

Pitches Left	AB	H	2B	3B	HR	RBI	BB	SO	AVG
Vs. RHB	730	177	37	3	19	80	88	149	.242
Vs. LHB	109	28	6	0	4	8	13	22	.257

	G	IP	W-L	Pct	H	SO	BB	ERA
At Home	17	125	9-3		99	103	50	3.03
On the Road	17	103	9-6		106	68	51	4.73
1991 Season	34	227	18-9	.667	205	171	101	3.80
Life 4.3 Years	44	234	16-12	.569	216	168	97	3.35

CARLTON FISK

CHICAGO CATCHER 44 Years Old

Runs Created: 52
Offensive Winning Percentage: .416
Batting Average: .241 Secondary Average: .243

Most Often Bats: 5th
Swings at First Pitch: 27%
Gets Ahead of the Pitcher: 49%
Hits Behind the Pitcher: 51%

1991 On Base Percentage: .299 Career: .342
1991 Slugging Percentage: .413 Career: .461
Batting Avg with Men in Scoring Position: .250

Bats Right-Handed	G	AB	R	H	2B	3B	HR	RBI	BB	SO	SB	AVG
Vs. RHP		303	35	75	17	0	13	46	23	62	1	.248
Vs. LHP		157	7	36	8	0	5	28	9	24	0	.229
At Home	71	233	21	55	13	0	9	39	18	41	0	.236
On the Road	63	227	21	56	12	0	9	35	14	45	1	.247
1991 Season	134	460	42	111	25	0	18	74	32	86	1	.241
Life 14.9 Years		572	85	155	28	3	25	88	55	90	8	.270

JULIO FRANCO

TEXAS SECOND BASE 30 Years Ol

Runs Created: 118
Offensive Winning Percentage: .699
Batting Average: .341 Secondary Average: .304

Most Often Bats: 4th
Swings at First Pitch: 20%
Gets Ahead of the Pitcher: 52%
Hits Behind the Pitcher: 48%

1991 On Base Percentage: .408 Career: .360
1991 Slugging Percentage: .474 Career: .410
Batting Avg with Men in Scoring Position: .322

Bats Right-Handed	G	AB	R	H	2B	3B	HR	RBI	BB	SO	SB	AVG
Vs. RHP		434	78	144	17	0	7	49	49	59	29	.332
Vs. LHP		155	30	57	10	3	8	29	16	19	7	.368
At Home	75	294	52	101	13	3	7	40	33	42	16	.344
On the Road	71	295	56	100	14	0	8	38	32	36	20	.339
1991 Season	146	589	108	201	27	3	15	78	65	78	36	.341
Life 8.4 Years		629	93	190	29	5	10	80	57	73	26	.302

STEVE FINLEY

HOUSTON CENTER FIELD 27 Years Old

Runs Created: 80
Offensive Winning Percentage: .560
Batting Average: .285 Secondary Average: .248

Most Often Bats: 1st
Swings at First Pitch: 26%
Gets Ahead of the Pitcher: 48%
Hits Behind the Pitcher: 52%

1991 On Base Percentage: .331 Career: .316
1991 Slugging Percentage: .406 Career: .363
Batting Avg with Men in Scoring Position: .311

Bats Left-Handed	G	AB	R	H	2B	3B	HR	RBI	BB	SO	SB	AVG
Vs. RHP		412	61	124	22	9	7	38	31	40	22	.301
Vs. LHP		184	23	46	6	1	1	16	11	25	12	.250
At Home	80	300	35	82	15	8	0	20	17	36	16	.273
On the Road	79	296	49	88	13	2	8	34	25	29	18	.297
1991 Season	159	596	84	170	28	10	8	54	42	65	34	.285
Life 2.4 Years		542	70	145	21	7	6	49	38	63	31	.269

MIKE FLANAGAN

BALTIMORE RELIEF PITCHER 40 Years Old

2-7 2.38 ERA 3 SAVES

Save Opportunities: 5 Blown Saves: 2 Holds: 14
Inherited Runners who Scored: 26%
Opponents Batting Average: .236
Double Play Support: 1.10 GDP Per Nine Innings

First Pitch is Hit: 15%
Gets Ahead of the Hitter: 47%
Gets Behind the Hitter: 53%
Gets First Batter Out: 67%

1991 On Base Pct Allowed: .289
Slugging Percentage: .323
Stolen Bases Allowed: 6 Caught Stealing: 3

Pitches Left	AB	H	2B	3B	HR	RBI	BB	SO	AVG
Vs. RHB	229	61	12	0	4	20	19	28	.266
Vs. LHB	127	23	1	0	2	10	6	27	.181

	G	IP	W-L	Pct	SO	BB	ERA	SV
1991 Season	64	98	2-7	.222	55	25	2.38	3
Life 12.0 Years	40	228	14-12	.539	123	72	3.84	0

TODD FROHWIRTH

BALTIMORE RELIEF PITCHER 29 Years Old

7-3 1.87 ERA 3 SAVES

Save Opportunities: 5 Blown Saves: 2 Holds: 10
Inherited Runners who Scored: 31%
Opponents Batting Average: .190
Double Play Support: .84 GDP Per Nine Innings

First Pitch is Hit: 12%
Gets Ahead of the Hitter: 49%
Gets Behind the Hitter: 51%
Gets First Batter Out: 84%

1991 On Base Pct Allowed: .255
Slugging Percentage: .267
Stolen Bases Allowed: 10 Caught Stealing: 4

Pitches Right	AB	H	2B	3B	HR	RBI	BB	SO	AVG
Vs. RHB	207	35	6	1	2	20	11	51	.169
Vs. LHB	130	29	8	2	0	16	18	26	.223

	G	IP	W-L	Pct	SO	BB	ERA	Sv
1991 Season	51	96	7-3	.700	77	29	1.87	3
Life 1.7 Years	74	110	6-4	.625	82	40	2.85	2

TRAVIS FRYMAN

DETROIT THIRD BASE 23 Years Old

Runs Created: 75
Offensive Winning Percentage: .460
Batting Average: .259 Secondary Average: .282

Most Often Bats: 7th
Swings at First Pitch: 35%
Gets Ahead of the Pitcher: 48%
Hits Behind the Pitcher: 52%

1991 On Base Percentage: .309 Career: .320
1991 Slugging Percentage: .447 Career: .454
Batting Avg with Men in Scoring Position: .290

Bats Right-Handed		AB	R	H	2B	3B	HR	RBI	BB	SO	SB	AVG
Vs. RHP		405	48	99	27	1	16	68	29	106	9	.244
Vs. LHP		152	17	45	9	2	5	23	11	43	3	.296
At Home	71	261	28	65	15	3	8	42	20	76	6	.249
On the Road	78	296	37	79	21	0	13	49	20	73	6	.267
1991 Season	149	557	65	144	36	3	21	91	40	149	12	.259
Life 1.3 Years		595	73	160	35	3	23	89	43	151	11	.270

GREG GAGNE

MINNESOTA SHORTSTOP 30 Years Old

Runs Created: 45
Offensive Winning Percentage: .409
Batting Average: .265 Secondary Average: .221

Most Often Bats: 9th
Swings at First Pitch: 35%
Gets Ahead of the Pitcher: 48%
Hits Behind the Pitcher: 52%

1991 On Base Percentage: .310 Career: .294
1991 Slugging Percentage: .395 Career: .391
Batting Avg with Men in Scoring Position: .252

Bats Right-Handed		AB	R	H	2B	3B	HR	RBI	BB	SO	SB	AVG
Vs. RHP		290	39	75	15	1	6	30	14	55	10	.259
Vs. LHP		118	13	33	8	2	2	12	12	17	1	.280
At Home	68	194	28	51	7	3	3	18	15	28	4	.263
On the Road	71	214	24	57	16	0	5	24	11	44	7	.266
1991 Season	139	408	52	108	23	3	8	42	26	72	11	.265
Life 6.1 Years		480	65	120	26	6	10	48	28	97	12	.250

RON GANT

ATLANTA CENTER FIELD 27 Years Old

Runs Created: 96
Offensive Winning Percentage: .646
Batting Average: .251 Secondary Average: .431

Most Often Bats: 4th
Swings at First Pitch: 28%
Gets Ahead of the Pitcher: 55%
Hits Behind the Pitcher: 45%

1991 On Base Percentage: .338 Career: .322
1991 Slugging Percentage: .496 Career: .467
Batting Avg with Men in Scoring Postion: .262

Bats Right-Handed		AB	R	H	2B	3B	HR	RBI	BB	SO	SB	AVG
Vs. RHP		397	63	94	19	3	22	68	46	81	22	.237
Vs. LHP		164	38	47	16	0	10	37	25	23	12	.287
At Home	73	258	53	72	16	1	18	52	36	52	14	.279
On the Road	81	303	48	69	19	2	14	53	35	52	20	.228
1991 Season	154	561	101	141	35	3	32	105	71	104	34	.251
Life 3.4 Years		604	97	156	32	5	28	84	56	113	29	.259

GARY GAETTI

CALIFORNIA THIRD BASE 33 Years Old

Runs Created: 63
Offensive Winning Percentage: .449
Batting Average: .246 Secondary Average: .198

Most Often Bats: 5th
Swings at First Pitch: 50%
Gets Ahead of the Pitcher: 47%
Hits Behind the Pitcher: 53%

1991 On Base Percentage: .293 Career: .306
1991 Slugging Percentage: .379 Career: .431
Batting Avg with Men in Scoring Position: .288

Bats Right-Handed		AB	R	H	2B	3B	HR	RBI	BB	SO	SB	AVG
Vs. RHP		427	39	106	15	1	12	40	20	79	5	.248
Vs. LHP		159	19	38	7	0	6	26	13	25	0	.239
At Home	76	280	29	77	5	1	12	31	20	59	2	.275
On the Road	76	306	29	67	17	0	6	35	13	45	3	.219
1991 Season	152	586	58	144	22	1	18	66	33	104	5	.246
Life 9.3 Years		597	75	152	29	3	23	88	42	105	8	.255

MIKE GALLEGO

OAKLAND SECOND BASE 31 Years Old

Runs Created: 63
Offensive Winning Percentage: .456
Batting Average: .247 Secondary Average: .274

Most Often Bats: 8th
Swings at First Pitch: 31%
Gets Ahead of the Pitcher: 51%
Hits Behind the Pitcher: 49%

1991 On Base Percentage: .343 Career: .314
1991 Slugging Percentage: .369 Career: .318
Batting Avg with Men in Scoring Position: .250

Bats Right-Handed		AB	R	H	2B	3B	HR	RBI	BB	SO	SB	AVG
Vs. RHP		360	46	81	9	3	7	36	47	68	5	.225
Vs. LHP		122	21	38	6	1	5	13	20	16	1	.311
At Home	79	230	30	62	8	3	6	20	40	34	1	.270
On the Road	80	252	37	57	7	1	6	29	27	50	5	.226
1991 Season	159	482	67	119	15	4	12	49	67	84	6	.247
Life 4.5 Years		387	49	90	14	2	5	36	44	60	5	.232

JIM GANTNER

MILWAUKEE THIRD BASE 38 Years Old

Runs Created: 58
Offensive Winning Percentage: .392
Batting Average: .283 Secondary Average: .137

Most Often Bats: 7th
Swings at First Pitch: 39%
Gets Ahead of the Pitcher: 51%
Hits Behind the Pitcher: 49%

1991 On Base Percentage: .320 Career: .321
1991 Slugging Percentage: .361 Career: .353
Batting Avg with Men in Scoring Position: .236

Bats Left-Handed		AB	R	H	2B	3B	HR	RBI	BB	SO	SB	AVG
Vs. RHP		387	51	112	24	4	2	34	21	26	2	.289
Vs. LHP		139	12	37	3	0	0	13	6	8	2	.266
At Home	69	254	31	73	14	1	1	20	15	15	2	.287
On the Road	71	272	32	76	13	3	1	27	12	19	2	.279
1991 Season	140	526	63	149	27	4	2	47	27	34	4	.283
Life 10.5 Years		565	67	156	24	4	4	52	35	46	12	.275

MIKE GARDINER

BOSTON STARTING PITCHER 26 Years Old
9-10 4.85 ERA

Opponents Batting Average: .274
Offensive Support: 6.23 Runs Per Nine Innings
Double Play Support: .76 GDP Per Nine Innings

First Pitch is Hit: 14%
Gets Ahead of the Hitter: 48%
Gets Behind the Hitter: 52%
Gets Leadoff Man Out: 61%

1991 On Base Pct Allowed: .333
Slugging Percentage: .438
Stolen Bases Allowed: 11 Caught Stealing: 5

Pitches Right	AB	H	2B	3B	HR	RBI	BB	SO	AVG
Vs. RHB	264	76	14	1	14	41	25	52	.288
Vs. LHB	247	64	12	1	4	23	22	39	.259

	G	IP	W-L	Pct	H	SO	BB	ERA
At Home	12	75	4-5		81	50	27	4.30
On the Road	10	55	5-5		59	41	20	5.60
1991 Season	22	130	9-10	.474	140	91	47	4.85
Life 0.7 Years	38	203	13-17	.429	231	138	74	5.36

MARK GARDNER

MONTREAL STARTING PITCHER 30 Years Old
9-11 3.85 ERA

Opponents Batting Average: .230
Offensive Support: 3.37 Runs Per Nine Innings
Double Play Support: .43 GDP Per Nine Innings

First Pitch is Hit: 10%
Gets Ahead of the Hitter: 41%
Gets Behind the Hitter: 59%
Gets Leadoff Man Out: 64%

1991 On Base Pct Allowed: .318
Slugging Percentage: .356
Stolen Bases Allowed: 13 Caught Stealing: 17

Pitches Right	AB	H	2B	3B	HR	RBI	BB	SO	AVG
Vs. RHB	223	52	8	0	7	27	24	46	.233
Vs. LHB	381	87	13	2	10	41	51	61	.228

	G	IP	W-L	Pct	H	SO	BB	ERA
At Home	10	65	4-4		52	46	30	2.51
On the Road	17	104	5-7		87	61	45	4.69
1991 Season	27	168	9-11	.450	139	107	75	3.85
Life 1.6 Years	38	218	10-14	.410	184	165	92	3.76

KIRK GIBSON

KANSAS CITY LEFT FIELD 35 Years Old

Runs Created: 68
Offensive Winning Percentage: .555
Batting Average: .236 Secondary Average: .355

Most Often Bats: 2nd
Swings at First Pitch: 25%
Gets Ahead of the Pitcher: 55%
Hits Behind the Pitcher: 45%

1991 On Base Percentage: .341 Career: .353
1991 Slugging Percentage: .403 Career: .463
Batting Avg with Men in Scoring Position: .231

Bats Left-Handed		AB	R	H	2B	3B	HR	RBI	BB	SO	SB	AVG
Vs. RHP		330	60	83	15	3	14	44	53	72	13	.252
Vs. LHP		132	21	26	2	3	2	11	16	31	5	.197
At Home	68	239	34	53	5	6	4	26	35	46	10	.222
On the Road	64	223	47	56	12	0	12	29	34	57	8	.251
1991 Season	132	462	81	109	17	6	16	55	69	103	18	.236
Life 8.2 Years		580	98	156	26	5	25	84	72	128	31	.269

PAUL GIBSON

DETROIT RELIEF PITCHER 32 Years Old
5-7 4.59 ERA 8 SAVES

Save Opportunities: 13 Blown Saves: 5 Holds: 10
Inherited Runners who Scored: 37%
Opponents Batting Average: .297
Double Play Support: 1.22 GDP Per Nine Innings

First Pitch is Hit: 11%
Gets Ahead of the Hitter: 52%
Gets Behind the Hitter: 48%
Gets First Batter Out: 60%

1991 On Base Pct Allowed: .379
Slugging Percentage: .424
Stolen Bases Allowed: 5 Caught Stealing: 5

Pitches Left	AB	H	2B	3B	HR	RBI	BB	SO	AVG
Vs. RHB	264	73	9	2	4	29	37	40	.277
Vs. LHB	113	39	1	2	6	30	11	12	.345

	G	IP	W-L	Pct	SO	BB	ERA	Sv
1991 Season	68	96	5-7	.417	52	48	4.59	8
Life 3.1 Years	69	135	6-7	.462	76	59	3.88	4

DAN GLADDEN

MINNESOTA LEFT FIELD 34 Years Old

Runs Created: 49
Offensive Winning Percentage: .383
Batting Average: .247 Secondary Average: .219

Most Often Bats: 1st
Swings at First Pitch: 28%
Gets Ahead of the Pitcher: 55%
Hits Behind the Pitcher: 45%

1991 On Base Percentage: .306 Career: .328
1991 Slugging Percentage: .356 Career: .380
Batting Avg with Men in Scoring Position: .222

Bats Right-Handed		AB	R	H	2B	3B	HR	RBI	BB	SO	SB	AVG
Vs. RHP		343	55	84	9	5	5	33	20	50	12	.245
Vs. LHP		118	10	30	5	4	1	19	16	10	3	.254
At Home	65	244	34	65	9	5	3	27	22	33	9	.266
On the Road	61	217	31	49	5	4	3	25	14	27	6	.226
1991 Season	126	461	65	114	14	9	6	52	36	60	15	.247
Life 6.1 Years		608	90	165	27	6	9	57	47	83	34	.272

TOM GLAVINE

ATLANTA STARTING PITCHER 26 Years Old
20-11 2.55 ERA

Opponents Batting Average: .222
Offensive Support: 4.71 Runs Per Nine Innings
Double Play Support: .69 GDP Per Nine Innings

First Pitch is Hit: 14%
Gets Ahead of the Hitter: 50%
Gets Behind the Hitter: 50%
Gets Leadoff Man Out: 77%

1991 On Base Pct Allowed: .277
Slugging Percentage: .330
Stolen Bases Allowed: 18 Caught Stealing: 10

Pitches Left	AB	H	2B	3B	HR	RBI	BB	SO	AVG
Vs. RHB	735	151	27	4	13	56	52	155	.205
Vs. LHB	170	50	8	2	4	18	17	37	.294

	G	IP	W-L	Pct	H	SO	BB	ERA
At Home	15	106	10-4		90	78	28	2.71
On the Road	19	140	10-7		111	114	41	2.44
1991 Season	34	247	20-11	.645	201	192	69	2.55
Life 3.8 Years	37	238	14-14	.505	229	137	75	3.81

LEO GOMEZ

BALTIMORE THIRD BASE 25 Years Old

Runs Created: 48
Offensive Winning Percentage: .437
Batting Average: .233 Secondary Average: .281

Most Often Bats: 7th
Swings at First Pitch: 26%
Gets Ahead of the Pitcher: 53%
Hits Behind the Pitcher: 47%

1991 On Base Percentage: .302 Career: .308
1991 Slugging Percentage: .409 Career: .393
Batting Avg with Men in Scoring Position: .188

Bats Right-Handed		AB	R	H	2B	3B	HR	RBI	BB	SO	SB	AVG
Vs. RHP		277	29	66	13	2	10	29	27	62	0	.238
Vs. LHP		114	11	25	4	0	6	16	13	20	1	.219
At Home	63	203	23	47	12	2	7	23	22	38	1	.232
On the Road	55	188	17	44	5	0	9	22	18	44	0	.234
1991 Season	118	391	40	91	17	2	16	45	40	82	1	.233
Life 0.8 Years		536	54	125	21	2	20	57	60	111	1	.233

LUIS GONZALEZ

HOUSTON LEFT FIELD 24 Years Old

Runs Created: 65
Offensive Winning Percentage: .568
Batting Average: .254 Secondary Average: .285

Most Often Bats: 4th
Swings at First Pitch: 37%
Gets Ahead of the Pitcher: 48%
Hits Behind the Pitcher: 52%

1991 On Base Percentage: .320 Career: .318
1991 Slugging Percentage: .433 Career: .427
Batting Avg with Men in Scoring Position: .272

Bats Left-Handed		AB	R	H	2B	3B	HR	RBI	BB	SO	SB	AVG
Vs. RHP		351	43	99	21	8	12	56	28	70	6	.282
Vs. LHP		122	8	21	7	1	1	13	12	31	4	.172
At Home	69	227	25	62	15	6	4	32	20	41	5	.273
On the Road	68	246	26	58	13	3	9	37	20	60	5	.236
1991 Season	137	473	51	120	28	9	13	69	40	101	10	.254
Life 0.9 Years		537	57	135	33	10	14	75	46	115	11	.251

TOM GORDON

KANSAS CITY RELIEF PITCHER 24 Years Old
9-14 3.87 ERA 1 SAVE

Save Opportunities: 4 Blown Saves: 3 Holds: 4
Inherited Runners who Scored: 35%
Opponents Batting Average: .221
Double Play Support: .46 GDP Per Nine Innings

First Pitch is Hit: 11%
Gets Ahead of the Hitter: 44%
Gets Behind the Hitter: 56%
Gets First Batter Out: 71%

1991 On Base Pct Allowed: .324
Slugging Percentage: .357
Stolen Bases Allowed: 9 Caught Stealing: 7

Pitches Right	AB	H	2B	3B	HR	RBI	BB	SO	AVG
Vs. RHB	283	54	9	3	12	32	45	86	.191
Vs. LHB	302	75	7	5	4	31	42	81	.248

	G	IP	W-L	Pct	SO	BB	ERA	Sv
1991 Season	45	158	9-14	.391	167	87	3.87	1
Life 2.6 Years	50	202	14-14	.514	195	106	3.79	1

JUAN GONZALEZ

TEXAS CENTER FIELD 22 Years Old

Runs Created: 82
Offensive Winning Percentage: .521
Batting Average: .264 Secondary Average: .299

Most Often Bats: 5th
Swings at First Pitch: 22%
Gets Ahead of the Pitcher: 50%
Hits Behind the Pitcher: 50%

1991 On Base Percentage: .321 Career: .312
1991 Slugging Percentage: .479 Career: .465
Batting Avg with Men in Scoring Position: .265

Bats Right-Handed		AB	R	H	2B	3B	HR	RBI	BB	SO	SB	AVG
Vs. RHP		398	54	100	27	1	18	75	26	90	3	.251
Vs. LHP		147	24	44	7	0	9	27	16	28	1	.299
At Home	73	262	37	70	16	0	7	40	19	62	1	.267
On the Road	69	283	41	74	18	1	20	62	23	56	3	.261
1991 Season	142	545	78	144	34	1	27	102	42	118	4	.264
Life 1.2 Years		589	81	152	37	2	27	103	42	130	3	.258

DWIGHT GOODEN

NEW YORK STARTING PITCHER 27 Years Old
13-7 3.60 ERA

Opponents Batting Average: .257
Offensive Support: 5.12 Runs Per Nine Innings
Double Play Support: .71 GDP Per Nine Innings

First Pitch is Hit: 15%
Gets Ahead of the Hitter: 50%
Gets Behind the Hitter: 50%
Gets Leadoff Man Out: 65%

1991 On Base Pct Allowed: .311
Slugging Percentage: .369
Stolen Bases Allowed: 33 Caught Stealing: 16

Pitches Right	AB	H	2B	3B	HR	RBI	BB	SO	AVG
Vs. RHB	309	81	11	4	8	38	14	75	.262
Vs. LHB	412	104	22	2	4	35	42	75	.252

	G	IP	W-L	Pct	H	SO	BB	ERA
At Home	15	106	9-3		98	85	29	3.55
On the Road	12	84	4-4		87	65	27	3.66
1991 Season	27	190	13-7	.650	185	150	56	3.60
Life 6.4 Years	37	268	21-8	.714	229	241	79	2.91

MARK GRACE

CHICAGO FIRST BASE 28 Years Old

Runs Created: 84
Offensive Winning Percentage: .536
Batting Average: .273 Secondary Average: .218

Most Often Bats: 2nd
Swings at First Pitch: 34%
Gets Ahead of the Pitcher: 52%
Hits Behind the Pitcher: 48%

1991 On Base Percentage: .346 Career: .372
1991 Slugging Percentage: .373 Career: .410
Batting Avg with Men in Scoring Position: .229

Bats Left-Handed		AB	R	H	2B	3B	HR	RBI	BB	SO	SB	AVG
Vs. RHP		367	61	101	21	2	6	39	47	20	3	.275
Vs. LHP		252	26	68	7	3	2	19	23	33	0	.270
At Home	83	322	57	93	18	1	5	32	38	28	1	.289
On the Road	77	297	30	76	10	4	3	26	32	25	2	.256
1991 Season	160	619	87	169	28	5	8	58	70	53	3	.273
Life 3.7 Years		602	81	179	30	4	10	75	73	52	10	.297

CRAIG GREBECK

CHICAGO SECOND BASE 27 Years Old

Runs Created: 42
Offensive Winning Percentage: .684
Batting Average: .281 Secondary Average: .353

Most Often Bats: 8th
Swings at First Pitch: 22%
Gets Ahead of the Pitcher: 51%
Hits Behind the Pitcher: 49%

1991 On Base Percentage: .386 Career: .333
1991 Slugging Percentage: .460 Career: .382
Batting Avg with Men in Scoring Position: .276

Bats Right-Handed		AB	R	H	2B	3B	HR	RBI	BB	SO	SB	AVG
Vs. RHP		109	21	28	8	1	1	10	18	18	1	.257
Vs. LHP		115	16	35	8	2	5	21	20	22	0	.304
At Home	55	109	17	32	8	0	3	12	19	19	1	.294
On the Road	52	115	20	31	8	3	3	19	19	21	0	.270
1991 Season	107	224	37	63	16	3	6	31	38	40	1	.281
Life 1.0 Years		335	43	81	19	4	7	39	45	62	1	.242

MIKE GREENWELL

BOSTON LEFT FIELD 28 Years Old

Runs Created: 81
Offensive Winning Percentage: .594
Batting Average: .300 Secondary Average: .226

Most Often Bats: 5th
Swings at First Pitch: 41%
Gets Ahead of the Pitcher: 57%
Hits Behind the Pitcher: 43%

1991 On Base Percentage: .350 Career: .378
1991 Slugging Percentage: .419 Career: .476
Batting Avg with Men in Scoring Position: .307

Bats Left-Handed		AB	R	H	2B	3B	HR	RBI	BB	SO	SB	AVG
Vs. RHP		376	50	108	17	4	5	49	35	23	11	.287
Vs. LHP		168	26	55	9	2	4	34	8	12	4	.327
At Home	71	255	35	77	17	3	5	42	27	13	5	.302
On the Road	76	289	41	86	9	3	4	41	16	22	10	.298
1991 Season	147	544	76	163	26	6	9	83	43	35	15	.300
Life 4.8 Years		580	83	180	34	5	17	98	61	44	12	.311

MARQUIS GRISSOM

MONTREAL CENTER FIELD 25 Years Ol

Runs Created: 69
Offensive Winning Percentage: .551
Batting Average: .267 Secondary Average: .303

Most Often Bats: 2nd
Swings at First Pitch: 28%
Gets Ahead of the Pitcher: 54%
Hits Behind the Pitcher: 46%

1991 On Base Percentage: .310 Career: .318
1991 Slugging Percentage: .373 Career: .362
Batting Avg with Men in Scoring Position: .286

Bats Right-Handed		AB	R	H	2B	3B	HR	RBI	BB	SO	SB	AVG
Vs. RHP		347	42	89	12	8	3	21	16	54	41	.256
Vs. LHP		211	31	60	11	1	3	18	18	35	35	.284
At Home	63	233	31	65	7	3	3	18	15	41	35	.279
On the Road	85	325	42	84	16	6	3	21	19	48	41	.258
1991 Season	148	558	73	149	23	9	6	39	34	89	76	.267
Life 1.7 Years		548	78	144	23	7	6	42	43	89	59	.263

TOMMY GREENE

PHILADELPHIA STARTING PITCHER 25 Years Old
13-7 3.38 ERA

Opponents Batting Average: .230
Offensive Support: 4.42 Runs Per Nine Innings
Double Play Support: .39 GDP Per Nine Innings

First Pitch is Hit: 13%
Gets Ahead of the Hitter: 46%
Gets Behind the Hitter: 54%
Gets Leadoff Man Out: 75%

1991 On Base Pct Allowed: .290
Slugging Percentage: .361
Stolen Bases Allowed: 18 Caught Stealing: 7

Pitches Right	AB	H	2B	3B	HR	RBI	BB	SO	AVG
Vs. RHB	315	61	12	0	7	30	21	72	.194
Vs. LHB	453	116	23	4	12	52	45	82	.256

	G	IP	W-L	Pct	H	SO	BB	ERA
At Home	19	109	6-4		95	89	34	3.31
On the Road	17	99	7-3		82	65	32	3.45
1991 Season	36	208	13-7	.650	177	154	66	3.38
Life 1.3 Years	43	222	13-9	.586	194	150	76	3.75

KEN GRIFFEY JR

SEATTLE CENTER FIELD 22 Years Old

Runs Created: 118
Offensive Winning Percentage: .781
Batting Average: .327 Secondary Average: .363

Most Often Bats: 3rd
Swings at First Pitch: 30%
Gets Ahead of the Pitcher: 52%
Hits Behind the Pitcher: 48%

1991 On Base Percentage: .399 Career: .367
1991 Slugging Percentage: .527 Career: .479
Batting Avg with Men in Scoring Position: .329

Bats Left-Handed		AB	R	H	2B	3B	HR	RBI	BB	SO	SB	AVG
Vs. RHP		389	56	129	32	1	17	74	51	52	17	.332
Vs. LHP		159	20	50	10	0	5	26	20	30	1	.314
At Home	79	282	44	103	23	0	16	59	36	47	9	.365
On the Road	75	266	32	76	19	1	6	41	35	35	9	.286
1991 Season	154	548	76	179	42	1	22	100	71	82	18	.327
Life 2.7 Years		594	85	178	35	3	22	90	66	91	19	.299

KEVIN GROSS

LOS ANGELES RELIEF PITCHER 31 Years Old
10-11 3.58 ERA 3 SAVES

Save Opportunities: 6 Blown Saves: 3 Holds: 4
Inherited Runners who Scored: 38%
Opponents Batting Average: .275
Double Play Support: .47 GDP Per Nine Innings

First Pitch is Hit: 13%
Gets Ahead of the Hitter: 49%
Gets Behind the Hitter: 51%
Gets First Batter Out: 56%

1991 On Base Pct Allowed: .348
Slugging Percentage: .380
Stolen Bases Allowed: 15 Caught Stealing: 6

Pitches Right	AB	H	2B	3B	HR	RBI	BB	SO	AVG
Vs. RHB	214	50	4	0	4	16	15	53	.234
Vs. LHB	233	73	9	2	6	32	35	42	.313

	G	IP	W-L	Pct	SO	BB	ERA	Sv
1991 Season	46	116	10-11	.476	95	50	3.58	3
Life 7.3 Years	42	216	12-14	.471	149	86	3.99	1

KELLY GRUBER

TORONTO THIRD BASE 30 Years Old

Runs Created: 58
Offensive Winning Percentage: .559
Batting Average: .252 Secondary Average: .291

Most Often Bats: 5th
Swings at First Pitch: 45%
Gets Ahead of the Pitcher: 43%
Hits Behind the Pitcher: 57%

1991 On Base Percentage: .308 Career: .312
1991 Slugging Percentage: .443 Career: .445
Batting Avg with Men in Scoring Position: .237

Bats Right-Handed		AB	R	H	2B	3B	HR	RBI	BB	SO	SB	AVG
Vs. RHP		317	45	77	14	2	12	47	23	55	11	.243
Vs. LHP		112	13	31	4	0	8	18	8	15	1	.277
At Home	59	221	32	58	6	0	8	31	18	34	7	.262
On the Road	54	208	26	50	12	2	12	34	13	36	5	.240
1991 Season	113	429	58	108	18	2	20	65	31	70	12	.252
Life 4.9 Years		536	77	141	26	4	21	79	34	85	15	.264

PEDRO GUERRERO

ST. LOUIS FIRST BASE 36 Years Old

Runs Created: 50
Offensive Winning Percentage: .509
Batting Average: .272 Secondary Average: .185

Most Often Bats: 4th
Swings at First Pitch: 35%
Gets Ahead of the Pitcher: 52%
Hits Behind the Pitcher: 48%

1991 On Base Percentage: .326 Career: .373
1991 Slugging Percentage: .361 Career: .485
Batting Avg with Men in Scoring Position: .350

Bats Right-Handed		AB	R	H	2B	3B	HR	RBI	BB	SO	SB	AVG
Vs. RHP		267	27	75	7	0	8	55	20	32	2	.281
Vs. LHP		160	14	41	5	1	0	15	17	14	2	.256
At Home	61	216	19	61	7	0	4	42	21	23	2	.282
On the Road	54	211	22	55	5	1	4	28	16	23	2	.261
1991 Season	115	427	41	116	12	1	8	70	37	46	4	.272
Life 9.2 Years		569	78	172	28	3	23	96	65	91	10	.302

OZZIE GUILLEN

CHICAGO SHORTSTOP 28 Years Old

Runs Created: 48
Offensive Winning Percentage: .323
Batting Average: .273 Secondary Average: .128

Most Often Bats: 9th
Swings at First Pitch: 57%
Gets Ahead of the Pitcher: 40%
Hits Behind the Pitcher: 60%

1991 On Base Percentage: .284 Career: .288
1991 Slugging Percentage: .340 Career: .333
Batting Avg with Men in Scoring Position: .248

Bats Left-Handed		AB	R	H	2B	3B	HR	RBI	BB	SO	SB	AVG
Vs. RHP		363	43	109	17	3	2	40	10	23	19	.300
Vs. LHP		161	9	34	3	0	1	9	1	15	2	.211
At Home	78	247	25	71	10	3	1	29	4	21	10	.287
On the Road	76	277	27	72	10	0	2	20	7	17	11	.260
1991 Season	154	524	52	143	20	3	3	49	11	38	21	.273
Life 6.7 Years		569	64	152	21	6	1	50	18	45	20	.267

MARK GUBICZA

KANSAS CITY STARTING PITCHER 29 Years Old
9-12 5.68 ERA

Opponents Batting Average: .308
Offensive Support: 4.26 Runs Per Nine Innings
Double Play Support: .95 GDP Per Nine Innings

First Pitch is Hit: 14%
Gets Ahead of the Hitter: 44%
Gets Behind the Hitter: 56%
Gets Leadoff Man Out: 68%

1991 On Base Pct Allowed: .361
Slugging Percentage: .424
Stolen Bases Allowed: 18 Caught Stealing: 6

Pitches Right	AB	H	2B	3B	HR	RBI	BB	SO	AVG
Vs. RHB	287	84	13	0	7	45	14	46	.293
Vs. LHB	258	84	14	3	3	36	28	43	.326

	G	IP	W-L	Pct	H	SO	BB	ERA
At Home	13	66	4-6		75	48	18	5.21
On the Road	13	67	5-6		93	41	24	6.15
1991 Season	26	133	9-12	.429	168	89	42	5.68
Life 6.4 Years	38	243	15-14	.530	232	159	92	3.76

LEE GUETTERMAN

NEW YORK RELIEF PITCHER 33 Years Old
3-4 3.68 ERA 6 SAVES

Save Opportunities: 9 Blown Saves: 3 Holds: 8
Inherited Runners who Scored: 30%
Opponents Batting Average: .268
Double Play Support: 1.13 GDP Per Nine Innings

First Pitch is Hit: 17%
Gets Ahead of the Hitter: 48%
Gets Behind the Hitter: 52%
Gets First Batter Out: 67%

1991 On Base Pct Allowed: .320
Slugging Percentage: .388
Stolen Bases Allowed: 4 Caught Stealing: 3

Pitches Left	AB	H	2B	3B	HR	RBI	BB	SO	AVG
Vs. RHB	243	74	14	2	4	31	18	22	.305
Vs. LHB	97	17	5	0	2	8	7	13	.175

	G	IP	W-L	Pct	SO	BB	ERA	Sv
1991 Season	64	88	3-4	.429	35	25	3.68	6
Life 4.2 Years	69	124	7-6	.544	55	38	4.03	5

BILL GULLICKSON

DETROIT STARTING PITCHER 33 Years Old
20-9 3.90 ERA

Opponents Batting Average: .288
Offensive Support: 5.81 Runs Per Nine Innings
Double Play Support: .87 GDP Per Nine Innings

First Pitch is Hit: 17%
Gets Ahead of the Hitter: 48%
Gets Behind the Hitter: 52%
Gets Leadoff Man Out: 72%

1991 On Base Pct Allowed: .321
Slugging Percentage: .435
Stolen Bases Allowed: 15 Caught Stealing: 8

Pitches Right	AB	H	2B	3B	HR	RBI	BB	SO	AVG
Vs. RHB	403	122	20	4	7	47	19	56	.303
Vs. LHB	487	134	31	3	15	55	25	35	.275

	G	IP	W-L	Pct	H	SO	BB	ERA
At Home	17	104	10-4		123	47	23	4.95
On the Road	18	123	10-5		133	44	21	3.01
1991 Season	35	226	20-9	.690	256	91	44	3.90
Life 8.4 Years	37	245	16-13	.546	248	128	60	3.66

MARK GUTHRIE

MINNESOTA RELIEF PITCHER 26 Years Old

7-5 4.32 ERA 2 SAVES

Save Opportunities: 2 Blown Saves: 0 Holds: 5
Inherited Runners who Scored: 36%
Opponents Batting Average: .303
Double Play Support: 1.47 GDP Per Nine Innings

First Pitch is Hit: 13%
Gets Ahead of the Hitter: 45%
Gets Behind the Hitter: 55%
Gets First Batter Out: 59%

1991 On Base Pct Allowed: .369
Slugging Percentage: .465
Stolen Bases Allowed: 9 Caught Stealing: 5

Pitches Left	AB	H	2B	3B	HR	RBI	BB	SO	AVG
Vs. RHB	297	87	17	5	7	36	34	58	.293
Vs. LHB	86	29	2	0	4	10	7	14	.337

	G	IP	W-L	Pct	SO	BB	ERA	Sv
1991 Season	41	98	7-5	.583	72	41	4.32	2
Life 1.6 Years	49	187	10-11	.471	131	63	4.11	1

JUAN GUZMAN

TORONTO STARTING PITCHER 25 Years Old

10-3 2.99 ERA

Opponents Batting Average: .197
Offensive Support: 5.97 Runs Per Nine Innings
Double Play Support: .45 GDP Per Nine Innings

First Pitch is Hit: 10%
Gets Ahead of the Hitter: 46%
Gets Behind the Hitter: 54%
Gets Leadoff Man Out: 66%

1991 On Base Pct Allowed: .294
Slugging Percentage: .268
Stolen Bases Allowed: 11 Caught Stealing: 6

Pitches Right	AB	H	2B	3B	HR	RBI	BB	SO	AVG
Vs. RHB	259	52	7	1	5	30	30	74	.201
Vs. LHB	238	46	6	1	1	15	36	49	.193

	G	IP	W-L	Pct	H	SO	BB	ERA
At Home	11	64	5-1		47	62	34	3.82
On the Road	12	75	5-2		51	61	32	2.28
1991 Season	23	139	10-3	.769	98	123	66	2.99
Life 0.6 Years	37	223	16-5	.769	158	198	106	2.99

MEL HALL

NEW YORK RIGHT FIELD 31 Years Old

Runs Created: 72
Offensive Winning Percentage: .583
Batting Average: .285 Secondary Average: .224

Most Often Bats: 4th
Swings at First Pitch: 40%
Gets Ahead of the Pitcher: 54%
Hits Behind the Pitcher: 46%

1991 On Base Percentage: .321 Career: .320
1991 Slugging Percentage: .455 Career: .441
Batting Avg with Men in Scoring Position: .250

Bats Left-Handed		AB	R	H	2B	3B	HR	RBI	BB	SO	SB	AVG
Vs. RHP		330	50	90	18	1	14	53	17	31	0	.273
Vs. LHP		162	17	50	5	1	5	27	9	9	0	.309
At Home	71	245	42	67	9	1	13	48	16	17	0	.273
On the Road	70	247	25	73	14	1	6	32	10	23	0	.296
1991 Season	141	492	67	140	23	2	19	80	26	40	0	.285
Life 6.8 Years		535	73	148	28	3	18	79	35	76	4	.277

JOSE GUZMAN

TEXAS STARTING PITCHER 29 Years Old

13-7 3.08 ERA

Opponents Batting Average: .239
Offensive Support: 5.20 Runs Per Nine Innings
Double Play Support: .58 GDP Per Nine Innings

First Pitch is Hit: 12%
Gets Ahead of the Hitter: 46%
Gets Behind the Hitter: 54%
Gets Leadoff Man Out: 66%

1991 On Base Pct Allowed: .330
Slugging Percentage: .341
Stolen Bases Allowed: 12 Caught Stealing: 13

Pitches Right	AB	H	2B	3B	HR	RBI	BB	SO	AVG
Vs. RHB	353	83	18	0	4	21	37	73	.235
Vs. LHB	283	69	15	1	6	30	47	52	.244

	G	IP	W-L	Pct	H	SO	BB	ERA
At Home	9	61	5-3		57	42	27	3.86
On the Road	16	109	8-4		95	83	57	2.64
1991 Season	25	170	13-7	.650	152	125	84	3.08
Life 3.3 Years	38	239	15-15	.495	228	162	97	3.97

TONY GWYNN

SAN DIEGO RIGHT FIELD 32 Years Old

Runs Created: 78
Offensive Winning Percentage: .655
Batting Average: .317 Secondary Average: .194

Most Often Bats: 3rd
Swings at First Pitch: 17%
Gets Ahead of the Pitcher: 53%
Hits Behind the Pitcher: 47%

1991 On Base Percentage: .355 Career: .382
1991 Slugging Percentage: .432 Career: .434
Batting Avg with Men in Scoring Position: .377

Bats Left-Handed		AB	R	H	2B	3B	HR	RBI	BB	SO	SB	AVG
Vs. RHP		319	40	106	20	7	2	43	21	12	6	.332
Vs. LHP		211	29	62	7	4	2	19	13	7	2	.294
At Home	63	244	32	75	13	4	1	21	17	12	5	.307
On the Road	71	286	37	93	14	7	3	41	17	7	3	.325
1991 Season	134	530	69	168	27	11	4	62	34	19	8	.317
Life 8.2 Years		629	93	206	30	9	6	67	56	33	30	.328

DARRYL HAMILTON

MILWAUKEE RIGHT FIELD 27 Years Old

Runs Created: 57
Offensive Winning Percentage: .531
Batting Average: .311 Secondary Average: .195

Most Often Bats: 3rd
Swings at First Pitch: 19%
Gets Ahead of the Pitcher: 53%
Hits Behind the Pitcher: 47%

1991 On Base Percentage: .361 Career: .340
1991 Slugging Percentage: .385 Career: .355
Batting Avg with Men in Scoring Position: .368

Bats Left-Handed		AB	R	H	2B	3B	HR	RBI	BB	SO	SB	AVG
Vs. RHP		318	57	102	13	5	1	46	29	26	15	.321
Vs. LHP		87	7	24	2	1	0	11	4	12	1	.276
At Home	63	195	33	67	10	4	0	24	21	21	7	.344
On the Road	59	210	31	59	5	2	1	33	12	17	9	.281
1991 Season	122	405	64	126	15	6	1	57	33	38	16	.311
Life 1.6 Years		422	67	121	15	4	2	55	34	37	21	.288

CHRIS HAMMOND

CINCINNATI STARTING PITCHER 26 Years Old

7-7 4.06 ERA

Opponents Batting Average: .250
Offensive Support: 3.52 Runs Per Nine Innings
Double Play Support: 1.17 GDP Per Nine Innings

First Pitch is Hit: 13%
Gets Ahead of the Hitter: 49%
Gets Behind the Hitter: 51%
Gets Leadoff Man Out: 65%

1991 On Base Pct Allowed: .339
Slugging Percentage: .340
Stolen Bases Allowed: 8 Caught Stealing: 3

Pitches Left	AB	H	2B	3B	HR	RBI	BB	SO	AVG
Vs. RHB	270	74	15	1	3	31	35	36	.274
Vs. LHB	98	18	2	1	1	11	13	14	.184

	G	IP	W-L	Pct	H	SO	BB	ERA
At Home	10	46	3-3		46	26	26	4.73
On the Road	10	54	4-4		46	24	22	3.50
1991 Season	20	100	7-7	.500	92	50	48	4.06
Life 0.6 Years	39	187	12-15	.438	177	91	101	4.30

PETE HARNISCH

HOUSTON STARTING PITCHER 25 Years Old

12-9 2.70 ERA

Opponents Batting Average: .212
Offensive Support: 3.49 Runs Per Nine Innings
Double Play Support: .25 GDP Per Nine Innings

First Pitch is Hit: 14%
Gets Ahead of the Hitter: 54%
Gets Behind the Hitter: 46%
Gets Leadoff Man Out: 70%

1991 On Base Pct Allowed: .288
Slugging Percentage: .313
Stolen Bases Allowed: 27 Caught Stealing: 6

Pitches Right	AB	H	2B	3B	HR	RBI	BB	SO	AVG
Vs. RHB	339	62	12	1	4	28	28	84	.183
Vs. LHB	457	107	16	4	10	35	55	88	.234

	G	IP	W-L	Pct	H	SO	BB	ERA
At Home	17	119	7-4		87	102	34	2.41
On the Road	16	97	5-5		82	70	49	3.05
1991 Season	33	217	12-9	.571	169	172	83	2.70
Life 2.3 Years	37	231	12-14	.475	207	166	107	3.74

GREG HARRIS

BOSTON RELIEF PITCHER 36 Years Old

11-12 3.85 ERA 2 SAVES

Save Opportunities: 5 Blown Saves: 3 Holds: 6
Inherited Runners who Scored: 33%
Opponents Batting Average: .243
Double Play Support: .88 GDP Per Nine Innings

First Pitch is Hit: 12%
Gets Ahead of the Hitter: 46%
Gets Behind the Hitter: 54%
Gets First Batter Out: 66%

1991 On Base Pct Allowed: .318
Slugging Percentage: .363
Stolen Bases Allowed: 1 Caught Stealing: 6

Pitches Right	AB	H	2B	3B	HR	RBI	BB	SO	AVG
Vs. RHB	342	83	16	2	8	40	35	69	.243
Vs. LHB	303	74	14	2	5	35	34	58	.244

	G	IP	W-L	Pct	SO	BB	ERA	Sv
1991 Season	53	173	11-12	.478	127	69	3.85	2
Life 7.6 Years	61	150	8-9	.472	114	64	3.64	5

ERIK HANSON

SEATTLE STARTING PITCHER 27 Years Old

8-8 3.81 ERA

Opponents Batting Average: .269
Offensive Support: 5.15 Runs Per Nine Innings
Double Play Support: .82 GDP Per Nine Innings

First Pitch is Hit: 14%
Gets Ahead of the Hitter: 47%
Gets Behind the Hitter: 53%
Gets Leadoff Man Out: 71%

1991 On Base Pct Allowed: .323
Slugging Percentage: .414
Stolen Bases Allowed: 11 Caught Stealing: 10

Pitches Right	AB	H	2B	3B	HR	RBI	BB	SO	AVG
Vs. RHB	321	97	15	2	6	22	38	59	.302
Vs. LHB	355	85	21	5	10	47	18	84	.239

	G	IP	W-L	Pct	H	SO	BB	ERA
At Home	14	89	4-5		100	80	19	4.25
On the Road	13	86	4-3		82	63	37	3.36
1991 Season	27	175	8-8	.500	182	143	56	3.81
Life 2.2 Years	37	252	16-11	.597	234	207	75	3.40

BRIAN HARPER

MINNESOTA CATCHER 32 Years Old

Runs Created: 62
Offensive Winning Percentage: .573
Batting Average: .311 Secondary Average: .170

Most Often Bats: 6th
Swings at First Pitch: 29%
Gets Ahead of the Pitcher: 53%
Hits Behind the Pitcher: 47%

1991 On Base Percentage: .336 Career: .322
1991 Slugging Percentage: .447 Career: .424
Batting Avg with Men in Scoring Position: .313

Bats Right-Handed	G	AB	R	H	2B	3B	HR	RBI	BB	SO	SB	AVG
Vs. RHP		327	39	101	21	0	8	55	9	14	1	.309
Vs. LHP		114	15	36	7	1	2	14	5	8	0	.316
At Home	60	217	27	74	14	1	4	35	7	12	1	.341
On the Road	63	224	27	63	14	0	6	34	7	10	0	.281
1991 Season	123	441	54	137	28	1	10	69	14	22	1	.311
Life 4.0 Years		465	52	136	30	2	10	63	17	30	2	.292

GREG W. HARRIS

SAN DIEGO STARTING PITCHER 28 Years Old

9–5 2.23 ERA

Opponents Batting Average: .233
Offensive Support: 3.32 Runs Per Nine Innings
Double Play Support: .20 GDP Per Nine Innings

First Pitch is Hit: 18%
Gets Ahead of the Hitter: 48%
Gets Behind the Hitter: 52%
Gets Leadoff Man Out: 75%

1991 On Base Pct Allowed: .273
Slugging Percentage: .363
Stolen Bases Allowed: 13 Caught Stealing: 8

Pitches Right	AB	H	2B	3B	HR	RBI	BB	SO	AVG
Vs. RHB	189	38	8	0	4	13	11	31	.201
Vs. LHB	309	78	9	0	12	27	16	64	.252

	G	IP	W-L	Pct	H	SO	BB	ERA
At Home	10	73	5-2		60	48	11	1.85
On the Road	10	60	4-3		56	47	16	2.70
1991 Season	20	133	9-5	.643	116	95	27	2.23
Life 2.4 Years	62	165	11-9	.551	134	128	54	2.34

LENNY HARRIS

LOS ANGELES THIRD BASE 27 Years Old

Runs Created: 52
Offensive Winning Percentage: .540
Batting Average: .287 Secondary Average: .177

Most Often Bats: 6th
Swings at First Pitch: 38%
Gets Ahead of the Pitcher: 54%
Hits Behind the Pitcher: 46%

1991 On Base Percentage: .349 Career: .334
1991 Slugging Percentage: .350 Career: .346
Batting Avg with Men in Scoring Position: .280

Bats Left-Handed		AB	R	H	2B	3B	HR	RBI	BB	SO	SB	AVG
Vs. RHP		342	44	102	16	1	2	29	31	24	12	.298
Vs. LHP		87	15	21	0	0	1	9	6	8	0	.241
At Home	70	211	30	58	6	0	1	17	18	18	5	.275
On the Road	75	218	29	65	10	1	2	21	19	14	7	.298
1991 Season	145	429	59	123	16	1	3	38	37	32	12	.287
Life 2.5 Years		486	64	137	17	2	3	40	36	39	18	.282

BILLY HATCHER

CINCINNATI LEFT FIELD 31 Years Old

Runs Created: 48
Offensive Winning Percentage: .427
Batting Average: .262 Secondary Average: .181

Most Often Bats: 2nd
Swings at First Pitch: 34%
Gets Ahead of the Pitcher: 49%
Hits Behind the Pitcher: 51%

1991 On Base Percentage: .312 Career: .315
1991 Slugging Percentage: .360 Career: .366
Batting Avg with Men in Scoring Position: .340

Bats Right-Handed		AB	R	H	2B	3B	HR	RBI	BB	SO	SB	AVG
Vs. RHP		312	31	80	18	2	3	30	18	35	10	.256
Vs. LHP		130	14	36	7	1	1	11	8	20	1	.277
At Home	72	216	25	58	16	1	2	17	16	24	8	.269
On the Road	66	226	20	58	9	2	2	24	10	31	3	.257
1991 Season	138	442	45	116	25	3	4	41	26	55	11	.262
Life 5.5 Years		569	78	151	28	4	7	51	36	64	35	.265

DAVE HENDERSON

OAKLAND CENTER FIELD 33 Years Old

Runs Created: 92
Offensive Winning Percentage: .599
Batting Average: .276 Secondary Average: .301

Most Often Bats: 2nd
Swings at First Pitch: 29%
Gets Ahead of the Pitcher: 50%
Hits Behind the Pitcher: 50%

1991 On Base Percentage: .346 Career: .327
1991 Slugging Percentage: .465 Career: .442
Batting Avg with Men in Scoring Position: .283

Bats Right-Handed		AB	R	H	2B	3B	HR	RBI	BB	SO	SB	AVG
Vs. RHP		428	59	107	19	0	17	61	43	90	5	.250
Vs. LHP		144	27	51	14	0	8	24	15	23	1	.354
At Home	76	282	40	73	9	0	15	39	29	57	1	.259
On the Road	74	290	46	85	24	0	10	46	29	56	5	.293
1991 Season	150	572	86	158	33	0	25	85	58	113	6	.276
Life 8.4 Years		536	77	141	30	2	21	74	50	113	6	.263

BRYAN HARVEY

CALIFORNIA RELIEF PITCHER 29 Years Old

2-4 1.60 ERA 46 SAVES

Save Opportunities: 52 Blown Saves: 6 Holds: 0
Inherited Runners who Scored: 27%
Opponents Batting Average: .178
Double Play Support: .34 GDP Per Nine Innings

First Pitch is Hit: 11%
Gets Ahead of the Hitter: 58%
Gets Behind the Hitter: 42%
Gets First Batter Out: 76%

1991 On Base Pct Allowed: .225
Slugging Percentage: .266
Stolen Bases Allowed: 12 Caught Stealing: 0

Pitches Right	AB	H	2B	3B	HR	RBI	BB	SO	AVG
Vs. RHB	122	21	1	0	2	11	6	39	.172
Vs. LHB	164	30	6	0	4	14	11	62	.183

	G	IP	W-L	Pct	SO	BB	ERA	Sv
1991 Season	67	79	2-4	.333	101	17	1.60	46
Life 3.0 Years	74	92	5-5	.500	109	38	2.45	37

CHARLIE HAYES

PHILADELPHIA THIRD BASE 27 Years Old

Runs Created: 39
Offensive Winning Percentage: .325
Batting Average: .230 Secondary Average: .174

Most Often Bats: 6th
Swings at First Pitch: 46%
Gets Ahead of the Pitcher: 44%
Hits Behind the Pitcher: 56%

1991 On Base Percentage: .257 Career: .276
1991 Slugging Percentage: .363 Career: .361
Batting Avg with Men in Scoring Position: .239

Bats Right-Handed		AB	R	H	2B	3B	HR	RBI	BB	SO	SB	AVG
Vs. RHP		270	21	57	9	1	8	31	10	45	2	.211
Vs. LHP		190	13	49	14	0	4	22	6	30	1	.258
At Home	75	248	20	65	16	1	6	34	10	36	2	.262
On the Road	67	212	14	41	7	0	6	19	6	39	1	.193
1991 Season	142	460	34	106	23	1	12	53	16	75	3	.230
Life 2.4 Years		558	48	138	24	1	13	64	23	91	4	.247

RICKEY HENDERSON

OAKLAND LEFT FIELD 33 Years Old

Runs Created: 91
Offensive Winning Percentage: .662
Batting Average: .268 Secondary Average: .487

Most Often Bats: 1st
Swings at First Pitch: 11%
Gets Ahead of the Pitcher: 57%
Hits Behind the Pitcher: 43%

1991 On Base Percentage: .400 Career: .403
1991 Slugging Percentage: .423 Career: .440
Batting Avg with Men in Scoring Position: .231

Bats Right-Handed		AB	R	H	2B	3B	HR	RBI	BB	SO	SB	AVG
Vs. RHP		356	74	93	14	1	10	40	77	54	50	.261
Vs. LHP		114	31	33	3	0	8	17	21	19	8	.289
At Home	71	248	54	69	10	0	8	28	48	36	27	.278
On the Road	63	222	51	57	7	1	10	29	50	37	31	.257
1991 Season	134	470	105	126	17	1	18	57	98	73	58	.268
Life 10.8 Years		603	130	176	29	5	17	63	111	81	92	.291

MIKE HENNEMAN

DETROIT RELIEF PITCHER 30 Years Old

10-2 2.88 ERA 21 SAVES

Save Opportunities: 24 Blown Saves: 3 Holds: 1
Inherited Runners who Scored: 20%
Opponents Batting Average: .258
Double Play Support: 1.07 GDP Per Nine Innings

First Pitch is Hit: 13%
Gets Ahead of the Hitter: 51%
Gets Behind the Hitter: 49%
Gets First Batter Out: 69%

1991 On Base Pct Allowed: .326
Slugging Percentage: .344
Stolen Bases Allowed: 3 Caught Stealing: 2

Pitches Right	AB	H	2B	3B	HR	RBI	BB	SO	AVG
Vs. RHB	187	47	8	2	2	24	11	44	.251
Vs. LHB	127	34	9	0	0	11	23	17	.268

	G	IP	W-L	Pct	SO	BB	ERA	Sv
1991 Season	60	84	10-2	.833	61	34	2.88	21
Life 4.2 Years	74	109	12-5	.700	75	41	2.90	19

OREL HERSHISER

LOS ANGELES STARTING PITCHER 33 Years Old

7-2 3.46 ERA

Opponents Batting Average: .259
Offensive Support: 6.19 Runs Per Nine Innings
Double Play Support: .64 GDP Per Nine Innings

First Pitch is Hit: 12%
Gets Ahead of the Hitter: 48%
Gets Behind the Hitter: 52%
Gets Leadoff Man Out: 71%

1991 On Base Pct Allowed: .316
Slugging Percentage: .330
Stolen Bases Allowed: 11 Caught Stealing: 2

Pitches Right	AB	H	2B	3B	HR	RBI	BB	SO	AVG
Vs. RHB	225	53	9	0	1	20	14	46	.236
Vs. LHB	208	59	9	2	2	20	18	27	.284

	G	IP	W-L	Pct	H	SO	BB	ERA
At Home	12	63	3-2		61	37	22	3.27
On the Road	9	49	4-0		51	36	10	3.70
1991 Season	21	112	7-2	.778	112	73	32	3.46
Life 6.4 Years	40	250	17-11	.613	216	172	74	2.77

JOE HESKETH

BOSTON RELIEF PITCHER 33 Years Old

12-4 3.29 ERA 0 SAVES

Save Opportunities: 0 Blown Saves: 0 Holds: 4
Inherited Runners who Scored: 42%
Opponents Batting Average: .250
Double Play Support: 1.12 GDP Per Nine Innings

First Pitch is Hit: 14%
Gets Ahead of the Hitter: 47%
Gets Behind the Hitter: 53%
Gets First Batter Out: 65%

1991 On Base Pct Allowed: .313
Slugging Percentage: .424
Stolen Bases Allowed: 7 Caught Stealing: 8

Pitches Left	AB	H	2B	3B	HR	RBI	BB	SO	AVG
Vs. RHB	481	121	25	5	17	44	41	86	.252
Vs. LHB	87	21	7	0	2	9	12	18	.241

	G	IP	W-L	Pct	SO	BB	ERA	Sv
1991 Season	39	153	12-4	.750	104	53	3.29	0
Life 4.3 Years	59	149	9-7	.586	117	57	3.46	4

GREG HIBBARD

CHICAGO STARTING PITCHER 27 Years Old

11-11 4.31 ERA

Opponents Batting Average: .266
Offensive Support: 4.87 Runs Per Nine Innings
Double Play Support: 1.25 GDP Per Nine Innings

First Pitch is Hit: 15%
Gets Ahead of the Hitter: 43%
Gets Behind the Hitter: 57%
Gets Leadoff Man Out: 67%

1991 On Base Pct Allowed: .320
Slugging Percentage: .402
Stolen Bases Allowed: 6 Caught Stealing: 8

Pitches Left	AB	H	2B	3B	HR	RBI	BB	SO	AVG
Vs. RHB	617	166	25	2	18	71	53	61	.269
Vs. LHB	120	30	2	0	5	19	4	10	.250

	G	IP	W-L	Pct	H	SO	BB	ERA
At Home	15	92	4-5		92	29	28	3.44
On the Road	17	102	7-6		104	42	29	5.10
1991 Season	32	194	11-11	.500	196	71	57	4.31
Life 2.3 Years	38	232	13-12	.534	231	93	65	3.58

KEN HILL

ST. LOUIS STARTING PITCHER 26 Years Old

11-10 3.57 ERA

Opponents Batting Average: .224
Offensive Support: 3.47 Runs Per Nine Innings
Double Play Support: .55 GDP Per Nine Innings

First Pitch is Hit: 14%
Gets Ahead of the Hitter: 48%
Gets Behind the Hitter: 52%
Gets Leadoff Man Out: 71%

1991 On Base Pct Allowed: .299
Slugging Percentage: .346
Stolen Bases Allowed: 19 Caught Stealing: 11

Pitches Right	AB	H	2B	3B	HR	RBI	BB	SO	AVG
Vs. RHB	289	60	15	3	7	33	30	59	.208
Vs. LHB	367	87	8	3	8	36	37	62	.237

	G	IP	W-L	Pct	H	SO	BB	ERA
At Home	14	88	6-4		63	60	34	3.18
On the Road	16	94	5-6		84	61	33	3.94
1991 Season	30	181	11-10	.524	147	121	67	3.57
Life 2.2 Years	38	215	11-15	.418	196	136	94	4.03

CHRIS HOILES

BALTIMORE CATCHER 27 Years Old

Runs Created: 37
Offensive Winning Percentage: .397
Batting Average: .243 Secondary Average: .226

Most Often Bats: 8th
Swings at First Pitch: 30%
Gets Ahead of the Pitcher: 52%
Hits Behind the Pitcher: 48%

1991 On Base Percentage: .304 Career: .293
1991 Slugging Percentage: .384 Career: .366
Batting Avg with Men in Scoring Position: .227

Bats Right-Handed		AB	R	H	2B	3B	HR	RBI	BB	SO	SB	AVG
Vs. RHP		228	26	54	9	0	5	23	18	45	0	.237
Vs. LHP		113	10	29	6	0	6	8	11	16	0	.257
At Home	52	153	16	35	7	0	5	12	16	26	0	.229
On the Road	55	188	20	48	8	0	6	19	13	35	0	.255
1991 Season	107	341	36	83	15	0	11	31	29	61	0	.243
Life 0.8 Years		492	51	114	23	0	14	45	42	91	0	.232

BRIAN HOLMAN

SEATTLE STARTING PITCHER 27 Years Old

13-14 3.69 ERA

Opponents Batting Average: .268
Offensive Support: 3.64 Runs Per Nine Innings
Double Play Support: 1.01 GDP Per Nine Innings

First Pitch is Hit: 14%
Gets Ahead of the Hitter: 44%
Gets Behind the Hitter: 56%
Gets Leadoff Man Out: 62%

1991 On Base Pct Allowed: .343
Slugging Percentage: .392
Stolen Bases Allowed: 4 Caught Stealing: 5

Pitches Right	AB	H	2B	3B	HR	RBI	BB	SO	AVG
Vs. RHB	352	88	15	2	10	35	31	60	.250
Vs. LHB	391	111	21	2	6	42	46	48	.284

	G	IP	W-L	Pct	H	SO	BB	ERA
At Home	17	119	9-7		106	74	32	2.65
On the Road	13	77	4-7		93	34	45	5.28
1991 Season	30	195	13-14	.481	199	108	77	3.69
Life 2.8 Years	39	241	13-16	.451	243	139	90	3.71

KENT HRBEK

MINNESOTA FIRST BASE 32 Years Old

Runs Created: 78
Offensive Winning Percentage: .647
Batting Average: .284 Secondary Average: .331

Most Often Bats: 4th
Swings at First Pitch: 36%
Gets Ahead of the Pitcher: 55%
Hits Behind the Pitcher: 45%

1991 On Base Percentage: .373 Career: .369
1991 Slugging Percentage: .461 Career: .490
Batting Avg with Men in Scoring Position: .310

Bats Left-Handed		AB	R	H	2B	3B	HR	RBI	BB	SO	SB	AVG
Vs. RHP		334	57	95	17	1	14	64	53	29	3	.284
Vs. LHP		128	15	36	3	0	6	25	14	19	1	.281
At Home	66	236	40	75	11	0	11	52	37	22	2	.318
On the Road	66	226	32	56	9	1	9	37	30	26	2	.248
1991 Season	132	462	72	131	20	1	20	89	67	48	4	.284
Life 8.8 Years		581	86	168	31	2	28	101	75	74	3	.289

DARRIN JACKSON

SAN DIEGO CENTER FIELD 28 Years Old

Runs Created: 54
Offensive Winning Percentage: .632
Batting Average: .262 Secondary Average: .304

Most Often Bats: 1st
Swings at First Pitch: 38%
Gets Ahead of the Pitcher: 45%
Hits Behind the Pitcher: 55%

1991 On Base Percentage: .315 Career: .296
1991 Slugging Percentage: .476 Career: .424
Batting Avg with Men in Scoring Position: .269

Bats Right-Handed		AB	R	H	2B	3B	HR	RBI	BB	SO	SB	AVG
Vs. RHP		196	23	51	7	1	10	23	15	42	4	.260
Vs. LHP		163	28	43	5	0	11	26	12	24	1	.264
At Home	60	174	26	45	3	1	12	24	13	29	3	.259
On the Road	62	185	25	49	9	0	9	25	14	37	2	.265
1991 Season	122	359	51	94	12	1	21	49	27	66	5	.262
Life 2.2 Years		379	49	96	15	2	15	44	22	69	6	.254

CHARLIE HOUGH

CHICAGO STARTING PITCHER 44 Years Old

9-10 4.02 ERA

Opponents Batting Average: .229
Offensive Support: 4.20 Runs Per Nine Innings
Double Play Support: .54 GDP Per Nine Innings

First Pitch is Hit: 12%
Gets Ahead of the Hitter: 44%
Gets Behind the Hitter: 56%
Gets Leadoff Man Out: 69%

1991 On Base Pct Allowed: .320
Slugging Percentage: .381
Stolen Bases Allowed: 10 Caught Stealing: 9

Pitches Right	AB	H	2B	3B	HR	RBI	BB	SO	AVG
Vs. RHB	374	83	17	3	13	45	50	59	.222
Vs. LHB	355	84	11	7	8	45	44	48	.237

	G	IP	W-L	Pct	H	SO	BB	ERA
At Home	15	107	5-5		89	59	41	3.38
On the Road	16	93	4-5		78	48	53	4.76
1991 Season	31	199	9-10	.474	167	107	94	4.02
Life 15.3 Years	51	216	13-12	.521	183	137	96	3.66

BRUCE HURST

SAN DIEGO STARTING PITCHER 34 Years Old

15-8 3.29 ERA

Opponents Batting Average: .241
Offensive Support: 4.71 Runs Per Nine Innings
Double Play Support: .57 GDP Per Nine Innings

First Pitch is Hit: 17%
Gets Ahead of the Hitter: 54%
Gets Behind the Hitter: 46%
Gets Leadoff Man Out: 76%

1991 On Base Pct Allowed: .292
Slugging Percentage: .340
Stolen Bases Allowed: 11 Caught Stealing: 6

Pitches Left	AB	H	2B	3B	HR	RBI	BB	SO	AVG
Vs. RHB	699	177	27	1	16	65	46	110	.253
Vs. LHB	136	24	3	0	1	10	13	31	.176

	G	IP	W-L	Pct	H	SO	BB	ERA
At Home	18	127	7-5		103	92	36	3.34
On the Road	13	95	8-3		98	49	23	3.22
1991 Season	31	222	15-8	.652	201	141	59	3.29
Life 8.8 Years	38	245	15-12	.561	248	174	76	3.84

MIKE JACKSON

SEATTLE RELIEF PITCHER 27 Years Old

7-7 3.25 ERA 14 SAVES

Save Opportunities: 22 Blown Saves: 8 Holds: 9
Inherited Runners who Scored: 19%
Opponents Batting Average: .201
Double Play Support: .51 GDP Per Nine Innings

First Pitch is Hit: 14%
Gets Ahead of the Hitter: 48%
Gets Behind the Hitter: 52%
Gets First Batter Out: 73%

1991 On Base Pct Allowed: .290
Slugging Percentage: .298
Stolen Bases Allowed: 5 Caught Stealing: 0

Pitches Right	AB	H	2B	3B	HR	RBI	BB	SO	AVG
Vs. RHB	200	34	4	1	3	21	17	51	.170
Vs. LHB	119	30	6	2	2	12	17	23	.252

	G	IP	W-L	Pct	SO	BB	ERA	Sv
1991 Season	72	89	7-7	.500	74	34	3.25	14
Life 4.5 Years	72	108	6-8	.417	91	52	3.53	6

CHRIS JAMES

CLEVELAND DESIGNATED HITTER 29 Years Old

Runs Created: 36
Offensive Winning Percentage: .313
Batting Average: .238 Secondary Average: .128

Most Often Bats: 2nd
Swings at First Pitch: 21%
Gets Ahead of the Pitcher: 52%
Hits Behind the Pitcher: 48%

1991 On Base Percentage: .273 Career: .303
1991 Slugging Percentage: .318 Career: .404
Batting Avg with Men in Scoring Position: .237

Bats Right-Handed		AB	R	H	2B	3B	HR	RBI	BB	SO	SB	AVG
Vs. RHP		306	23	78	11	1	3	29	11	41	1	.255
Vs. LHP		131	8	26	5	1	2	12	7	20	2	.198
At Home	60	221	14	64	8	2	1	21	10	20	1	.290
On the Road	55	216	17	40	8	0	4	20	8	41	2	.185
1991 Season	115	437	31	104	16	2	5	41	18	61	3	.238
Life 4.1 Years		586	63	154	27	4	16	73	32	86	5	.262

HOWARD JOHNSON

NEW YORK THIRD BASE 31 Years Old

Runs Created: 107
Offensive Winning Percentage: .718
Batting Average: .259 Secondary Average: .468

Most Often Bats: 5th
Swings at First Pitch: 27%
Gets Ahead of the Pitcher: 54%
Hits Behind the Pitcher: 46%

1991 On Base Percentage: .342 Career: .341
1991 Slugging Percentage: .535 Career: .466
Batting Avg with Men in Scoring Position: .276

Switch Hitter		AB	R	H	2B	3B	HR	RBI	BB	SO	SB	AVG
Vs. RHP		347	74	91	25	3	24	77	54	61	18	.262
Vs. LHP		217	34	55	9	1	14	40	24	59	12	.253
At Home	79	280	58	75	12	3	21	64	38	60	14	.268
On the Road	77	284	50	71	22	1	17	53	40	60	16	.250
1991 Season	156	564	108	146	34	4	38	117	78	120	30	.259
Life 7.3 Years		544	86	139	28	2	27	86	72	112	26	.256

LANCE JOHNSON

CHICAGO CENTER FIELD 28 Years Old

Runs Created: 59
Offensive Winning Percentage: .381
Batting Average: .274 Secondary Average: .156

Most Often Bats: 7th
Swings at First Pitch: 42%
Gets Ahead of the Pitcher: 47%
Hits Behind the Pitcher: 53%

1991 On Base Percentage: .304 Career: .311
1991 Slugging Percentage: .342 Career: .339
Batting Avg with Men in Scoring Position: .246

Bats Left-Handed		AB	R	H	2B	3B	HR	RBI	BB	SO	SB	AVG
Vs. RHP		424	52	121	11	12	0	41	16	37	19	.285
Vs. LHP		164	20	40	3	1	0	8	10	21	7	.244
At Home	80	286	33	76	5	6	0	22	14	26	12	.266
On the Road	80	302	39	85	9	7	0	27	12	32	14	.281
1991 Season	160	588	72	161	14	13	0	49	26	58	26	.274
Life 2.6 Years		566	72	154	17	10	0	49	33	55	34	.271

GREGG JEFFERIES

NEW YORK SECOND BASE 24 Years Old

Runs Created: 64
Offensive Winning Percentage: .570
Batting Average: .272 Secondary Average: .253

Most Often Bats: 3rd
Swings at First Pitch: 15%
Gets Ahead of the Pitcher: 58%
Hits Behind the Pitcher: 42%

1991 On Base Percentage: .336 Career: .332
1991 Slugging Percentage: .374 Career: .416
Batting Avg with Men in Scoring Position: .306

Switch Hitter		AB	R	H	2B	3B	HR	RBI	BB	SO	SB	AVG
Vs. RHP		312	34	81	9	1	8	44	32	29	17	.260
Vs. LHP		174	25	51	10	1	1	18	15	9	9	.293
At Home	69	244	35	72	10	1	5	28	30	21	14	.295
On the Road	67	242	24	60	9	1	4	34	17	17	12	.248
1991 Season	136	486	59	132	19	2	9	62	47	38	26	.272
Life 2.9 Years		597	86	164	33	3	15	71	49	47	22	.276

JEFF JOHNSON

NEW YORK STARTING PITCHER 25 Years Old
6-11 5.95 ERA

Opponents Batting Average: .305
Offensive Support: 4.18 Runs Per Nine Innings
Double Play Support: .92 GDP Per Nine Innings

First Pitch is Hit: 17%
Gets Ahead of the Hitter: 47%
Gets Behind the Hitter: 53%
Gets Leadoff Man Out: 67%

1991 On Base Pct Allowed: .351
Slugging Percentage: .453
Stolen Bases Allowed: 18 Caught Stealing: 4

Pitches Left	AB	H	2B	3B	HR	RBI	BB	SO	AVG
Vs. RHB	460	144	20	5	14	70	26	55	.313
Vs. LHB	52	12	1	0	1	7	7	7	.231

	G	IP	W-L	Pct	H	SO	BB	ERA
At Home	11	65	2-6		83	26	9	5.57
On the Road	12	62	4-5		73	36	24	6.35
1991 Season	23	127	6-11	.353	156	62	33	5.95
Life 0.6 Years	37	204	10-18	.353	251	100	53	5.88

RANDY JOHNSON

SEATTLE STARTING PITCHER 28 Years Old
13-10 3.98 ERA

Opponents Batting Average: .213
Offensive Support: 5.01 Runs Per Nine Innings
Double Play Support: .98 GDP Per Nine Innings

First Pitch is Hit: 8%
Gets Ahead of the Hitter: 45%
Gets Behind the Hitter: 55%
Gets Leadoff Man Out: 64%

1991 On Base Pct Allowed: .358
Slugging Percentage: .325
Stolen Bases Allowed: 18 Caught Stealing: 9

Pitches Left	AB	H	2B	3B	HR	RBI	BB	SO	AVG
Vs. RHB	623	133	30	1	13	67	137	203	.213
Vs. LHB	85	18	2	0	2	14	15	25	.212

	G	IP	W-L	Pct	H	SO	BB	ERA
At Home	17	106	6-5		85	114	72	3.92
On the Road	16	96	7-5		66	114	80	4.05
1991 Season	33	201	13-10	.565	151	228	152	3.98
Life 2.7 Years	37	228	14-13	.521	186	217	141	4.01

JIMMY JONES

HOUSTON STARTING PITCHER 28 Years Old

6-8 4.39 ERA

Opponents Batting Average: .270
Offensive Support: 3.86 Runs Per Nine Innings
Double Play Support: .60 GDP Per Nine Innings

First Pitch is Hit: 16%
Gets Ahead of the Hitter: 49%
Gets Behind the Hitter: 51%
Gets Leadoff Man Out: 70%

1991 On Base Pct Allowed: .336
Slugging Percentage: .374
Stolen Bases Allowed: 18 Caught Stealing: 6

Pitches Right	AB	H	2B	3B	HR	RBI	BB	SO	AVG
Vs. RHB	182	38	5	1	3	19	14	31	.209
Vs. LHB	348	105	13	4	6	40	37	57	.302

	G	IP	W-L	Pct	H	SO	BB	ERA
At Home	16	96	4-3		82	64	35	3.08
On the Road	10	39	2-5		61	24	16	7.62
1991 Season	26	135	6-8	.429	143	88	51	4.39
Life 2.8 Years	42	208	10-12	.475	226	103	69	4.42

WALLY JOYNER

CALIFORNIA FIRST BASE 30 Years Old

Runs Created: 98
Offensive Winning Percentage: .725
Batting Average: .301 Secondary Average: .285

Most Often Bats: 3rd
Swings at First Pitch: 27%
Gets Ahead of the Pitcher: 56%
Hits Behind the Pitcher: 44%

1991 On Base Percentage: .360 Career: .353
1991 Slugging Percentage: .488 Career: .455
Batting Avg with Men in Scoring Position: .331

Bats Left-Handed	G	AB	R	H	2B	3B	HR	RBI	BB	SO	SB	AVG
Vs. RHP		362	56	114	19	2	16	68	43	35	2	.315
Vs. LHP		189	23	52	15	1	5	28	9	31	0	.275
At Home	73	268	34	74	14	1	10	39	29	30	0	.276
On the Road	70	283	45	92	20	2	11	57	23	36	2	.325
1991 Season	143	551	79	166	34	3	21	96	52	66	2	.301
Life 5.2 Years		614	87	177	33	2	22	99	62	63	5	.288

ROBERTO KELLY

NEW YORK CENTER FIELD 27 Years Old

Runs Created: 72
Offensive Winning Percentage: .558
Batting Average: .267 Secondary Average: .335

Most Often Bats: 1st
Swings at First Pitch: 36%
Gets Ahead of the Pitcher: 50%
Hits Behind the Pitcher: 50%

1991 On Base Percentage: .333 Career: .336
1991 Slugging Percentage: .444 Career: .422
Batting Avg with Men in Scoring Position: .299

Bats Right-Handed	G	AB	R	H	2B	3B	HR	RBI	BB	SO	SB	AVG
Vs. RHP		327	39	83	18	1	11	43	25	59	22	.254
Vs. LHP		159	29	47	4	1	9	26	20	18	10	.296
At Home	63	232	40	72	11	0	11	30	21	32	23	.310
On the Road	63	254	28	58	11	2	9	39	24	45	9	.228
1991 Season	126	486	68	130	22	2	20	69	45	77	32	.267
Life 3.0 Years		566	80	160	26	3	15	64	42	115	41	.282

FELIX JOSE

ST. LOUIS RIGHT FIELD 27 Years Old

Runs Created: 88
Offensive Winning Percentage: .661
Batting Average: .305 Secondary Average: .257

Most Often Bats: 5th
Swings at First Pitch: 45%
Gets Ahead of the Pitcher: 43%
Hits Behind the Pitcher: 57%

1991 On Base Percentage: .360 Career: .334
1991 Slugging Percentage: .438 Career: .406
Batting Avg with Men in Scoring Position: .343

Switch Hitter	G	AB	R	H	2B	3B	HR	RBI	BB	SO	SB	AVG
Vs. RHP		306	34	95	22	4	6	47	27	62	10	.310
Vs. LHP		262	35	78	18	2	2	30	23	51	10	.298
At Home	78	280	34	83	16	5	3	39	25	48	9	.296
On the Road	76	288	35	90	24	1	5	38	25	65	11	.313
1991 Season	154	568	69	173	40	6	8	77	50	113	20	.305
Life 1.9 Years		556	67	157	31	4	10	71	41	109	17	.283

DAVE JUSTICE

ATLANTA RIGHT FIELD 26 Years Old

Runs Created: 78
Offensive Winning Percentage: .718
Batting Average: .275 Secondary Average: .412

Most Often Bats: 4th
Swings at First Pitch: 31%
Gets Ahead of the Pitcher: 50%
Hits Behind the Pitcher: 50%

1991 On Base Percentage: .377 Career: .371
1991 Slugging Percentage: .503 Career: .510
Batting Avg with Men in Scoring Position: .347

Bats Left-Handed	G	AB	R	H	2B	3B	HR	RBI	BB	SO	SB	AVG
Vs. RHP		241	50	66	19	0	14	48	51	57	8	.274
Vs. LHP		155	17	43	6	1	7	39	14	24	0	.277
At Home	49	175	34	47	12	1	11	41	30	39	5	.269
On the Road	60	221	33	62	13	0	10	46	35	42	3	.281
1991 Season	109	396	67	109	25	1	21	87	65	81	8	.275
Life 1.6 Years		570	96	158	33	2	32	108	85	117	14	.277

JIMMY KEY

TORONTO STARTING PITCHER 31 Years Old

16-12 3.05 ERA

Opponents Batting Average: .254
Offensive Support: 4.60 Runs Per Nine Innings
Double Play Support: .60 GDP Per Nine Innings

First Pitch is Hit: 12%
Gets Ahead of the Hitter: 52%
Gets Behind the Hitter: 48%
Gets Leadoff Man Out: 72%

1991 On Base Pct Allowed: .293
Slugging Percentage: .347
Stolen Bases Allowed: 6 Caught Stealing: 2

Pitches Left	AB	H	2B	3B	HR	RBI	BB	SO	AVG
Vs. RHB	703	175	34	2	10	57	38	106	.249
Vs. LHB	112	32	2	0	2	9	6	19	.286

	G	IP	W-L	Pct	H	SO	BB	ERA
At Home	18	110	7-8		120	66	27	3.43
On the Road	15	99	9-4		87	59	17	2.64
1991 Season	33	209	16-12	.571	207	125	44	3.05
Life 6.8 Years	42	218	15-10	.602	210	122	51	3.41

DARRYL KILE

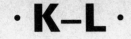

HOUSTON STARTING PITCHER 23 Years Old
7-11 3.69 ERA

Opponents Batting Average: .246
Offensive Support: 4.45 Runs Per Nine Innings
Double Play Support: .41 GDP Per Nine Innings

First Pitch is Hit: 16%
Gets Ahead of the Hitter: 45%
Gets Behind the Hitter: 55%
Gets Leadoff Man Out: 67%

1991 On Base Pct Allowed: .344
Slugging Percentage: .393
Stolen Bases Allowed: 12 Caught Stealing: 3

Pitches Right	AB	H	2B	3B	HR	RBI	BB	SO	AVG
Vs. RHB	242	54	8	2	9	34	28	36	.223
Vs. LHB	343	90	20	3	7	36	56	64	.262

	G	IP	W-L	Pct	H	SO	BB	ERA
At Home	18	78	4-5		68	49	45	3.36
On the Road	19	76	3-6		76	51	39	4.03
1991 Season	37	154	7-11	.389	144	100	84	3.69
Life 0.8 Years	46	193	9-14	.389	181	125	105	3.69

CHUCK KNOBLAUCH

MINNESOTA SECOND BASE 23 Years Old

Runs Created: 76
Offensive Winning Percentage: .545
Batting Average: .281 Secondary Average: .218

Most Often Bats: 2nd
Swings at First Pitch: 25%
Gets Ahead of the Pitcher: 53%
Hits Behind the Pitcher: 47%

1991 On Base Percentage: .351 Career: .351
1991 Slugging Percentage: .350 Career: .350
Batting Avg with Men in Scoring Position: .308

Bats Right-Handed		AB	R	H	2B	3B	HR	RBI	BB	SO	SB	AVG
Vs. RHP		417	53	121	16	5	1	44	45	30	23	.290
Vs. LHP		148	25	38	8	1	0	6	14	10	2	.257
At Home	75	287	43	94	12	5	1	26	30	18	17	.328
On the Road	76	278	35	65	12	1	0	24	29	22	8	.234
1991 Season	151	565	78	159	24	6	1	50	59	40	25	.281
Life 0.9 Years		606	84	171	26	6	1	54	63	43	27	.281

JOHN KRUK

PHILADELPHIA FIRST BASE 31 Years Old

Runs Created: 99
Offensive Winning Percentage: .733
Batting Average: .294 Secondary Average: .327

Most Often Bats: 4th
Swings at First Pitch: 26%
Gets Ahead of the Pitcher: 57%
Hits Behind the Pitcher: 43%

1991 On Base Percentage: .367 Career: .383
1991 Slugging Percentage: .483 Career: .442
Batting Avg with Men in Scoring Position: .275

Bats Left-Handed		AB	R	H	2B	3B	HR	RBI	BB	SO	SB	AVG
Vs. RHP		336	58	98	15	4	17	57	49	62	5	.292
Vs. LHP		202	26	60	12	2	4	35	18	38	2	.297
At Home	78	276	41	79	17	1	8	48	35	50	4	.286
On the Road	74	262	43	79	10	5	13	44	32	50	3	.302
1991 Season	152	538	84	158	27	6	21	92	67	100	7	.294
Life 4.9 Years		503	72	147	23	5	14	77	78	91	9	.291

ERIC KING

CLEVELAND STARTING PITCHER 28 Years Old
6-11 4.60 ERA

Opponents Batting Average: .279
Offensive Support: 4.06 Runs Per Nine Innings
Double Play Support: .54 GDP Per Nine Innings

First Pitch is Hit: 17%
Gets Ahead of the Hitter: 50%
Gets Behind the Hitter: 50%
Gets Leadoff Man Out: 68%

1991 On Base Pct Allowed: .328
Slugging Percentage: .384
Stolen Bases Allowed: 8 Caught Stealing: 3

Pitches Right	AB	H	2B	3B	HR	RBI	BB	SO	AVG
Vs. RHB	268	73	21	0	2	28	18	26	.272
Vs. LHB	326	93	12	4	5	44	26	33	.285

	G	IP	W-L	Pct	H	SO	BB	ERA
At Home	12	65	2-7		89	26	22	5.95
On the Road	13	86	4-4		77	33	22	3.57
1991 Season	25	151	6-11	.353	166	59	44	4.60
Life 3.9 Years	48	204	12-10	.552	188	107	79	3.85

BILL KRUEGER

SEATTLE STARTING PITCHER 34 Years Old
11-8 3.60 ERA

Opponents Batting Average: .289
Offensive Support: 4.17 Runs Per Nine Innings
Double Play Support: .98 GDP Per Nine Innings

First Pitch is Hit: 17%
Gets Ahead of the Hitter: 45%
Gets Behind the Hitter: 55%
Gets Leadoff Man Out: 65%

1991 On Base Pct Allowed: .346
Slugging Percentage: .418
Stolen Bases Allowed: 11 Caught Stealing: 5

Pitches Left	AB	H	2B	3B	HR	RBI	BB	SO	AVG
Vs. RHB	532	151	27	3	13	56	50	72	.284
Vs. LHB	140	43	7	1	2	16	10	19	.307

	G	IP	W-L	Pct	H	SO	BB	ERA
At Home	19	94	7-3		100	52	31	3.73
On the Road	16	81	4-5		94	39	29	3.44
1991 Season	35	175	11-8	.579	194	91	60	3.60
Life 4.2 Years	47	201	11-12	.490	216	99	90	4.19

LES LANCASTER

CHICAGO RELIEF PITCHER 30 Years Old
9-7 3.52 ERA 3 SAVES

Save Opportunities: 6 Blown Saves: 3 Holds: 4
Inherited Runners who Scored: 41%
Opponents Batting Average: .256
Double Play Support: .35 GDP Per Nine Innings

First Pitch is Hit: 15%
Gets Ahead of the Hitter: 46%
Gets Behind the Hitter: 54%
Gets First Batter Out: 63%

1991 On Base Pct Allowed: .315
Slugging Percentage: .376
Stolen Bases Allowed: 14 Caught Stealing: 14

Pitches Right	AB	H	2B	3B	HR	RBI	BB	SO	AVG
Vs. RHB	277	69	11	2	7	36	15	56	.249
Vs. LHB	310	81	15	1	6	36	34	46	.261

	G	IP	W-L	Pct	SO	BB	ERA	Sv
1991 Season	64	156	9-7	.563	102	49	3.52	3
Life 3.6 Years	64	152	9-6	.596	92	52	3.82	6

BILL LANDRUM

PITTSBURGH RELIEF PITCHER 33 Years Old

4-4 3.18 ERA 17 SAVES

Save Opportunities: 22 Blown Saves: 5 Holds: 4
Inherited Runners who Scored: 29%
Opponents Batting Average: .252
Double Play Support: .35 GDP Per Nine Innings

First Pitch is Hit: 15%
Gets Ahead of the Hitter: 52%
Gets Behind the Hitter: 48%
Gets First Batter Out: 80%

1991 On Base Pct Allowed: .296
Slugging Percentage: .329
Stolen Bases Allowed: 9 Caught Stealing: 1

Pitches Right	AB	H	2B	3B	HR	RBI	BB	SO	AVG
Vs. RHB	162	38	3	1	2	18	6	26	.235
Vs. LHB	139	38	4	1	2	18	13	19	.273

	G	IP	W-L	Pct	SO	BB	ERA	Sv
1991 Season	61	76	4-4	.500	45	19	3.18	17
Life 3.2 Years	73	101	5-4	.586	62	34	3.13	18

MARK LANGSTON

CALIFORNIA STARTING PITCHER 31 Years Old

19-8 3.00 ERA

Opponents Batting Average: .215
Offensive Support: 4.57 Runs Per Nine Innings
Double Play Support: .58 GDP Per Nine Innings

First Pitch is Hit: 13%
Gets Ahead of the Hitter: 50%
Gets Behind the Hitter: 50%
Gets Leadoff Man Out: 68%

1991 On Base Pct Allowed: .291
Slugging Percentage: .360
Stolen Bases Allowed: 10 Caught Stealing: 15

Pitches Left	AB	H	2B	3B	HR	RBI	BB	SO	AVG
Vs. RHB	755	162	29	1	29	75	82	156	.215
Vs. LHB	129	28	5	1	1	7	14	27	.217

	G	IP	W-L	Pct	H	SO	BB	ERA
At Home	18	127	9-3		103	105	45	3.33
On the Road	16	119	10-5		87	78	51	2.64
1991 Season	34	246	19-8	.704	190	183	96	3.00
Life 7.2 Years	37	257	16-14	.532	225	227	121	3.76

RAY LANKFORD

ST. LOUIS CENTER FIELD 25 Years Old

Runs Created: 67
Offensive Winning Percentage: .499
Batting Average: .251 Secondary Average: .292

Most Often Bats: 1st
Swings at First Pitch: 30%
Gets Ahead of the Pitcher: 51%
Hits Behind the Pitcher: 49%

1991 On Base Percentage: .301 Career: .311
1991 Slugging Percentage: .392 Career: .403
Batting Avg with Men in Scoring Position: .286

Bats Left-Handed		AB	R	H	2B	3B	HR	RBI	BB	SO	SB	AVG
Vs. RHP		346	52	90	12	8	9	43	25	66	24	.260
Vs. LHP		220	31	52	11	7	0	26	16	48	20	.236
At Home	79	283	47	67	10	10	4	33	23	53	28	.237
On the Road	72	283	36	75	13	5	5	36	18	61	16	.265
1991 Season	151	566	83	142	23	15	9	69	41	114	44	.251
Life 1.2 Years		590	81	152	28	14	10	69	46	120	44	.257

BARRY LARKIN

CINCINNATI SHORTSTOP 28 Years Old

Runs Created: 93
Offensive Winning Percentage: .748
Batting Average: .302 Secondary Average: .375

Most Often Bats: 3rd
Swings at First Pitch: 11%
Gets Ahead of the Pitcher: 55%
Hits Behind the Pitcher: 45%

1991 On Base Percentage: .378 Career: .350
1991 Slugging Percentage: .506 Career: .426
Batting Avg with Men in Scoring Position: .288

Bats Right-Handed		AB	R	H	2B	3B	HR	RBI	BB	SO	SB	AVG
Vs. RHP		329	56	96	20	2	12	47	27	49	16	.292
Vs. LHP		135	32	44	7	2	8	22	28	15	8	.326
At Home	64	242	55	79	17	2	16	48	30	37	17	.326
On the Road	59	222	33	61	10	2	4	21	25	27	7	.275
1991 Season	123	464	88	140	27	4	20	69	55	64	24	.302
Life 4.3 Years		603	94	178	28	6	14	68	49	54	31	.294

MIKE LaVALLIERE

PITTSBURGH CATCHER 31 Years Old

Runs Created: 43
Offensive Winning Percentage: .521
Batting Average: .289 Secondary Average: .176

Most Often Bats: 7th
Swings at First Pitch: 32%
Gets Ahead of the Pitcher: 54%
Hits Behind the Pitcher: 46%

1991 On Base Percentage: .351 Career: .356
1991 Slugging Percentage: .360 Career: .344
Batting Avg with Men in Scoring Position: .263

Bats Left-Handed		AB	R	H	2B	3B	HR	RBI	BB	SO	SB	AVG
Vs. RHP		282	22	85	9	1	3	27	30	18	2	.301
Vs. LHP		54	3	12	2	1	0	14	3	9	0	.222
At Home	56	163	10	54	5	1	1	22	20	13	2	.331
On the Road	52	173	15	43	6	1	2	19	13	14	0	.249
1991 Season	108	336	25	97	11	2	3	41	33	27	2	.289
Life 4.0 Years		465	36	126	21	1	4	54	62	45	1	.271

TIM LEARY

NEW YORK STARTING PITCHER 33 Years Old

4-10 6.49 ERA

Opponents Batting Average: .312
Offensive Support: 4.77 Runs Per Nine Innings
Double Play Support: .97 GDP Per Nine Innings

First Pitch is Hit: 14%
Gets Ahead of the Hitter: 44%
Gets Behind the Hitter: 56%
Gets Leadoff Man Out: 63%

1991 On Base Pct Allowed: .388
Slugging Percentage: .511
Stolen Bases Allowed: 10 Caught Stealing: 5

Pitches Right	AB	H	2B	3B	HR	RBI	BB	SO	AVG
Vs. RHB	214	69	13	0	11	37	27	41	.322
Vs. LHB	267	81	19	2	9	38	30	42	.303

	G	IP	W-L	Pct	H	SO	BB	ERA
At Home	12	56	1-4		62	39	26	5.75
On the Road	16	64	3-6		88	44	31	7.13
1991 Season	28	121	4-10	.286	150	83	57	6.49
Life 5.4 Years	42	216	11-16	.406	225	142	70	4.07

MANUEL LEE

TORONTO SHORTSTOP 27 Years Old

Runs Created: 35
Offensive Winning Percentage: .295
Batting Average: .234 Secondary Average: .124

Most Often Bats: 9th
Swings at First Pitch: 35%
Gets Ahead of the Pitcher: 48%
Hits Behind the Pitcher: 52%

1991 On Base Percentage: .274 Career: .294
1991 Slugging Percentage: .288 Career: .325
Batting Avg with Men in Scoring Position: .219

Switch Hitter		AB	R	H	2B	3B	HR	RBI	BB	SO	SB	AVG
Vs. RHP		301	27	63	9	3	0	18	14	82	7	.209
Vs. LHP		144	14	41	9	0	0	11	10	25	0	.285
At Home	69	213	25	53	12	2	0	12	18	50	3	.249
On the Road	69	232	16	51	6	1	0	17	6	57	4	.220
1991 Season	138	445	41	104	18	3	0	29	24	107	7	.234
Life 3.9 Years		455	47	115	15	4	3	41	28	91	5	.252

CHARLIE LEIBRANDT

ATLANTA STARTING PITCHER 35 Years Old
15-13 3.49 ERA

Opponents Batting Average: .245
Offensive Support: 4.04 Runs Per Nine Innings
Double Play Support: .24 GDP Per Nine Innings

First Pitch is Hit: 14%
Gets Ahead of the Hitter: 57%
Gets Behind the Hitter: 43%
Gets Leadoff Man Out: 74%

1991 On Base Pct Allowed: .292
Slugging Percentage: .363
Stolen Bases Allowed: 35 Caught Stealing: 11

Pitches Left	AB	H	2B	3B	HR	RBI	BB	SO	AVG
Vs. RHB	674	160	24	4	16	71	43	97	.237
Vs. LHB	190	52	14	1	2	20	13	31	.274

	G	IP	W-L	Pct	H	SO	BB	ERA
At Home	16	101	6-8		105	55	28	4.35
On the Road	20	128	9-5		107	73	28	2.81
1991 Season	36	230	15-13	.536	212	128	56	3.49
Life 8.4 Years	40	233	14-12	.532	240	110	67	3.68

DARREN LEWIS

SAN FRANCISCO CENTER FIELD 24 Years Old

Runs Created: 28
Offensive Winning Percentage: .507
Batting Average: .248 Secondary Average: .284

Most Often Bats: 1st
Swings at First Pitch: 20%
Gets Ahead of the Pitcher: 55%
Hits Behind the Pitcher: 45%

1991 On Base Percentage: .358 Career: .360
1991 Slugging Percentage: .311 Career: .300
Batting Avg with Men in Scoring Position: .229

Bats Right-Handed		AB	R	H	2B	3B	HR	RBI	BB	SO	SB	AVG
Vs. RHP		147	25	34	1	2	0	9	24	22	8	.231
Vs. LHP		75	16	21	4	1	1	6	12	8	5	.280
At Home	38	121	21	28	2	0	0	6	21	15	8	.231
On the Road	34	101	20	27	3	3	1	9	15	15	5	.267
1991 Season	72	222	41	55	5	3	1	15	36	30	13	.248
Life 0.6 Years		429	75	105	8	5	2	27	72	57	25	.245

CRAIG LEFFERTS

SAN DIEGO RELIEF PITCHER 34 Years Old
1-6 3.91 ERA 23 SAVES

Save Opportunities: 30 Blown Saves: 7 Holds: 3
Inherited Runners who Scored: 33%
Opponents Batting Average: .285
Double Play Support: .52 GDP Per Nine Innings

First Pitch is Hit: 16%
Gets Ahead of the Hitter: 58%
Gets Behind the Hitter: 42%
Gets First Batter Out: 65%

1991 On Base Pct Allowed: .318
Slugging Percentage: .408
Stolen Bases Allowed: 6 Caught Stealing: 4

Pitches Left	AB	H	2B	3B	HR	RBI	BB	SO	AVG
Vs. RHB	196	56	9	1	4	25	11	32	.286
Vs. LHB	64	18	2	2	1	17	3	16	.281

	G	IP	W-L	Pct	SO	BB	ERA	Sv
1991 Season	54	69	1-6	.143	48	14	3.91	23
Life 7.9 Years	73	105	5-6	.444	67	30	3.03	13

MARK LEITER

DETROIT RELIEF PITCHER 29 Years Old
9-7 4.21 ERA 1 SAVE

Save Opportunities: 2 Blown Saves: 1 Holds: 2
Inherited Runners who Scored: 40%
Opponents Batting Average: .245
Double Play Support: .53 GDP Per Nine Innings

First Pitch is Hit: 13%
Gets Ahead of the Hitter: 48%
Gets Behind the Hitter: 52%
Gets First Batter Out: 52%

1991 On Base Pct Allowed: .316
Slugging Percentage: .397
Stolen Bases Allowed: 6 Caught Stealing: 6

Pitches Right	AB	H	2B	3B	HR	RBI	BB	SO	AVG
Vs. RHB	281	70	10	3	7	41	24	70	.249
Vs. LHB	230	55	10	2	9	26	26	33	.239

	G	IP	W-L	Pct	SO	BB	ERA	Sv
1991 Season	38	135	9-7	.563	103	50	4.21	1
Life 0.9 Years	53	186	12-9	.556	143	68	4.64	1

JOSE LIND

PITTSBURGH SECOND BASE 28 Years Old

Runs Created: 48
Offensive Winning Percentage: .359
Batting Average: .265 Secondary Average: .147

Most Often Bats: 8th
Swings at First Pitch: 30%
Gets Ahead of the Pitcher: 48%
Hits Behind the Pitcher: 52%

1991 On Base Percentage: .306 Career: .303
1991 Slugging Percentage: .339 Career: .329
Batting Avg with Men in Scoring Position: .280

Bats Right-Handed		AB	R	H	2B	3B	HR	RBI	BB	SO	SB	AVG
Vs. RHP		335	34	88	14	5	1	39	16	36	5	.263
Vs. LHP		167	19	45	2	1	2	15	14	20	2	.269
At Home	80	262	24	64	7	5	2	30	17	32	4	.244
On the Road	70	240	29	69	9	1	1	24	13	24	3	.287
1991 Season	150	502	53	133	16	6	3	54	30	56	7	.265
Life 4.0 Years		591	64	153	24	6	2	53	39	65	12	.259

KEVIN MAAS

NEW YORK DESIGNATED HITTER 27 Years Old

Runs Created: 72
Offensive Winning Percentage: .541
Batting Average: .220 Secondary Average: .346

Most Often Bats: 4th
Swings at First Pitch: 19%
Gets Ahead of the Pitcher: 55%
Hits Behind the Pitcher: 45%

1991 On Base Percentage: .333 Career: .344
1991 Slugging Percentage: .390 Career: .439
Batting Avg with Men in Scoring Position: .179

Bats Left-Handed		AB	R	H	2B	3B	HR	RBI	BB	SO	SB	AVG
Vs. RHP		319	45	70	7	1	14	32	53	77	4	.219
Vs. LHP		181	24	40	7	0	9	31	30	51	1	.221
At Home	73	236	28	42	8	0	8	25	40	55	3	.178
On the Road	75	264	41	68	6	1	15	38	43	73	2	.258
1991 Season	148	500	69	110	14	1	23	63	83	128	5	.220
Life 1.4 Years		538	79	124	16	1	31	74	90	146	4	.231

MIKE MACFARLANE

KANSAS CITY CATCHER 28 Years Old

Runs Created: 45
Offensive Winning Percentage: .648
Batting Average: .277 Secondary Average: .296

Most Often Bats: 7th
Swings at First Pitch: 34%
Gets Ahead of the Pitcher: 47%
Hits Behind the Pitcher: 53%

1991 On Base Percentage: .330 Career: .311
1991 Slugging Percentage: .506 Career: .400
Batting Avg with Men in Scoring Position: .278

Bats Right-Handed		AB	R	H	2B	3B	HR	RBI	BB	SO	SB	AVG
Vs. RHP		155	21	38	8	1	8	27	10	33	1	.245
Vs. LHP		112	13	36	10	1	5	14	7	19	0	.321
At Home	43	126	14	36	7	2	6	17	9	20	0	.286
On the Road	41	141	20	38	11	0	7	24	8	32	1	.270
1991 Season	84	267	34	74	18	2	13	41	17	52	1	.277
Life 2.2 Years		481	50	124	29	3	11	67	33	85	1	.257

DAVE MAGADAN

NEW YORK FIRST BASE 29 Years Old

Runs Created: 62
Offensive Winning Percentage: .619
Batting Average: .258 Secondary Average: .285

Most Often Bats: 2nd
Swings at First Pitch: 21%
Gets Ahead of the Pitcher: 52%
Hits Behind the Pitcher: 48%

1991 On Base Percentage: .378 Career: .391
1991 Slugging Percentage: .342 Career: .393
Batting Avg with Men in Scoring Position: .291

Bats Left-Handed		AB	R	H	2B	3B	HR	RBI	BB	SO	SB	AVG
Vs. RHP		267	44	71	19	0	4	39	59	36	1	.266
Vs. LHP		151	14	37	4	0	0	12	24	14	0	.245
At Home	62	202	30	49	10	0	2	25	38	27	1	.243
On the Road	62	216	28	59	13	0	2	26	45	23	0	.273
1991 Season	124	418	58	108	23	0	4	51	83	50	1	.258
Life 3.7 Years		476	65	140	27	3	5	61	78	55	1	.294

SHANE MACK

MINNESOTA RIGHT FIELD 28 Years Old

Runs Created: 82
Offensive Winning Percentage: .695
Batting Average: .310 Secondary Average: .326

Most Often Bats: 7th
Swings at First Pitch: 44%
Gets Ahead of the Pitcher: 49%
Hits Behind the Pitcher: 51%

1991 On Base Percentage: .363 Career: .355
1991 Slugging Percentage: .529 Career: .446
Batting Avg with Men in Scoring Position: .265

Bats Right-Handed		AB	R	H	2B	3B	HR	RBI	BB	SO	SB	AVG
Vs. RHP		305	50	89	14	4	9	45	20	60	12	.292
Vs. LHP		137	29	48	13	4	9	29	14	19	1	.350
At Home	72	213	37	71	16	7	4	34	15	35	5	.333
On the Road	71	229	42	66	11	1	14	40	19	44	8	.288
1991 Season	143	442	79	137	27	8	18	74	34	79	13	.310
Life 2.6 Years		420	64	123	19	6	11	59	36	82	13	.292

GREG MADDUX

CHICAGO STARTING PITCHER 26 Years Old
15-11 3.35 ERA

Opponents Batting Average: .237
Offensive Support: 4.45 Runs Per Nine Innings
Double Play Support: .48 GDP Per Nine Innings

First Pitch is Hit: 16%
Gets Ahead of the Hitter: 53%
Gets Behind the Hitter: 47%
Gets Leadoff Man Out: 71%

1991 On Base Pct Allowed: .288
Slugging Percentage: .345
Stolen Bases Allowed: 25 Caught Stealing: 7

Pitches Right	AB	H	2B	3B	HR	RBI	BB	SO	AVG
Vs. RHB	392	84	16	2	4	29	22	85	.214
Vs. LHB	587	148	18	7	14	65	44	113	.252

	G	IP	W-L	Pct	H	SO	BB	ERA
At Home	18	128	7-5		118	94	36	3.45
On the Road	19	135	8-6		114	104	30	3.26
1991 Season	37	263	15-11	.577	232	198	66	3.35
Life 4.7 Years	37	248	16-14	.540	243	156	81	3.61

DAVE MARTINEZ

MONTREAL RIGHT FIELD 27 Years Old

Runs Created: 56
Offensive Winning Percentage: .638
Batting Average: .295 Secondary Average: .215

Most Often Bats: 5th
Swings at First Pitch: 24%
Gets Ahead of the Pitcher: 52%
Hits Behind the Pitcher: 48%

1991 On Base Percentage: .332 Career: .326
1991 Slugging Percentage: .419 Career: .388
Batting Avg with Men in Scoring Position: .302

Bats Left-Handed		AB	R	H	2B	3B	HR	RBI	BB	SO	SB	AVG
Vs. RHP		303	34	95	12	4	7	34	15	32	14	.314
Vs. LHP		93	13	22	6	1	0	8	5	22	2	.237
At Home	57	173	15	49	9	2	3	21	8	19	7	.283
On the Road	67	223	32	68	9	3	4	21	12	35	9	.305
1991 Season	124	396	47	117	18	5	7	42	20	54	16	.295
Life 4.3 Years		500	65	136	18	7	8	46	40	86	22	.272

DENNIS MARTINEZ

MONTREAL STARTING PITCHER 37 Years Old

14-11 2.39 ERA

Opponents Batting Average: .226
Offensive Support: 3.69 Runs Per Nine Innings
Double Play Support: .57 GDP Per Nine Innings

First Pitch is Hit: 14%
Gets Ahead of the Hitter: 53%
Gets Behind the Hitter: 47%
Gets Leadoff Man Out: 75%

1991 On Base Pct Allowed: .282
Slugging Percentage: .311
Stolen Bases Allowed: 22 Caught Stealing: 4

Pitches Right	AB	H	2B	3B	HR	RBI	BB	SO	AVG
Vs. RHB	340	73	15	4	5	28	11	50	.215
Vs. LHB	489	114	17	2	4	34	51	73	.233

	G	IP	W-L	Pct	H	SO	BB	ERA
At Home	13	96	7-4		86	51	21	2.16
On the Road	18	126	7-7		101	72	41	2.57
1991 Season	31	222	14-11	.560	187	123	62	2.39
Life 12.2 Years	40	241	15-12	.550	236	127	71	3.71

RAMON MARTINEZ

LOS ANGELES STARTING PITCHER 24 Years Old

17-13 3.27 ERA

Opponents Batting Average: .229
Offensive Support: 4.94 Runs Per Nine Innings
Double Play Support: .25 GDP Per Nine Innings

First Pitch is Hit: 12%
Gets Ahead of the Hitter: 49%
Gets Behind the Hitter: 51%
Gets Leadoff Man Out: 72%

1991 On Base Pct Allowed: .293
Slugging Percentage: .337
Stolen Bases Allowed: 16 Caught Stealing: 9

Pitches Right	AB	H	2B	3B	HR	RBI	BB	SO	AVG
Vs. RHB	375	88	12	1	11	40	21	69	.235
Vs. LHB	453	102	21	0	7	39	48	81	.225

	G	IP	W-L	Pct	H	SO	BB	ERA
At Home	15	105	9-4		82	85	37	2.91
On the Road	18	115	8-9		108	65	32	3.59
1991 Season	33	220	17-13	.567	190	150	69	3.27
Life 2.4 Years	38	246	18-11	.629	204	203	83	3.15

KIRK McCASKILL

CALIFORNIA STARTING PITCHER 31 Years Old

10-19 4.26 ERA

Opponents Batting Average: .283
Offensive Support: 3.14 Runs Per Nine Innings
Double Play Support: 1.11 GDP Per Nine Innings

First Pitch is Hit: 13%
Gets Ahead of the Hitter: 47%
Gets Behind the Hitter: 53%
Gets Leadoff Man Out: 65%

1991 On Base Pct Allowed: .347
Slugging Percentage: .435
Stolen Bases Allowed: 8 Caught Stealing: 6

Pitches Right	AB	H	2B	3B	HR	RBI	BB	SO	AVG
Vs. RHB	330	83	19	3	8	33	44	47	.252
Vs. LHB	351	110	17	2	11	50	22	24	.313

	G	IP	W-L	Pct	H	SO	BB	ERA
At Home	15	93	4-10		94	38	27	4.08
On the Road	15	85	6-9		99	33	39	4.45
1991 Season	30	178	10-19	.345	193	71	66	4.26
Life 5.1 Years	37	237	15-14	.513	231	139	87	3.86

EDGAR MARTINEZ

SEATTLE THIRD BASE 29 Years Old

Runs Created: 100
Offensive Winning Percentage: .711
Batting Average: .307 Secondary Average: .300

Most Often Bats: 1st
Swings at First Pitch: 14%
Gets Ahead of the Pitcher: 48%
Hits Behind the Pitcher: 52%

1991 On Base Percentage: .405 Career: .389
1991 Slugging Percentage: .452 Career: .428
Batting Avg with Men in Scoring Position: .219

Bats Right-Handed	G	AB	R	H	2B	3B	HR	RBI	BB	SO	SB	AVG
Vs. RHP		388	71	111	22	1	12	40	60	61	0	.286
Vs. LHP		156	27	56	13	0	2	12	24	11	0	.359
At Home	72	250	47	80	14	1	8	28	45	33	0	.320
On the Road	78	294	51	87	21	0	6	24	39	39	0	.296
1991 Season	150	544	98	167	35	1	14	52	84	72	0	.307
Life 2.4 Years		536	82	159	32	2	11	55	76	72	1	.298

DON MATTINGLY

NEW YORK FIRST BASE 31 Years Old

Runs Created: 76
Offensive Winning Percentage: .509
Batting Average: .288 Secondary Average: .187

Most Often Bats: 3rd
Swings at First Pitch: 15%
Gets Ahead of the Pitcher: 58%
Hits Behind the Pitcher: 42%

1991 On Base Percentage: .339 Career: .360
1991 Slugging Percentage: .394 Career: .491
Batting Avg with Men in Scoring Position: .292

Bats Left-Handed	G	AB	R	H	2B	3B	HR	RBI	BB	SO	SB	AVG
Vs. RHP		360	36	109	23	0	4	39	28	22	0	.303
Vs. LHP		227	28	60	12	0	5	29	18	20	2	.264
At Home	71	266	34	81	21	0	7	40	22	20	0	.305
On the Road	81	321	30	88	14	0	2	28	24	22	2	.274
1991 Season	152	587	64	169	35	0	9	68	46	42	2	.288
Life 7.8 Years		639	92	200	41	2	23	106	50	38	1	.314

BEN McDONALD

BALTIMORE STARTING PITCHER 24 Years Old

6-8 4.84 ERA

Opponents Batting Average: .261
Offensive Support: 5.06 Runs Per Nine Innings
Double Play Support: .78 GDP Per Nine Innings

First Pitch is Hit: 12%
Gets Ahead of the Hitter: 48%
Gets Behind the Hitter: 52%
Gets Leadoff Man Out: 75%

1991 On Base Pct Allowed: .321
Slugging Percentage: .418
Stolen Bases Allowed: 14 Caught Stealing: 3

Pitches Right	AB	H	2B	3B	HR	RBI	BB	SO	AVG
Vs. RHB	227	71	14	2	8	32	17	35	.313
Vs. LHB	256	55	8	1	8	30	26	50	.215

	G	IP	W-L	Pct	H	SO	BB	ERA
At Home	10	73	2-4		75	50	12	3.70
On the Road	11	53	4-4		51	35	31	6.41
1991 Season	21	126	6-8	.429	126	85	43	4.84
Life 1.1 Years	42	222	13-11	.536	196	135	72	3.82

JACK McDOWELL

CHICAGO STARTING PITCHER 26 Years Old

17-10 3.41 ERA

Opponents Batting Average: .228
Offensive Support: 5.53 Runs Per Nine Innings
Double Play Support: .43 GDP Per Nine Innings

First Pitch is Hit: 13%
Gets Ahead of the Hitter: 52%
Gets Behind the Hitter: 48%
Gets Leadoff Man Out: 74%

1991 On Base Pct Allowed: .292
Slugging Percentage: .347
Stolen Bases Allowed: 22 Caught Stealing: 10

Pitches Right	AB	H	2B	3B	HR	RBI	BB	SO	AVG
Vs. RHB	445	103	21	3	12	49	40	107	.231
Vs. LHB	485	109	23	2	7	40	42	84	.225

	G	IP	W-L	Pct	H	SO	BB	ERA
At Home	20	139	10-6		134	101	48	3.89
On the Road	15	115	7-4		78	90	34	2.82
1991 Season	35	254	17-10	.630	212	191	82	3.41
Life 2.6 Years	37	244	15-11	.574	213	172	88	3.61

ROGER McDOWELL

LOS ANGELES RELIEF PITCHER 31 Years Old

9-9 2.93 ERA 10 SAVES

Save Opportunities: 15 Blown Saves: 5 Holds: 10
Inherited Runners who Scored: 33%
Opponents Batting Average: .262
Double Play Support: .89 GDP Per Nine Innings

First Pitch is Hit: 16%
Gets Ahead of the Hitter: 48%
Gets Behind the Hitter: 52%
Gets First Batter Out: 60%

1991 On Base Pct Allowed: .346
Slugging Percentage: .357
Stolen Bases Allowed: 12 Caught Stealing: 4

Pitches Right	AB	H	2B	3B	HR	RBI	BB	SO	AVG
Vs. RHB	185	47	10	0	2	21	12	25	.254
Vs. LHB	196	53	10	2	2	26	36	25	.270

	G	IP	W-L	Pct	SO	BB	ERA	Sv
1991 Season	71	101	9-9	.500	50	48	2.93	10
Life 6.3 Years	74	112	8-8	.510	55	41	3.03	21

CHUCK McELROY

CHICAGO RELIEF PITCHER 24 Years Old

6-2 1.95 ERA 3 SAVES

Save Opportunities: 6 Blown Saves: 3 Holds: 10
Inherited Runners who Scored: 36%
Opponents Batting Average: .210
Double Play Support: .53 GDP Per Nine Innings

First Pitch is Hit: 11%
Gets Ahead of the Hitter: 49%
Gets Behind the Hitter: 51%
Gets First Batter Out: 68%

1991 On Base Pct Allowed: .317
Slugging Percentage: .305
Stolen Bases Allowed: 12 Caught Stealing: 10

Pitches Left	AB	H	2B	3B	HR	RBI	BB	SO	AVG
Vs. RHB	225	52	7	1	4	23	38	50	.231
Vs. LHB	122	21	3	0	3	15	19	42	.172

	G	IP	W-L	Pct	SO	BB	ERA	Sv
1991 Season	71	101	6-2	.750	92	57	1.95	3
Life 1.3 Years	74	95	5-2	.667	88	54	2.58	2

WILLIE McGEE

SAN FRANCISCO CENTER FIELD 33 Years Old

Runs Created: 71
Offensive Winning Percentage: .606
Batting Average: .312 Secondary Average: .199

Most Often Bats: 2nd
Swings at First Pitch: 41%
Gets Ahead of the Pitcher: 45%
Hits Behind the Pitcher: 55%

1991 On Base Percentage: .357 Career: .334
1991 Slugging Percentage: .408 Career: .407
Batting Avg with Men in Scoring Position: .343

Switch Hitter	G	AB	R	H	2B	3B	HR	RBI	BB	SO	SB	AVG
Vs. RHP		343	45	103	19	3	2	23	24	50	11	.300
Vs. LHP		154	22	52	11	0	2	20	10	24	6	.338
At Home	61	222	25	60	12	0	2	20	12	29	6	.270
On the Road	70	275	42	95	18	3	2	23	22	45	11	.345
1991 Season	131	497	67	155	30	3	4	43	34	74	17	.312
Life 8.2 Years		636	88	189	29	10	7	74	35	97	36	.298

FRED McGRIFF

SAN DIEGO FIRST BASE 28 Years Old

Runs Created: 107
Offensive Winning Percentage: .767
Batting Average: .278 Secondary Average: .422

Most Often Bats: 4th
Swings at First Pitch: 31%
Gets Ahead of the Pitcher: 51%
Hits Behind the Pitcher: 49%

1991 On Base Percentage: .396 Career: .391
1991 Slugging Percentage: .494 Career: .522
Batting Avg with Men in Scoring Position: .271

Bats Left-Handed	G	AB	R	H	2B	3B	HR	RBI	BB	SO	SB	AVG
Vs. RHP		315	50	89	12	0	17	58	66	79	2	.283
Vs. LHP		213	34	58	7	1	14	48	39	56	2	.272
At Home	74	239	46	67	7	0	18	53	60	68	4	.280
On the Road	79	289	38	80	12	1	13	53	45	67	0	.277
1991 Season	153	528	84	147	19	1	31	106	105	135	4	.278
Life 4.5 Years		548	96	152	26	2	35	91	101	140	6	.278

MARK McGWIRE

OAKLAND FIRST BASE 28 Years Old

Runs Created: 65
Offensive Winning Percentage: .456
Batting Average: .201 Secondary Average: .379

Most Often Bats: 6th
Swings at First Pitch: 43%
Gets Ahead of the Pitcher: 49%
Hits Behind the Pitcher: 51%

1991 On Base Percentage: .330 Career: .351
1991 Slugging Percentage: .383 Career: .488
Batting Avg with Men in Scoring Position: .240

Bats Right-Handed	G	AB	R	H	2B	3B	HR	RBI	BB	SO	SB	AVG
Vs. RHP		353	46	71	17	0	17	56	70	88	2	.201
Vs. LHP		130	16	26	5	0	5	19	23	28	0	.200
At Home	77	243	34	45	10	0	15	48	52	55	1	.185
On the Road	77	240	28	52	12	0	7	27	41	61	1	.217
1991 Season	154	483	62	97	22	0	22	75	93	116	2	.201
Life 4.8 Years		554	87	135	22	1	37	105	91	123	1	.244

BRIAN McRAE

KANSAS CITY CENTER FIELD 24 Years Old

Runs Created: 64
Offensive Winning Percentage: .379
Batting Average: .261 Secondary Average: .181

Most Often Bats: 1st
Swings at First Pitch: 32%
Gets Ahead of the Pitcher: 47%
Hits Behind the Pitcher: 53%

1991 On Base Percentage: .288 Career: .294
1991 Slugging Percentage: .372 Career: .379
Batting Avg with Men in Scoring Position: .259

Switch Hitter		AB	R	H	2B	3B	HR	RBI	BB	SO	SB	AVG
Vs. RHP		425	56	104	15	7	6	45	15	83	13	.245
Vs. LHP		204	30	60	13	2	2	19	9	16	7	.294
At Home	78	318	46	85	16	6	3	29	17	52	10	.267
On the Road	74	311	40	79	12	3	5	35	7	47	10	.254
1991 Season	152	629	86	164	28	9	8	64	24	99	20	.261
Life 1.2 Years		652	88	173	29	10	8	71	27	105	20	.266

KEVIN McREYNOLDS

NEW YORK LEFT FIELD 32 Years Old

Runs Created: 70
Offensive Winning Percentage: .574
Batting Average: .259 Secondary Average: .262

Most Often Bats: 4th
Swings at First Pitch: 28%
Gets Ahead of the Pitcher: 47%
Hits Behind the Pitcher: 53%

1991 On Base Percentage: .322 Career: .326
1991 Slugging Percentage: .416 Career: .453
Batting Avg with Men in Scoring Position: .308

Bats Right-Handed		AB	R	H	2B	3B	HR	RBI	BB	SO	SB	AVG
Vs. RHP		333	41	86	22	0	10	53	35	29	3	.258
Vs. LHP		189	24	49	10	1	6	21	14	17	3	.259
At Home	67	236	27	56	12	1	7	33	17	14	3	.237
On the Road	76	286	38	79	20	0	9	41	32	32	3	.276
1991 Season	143	522	65	135	32	1	16	74	49	46	6	.259
Life 7.6 Years		594	81	160	30	4	24	91	52	75	11	.269

ORLANDO MERCED

PITTSBURGH FIRST BASE 25 Years Old

Runs Created: 65
Offensive Winning Percentage: .632
Batting Average: .275 Secondary Average: .299

Most Often Bats: 1st
Swings at First Pitch: 16%
Gets Ahead of the Pitcher: 59%
Hits Behind the Pitcher: 41%

1991 On Base Percentage: .373 Career: .367
1991 Slugging Percentage: .399 Career: .391
Batting Avg with Men in Scoring Position: .326

Switch Hitter		AB	R	H	2B	3B	HR	RBI	BB	SO	SB	AVG
Vs. RHP		358	74	102	14	1	10	44	61	71	7	.285
Vs. LHP		53	9	11	3	1	0	6	3	10	1	.208
At Home	58	192	41	49	9	1	5	22	35	41	3	.255
On the Road	62	219	42	64	8	1	5	28	29	40	5	.292
1991 Season	120	411	83	113	17	2	10	50	64	81	8	.275
Life 0.9 Years		486	96	132	20	2	11	56	73	101	9	.271

KENT MERCKER

ATLANTA RELIEF PITCHER 24 Years Old
5-3 2.58 ERA 6 SAVES

Save Opportunities: 8 Blown Saves: 2 Holds: 3
Inherited Runners who Scored: 54%
Opponents Batting Average: .211
Double Play Support: .61 GDP Per Nine Innings

First Pitch is Hit: 7%
Gets Ahead of the Hitter: 47%
Gets Behind the Hitter: 53%
Gets First Batter Out: 63%

1991 On Base Pct Allowed: .303
Slugging Percentage: .316
Stolen Bases Allowed: 10 Caught Stealing: 0

Pitches Left	AB	H	2B	3B	HR	RBI	BB	SO	AVG
Vs. RHB	194	42	8	2	4	18	22	42	.216
Vs. LHB	72	14	1	0	1	6	13	20	.194

	G	IP	W-L	Pct	SO	BB	ERA	Sv
1991 Season	50	73	5-3	.625	62	35	2.58	6
Life 1.3 Years	70	100	7-8	.474	84	52	3.14	10

JOSE MESA

BALTIMORE STARTING PITCHER 26 Years Old
6-11 5.97 ERA

Opponents Batting Average: .307
Offensive Support: 5.46 Runs Per Nine Innings
Double Play Support: .65 GDP Per Nine Innings

First Pitch is Hit: 14%
Gets Ahead of the Hitter: 47%
Gets Behind the Hitter: 53%
Gets Leadoff Man Out: 60%

1991 On Base Pct Allowed: .385
Slugging Percentage: .449
Stolen Bases Allowed: 12 Caught Stealing: 5

Pitches Right	AB	H	2B	3B	HR	RBI	BB	SO	AVG
Vs. RHB	234	73	18	2	7	36	28	41	.312
Vs. LHB	258	78	15	0	4	28	34	23	.302

	G	IP	W-L	Pct	H	SO	BB	ERA
At Home	12	59	2-8		67	32	34	5.68
On the Road	11	65	4-3		84	32	28	6.23
1991 Season	23	124	6-11	.353	151	64	62	5.97
Life 1.0 Years	38	210	10-17	.385	236	109	108	5.49

BOB MILACKI

BALTIMORE STARTING PITCHER 27 Years Old
10-9 4.01 ERA

Opponents Batting Average: .253
Offensive Support: 4.11 Runs Per Nine Innings
Double Play Support: .88 GDP Per Nine Innings

First Pitch is Hit: 16%
Gets Ahead of the Hitter: 51%
Gets Behind the Hitter: 49%
Gets Leadoff Man Out: 65%

1991 On Base Pct Allowed: .305
Slugging Percentage: .383
Stolen Bases Allowed: 12 Caught Stealing: 6

Pitches Right	AB	H	2B	3B	HR	RBI	BB	SO	AVG
Vs. RHB	332	83	20	0	12	41	25	52	.250
Vs. LHB	360	92	19	0	5	41	28	56	.256

	G	IP	W-L	Pct	H	SO	BB	ERA
At Home	15	84	4-4		98	50	18	5.16
On the Road	16	100	6-5		77	58	35	3.05
1991 Season	31	184	10-9	.526	175	108	53	4.01
Life 2.5 Years	39	232	12-11	.517	222	118	83	3.86

KEITH MILLER

NEW YORK SECOND BASE 29 Years Old

Runs Created: 42
Offensive Winning Percentage: .654
Batting Average: .280 Secondary Average: .265

Most Often Bats: 1st
Swings at First Pitch: 35%
Gets Ahead of the Pitcher: 48%
Hits Behind the Pitcher: 52%

1991 On Base Percentage: .345 Career: .323
1991 Slugging Percentage: .411 Career: .354
Batting Avg with Men in Scoring Position: .345

Bats Right-Handed		AB	R	H	2B	3B	HR	RBI	BB	SO	SB	AVG
Vs. RHP		129	28	41	11	1	3	16	14	18	9	.318
Vs. LHP		146	13	36	11	0	1	7	9	26	5	.247
At Home	57	158	23	46	12	0	2	10	13	23	10	.291
On the Road	41	117	18	31	10	1	2	13	10	21	4	.265
1991 Season	98	275	41	77	22	1	4	23	23	44	14	.280
Life 1.9 Years		406	64	107	21	2	4	25	31	70	23	.264

KEVIN MITCHELL

SAN FRANCISCO LEFT FIELD 30 Years Old

Runs Created: 65
Offensive Winning Percentage: .680
Batting Average: .256 Secondary Average: .380

Most Often Bats: 4th
Swings at First Pitch: 40%
Gets Ahead of the Pitcher: 51%
Hits Behind the Pitcher: 49%

1991 On Base Percentage: .338 Career: .351
1991 Slugging Percentage: .515 Career: .517
Batting Avg with Men in Scoring Position: .242

Bats Right-Handed		AB	R	H	2B	3B	HR	RBI	BB	SO	SB	AVG
Vs. RHP		257	37	64	9	1	20	47	26	50	2	.249
Vs. LHP		114	15	31	4	0	7	22	17	7	0	.272
At Home	58	190	21	46	7	1	9	30	17	26	1	.242
On the Road	55	181	31	49	6	0	18	39	26	31	1	.271
1991 Season	113	371	52	95	13	1	27	69	43	57	2	.256
Life 4.9 Years		556	85	153	28	4	33	97	64	100	5	.275

MIKE MOORE

OAKLAND STARTING PITCHER 32 Years Old
17-8 2.96 ERA

Opponents Batting Average: .229
Offensive Support: 4.37 Runs Per Nine Innings
Double Play Support: .81 GDP Per Nine Innings

First Pitch is Hit: 11%
Gets Ahead of the Hitter: 50%
Gets Behind the Hitter: 50%
Gets Leadoff Man Out: 68%

1991 On Base Pct Allowed: .324
Slugging Percentage: .318
Stolen Bases Allowed: 19 Caught Stealing: 12

Pitches Right	AB	H	2B	3B	HR	RBI	BB	SO	AVG
Vs. RHB	374	86	16	0	7	33	49	88	.230
Vs. LHB	394	90	19	0	4	32	56	65	.228

	G	IP	W-L	Pct	H	SO	BB	ERA
At Home	18	118	11-3		81	81	54	2.14
On the Road	15	92	6-5		95	72	51	4.00
1991 Season	33	210	17-8	.680	176	153	105	2.96
Life 8.7 Years	38	241	13-15	.469	237	153	92	4.06

RANDY MILLIGAN

BALTIMORE FIRST BASE 30 Years Old

Runs Created: 71
Offensive Winning Percentage: .539
Batting Average: .263 Secondary Average: .317

Most Often Bats: 5th
Swings at First Pitch: 24%
Gets Ahead of the Pitcher: 52%
Hits Behind the Pitcher: 48%

1991 On Base Percentage: .373 Career: .390
1991 Slugging Percentage: .406 Career: .443
Batting Avg with Men in Scoring Position: .305

Bats Right-Handed		AB	R	H	2B	3B	HR	RBI	BB	SO	SB	AVG
Vs. RHP		343	36	95	14	1	11	51	58	73	0	.277
Vs. LHP		140	21	32	3	1	5	19	26	35	0	.229
At Home	72	237	24	59	9	0	8	33	41	51	0	.249
On the Road	69	246	33	68	8	2	8	37	43	57	0	.276
1991 Season	141	483	57	127	17	2	16	70	84	108	0	.263
Life 2.6 Years		502	73	132	25	3	20	71	104	107	6	.262

PAUL MOLITOR

MILWAUKEE DESIGNATED HITTER 35 Years Old

Runs Created: 132
Offensive Winning Percentage: .718
Batting Average: .325 Secondary Average: .308

Most Often Bats: 1st
Swings at First Pitch: 35%
Gets Ahead of the Pitcher: 49%
Hits Behind the Pitcher: 51%

1991 On Base Percentage: .399 Career: .365
1991 Slugging Percentage: .489 Career: .442
Batting Avg with Men in Scoring Position: .326

Bats Right-Handed		AB	R	H	2B	3B	HR	RBI	BB	SO	SB	AVG
Vs. RHP		491	94	160	24	10	12	58	53	49	13	.326
Vs. LHP		174	39	56	8	3	5	17	24	13	6	.322
At Home	76	315	63	92	14	8	7	38	39	23	6	.292
On the Road	82	350	70	124	18	5	10	37	38	39	13	.354
1991 Season	158	665	133	216	32	13	17	75	77	62	19	.325
Life 10.5 Years		659	113	199	35	8	14	67	65	78	36	.302

MICKEY MORANDINI

PHILADELPHIA SECOND BASE 26 Years Old

Runs Created: 35
Offensive Winning Percentage: .439
Batting Average: .249 Secondary Average: .197

Most Often Bats: 2nd
Swings at First Pitch: 28%
Gets Ahead of the Pitcher: 51%
Hits Behind the Pitcher: 49%

1991 On Base Percentage: .313 Career: .309
1991 Slugging Percentage: .317 Career: .319
Batting Avg with Men in Scoring Position: .266

Bats Left-Handed		AB	R	H	2B	3B	HR	RBI	BB	SO	SB	AVG
Vs. RHP		260	31	69	11	4	1	17	26	34	13	.265
Vs. LHP		65	7	12	0	0	0	3	3	11	0	.185
At Home	54	166	19	39	4	3	1	10	14	22	5	.235
On the Road	44	159	19	42	7	1	0	10	15	23	8	.264
1991 Season	98	325	38	81	11	4	1	20	29	45	13	.249
Life 0.8 Years		532	62	132	20	5	3	30	46	84	21	.248

MIKE MORGAN

LOS ANGELES STARTING PITCHER 32 Years Old
14-10 2.78 ERA

Opponents Batting Average: .226
Offensive Support: 3.66 Runs Per Nine Innings
Double Play Support: .88 GDP Per Nine Innings

First Pitch is Hit: 16%
Gets Ahead of the Hitter: 52%
Gets Behind the Hitter: 48%
Gets Leadoff Man Out: 75%

1991 On Base Pct Allowed: .278
Slugging Percentage: .307
Stolen Bases Allowed: 24 Caught Stealing: 7

Pitches Right	AB	H	2B	3B	HR	RBI	BB	SO	AVG
Vs. RHB	376	84	9	3	3	29	18	62	.223
Vs. LHB	495	113	13	3	9	41	43	78	.228

	G	IP	W-L	Pct	H	SO	BB	ERA
At Home	17	119	6-5		100	71	32	3.32
On the Road	17	117	8-5		97	69	29	2.23
1991 Season	34	236	14-10	.583	197	140	61	2.78
Life 6.3 Years	42	219	11-16	.392	229	104	74	4.10

JACK MORRIS

MINNESOTA STARTING PITCHER 37 Years Old
18-12 3.43 ERA

Opponents Batting Average: .245
Offensive Support: 5.14 Runs Per Nine Innings
Double Play Support: .84 GDP Per Nine Innings

First Pitch is Hit: 14%
Gets Ahead of the Hitter: 51%
Gets Behind the Hitter: 49%
Gets Leadoff Man Out: 70%

1991 On Base Pct Allowed: .315
Slugging Percentage: .347
Stolen Bases Allowed: 32 Caught Stealing: 8

Pitches Right	AB	H	2B	3B	HR	RBI	BB	SO	AVG
Vs. RHB	466	98	10	3	9	45	34	100	.210
Vs. LHB	456	128	18	3	9	52	58	63	.281

	G	IP	W-L	Pct	H	SO	BB	ERA
At Home	18	133	13-3		120	85	42	3.31
On the Road	17	113	5-9		106	78	50	3.57
1991 Season	35	247	18-12	.600	226	163	92	3.43
Life 12.3 Years	38	268	18-13	.571	244	175	96	3.71

DALE MURPHY

PHILADELPHIA RIGHT FIELD 36 Years Old

Runs Created: 67
Offensive Winning Percentage: .513
Batting Average: .252 Secondary Average: .254

Most Often Bats: 5th
Swings at First Pitch: 44%
Gets Ahead of the Pitcher: 47%
Hits Behind the Pitcher: 53%

1991 On Base Percentage: .309 Career: .348
1991 Slugging Percentage: .415 Career: .472
Batting Avg with Men in Scoring Position: .239

Bats Right-Handed		AB	R	H	2B	3B	HR	RBI	BB	SO	SB	AVG
Vs. RHP		352	38	80	20	1	13	56	31	60	0	.227
Vs. LHP		192	28	57	13	0	5	25	17	33	1	.297
At Home	82	279	38	78	21	0	9	54	29	48	1	.280
On the Road	71	265	28	59	12	1	9	27	19	45	0	.223
1991 Season	153	544	66	137	33	1	18	81	48	93	1	.252
Life 13.2 Years		596	90	159	26	3	30	95	74	130	12	.267

HAL MORRIS

CINCINNATI FIRST BASE 27 Years Old

Runs Created: 89
Offensive Winning Percentage: .728
Batting Average: .318 Secondary Average: .278

Most Often Bats: 3rd
Swings at First Pitch: 31%
Gets Ahead of the Pitcher: 49%
Hits Behind the Pitcher: 51%

1991 On Base Percentage: .374 Career: .369
1991 Slugging Percentage: .479 Career: .473
Batting Avg with Men in Scoring Position: .284

Bats Left-Handed		AB	R	H	2B	3B	HR	RBI	BB	SO	SB	AVG
Vs. RHP		375	60	126	25	0	13	47	40	36	10	.336
Vs. LHP		103	12	26	8	1	1	12	6	25	0	.252
At Home	68	238	33	76	20	1	9	33	21	31	0	.319
On the Road	68	240	39	76	13	0	5	26	25	30	10	.317
1991 Season	136	478	72	152	33	1	14	59	46	61	10	.318
Life 1.7 Years		490	74	157	33	2	12	59	40	63	11	.320

TERRY MULHOLLAND

PHILADELPHIA STARTING PITCHER 29 Years Old
16-13 3.61 ERA

Opponents Batting Average: .260
Offensive Support: 4.27 Runs Per Nine Innings
Double Play Support: .62 GDP Per Nine Innings

First Pitch is Hit: 15%
Gets Ahead of the Hitter: 48%
Gets Behind the Hitter: 52%
Gets Leadoff Man Out: 71%

1991 On Base Pct Allowed: .299
Slugging Percentage: .374
Stolen Bases Allowed: 6 Caught Stealing: 5

Pitches Left	AB	H	2B	3B	HR	RBI	BB	SO	AVG
Vs. RHB	730	191	39	5	9	69	43	123	.262
Vs. LHB	157	40	3	2	6	20	6	19	.255

	G	IP	W-L	Pct	H	SO	BB	ERA
At Home	18	131	11-2		121	83	28	2.96
On the Road	16	101	5-11		110	59	21	4.44
1991 Season	34	232	16-13	.552	231	142	49	3.61
Life 2.8 Years	41	222	11-13	.457	226	116	60	3.89

EDDIE MURRAY

LOS ANGELES FIRST BASE 36 Years Old

Runs Created: 73
Offensive Winning Percentage: .565
Batting Average: .260 Secondary Average: .255

Most Often Bats: 4th
Swings at First Pitch: 39%
Gets Ahead of the Pitcher: 49%
Hits Behind the Pitcher: 51%

1991 On Base Percentage: .321 Career: .369
1991 Slugging Percentage: .403 Career: .488
Batting Avg with Men in Scoring Position: .258

Switch Hitter		AB	R	H	2B	3B	HR	RBI	BB	SO	SB	AVG
Vs. RHP		322	43	95	13	1	13	56	35	44	5	.295
Vs. LHP		254	26	55	10	0	6	40	20	30	5	.217
At Home	79	282	41	76	9	1	11	50	35	41	3	.270
On the Road	74	294	28	74	14	0	8	46	20	33	7	.252
1991 Season	153	576	69	150	23	1	19	96	55	74	10	.260
Life 14.1 Years		607	91	177	30	2	28	104	77	81	6	.292

MIKE MUSSINA

BALTIMORE STARTING PITCHER 23 Years Old

4-5 2.87 ERA

Opponents Batting Average: .239
Offensive Support: 3.90 Runs Per Nine Innings
Double Play Support: .92 GDP Per Nine Innings

First Pitch is Hit: 15%
Gets Ahead of the Hitter: 51%
Gets Behind the Hitter: 49%
Gets Leadoff Man Out: 74%

1991 On Base Pct Allowed: .286
Slugging Percentage: .354
Stolen Bases Allowed: 4 Caught Stealing: 4

Pitches Right	AB	H	2B	3B	HR	RBI	BB	SO	AVG
Vs. RHB	140	38	7	1	4	12	7	23	.271
Vs. LHB	182	39	7	0	3	17	14	29	.214

	G	IP	W-L	Pct	H	SO	BB	ERA
At Home	6	43	3-1		36	30	11	2.74
On the Road	6	45	1-4		41	22	10	3.00
1991 Season	12	88	4-5	.444	77	52	21	2.87
Life 0.3 Years	37	270	12-15	.444	237	160	65	2.87

RANDY MYERS

CINCINNATI RELIEF PITCHER 29 Years Old

6-13 3.55 ERA 6 SAVES

Save Opportunities: 10 Blown Saves: 4 Holds: 8
Inherited Runners who Scored: 21%
Opponents Batting Average: .242
Double Play Support: .95 GDP Per Nine Innings

First Pitch is Hit: 9%
Gets Ahead of the Hitter: 47%
Gets Behind the Hitter: 53%
Gets First Batter Out: 65%

1991 On Base Pct Allowed: .347
Slugging Percentage: .342
Stolen Bases Allowed: 4 Caught Stealing: 7

Pitches Left	AB	H	2B	3B	HR	RBI	BB	SO	AVG
Vs. RHB	358	81	12	2	5	40	54	70	.226
Vs. LHB	122	35	6	1	3	18	26	38	.287

	G	IP	W-L	Pct	SO	BB	ERA	Sv
1991 Season	58	132	6-13	.316	108	80	3.55	6
Life 4.3 Years	71	106	6-7	.458	108	50	2.85	21

CHARLES NAGY

CLEVELAND STARTING PITCHER 25 Years Old

10-15 4.13 ERA

Opponents Batting Average: .275
Offensive Support: 3.41 Runs Per Nine Innings
Double Play Support: .94 GDP Per Nine Innings

First Pitch is Hit: 13%
Gets Ahead of the Hitter: 47%
Gets Behind the Hitter: 53%
Gets Leadoff Man Out: 67%

1991 On Base Pct Allowed: .330
Slugging Percentage: .403
Stolen Bases Allowed: 23 Caught Stealing: 7

Pitches Right	AB	H	2B	3B	HR	RBI	BB	SO	AVG
Vs. RHB	368	95	19	2	8	42	29	47	.258
Vs. LHB	460	133	26	6	7	47	37	62	.289

	G	IP	W-L	Pct	H	SO	BB	ERA
At Home	13	94	6-5		92	55	25	3.56
On the Road	20	118	4-10		136	54	41	4.59
1991 Season	33	211	10-15	.400	228	109	66	4.13
Life 1.1 Years	37	229	11-17	.387	255	120	78	4.45

GREG MYERS

TORONTO CATCHER 26 Years Old

Runs Created: 36
Offensive Winning Percentage: .488
Batting Average: .262 Secondary Average: .217

Most Often Bats: 7th
Swings at First Pitch: 44%
Gets Ahead of the Pitcher: 47%
Hits Behind the Pitcher: 53%

1991 On Base Percentage: .306 Career: .288
1991 Slugging Percentage: .411 Career: .356
Batting Avg with Men in Scoring Position: .235

Bats Left-Handed		AB	R	H	2B	3B	HR	RBI	BB	SO	SB	AVG
Vs. RHP		274	23	75	21	0	7	33	19	38	0	.274
Vs. LHP		35	2	6	1	0	1	3	2	7	0	.171
At Home	54	145	11	42	14	0	5	20	16	21	0	.290
On the Road	53	164	14	39	8	0	3	16	5	24	0	.238
1991 Season	107	309	25	81	22	0	8	36	21	45	0	.262
Life 1.3 Years		455	44	108	23	1	10	44	33	67	0	.239

CHRIS NABHOLZ

MONTREAL STARTING PITCHER 25 Years Old

8-7 3.63 ERA

Opponents Batting Average: .237
Offensive Support: 4.51 Runs Per Nine Innings
Double Play Support: .53 GDP Per Nine Innings

First Pitch is Hit: 15%
Gets Ahead of the Hitter: 49%
Gets Behind the Hitter: 51%
Gets Leadoff Man Out: 68%

1991 On Base Pct Allowed: .307
Slugging Percentage: .336
Stolen Bases Allowed: 15 Caught Stealing: 11

Pitches Left	AB	H	2B	3B	HR	RBI	BB	SO	AVG
Vs. RHB	471	112	29	1	3	43	47	73	.238
Vs. LHB	95	22	6	2	2	8	10	26	.232

	G	IP	W-L	Pct	H	SO	BB	ERA
At Home	11	75	3-5		59	51	29	3.36
On the Road	13	79	5-2		75	48	28	3.89
1991 Season	24	154	8-7	.533	134	99	57	3.63
Life 0.9 Years	37	236	15-10	.609	187	161	94	3.38

JAIME NAVARRO

MILWAUKEE STARTING PITCHER 25 Years Old

15-12 3.92 ERA

Opponents Batting Average: .261
Offensive Support: 4.88 Runs Per Nine Innings
Double Play Support: .77 GDP Per Nine Innings

First Pitch is Hit: 14%
Gets Ahead of the Hitter: 47%
Gets Behind the Hitter: 53%
Gets Leadoff Man Out: 70%

1991 On Base Pct Allowed: .318
Slugging Percentage: .370
Stolen Bases Allowed: 23 Caught Stealing: 7

Pitches Right	AB	H	2B	3B	HR	RBI	BB	SO	AVG
Vs. RHB	428	107	22	2	5	45	30	62	.250
Vs. LHB	480	130	17	1	13	59	43	52	.271

	G	IP	W-L	Pct	H	SO	BB	ERA
At Home	16	113	9-3		111	60	34	3.58
On the Road	18	121	6-9		126	54	39	4.24
1991 Season	34	234	15-12	.556	237	114	73	3.92
Life 2.1 Years	40	231	14-13	.526	249	115	68	3.91

ROD NICHOLS

CLEVELAND STARTING PITCHER 27 Years Old

2-11 3.54 ERA

Opponents Batting Average: .273
Offensive Support: 2.62 Runs Per Nine Innings
Double Play Support: .66 GDP Per Nine Innings

First Pitch is Hit: 15%
Gets Ahead of the Hitter: 51%
Gets Behind the Hitter: 49%
Gets Leadoff Man Out: 72%

1991 On Base Pct Allowed: .316
Slugging Percentage: .344
Stolen Bases Allowed: 16 Caught Stealing: 8

Pitches Right	AB	H	2B	3B	HR	RBI	BB	SO	AVG
Vs. RHB	260	64	5	0	4	25	10	42	.246
Vs. LHB	272	81	13	1	2	35	20	34	.298

	G	IP	W-L	Pct	H	SO	BB	ERA
At Home	15	75	1-7		87	35	22	4.08
On the Road	16	62	1-4		58	41	8	2.89
1991 Season	31	137	2-11	.154	145	76	30	3.54
Life 1.4 Years	45	218	5-20	.206	239	112	61	4.34

MATT NOKES

NEW YORK CATCHER 28 Years Old

Runs Created: 66
Offensive Winning Percentage: .565
Batting Average: .268 Secondary Average: .263

Most Often Bats: 6th
Swings at First Pitch: 44%
Gets Ahead of the Pitcher: 50%
Hits Behind the Pitcher: 50%

1991 On Base Percentage: .308 Career: .315
1991 Slugging Percentage: .469 Career: .446
Batting Avg with Men in Scoring Position: .256

Bats Left-Handed		AB	R	H	2B	3B	HR	RBI	BB	SO	SB	AVG
Vs. RHP		345	39	93	19	0	17	54	19	37	1	.270
Vs. LHP		111	13	29	1	0	7	23	6	12	2	.261
At Home	61	200	27	52	8	0	13	43	12	26	1	.260
On the Road	74	256	25	70	12	0	11	34	13	23	2	.273
1991 Season	135	456	52	122	20	0	24	77	25	49	3	.268
Life 4.0 Years		504	57	132	19	1	24	77	35	68	2	.263

BOBBY OJEDA

LOS ANGELES STARTING PITCHER 34 Years Old

12-9 3.18 ERA

Opponents Batting Average: .257
Offensive Support: 3.42 Runs Per Nine Innings
Double Play Support: .57 GDP Per Nine Innings

First Pitch is Hit: 14%
Gets Ahead of the Hitter: 47%
Gets Behind the Hitter: 53%
Gets Leadoff Man Out: 69%

1991 On Base Pct Allowed: .323
Slugging Percentage: .376
Stolen Bases Allowed: 23 Caught Stealing: 15

Pitches Left	AB	H	2B	3B	HR	RBI	BB	SO	AVG
Vs. RHB	569	146	27	3	14	61	63	84	.257
Vs. LHB	136	35	4	1	1	11	7	36	.257

	G	IP	W-L	Pct	H	SO	BB	ERA
At Home	15	99	6-4		95	67	34	3.01
On the Road	16	91	6-5		86	53	36	3.38
1991 Season	31	189	12-9	.571	181	120	70	3.18
Life 7.6 Years	41	219	14-12	.549	211	132	75	3.60

OTIS NIXON

ATLANTA RIGHT FIELD 33 Years Old

Runs Created: 57
Offensive Winning Percentage: .558
Batting Average: .297 Secondary Average: .327

Most Often Bats: 1st
Swings at First Pitch: 33%
Gets Ahead of the Pitcher: 56%
Hits Behind the Pitcher: 44%

1991 On Base Percentage: .371 Career: .320
1991 Slugging Percentage: .327 Career: .290
Batting Avg with Men in Scoring Position: .312

Switch Hitter		AB	R	H	2B	3B	HR	RBI	BB	SO	SB	AVG
Vs. RHP		306	58	90	5	1	0	19	33	33	50	.294
Vs. LHP		95	23	29	5	0	0	7	14	7	22	.305
At Home	67	207	44	68	8	0	0	15	26	18	38	.329
On the Road	57	194	37	51	2	1	0	11	21	22	34	.263
1991 Season	124	401	81	119	10	1	0	26	47	40	72	.297
Life 4.6 Years		333	65	82	8	2	1	22	37	45	57	.246

PETE O'BRIEN

SEATTLE FIRST BASE 34 Years Old

Runs Created: 66
Offensive Winning Percentage: .468
Batting Average: .248 Secondary Average: .232

Most Often Bats: 4th
Swings at First Pitch: 16%
Gets Ahead of the Pitcher: 50%
Hits Behind the Pitcher: 50%

1991 On Base Percentage: .300 Career: .340
1991 Slugging Percentage: .402 Career: .413
Batting Avg with Men in Scoring Position: .287

Bats Left-Handed		AB	R	H	2B	3B	HR	RBI	BB	SO	SB	AVG
Vs. RHP		381	42	97	18	3	13	61	33	39	0	.255
Vs. LHP		179	16	42	11	0	4	27	11	22	0	.235
At Home	77	290	32	69	17	3	12	53	19	30	0	.238
On the Road	75	270	26	70	12	0	5	35	25	31	0	.259
1991 Season	152	560	58	139	29	3	17	88	44	61	0	.248
Life 8.4 Years		575	70	152	28	2	18	78	68	61	3	.265

JOHN OLERUD

TORONTO FIRST BASE 23 Years Old

Runs Created: 72
Offensive Winning Percentage: .639
Batting Average: .256 Secondary Average: .333

Most Often Bats: 4th
Swings at First Pitch: 26%
Gets Ahead of the Pitcher: 54%
Hits Behind the Pitcher: 46%

1991 On Base Percentage: .353 Career: .358
1991 Slugging Percentage: .438 Career: .434
Batting Avg with Men in Scoring Position: .233

Bats Left-Handed		AB	R	H	2B	3B	HR	RBI	BB	SO	SB	AVG
Vs. RHP		371	49	98	27	0	14	52	51	65	0	.264
Vs. LHP		83	15	18	3	1	3	16	17	19	0	.217
At Home	70	226	27	61	17	1	7	39	36	36	0	.270
On the Road	69	228	37	55	13	0	10	29	32	48	0	.241
1991 Season	139	454	64	116	30	1	17	68	68	84	0	.256
Life 1.6 Years		519	69	135	28	1	20	73	79	101	0	.261

OMAR OLIVARES

ST. LOUIS STARTING PITCHER 24 Years Old

11-7 3.71 ERA

Opponents Batting Average: .243
Offensive Support: 4.20 Runs Per Nine Innings
Double Play Support: .65 GDP Per Nine Innings

First Pitch is Hit: 15%
Gets Ahead of the Hitter: 47%
Gets Behind the Hitter: 53%
Gets Leadoff Man Out: 74%

1991 On Base Pct Allowed: .316
Slugging Percentage: .356
Stolen Bases Allowed: 10 Caught Stealing: 11

Pitches Right	AB	H	2B	3B	HR	RBI	BB	SO	AVG
Vs. RHB	264	67	13	1	8	32	19	43	.254
Vs. LHB	345	81	9	3	5	32	42	48	.235

	G	IP	W-L	Pct	H	SO	BB	ERA
At Home	16	97	7-5		88	51	31	3.33
On the Road	12	70	4-2		60	40	30	4.24
1991 Season	28	167	11-7	.611	148	91	61	3.71
Life 0.9 Years	41	239	13-9	.600	213	123	86	3.53

GREGG OLSON

BALTIMORE RELIEF PITCHER 25 Years Old

4-6 3.18 ERA 31 SAVES

Save Opportunities: 39 Blown Saves: 8 Holds: 1
Inherited Runners who Scored: 40%
Opponents Batting Average: .262
Double Play Support: .61 GDP Per Nine Innings

First Pitch is Hit: 12%
Gets Ahead of the Hitter: 47%
Gets Behind the Hitter: 53%
Gets First Batter Out: 77%

1991 On Base Pct Allowed: .332
Slugging Percentage: .305
Stolen Bases Allowed: 13 Caught Stealing: 1

Pitches Right	AB	H	2B	3B	HR	RBI	BB	SO	AVG
Vs. RHB	143	42	3	2	0	21	12	33	.294
Vs. LHB	139	32	2	0	1	15	17	39	.230

	G	IP	W-L	Pct	SO	BB	ERA	Sv
1991 Season	72	74	4-6	.400	72	29	3.18	31
Life 2.8 Years	74	86	6-5	.533	86	41	2.43	33

JOSE OQUENDO

ST. LOUIS SECOND BASE 28 Years Ol

Runs Created: 43
Offensive Winning Percentage: .500
Batting Average: .240 Secondary Average: .246

Most Often Bats: 8th
Swings at First Pitch: 28%
Gets Ahead of the Pitcher: 54%
Hits Behind the Pitcher: 46%

1991 On Base Percentage: .357 Career: .348
1991 Slugging Percentage: .301 Career: .321
Batting Avg with Men in Scoring Position: .250

Switch Hitter		AB	R	H	2B	3B	HR	RBI	BB	SO	SB	AVG
Vs. RHP		216	23	52	3	3	0	11	38	27	1	.241
Vs. LHP		150	14	36	8	1	1	15	29	21	0	.240
At Home	67	184	21	48	3	2	0	14	32	19	1	.261
On the Road	60	182	16	40	8	2	1	12	35	29	0	.220
1991 Season	127	366	37	88	11	4	1	26	67	48	1	.240
Life 6.1 Years		451	47	118	15	3	2	36	62	54	5	.261

JOE OLIVER

CINCINNATI CATCHER 26 Years Old

Runs Created: 23
Offensive Winning Percentage: .287
Batting Average: .216 Secondary Average: .230

Most Often Bats: 8th
Swings at First Pitch: 44%
Gets Ahead of the Pitcher: 46%
Hits Behind the Pitcher: 54%

1991 On Base Percentage: .265 Career: .290
1991 Slugging Percentage: .379 Career: .371
Batting Avg with Men in Scoring Position: .258

Bats Right-Handed		AB	R	H	2B	3B	HR	RBI	BB	SO	SB	AVG
Vs. RHP		138	9	28	6	0	3	14	3	29	0	.203
Vs. LHP		131	12	30	5	0	8	27	15	24	0	.229
At Home	50	145	14	29	6	0	7	17	11	27	0	.200
On the Road	44	124	7	29	5	0	4	24	7	26	0	.234
1991 Season	94	269	21	58	11	0	11	41	18	53	0	.216
Life 1.6 Years		481	42	112	26	0	14	71	37	96	1	.233

PAUL O'NEILL

CINCINNATI RIGHT FIELD 29 Years Old

Runs Created: 89
Offensive Winning Percentage: .654
Batting Average: .256 Secondary Average: .385

Most Often Bats: 4th
Swings at First Pitch: 29%
Gets Ahead of the Pitcher: 50%
Hits Behind the Pitcher: 50%

1991 On Base Percentage: .346 Career: .334
1991 Slugging Percentage: .481 Career: .444
Batting Avg with Men in Scoring Position: .262

Bats Left-Handed		AB	R	H	2B	3B	HR	RBI	BB	SO	SB	AVG
Vs. RHP		363	55	102	27	0	25	76	62	55	11	.281
Vs. LHP		169	16	34	9	0	3	15	11	52	1	.201
At Home	74	268	42	76	21	0	20	59	32	45	8	.284
On the Road	78	264	29	60	15	0	8	32	41	62	4	.227
1991 Season	152	532	71	136	36	0	28	91	73	107	12	.256
Life 4.0 Years		528	65	139	32	1	20	86	57	92	14	.262

JOE ORSULAK

BALTIMORE LEFT FIELD 30 Years Old

Runs Created: 56
Offensive Winning Percentage: .450
Batting Average: .278 Secondary Average: .150

Most Often Bats: 2nd
Swings at First Pitch: 35%
Gets Ahead of the Pitcher: 52%
Hits Behind the Pitcher: 48%

1991 On Base Percentage: .321 Career: .329
1991 Slugging Percentage: .358 Career: .381
Batting Avg with Men in Scoring Position: .241

Bats Left-Handed		AB	R	H	2B	3B	HR	RBI	BB	SO	SB	AVG
Vs. RHP		422	49	120	19	1	5	37	24	37	6	.284
Vs. LHP		64	8	15	3	0	0	6	4	8	0	.234
At Home	71	235	29	65	10	0	3	21	14	23	2	.277
On the Road	72	251	28	70	12	1	2	22	14	22	4	.279
1991 Season	143	486	57	135	22	1	5	43	28	45	6	.278
Life 5.0 Years		507	68	140	23	5	7	45	38	46	15	.277

DAVE OTTO

CLEVELAND STARTING PITCHER 27 Years Old

2-8 4.23 ERA

Opponents Batting Average: .283
Offensive Support: 3.96 Runs Per Nine Innings
Double Play Support: .99 GDP Per Nine Innings

First Pitch is Hit: 14%
Gets Ahead of the Hitter: 45%
Gets Behind the Hitter: 55%
Gets Leadoff Man Out: 67%

1991 On Base Pct Allowed: .333
Slugging Percentage: .395
Stolen Bases Allowed: 4 Caught Stealing: 4

Pitches Left	AB	H	2B	3B	HR	RBI	BB	SO	AVG
Vs. RHB	313	87	12	4	7	31	23	44	.278
Vs. LHB	69	21	2	0	0	11	4	3	.304

	G	IP	W-L	Pct	H	SO	BB	ERA
At Home	9	59	1-6		63	31	11	4.12
On the Road	9	41	1-2		45	16	16	4.39
1991 Season	18	100	2-8	.200	108	47	27	4.23
Life 0.6 Years	45	210	3-13	.200	224	106	66	4.25

SPIKE OWEN

MONTREAL SHORTSTOP 31 Years Old

Runs Created: 48
Offensive Winning Percentage: .491
Batting Average: .255 Secondary Average: .215

Most Often Bats: 8th
Swings at First Pitch: 24%
Gets Ahead of the Pitcher: 48%
Hits Behind the Pitcher: 52%

1991 On Base Percentage: .321 Career: .318
1991 Slugging Percentage: .366 Career: .336
Batting Avg with Men in Scoring Position: .215

Switch Hitter		AB	R	H	2B	3B	HR	RBI	BB	SO	SB	AVG
Vs. RHP		224	19	47	4	6	2	14	28	36	1	.210
Vs. LHP		200	20	61	18	2	1	12	14	25	1	.305
At Home	58	161	8	34	6	1	1	7	19	26	2	.211
On the Road	81	263	31	74	16	7	2	19	23	35	0	.281
1991 Season	139	424	39	108	22	8	3	26	42	61	2	.255
Life 7.1 Years		522	63	126	22	7	5	44	59	59	9	.241

MIKE PAGLIARULO

MINNESOTA THIRD BASE 32 Years Old

Runs Created: 43
Offensive Winning Percentage: .477
Batting Average: .279 Secondary Average: .164

Most Often Bats: 8th
Swings at First Pitch: 37%
Gets Ahead of the Pitcher: 46%
Hits Behind the Pitcher: 54%

1991 On Base Percentage: .322 Career: .305
1991 Slugging Percentage: .384 Career: .410
Batting Avg with Men in Scoring Position: .195

Bats Left-Handed		AB	R	H	2B	3B	HR	RBI	BB	SO	SB	AVG
Vs. RHP		349	38	99	19	0	6	35	18	54	1	.284
Vs. LHP		16	0	3	1	0	0	1	3	1	0	.188
At Home	66	190	19	54	11	0	4	27	13	32	1	.284
On the Road	55	175	19	48	9	0	2	9	8	23	0	.274
1991 Season	121	365	38	102	20	0	6	36	21	55	1	.279
Life 6.2 Years		515	60	122	26	2	20	69	49	108	2	.236

TOM PAGNOZZI

ST. LOUIS CATCHER 29 Years Old

Runs Created: 49
Offensive Winning Percentage: .438
Batting Average: .264 Secondary Average: .185

Most Often Bats: 7th
Swings at First Pitch: 37%
Gets Ahead of the Pitcher: 46%
Hits Behind the Pitcher: 54%

1991 On Base Percentage: .319 Career: .308
1991 Slugging Percentage: .351 Career: .336
Batting Avg with Men in Scoring Position: .261

Bats Right-Handed		AB	R	H	2B	3B	HR	RBI	BB	SO	SB	AVG
Vs. RHP		258	20	70	13	3	0	32	18	34	6	.271
Vs. LHP		201	18	51	11	2	2	25	18	29	3	.254
At Home	71	221	20	50	11	2	2	23	23	29	3	.226
On the Road	69	238	18	71	13	3	0	34	13	34	6	.298
1991 Season	140	459	38	121	24	5	2	57	36	63	9	.264
Life 2.3 Years		440	38	113	22	2	3	47	31	72	5	.257

RAFAEL PALMEIRO

TEXAS FIRST BASE 27 Years Old

Runs Created: 129
Offensive Winning Percentage: .692
Batting Average: .322 Secondary Average: .325

Most Often Bats: 2nd
Swings at First Pitch: 19%
Gets Ahead of the Pitcher: 56%
Hits Behind the Pitcher: 44%

1991 On Base Percentage: .389 Career: .360
1991 Slugging Percentage: .532 Career: .462
Batting Avg with Men in Scoring Position: .232

Bats Left-Handed		AB	R	H	2B	3B	HR	RBI	BB	SO	SB	AVG
Vs. RHP		445	89	152	41	2	17	62	54	46	2	.342
Vs. LHP		186	26	51	8	1	9	26	14	26	2	.274
At Home	79	298	55	101	22	1	12	43	34	36	2	.339
On the Road	80	333	60	102	27	2	14	45	34	36	2	.306
1991 Season	159	631	115	203	49	3	26	88	68	72	4	.322
Life 4.5 Years		593	84	179	37	4	16	75	52	55	6	.302

DEAN PALMER

TEXAS THIRD BASE 23 Years Old

Runs Created: 31
Offensive Winning Percentage: .343
Batting Average: .187 Secondary Average: .336

Most Often Bats: 7th
Swings at First Pitch: 15%
Gets Ahead of the Pitcher: 53%
Hits Behind the Pitcher: 47%

1991 On Base Percentage: .281 Career: .269
1991 Slugging Percentage: .403 Career: .390
Batting Avg with Men in Scoring Position: .236

Bats Right-Handed		AB	R	H	2B	3B	HR	RBI	BB	SO	SB	AVG
Vs. RHP		187	23	30	6	2	6	21	21	68	0	.160
Vs. LHP		81	15	20	3	0	9	16	11	30	0	.247
At Home	39	114	17	16	3	1	6	11	19	43	0	.140
On the Road	42	154	21	34	6	1	9	26	13	55	0	.221
1991 Season	81	268	38	50	9	2	15	37	32	98	0	.187
Life 0.6 Years		479	63	87	18	3	25	63	53	184	0	.181

DAVE PARKER

TORONTO — DESIGNATED HITTER — 41 Years Old

Runs Created: 52
Offensive Winning Percentage: .433
Batting Average: .239 Secondary Average: .197

Most Often Bats: 4th
Swings at First Pitch: 43%
Gets Ahead of the Pitcher: 48%
Hits Behind the Pitcher: 52%

1991 On Base Percentage: .288 Career: .339
1991 Slugging Percentage: .365 Career: .471
Batting Avg with Men in Scoring Position: .254

Bats Left-Handed	G	AB	R	H	2B	3B	HR	RBI	BB	SO	SB	AVG
Vs. RHP		369	33	89	20	1	7	42	30	72	3	.241
Vs. LHP		133	14	31	6	1	4	17	3	26	0	.233
At Home	63	229	20	49	11	1	6	23	19	39	1	.214
On the Road	69	273	27	71	15	1	5	36	14	59	2	.260
1991 Season	132	502	47	120	26	2	11	59	33	98	3	.239
Life 15.2 Years		615	84	178	35	5	22	98	45	101	10	.290

DAN PASQUA

CHICAGO — FIRST BASE — 30 Years Old

Runs Created: 71
Offensive Winning Percentage: .640
Batting Average: .259 Secondary Average: .355

Most Often Bats: 4th
Swings at First Pitch: 29%
Gets Ahead of the Pitcher: 54%
Hits Behind the Pitcher: 46%

1991 On Base Percentage: .358 Career: .337
1991 Slugging Percentage: .465 Career: .455
Batting Avg with Men in Scoring Position: .243

Bats Left-Handed	G	AB	R	H	2B	3B	HR	RBI	BB	SO	SB	AVG
Vs. RHP		368	62	95	20	4	15	58	53	74	0	.258
Vs. LHP		49	9	13	2	1	3	8	9	12	0	.265
At Home	66	196	39	57	11	3	10	29	36	34	0	.291
On the Road	68	221	32	51	11	2	8	37	26	52	0	.231
1991 Season	134	417	71	108	22	5	18	66	62	86	0	.259
Life 4.5 Years		483	65	121	23	3	23	75	61	118	1	.251

ALEJANDRO PENA

ATLANTA — RELIEF PITCHER — 33 Years Ol

8-1 2.40 ERA 15 SAVES

Save Opportunities: 20 Blown Saves: 5 Holds:
Inherited Runners who Scored: 29%
Opponents Batting Average: .245
Double Play Support: .66 GDP Per Nine Innings

First Pitch is Hit: 11%
Gets Ahead of the Hitter: 59%
Gets Behind the Hitter: 41%
Gets First Batter Out: 78%

1991 On Base Pct Allowed: .293
Slugging Percentage: .341
Stolen Bases Allowed: 8 Caught Stealing:

Pitches Right	AB	H	2B	3B	HR	RBI	BB	SO	AVG
Vs. RHB	152	45	5	1	3	16	9	27	.296
Vs. LHB	150	29	4	0	3	14	13	35	.193

	G	IP	W-L	Pct	SO	BB	ERA	Sv
1991 Season	59	82	8-1	.889	62	22	2.40	15
Life 6.3 Years	63	148	8-7	.538	113	46	2.90	8

LANCE PARRISH

CALIFORNIA — CATCHER — 36 Years Old

Runs Created: 45
Offensive Winning Percentage: .460
Batting Average: .216 Secondary Average: .259

Most Often Bats: 6th
Swings at First Pitch: 28%
Gets Ahead of the Pitcher: 50%
Hits Behind the Pitcher: 50%

1991 On Base Percentage: .285 Career: .314
1991 Slugging Percentage: .388 Career: .446
Batting Avg with Men in Scoring Position: .250

Bats Right-Handed	G	AB	R	H	2B	3B	HR	RBI	BB	SO	SB	AVG
Vs. RHP		297	29	64	11	0	16	41	23	92	0	.215
Vs. LHP		105	9	23	1	0	3	10	12	25	0	.219
At Home	64	216	15	49	6	0	9	24	15	51	0	.227
On the Road	55	186	23	38	6	0	10	27	20	66	0	.204
1991 Season	119	402	38	87	12	0	19	51	35	117	0	.216
Life 11.C Years		590	73	150	25	2	28	91	50	125	2	.254

BILL PECOTA

KANSAS CITY — THIRD BASE — 32 Years Old

Runs Created: 56
Offensive Winning Percentage: .540
Batting Average: .286 Secondary Average: .256

Most Often Bats: 6th
Swings at First Pitch: 17%
Gets Ahead of the Pitcher: 52%
Hits Behind the Pitcher: 48%

1991 On Base Percentage: .356 Career: .330
1991 Slugging Percentage: .399 Career: .370
Batting Avg with Men in Scoring Position: .323

Bats Right-Handed	G	AB	R	H	2B	3B	HR	RBI	BB	SO	SB	AVG
Vs. RHP		270	30	71	13	2	4	28	24	32	12	.263
Vs. LHP		128	23	43	10	0	2	17	17	13	4	.336
At Home	65	203	34	60	12	0	4	25	25	20	13	.296
On the Road	60	195	19	54	11	2	2	20	16	25	3	.277
1991 Season	125	398	53	114	23	2	6	45	41	45	16	.286
Life 2.7 Years		395	61	100	19	4	7	37	43	56	15	.254

TONY PENA

BOSTON — CATCHER — 35 Years Ol

Runs Created: 40
Offensive Winning Percentage: .277
Batting Average: .231 Secondary Average: .188

Most Often Bats: 8th
Swings at First Pitch: 37%
Gets Ahead of the Pitcher: 50%
Hits Behind the Pitcher: 50%

1991 On Base Percentage: .291 Career: .317
1991 Slugging Percentage: .321 Career: .379
Batting Avg with Men in Scoring Position: .238

Bats Right-Handed	G	AB	R	H	2B	3B	HR	RBI	BB	SO	SB	AVG
Vs. RHP		358	32	77	19	2	1	31	28	42	4	.215
Vs. LHP		106	13	30	4	0	4	17	9	11	4	.283
At Home	73	230	24	51	13	1	2	22	19	27	5	.222
On the Road	68	234	21	56	10	1	3	26	18	26	3	.239
1991 Season	141	464	45	107	23	2	5	48	37	53	8	.231
Life 9.2 Years		558	59	150	26	3	10	63	39	70	8	.269

TERRY PENDLETON

ATLANTA THIRD BASE 31 Years Old

Runs Created: 107
Offensive Winning Percentage: .708
Batting Average: .319 Secondary Average: .288

Most Often Bats: 3rd
Swings at First Pitch: 33%
Gets Ahead of the Pitcher: 50%
Hits Behind the Pitcher: 50%

1991 On Base Percentage: .363 Career: .316
1991 Slugging Percentage: .517 Career: .380
Batting Avg with Men in Scoring Position: .320

Switch Hitter		AB	R	H	2B	3B	HR	RBI	BB	SO	SB	AVG
Vs. RHP		409	63	134	24	5	18	63	28	61	5	.328
Vs. LHP		177	31	53	10	3	4	23	15	9	5	.299
At Home	75	285	51	97	18	3	13	48	18	30	6	.340
On the Road	78	301	43	90	16	5	9	38	25	40	4	.299
1991 Season	153	586	94	187	34	8	22	86	43	70	10	.319
Life 6.7 Years		603	75	161	28	5	10	79	44	75	16	.267

MELIDO PEREZ

CHICAGO RELIEF PITCHER 26 Years Old
8-7 3.12 ERA 1 SAVE

Save Opportunities: 5 Blown Saves: 4 Holds: 9
Inherited Runners who Scored: 39%
Opponents Batting Average: .224
Double Play Support: .66 GDP Per Nine Innings

First Pitch is Hit: 11%
Gets Ahead of the Hitter: 50%
Gets Behind the Hitter: 50%
Gets First Batter Out: 61%

1991 On Base Pct Allowed: .299
Slugging Percentage: .352
Stolen Bases Allowed: 15 Caught Stealing: 5

Pitches Right	AB	H	2B	3B	HR	RBI	BB	SO	AVG
Vs. RHB	272	66	7	0	9	25	28	62	.243
Vs. LHB	223	45	9	1	6	25	24	66	.202

	G	IP	W-L	Pct	SO	BB	ERA	Sv
1991 Season	49	136	8-7	.533	128	52	3.12	1
Life 3.5 Years	43	207	13-13	.495	164	87	4.26	0

TONY PHILLIPS

DETROIT THIRD BASE 33 Years Old

Runs Created: 97
Offensive Winning Percentage: .604
Batting Average: .284 Secondary Average: .312

Most Often Bats: 1st
Swings at First Pitch: 25%
Gets Ahead of the Pitcher: 53%
Hits Behind the Pitcher: 47%

1991 On Base Percentage: .371 Career: .347
1991 Slugging Percentage: .438 Career: .363
Batting Avg with Men in Scoring Position: .322

Switch Hitter		AB	R	H	2B	3B	HR	RBI	BB	SO	SB	AVG
Vs. RHP		410	56	105	21	4	6	47	47	77	8	.256
Vs. LHP		154	31	55	7	0	11	25	32	18	2	.357
At Home	76	292	53	86	13	1	9	42	50	43	9	.295
On the Road	70	272	34	74	15	3	8	30	29	52	1	.272
1991 Season	146	564	87	160	28	4	17	72	79	95	10	.284
Life 7.0 Years		533	77	136	23	5	8	55	74	96	12	.256

DAN PLESAC

MILWAUKEE RELIEF PITCHER 30 Years Old
2-7 4.29 ERA 8 SAVES

Save Opportunities: 12 Blown Saves: 4 Holds: 1
Inherited Runners who Scored: 18%
Opponents Batting Average: .263
Double Play Support: .68 GDP Per Nine Innings

First Pitch is Hit: 15%
Gets Ahead of the Hitter: 47%
Gets Behind the Hitter: 53%
Gets First Batter Out: 76%

1991 On Base Pct Allowed: .336
Slugging Percentage: .434
Stolen Bases Allowed: 4 Caught Stealing: 5

Pitches Left	AB	H	2B	3B	HR	RBI	BB	SO	AVG
Vs. RHB	286	73	18	2	8	38	32	49	.255
Vs. LHB	64	19	2	0	4	14	7	12	.297

	G	IP	W-L	Pct	SO	BB	ERA	Sv
1991 Season	45	92	2-7	.222	61	39	4.29	8
Life 4.5 Years	72	100	5-7	.421	88	34	3.25	30

ERIC PLUNK

NEW YORK RELIEF PITCHER 28 Years Old
2-5 4.76 ERA 0 SAVES

Save Opportunities: 0 Blown Saves: 0 Holds: 2
Inherited Runners who Scored: 46%
Opponents Batting Average: .286
Double Play Support: .56 GDP Per Nine Innings

First Pitch is Hit: 12%
Gets Ahead of the Hitter: 47%
Gets Behind the Hitter: 53%
Gets First Batter Out: 69%

1991 On Base Pct Allowed: .371
Slugging Percentage: .478
Stolen Bases Allowed: 28 Caught Stealing: 3

Pitches Right	AB	H	2B	3B	HR	RBI	BB	SO	AVG
Vs. RHB	225	63	13	1	8	40	27	59	.280
Vs. LHB	223	65	9	4	10	30	35	44	.291

	G	IP	W-L	Pct	SO	BB	ERA	Sv
1991 Season	43	112	2-5	.286	103	62	4.76	0
Life 3.9 Years	63	150	8-7	.517	134	96	4.11	2

LUIS POLONIA

CALIFORNIA LEFT FIELD 27 Years Old

Runs Created: 81
Offensive Winning Percentage: .576
Batting Average: .296 Secondary Average: .248

Most Often Bats: 1st
Swings at First Pitch: 33%
Gets Ahead of the Pitcher: 47%
Hits Behind the Pitcher: 53%

1991 On Base Percentage: .352 Career: .348
1991 Slugging Percentage: .379 Career: .391
Batting Avg with Men in Scoring Position: .333

Bats Left-Handed		AB	R	H	2B	3B	HR	RBI	BB	SO	SB	AVG
Vs. RHP		436	70	139	20	7	2	33	41	49	37	.319
Vs. LHP		168	22	40	8	1	0	17	11	25	11	.238
At Home	77	303	38	79	11	4	1	20	30	36	17	.261
On the Road	73	301	54	100	17	4	1	30	22	38	31	.332
1991 Season	150	604	92	179	28	8	2	50	52	74	48	.296
Life 3.7 Years		580	92	175	21	10	3	56	42	71	39	.302

MARK PORTUGAL

HOUSTON STARTING PITCHER 29 Years Old

10-12 4.49 ERA

Opponents Batting Average: .256
Offensive Support: 4.54 Runs Per Nine Innings
Double Play Support: .80 GDP Per Nine Innings

First Pitch is Hit: 15%
Gets Ahead of the Hitter: 49%
Gets Behind the Hitter: 51%
Gets Leadoff Man Out: 66%

1991 On Base Pct Allowed: .318
Slugging Percentage: .400
Stolen Bases Allowed: 12 Caught Stealing: 7

Pitches Right	AB	H	2B	3B	HR	RBI	BB	SO	AVG
Vs. RHB	271	74	15	0	9	34	22	41	.273
Vs. LHB	366	89	14	3	10	45	37	79	.243

	G	IP	W-L	Pct	H	SO	BB	ERA
At Home	16	79	4-5		71	58	24	3.06
On the Road	16	89	6-7		92	62	35	5.76
1991 Season	32	168	10-12	.455	163	120	59	4.49
Life 3.5 Years	45	206	11-12	.481	201	139	77	4.20

CARLOS QUINTANA

BOSTON FIRST BASE 26 Years Old

Runs Created: 74
Offensive Winning Percentage: .605
Batting Average: .295 Secondary Average: .247

Most Often Bats: 3rd
Swings at First Pitch: 31%
Gets Ahead of the Pitcher: 50%
Hits Behind the Pitcher: 50%

1991 On Base Percentage: .375 Career: .359
1991 Slugging Percentage: .412 Career: .388
Batting Avg with Men in Scoring Position: .277

Bats Right-Handed		AB	R	H	2B	3B	HR	RBI	BB	SO	SB	AVG
Vs. RHP		325	39	89	14	1	6	45	35	45	1	.274
Vs. LHP		153	30	52	7	0	5	26	26	21	0	.340
At Home	74	236	31	69	10	0	2	30	34	31	1	.292
On the Road	75	242	38	72	11	1	9	41	27	35	0	.298
1991 Season	149	478	69	141	21	1	11	71	61	66	1	.295
Life 2.1 Years		516	63	147	26	0	9	70	59	75	1	.285

TIM RAINES

CHICAGO LEFT FIELD 32 Years Old

Runs Created: 85
Offensive Winning Percentage: .537
Batting Average: .268 Secondary Average: .297

Most Often Bats: 1st
Swings at First Pitch: 28%
Gets Ahead of the Pitcher: 57%
Hits Behind the Pitcher: 43%

1991 On Base Percentage: .359 Career: .387
1991 Slugging Percentage: .345 Career: .428
Batting Avg with Men in Scoring Position: .286

Switch Hitter		AB	R	H	2B	3B	HR	RBI	BB	SO	SB	AVG
Vs. RHP		401	76	105	14	5	3	33	62	47	37	.262
Vs. LHP		208	26	58	6	1	2	17	21	21	14	.279
At Home	77	284	44	72	7	2	1	21	39	30	21	.254
On the Road	78	325	58	91	13	4	4	29	44	38	30	.280
1991 Season	155	609	102	163	20	6	5	50	83	68	51	.268
Life 9.6 Years		614	108	183	30	9	10	63	89	66	71	.298

KIRBY PUCKETT

MINNESOTA CENTER FIELD 31 Years Old

Runs Created: 91
Offensive Winning Percentage: .590
Batting Average: .319 Secondary Average: .209

Most Often Bats: 3rd
Swings at First Pitch: 45%
Gets Ahead of the Pitcher: 47%
Hits Behind the Pitcher: 53%

1991 On Base Percentage: .352 Career: .357
1991 Slugging Percentage: .460 Career: .466
Batting Avg with Men in Scoring Position: .301

Bats Right-Handed		AB	R	H	2B	3B	HR	RBI	BB	SO	SB	AVG
Vs. RHP		456	58	132	21	1	8	65	23	59	8	.289
Vs. LHP		155	34	63	8	5	7	24	8	19	3	.406
At Home	80	328	54	107	16	4	7	45	16	45	6	.326
On the Road	72	283	38	88	13	2	8	44	15	33	5	.311
1991 Season	152	611	92	195	29	6	15	89	31	78	11	.319
Life 7.5 Years		664	95	212	35	6	16	89	36	85	13	.320

SCOTT RADINSKY

CHICAGO RELIEF PITCHER 24 Years Old

5-5 2.02 ERA 8 SAVES

Save Opportunities: 15 Blown Saves: 7 Holds: 15
Inherited Runners who Scored: 25%
Opponents Batting Average: .206
Double Play Support: .50 GDP Per Nine Innings

First Pitch is Hit: 16%
Gets Ahead of the Hitter: 54%
Gets Behind the Hitter: 46%
Gets First Batter Out: 75%

1991 On Base Pct Allowed: .270
Slugging Percentage: .288
Stolen Bases Allowed: 1 Caught Stealing: 0

Pitches Left	AB	H	2B	3B	HR	RBI	BB	SO	AVG
Vs. RHB	179	37	7	0	1	13	21	31	.207
Vs. LHB	78	16	2	0	3	11	2	18	.205

	G	IP	W-L	Pct	SO	BB	ERA	Sv
1991 Season	67	71	5-5	.500	49	23	2.02	8
Life 1.7 Years	74	71	6-3	.647	54	34	3.20	7

WILLIE RANDOLPH

MILWAUKEE SECOND BASE 37 Years Old

Runs Created: 72
Offensive Winning Percentage: .633
Batting Average: .327 Secondary Average: .230

Most Often Bats: 2nd
Swings at First Pitch: 25%
Gets Ahead of the Pitcher: 55%
Hits Behind the Pitcher: 45%

1991 On Base Percentage: .424 Career: .374
1991 Slugging Percentage: .374 Career: .353
Batting Avg with Men in Scoring Position: .373

Bats Right-Handed		AB	R	H	2B	3B	HR	RBI	BB	SO	SB	AVG
Vs. RHP		283	42	88	9	2	0	33	48	28	4	.311
Vs. LHP		148	18	53	5	1	0	21	27	10	0	.358
At Home	61	220	24	74	10	2	0	31	28	20	1	.336
On the Road	63	211	36	67	4	1	0	23	47	18	3	.318
1991 Season	124	431	60	141	14	3	0	54	75	38	4	.327
Life 13.0 Years		593	93	164	23	5	4	52	92	49	21	.277

DENNIS RASMUSSEN

AN DIEGO STARTING PITCHER 33 Years Old
6-13 3.74 ERA

pponents Batting Average: .271
ffensive Support: 3.56 Runs Per Nine Innings
ouble Play Support: .80 GDP Per Nine Innings

irst Pitch is Hit: 17%
ets Ahead of the Hitter: 51%
ets Behind the Hitter: 49%
ets Leadoff Man Out: 66%

991 On Base Pct Allowed: .328
lugging Percentage: .385
tolen Bases Allowed: 21 Caught Stealing: 6

Pitches Left	AB	H	2B	3B	HR	RBI	BB	SO	AVG
Vs. RHB	468	131	15	5	10	53	41	56	.280
Vs. LHB	104	24	2	1	2	10	8	19	.231

	G	IP	W-L	Pct	H	SO	BB	ERA
At Home	10	60	4-5		62	30	18	3.88
On the Road	14	86	2-8		93	45	31	3.65
1991 Season	24	147	6-13	.316	155	75	49	3.74
Life 6.2 Years	38	223	14-12	.541	216	130	79	4.09

JEFF REED

CINCINNATI CATCHER 29 Years Old

Runs Created: 32
Offensive Winning Percentage: .484
Batting Average: .267 Secondary Average: .189

Most Often Bats: 8th
Swings at First Pitch: 17%
Gets Ahead of the Pitcher: 57%
Hits Behind the Pitcher: 43%

1991 On Base Percentage: .321 Career: .303
1991 Slugging Percentage: .370 Career: .316
Batting Avg with Men in Scoring Position: .203

Bats Left-Handed		AB	R	H	2B	3B	HR	RBI	BB	SO	SB	AVG
Vs. RHP		244	18	67	13	2	3	26	20	32	0	.275
Vs. LHP		26	2	5	2	0	0	5	3	6	0	.192
At Home	39	115	11	30	9	2	1	15	13	19	0	.261
On the Road	52	155	9	42	6	0	2	16	10	19	0	.271
1991 Season	91	270	20	72	15	2	3	31	23	38	0	.267
Life 3.2 Years		432	31	101	19	2	4	36	43	61	1	.234

KEVIN REIMER

TEXAS LEFT FIELD 28 Years Old

Runs Created: 60
Offensive Winning Percentage: .524
Batting Average: .269 Secondary Average: .292

Most Often Bats: 5th
Swings at First Pitch: 40%
Gets Ahead of the Pitcher: 44%
Hits Behind the Pitcher: 56%

1991 On Base Percentage: .332 Career: .320
1991 Slugging Percentage: .477 Career: .452
Batting Avg with Men in Scoring Position: .284

Bats Left-Handed		AB	R	H	2B	3B	HR	RBI	BB	SO	SB	AVG
Vs. RHP		358	44	98	21	0	19	65	31	84	0	.274
Vs. LHP		36	2	8	1	0	1	4	2	9	0	.222
At Home	65	184	25	50	15	0	13	41	16	56	0	.272
On the Road	71	210	21	56	7	0	7	28	17	37	0	.267
1991 Season	136	394	46	106	22	0	20	69	33	93	0	.269
Life 1.3 Years		395	40	102	23	1	17	65	32	92	0	.258

GARY REDUS

PITTSBURGH FIRST BASE 35 Years Old

Runs Created: 37
Offensive Winning Percentage: .575
Batting Average: .246 Secondary Average: .325

Most Often Bats: 1st
Swings at First Pitch: 23%
Gets Ahead of the Pitcher: 62%
Hits Behind the Pitcher: 38%

1991 On Base Percentage: .324 Career: .342
1991 Slugging Percentage: .393 Career: .409
Batting Avg with Men in Scoring Position: .143

Bats Right-Handed		AB	R	H	2B	3B	HR	RBI	BB	SO	SB	AVG
Vs. RHP		79	16	19	5	0	2	9	13	12	4	.241
Vs. LHP		173	29	43	7	2	5	15	15	27	13	.249
At Home	49	125	24	35	8	2	3	11	12	18	8	.280
On the Road	49	127	21	27	4	0	4	13	16	21	9	.213
1991 Season	98	252	45	62	12	2	7	24	28	39	17	.246
Life 6.1 Years		505	88	126	27	7	13	50	72	102	50	.249

JODY REED

BOSTON SECOND BASE 29 Years Old

Runs Created: 83
Offensive Winning Percentage: .524
Batting Average: .283 Secondary Average: .206

Most Often Bats: 2nd
Swings at First Pitch: 16%
Gets Ahead of the Pitcher: 51%
Hits Behind the Pitcher: 49%

1991 On Base Percentage: .349 Career: .368
1991 Slugging Percentage: .382 Career: .386
Batting Avg with Men in Scoring Position: .304

Bats Right-Handed		AB	R	H	2B	3B	HR	RBI	BB	SO	SB	AVG
Vs. RHP		453	59	131	33	2	5	54	44	42	5	.289
Vs. LHP		165	28	44	9	0	0	6	16	11	1	.267
At Home	78	312	46	82	27	1	3	37	34	27	2	.263
On the Road	75	306	41	93	15	1	2	23	26	26	4	.304
1991 Season	153	618	87	175	42	2	5	60	60	53	6	.283
Life 3.5 Years		597	84	172	43	2	4	53	73	52	5	.288

HAROLD REYNOLDS

SEATTLE SECOND BASE 31 Years Old

Runs Created: 78
Offensive Winning Percentage: .484
Batting Average: .254 Secondary Average: .246

Most Often Bats: 2nd
Swings at First Pitch: 16%
Gets Ahead of the Pitcher: 57%
Hits Behind the Pitcher: 43%

1991 On Base Percentage: .332 Career: .327
1991 Slugging Percentage: .341 Career: .347
Batting Avg with Men in Scoring Position: .322

Switch Hitter		AB	R	H	2B	3B	HR	RBI	BB	SO	SB	AVG
Vs. RHP		457	74	114	27	6	2	41	55	49	23	.249
Vs. LHP		174	21	46	7	0	1	16	17	14	5	.264
At Home	81	314	58	94	20	5	1	27	42	27	15	.299
On the Road	80	317	37	66	14	1	2	30	30	36	13	.208
1991 Season	161	631	95	160	34	6	3	57	72	63	28	.254
Life 6.3 Years		580	78	152	28	7	2	42	55	50	34	.262

DAVE RIGHETTI

SAN FRANCISCO RELIEF PITCHER 33 Years Old

2-7 3.39 ERA 24 SAVES

Save Opportunities: 29 Blown Saves: 5 Holds: 5
Inherited Runners who Scored: 16%
Opponents Batting Average: .240
Double Play Support: .63 GDP Per Nine Innings

First Pitch is Hit: 13%
Gets Ahead of the Hitter: 48%
Gets Behind the Hitter: 52%
Gets First Batter Out: 85%

1991 On Base Pct Allowed: .317
Slugging Percentage: .330
Stolen Bases Allowed: 8 Caught Stealing: 4

Pitches Left	AB	H	2B	3B	HR	RBI	BB	SO	AVG
Vs. RHB	195	52	12	0	4	23	26	38	.267
Vs. LHB	72	12	0	0	0	9	2	13	.167

	G	IP	W-L	Pct	SO	BB	ERA	Sv
1991 Season	61	72	2-7	.222	51	28	3.39	24
Life 8.9 Years	65	136	9-8	.528	111	56	3.13	28

JOSE RIJO

CINCINNATI STARTING PITCHER 27 Years Old

15-6 2.51 ERA

Opponents Batting Average: .219
Offensive Support: 5.64 Runs Per Nine Innings
Double Play Support: .66 GDP Per Nine Innings

First Pitch is Hit: 15%
Gets Ahead of the Hitter: 53%
Gets Behind the Hitter: 47%
Gets Leadoff Man Out: 76%

1991 On Base Pct Allowed: .272
Slugging Percentage: .305
Stolen Bases Allowed: 16 Caught Stealing: 3

Pitches Right	AB	H	2B	3B	HR	RBI	BB	SO	AVG
Vs. RHB	319	55	12	0	3	16	17	80	.172
Vs. LHB	436	110	21	4	5	45	38	92	.252

	G	IP	W-L	Pct	H	SO	BB	ERA
At Home	15	99	9-0		73	74	35	2.99
On the Road	15	105	6-6		92	98	20	2.06
1991 Season	30	204	15-6	.714	165	172	55	2.51
Life 5.1 Years	44	213	13-11	.540	187	183	90	3.39

CAL RIPKEN

BALTIMORE SHORTSTOP 31 Years Old

Runs Created: 134
Offensive Winning Percentage: .739
Batting Average: .323 Secondary Average: .334

Most Often Bats: 3rd
Swings at First Pitch: 36%
Gets Ahead of the Pitcher: 49%
Hits Behind the Pitcher: 51%

1991 On Base Percentage: .374 Career: .349
1991 Slugging Percentage: .566 Career: .467
Batting Avg with Men in Scoring Position: .315

Bats Right-Handed		AB	R	H	2B	3B	HR	RBI	BB	SO	SB	AVG
Vs. RHP		486	74	153	32	3	22	83	34	31	5	.315
Vs. LHP		164	25	57	14	2	12	31	19	15	1	.348
At Home	81	315	44	90	19	1	16	52	28	23	3	.286
On the Road	81	335	55	120	27	4	18	62	25	23	3	.358
1991 Season	162	650	99	210	46	5	34	114	53	46	6	.323
Life 10.1 Years		624	96	174	34	3	26	93	68	74	3	.279

LUIS RIVERA

BOSTON SHORTSTOP 28 Years Old

Runs Created: 50
Offensive Winning Percentage: .449
Batting Average: .258 Secondary Average: .220

Most Often Bats: 9th
Swings at First Pitch: 34%
Gets Ahead of the Pitcher: 52%
Hits Behind the Pitcher: 48%

1991 On Base Percentage: .318 Career: .290
1991 Slugging Percentage: .384 Career: .343
Batting Avg with Men in Scoring Position: .202

Bats Right-Handed		AB	R	H	2B	3B	HR	RBI	BB	SO	SB	AVG
Vs. RHP		306	46	73	12	2	4	24	29	61	3	.239
Vs. LHP		108	18	34	10	1	4	16	6	25	1	.315
At Home	66	204	32	52	13	0	4	16	23	43	2	.255
On the Road	63	210	32	55	9	3	4	24	12	43	2	.262
1991 Season	129	414	64	107	22	3	8	40	35	86	4	.258
Life 3.3 Years		499	58	118	27	2	7	48	37	95	4	.236

BIP ROBERTS

SAN DIEGO SECOND BASE 28 Years O

Runs Created: 53
Offensive Winning Percentage: .547
Batting Average: .281 Secondary Average: .215

Most Often Bats: 1st
Swings at First Pitch: 37%
Gets Ahead of the Pitcher: 48%
Hits Behind the Pitcher: 52%

1991 On Base Percentage: .342 Career: .358
1991 Slugging Percentage: .347 Career: .387
Batting Avg with Men in Scoring Position: .316

Switch Hitter		AB	R	H	2B	3B	HR	RBI	BB	SO	SB	AV
Vs. RHP		305	49	89	10	2	3	24	30	58	23	.29
Vs. LHP		119	17	30	3	1	0	8	7	13	3	.25
At Home	62	223	31	64	4	1	3	17	12	32	9	.28
On the Road	55	201	35	55	9	2	0	15	25	39	17	.27
1991 Season	117	424	66	119	13	3	3	32	37	71	26	.28
Life 3.0 Years		516	95	150	23	5	5	37	52	70	35	.29

JEFF M. ROBINSON

BALTIMORE STARTING PITCHER 30 Years Ol

4-9 5.18 ERA

Opponents Batting Average: .289
Offensive Support: 3.80 Runs Per Nine Innings
Double Play Support: 1.04 GDP Per Nine Innings

First Pitch is Hit: 13%
Gets Ahead of the Hitter: 50%
Gets Behind the Hitter: 50%
Gets Leadoff Man Out: 72%

1991 On Base Pct Allowed: .375
Slugging Percentage: .434
Stolen Bases Allowed: 10 Caught Stealing:

Pitches Right	AB	H	2B	3B	HR	RBI	BB	SO	AVG
Vs. RHB	198	44	8	1	1	19	20	37	.222
Vs. LHB	214	75	14	0	11	31	31	28	.350

	G	IP	W-L	Pct	H	SO	BB	ERA
At Home	11	69	3-3		72	40	28	3.78
On the Road	10	35	1-6		47	25	23	7.90
1991 Season	21	104	4-9	.308	119	65	51	5.18
Life 3.0 Years	39	208	13-12	.533	195	130	103	4.74

IVAN RODRIGUEZ

EXAS CATCHER 20 Years Old

uns Created: 24
ffensive Winning Percentage: .253
atting Average: .264 Secondary Average: .107

lost Often Bats: 8th
wings at First Pitch: 28%
ets Ahead of the Pitcher: 50%
lits Behind the Pitcher: 50%

991 On Base Percentage: .276 Career: .276
991 Slugging Percentage: .354 Career: .354
atting Avg with Men in Scoring Position: .333

Bats Right-Handed		AB	R	H	2B	3B	HR	RBI	BB	SO	SB	AVG
Vs. RHP		209	17	57	10	0	2	18	3	33	0	.273
Vs. LHP		71	7	17	6	0	1	9	2	9	0	.239
At Home	41	135	11	32	9	0	3	18	2	23	0	.237
On the Road	47	145	13	42	7	0	0	9	3	19	0	.290
1991 Season	88	280	24	74	16	0	3	27	5	42	0	.264
Life 0.5 Years		515	44	136	29	0	6	50	9	77	0	.264

BRUCE RUFFIN

PHILADELPHIA RELIEF PITCHER 28 Years Old
4-7 3.78 ERA 0 SAVES

Save Opportunities: 0 Blown Saves: 0 Holds: 5
Inherited Runners who Scored: 29%
Opponents Batting Average: .272
Double Play Support: .91 GDP Per Nine Innings

First Pitch is Hit: 16%
Gets Ahead of the Hitter: 49%
Gets Behind the Hitter: 51%
Gets First Batter Out: 75%

1991 On Base Pct Allowed: .327
Slugging Percentage: .386
Stolen Bases Allowed: 7 Caught Stealing: 4

Pitches Left	AB	H	2B	3B	HR	RBI	BB	SO	AVG
Vs. RHB	348	97	22	3	5	35	32	63	.279
Vs. LHB	111	28	6	0	1	12	6	22	.252

	G	IP	W-L	Pct	SO	BB	ERA	Sv
1991 Season	31	119	4-7	.364	85	38	3.78	0
Life 4.5 Years	44	198	9-13	.420	107	80	4.16	1

JEFF RUSSELL

TEXAS RELIEF PITCHER 30 Years Old
6-4 3.29 ERA 30 SAVES

Save Opportunities: 40 Blown Saves: 10 Holds: 0
Inherited Runners who Scored: 40%
Opponents Batting Average: .236
Double Play Support: 1.13 GDP Per Nine Innings

First Pitch is Hit: 17%
Gets Ahead of the Hitter: 46%
Gets Behind the Hitter: 54%
Gets First Batter Out: 55%

1991 On Base Pct Allowed: .295
Slugging Percentage: .365
Stolen Bases Allowed: 1 Caught Stealing: 0

Pitches Right	AB	H	2B	3B	HR	RBI	BB	SO	AVG
Vs. RHB	156	36	4	0	9	24	9	32	.231
Vs. LHB	145	35	2	0	2	28	17	20	.241

	G	IP	W-L	Pct	SO	BB	ERA	Sv
1991 Season	68	79	6-4	.600	52	26	3.29	30
Life 5.7 Years	60	150	8-10	.447	92	57	3.96	14

NOLAN RYAN

TEXAS STARTING PITCHER 45 Years Old
12-6 2.91 ERA

Opponents Batting Average: .172
Offensive Support: 4.94 Runs Per Nine Innings
Double Play Support: .31 GDP Per Nine Innings

First Pitch is Hit: 10%
Gets Ahead of the Hitter: 52%
Gets Behind the Hitter: 48%
Gets Leadoff Man Out: 77%

1991 On Base Pct Allowed: .263
Slugging Percentage: .285
Stolen Bases Allowed: 24 Caught Stealing: 8

Pitches Right	AB	H	2B	3B	HR	RBI	BB	SO	AVG
Vs. RHB	249	39	12	0	7	27	38	98	.157
Vs. LHB	345	63	13	3	5	27	34	105	.183

	G	IP	W-L	Pct	H	SO	BB	ERA
At Home	20	132	10-4		75	157	53	3.08
On the Road	7	41	2-2		27	46	19	2.40
1991 Season	27	173	12-6	.667	102	203	72	2.91
Life 20.3 Years	38	255	15-14	.530	184	272	133	3.15

BRET SABERHAGEN

KANSAS CITY STARTING PITCHER 28 Years Old
13-8 3.07 ERA

Opponents Batting Average: .228
Offensive Support: 4.31 Runs Per Nine Innings
Double Play Support: .64 GDP Per Nine Innings

First Pitch is Hit: 14%
Gets Ahead of the Hitter: 52%
Gets Behind the Hitter: 48%
Gets Leadoff Man Out: 72%

1991 On Base Pct Allowed: .280
Slugging Percentage: .327
Stolen Bases Allowed: 9 Caught Stealing: 9

Pitches Right	AB	H	2B	3B	HR	RBI	BB	SO	AVG
Vs. RHB	370	89	17	2	3	27	18	68	.241
Vs. LHB	354	76	11	2	9	36	27	68	.215

	G	IP	W-L	Pct	H	SO	BB	ERA
At Home	14	95	7-3		70	62	25	2.76
On the Road	14	102	6-5		95	74	20	3.36
1991 Season	28	196	13-8	.619	165	136	45	3.07
Life 6.5 Years	39	257	17-12	.585	240	169	51	3.21

CHRIS SABO

CINCINNATI THIRD BASE 30 Years Old

Runs Created: 103
Offensive Winning Percentage: .694
Batting Average: .301 Secondary Average: .313

Most Often Bats: 5th
Swings at First Pitch: 28%
Gets Ahead of the Pitcher: 53%
Hits Behind the Pitcher: 47%

1991 On Base Percentage: .354 Career: .335
1991 Slugging Percentage: .505 Career: .456
Batting Avg with Men in Scoring Position: .303

Bats Right-Handed		AB	R	H	2B	3B	HR	RBI	BB	SO	SB	AVG
Vs. RHP		389	54	106	18	2	17	59	28	56	12	.272
Vs. LHP		193	37	69	17	1	9	29	16	23	7	.358
At Home	79	298	48	101	24	2	15	45	25	37	9	.339
On the Road	74	284	43	74	11	1	11	43	19	42	10	.261
1991 Season	153	582	91	175	35	3	26	88	44	79	19	.301
Life 3.2 Years		620	93	172	42	2	21	72	50	69	32	.278

LUIS SALAZAR

CHICAGO THIRD BASE 36 Years Old

Runs Created: 39
Offensive Winning Percentage: .443
Batting Average: .258 Secondary Average: .219

Most Often Bats: 6th
Swings at First Pitch: 23%
Gets Ahead of the Pitcher: 46%
Hits Behind the Pitcher: 54%

1991 On Base Percentage: .292 Career: .296
1991 Slugging Percentage: .432 Career: .386
Batting Avg with Men in Scoring Position: .192

Bats Right-Handed		AB	R	H	2B	3B	HR	RBI	BB	SO	SB	AVG
Vs. RHP		167	13	41	6	1	4	13	7	27	0	.246
Vs. LHP		166	21	45	8	0	10	25	8	18	0	.271
At Home	52	165	16	43	11	0	8	20	4	22	0	.261
On the Road	51	168	18	43	3	1	6	18	11	23	0	.256
1991 Season	103	333	34	86	14	1	14	38	15	45	0	.258
Life 7.4 Years		517	56	137	18	4	12	58	23	83	16	.264

RYNE SANDBERG

CHICAGO SECOND BASE 32 Years Old

Runs Created: 114
Offensive Winning Percentage: .707
Batting Average: .291 Secondary Average: .381

Most Often Bats: 3rd
Swings at First Pitch: 10%
Gets Ahead of the Pitcher: 51%
Hits Behind the Pitcher: 49%

1991 On Base Percentage: .379 Career: .346
1991 Slugging Percentage: .485 Career: .455
Batting Avg with Men in Scoring Position: .338

Bats Right-Handed		AB	R	H	2B	3B	HR	RBI	BB	SO	SB	AVG
Vs. RHP		376	63	95	13	2	18	73	48	66	15	.253
Vs. LHP		209	41	75	19	0	8	27	39	23	7	.359
At Home	81	291	57	90	14	2	15	54	43	39	11	.309
On the Road	77	294	47	80	18	0	11	46	44	50	11	.272
1991 Season	158	585	104	170	32	2	26	100	87	89	22	.291
Life 9.5 Years		638	102	184	30	6	21	78	58	92	31	.288

BENITO SANTIAGO

SAN DIEGO CATCHER 27 Years Old

Runs Created: 61
Offensive Winning Percentage: .446
Batting Average: .267 Secondary Average: .190

Most Often Bats: 5th
Swings at First Pitch: 47%
Gets Ahead of the Pitcher: 48%
Hits Behind the Pitcher: 52%

1991 On Base Percentage: .296 Career: .300
1991 Slugging Percentage: .403 Career: .410
Batting Avg with Men in Scoring Position: .275

Bats Right-Handed		AB	R	H	2B	3B	HR	RBI	BB	SO	SB	AVG
Vs. RHP		376	32	97	10	1	9	52	13	73	5	.258
Vs. LHP		204	28	58	12	2	8	35	10	41	3	.284
At Home	76	287	23	70	8	0	6	34	8	49	4	.244
On the Road	76	293	37	85	14	3	11	53	15	65	4	.290
1991 Season	152	580	60	155	22	3	17	87	23	114	8	.267
Life 4.2 Years		590	65	157	24	4	18	79	28	110	14	.266

JUAN SAMUEL

LOS ANGELES SECOND BASE 31 Years Old

Runs Created: 78
Offensive Winning Percentage: .593
Batting Average: .271 Secondary Average: .239

Most Often Bats: 2nd
Swings at First Pitch: 29%
Gets Ahead of the Pitcher: 53%
Hits Behind the Pitcher: 47%

1991 On Base Percentage: .328 Career: .312
1991 Slugging Percentage: .389 Career: .418
Batting Avg with Men in Scoring Position: .248

Bats Right-Handed		AB	R	H	2B	3B	HR	RBI	BB	SO	SB	AVG
Vs. RHP		344	36	98	11	4	5	31	35	74	16	.285
Vs. LHP		250	38	63	11	2	7	27	14	59	7	.252
At Home	77	295	37	75	12	1	4	26	25	67	11	.254
On the Road	76	299	37	86	10	5	8	32	24	66	12	.288
1991 Season	153	594	74	161	22	6	12	58	49	133	23	.271
Life 7.6 Years		646	91	168	31	11	17	72	44	152	45	.259

SCOTT SANDERSON

NEW YORK STARTING PITCHER 35 Years Old
16-10 3.81 ERA

Opponents Batting Average: .252
Offensive Support: 4.98 Runs Per Nine Innings
Double Play Support: .82 GDP Per Nine Innings

First Pitch is Hit: 11%
Gets Ahead of the Hitter: 57%
Gets Behind the Hitter: 43%
Gets Leadoff Man Out: 69%

1991 On Base Pct Allowed: .279
Slugging Percentage: .405
Stolen Bases Allowed: 16 Caught Stealing: 7

Pitches Right	AB	H	2B	3B	HR	RBI	BB	SO	AVG
Vs. RHB	358	86	22	1	7	35	12	56	.240
Vs. LHB	437	114	24	4	15	54	17	74	.261

	G	IP	W-L	Pct	H	SO	BB	ERA
At Home	15	93	7-6		102	55	16	4.66
On the Road	19	115	9-4		98	75	13	3.12
1991 Season	34	208	16-10	.615	200	130	29	3.81
Life 9.4 Years	40	216	14-12	.544	209	142	54	3.61

STEVE SAX

NEW YORK SECOND BASE 32 Years Old

Runs Created: 92
Offensive Winning Percentage: .560
Batting Average: .304 Secondary Average: .221

Most Often Bats: 2nd
Swings at First Pitch: 19%
Gets Ahead of the Pitcher: 50%
Hits Behind the Pitcher: 50%

1991 On Base Percentage: .345 Career: .340
1991 Slugging Percentage: .414 Career: .363
Batting Avg with Men in Scoring Position: .318

Bats Right-Handed		AB	R	H	2B	3B	HR	RBI	BB	SO	SB	AVG
Vs. RHP		437	42	124	18	2	5	36	24	32	19	.284
Vs. LHP		215	43	74	20	0	5	20	17	6	12	.344
At Home	81	327	44	95	20	1	6	27	25	19	13	.291
On the Road	77	325	41	103	18	1	4	29	16	19	18	.317
1991 Season	158	652	85	198	38	2	10	56	41	38	31	.304
Life 9.6 Years		646	85	185	26	4	5	51	52	55	42	.286

BOB SCANLAN

CHICAGO RELIEF PITCHER 25 Years Old

7-8 3.89 ERA 1 SAVE

Save Opportunities: 2 Blown Saves: 1 Holds: 2
Inherited Runners who Scored: 33%
Opponents Batting Average: .269
Double Play Support: .89 GDP Per Nine Innings

First Pitch is Hit: 14%
Gets Ahead of the Hitter: 49%
Gets Behind the Hitter: 51%
Gets First Batter Out: 56%

1991 On Base Pct Allowed: .332
Slugging Percentage: .373
Stolen Bases Allowed: 5 Caught Stealing: 7

Pitches Right	AB	H	2B	3B	HR	RBI	BB	SO	AVG
Vs. RHB	199	56	7	2	3	30	19	24	.281
Vs. LHB	225	58	12	3	2	25	21	20	.258

	G	IP	W-L	Pct	SO	BB	ERA	Sv
1991 Season	40	111	7-8	.467	44	40	3.89	1
Life 0.7 Years	56	155	10-11	.467	61	56	3.89	1

MIKE SCIOSCIA

LOS ANGELES CATCHER 33 Years Old

Runs Created: 51
Offensive Winning Percentage: .639
Batting Average: .264 Secondary Average: .275

Most Often Bats: 7th
Swings at First Pitch: 14%
Gets Ahead of the Pitcher: 55%
Hits Behind the Pitcher: 45%

1991 On Base Percentage: .353 Career: .349
1991 Slugging Percentage: .391 Career: .362
Batting Avg with Men in Scoring Position: .276

Bats Left-Handed		AB	R	H	2B	3B	HR	RBI	BB	SO	SB	AVG
Vs. RHP		239	25	71	14	2	5	27	36	20	1	.297
Vs. LHP		106	14	20	2	0	3	13	11	12	3	.189
At Home	62	163	15	47	9	0	3	22	26	15	1	.288
On the Road	57	182	24	44	7	2	5	18	21	17	3	.242
1991 Season	119	345	39	91	16	2	8	40	47	32	4	.264
Life 8.2 Years		492	46	129	23	1	8	52	65	34	3	.262

KEVIN SEITZER

KANSAS CITY THIRD BASE 30 Years Old

Runs Created: 30
Offensive Winning Percentage: .513
Batting Average: .265 Secondary Average: .226

Most Often Bats: 6th
Swings at First Pitch: 17%
Gets Ahead of the Pitcher: 54%
Hits Behind the Pitcher: 46%

1991 On Base Percentage: .350 Career: .380
1991 Slugging Percentage: .350 Career: .394
Batting Avg with Men in Scoring Position: .242

Bats Right-Handed		AB	R	H	2B	3B	HR	RBI	BB	SO	SB	AVG
Vs. RHP		168	19	40	8	3	0	18	18	18	4	.238
Vs. LHP		66	9	22	3	0	1	7	11	3	0	.333
At Home	42	117	12	32	7	2	0	15	11	10	2	.274
On the Road	43	117	16	30	4	1	1	10	18	11	2	.256
1991 Season	85	234	28	62	11	3	1	25	29	21	4	.265
Life 4.6 Years		601	89	177	28	5	7	58	81	71	11	.294

DICK SCHOFIELD

CALIFORNIA SHORTSTOP 29 Years Old

Runs Created: 39
Offensive Winning Percentage: .360
Batting Average: .225 Secondary Average: .171

Most Often Bats: 9th
Swings at First Pitch: 26%
Gets Ahead of the Pitcher: 53%
Hits Behind the Pitcher: 47%

1991 On Base Percentage: .310 Career: .305
1991 Slugging Percentage: .260 Career: .321
Batting Avg with Men in Scoring Position: .255

Bats Right-Handed		AB	R	H	2B	3B	HR	RBI	BB	SO	SB	AVG
Vs. RHP		312	29	75	8	3	0	23	28	54	5	.240
Vs. LHP		115	15	21	1	0	0	8	22	15	3	.183
At Home	68	211	17	44	4	1	0	19	22	29	5	.209
On the Road	66	216	27	52	5	2	0	12	28	40	3	.241
1991 Season	134	427	44	96	9	3	0	31	50	69	8	.225
Life 6.5 Years		519	61	120	16	4	7	42	50	78	15	.232

SCOTT SCUDDER

CINCINNATI STARTING PITCHER 24 Years Old

6-9 4.35 ERA

Opponents Batting Average: .246
Offensive Support: 4.53 Runs Per Nine Innings
Double Play Support: .53 GDP Per Nine Innings

First Pitch is Hit: 15%
Gets Ahead of the Hitter: 47%
Gets Behind the Hitter: 53%
Gets Leadoff Man Out: 63%

1991 On Base Pct Allowed: .352
Slugging Percentage: .362
Stolen Bases Allowed: 12 Caught Stealing: 6

Pitches Right	AB	H	2B	3B	HR	RBI	BB	SO	AVG
Vs. RHB	155	37	6	0	3	18	18	21	.239
Vs. LHB	215	54	13	3	3	23	38	30	.251

	G	IP	W-L	Pct	H	SO	BB	ERA
At Home	14	56	3-6		52	29	33	5.34
On the Road	13	46	3-3		39	22	23	3.15
1991 Season	27	101	6-9	.400	91	51	56	4.35
Life 1.5 Years	47	181	10-15	.395	169	105	97	4.54

TERRY SHUMPERT

KANSAS CITY SECOND BASE 25 Years Old

Runs Created: 32
Offensive Winning Percentage: .268
Batting Average: .217 Secondary Average: .233

Most Often Bats: 9th
Swings at First Pitch: 37%
Gets Ahead of the Pitcher: 41%
Hits Behind the Pitcher: 59%

1991 On Base Percentage: .283 Career: .284
1991 Slugging Percentage: .322 Career: .330
Batting Avg with Men in Scoring Position: .266

Bats Right-Handed		AB	R	H	2B	3B	HR	RBI	BB	SO	SB	AVG
Vs. RHP		234	29	52	10	4	3	22	21	50	9	.222
Vs. LHP		135	16	28	6	0	2	12	9	25	8	.207
At Home	74	183	19	40	8	3	1	16	14	35	11	.219
On the Road	70	186	26	40	8	1	4	18	16	40	6	.215
1991 Season	144	369	45	80	16	4	5	34	30	75	17	.217
Life 1.1 Years		423	48	97	20	5	5	39	29	85	18	.228

RUBEN SIERRA

TEXAS RIGHT FIELD 26 Years Old

Runs Created: 117
Offensive Winning Percentage: .621
Batting Average: .307 Secondary Average: .304

Most Often Bats: 3rd
Swings at First Pitch: 15%
Gets Ahead of the Pitcher: 58%
Hits Behind the Pitcher: 42%

1991 On Base Percentage: .357 Career: .325
1991 Slugging Percentage: .502 Career: .474
Batting Avg with Men in Scoring Position: .342

Switch Hitter	G	AB	R	H	2B	3B	HR	RBI	BB	SO	SB	AVG
Vs. RHP		473	76	140	29	3	18	84	36	69	12	.296
Vs. LHP		188	34	63	15	2	7	32	20	22	4	.335
At Home	80	328	54	105	22	4	12	61	18	44	10	.320
On the Road	81	333	56	98	22	1	13	55	38	47	6	.294
1991 Season	161	661	110	203	44	5	25	116	56	91	16	.307
Life 5.6 Years		631	90	177	35	7	25	104	45	94	13	.280

JOHN SMILEY

PITTSBURGH STARTING PITCHER 27 Years Old
20-8 3.08 ERA

Opponents Batting Average: .251
Offensive Support: 4.77 Runs Per Nine Innings
Double Play Support: .48 GDP Per Nine Innings

First Pitch is Hit: 14%
Gets Ahead of the Hitter: 55%
Gets Behind the Hitter: 45%
Gets Leadoff Man Out: 70%

1991 On Base Pct Allowed: .292
Slugging Percentage: .381
Stolen Bases Allowed: 18 Caught Stealing: 13

Pitches Left	AB	H	2B	3B	HR	RBI	BB	SO	AVG
Vs. RHB	621	164	34	3	14	59	39	99	.264
Vs. LHB	153	30	4	3	3	12	5	30	.196

	G	IP	W-L	Pct	H	SO	BB	ERA
At Home	16	100	10-5		90	60	24	2.98
On the Road	17	108	10-3		104	69	20	3.17
1991 Season	33	208	20-8	.714	194	129	44	3.08
Life 4.2 Years	46	202	14-10	.588	186	126	54	3.57

LEE SMITH

ST. LOUIS RELIEF PITCHER 34 Years Old
6-3 2.34 ERA 47 SAVES

Save Opportunities: 53 Blown Saves: 6 Holds: 0
Inherited Runners who Scored: 46%
Opponents Batting Average: .249
Double Play Support: .37 GDP Per Nine Innings

First Pitch is Hit: 13%
Gets Ahead of the Hitter: 54%
Gets Behind the Hitter: 46%
Gets First Batter Out: 70%

1991 On Base Pct Allowed: .281
Slugging Percentage: .352
Stolen Bases Allowed: 10 Caught Stealing: 2

Pitches Right	AB	H	2B	3B	HR	RBI	BB	SO	AVG
Vs. RHB	116	28	3	1	2	12	2	24	.241
Vs. LHB	165	42	5	2	3	19	11	43	.255

	G	IP	W-L	Pct	SO	BB	ERA	SV
1991 Season	67	73	6-3	.667	67	13	2.34	47
Life 9.8 Years	73	102	6-7	.484	101	38	2.84	32

JOE SLUSARSKI

OAKLAND STARTING PITCHER 25 Years Old
5-7 5.27 ERA

Opponents Batting Average: .283
Offensive Support: 5.19 Runs Per Nine Innings
Double Play Support: .91 GDP Per Nine Innings

First Pitch is Hit: 14%
Gets Ahead of the Hitter: 49%
Gets Behind the Hitter: 51%
Gets Leadoff Man Out: 70%

1991 On Base Pct Allowed: .364
Slugging Percentage: .436
Stolen Bases Allowed: 5 Caught Stealing: 5

Pitches Right	AB	H	2B	3B	HR	RBI	BB	SO	AVG
Vs. RHB	174	46	7	0	7	28	30	31	.264
Vs. LHB	253	75	10	3	7	25	22	29	.296

	G	IP	W-L	Pct	H	SO	BB	ERA
At Home	7	44	2-3		46	24	17	5.36
On the Road	13	66	3-4		75	36	35	5.21
1991 Season	20	109	5-7	.417	121	60	52	5.27
Life 0.5 Years	38	207	9-13	.417	230	114	99	5.27

BRYN SMITH

ST. LOUIS STARTING PITCHER 36 Years Old
12-9 3.85 ERA

Opponents Batting Average: .251
Offensive Support: 5.48 Runs Per Nine Innings
Double Play Support: .50 GDP Per Nine Innings

First Pitch is Hit: 18%
Gets Ahead of the Hitter: 57%
Gets Behind the Hitter: 43%
Gets Leadoff Man Out: 70%

1991 On Base Pct Allowed: .297
Slugging Percentage: .381
Stolen Bases Allowed: 19 Caught Stealing: 8

Pitches Right	AB	H	2B	3B	HR	RBI	BB	SO	AVG
Vs. RHB	308	68	11	1	9	34	17	53	.221
Vs. LHB	441	120	28	4	7	50	28	41	.272

	G	IP	W-L	Pct	H	SO	BB	ERA
At Home	16	107	5-4		95	46	25	3.52
On the Road	15	91	7-5		93	48	20	4.24
1991 Season	31	199	12-9	.571	188	94	45	3.85
Life 8.0 Years	43	218	13-11	.537	208	127	52	3.43

LONNIE SMITH

ATLANTA LEFT FIELD 36 Years Old

Runs Created: 57
Offensive Winning Percentage: .633
Batting Average: .275 Secondary Average: .286

Most Often Bats: 1st
Swings at First Pitch: 43%
Gets Ahead of the Pitcher: 51%
Hits Behind the Pitcher: 49%

1991 On Base Percentage: .377 Career: .371
1991 Slugging Percentage: .394 Career: .420
Batting Avg with Men in Scoring Position: .292

Bats Right-Handed	G	AB	R	H	2B	3B	HR	RBI	BB	SO	SB	AVG
Vs. RHP		238	33	58	10	0	7	33	32	42	8	.244
Vs. LHP		115	25	39	9	1	0	11	18	22	1	.339
At Home	63	193	33	56	10	0	6	31	23	35	2	.290
On the Road	59	160	25	41	9	1	1	13	27	29	7	.256
1991 Season	122	353	58	97	19	1	7	44	50	64	9	.275
Life 8.6 Years		551	97	160	30	6	10	55	63	86	41	.291

OZZIE SMITH

ST. LOUIS SHORTSTOP 37 Years Old

Runs Created: 86
Offensive Winning Percentage: .657
Batting Average: .285 Secondary Average: .296

Most Often Bats: 2nd
Swings at First Pitch: 24%
Gets Ahead of the Pitcher: 56%
Hits Behind the Pitcher: 44%

1991 On Base Percentage: .380 Career: .337
1991 Slugging Percentage: .367 Career: .325
Batting Avg with Men in Scoring Position: .275

Switch Hitter	G	AB	R	H	2B	3B	HR	RBI	BB	SO	SB	AVG
Vs. RHP		302	58	92	12	1	0	25	48	16	24	.305
Vs. LHP		248	38	65	18	2	3	25	35	20	11	.262
At Home	81	291	55	94	19	1	2	28	46	18	19	.323
On the Road	69	259	41	63	11	2	1	22	37	18	16	.243
1991 Season	150	550	96	157	30	3	3	50	83	36	35	.285
Life 12.8 Years		591	79	153	26	4	2	51	69	38	39	.258

JOHN SMOLTZ

ATLANTA STARTING PITCHER 25 Years Old
14-13 3.80 ERA

Opponents Batting Average: .243
Offensive Support: 4.47 Runs Per Nine Innings
Double Play Support: .71 GDP Per Nine Innings

First Pitch is Hit: 14%
Gets Ahead of the Hitter: 46%
Gets Behind the Hitter: 54%
Gets Leadoff Man Out: 67%

1991 On Base Pct Allowed: .305
Slugging Percentage: .360
Stolen Bases Allowed: 14 Caught Stealing: 13

Pitches Right	AB	H	2B	3B	HR	RBI	BB	SO	AVG
Vs. RHB	363	66	15	1	6	33	17	79	.182
Vs. LHB	486	140	23	6	10	56	60	69	.288

	G	IP	W-L	Pct	H	SO	BB	ERA
At Home	21	136	9-7		138	81	32	4.10
On the Road	15	94	5-6		68	67	45	3.36
1991 Season	36	230	14-13	.519	206	148	77	3.80
Life 3.0 Years	37	244	14-14	.500	215	174	91	3.72

BILL SPIERS

MILWAUKEE SHORTSTOP 26 Years Old

Runs Created: 56
Offensive Winning Percentage: .481
Batting Average: .283 Secondary Average: .234

Most Often Bats: 9th
Swings at First Pitch: 28%
Gets Ahead of the Pitcher: 54%
Hits Behind the Pitcher: 46%

1991 On Base Percentage: .337 Career: .305
1991 Slugging Percentage: .401 Career: .353
Batting Avg with Men in Scoring Position: .320

Bats Left-Handed	G	AB	R	H	2B	3B	HR	RBI	BB	SO	SB	AVG
Vs. RHP		297	61	91	12	6	6	42	21	39	11	.306
Vs. LHP		117	10	26	1	0	2	12	13	16	3	.222
At Home	66	187	34	56	6	2	1	24	21	30	5	.299
On the Road	67	227	37	61	7	4	7	30	13	25	9	.269
1991 Season	133	414	71	117	13	6	8	54	34	55	14	.283
Life 2.2 Years		506	72	132	17	5	6	56	32	74	16	.261

ZANE SMITH

PITTSBURGH STARTING PITCHER 31 Years Old
16-10 3.20 ERA

Opponents Batting Average: .268
Offensive Support: 5.13 Runs Per Nine Innings
Double Play Support: 1.07 GDP Per Nine Innings

First Pitch is Hit: 15%
Gets Ahead of the Hitter: 55%
Gets Behind the Hitter: 45%
Gets Leadoff Man Out: 70%

1991 On Base Pct Allowed: .292
Slugging Percentage: .370
Stolen Bases Allowed: 26 Caught Stealing: 8

Pitches Left	AB	H	2B	3B	HR	RBI	BB	SO	AVG
Vs. RHB	727	195	36	2	14	76	24	88	.268
Vs. LHB	146	39	0	2	1	12	5	32	.267

	G	IP	W-L	Pct	H	SO	BB	ERA
At Home	19	129	11-3		132	69	14	2.78
On the Road	16	99	5-7		102	51	15	3.74
1991 Season	35	228	16-10	.615	234	120	29	3.20
Life 6.1 Years	42	220	11-13	.462	219	126	76	3.58

LUIS SOJO

CALIFORNIA SECOND BASE 26 Years Old

Runs Created: 33
Offensive Winning Percentage: .355
Batting Average: .258 Secondary Average: .118

Most Often Bats: 8th
Swings at First Pitch: 25%
Gets Ahead of the Pitcher: 50%
Hits Behind the Pitcher: 50%

1991 On Base Percentage: .295 Career: .291
1991 Slugging Percentage: .327 Career: .322
Batting Avg with Men in Scoring Position: .225

Bats Right-Handed	G	AB	R	H	2B	3B	HR	RBI	BB	SO	SB	AVG
Vs. RHP		250	22	60	7	0	3	15	9	20	4	.240
Vs. LHP		114	16	34	7	1	0	5	5	6	0	.298
At Home	56	176	16	42	5	0	1	6	11	11	2	.239
On the Road	57	188	22	52	9	1	2	14	3	15	2	.277
1991 Season	113	364	38	94	14	1	3	20	14	26	4	.258
Life 0.9 Years		493	58	124	19	1	4	32	21	34	6	.252

TERRY STEINBACH

OAKLAND CATCHER 30 Years Old

Runs Created: 52
Offensive Winning Percentage: .409
Batting Average: .274 Secondary Average: .164

Most Often Bats: 5th
Swings at First Pitch: 32%
Gets Ahead of the Pitcher: 52%
Hits Behind the Pitcher: 48%

1991 On Base Percentage: .312 Career: .321
1991 Slugging Percentage: .386 Career: .396
Batting Avg with Men in Scoring Position: .285

Bats Right-Handed	G	AB	R	H	2B	3B	HR	RBI	BB	SO	SB	AVG
Vs. RHP		317	39	88	20	1	3	52	15	53	2	.278
Vs. LHP		139	11	37	11	0	3	15	7	17	0	.266
At Home	66	220	23	61	19	0	1	31	14	29	2	.277
On the Road	63	236	27	64	12	1	5	36	8	41	0	.271
1991 Season	129	456	50	125	31	1	6	67	22	70	2	.274
Life 3.7 Years		548	62	148	25	2	13	74	37	84	2	.270

DAVE STEWART

OAKLAND STARTING PITCHER 35 Years Old

11-11 5.18 ERA

Opponents Batting Average: .278
Offensive Support: 6.13 Runs Per Nine Innings
Double Play Support: .76 GDP Per Nine Innings

First Pitch is Hit: 12%
Gets Ahead of the Hitter: 45%
Gets Behind the Hitter: 55%
Gets Leadoff Man Out: 68%

1991 On Base Pct Allowed: .356
Slugging Percentage: .428
Stolen Bases Allowed: 23 Caught Stealing: 9

Pitches Right	AB	H	2B	3B	HR	RBI	BB	SO	AVG
Vs. RHB	436	111	22	3	16	55	59	93	.255
Vs. LHB	444	134	22	5	8	71	46	51	.302

	G	IP	W-L	Pct	H	SO	BB	ERA
At Home	18	115	8-3		118	72	45	4.21
On the Road	17	111	3-8		127	72	60	6.18
1991 Season	35	226	11-11	.500	245	144	105	5.18
Life 9.2 Years	47	223	15-10	.583	209	146	85	3.70

TODD STOTTLEMYRE

TORONTO STARTING PITCHER 27 Years Old

15-8 3.78 ERA

Opponents Batting Average: .235
Offensive Support: 4.52 Runs Per Nine Innings
Double Play Support: .45 GDP Per Nine Innings

First Pitch is Hit: 13%
Gets Ahead of the Hitter: 51%
Gets Behind the Hitter: 49%
Gets Leadoff Man Out: 68%

1991 On Base Pct Allowed: .305
Slugging Percentage: .356
Stolen Bases Allowed: 24 Caught Stealing: 3

Pitches Right	AB	H	2B	3B	HR	RBI	BB	SO	AVG
Vs. RHB	404	92	18	2	10	51	35	65	.228
Vs. LHB	422	102	9	3	11	33	40	51	.242

	G	IP	W-L	Pct	H	SO	BB	ERA
At Home	17	116	9-3		99	51	28	3.96
On the Road	17	103	6-5		95	65	47	3.58
1991 Season	34	219	15-8	.652	194	116	75	3.78
Life 3.0 Years	40	215	13-13	.494	217	120	78	4.27

B. J. SURHOFF

MILWAUKEE CATCHER 27 Years Old

Runs Created: 54
Offensive Winning Percentage: .357
Batting Average: .289 Secondary Average: .145

Most Often Bats: 3rd
Swings at First Pitch: 24%
Gets Ahead of the Pitcher: 56%
Hits Behind the Pitcher: 44%

1991 On Base Percentage: .319 Career: .315
1991 Slugging Percentage: .372 Career: .364
Batting Avg with Men in Scoring Position: .313

Bats Left-Handed	G	AB	R	H	2B	3B	HR	RBI	BB	SO	SB	AVG
Vs. RHP		403	49	120	17	3	5	57	20	21	4	.298
Vs. LHP		102	8	26	2	1	0	11	6	12	1	.255
At Home	69	236	25	63	8	3	3	34	14	13	1	.267
On the Road	74	269	32	83	11	1	2	34	12	20	4	.309
1991 Season	143	505	57	146	19	4	5	68	26	33	5	.289
Life 4.1 Years		567	62	154	25	4	7	71	39	44	17	.271

KURT STILLWELL

KANSAS CITY SHORTSTOP 27 Years Old

Runs Created: 44
Offensive Winning Percentage: .436
Batting Average: .265 Secondary Average: .190

Most Often Bats: 8th
Swings at First Pitch: 24%
Gets Ahead of the Pitcher: 53%
Hits Behind the Pitcher: 47%

1991 On Base Percentage: .322 Career: .316
1991 Slugging Percentage: .361 Career: .360
Batting Avg with Men in Scoring Position: .297

Switch Hitter	G	AB	R	H	2B	3B	HR	RBI	BB	SO	SB	AVG
Vs. RHP		276	33	73	11	0	5	36	27	39	2	.264
Vs. LHP		109	11	29	6	1	1	15	6	17	1	.266
At Home	59	183	22	47	10	1	1	24	18	23	1	.257
On the Road	63	202	22	55	7	0	5	27	15	33	2	.272
1991 Season	122	385	44	102	17	1	6	51	33	56	3	.265
Life 4.7 Years		531	65	134	27	5	6	57	48	75	6	.253

DARRYL STRAWBERRY

LOS ANGELES RIGHT FIELD 30 Years Old

Runs Created: 92
Offensive Winning Percentage: .735
Batting Average: .265 Secondary Average: .394

Most Often Bats: 3rd
Swings at First Pitch: 26%
Gets Ahead of the Pitcher: 56%
Hits Behind the Pitcher: 44%

1991 On Base Percentage: .361 Career: .359
1991 Slugging Percentage: .491 Career: .516
Batting Avg with Men in Scoring Position: .285

Bats Left-Handed	G	AB	R	H	2B	3B	HR	RBI	BB	SO	SB	AVG
Vs. RHP		277	52	71	13	2	17	56	41	66	5	.256
Vs. LHP		228	34	63	9	2	11	43	34	59	5	.276
At Home	71	257	44	73	12	2	14	54	38	55	9	.284
On the Road	68	248	42	61	10	2	14	45	37	70	1	.246
1991 Season	139	505	86	134	22	4	28	99	75	125	10	.265
Life 7.7 Years		572	97	150	27	4	36	108	85	141	26	.263

RICK SUTCLIFFE

CHICAGO STARTING PITCHER 36 Years Old

6-5 4.10 ERA

Opponents Batting Average: .264
Offensive Support: 4.56 Runs Per Nine Innings
Double Play Support: 1.12 GDP Per Nine Innings

First Pitch is Hit: 12%
Gets Ahead of the Hitter: 41%
Gets Behind the Hitter: 59%
Gets Leadoff Man Out: 65%

1991 On Base Pct Allowed: .338
Slugging Percentage: .379
Stolen Bases Allowed: 21 Caught Stealing: 2

Pitches Right	AB	H	2B	3B	HR	RBI	BB	SO	AVG
Vs. RHB	146	33	8	1	0	14	15	28	.226
Vs. LHB	218	63	12	4	4	30	30	24	.289

	G	IP	W-L	Pct	H	SO	BB	ERA
At Home	10	57	3-1		47	37	18	3.18
On the Road	9	40	3-4		49	15	27	5.40
1991 Season	19	97	6-5	.545	96	52	45	4.10
Life 9.3 Years	40	239	15-12	.558	226	157	97	3.84

GREG SWINDELL

CLEVELAND STARTING PITCHER 27 Years Old

9-16 3.48 ERA

Opponents Batting Average: .263
Offensive Support: 3.63 Runs Per Nine Innings
Double Play Support: .57 GDP Per Nine Innings

First Pitch is Hit: 18%
Gets Ahead of the Hitter: 59%
Gets Behind the Hitter: 41%
Gets Leadoff Man Out: 73%

1991 On Base Pct Allowed: .287
Slugging Percentage: .393
Stolen Bases Allowed: 9 Caught Stealing: 11

Pitches Left	AB	H	2B	3B	HR	RBI	BB	SO	AVG
Vs. RHB	763	199	40	2	20	88	24	141	.261
Vs. LHB	153	42	8	2	1	14	7	28	.275

	G	IP	W-L	Pct	H	SO	BB	ERA
At Home	20	153	7-9		139	107	18	2.52
On the Road	13	85	2-7		102	62	13	5.21
1991 Season	33	238	9-16	.360	241	169	31	3.48
Life 4.1 Years	37	253	15-13	.522	257	183	55	3.79

FRANK TANANA

DETROIT STARTING PITCHER 38 Years Old

13-12 3.77 ERA

Opponents Batting Average: .265
Offensive Support: 5.18 Runs Per Nine Innings
Double Play Support: .70 GDP Per Nine Innings

First Pitch is Hit: 13%
Gets Ahead of the Hitter: 49%
Gets Behind the Hitter: 51%
Gets Leadoff Man Out: 63%

1991 On Base Pct Allowed: .327
Slugging Percentage: .412
Stolen Bases Allowed: 17 Caught Stealing: 14

Pitches Left	AB	H	2B	3B	HR	RBI	BB	SO	AVG
Vs. RHB	659	180	29	3	21	70	67	82	.273
Vs. LHB	159	37	5	1	5	17	11	25	.233

	G	IP	W-L	Pct	H	SO	BB	ERA
At Home	18	121	7-5		122	62	49	4.10
On the Road	15	97	6-7		95	45	29	3.35
1991 Season	33	217	13-12	.520	217	107	78	3.77
Life 15.2 Years	38	249	14-14	.514	240	168	73	3.59

KEVIN TAPANI

MINNESOTA STARTING PITCHER 28 Years Old

16-9 2.99 ERA

Opponents Batting Average: .245
Offensive Support: 5.31 Runs Per Nine Innings
Double Play Support: .52 GDP Per Nine Innings

First Pitch is Hit: 18%
Gets Ahead of the Hitter: 54%
Gets Behind the Hitter: 46%
Gets Leadoff Man Out: 69%

1991 On Base Pct Allowed: .277
Slugging Percentage: .382
Stolen Bases Allowed: 18 Caught Stealing: 3

Pitches Right	AB	H	2B	3B	HR	RBI	BB	SO	AVG
Vs. RHB	397	103	22	1	15	34	24	66	.259
Vs. LHB	520	122	26	3	8	42	16	69	.235

	G	IP	W-L	Pct	H	SO	BB	ERA
At Home	18	132	10-5		117	80	25	2.79
On the Road	16	112	6-4		108	55	15	3.22
1991 Season	34	244	16-9	.640	225	135	40	2.99
Life 1.9 Years	38	239	16-10	.612	231	140	44	3.45

DANNY TARTABULL

KANSAS CITY RIGHT FIELD 29 Years Old

Runs Created: 116
Offensive Winning Percentage: .802
Batting Average: .316 Secondary Average: .424

Most Often Bats: 4th
Swings at First Pitch: 32%
Gets Ahead of the Pitcher: 54%
Hits Behind the Pitcher: 46%

1991 On Base Percentage: .397 Career: .372
1991 Slugging Percentage: .593 Career: .514
Batting Avg with Men in Scoring Position: .374

Bats Right-Handed		AB	R	H	2B	3B	HR	RBI	BB	SO	SB	AVG
Vs. RHP		342	56	111	26	2	23	78	38	90	5	.325
Vs. LHP		142	22	42	9	1	8	22	27	31	1	.296
At Home	62	226	34	71	15	2	13	35	30	54	1	.314
On the Road	70	258	44	82	20	1	18	65	35	67	5	.318
1991 Season	132	484	78	153	35	3	31	100	65	121	6	.316
Life 5.1 Years		575	86	165	34	3	30	105	78	151	6	.287

WADE TAYLOR

NEW YORK STARTING PITCHER 26 Years Old

7-12 6.27 ERA

Opponents Batting Average: .314
Offensive Support: 5.26 Runs Per Nine Innings
Double Play Support: 1.32 GDP Per Nine Innings

First Pitch is Hit: 12%
Gets Ahead of the Hitter: 48%
Gets Behind the Hitter: 52%
Gets Leadoff Man Out: 57%

1991 On Base Pct Allowed: .388
Slugging Percentage: .477
Stolen Bases Allowed: 12 Caught Stealing: 6

Pitches Right	AB	H	2B	3B	HR	RBI	BB	SO	AVG
Vs. RHB	253	77	15	3	7	43	22	43	.304
Vs. LHB	206	67	13	1	6	30	31	29	.325

	G	IP	W-L	Pct	H	SO	BB	ERA
At Home	11	62	5-6		81	36	19	5.34
On the Road	12	54	2-6		63	36	34	7.33
1991 Season	23	116	7-12	.368	144	72	53	6.27
Life 0.6 Years	38	191	12-20	.368	237	118	87	6.27

WALT TERRELL

DETROIT STARTING PITCHER 34 Years Old

12-14 4.24 ERA

Opponents Batting Average: .301
Offensive Support: 4.53 Runs Per Nine Innings
Double Play Support: 1.44 GDP Per Nine Innings

First Pitch is Hit: 15%
Gets Ahead of the Hitter: 47%
Gets Behind the Hitter: 53%
Gets Leadoff Man Out: 65%

1991 On Base Pct Allowed: .358
Slugging Percentage: .433
Stolen Bases Allowed: 6 Caught Stealing: 5

Pitches Right	AB	H	2B	3B	HR	RBI	BB	SO	AVG
Vs. RHB	392	116	21	4	7	44	29	49	.296
Vs. LHB	461	141	27	4	9	55	50	31	.306

	G	IP	W-L	Pct	H	SO	BB	ERA
At Home	19	112	9-7		138	38	36	4.84
On the Road	16	107	3-7		119	42	43	3.62
1991 Season	35	219	12-14	.462	257	80	79	4.24
Life 7.6 Years	37	242	14-15	.477	252	114	92	4.14

MICKEY TETTLETON

DETROIT CATCHER 31 Years Old

Runs Created: 99
Offensive Winning Percentage: .658
Batting Average: .263 Secondary Average: .435

Most Often Bats: 5th
Swings at First Pitch: 21%
Gets Ahead of the Pitcher: 55%
Hits Behind the Pitcher: 45%

1991 On Base Percentage: .387 Career: .356
1991 Slugging Percentage: .491 Career: .424
Batting Avg with Men in Scoring Position: .283

Switch Hitter		AB	R	H	2B	3B	HR	RBI	BB	SO	SB	AVG
Vs. RHP		392	69	105	13	2	22	64	84	99	3	.268
Vs. LHP		109	16	27	4	0	9	25	17	32	0	.248
At Home	77	239	42	63	7	2	15	44	56	63	2	.264
On the Road	77	262	43	69	10	0	16	45	45	68	1	.263
1991 Season	154	501	85	132	17	2	31	89	101	131	3	.263
Life 4.8 Years		491	70	119	20	2	22	68	87	141	4	.242

BOBBY THIGPEN

CHICAGO RELIEF PITCHER 28 Years Old
7-5 3.49 ERA 30 SAVES

Save Opportunities: 39 Blown Saves: 9 Holds: 0
Inherited Runners who Scored: 29%
Opponents Batting Average: .245
Double Play Support: .52 GDP Per Nine Innings

First Pitch is Hit: 14%
Gets Ahead of the Hitter: 39%
Gets Behind the Hitter: 61%
Gets First Batter Out: 71%

1991 On Base Pct Allowed: .348
Slugging Percentage: .409
Stolen Bases Allowed: 8 Caught Stealing: 5

Pitches Right	AB	H	2B	3B	HR	RBI	BB	SO	AVG
Vs. RHB	133	31	4	0	4	19	17	29	.233
Vs. LHB	124	32	4	2	6	23	21	18	.258

	G	IP	W-L	Pct	SO	BB	ERA	Sv
1991 Season	67	70	7-5	.583	47	38	3.49	30
Life 4.6 Years	74	97	6-6	.474	64	39	2.89	38

ROBBY THOMPSON

SAN FRANCISCO SECOND BASE 30 Years Old

Runs Created: 81
Offensive Winning Percentage: .652
Batting Average: .262 Secondary Average: .341

Most Often Bats: 6th
Swings at First Pitch: 26%
Gets Ahead of the Pitcher: 57%
Hits Behind the Pitcher: 43%

1991 On Base Percentage: .352 Career: .327
1991 Slugging Percentage: .447 Career: .401
Batting Avg with Men in Scoring Position: .229

Bats Right-Handed		AB	R	H	2B	3B	HR	RBI	BB	SO	SB	AVG
Vs. RHP		357	48	91	16	4	12	32	43	69	12	.255
Vs. LHP		135	26	38	8	1	7	16	20	26	2	.281
At Home	72	241	45	71	13	4	11	26	38	43	6	.295
On the Road	72	251	29	58	11	1	8	22	25	52	8	.231
1991 Season	144	492	74	129	24	5	19	48	63	95	14	.262
Life 5.3 Years		565	82	146	28	6	13	56	51	121	16	.257

BOB TEWKSBURY

ST. LOUIS STARTING PITCHER 31 Years Old
11-12 3.25 ERA

Opponents Batting Average: .281
Offensive Support: 4.38 Runs Per Nine Innings
Double Play Support: .90 GDP Per Nine Innings

First Pitch is Hit: 20%
Gets Ahead of the Hitter: 54%
Gets Behind the Hitter: 46%
Gets Leadoff Man Out: 68%

1991 On Base Pct Allowed: .317
Slugging Percentage: .413
Stolen Bases Allowed: 10 Caught Stealing: 10

Pitches Right	AB	H	2B	3B	HR	RBI	BB	SO	AVG
Vs. RHB	327	93	14	5	9	41	7	44	.284
Vs. LHB	406	113	28	3	4	38	31	31	.278

	G	IP	W-L	Pct	H	SO	BB	ERA
At Home	14	94	6-3		93	34	18	3.24
On the Road	16	97	5-9		113	41	20	3.26
1991 Season	30	191	11-12	.478	206	75	38	3.25
Life 2.5 Years	41	217	13-13	.485	241	84	46	3.67

FRANK THOMAS

CHICAGO DESIGNATED HITTER 24 Years Old

Runs Created: 145
Offensive Winning Percentage: .825
Batting Average: .318 Secondary Average: .483

Most Often Bats: 3rd
Swings at First Pitch: 14%
Gets Ahead of the Pitcher: 55%
Hits Behind the Pitcher: 45%

1991 On Base Percentage: .453 Career: .453
1991 Slugging Percentage: .553 Career: .547
Batting Avg with Men in Scoring Position: .347

Bats Right-Handed		AB	R	H	2B	3B	HR	RBI	BB	SO	SB	AVG
Vs. RHP		389	78	114	22	2	21	74	96	85	0	.293
Vs. LHP		170	26	64	9	0	11	35	42	27	1	.376
At Home	81	267	65	99	16	1	24	61	76	60	1	.371
On the Road	77	292	39	79	15	1	8	48	62	52	0	.271
1991 Season	158	559	104	178	31	2	32	109	138	112	1	.318
Life 1.3 Years		557	106	179	31	4	29	104	135	123	1	.321

DICKIE THON

PHILADELPHIA SHORTSTOP 34 Years Old

Runs Created: 52
Offensive Winning Percentage: .406
Batting Average: .252 Secondary Average: .165

Most Often Bats: 8th
Swings at First Pitch: 50%
Gets Ahead of the Pitcher: 42%
Hits Behind the Pitcher: 58%

1991 On Base Percentage: .283 Career: .318
1991 Slugging Percentage: .351 Career: .378
Batting Avg with Men in Scoring Position: .220

Bats Right-Handed		AB	R	H	2B	3B	HR	RBI	BB	SO	SB	AVG
Vs. RHP		334	24	83	11	2	7	30	11	61	7	.249
Vs. LHP		205	20	53	7	2	2	14	14	23	4	.259
At Home	74	270	21	73	8	2	4	25	12	44	5	.270
On the Road	72	269	23	63	10	2	5	19	13	40	6	.234
1991 Season	146	539	44	136	18	4	9	44	25	84	11	.252
Life 7.5 Years		527	59	140	23	5	9	49	41	78	20	.265

MIKE TIMLIN

TORONTO RELIEF PITCHER 26 Years Old

11-6 3.16 ERA 3 SAVES

Save Opportunities: 8 Blown Saves: 5 Holds: 9
Inherited Runners who Scored: 45%
Opponents Batting Average: .233
Double Play Support: .66 GDP Per Nine Innings

First Pitch is Hit: 11%
Gets Ahead of the Hitter: 49%
Gets Behind the Hitter: 51%
Gets First Batter Out: 61%

1991 On Base Pct Allowed: .317
Slugging Percentage: .297
Stolen Bases Allowed: 11 Caught Stealing: 5

Pitches Right	AB	H	2B	3B	HR	RBI	BB	SO	AVG
Vs. RHB	235	44	4	0	3	30	23	58	.187
Vs. LHB	169	50	2	1	3	22	27	27	.296

	G	IP	W-L	Pct	SO	BB	ERA	Sv
1991 Season	63	108	11-6	.647	85	50	3.16	3
Life 0.9 Years	71	121	12-7	.647	95	56	3.16	3

RANDY TOMLIN

PITTSBURGH STARTING PITCHER 26 Years Old

8-7 2.98 ERA

Opponents Batting Average: .254
Offensive Support: 4.37 Runs Per Nine Innings
Double Play Support: .77 GDP Per Nine Innings

First Pitch is Hit: 13%
Gets Ahead of the Hitter: 54%
Gets Behind the Hitter: 46%
Gets Leadoff Man Out: 66%

1991 On Base Pct Allowed: .315
Slugging Percentage: .354
Stolen Bases Allowed: 17 Caught Stealing: 12

Pitches Left	AB	H	2B	3B	HR	RBI	BB	SO	AVG
Vs. RHB	535	147	25	6	8	53	41	74	.275
Vs. LHB	134	23	3	0	1	10	13	30	.172

	G	IP	W-L	Pct	H	SO	BB	ERA
At Home	16	92	5-4		86	64	25	2.83
On the Road	15	83	3-3		84	40	29	3.16
1991 Season	31	175	8-7	.533	170	104	54	2.98
Life 1.1 Years	39	228	11-10	.522	209	132	60	2.85

ALAN TRAMMELL

DETROIT SHORTSTOP 34 Years Old

Runs Created: 47
Offensive Winning Percentage: .423
Batting Average: .248 Secondary Average: .253

Most Often Bats: 3rd
Swings at First Pitch: 21%
Gets Ahead of the Pitcher: 57%
Hits Behind the Pitcher: 43%

1991 On Base Percentage: .320 Career: .353
1991 Slugging Percentage: .373 Career: .417
Batting Avg with Men in Scoring Position: .270

Bats Right-Handed		AB	R	H	2B	3B	HR	RBI	BB	SO	SB	AVG
Vs. RHP		262	40	69	14	0	5	38	29	29	11	.263
Vs. LHP		113	17	24	6	0	4	17	8	10	0	.212
At Home	59	218	33	53	11	0	6	39	22	17	6	.243
On the Road	42	157	24	40	9	0	3	16	15	22	5	.255
1991 Season	101	375	57	93	20	0	9	55	37	39	11	.248
Life 12.0 Years		592	89	169	29	4	13	72	62	63	18	.286

JEFF TREADWAY

ATLANTA SECOND BASE 29 Years Old

Runs Created: 46
Offensive Winning Percentage: .627
Batting Average: .320 Secondary Average: .180

Most Often Bats: 2nd
Swings at First Pitch: 32%
Gets Ahead of the Pitcher: 57%
Hits Behind the Pitcher: 43%

1991 On Base Percentage: .368 Career: .329
1991 Slugging Percentage: .418 Career: .394
Batting Avg with Men in Scoring Position: .333

Bats Left-Handed		AB	R	H	2B	3B	HR	RBI	BB	SO	SB	AVG
Vs. RHP		286	39	93	17	2	3	32	23	17	2	.325
Vs. LHP		20	2	5	0	0	0	0	0	2	0	.250
At Home	56	159	25	42	7	1	1	12	18	8	1	.264
On the Road	50	147	16	56	10	1	2	20	5	11	1	.381
1991 Season	106	306	41	98	17	2	3	32	23	19	2	.320
Life 3.0 Years		537	64	153	26	4	9	52	35	44	4	.285

DAVE VALLE

SEATTLE CATCHER 31 Years Old

Runs Created: 26
Offensive Winning Percentage: .237
Batting Average: .194 Secondary Average: .210

Most Often Bats: 9th
Swings at First Pitch: 26%
Gets Ahead of the Pitcher: 50%
Hits Behind the Pitcher: 50%

1991 On Base Percentage: .286 Career: .302
1991 Slugging Percentage: .299 Career: .367
Batting Avg with Men in Scoring Position: .163

Bats Right-Handed		AB	R	H	2B	3B	HR	RBI	BB	SO	SB	AVG
Vs. RHP		212	21	37	7	1	2	15	24	35	0	.175
Vs. LHP		112	17	26	1	0	6	17	10	14	0	.232
At Home	72	173	15	28	4	1	0	8	17	27	0	.162
On the Road	60	151	23	35	4	0	8	24	17	22	0	.232
1991 Season	132	324	38	63	8	1	8	32	34	49	0	.194
Life 3.6 Years		473	53	108	19	2	14	62	41	67	1	.228

ANDY VAN SLYKE

PITTSBURGH CENTER FIELD 31 Years Old

Runs Created: 85
Offensive Winning Percentage: .662
Batting Average: .265 Secondary Average: .346

Most Often Bats: 3rd
Swings at First Pitch: 28%
Gets Ahead of the Pitcher: 51%
Hits Behind the Pitcher: 49%

1991 On Base Percentage: .355 Career: .347
1991 Slugging Percentage: .446 Career: .447
Batting Avg with Men in Scoring Position: .280

Bats Left-Handed		AB	R	H	2B	3B	HR	RBI	BB	SO	SB	AVG
Vs. RHP		306	57	94	15	5	13	60	48	45	8	.307
Vs. LHP		185	30	36	9	2	4	23	23	40	2	.195
At Home	77	265	41	60	9	4	9	46	37	44	3	.226
On the Road	61	226	46	70	15	3	8	37	34	41	7	.310
1991 Season	138	491	87	130	24	7	17	83	71	85	10	.265
Life 7.6 Years		540	81	145	27	9	17	79	66	104	27	.269

GREG VAUGHN

MILWAUKEE LEFT FIELD 26 Years Old

Runs Created: 82
Offensive Winning Percentage: .545
Batting Average: .244 Secondary Average: .330

Most Often Bats: 5th
Swings at First Pitch: 36%
Gets Ahead of the Pitcher: 54%
Hits Behind the Pitcher: 46%

1991 On Base Percentage: .319 Career: .306
1991 Slugging Percentage: .456 Career: .444
Batting Avg with Men in Scoring Position: .277

Bats Right-Handed	G	AB	R	H	2B	3B	HR	RBI	BB	SO	SB	AVG
Vs. RHP		388	57	97	18	4	22	76	43	90	1	.250
Vs. LHP		154	24	35	6	1	5	22	19	35	1	.227
At Home	72	256	42	63	16	1	16	54	34	58	1	.246
On the Road	73	286	39	69	8	4	11	44	28	67	1	.241
1991 Season	145	542	81	132	24	5	27	98	62	125	2	.244
Life 1.9 Years		554	80	132	28	4	26	97	58	128	7	.237

FRANK VIOLA

NEW YORK STARTING PITCHER 32 Years Old
13-15 3.97 ERA

Opponents Batting Average: .286
Offensive Support: 3.50 Runs Per Nine Innings
Double Play Support: .62 GDP Per Nine Innings

First Pitch is Hit: 14%
Gets Ahead of the Hitter: 48%
Gets Behind the Hitter: 52%
Gets Leadoff Man Out: 69%

1991 On Base Pct Allowed: .325
Slugging Percentage: .423
Stolen Bases Allowed: 6 Caught Stealing: 16

Pitches Left	AB	H	2B	3B	HR	RBI	BB	SO	AVG
Vs. RHB	712	214	33	3	20	77	43	97	.301
Vs. LHB	193	45	8	1	5	22	11	35	.233

	G	IP	W-L	Pct	H	SO	BB	ERA
At Home	19	123	8-8		142	65	28	4.26
On the Road	16	109	5-7		117	67	26	3.64
1991 Season	35	231	13-15	.464	259	132	54	3.97
Life 9.2 Years	37	253	16-14	.545	253	173	72	3.72

BOB WALK

PITTSBURGH STARTING PITCHER 35 Years Old
9-2 3.60 ERA

Opponents Batting Average: .240
Offensive Support: 5.71 Runs Per Nine Innings
Double Play Support: .55 GDP Per Nine Innings

First Pitch is Hit: 11%
Gets Ahead of the Hitter: 52%
Gets Behind the Hitter: 48%
Gets Leadoff Man Out: 72%

1991 On Base Pct Allowed: .302
Slugging Percentage: .363
Stolen Bases Allowed: 7 Caught Stealing: 4

Pitches Right	AB	H	2B	3B	HR	RBI	BB	SO	AVG
Vs. RHB	189	41	7	0	5	24	14	37	.217
Vs. LHB	244	63	14	1	5	24	21	30	.258

	G	IP	W-L	Pct	H	SO	BB	ERA
At Home	12	62	4-2		56	39	18	3.48
On the Road	13	53	5-0		48	28	17	3.74
1991 Season	25	115	9-2	.818	104	67	35	3.60
Life 6.6 Years	43	203	12-9	.573	200	107	74	3.88

ROBIN VENTURA

CHICAGO THIRD BASE 24 Years Old

Runs Created: 97
Offensive Winning Percentage: .607
Batting Average: .284 Secondary Average: .294

Most Often Bats: 2nd
Swings at First Pitch: 15%
Gets Ahead of the Pitcher: 56%
Hits Behind the Pitcher: 44%

1991 On Base Percentage: .367 Career: .346
1991 Slugging Percentage: .442 Career: .381
Batting Avg with Men in Scoring Position: .333

Bats Left-Handed	G	AB	R	H	2B	3B	HR	RBI	BB	SO	SB	AVG
Vs. RHP		414	69	122	19	1	18	80	49	38	2	.295
Vs. LHP		192	23	50	6	0	5	20	31	29	0	.260
At Home	81	304	52	88	13	0	16	58	37	37	1	.289
On the Road	76	302	40	84	12	1	7	42	43	30	1	.278
1991 Season	157	606	92	172	25	1	23	100	80	67	2	.284
Life 2.0 Years		574	73	152	23	1	14	81	72	63	2	.265

OMAR VIZQUEL

SEATTLE SHORTSTOP 25 Years Old

Runs Created: 40
Offensive Winning Percentage: .350
Batting Average: .230 Secondary Average: .185

Most Often Bats: 9th
Swings at First Pitch: 34%
Gets Ahead of the Pitcher: 48%
Hits Behind the Pitcher: 52%

1991 On Base Percentage: .302 Career: .290
1991 Slugging Percentage: .293 Career: .283
Batting Avg with Men in Scoring Position: .312

Switch Hitter	G	AB	R	H	2B	3B	HR	RBI	BB	SO	SB	AVG
Vs. RHP		339	30	78	12	4	1	30	38	32	6	.230
Vs. LHP		87	12	20	4	0	0	11	7	5	1	.230
At Home	69	206	24	52	11	4	1	24	21	21	1	.252
On the Road	73	220	18	46	5	0	0	17	24	16	6	.209
1991 Season	142	426	42	98	16	4	1	41	45	37	7	.230
Life 2.3 Years		473	47	109	12	4	2	35	40	44	5	.230

CHICO WALKER

CHICAGO THIRD BASE 34 Years Old

Runs Created: 42
Offensive Winning Percentage: .432
Batting Average: .257 Secondary Average: .203

Most Often Bats: 1st
Swings at First Pitch: 35%
Gets Ahead of the Pitcher: 51%
Hits Behind the Pitcher: 49%

1991 On Base Percentage: .315 Career: .298
1991 Slugging Percentage: .337 Career: .306
Batting Avg with Men in Scoring Position: .286

Switch Hitter	G	AB	R	H	2B	3B	HR	RBI	BB	SO	SB	AVG
Vs. RHP		255	41	71	8	0	3	22	25	40	10	.278
Vs. LHP		119	10	25	2	1	3	12	8	17	3	.210
At Home	65	200	28	54	5	1	4	19	17	27	7	.270
On the Road	59	174	23	42	5	0	2	15	16	30	6	.241
1991 Season	124	374	51	96	10	1	6	34	33	57	13	.257
Life 1.8 Years		427	60	101	10	3	5	34	39	76	26	.237

LARRY WALKER

MONTREAL RIGHT FIELD 25 Years Old

Runs Created: 78
Offensive Winning Percentage: .692
Batting Average: .290 Secondary Average: .283

Most Often Bats: 5th
Swings at First Pitch: 49%
Gets Ahead of the Pitcher: 45%
Hits Behind the Pitcher: 55%

1991 On Base Percentage: .349 Career: .335
1991 Slugging Percentage: .458 Career: .433
Batting Avg with Men in Scoring Position: .269

Bats Left-Handed	G	AB	R	H	2B	3B	HR	RBI	BB	SO	SB	AVG
Vs. RHP		327	42	95	21	2	12	39	29	63	11	.291
Vs. LHP		160	17	46	9	0	4	25	13	39	3	.287
At Home	54	187	24	51	14	0	5	24	14	46	7	.273
On the Road	83	300	35	90	16	2	11	40	28	56	7	.300
1991 Season	137	487	59	141	30	2	16	64	42	102	14	.290
Life 1.8 Years		532	68	140	27	3	20	66	54	127	20	.262

DUANE WARD

TORONTO RELIEF PITCHER 28 Years Old
7-6 2.77 ERA 23 SAVES

Save Opportunities: 27 Blown Saves: 4 Holds: 17
Inherited Runners who Scored: 28%
Opponents Batting Average: .207
Double Play Support: .59 GDP Per Nine Innings

First Pitch is Hit: 7%
Gets Ahead of the Hitter: 50%
Gets Behind the Hitter: 50%
Gets First Batter Out: 76%

1991 On Base Pct Allowed: .271
Slugging Percentage: .262
Stolen Bases Allowed: 7 Caught Stealing: 4

Pitches Right	AB	H	2B	3B	HR	RBI	BB	SO	AVG
Vs. RHB	199	44	5	0	0	20	12	56	.221
Vs. LHB	187	36	5	1	3	18	21	76	.193

	G	IP	W-L	Pct	SO	BB	ERA	Sv
1991 Season	81	107	7-6	.538	132	33	2.77	23
Life 4.2 Years	74	117	5-7	.442	114	52	3.59	15

BOB WELCH

OAKLAND STARTING PITCHER 35 Years Old
12-13 4.58 ERA

Opponents Batting Average: .263
Offensive Support: 4.17 Runs Per Nine Innings
Double Play Support: .70 GDP Per Nine Innings

First Pitch is Hit: 13%
Gets Ahead of the Hitter: 49%
Gets Behind the Hitter: 51%
Gets Leadoff Man Out: 64%

1991 On Base Pct Allowed: .341
Slugging Percentage: .404
Stolen Bases Allowed: 12 Caught Stealing: 16

Pitches Right	AB	H	2B	3B	HR	RBI	BB	SO	AVG
Vs. RHB	405	103	17	2	17	55	40	52	.254
Vs. LHB	430	117	17	2	8	57	51	49	.272

	G	IP	W-L	Pct	H	SO	BB	ERA
At Home	18	125	8-7		112	65	43	3.60
On the Road	17	95	4-6		108	36	48	5.87
1991 Season	35	220	12-13	.480	220	101	91	4.58
Life 11.3 Years	38	242	17-11	.606	220	160	79	3.27

TIM WALLACH

MONTREAL THIRD BASE 34 Years Old

Runs Created: 56
Offensive Winning Percentage: .414
Batting Average: .225 Secondary Average: .199

Most Often Bats: 4th
Swings at First Pitch: 36%
Gets Ahead of the Pitcher: 50%
Hits Behind the Pitcher: 50%

1991 On Base Percentage: .292 Career: .319
1991 Slugging Percentage: .334 Career: .426
Batting Avg with Men in Scoring Position: .240

Bats Right-Handed	G	AB	R	H	2B	3B	HR	RBI	BB	SO	SB	AVG
Vs. RHP		392	42	89	14	1	8	52	32	71	2	.227
Vs. LHP		185	18	41	8	0	5	21	18	29	0	.222
At Home	63	230	19	49	9	0	5	23	26	36	1	.213
On the Road	88	347	41	81	13	1	8	50	24	64	1	.233
1991 Season	151	577	60	130	22	1	13	73	50	100	2	.225
Life 10.0 Years		600	69	158	33	3	20	85	46	92	5	.263

BILL WEGMAN

MILWAUKEE STARTING PITCHER 29 Years Old
15-7 2.84 ERA

Opponents Batting Average: .242
Offensive Support: 5.21 Runs Per Nine Innings
Double Play Support: .79 GDP Per Nine Innings

First Pitch is Hit: 16%
Gets Ahead of the Hitter: 51%
Gets Behind the Hitter: 49%
Gets Leadoff Man Out: 70%

1991 On Base Pct Allowed: .286
Slugging Percentage: .356
Stolen Bases Allowed: 10 Caught Stealing: 7

Pitches Right	AB	H	2B	3B	HR	RBI	BB	SO	AVG
Vs. RHB	344	91	16	2	10	28	14	56	.265
Vs. LHB	384	85	13	1	6	34	26	33	.221

	G	IP	W-L	Pct	H	SO	BB	ERA
At Home	15	103	7-4		91	51	21	2.62
On the Road	13	90	8-3		85	38	19	3.09
1991 Season	28	193	15-7	.682	176	89	40	2.84
Life 3.9 Years	38	232	13-13	.500	242	104	55	4.25

DAVID WELLS

TORONTO STARTING PITCHER 29 Years Old
15-10 3.72 ERA

Opponents Batting Average: .252
Offensive Support: 4.49 Runs Per Nine Innings
Double Play Support: .50 GDP Per Nine Innings

First Pitch is Hit: 11%
Gets Ahead of the Hitter: 49%
Gets Behind the Hitter: 51%
Gets Leadoff Man Out: 70%

1991 On Base Pct Allowed: .297
Slugging Percentage: .403
Stolen Bases Allowed: 8 Caught Stealing: 13

Pitches Left	AB	H	2B	3B	HR	RBI	BB	SO	AVG
Vs. RHB	617	161	34	1	21	61	43	92	.261
Vs. LHB	130	27	3	1	3	9	6	14	.208

	G	IP	W-L	Pct	H	SO	BB	ERA
At Home	18	86	6-5		89	49	24	4.81
On the Road	22	112	9-5		99	57	25	2.88
1991 Season	40	198	15-10	.600	188	106	49	3.72
Life 3.4 Years	58	167	12-8	.588	154	114	49	3.44

WALLY WHITEHURST

NEW YORK STARTING PITCHER 28 Years Old

7-12 4.18 ERA

Opponents Batting Average: .274
Offensive Support: 5.40 Runs Per Nine Innings
Double Play Support: .81 GDP Per Nine Innings

First Pitch is Hit: 18%
Gets Ahead of the Hitter: 51%
Gets Behind the Hitter: 49%
Gets Leadoff Man Out: 71%

1991 On Base Pct Allowed: .311
Slugging Percentage: .409
Stolen Bases Allowed: 9 Caught Stealing: 8

Pitches Right	AB	H	2B	3B	HR	RBI	BB	SO	AVG
Vs. RHB	248	62	9	2	5	30	10	41	.250
Vs. LHB	270	80	15	3	7	30	15	46	.296

	G	IP	W-L	Pct	H	SO	BB	ERA
At Home	18	61	3-7		68	44	12	4.43
On the Road	18	72	4-5		74	43	13	3.98
1991 Season	36	133	7-12	.368	142	87	25	4.18
Life 1.4 Years	59	152	6-9	.381	158	101	28	3.93

MATT D. WILLIAMS

SAN FRANCISCO THIRD BASE 26 Years Old

Runs Created: 88
Offensive Winning Percentage: .614
Batting Average: .268 Secondary Average: .295

Most Often Bats: 5th
Swings at First Pitch: 46%
Gets Ahead of the Pitcher: 46%
Hits Behind the Pitcher: 54%

1991 On Base Percentage: .310 Career: .289
1991 Slugging Percentage: .499 Career: .461
Batting Avg with Men in Scoring Position: .243

Bats Right-Handed	G	AB	R	H	2B	3B	HR	RBI	BB	SO	SB	AVG
Vs. RHP		424	51	112	16	5	27	73	24	94	3	.264
Vs. LHP		165	21	46	8	0	7	25	9	34	2	.279
At Home	78	289	35	83	12	3	17	46	16	60	3	.287
On the Road	79	300	37	75	12	2	17	52	17	68	2	.250
1991 Season	157	589	72	158	24	5	34	98	33	128	5	.268
Life 3.3 Years		574	71	141	25	3	31	94	31	135	5	.245

MITCH WILLIAMS

PHILADELPHIA RELIEF PITCHER 27 Years Old

12-5 2.34 ERA 30 SAVES

Save Opportunities: 39 Blown Saves: 9 Holds: 1
Inherited Runners who Scored: 25%
Opponents Batting Average: .182
Double Play Support: .31 GDP Per Nine Innings

First Pitch is Hit: 11%
Gets Ahead of the Hitter: 47%
Gets Behind the Hitter: 53%
Gets First Batter Out: 68%

1991 On Base Pct Allowed: .330
Slugging Percentage: .266
Stolen Bases Allowed: 12 Caught Stealing: 2

Pitches Left	AB	H	2B	3B	HR	RBI	BB	SO	AVG
Vs. RHB	240	43	8	0	4	21	50	67	.179
Vs. LHB	68	13	4	1	0	6	12	17	.191

	G	IP	W-L	Pct	SO	BB	ERA	Sv
1991 Season	69	88	12-5	.706	84	62	2.34	30
Life 5.9 Years	73	86	6-6	.493	82	65	3.33	19

CARL WILLIS

MINNESOTA RELIEF PITCHER 31 Years Old

8-3 2.63 ERA 2 SAVES

Save Opportunities: 3 Blown Saves: 1 Holds: 5
Inherited Runners who Scored: 21%
Opponents Batting Average: .232
Double Play Support: .81 GDP Per Nine Innings

First Pitch is Hit: 19%
Gets Ahead of the Hitter: 48%
Gets Behind the Hitter: 52%
Gets First Batter Out: 85%

1991 On Base Pct Allowed: .273
Slugging Percentage: .311
Stolen Bases Allowed: 5 Caught Stealing: 3

Pitches Right	AB	H	2B	3B	HR	RBI	BB	SO	AVG
Vs. RHB	198	39	4	0	4	19	9	38	.197
Vs. LHB	130	37	8	1	0	10	10	15	.285

	G	IP	W-L	Pct	SO	BB	ERA	Sv
1991 Season	40	89	8-3	.727	53	19	2.63	2
Life 1.4 Years	73	136	7-6	.526	68	49	4.39	3

TREVOR WILSON

SAN FRANCISCO STARTING PITCHER 26 Years Old

13-11 3.56 ERA

Opponents Batting Average: .234
Offensive Support: 4.41 Runs Per Nine Innings
Double Play Support: .80 GDP Per Nine Innings

First Pitch is Hit: 12%
Gets Ahead of the Hitter: 47%
Gets Behind the Hitter: 53%
Gets Leadoff Man Out: 69%

1991 On Base Pct Allowed: .308
Slugging Percentage: .343
Stolen Bases Allowed: 8 Caught Stealing: 12

Pitches Left	AB	H	2B	3B	HR	RBI	BB	SO	AVG
Vs. RHB	580	146	30	4	12	62	55	100	.252
Vs. LHB	160	27	2	1	1	13	22	39	.169

	G	IP	W-L	Pct	H	SO	BB	ERA
At Home	20	120	8-4		91	78	43	2.71
On the Road	24	82	5-7		82	61	34	4.81
1991 Season	44	202	13-11	.542	173	139	77	3.56
Life 1.9 Years	46	193	12-12	.500	162	125	82	3.81

DEVON WHITE

TORONTO CENTER FIELD 29 Years Old

Runs Created: 105
Offensive Winning Percentage: .672
Batting Average: .282 Secondary Average: .310

Most Often Bats: 1st
Swings at First Pitch: 30%
Gets Ahead of the Pitcher: 49%
Hits Behind the Pitcher: 51%

1991 On Base Percentage: .342 Career: .306
1991 Slugging Percentage: .455 Career: .403
Batting Avg with Men in Scoring Position: .172

Switch Hitter	G	AB	R	H	2B	3B	HR	RBI	BB	SO	SB	AVG
Vs. RHP		443	71	121	25	8	9	40	39	103	22	.273
Vs. LHP		199	39	60	15	2	8	20	16	32	11	.302
At Home	79	326	58	97	26	6	9	33	25	61	18	.298
On the Road	77	316	52	84	14	4	8	27	30	74	15	.266
1991 Season	156	642	110	181	40	10	17	60	55	135	33	.282
Life 4.7 Years		606	94	154	28	7	16	63	42	129	33	.255

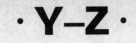

DAVE WINFIELD

CALIFORNIA RIGHT FIELD 40 Years Old

Runs Created: 84
Offensive Winning Percentage: .610
Batting Average: .262 Secondary Average: .320

Most Often Bats: 4th
Swings at First Pitch: 20%
Gets Ahead of the Pitcher: 55%
Hits Behind the Pitcher: 45%

1991 On Base Percentage: .326 Career: .354
1991 Slugging Percentage: .472 Career: .479
Batting Avg with Men in Scoring Position: .275

Bats Right-Handed		AB	R	H	2B	3B	HR	RBI	BB	SO	SB	AVG
Vs. RHP		408	51	101	18	3	17	59	36	85	6	.248
Vs. LHP		160	24	48	9	1	11	27	20	24	1	.300
At Home	73	271	33	66	10	1	13	33	25	54	4	.244
On the Road	77	297	42	83	17	3	15	53	31	55	3	.279
1991 Season	150	568	75	149	27	4	28	86	56	109	7	.262
Life 15.7 Years		601	93	171	29	5	26	102	66	90	14	.285

LOU WHITAKER

DETROIT SECOND BASE 35 Years Old

Runs Created: 99
Offensive Winning Percentage: .697
Batting Average: .279 Secondary Average: .411

Most Often Bats: 2nd
Swings at First Pitch: 22%
Gets Ahead of the Pitcher: 56%
Hits Behind the Pitcher: 44%

1991 On Base Percentage: .391 Career: .358
1991 Slugging Percentage: .489 Career: .416
Batting Avg with Men in Scoring Position: .284

Bats Left-Handed		AB	R	H	2B	3B	HR	RBI	BB	SO	SB	AVG
Vs. RHP		373	78	107	23	2	21	64	75	30	4	.287
Vs. LHP		97	16	24	3	0	2	14	15	15	0	.247
At Home	72	237	56	72	13	1	15	51	61	23	2	.304
On the Road	66	233	38	59	13	1	8	27	29	22	2	.253
1991 Season	138	470	94	131	26	2	23	78	90	45	4	.279
Life 12.1 Years		591	93	162	27	5	16	71	80	76	11	.274

MARK WHITEN

CLEVELAND RIGHT FIELD 25 Years Old

Runs Created: 45
Offensive Winning Percentage: .446
Batting Average: .243 Secondary Average: .229

Most Often Bats: 5th
Swings at First Pitch: 40%
Gets Ahead of the Pitcher: 50%
Hits Behind the Pitcher: 50%

1991 On Base Percentage: .297 Career: .301
1991 Slugging Percentage: .388 Career: .386
Batting Avg with Men in Scoring Position: .232

Switch Hitter		AB	R	H	2B	3B	HR	RBI	BB	SO	SB	AVG
Vs. RHP		298	34	71	11	5	7	35	21	59	2	.238
Vs. LHP		109	12	28	7	2	2	10	9	26	2	.257
At Home	57	197	24	49	8	5	4	16	16	40	1	.249
On the Road	59	210	22	50	10	2	5	29	14	45	3	.238
1991 Season	116	407	46	99	18	7	9	45	30	85	4	.243
Life 0.9 Years		538	63	134	21	9	12	57	40	108	7	.248

BOBBY WITT

TEXAS STARTING PITCHER 28 Years Old
3-7 6.09 ERA

Opponents Batting Average: .254
Offensive Support: 4.97 Runs Per Nine Innings
Double Play Support: .51 GDP Per Nine Innings

First Pitch is Hit: 9%
Gets Ahead of the Hitter: 44%
Gets Behind the Hitter: 56%
Gets Leadoff Man Out: 59%

1991 On Base Pct Allowed: .388
Slugging Percentage: .356
Stolen Bases Allowed: 18 Caught Stealing: 4

Pitches Right	AB	H	2B	3B	HR	RBI	BB	SO	AVG
Vs. RHB	180	49	13	0	2	33	37	42	.272
Vs. LHB	151	35	5	2	2	21	37	40	.232

	G	IP	W-L	Pct	H	SO	BB	ERA
At Home	8	40	0-5		42	40	30	6.30
On the Road	9	49	3-2		42	42	44	5.92
1991 Season	17	89	3-7	.300	84	82	74	6.09
Life 4.3 Years	37	229	14-14	.500	196	222	159	4.63

ROBIN YOUNT

MILWAUKEE CENTER FIELD 36 Years Old

Runs Created: 63
Offensive Winning Percentage: .448
Batting Average: .260 Secondary Average: .235

Most Often Bats: 4th
Swings at First Pitch: 28%
Gets Ahead of the Pitcher: 52%
Hits Behind the Pitcher: 48%

1991 On Base Percentage: .332 Career: .344
1991 Slugging Percentage: .376 Career: .434
Batting Avg with Men in Scoring Position: .297

Bats Right-Handed		AB	R	H	2B	3B	HR	RBI	BB	SO	SB	AVG
Vs. RHP		374	47	98	15	4	8	59	28	63	5	.262
Vs. LHP		129	19	33	5	0	2	18	26	16	1	.256
At Home	67	250	35	59	10	3	8	42	26	43	3	.236
On the Road	63	253	31	72	10	1	2	35	28	36	3	.285
1991 Season	130	503	66	131	20	4	10	77	54	79	6	.260
Life 15.9 Years		628	94	181	33	8	15	80	55	74	16	.288

TODD ZEILE

ST. LOUIS THIRD BASE 26 Years Old

Runs Created: 82
Offensive Winning Percentage: .610
Batting Average: .280 Secondary Average: .273

Most Often Bats: 6th
Swings at First Pitch: 19%
Gets Ahead of the Pitcher: 51%
Hits Behind the Pitcher: 49%

1991 On Base Percentage: .353 Career: .342
1991 Slugging Percentage: .412 Career: .402
Batting Avg with Men in Scoring Position: .304

Bats Right-Handed		AB	R	H	2B	3B	HR	RBI	BB	SO	SB	AVG
Vs. RHP		328	38	86	21	2	6	48	36	50	9	.262
Vs. LHP		237	38	72	15	1	5	33	26	44	8	.304
At Home	80	279	40	83	20	2	7	50	33	40	8	.297
On the Road	75	286	36	75	16	1	4	31	29	54	9	.262
1991 Season	155	565	76	158	36	3	11	81	62	94	17	.280
Life 2.0 Years		566	72	149	32	3	13	72	68	92	9	.263

PART FOUR

THE BIOGRAPHIC ENCYCLOPEDIA OF BASEBALL

THIRD INSTALLMENT

NOTE TO THE READERS

This is the third installment of the *Biographic Encyclopedia of Baseball*, which began with *The Baseball Book* in 1990, and has reached so far from Henry Aaron to Frank Baker. The idea is simple: to outline the basic stories of every person who has had a significant impact on the game of baseball, from its origins to the present.

This, of course, is an enormous undertaking, and I won't live long enough to complete it.

The *Biographic Encyclopedia* is essentially the work of three people: myself, Rob Neyer (R.N.) and Mike Kopf (M.K.) Rob does more of the hard research than the rest of us. If somebody has gone to the library to try to find an article about a minor player who played 48 games in the 1920s, that's Rob. Rob and Mike do most of the writing; I don't do the first draft of many of the articles, but in order to create a kind of evenness and consistency in tone, I do the final edit on everything.

The artworks, the drawings of the players, are the work of my wife, Susan McCarthy.

This will be the last installment of the *Biographic Encyclopedia* to appear in annual editions of *The Baseball Book*. We are not discontinuing the effort; we are merely going to continue it in some other form. We have reached the conclusion that the nature of the *Biographic Encyclopedia* is such that it doesn't really fit in a spring annual. A spring annual is by nature very *current*; the biographic entries are *historical*. The material has different needs than the rest of the book. We're breaking it out into its own publication in order to provide this material with the production values and work schedule which are appropriate to it.

The material in this book, beginning with Rick Auerbach and ending with George Baker, runs 35,000 words. That's one "unit", one "installment". What we plan to do is four installments per year, 35,000 each, each printed and distributed as its own publication. We will continue the slow march through the alphabet, and even at this accelerated pace we won't live long enough to complete it, but we will be able to move a lot faster.

What we do not know, at this time, is
a) who will be publishing this, and
b) when exactly the first installment will be published.

When we made the decision to break the material out of *The Baseball Book*, we planned to continue the *Biographic Encyclopedia* as a very small publication, printing 2500, 3000 copies of each issue. Our assumption was that Random House or Villard would not be interested in participating in the project, but we informed them of what we were doing anyway, mostly as a courtesy. To our surprise, they informed us that they *were* interested in being our publisher, and thought we were seriously under-publishing it at 2500 copies. At this point, however, no arrangement has been made, so we simply don't know who will be publishing it or how it will be made available to you.

If you enjoy this part of the book and want to continue to read the biographies as they are published, please send a card with your address to:

Bill James
The Biographic Encyclopedia of Baseball
901 Kentucky Suite 304
Lawrence, Kansas 66044

We will collect these cards in a corner, and when we have a clearer idea what we are doing we will let you know. If you just send a card, we won't forget you. If you send anything *else* to this address—a letter, a manuscript, a treasured work of art, a check for $73,000—then it's anybody's guess what might happen to it.

Thanks. This is my favorite part of the book. We enjoy doing these things; we enjoy piecing together the story of Del Baker, who was a part of the game for half a century, and trying to re-create an image of him. I know that for many of you it is also your favorite part of the book, because many of you have told me so. We're going to keep plugging away at it.

• A •

(continues)

Rick Auerbach, utility infielder of the 1970s.

Rick Auerbach was one of the first players signed by the Seattle Pilots when they began constructing their farm system; he had been drafted by the Angels, didn't sign with them, went to college briefly and became eligible for the January draft in 1969. By mid-1971 the Pilots had flown to Milwaukee, and Auerbach had become their regular shortstop. He held the job for a year and a half, didn't hit a lick and was traded to the Dodgers, where he backed up Bill Russell in the mid-seventies. Later he served the same function for Dave Concepcion of the Reds.

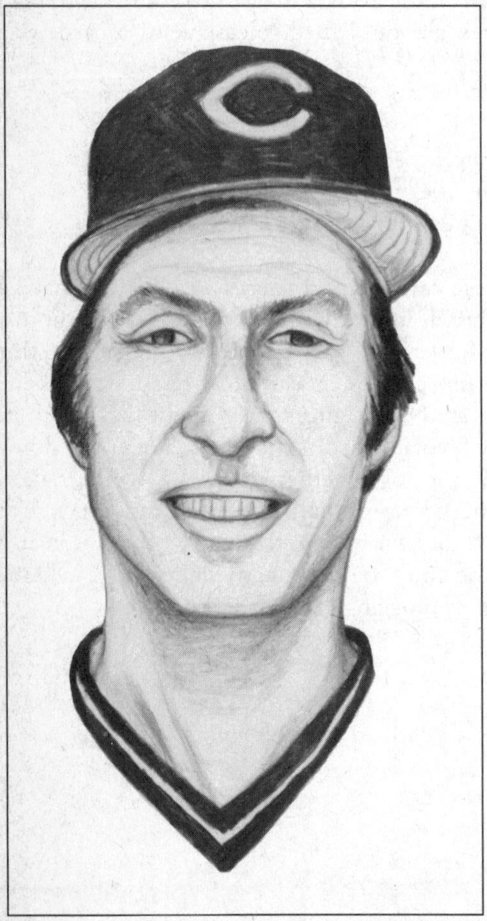

Susan McCarthy

Rick AUERBACH

Auerbach, who listed taxidermy among his hobbies in *The Baseball Register,* was a fine defensive shortstop. Vin Scully said that he played shortstop like a crab, hugging the ground. He had periodic chances to grab a job, when Russell or Concepcion was hurt, but never hit consistently.

The following note appeared in the August 2, 1980 *Sporting News:*

> Because a storm knocked out the lights in the Zion Lutheran Church at Hamilton, O., infielder Rick Auerbach began his marriage to Marlene Moore in the dark. "I had to do the service completely from memory," said the Rev. Daniel Snider, pastor. "It was very quiet, with the exception of the claps of thunder which continually interrupted. Everything went off without a hitch, though."

Uh . . . I thought there was *supposed* to be a hitch there. Auerbach was traded to the Rangers a few days later for a player to be named later, and was out of the majors after one more season.

Jerry Augustine, pitcher with the Milwaukee Brewers from 1975 to 1984.

Augustine, a native of Wisconsin, graduated from the University of Wisconsin-La-Crosse in 1974, and was working in a lumber mill that summer when he was drafted by the Brewers in the fifteenth round. Sent to Danville in the Midwest League, he pitched so well in 1974 that he was in the Brewers' major league camp the next spring. On the first day of spring training, however, he twisted his knee covering first base in a drill, and was flown from Arizona to Milwaukee, where he underwent knee surgery a few days later. He was told he would be out six months.

He was back in uniform by June, and arrived in the majors that September. He never returned to the minor leagues. Opening the 1976 season in the bullpen, Augustine was moved into the rotation by manager Alex Grammas after Pete Broberg went 1-7. At first Augustine seemed bound for glory. Changing speeds with a slow curve and a slider off an 87-MPH fastball, Augustine placed his ERA among the American League leaders for most of the summer, losing his spot there in September but winding up with a fine 3.30 ERA.

As often happens to finesse pitchers, Augustine's effectiveness slipped in 1977 and 1978, but in 1978 he went 13-12 with a 4.54 ERA, and was rewarded by Brewers general manager Harry Dalton with a guaranteed five-year contract at $180,000 a year. He spent the entire five years in the bullpen, becoming, as Dan Okrent wrote in *Nine Innings,* "an inning eater, an omnivore who could occupy the mound when it was hopeless to waste a truly valuable pitcher." His career ended as soon as the contract has run its course.

Eldon Auker, who started the seventh game of the World Series for the Detroit Tigers in 1934.

Auker was born in Norcatur, Kansas, on September 21, 1910. His father was a rural mail carrier, driving a team of horses around a daily route surrounding the small town. In high school Auker filled in on the route, and was such an outstanding multisport athlete that he received numerous offers from colleges and professional baseball teams.

In the fall of 1928 Auker enrolled at Kansas State (now Kansas State University, at that time Kansas State Agricultural College) in Manhattan, Kansas. He had a formidable career as a college athlete, emerging as one of the outstanding running backs in the midwest, and playing basketball so well that twenty years later Phog Allen, the great basketball coach at the University of Kansas, would choose Auker to his all-opponents team. He studied pre-med, and was all-conference in three sports.

As a running back, Auker suffered a separated shoulder which left him unable to throw hard overhanded. He began throwing underhanded, sometimes scooping up pebbles as his arm sped over the mound. Auker completed his college education, graduating from Kansas State in June, 1932. He was offered contracts by the Chicago Bears and the Detroit Tigers, and wanted to accept both; he wanted to play baseball in the summer and football in the fall. Frank Navin, however, said no; if he signed the baseball contract he couldn't play football. Auker liked football better and would have preferred to play football, but the money was better in baseball, plus the money was *immediate*, since the baseball season was already underway. It was 1932, the depth of the depression, and Auker could ill afford to turn down the $450 a month the Tigers were willing to pay to wait for lower wages in the fall.

Susan McCarthy

Eldon AUKER

Auker signed with the Tigers, and reported to Decatur in the Three-I League. After his injury healed Auker had returned to throwing overhand, and was getting his brains beat out in the Three-I League. His manager suggested that he try the underhand delivery in a game. "The first-place team came to town, and I beat them, 1-0. I gave up two hits and struck out twelve. From then on I pitched that way until it seemed a natural way to throw." By mid-1933 he was in the major leagues, reporting to Detroit in early August after winning 16 games in the Texas League.

He joined the Tigers at a good time; Hank Greenberg and Schoolboy Rowe were also in their rookie seasons (see entry on Del Baker). The Tigers, a fifth-place team in 1933, won their first pennant in 25 years in 1934. Auker emerged as the number three pitcher on the team, behind Tommy Bridges (22-11) and Schoolboy Rowe (24-8). Auker was 15-7, and had the best ERA on the staff (3.42).

He threw underhand, but very hard, and the combination was frightening to a right-handed hitter. "When I throw a fastball, it rises and sinks," he said. "When I turn my wrist, it rises as it breaks." (Quoted from *The Crooked Pitch,* Martin Quigley.)

"The submarine ball comes up from below and explodes as it passes the batter," reported *Who's Who in the Major Leagues* in 1939. "Sometimes the batter explodes, because it's hard to hit what you don't see." Babe Ruth told Auker in 1933 that he'd been struck out many times, but never before by a girl. On the other hand, Birdie Tebbets said that "the easiest pitcher I ever caught was Elden Auker. His underhand deliveries came over the plate nice and soft." Elden—it was always spelled that way while he was playing.

Auker started, completed and won Game Four of the 1934 series, beating the Cardinals in St. Louis, 10-4. At that time they didn't take a travel day to move the series to Detroit; they played October 7 in St. Louis and October 8 in Detroit. When Bridges and Rowe pitched games five and six, Auker came back on two days rest to start Game Seven.

Dizzy Dean spotted him warming up. "Hey, podnah," said Dean. "You don't expect to get anybody out with that shit, do you?" He did for two innings, but in the third Dean ignited a seven-run explosion with a leg double. Auker left in the middle of that inning, setting the stage for an 11-0 Cardinal win enlivened by the famous Joe Medwick flying fruit incident.

The Tigers repeated in 1935, Auker going 18-7 with a 3.83 ERA; he led the American League in winning percentage. Bridges and Rowe won 40 games between them, again making Eldon the third starter on the Tiger staff. He started the third game of the 1935 series and pitched well; had that series gone seven games he would almost certainly have become the first pitcher to start Game Seven more than once. The Tigers won in six, avoiding the need.

Greenberg was hurt in 1936, and the Tigers dropped to second place. With off seasons from Bridges and Rowe, Auker emerged as the ace of the staff in 1937, going 17-9 with an excellent 3.88 ERA; the Tigers again finished second. After two subpar seasons he found himself with the St. Louis Browns, where he had perhaps his best season in 1940, going 16-11 with a 3.95 ERA—for an awful ballclub in a park where 5.50 ERAs were more the rule than the exception. After two more solid seasons his career was ended by the war. He was 31 years old, and had won 130 games.

Now in his early eighties, Auker at this writing is living in Florida.

(Some information and two quotes for this article comes from a new book, *Cobb Would Have Caught It,* by Richard Bak. The book may be hard to find but is outstanding.)

Doug Ault, who hit the first home run in Toronto Blue Jays history.

Born in 1950, Ault attended Junior College and then Texas Tech, and was drafted by the Pirates, Padres and Indians as an underclassman. He stayed to finish his education, and was apparently injured in his senior year, as he was undrafted coming out of college. He got a job with the Glacier Pilots of Anchorage, Alaska. Years later, playing for the Blue Jays in the coldest major league stadium God ever made, he would recall that the Pilots sometimes had sleet during their games. The Pilots won the National Baseball Congress (semi-pro) championship in 1972, Ault in the process earning a chance to play with the Texas Rangers' system in 1973.

He led the Western Carolina League in home runs and RBI his first year. Ault was 23 years old before he entered professional baseball, and 26 years old when he hit .313 with 25 homers in the Pacific Coast League in 1976. He was called up late that year by the Rangers, and then claimed by the Blue Jays in the expansion draft. The Blue Jays played their first game on April 7, 1977. Ault homered twice and singled, driving in four runs (4 2 3 4), leading the Jays to a 9-5 victory over the White Sox. The two home runs were hit in his first two at bats as a Blue Jay.

Ault stayed hot for a month, hitting .379 with 5 homers, 17 RBI through his first 18 games. On May 9 he was struck over the right eye by a ball thrown by third baseman Dave McKay during infield warmups, the cut requiring two stitches. He played the game anyway, and hit a three-run homer—his sixth—in the first inning. "A little knock on the head never hurt anyone," he said after the game, but a few days later he sprained his hand, and pitched into an 0-for-14 slump. After playing every inning of the Jays' first 36 games, he was benched on May 19. He never really did pull out of the slump, finishing the season at .245 with 11 home runs. The Blue Jays acquired John Mayberry in spring training, 1978, and Ault was out of a job. He went back to the minors, earned another chance in 1980, but hit below .200.

Retiring as a player following the 1982 season, Ault signed to manage in the Blue Jays' farm system, where he remains to this day. In the last ten years he has managed at Dunedin (Florida State League), at Kinston (Class A) and at Syracuse (AAA), and in 1990 and 1991 at St. Catharines (Class A). This winter he managed the Sydney Blues in the Australian winter league, with whom the Blue Jays have a working agreement. He is now 42 years old.

Jimmy "Pepper" Austin, long-time third baseman and coach for the St. Louis Browns.

Austin was born in Swansea, Wales, and came to the United States with his family at the age of eight. He grew up in Cleveland, the oldest of eight children, and after finishing school became a machinist-apprentice at the local Westinghouse plant. He played baseball for a hometown athletic club, but had no notion of becoming a professional until, one month after his apprenticeship ended, the Westinghouse machinists went out on strike. This led him to accept an offer to play ball (and work) for a factory team in nearby Warren, Ohio, taking with him another future major leaguer named Dode Paskert.

Austin returned to Westinghouse in the fall, but in the spring of 1904 was contacted by Dayton of the Central League, and at age twenty-four cast his lot with baseball. In 1907 he was sold to Omaha of the Western League, where in 1908 he stole ninety-seven bases. He joined the New York Highlanders—the Yankees—in 1909; he was already 29 years old.

Kid Elberfeld was the Highlanders' third baseman at the start of the 1909 season, but was suspended after a fight with an umpire, Austin getting a chance to play. He would be a regular for eleven years. Interviewed many years later for the classic book *The Glory of Their Times*, he recalled that, unlike many rookies of that era, he was not hazed by the veterans, Elberfeld even insisting that he take the lower berth on trains (which were reserved for regulars) as soon as he won the third base job.

Susan McCarthy

In 1910 manager George Stallings led the Highlanders to a second place finish. Austin hit poorly, but Stallings, who liked his glove and his constant hustle, dubbed him "The Pepper Kid". Late in the 1910 season, however, Stallings was cashiered in favor of Hal Chase, who had no use for anyone who had found favor with Stallings. Austin was traded to the St. Louis Browns, where he would find a home for more than twenty years.

Austin hit better in St. Louis, and emerged as one of the finest third basemen of his era. In 1913, Browns manager George Stovall was suspended for expectorating tobacco all over an umpire. ("George always did chew an uncommonly large wad, you know," Austin commented.) Austin became interim manager. Branch Rickey arrived to take the helm later that year, but since Rickey never went to the ballpark on Sunday, Austin remained as the Browns' "Sunday Manager" through Rickey's term as a field manager, which lasted two years. Pepper served two more stints as interim manager, and coached for St. Louis after his playing days were over. A trim little man bursting with nervous energy, he would continue to make occasional appearances in a game, playing one game in 1923, 1925, 1926 and 1929. In 1926, at age 46, he doubled and stole third base. In his last appearance, 1929, he was almost 50 years old.

Rogers Hornsby took over the Browns in 1933, and brought in a new coaching staff. Austin moved to the White Sox, coaching for Jimmie Dykes until his wife's ill-health forced him into retirement. He was still full of enthusiasm for baseball at age eighty-five when Lawrence Ritter transcribed his reminiscences for *The Glory of Their Times.* His wife's Christmas present was always a subscription to *The Sporting News,* and he read it cover to cover. He said he didn't come to this country until he was eight years old, and he'd missed a lot of baseball by that time. He didn't want to miss any more. Austin died at his home in Laguna Beach, California, in 1965.

(—Mike)

Rick Austin, a left-handed spot reliever in the American League in the 1970s.

Gene Autry, cowboy star and owner of the California Angels.

Autry was born in 1907 in Tioga, Texas. At age nineteen he tried out as a shortstop with Tulsa, in the St. Louis Cardinals organization. He was offered a contract for $100 a month, but elected to keep instead his $150 a month job as a railroad telegrapher. One night, he was passing the time playing his guitar in the telegraph office at Chelsea, Oklahoma. A customer asked him to continue the entertainment while he composed a message, and Autry began to sing. "You know," said the customer, "with some hard work, young man, you might have something. You ought to think about going to New York and get yourself a job on radio." Autry did. The customer was Will Rogers.

Autry had begun his radio career in 1928, and recordings and movies soon followed. In 1934 the Theater Exhibitors of America voted him "America's Favorite Cowboy", and in 1940 a poll placed him fourth in popularity among all movie stars. He became the first recording artist to sell over a million copies of a song, and the success of "Rudolph the Red-Nosed Reindeer" (which he initially did not want to record) became an international phenomenon. His radio show "Melody Ranch" lasted for sixteen years on CBS radio, and he became, in 1950, one of the first major stars to have his own television show.

Susan McCarthy

Gene AUTRY (Rudolph)

The millions of dollars he earned in show business were wisely invested in what eventually became Golden West Broadcasting, an empire of radio and television stations. It was radio that led Autry to become the owner of a baseball team. He was angered when, in 1960, Los Angeles Dodgers owner Walter O'Malley, without warning, announced his intention to pull Dodger broadcasts off Autry's station, KMPC. At the same time O'Malley was waging war to keep the American League from invading his Southern California gold mine, most particularly the American League in the persons of Bill Veeck and Hank Greenberg. Eventually a deal was reached that allowed the National League to expand into New York and the American League to expand into Los Angeles. In part to make sure that their radio station would have the rights to broadcast the games, Autry and his partner Robert Reynolds (with the backing of other investors) made a bid for the new Los Angeles franchise, and were accepted by American League owners on December 7, 1960.

The deal Autry *et al* were forced to cut O'Malley (a $350,000 indemnity payment, one year's tenancy at inadequate Wrigley Field, to be followed by four years at the new Dodger Stadium) became the origin of what many regarded as a long-term Angel inferiority complex. Another $2.1 million had to be shelled out to purchase expansion players. With Fred Haney installed as General Manager the Angels selected wisely, and posted a respectable 70-91 mark in their first year, 1961. The team even finished in the black, but instead of pouring the profits back into player development and scouting, Autry and Reynolds felt obligated to return it to the original investors. The Angels did even better in 1962, battling for the pennant until September and drawing over a million fans.

And yet that very success in a way sowed the seeds of their future frustrations. Robert Reynolds said years later that "In its final form the effect of 1962 was harmful. From top to bottom, we overestimated what we had and underestimated what we had to do. We were lulled into a false sense of security."

A veteran Angels scout concurred. "This organization has never had a firm conviction, a firm belief, that the way to build a successful team is through the scouting and farm system."

In 1966 the Angels ended their service to the Dodgers by moving into Anaheim Stadium, but the team was now unsuccessful on the field. Haney was eased out after 1968, and after three years of mediocrity and chaos under Dick Walsh, Harry Dalton became the Angels' General Manager. Dalton had built his reputation as the architect of the Baltimore Orioles' success, the Orioles being then the dominant team in the American League East.

The Angels had a different theory of how they were going to win every year. One year they were going to steal bases; the next year it was power hitting. They hired Dick Williams, who had been successful in Boston and Oakland, and later would be successful in Montreal and San Diego. He couldn't do anything with the Angels.

The Angels were still struggling in 1976 when the baseball world was turned upside down by free agency. According to Ross Newhan (whose *The California Angels* is a major source for this work), Autry was initially opposed to entering the free agent market, but was convinced by Dalton that it was necessary. Autry became the biggest spender of the early years of free agency, signing Don Baylor, Bobby Grich and Joe Rudi in 1977, Lyman Bostock in 1978. Grich and Rudi were injured shortly after they signed; Bostock, of course, was murdered.

Success arrived, fleetingly, in 1979, as the Angels won their first division title under

Jim Fregosi. But decline set in the next two years, and when Fregosi was unloaded in 1981, he unloaded in turn. "One year they're building through the farm system," he told a reporter. "The next year it's with free agents." He also alluded to the pressure to get the team in the World Series before "poor old Gene Autry" died. The Angels had fired their manager **in mid-season** in 1974 (Bobby Winkles), 1976 (Dick Williams), 1977 (Norm Sherry), 1978 (Dave Garcia) and 1981 (Jim Fregosi). What would typically happen was that they would start poorly, fire the manager in mid-season, name an interim manager, play better the last half the season, decide to let the interim manager keep his job, and play badly the first half the next year.

The acquisition of star players continued. Buzzy Bavasi, who had replaced Dalton as GM in 1977, wrote of Autry in *Off the Record:*

> His own brilliant career was the impetus behind his insistence on signing or trading for stars. He knew the value of having recognizable names on the marquee . . . The Angels are in competition with the Dodgers, which is why Mr. Autry invested so heavily in name players . . . If we were to put nine unknown youngsters on the field and try to compete with the Dodgers we might just as well have folded the tent.

Don Baylor, however, took a dimmer view of this keep-up-with-the-Dodgers syndrome.

> As soon as [he and Bobby Grich and Joe Rudi] arrived we felt the burden of not being the Dodgers. Why the Angels wanted to be Dodger clones was beyond me, but the emulation never ended . . . The Angels had such an inferiority complex they actually attached significance to spring training games—their big Freeway Series linking Anaheim and Los Angeles at the end of the exhibition season.

In spite of the constant infusion of stars (Fred Lynn, Doug DeCinces, and Reggie Jackson arrived in the early eighties), the pennant remained elusive to Autry, and the one-strike-away defeat by Boston in 1986 must have been particularly galling. Through difficult defeats, Autry has maintained his dignity, and maintained the affection of his organization. Ross Newhan has written:

> . . . with baseball, both before and after 1961, he would always be just a fan, a boy of summer, an owner who writes a letter of appreciation to just about every player who leaves his organization, and who has made innumerable trips to the clubhouse to visit with his players, to sit on a stool and reminisce . . .

Reggie and Baylor, who have little in common besides their talent and unpleasant dealings with Steinbrenner and Charles Finley, both paid tribute to Autry in their autobiographies. "He is . . . one of the kindest, sweetest human beings I have ever met," wrote Reggie. "He cares." Baylor concurs. "From the beginning I felt from him a genuine affection. He loved his baseball players."

As the eighties came to a close, Autry had signed yet another star player, Mark Langston. The dream of going to the World Series still burned bright in spite of many disappointments. One other long-cherished dream has come to fruition with the opening of the Gene Autry Western Heritage Museum in November of 1988.

(—Mike)

Earl Averill, Hall of Fame centerfielder for the Cleveland Indians from 1929 to 1939.

Howard Earl Averill was born on May 21, 1902, in Snohomish, Washington, which is how he came to be known as "The Earl of Snohomish". He was the son of a logger and a local pioneer. His father died when he was two, and Earl ended up working his way through both grammar and high school, pitching for the latter's baseball team. After graduation he played for the local Snohomish team, the Snohomish Pilchuckers. The home folks, convinced he had ability, raised money to finance the thirty-five-mile trip to Seattle so that Averill might try out with the Pacific Coast League team in Seattle. He was not offered a contract by the Rainiers, and went on to play semi-pro ball for Bellingham (Washington) and Anaconda (Montana), the latter in the Butte Mines League. He was playing winter ball in California after the 1925 season when he was spotted, and signed, by the San Francisco Seals of the Pacific Coast League.

In many ways the career of Earl Averill would foreshadow that of Joe DiMaggio, who began his career as a center fielder for the Seals in 1932. The most important difference, however, was this: that DiMaggio began playing for the Seals at age 17, and was in the majors at 21. Averill was almost 24 when he played his first game for the Seals.

The Seals at that time were an incredible organization, playing in the strongest minor league that ever was. In 1927 they had four outfielders—Averill, Lefty O'Doul, Smead Jolley and Roy Johnson, all four outstanding major league hitters, all four in their prime. The first baseman on that team was Dolph Camilli, later a major league MVP and perennial 100-RBI man. The second baseman was Gus Suhr, who would also drive in a hundred runs in the National League several times. And the Seals didn't win the pennant. They finished second behind Oakland.

Anyway, Averill was an immediate success with the Seals, playing center field and hitting for both average and power. Roger Peckinpaugh, the Indians' manager in 1928, related in *The Man in the Dugout* that "Billy Evans made a trip out to the Coast League to look at an outfielder named Roy Johnson. When Billy got there, he learned that Johnson had already been sold to Detroit. But in talking with the players out there, he kept hearing that the best ballplayer in the league

Susan McCarthy

Earl AVERILL

was a fellow named Earl Averill. So he wound up buying Averill, who became one of the Cleveland greats." Averill was sold for a reported $45,000, $5,000 of which went to Averill himself.

Averill made his major league debut on April 16, 1929, and homered in his first at bat, off Tiger left-hander Earl Whitehill. Another homer followed in his second game, and his career was fairly launched. The short right field wall of Cleveland's League Park was tailor-made for the pull hitting Averill. "I played five or six seasons before I found out there were three fields to hit the ball to," Averill recalled. 1929 was a year of great rookies, so Averill's stunning numbers in his first year in the American League (.330 with 43 doubles, 18 homers, 97 RBI) were actually no better than those of several other rookies that year—Dale Alexander, Bob Johnson, Johnny Frederick, Wes Ferrell. Averill was different from the others in that

a) he could also play defense, and

b) he could do it every year.

In a typical year Averill would hit about .330 with 40 doubles, 15 triples and 30 homers. He was annually among the league leaders in doubles and triples. His best year is hard to spot—perhaps 1936, when he hit .378 with 232 hits, 126 RBI, but then in 1931 he had driven in 143 runs and scored 140.

Averill was small for a power hitter, five foot nine and a half, 172 pounds. He had, according to Franklin Lewis in *The Cleveland Indians*, "a strange batting stance. He stood with feet fairly close together, crowding the plate, and he swung his bat with his body, it seemed, instead of 'stepping into' the pitch with a snap and lash of the wrists." On the other hand Ira Smith, in *Baseball's Famous Outfielders*, ventured that Averill "got his power as result of perfect timing and fine wrist action. Used heavy bat. Stood quietly in box, awaiting pitch without wagging his bat."

Whatever the cause, the results were impressive. In a doubleheader on September 17, 1930, against the Senators, Averill cranked a then-record four homers, three of them consecutive in the first game, with a potential fourth consecutive home run barely carrying foul. He wound up with eleven RBI for the two games, including eight in the first game, his second eight-RBI game of the season. This is a record that he shares to this day with Lou Gehrig, two eight-RBI games in one year; both accomplished it in 1930.

His durability was remarkable. In seven of his first nine seasons he appeared in 150 or more games. It might have been eight of nine but for a freak accident on June 26, 1935, when, preparing for the Fourth of July, he held a firecracker too long and ended up with a burned and lacerated left hand. (It was apparently this incident which earned Averill the nickname "Rock".) In 1931 Averill toured the country with the Babe Ruth All-Stars, and in 1934 was part of an All-Star contingent (including Ruth, Gehrig, and Foxx) that toured the Orient.

Averill became the only outfielder to be selected for the first six All-Star games. In 1934 he was the fans' choice to be in the starting lineup, but American League manager Joe Cronin elected instead to go with Al Simmons. In the 1937 All-Star game, played in Washington, Averill stepped to the plate in the third inning against Dizzy Dean. He sent a liner back at Dean that caromed off Dizzy's left big toe, breaking it, and eventually leading to the early end of Dizzy's career.

No one knew it at the time, but Averill's career was also about to begin a swift downward descent. After seriously challenging for the batting title in '36 (Luke Appling beat him out, .388 to .378), Averill was hitting .394 on June 26, 1937, when, in his own words, "my back went haywire." He finished the 1937 season at .299. He came back to hit .330 in 1938, batting only 482 times, and after that season he was no longer effective.

In 1939, perhaps sensing that the end was near, he tried squeezing every last penny out of the Indians with a holdout. The Indians' brass, perhaps also sensing that his best days were behind him, were less than solicitous. Club President Alva Bradley publicly branded Averill a "quitter" who had attempted to jump ship in late 1938, when the team still had a shot at second place. Agreement was eventually reached, but on June 22 Earl was traded to the Detroit Tigers for a pitcher, Harry Eisenstat, and cash. Averill professed himself relieved: "I'm damned glad to go someplace where I'm wanted." Bob Feller, in *Strikeout Story*, reports that as Averill left he warned his now ex-teammates: "I'll see you fellows on the night of June 27." On that date the Tigers and Indians would meet in the first night game ever played in Cleveland. After giving Averill a generous ovation on his first at bat, the crowd of 55,000 watched as Feller carried a no-hitter into the sixth, only to see their erstwhile hero Averill rip a single to center for the only Detroit hit of the game.

Averill was fortunate enough to hang on with the Tigers through 1940, giving him the double satisfaction of edging out the Indians in a tight pennant race, and making an appearance in the World Series. The next year saw a cup of coffee with the Boston Braves and the end of his major league career.

Averill had married Gladys Hyatt as a young man, and they eventually had four sons, one of whom, Earl Douglas, would have a major league career of his own. Averill returned to Snohomish to spend the remainder of his life.

Averill was elected to the Hall of Fame by the Veterans' Committee in 1975. In the voting of the BBWAA Averill had drawn almost no support, never more than 14 votes, which is about one-tenth what would have been required to elect him. A Seattle-based publication called *Sports Scoop* had campaigned for Averill's election, and had helped push him to the top of the Veterans' Committee's list.

Well, immediately after the Hall of Fame induction ceremony, Averill and *Sports Scoop* handed out copies of a pre-printed news release, blasting the BBWAA for their failure to recognize Averill and other equally qualified candidates. Rather than being appreciative of the honor, Averill was angry that he had not been selected sooner. According to Bob Broeg in *The Sporting News*, September 13, 1975, Averill revealed that, had election to the Hall come after his death, he had instructed his family to refuse to accept the honor.

Averill and his fellow travelers held the

members of the BBWAA *personally* accountable for what was in truth a *structural* problem with the Hall of Fame vote: that at the time Averill could have been elected by the BBWAA, the writers had before them such an extensive backlog of qualified candidates that the inevitable consequence was that the vote would be split fifty different ways, and it would be almost impossible for anyone to clear the 75% barrier, meaning that everyone remained in the pot to further complicate next year's vote. In any case, Averill had eight years to enjoy his Hall of Fame status before he died of pneumonia on August 16, 1983.

(—M.K.)

Earl Averill, son of Earl Averill and catcher for the first edition of the Los Angeles (now California) Angels.

A right-handed hitter who was similar in build to his father, but stockier and lacking his father's speed, Averill got a degree from the University of Oregon in Eugene before entering baseball in 1953. After a substantial minor league internship he had a good year with San Diego in 1958, then hit 10 homers in 186 at bats for the 1959 Cubs. He was traded to the White Sox the next year anyway, and taken in the expansion draft. For the expansion Angels he hit 21 homers in 323 at bats, but lost his job in '62 to Buck Rodgers, now the manager of the team.

Bobby Avila, star second baseman of the Cleveland Indians in the fifties, and the American League's batting champion in 1954.

Roberto Francisco Avila (Gonzalez) was born in Vera Cruz, Mexico on April 2, 1924, the ninth and last child of a well-to-do lawyer. (During his career his date of birth was listed as June 7, 1926.) A soccer star as a youth, Avila was encouraged to try baseball by an older brother, Pedro; at Vera Cruz Preparatory High School he pitched and played shortstop. He found a book on playing baseball by Jack Coombs, former pitcher, and studied that. At the age of sixteen he played professional soccer, earning fifty dollars a month, and dreamed of perhaps being a great bullfighter.

His father didn't care for Roberto's soccer playing; he wanted his son to become a professional man. "Some day they will kick your head instead of the ball," he told him once, "and I will be hauled into court for having a son with rocks where his brains should be." Over the objections of his father Avila decided to pursue a career in baseball, and signed as a third baseman for Cordoba in the Vera Cruz State League, which operated during the off-season of the dominant Mexican League. The arrival of Luis Molinero, a veteran Mexican League star, forced Avila to switch to second base; Molinero was the best third baseman in Mexico. Molinero apparently took the youngster under his wing, and they were soon teammates for Puebla in the Mexican League. After batting .250 in his rookie season there, Avila went on to post batting marks of .334, .336, .360 and .347. In 1946 Jorge Pasquel induced a number of quality major-league players to defect to Mexico (see entry on Ace Adams, 1990 *Baseball Book*). Avila welcomed the Americans, figuring they would raise the pay all around the league, and when he saw them play he knew he could make it in the United States. "He's a real nice little guy and a helluva hitter,"

Susan McCarthy

Bobby AVILA

said Sal Maglie in 1950, recalling Avila from the Mexican League. "He's so good I think I will knock him down with my first pitch, just to be on the safe side."

In the winter of 1946–47 Avila played in Cuba, where, according to one account, Leo Durocher was impressed enough to offer Avila $10,000 to sign with the Dodgers. (Another account has the offer coming from Branch Rickey, at—predictably—a lower figure.) Avila, hardly the stereotype of a hungry Latin player looking for a way out of poverty, turned that offer down and also rejected overtures from the Senators' famous man in Havana, Joe Cambria. Another legendary scout, the Indians' Cy Slapnicka, shadowed him—supposedly secretly, although it's hard to imagine how—as his team made the rounds of the Mexican League. They met in Mexico City, where Avila demanded $17,500 to sign. Slapnicka reportedly had been prepared to go higher, and Avila signed with the Indians.

It must have seemed money ill-spent to the Tribe in 1948, for at Baltimore, Cleveland's top farm team, Avila batted a mere .220. He spoke no English, and his manager recalled that it took him a month to get Avila to understand that he needed to report to the park in time for batting and fielding drills; in the Mexican League, they just showed up and played the games. In the field he seemed lethargic. The Orioles' team doctor examined him and found a severe hernia. Going home to Vera Cruz in mid-season, he was operated on by one of his older brothers. Adding to a miserable season, Avila's father died suddenly of a heart attack in the fall of 1948.

The bonus rule in effect at that time allowed only a one-year minor league option for a player who had received a substantial bonus; after that the bonus baby had to spend two years on the major league roster (see entry on Johnny Antonelli, 1991 *Baseball Book*). Avila was assigned to room with Mike Garcia, whose parents were from Mexico. Garcia was the only person in his world that Avila could talk to, and Bobby nearly drove him nuts asking questions, trying to learn the language. Avila, twenty-five years old and ready to play—Lou Boudreau said that he'd never seen a rookie with as good a grasp of fundamentals—spent a year and a half on the Indians' bench, watching the brilliant Joe Gordon play second, and occasionally falling asleep. He talked about that to coach Muddy Ruel.

"Moddy," he said, "I no wanna sleep. I wanna learn."

"Chew tobacco," Ruel told him. "It won't let you fall asleep. If you do you'll choke."

One fundamental they apparently didn't teach in the Mexican League. Avila took up chewing tobacco, which he quit as soon as he got in the lineup. Fighting off Morpheus became easier in '50, when Gordon suddenly ran out of gas, and Avila replaced him late in the season. The Lou Boudreau years ended in Cleveland after 1950 and the Al Lopez years began, and with that Gordon was released.

From the day Avila stepped into the lineup, he hit, keeping his average within a few points of three hundred for several years. He walked twice as often as he struck out, and had a little line-drive power. On June 20, 1951, he hit three home runs, a single and a double in one game (6 4 5 4). Avila hit the ball where it was pitched, pulled the ball when the opportunity arose and bunted frequently and well. One of the fastest men in the league, Avila was also alert and extremely aggressive on the base paths, this being in fact what he was best known for before 1954. Using his soccer background, he perfected a "scissors-kick" slide; sliding into the base with his left leg extended and his right leg tucked against his body, he would lash out at the last moment with his right leg, knocking the ball, and sometimes the glove, away from the startled defender.

Earning a good salary, Roberto sent money back home to Mexico to support his mother and a widowed sister, maintaining the family's position by sending a nephew through law school. He began his own family, having several children; he spent much of his time writing letters to the people back home. He said he didn't want his son to grow up to be a ballplayer. "Is a fine game for a single man. But for a married man is no good. Too much travel around. Too much away from the family."

Avila was not a good defensive player in his early years. He made many errors, had an indifferent arm and was criticized for shying away from oncoming baserunners, as a consequence of which he turned few double plays. He had small, tender hands, a violinist's hands, but not much use to a second baseman. In 1952 the Indians suffered a general defensive collapse, to which Avila made a healthy contribution: he led all major league second basemen in errors. The Indians as a team were last in the league in double plays and first in errors, and so a team with the league's best offense and best pitching staff finished two games behind the Yankees.

In 1953 the Indians replaced the men on either side of Avila. Ray Boone, a good-hitting shortstop who later became a slugging third baseman, was replaced by George Strickland, and Luke Easter, a power hitting first baseman, was supplanted by Bill Glynn, a glove man who was supposed to hit more than he did. Avila, concentrating on his defense, slipped below three hundred, but led the league in fielding percentage and assists. The Indians vaulted from last in the league in double plays to first—and posted almost the same won-lost record as the year before, holding second place. For four straight years (1950–53) the Indians won 92 or 93 games, while the Yankees hung in the high nineties.

Well, you all know what happened in 1954. After starting out three and six—they were dead last—the Tribe then won more than three-fourths of their games the rest of the way, breaking the 1927 Yankees' American League record for wins. (For some odd reason, one very often hears the Indians' 111 wins that year referred to as the *major league* record, which it is not.) The Indians pulled off this remarkable feat despite suffering significant injuries to all four regular infielders. Third baseman Al Rosen chipped his right index finger on May 25, and couldn't swing the bat up to his ability the rest of the year. Shortstop Strickland missed five weeks with a fractured jaw, first baseman Glynn was slowed by hamstrings and replaced in midseason by Vic Wertz (who missed twenty games with various injuries himself), and Avila, hitting .391 in June, suffered a broken thumb in a collision at second base with Hank Bauer.

Avila reported to spring training in 1954 with ulcers, and was ordered to drink milk. He drank two quarts a day, and it turned out to be power lunch. Avila scored 112 runs that year, went three-for-three in the All-Star game and hit fifteen home runs, thirteen of which either tied or won the game for the Indians. Avila was also the Mike Hargrove of his day, going through a series of motions before he would get into the batter's box—hitching his sleeves, spitting on his hands, getting just the right stance. "He used to drive me nuts when I was umpiring," said Cal Hubbard. "He's the most careful batter in the game." Avila said that until it was pointed out to him, he didn't know that he did all that stuff.

On opening day, 1954, with Ted Williams sidelined by a broken collarbone, Dizzy Dean had wagered a $50 Texas hat that Avila would win the AL batting championship. Despite slumping badly in June with the broken thumb, Avila won Dean his hat. With left fielder Al Smith reaching base constantly as the leadoff man, Avila, hitting second, won the batting title with a mark of .341. The batting title led to a controversy, and thus to a rules change, leaving Avila's image on the game. Ted Williams returned to the lineup in mid-May, and finished with a .345 average in 117 games. At the time the rule was that a player had to bat 400 times to be eligible for the batting title, and The Splinter just missed that, with 386. Williams, however, had also walked 136 times; altogether he had 526 plate appearances. The rule, said Casey Stengel, "was never meant for a guy like Ted Williams, it's for humpty-dumpties trying to steal a batting championship on half a season's work."

Avila offered the opinion that if it hadn't been for his broken thumb there would have been no question as to who deserved the batting championship, leaving open the question of what Ted Williams would have hit had it not been for that painful steel pin in his shoulder. The rule was changed, anyway, so that eligibility for the batting championship was based on plate appearances rather than at bats. Avila could have been the MVP that year, as well as the batting champion, but three Cleveland players (Larry Doby, Avila and Bob Lemon) split the vote, leaving Yogi Berra on top of a rather weird vote.

Another thing that had helped him that season, Avila reported, was rooming with Hank Majeski, a veteran outfielder who worked with him on his swing and on "thinking baseball"; he came to regard Majeski almost as an older brother. Majeski was traded in early 1955, and Avila never again came close to matching his 1954 season. Over the next four years as a regular for Cleveland his offensive numbers slipped back as the Indians slipped gradually away from the pennant race. His defensive problems returned. On December 2, 1958, the Tribe traded Avila to Baltimore for Russ Heman and $30,000. He bounced from Baltimore to Boston to Milwaukee, becoming a part of the Braves' desperate search for a second baseman (see entry on Henry Aaron, 1990 *Baseball Book*). In his first appearance as a Brave he hit a game-winning home run to break a seven-game Milwaukee losing streak, and though he held his job the rest of the year, the playoff resulting from the Milwaukee-Los Angeles tie was his final major league appearance.

In his prime Avila had become a national hero in Mexico, more popular, it was said, than even the greatest bullfighters. Sometime in the fifties he became the owner/manager/second baseman of a Mexico City winter league team. "It's terrible," he said. "You playing game and players ask you for money right on the bench." He said that once his major league career was over he would sever his connections with baseball. He didn't, of course; in 1960, his first year out of the majors, he played for (but did not manage) the Mexico City Tigers, and had an excellent season, hitting .333 and leading the league in runs scored and walks. He remained active in baseball as an owner, later as president of the Vera Cruz Eagles. In the early 1980s he became President of the Mexican League. After a year in that job (September 1981–August 1982), he resigned to devote more time to his business interests. Avila still lives in the Mexico City area.

(Most of the work on this article was done by Mike Kopf. Background articles include *Viva Avila*, by Gordon Cobbledick, in the September, 1953, edition of *Sport* magazine, an article by Hal Lebovitz in the June, 1955, *Baseball Digest*, a profile of Avila by Harry Jones in *Baseball Stars of 1955*, and another Lebovitz article, *Avila's Flying Feet*, in the 1952 edition of *Best Sports Stories*.)

Ramon Aviles, utility infielder for the World Champion 1980 Philadelphia Phillies.

The Puerto Rican-born Aviles was signed out of high school by the Boston Red Sox in 1969, and seemed on his way to being a career minor leaguer (he'd appeared in one game for Boston) when Phillies second baseman Manny Trillo broke a bone in his forearm. Aviles was called up in May of 1979. "I'm just going to try my best," he said. "I've waited a long time for this chance; I don't want to blow it."

He didn't. He showed well enough to get the call again early in 1980, and this time stuck through 1981, seeing action in two post-seasons, and earning a World Series ring.

Aviles has coached and managed in the Phillies' minor league system since 1983. He will manage the Batavia team (New York-Penn League) in 1992.

(—Mike)

Pete Axthelm, sportswriter and TV commentator.

Axthelm graduated from Yale University (where he studied with Robert Penn Warren) in 1965 and began a series of journalistic assignments which included racing columnist for *The New York Herald-Tribune*, staff writer for *Sports Illustrated*, and sports editor for *Newsweek*. He wrote three books, *The City Game*, about basketball in New York City; *The Kid*, a portrait of jockey Steve Cauthen; and *O.J.: The Education of a Rich Rookie* (in collaboration with O.J. Simpson).

Axthlem was a tremendous writer; his *Newsweek* columns are quick combinations of wit, images and genuine insight, still fun to read fifteen years after the subject has grown cold. I knew Axthelm in the late seventies and early eighties, not real well but it would seem like I'd run into him whenever I went to New York. You'd see him in bars, in Charley O's or P.J. Clarke's, often sitting with a young woman or a research assistant having a drink and making notes about a column. He had a clear version of the good life: he liked to gamble, and drink, and go to horseraces and bars and ballgames. He was utterly unapologetic about all of this, and such a delightful man that he served as an advertisement for his own vaguely dissolute lifestyle.

In the early eighties NBC hired him to be an on-air person. Axthelm didn't *look* or *sound* like a broadcast journalist; he was a balding, heavy-set guy with thick glasses and a thin voice. It is to the credit of NBC television that they would try to break out of the mold a little, and let Axthelm's enthusiasm and wit take the place of a good coiffure. I always thought it was a mistake, from his standpoint and their's. What Axthelm did well was *write*. On television, giving on-the-spot reactions to breaking events and concentrating on speaking in complete sentences, he seemed no more insightful than the guys with the good hair. The job robbed him of his anonymity. I never saw him in the bars anymore; I wasn't sure whether he'd stopped going or I had. I wondered whether he was drinking in private now, and I still don't know the answer to that. He moved to ESPN in the late eighties.

On February 2, 1991, Pete Axthelm died in a Pittsburgh hospital. His liver had failed him, and he had gone to Pittsburgh to await a transplant. He was 47.

Benny Ayala, one of Earl Weaver's role players with the Orioles of the late seventies and early eighties.

Born in Yauco, Puerto Rico, Ayala entered pro baseball in the Mets system in 1971. He reached the majors on August 27, 1974, and hit a home run off Tom Griffin in his first major league at bat, becoming the first Met to do that. He failed to stick, and after hitting .225 at Tidewater in 1976 was sent to the Cardinals. The Cardinals loaned him to Pittsburgh; the Pirates looked and returned him.

As was his custom, after the '78 season Ayala played in the Puerto Rican Winter League. Doc Edwards, then the manager of Baltimore's Rochester farm club (and now a coach with the Mets), saw him, and sent word to the Orioles' front office that they ought to take a look at this guy. They did, and a trade was quickly worked out; the O's got Ayala from the Cardinals in exchange for outfielder Mike Dimmel.

Ayala began the '79 season in Rochester, but was called up when Doug Decinces was hurt. When Decinces was ready to play again, Hank Peters wanted to send Ayala back down. Earl Weaver, impressed by Ayala's bat, urged Peters to dump back-up outfielder Larry Harlow instead.

There were many things that Ayala *couldn't* do. He couldn't run, he couldn't field, and he couldn't make contact consistently against a right-handed pitcher. He could be overpowered by a left-hander with a good enough fastball. To most managers, that meant that Ayala couldn't play. Earl Weaver was a little different: he focused on what Ayala *could* do. Ayala could hit with power against a left-handed pitcher in a limited role. Between 1979 and 1982 Ayala batted only 470 times—but hit .277 with 25 homers, 83 RBI.

Susan McCarthy

Benny AYALA

Ayala stopped hitting after Weaver left the Orioles in 1983, and dropped out of the majors by the mid-eighties.

(—Rob)

Dr. Jose Aybar, dean of the University of Santo Domingo, Dominican Republic, who was assigned by President Rafael Trujillo to assemble the best possible baseball team to defeat the team of a political rival. Aybar brought in a team including Satchel Paige, Cool Papa Bell and Josh Gibson.

Jake Aydelott, pitcher in the American Association in the 1880s.

William O. Ayers, who pitched briefly for the Giants in 1947.

Ayers first pitched professionally in 1938, going 9-1 for Gastonia in the North Carolina State League. Despite this promising beginning he dropped out of baseball for several years, and pitched only semi-pro ball until the War created a shortage of professionals, when he was signed with Savannah in the Sally League. He won 19 games for Savannah in 1942, then had 15 wins for Atlanta by mid-season, 1943, before reporting for military duty. In 1946 he won 21 games with a 1.95 ERA for Atlanta, earning his brief major league trial.

Yancy Wyatt (Doc) Ayers, a pitcher with the Washington Senators in the Walter Johnson era.

Ayers, who was nicknamed "Doc" because he had studied medicine, had his best season in 1915, going 16-9 with a 2.22 ERA. He was a spitball pitcher, and became one of the nine American Leaguers who were protected by the grandfather clause included when the spitball was banned in 1920.

Jose Azcue, American League catcher of the sixties.

Azcue began his professional career in 1956, and had a cup of coffee with the Cincinnati Reds in 1960, returning to AAA in the Milwaukee organization before being traded to Kansas City in the winter of 1961. Birdie Tebbetts, Braves' manager, said of him, "He's got a fireball arm. No more than average in catching ability but good power with the bat."

Azcue's season with Kansas City was injury-plagued, and on May 25, 1963, Azcue and Dick Howser were traded to Cleveland for Doc Edwards and cash. For two months after that he was red hot; every swing was a line drive. The Cleveland fans began calling him "The Immortal Azcue". He wound up the 1963 season, his best in the majors, at .281 with 14 homers, 46 RBI.

For several years after that Azcue was one of the better platoon catchers in the majors, hitting .250–.270 with some power and good defense. In April, 1969, Azcue was part of a controversial trade that brought Hawk Harrelson to the Indians. Harrelson, however, initially refused to report to Cleveland, leaving Azcue and teammate Sonny Siebert, bound for Boston, in a sort of roster limbo.

Susan McCarthy

Joe AZCUE

For a time it appeared the deal would have to be rescinded, but Azcue and Siebert, figuring if it worked for Harrelson it was worth a shot, announced that they had served their time with the Indians, and didn't intend to go back. Eventually Harrelson reached an agreement with the Indians and reported to Cleveland, and Azcue resumed his career with the Red Sox.

Disenchantment, however, had begun to seep through the plumbing of Azcue's career, and would swamp him within three years. He didn't get along with Dick Williams, then managing the Red Sox. This wasn't unusual—nobody including his wife was getting along with Williams very well at that time—but when Williams benched Azcue in favor of Russ Gibson, Azcue jumped the team. He was traded to the California Angels, and caught regularly for the Angels over the last four months of the 1969 season and through 1970.

Azcue, however, didn't get along with California manager Lefty Phillips, either, and also didn't hit the way he had earlier in his career. Unhappy with his contract offer in 1971, Azcue sat out the entire season, returning to the Angels in 1972 after Phillips had been fired. After three games the Angels traded him to Milwaukee, Milwaukee released him, and his career ended in 1972.

Azcue now lives in the Kansas City area, where he was part owner of a bar for several years.

(—Mike)

• B •

Charlie Babb, a regular shortstop for two seasons in the early part of this century.

Babb debuted in 1903 with the Giants as a thirty-year-old rookie. On August 24, 1903, he set the modern National League record with five errors in one game. Ten months later, he tied his own record, which still stands.

On December 12, 1903, the Giants traded Babb and pitcher Jack Cronin to the Dodgers for Bill Dahlen, one of the finest defensive shortstops of all time. John McGraw, who had just completed his first full season as manager of the Giants, said of the trade: "Babb is a fine young player. I'm sure Brooklyn will like him. Babb will be playing long after Dahlen has retired. After all, he's two years younger."

McGraw knew better, of course. He later said that Dahlen, who played regularly through 1908, was the difference between his 1903 squad and the '04 and '05 pennant winners. Babb had disappeared from the majors by 1906.

(—R.N.)

Bob Babcock, briefly a pitcher with the Texas Rangers.

Babcock spent eleven years in the minors before making his major league debut in 1979 with the Rangers, for whom he appeared thirty-nine times in relief over the next three seasons.

Loren Babe, third baseman for the Philadelphia Athletics in 1953.

Babe started his career as a 17-year-old wartime minor leaguer, hitting .330 for Norfolk in the Piedmont League and playing a month in the Eastern League and a few games in the American Association. His best minor league season was 1950, when he hit .335 with Muskegon in the Central League. He jumped to the International League in 1951, and earned a major league job after hitting .305 for Syracuse in 1952.

With the A's in 1953 Babe hit only .230 with two home runs in 108 games, so he never played in the major leagues again. Back to the International League, he played four years with Toronto and one with Rochester, retiring after the 1958 season.

In 1961 Babe was hired to manage in the Yankee system, which he did for six years with considerable success, winning the Pioneer League (1963) and the Southern League (1965). In 1966, Babe's last as a manager, the ace of his Toledo staff was Stan Bahnsen (see **Bahnsen**). He coached the major league Yankees in 1967 before shifting into scouting, first for the Yanks and later the White Sox.

In April of 1983 Babe was working for the White Sox as a roving scout at the major and minor league levels, writing player reports for the front office, when he found out that he had cancer. According to Jerome Holtzman in his column of March 20, 1984,

> Babe needed 57 days of major-league service time to qualify as a vested member of the players' pension plan, which also provides medical benefits. The Sox management decided to bring him up as a coach. Not only would his hospital costs be covered, but Babe, if he survived, or his widow, would be entitled to a pension and death benefits.
>
> No more than four coaches, simultaneously, can earn pension credits. [Charlie] Lau, already vested, volunteered to be taken off the list. This was on May 6 . . .

A month or so later, Charlie Lau was diagnosed as having cancer of the colon. Babe and Lau both made it through the season while undergoing treatment for their illnesses, each of them occasionally missing Sox series. Holtzman compared the compassion exhibited by the club to that in the film "Bang the Drum Slowly", something he thought impossible on a real team.

Babe died on February 14, 1984, Lau just over a month later.

(—R.N.
The main sources for this entry were various editions of *The Chicago Tribune*)

Johnny Babich, whose brilliant pitching against the Yankees prevented them from winning their fifth consecutive American League pennant in 1940.

The 1935 *Who's Who in Baseball* contains a factual summary of Babich's early career which would be difficult to improve:

> Vernon Gomez, who was one of Johnny's schoolmates, was among the many individuals to sing the praises of the latter before he advanced to the Dodgers in 1934. Babich, who pitches and bats right-handed, was born in Albion, Calif., May 14, 1913. He is 6 feet 2½ inches tall, weighs 187; is of Austrian descent, with blue eyes and brown hair; married, and lives near Richmond, Calif. Babich first signed with San Francisco after attracting attention in semi-pro circles and was sent to Globe, Ariz., in 1931. He was with Tucson in 1932 and was recalled by the Seals, who permitted him to go to the Missions of the Coast League. In 1933 Johnny won 20 games and lost 15.

The San Francisco Seals were the dominant team in the Bay Area; they had signed Vince DiMaggio at about the same time they signed Babich, optioned the two of them out, and recalled them at about the same time in late 1932. It was just after this recall that Vince had encouraged the Seals to take a look at his little brother, Joe, which they did in November, 1932. When the Seals allowed Babich to go to their competitors over in Mission in early 1933 that was a type of rejection, a statement that they didn't believe he was destined to be *really* good. With limited space for young, untried players, the Seals may in a sense have been forced to choose between Babich and DiMaggio's younger brother, and chose the little brother. In the summer of 1933 Joe DiMaggio, then 18 years old, hit in 61 consecutive Coast League games for the Seals, a PCL record which still stands. According to Mike Seidel's book *Streak:*

Susan McCarthy

Johnny BABICH

> Johnny Babich that year had been traded from the San Francisco Seals to their crosstown rivals, the Missions, just before a young Joe DiMaggio began his Pacific Coast League hitting streak. Babich was always especially keyed up when he pitched against the Seals during DiMaggio's 1933 streak; the local papers at the time were filled with mutterings about what he intended to do to his former mates. He wanted to beat them badly, and DiMaggio, who was hotter than a pistol, made that difficult.

While Babich was unable to stop DiMaggio's 1933 streak, his twenty wins with a bad team earned him the attention of major league teams, and when he started the 1934 season 10-3 with a league-leading 2.03 ERA he was purchased by Casey Stengel's Brooklyn Dodgers. Only 21 years old, he pitched well at times, and pitched a brilliant game against the pennant-bound Cardinals, a four-hitter in which he struck out three straight left-handed hitters on eleven pitches.

He slipped badly in 1935, however, his ERA jumping to the devil's number (6.66). He dropped to the lower minors, but by 1937 was back with Mission, where he went 12-8 with a last-place team. In 1938 he was with Hollywood, the seventh-place team in the PCL, and went 19-17.

He was purchased by the Yankees after the 1938 season, and so finally got to pitch for a good team: the 1939 Kansas City Blues. Led by Vince DiMaggio's 46 homers, 136 RBI and the double play combination of Gerry Priddy and Phil Rizzuto, the Blues won 107 games in a 154-game schedule. Babich went 17-6 with a 2.55 ERA. The Yankees couldn't use him and couldn't hold him forever, so they sent him someplace they figured he could never hurt them: they sold him to the Philadelphia Athletics.

The A's by this time were an awful team. Babich was used to that; he'd been pitching for awful teams almost all of his career. In 1940, pitching for the last-place Athletics, Babich beat the Yankees five times, almost single-handedly preventing them from winning their fifth consecutive title. The Yankees finished 88-66, two games out of first place (see entry on Del Baker). According to Al Silverman's book *Joe DiMaggio: His Golden Year (1941):*

> His fifth victory knocked the Yankees out of the American League pennant. After that game Joe McCarthy came into the clubhouse growling, Babich . . . Babich . . . BABICH! Who in the hell ever heard of Babich?
>
> Joe Gordon looked up calmly and said, "Well, apparently our scouts didn't."

Babich, having by far his best major league season, finished 14-13 with a 3.73 ERA for a team which finished 54-100 with a 5.22 ERA.

Babich lost his effectiveness in 1941, but is remembered for his attempt to stop DiMaggio's 1941 streak at 39 games. According to Jack B. Moore's *Joe DiMaggio:*

> In game 40, the Yankees faced Johnny Babich of the Philadelphia Athletics. Babich had played for the Yankees in the minor leagues, but they had never brought him up to the majors, and according to Silverman, he "had a reputation as a Yankee killer." Babich plays a villainous role in streak narratives, and is punished accordingly. Having beaten the Yankees five times in 1940, his revenge, so the story goes, would be complete only if he could thwart DiMaggio. In the third inning Babich pitched to the hitless DiMaggio for the second time and threw him three straight balls far out of the strike zone. The fourth pitch would also have been a ball but DiMaggio had received the hit sign, and as Silverman says, the ball "went on a vengeful line directly at the pitcher . . . through his legs and out into center field." DiMaggio had hit safely and Babich was "white as a sheet."

According to Seidel's *Streak*, Babich "had made it known that he intended to give DiMaggio garbage to hit at the plate whether ahead or behind in the count . . . DiMaggio was genuinely miffed at Babich's tactics because his experience around the league had shown him that most pitchers wanted to get him out with their best stuff, not walk him with their worst." Seidel traced the bad blood between DiMaggio and Babich back to the Pacific Coast League competition in 1933. In any case, DiMaggio cited the hit off of Babich as the most satisfying hit of the streak, because Babich had tried so hard to stop him. Babich faced DiMaggio again a week later, with the streak at 47 games, and this time elected to pitch to him.

Babich left the majors after the 1941 season, and still lives today in the San Francisco area.

Charlie Babington, who got into 28 games as a pinch-hitter and spare outfielder with the 1915 New York Giants.

Shooty Babitt, a part-time second baseman for the Oakland A's in 1981. His manager was Billy Martin, who reportedly told Earl Weaver, "If you ever see Shooty Babitt play second base for me again, I want you to shooty me."

Les Backman, a pitcher with the St. Louis Cardinals in 1909 and 1910.

Backman (usually spelled Bachman while he was active) reached the majors on the Fourth of July, 1909, starting against the Reds in the first game of a holiday doubleheader. The next day's *St. Louis Post-Dispatch* noted:

> Young Bachman has the markings of a splendid athlete. He has weight and speed and a fancy drop curve that perplexed the Cincinnati batsmen continually. For five innings, he mowed down the opposing players with regularity and created quite a sensation in one instance by fanning Hoblitzell, the best hitter, when the bases were filled.

Backman lost that game after Roger Bresnahan, Cardinals catcher-manager, was kicked out of the game in the fourth inning for arguing balls and strikes with the umpire. Despite his speed and fancy drop curve, he lost 18 of 27 career decisions.

(—R.N.)

Wally Backman, second baseman for the Mets through the 1980s.

Backman was the Mets' #1 pick in the 1977 draft (sixteenth overall), played in the New York-Penn League and was named by the NY-P managers as the player most likely to make it to the majors. Backman moved up steadily, a rung at a time. By 1980 he played for Tidewater, then hit .323 for the Mets in a September call-up, but went back to Tidewater in 1981.

Called up late in 1981, Backman again hit well (.278) in a few games. In 1982 he played 96 games for the Mets and hit .272. They sent him back to Tidewater anyway, and he spent the 1983 season back at AAA.

The Mets at that time had a firm grip on last place, and one might think they could find a use for a middle infielder with an on base percentage of .380. Wally's reputation as a defensive player was along the lines of David Duke's reputation as a statesman. It was in 1983 that a comparison of Backman to Eddie Stanky drew the wrath of Howard Cosell on a national radio show. "Imagine comparing Backman to Eddie Stanky—ridiculous!" Cosell said. Backman's manager at Tidewater in '83 was Davey Johnson, who admired Backman's not-so-obvious talents in much the same way that Leo Durocher had admired Stanky's:

> He's not slick. His arm is average and he throws funny, which makes it look worse. He's an average runner with good instincts and an above average on-base percentage. But Wally's chemistry and drive go off the Richter scale. Put it all together and you have a good second baseman.

When Johnson moved up to manage the Mets in '84 he took Backman with him, this time to stay.

Backman is a small man (5-9, 160) and a switch hitter, but could never hit at all right-handed. An excellent bunter, he would try to bunt against left-handers, and sometimes would forget the switch hitting and try to hit left-handed against left-handers. He was platooned with Kelvin Chapman until late July 1985, when Chapman was sent down and Backman was given the full-time job for the rest of the season. It was the last time in his career Backman would start regularly against southpaws. He hit only .122 against them that season, which in fact is in the vicinity of his lifetime average against left-handers.

So it was back to platooning in '86, this time with Tim Teufel. When Backman *was* in the lineup he formed, along with newly installed leadoff man Lenny Dykstra, the most feared one-two combination in the league. The two were masters of the dirty uniform, the headfirst slide. They figured out ways to score runs. Backman hit .320 to lead the Mets in batting. In the playoffs against the Astros that fall Backman was in the middle of everything. In the ninth inning of Game Three, with the Mets down 5-4, he led off with a drag bunt, avoiding a sweeping tag by Glenn Davis with a slide that may or may not have been wider of the baseline than the rules allow. Two batters later, Dykstra hit a game-winning homer. In the dramatic Game Six, which went sixteen innings, Backman scored what proved to be the winning run in the top of the sixteenth. He continued to play well through the World Series, so well in fact that during the series Brent Musburger, probably not knowing or caring what the facts were, ripped Dave Johnson for not playing Backman against left-handers.

Backman was described by Mike Lupica in *Wait Till Next Year* as "a baseball citizen from some bygone, dirty uniform era, incapable of ducking a reporter's question, of giving a dishonest answer." In the spring of 1987, Backman was asked what it would take for the Mets *not* to repeat their World Championship. "Fifteen or twenty fucking car wrecks," was the reply. Actually, all it took was Dwight Gooden's drug problem, Bob Ojeda's elbow injury and the St. Louis Cardinals. Backman's .250 batting average didn't help.

Backman rebounded to hit three hundred again in 1988 before moving to Minnesota for a one-year stint. In 1990 he served as a platoon third baseman with the Pirates, where he again posted a .377 on base percentage for a championship team. He played for the Phillies in 1991, where he did not have a good season, and opens 1992 with his career in doubt.

(—R.N.

Sources for this article include *The Sporting News* articles of 8/6/84 and 9/2/85, *The Sporting News Official 1987 Baseball Guide*, and a *New York Times* article of 10/11/86.)

Eddie Bacon, pitcher who made his only major league appearance at the age of 32.

On August 13, 1917, Bacon relieved for the Athletics and gave up four earned runs in six innings. His height and weight remain unknown.

Mike Bacsik, right-handed relief pitcher who received trials with the Rangers and Brewers in the late seventies.

Bacsik saw the most action with Milwaukee in 1979, getting into 31 games and winning four of them. Ranger pitching coach Sid Hudson said of Bacsik that he was "one of those kids who didn't quite have enough to make it."

Fred Baczewski, who won eleven games in just over half a season for the 1953 Cincinnati Redlegs.

Baczewski (pronounced Bah-JESS-kee; contemporary sportswriters called him Pollock) was discovered by Bonneau Peters, president of the Shreveport team in the Texas League. Peters saw the pitcher-outfielder hit two home runs in a game for the Barksdale Field, Louisiana, Army team, signed him and optioned him to a lower league. In 1947 he began his professional career with Alexandria (Evangeline League), and went 16-10 with 242 strikeouts in 240 innings. He also led the league with 139 walks, and spent the next five years battling his control as well as minor league hitters of gradually ascending quality.

In 1953 Baczewski opened the season in the Chicago Cubs bullpen. Ten innings, twenty hits, and no decisions later, he and right-hander Bob Kelly were sent to Cincinnati for Bubba Church; that was on June 12. By the end of the season, Baczewski had won eleven games and lost only four, one of the wins being an eleven-hit shutout of Pittsburgh.

Rogers Hornsby managed the Redlegs that season, and Baczewski gave the Rajah much of the credit for his success.

> I became a pitcher when I learned to throw the ball over the plate and forgot about worrying whether the batter was going to knock the ball out of the park.
>
> Hornsby told me he would never blame me if I were knocked out of the box, but he would if I walked myself out of the game. I followed his philosophy and it worked.

After that season, the trade involving Baczewski was hailed as yet another of Gabe Paul's brilliant deals. Baczewski went on to win only six more major league games.

(—R.N.

The primary source for this entry is the article "Baczewski—The Surprise Package" in the June 1954 edition of *Baseball Digest*.)

Art Bader, who played in two games for the 1904 St. Louis Browns.

Bader, a seventeen-year-old outfielder, got his only start on August 2. The opposing pitcher was Rube Waddell. Bader went oh-for-two with a walk, then had a pinch-hit at-bat a day or two later. The *St. Louis Globe-Democrat* noted that even if Bader was "as yet too young and light for major league company, [he] should eventually make good even there."

Lore (King) Bader, career minor league pitcher whose misfortune it was to get his major league trials with pitching-rich teams.

Bader, who was from Bader, Illinois, made his major league debut for John McGraw's New York Giants on September 30, 1912, and pitched a nine-hitter to beat the Phils, 4-2. Both Phillie runs were unearned, and the *Tribune* noted that Bader "was invincible in the pinches." He picked up another win in relief before season's end, but the Giants' starters already included Christy Mathewson, Rube Marquard, Jeff Tesreau, Red Ames and Hooks Wiltse. Bader headed back to the bushes.

Up with the Red Sox for a while in 1917, Bader, pitching mostly in relief, ran his career record to 4-0 over the course of six years. The next June Bader finally got a shot at joining a starting rotation when Babe Ruth was unable to pitch due to a sore wrist. Bader pitched decently in four starts, but again there were five excellent pitchers ahead of him, and he wasn't able to break through.

Bader was a coach with the Boston Braves in 1926.

(—R.N.

An additional source for this article was Bob Creamer's *Babe*)

Red Badgro, a Hall of Fame football player who played for the St. Louis Browns in 1929 and 1930.

Badgro was a standout end at USC before playing with the Yankees, Giants and Dodgers, the three New York *football* teams, from 1927 through 1936. As Jim Thorpe, Ernie Nevers, and George Halas had before him, Badgro also tried his hand at baseball, and in 1930 was a semi-regular outfielder with the St. Louis Browns. He was enshrined in the Pro Football Hall of Fame in 1981.

Ed Baecht, who was the outstanding pitcher in the Pacific Coast League in 1930.

"Big Ed" (he was six-three) was in the major leagues at the age of 18, pitching for the Phillies on April 24, 1926, three weeks before his nineteenth birthday. He appeared in 28 games for the 1926 Phillies, all but one in relief, but his ERA was over six, and after spot appearances the next two years he was sent to the Pacific Coast League.

Baecht was one of the best pitchers in the PCL in 1929 (14-7, 3.44 ERA) and in 1930 was purchased by the Los Angeles Angels, who were the property of Cubs owner William Wrigley. In 1930 he led the PCL in ERA (3.23) and wins (actually, both Baecht and Jimmy Zinn were 26-12, although no one else in the league was close to that record). Cubs first baseman Charlie Grimm remembered in his autobiography that the Cubs "had high hopes that Ed Baecht, up from our Los Angeles club, would lead us on high, but he was a bust." He continued to receive major league trials until 1937, but wound up with only five major league wins in six seasons.

Bugs Baer, long-time columnist and cartoonist for King Features Syndicate, and apparently a loose model for the Max Mercy character in Bernard Malamud's *The Natural*.

Shirley Povich told this story in *The Washington Senators:*

> The 1912 season was notable for one incident. A full complement of Washington baseball writers accompanied the Senators to Charlottesville, and one enterprising newspaper sent a cartoonist as well as its sports editor to the camp. The cartoonist was a young man then nursing the ambition to draw his way to journalistic fame—Arthur (Bugs) Baer.
>
> Young Baer found himself not only drawing daily cartoons in the training camp, but also writing the stories for his sports editor who was busily engaged on another mission—a bit of research to discover if the Virginia moonshiners could produce their famed "corn likker" as fast as he could drink it.
>
> Young Baer's boss was holding his own, too, in the big test and was no bad bet to win the decision. Faithfully Baer protected the fellow with daily stories as well as cartoons. Apparently Baer did his boss's work well. At the end of the first fortnight, the sports editor received the following congratulatory message from the managing editor in Washington: "Your stories during the first two weeks in training have been the best to appear in any Washington newspaper. You are to be commended and I have already increased your salary. But tell that damn cartoonist if his work doesn't improve, we're calling him home."

Baer went on from there to compose some of the more memorable journalistic one-liners of all time, including "Bodie was out trying to steal second. His head was full of larceny, but his feet were honest." Baer's column, "One Word Led to Another", ran for years in the New York papers, ending only when the *World-Journal-Tribune* folded in 1966.

(—R.N.)

Jose Baez, the Seattle Mariners' first second baseman. Baez went two for four in the Mariners' first game and hit a respectable .259 as a rookie (1977), but was replaced by Julio Cruz in 1978.

Jim Bagby Sr., who won thirty-one games with the Cleveland Indians in 1920.

Born in rural Georgia in 1889, Bagby began his professional career with Augusta of the South Atlantic League in 1910. He won 22 games for Hattiesburg in 1911, leading the Cotton States League, and was drafted by the Cincinnati Reds. He pitched well in five games for the Reds in 1912, but the Reds unaccountably farmed him out anyway, and he spent four years (1912–1915) in the Southern Association. It was during this second minor league stint, he recalled later, that while filling in in the outfield he broke his forearm in a collision with former (and future) major leaguer Tim Hendryx. When the bone healed he found that his curve ball was dramatically improved, and he won 20 games for New Orleans in 1914 (20-9), 19 more in 1915.

The Cleveland Indians, after a 57-95 campaign in 1915, scoured the minors for pitching help and struck paydirt with the purchase of Bagby from New Orleans and Stan Coveleski from Portland. Both immediately entered the rotation and both were workhorses. Lee Fohl, Bagby's first manager in Cleveland, once said:

> They told me when I came into the Big Leagues, that the manager with one player on his staff who could think was lucky. I must be uncommonly lucky for I have at least two such players and their names are Tris Speaker and Jim Bagby.

Ty Cobb said that Bagby was the smartest pitcher he ever faced. Bagby himself credited his success to learning the weaknesses of every hitter, outstanding control, and a penchant for constant experimentation which was a reflection of his "restless disposition". He was practicing the knuckleball as a teen, and at 21 took up the "fade-away", or screwball. In Bagby's words:

> I threw it with my full speed and noticed that it had a very satisfactory break. About that time my arm began to get sore and I discovered that this 'fade-away' was a pretty tough delivery on the old soup bone. So I eased up on the speed and experimented some more. To my satisfaction I found that when I threw it with less speed it broke even better, and when I had succeeded in toning it down to a pretty slow, it broke better still.

The fade-away became, in Bagby's mind, his most effective pitch, the one he held back for use in tight situations.

Along with his reputation, Bagby also acquired the nickname "Sarge", which was not a reference to his military career (he never served) but rather, according to James Skipper, was borrowed from a character in a Broadway play named "Sgt. Jerry Bagby".

The acquisition of Coveleski and Bagby helped turn Cleveland's fortunes around almost immediately, and by 1918 they were

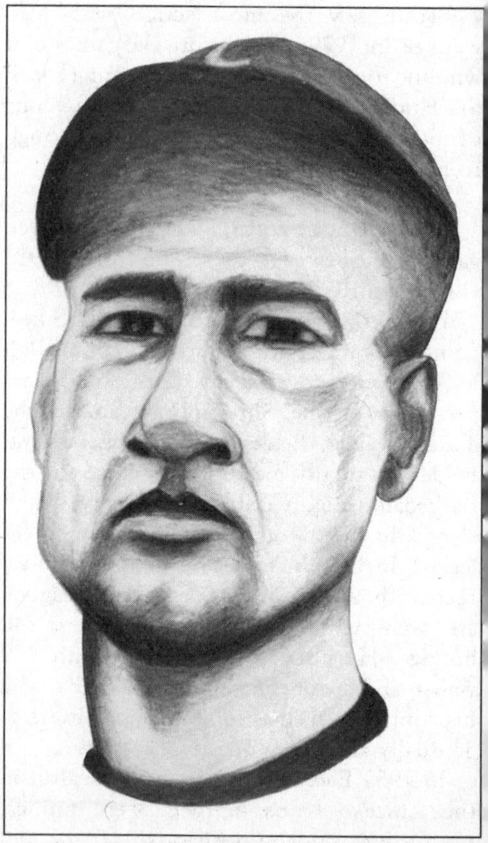

Susan McCarthy

Jim BAGBY Sr.

pennant contenders. The 1920 AL race, one of the most desperate in history (highlighted by the beaning death of Ray Chapman and the revelation of the 1919 World Series fix) saw Bagby shoulder an even heavier than usual workload. He led the league in games (48), starts (39), complete games (30), and innings pitched (340) as well as wins, 31. He also led the league in hits allowed (for the second time), perhaps fueling the widespread belief that Bagby was, besides a workhorse, a very lucky pitcher in 1920. The writer's grandfather, a Cleveland resident throughout Bagby's career, regaled his grandson with tales of Tribe offensive outbursts whenever the Sarge took the mound, and Franklin Lewis, in *The Cleveland Indians*, conceded that Bagby's loss in the second World Series game "was one of the few times that the Indians were unable to get Sarge Jim a big batch of runs." He also noted that "Batters, two and three in a row, were forever singling off Bagby, it seemed." A typical Bagby performance, apparently, was the pennant-clinching victory over Detroit—eleven hits surrendered en route to an easy 10-1 victory. Bagby himself was an excellent hitter.

After the loss in the second game of the Series, the Bagby pattern seemed to reassert itself in Game Five at Cleveland. Fortune smiled on all aspects of the Sarge's game that day. In order to increase attendance, owner Jim Dunn had shrunk the field of play by installing temporary bleachers in center and right field. When manager Tris Speaker warned Bagby before the game to pitch with extra care to the Dodger home run threats, he replied, "Ah think ah'll bust one out to those wooden seats. They seem just about right for me to hit." In the fourth inning, with two men on, Bagby was as good as his word, sending a fly to right center that barely made the bleachers for the first World Series home run ever hit by a pitcher.

The home run staked him to a 7-0 lead, but he still managed to make things interesting. The first two Dodgers singled to start the fifth before pitcher Clarence Mitchell hit a liner over second that was miraculously speared by Bill Wambsganss and converted into the famous unassisted triple play. By game's end Bagby had scattered thirteen hits but allowed only one run as the Indians took command of a Series they eventually won, five games to two.

To those who felt that Bagby had used up a lifetime's worth of luck in 1920, the rest of his career must have seemed a confirmation of their theory. In the deadball era the workload that Bagby shouldered in 1920 wouldn't have been unusual, and as a consequence of that 30-win seasons were not especially rare. But the 1920 season is the most significant dividing line in baseball history; after 1920 everything is different than before. Beginning in 1920 there was the constant danger of a home run at any moment, which made it impossible for a pitcher to coast through a certain number of easy innings, as Walter Johnson and Pete Alexander had done just a few years earlier. The workload Bagby endured in 1920 was probably unwise and probably destroyed his arm. In any case, he was never an effective pitcher again, and in October, 1923, was sold to Seattle of the Pacific Coast League. He went 16-10 for Seattle in '24, and began stumbling gradually down the option ladder. He could win as many as he lost in the minor leagues simply by not walking anybody, and he did that for the better part of a decade before concluding his career with York of the New York-Penn League in 1930.

Bagby later had a fling as a minor league umpire (1941–42) and operated a cleaning and dyeing shop in Atlanta. He helped his son, Jim Jr., get his first major league tryout, and lived to see him become a major league pitcher in his own right (see below). The Sarge died in Marietta, Georgia, in 1954.

(—M.K.
A major source for this article
is F.C. Lane's "James Bagby, a Pitcher
Who Can 'Think' " in *Baseball Magazine*,
October 1920.)

Jim Bagby Jr., the pitcher who stopped Joe DiMaggio's hitting streak on July 17, 1941.

In a 1943 *Baseball Digest* article, Frank Graham wrote:

> The conversation was repeated many times. Often enough to impress Jim Bagby, Junior, young as he was.
>
> "I don't see why you want him to grow up to be a ballplayer," his mother would say. "What has baseball ever done for you, Jim? You worked hard in the minor leagues for years, and then you were in the majors for a spell, and here you are in the minors again. After all those years, what have you got to show for it? First I want our boy to have a good education, and then a job in some reliable business."
>
> The talk would die down, and then, when his mother had left the room, his father would say, "Ready, Jim?" And Jim would nod eagerly and the two would go out behind the little house in Atlanta and play ball.

The younger Bagby may have been especially inclined toward a baseball career because of a harelip, which affected his speech as well as appearance. Did people thus afflicted fifty years ago have much of a chance at "a job in a reliable business"? At age twelve, it appeared he might find out because his pitching arm went dead. Bagby virtually grew up around the Atlanta ballpark, where his father had pitched when he was small, but for three years he didn't play baseball. At fifteen he made a comeback, pitching successfully in American Legion ball, and later at the semi-pro level in Montgomery.

In the spring of 1935 Bagby Sr. arranged a trial for his eighteen-year-old son with the Cincinnati Reds. His mother had mellowed by this time, and was there to see him off at the train station. He was back in Atlanta in three weeks, having made no impression on manager Charlie Dressen or anyone else. His professional career might have ended there, but the father, probably remembering his failed trial with the Reds twenty years before, refused to let the matter rest. When the Boston Red Sox stopped in Atlanta later that spring, he buttonholed player-manager Joe Cronin, who instead of watching Bagby Jr. pitch, stood in against him at the plate. The result of this unconventional trial was a telegram from Cronin to General Manager Eddie Collins urging that young Bagby be signed.

Bagby won 21 games in the NYP League in 1937, and joined the Red Sox in 1938.

He pitched the season opener for the Sox, beating the world champion Yankees, and went on to a rookie record of 15-11, helping the Red Sox jump from sixth place to second. He was only 21 years old. For two years after that he was ineffective, bounced back to the minor leagues and was traded to Cleveland. Neither success nor failure seemed to stifle his extrovert personality. Ted Williams, in *My Turn at Bat*, recalls Bagby warning Hank Greenberg in early '39 not to play in close against the newly arrived Splendid Splinter:

> So Bagby's yelling at him, "Well, Hank, you had better get back. You don't know this guy, you . . . better . . . get . . . back." Greenberg wasn't paying any attention. Bagby yelled at him four or five times and Greenberg paid absolutely no attention. Finally, and I can still hear Bagby loud and clear, "All right, Hank, if you want to look like me and talk like me, stand right where you are!"

Bagby was traded to Cleveland on December 12, 1940, a six-player deal in which the key figures were Bagby and Joe Dobson, who would be a rotation starter, and a consistent winner, until 1952.

In 1941 Joe DiMaggio hit in 56 straight games. He faced Bagby (as a starter) once during the streak, in the middle game, the 28th game. He hit a home run in that game. On July 17 the starting pitcher for the Indians was Al Smith, a left-hander. There were 67,468 people in the stands, watching DiMaggio try to hit in his 57th consecutive game. In three trips to the plate DiMaggio walked once and hit two screaming drives to third base, both turned into outs by third baseman Ken Keltner. When DiMaggio came to bat in the eighth the Yankees had runners on first and second, one out, a 4-1 lead. Cleveland manager Roger Peckinpaugh took Smith out, and brought in Bagby to pitch to DiMaggio.

> DiMaggio took the first pitch. Ball one.
>
> He took the second pitch, called a strike. One and one.
>
> The third pitch was outside, two and one.
>
> On the fourth pitch DiMaggio ripped a hard ground ball toward center field. Boudreau jumped in front of it. The ball took a bad hop, but Boudreau covered it and flipped to second.
>
> Second baseman Ray Mack relayed it to first for a double play.
>
> The streak was over.

Bagby finished 9-15 in 1941, a kid pitcher with some ability but no real idea what he was doing. After the season the Indians hired Lou Boudreau, a year younger than Bagby, to be their manager. Boudreau had an idea about how to handle Bagby, and he worked at the task. As he wrote in his autobiography, *Player-Manager:*

> He (Bagby) was my first, and my most persistent, disciplinary problem. Jim had his own ideas about training and he was reluctant to change them for mine. It was inevitable that we should cross swords frequently. He was the subject of the first fine I levied as manager of the Indians. I thought he was out of condition and I ordered him to take specific corrective measures and he refused. I had no choice but to fine him $100 for disobedience. We were destined to work at cross-purposes throughout our relationship.

Boudreau also told a story about discovering that Bagby's roommate, anonymous, was out on the town late at night. He called the room, and Bagby answered. Is (John Smith) there? asked Boudreau. Yup, said Bagby, sleeping right here.

Wake him up, said Boudreau. I want to talk to him.

Uh, don't think we should do that, boss.

Wake him up, Jim.

Bagby put down the phone, waited a few minutes, and gamely tried to pretend to be his roommate. Unfortunately he had a serious speech impediment, so this was quite impossible, but ballplayer roommate ethics required that he make the effort:

> "You're all set for the night?" I asked.
>
> "Yup. Sure am. Everything's okay, Lou." It was so obviously Bagby that I really had to restrain myself. I wanted to laugh out loud.
>
> "Good," I said, firmly. "I'm coming right up to see you."
>
> With that, I hung up and went straight up to the room. I just barely knocked on the door when it opened wide and Jim Bagby stood there, looking at me with his usual distaste.
>
> "Aw," he said, angrily. "You knew he wasn't here all the time."
>
> So far as I know, there was only one time when Jim said anything complimentary about me. "That no good so-and-so," he told a reporter, "is the best goddamned shortstop who ever lived."

The short-leash approach worked with Bagby, who won 17 games in 1942 and again in 1943, leading the American League in games started both seasons. In 1943 he beat one team (the Tigers) three times by a score of one to nothing, tying a major league record previously held by Walter Johnson.

Bagby Jr's. career pattern is similar to his father's. Like his father he lived by his control, and like his father he became a workhorse in his peak years, leading the American League with 273 innings pitched in 1943. As had happened to his dad, he lost it suddenly the next year, 1944.

Bagby joined the Merchant Marine in mid-season, 1944. After a losing record in '45 Boudreau traded him back to Boston, where he did creditable work as a swingman for the '46 pennant winners, and made his only World Series appearance in mop-up relief.

The '47 season found him toiling for the Pittsburgh Pirates, and in the company of his old American League adversary Hank Greenberg. In his autobiography, Greenberg described Bagby as

> the worst dumb son of a bitch . . . When he played for the Boston Red Sox . . . I hit him very well, and he was a clown then. But when he came over to Pittsburgh, I guess things were tough on him. The whole team was inferior and Jim had difficulty holding his own on the mound. I wasn't much help to him, because by this time I was an inadequate first baseman.

One afternoon, with Bagby on the mound, Greenberg bobbled an easy ground ball. "Hey, you big Jew son of a bitch," said Bagby thoughtfully. "You make enough money to catch that kind of ball." Greenberg informed Bagby that when the game was over he intended to kill him.

Bagby, removed from the contest and waiting in the clubhouse, proved a little smarter than Greenberg had figured. He changed to tennis shoes and was waiting in the men's room when the game ended. The men's room had a slick new tile floor, and when the still furious Greenberg charged him without removing his spikes his feet flew out from under him, making him an easy target for the much lighter Bagby, who promptly blackened his eye. Almost forty years later Greenberg ruefully conceded, "I guess I lost that one."

Unfortunately for Bagby, ineffective mound work combined with dishing out a shiner to a Hall of Famer proved not to be a recipe for an extended major league career. He returned to the minors in '48, posting a 16-9 record with Indianapolis (almost exactly the same record his father had posted in *his* first year back in the minors, 1924). Again like his father, he hung on for several years, retiring in 1952. Like his father, he died in Marietta, Georgia, in his early sixties.

(—M.K.)

Bill Bagwell, a lifetime .360 hitter in the minor leagues.

Bagwell, who was born and died in Choudrant, Louisiana, was a left-handed hitting outfielder who won three batting titles, hitting .357 in the Southwest League (1921), .402 in the same league (1922) and .391 in the Pacific Coast League (1926). He also hit:

- .453 in the Eastern League, in 49 games,
- .367 in the Texas League, with 27 homers and 111 RBI, and
- .353 in the American Association (1929).

He had two major league trials, and wasn't exactly a disaster, hitting .290 and .300. In fact, his major league batting average, not counting pinch hitting attempts, was .363 (29 for 80), but he had almost as many at bats as a pinch hitter as he did in the lineup, and as we all know now, pinch hitting drags your average down.

In any case, he didn't stick in the majors. His professional career is detailed in the SABR publication, *Minor League Baseball Stars.*

—R.N.

Jeff Bagwell, National League Rookie of the Year in 1991.

A native New Englander and third baseman by trade, Bagwell was drafted out of the University of Hartford by the Boston Red Sox in the fourth round of the 1989 June draft. He was the Eastern League MVP in 1990, but was traded to the Astros on August 30 of that year, made the Astros in spring training and went on to become the Rookie of the Year.

Stan Bahnsen, the American League Rookie of the Year in 1968.

Bahnsen, who was born in Iowa and attended the University of Nebraska, was the fourth-round draft pick of the Yankees in the first amateur draft in June, 1965. He received a $30,000 bonus and was assigned to the Southern League, where he pitched well in 1965. He threw a no-hitter with Toledo in 1966, and a perfect game with Syracuse in 1967, each lasting seven innings.

Joining the Yankees in 1968, Bahnsen won 17 games as a rookie with a 2.06 ERA, giving him 85% of the vote in the Rookie of the Year balloting. The Yankee empire had collapsed in 1965 after dominating the American League for as long as almost anyone living could remember, so in 1968 there was still a vital suspicion that they would be back on top soon. The '68 Yankees finished over .500 for the first time since 1964, and Bahnsen was looked to as the Whitey Ford of the seventies, the pitcher who would lead the Yankees back to the top.

Baseball in the 1960s was dominated by pitching, to such an extent that the game became a little boring. It was a tough decade for the game, attendance stagnant, profits down. After the 1968 season the decision was made to put more offense in the game. One of the things that was done to this end was to lower the pitching mound. This helped hitters in general and hurt pitchers in general, but in specific it was devastating to Bahnsen.

"In my rookie year," Bahnsen told Jim Ogle of *The Sporting News* in 1971, "I had a good fast ball that would rise, plus a big curve and the combination made me fortunate enough to win Rookie of the Year honors . . . Not only did the lower mound take something off my fast ball, but my curve started to hang." Bahnsen dropped to 9-16 in 1969, then began to experiment with ways to get his effectiveness back. He began to spin the curve ball off his forefinger and the slider off his index finger, rather than the opposite, which is the normal pattern. He switched his delivery from straight overhand to three-quarters. He developed a changeup, giving him four pitches.

He wasn't Whitey Ford, but Bahnsen pitched well through 1970 (14-11) and 1971 (14-12). He was a very quiet man, almost dour in appearance. Reporters sometimes thought he seemed lethargic, but he was also a practical joker. When Mike Kekich purchased a water bed in Minnesota—water beds were rather outreé at that time—Bahnsen and Fritz Peterson swiped the thing from his hotel room in Milwaukee, took it to the ballpark and draped it from the top of the scoreboard. He bought an over-sized padlock and padlocked things together in inconvenient ways. Mel Stottlemyre, picking up his bags to depart the hotel room, found them padlocked to the TV set.

At the winter meetings in 1971 Bahnsen was traded to the White Sox, a trade that General Manager Lee MacPhail would describe in his autobiography as the worst of his long career. Chuck Tanner was trying to dance an overmatched White Sox team to a division title by being nice to Dick Allen (see *Dick Allen*, 1990 Baseball Book) and pumping as many innings as possible out of his three or four decent pitchers. Bahnsen was the number two man on the staff, behind Wilbur Wood. The 1972 season was delayed by a strike, cutting the White Sox schedule to 154 games, but despite the missing games Wood started 49 times in 1972, going 24-17, and Bahnsen started 41 times (and relieved twice), going 21-16. The 49 starts by Wood and the 90 starts by Wood and Bahnsen combined were the highest totals in the major leagues in many years, while a third starter, Tom Bradley, started 40 times and went 15-14. The three pitchers accounted for 84% of the White Sox' starts.

Bahnsen with the White Sox often didn't look good, but survived by pitching out of jams. Richard Lindberg in *Who's On 3rd* referred to him as "Stanley Struggle". On June 21, 1973, he pitched a 12-hit shutout against the Oakland A's. On August 21, 1973, just after his father had died, Bahnsen pitched no-hit ball for eight and two-thirds, losing the no-hitter when Walt Williams bounced a single over Bill Melton at third. Melton was playing in, inexplicably protecting against the bunt although there were two out.

Bahnsen pitched even more in 1973 than he had in 1972 (42 starts, 282 innings, won-lost record of 18-21), and although his ERA remained almost the same there was a sudden, drastic deterioration in his strikeout to walk ratio, from 157-73 in 1972 to 120-117 in 1973. Bahnsen was strictly hanging on from then on. In 1974 he was 12-15 with a 4.71 ERA. At the trading deadline in 1975 (June 15) Bahnsen was traded to the Oakland A's, who were trying to patch a starting rotation punctured by the loss of Catfish Hunter, the first free agent, and the ineffectiveness of Blue Moon Odom. Bahnsen pitched .500 ball as a sixth man for Oakland for two years, but stepped on a sprinkler while running in the outfield in spring training, 1976, and the injury took what was left of his fastball. He was traded to Montreal, where he fell from the rotation but pitched well as a middle reliever from 1978 to 1980, extending his career to 1982. Altogether he won 146 games, losing 149.

Ed Bahr, a Saskatchewan native who pitched for the Pittsburgh Pirates in 1946 and '47.

Bahr was signed by Joe Devine, a scout for the Yankees, in 1939. Optioned to the West Texas/New Mexico League, he walked 154 men in 191 innings in '39, giving him a 6.36 ERA, but still managed a 14-9 won-lost record. He dropped out of baseball for three years (1942–44) for service in the Canadian military, returned to Kansas City in 1945, where he was a teammate of Loren Babe, and pitched himself into a major league job. He pitched well in 1946 (2.63 ERA), then lost it in 1947 and returned to the minors, where he was a teammate of Jim Bagby's in 1948. He was never able to pitch himself back into the majors.

Frank Bahret, who played two games in the outfield for the Boston Monumentals of the Union Association.

The only scrap of biographical information we have on Bahret is that he is believed to have been born in Baltimore. His date of birth, date of death, height, weight, which hand he threw with, and how he batted are all unknown.

Grover Baichley, who pitched in four games for the 1914 St. Louis Browns.

Scott Bailes, contemporary pitcher.

Bailes, pitching in the Pittsburgh system, was selected by the Cleveland Indians when they were owed a player as part of a minor trade. He has always been regarded as having fairly good stuff—a hard slider and a sinking fastball—but has never been successful due to a lack of confidence and consequent inconsistency.

Bill Bailey, an outfielder whose major league experience consisted of nine at bats with the 1911 New York Highlanders.

Bill Bailey, who went 3-18 with the St. Louis Browns in 1910 but won 242 minor league games.

Bailey, a raw left-hander from Fort Smith, Arkansas, joined the Browns as an 18-year-old in 1907 and pitched impressively, going 4-1 with a 2.42 ERA. After a start against Washington the *St. Louis Post-Dispatch* noted that "Bill Bailey is a very deliberate young man. He is not in any hurry about delivering the ball to the plate and acts as though he might make a good pitcher, though he still lacks considerable experience." The Browns were flowing toward the bottom of the American League, where they would be for most of the next forty years, and Bailey was unable to swim against the tide, posting losing records in 1908 and 1909, followed by the 3-18 season in 1910.

Bailey was optioned to Montgomery in 1911, beginning a long minor league career in which he would go 17-6 (Montgomery 1911), 24-21 (Beaumont, Texas League, 1919) and 23-15 (Omaha, Western League, 1924). He had occasional looks by major league teams throughout his career, and added two years of quasi-major league service by pitching in the Federal League in 1914–1915, giving him a major league record of 37–76.

According to Robert Creamer's *Babe*, Bailey's move to the Federal League had an indirect impact on the career of Babe Ruth. In July, 1914, Bailey was in the midst of another fine year for Providence when he jumped the team in favor of Baltimore's Federal League entry. This, along with the sale of star pitcher Red Oldham, had Providence fans up in arms. The Providence team was owned by Joe Lannin, who also owned the Red Sox.

As Robert Creamer writes in *Babe*, "To placate the Providence fans, Lannin announced on August 1 that he would send a lefthanded pitcher down from the Red Sox to take Oldham's place. Ruth was the pitcher chosen." Several other major league teams filed waiver claims for Ruth, and Lannin and American League President Ban Johnson had to write letters clearing the way for Ruth to return to Providence, where he pitched a few games in late 1914.

Meanwhile, in 1915 Bailey lost twenty games for the Baltimore Federals and the ChiFeds. After a brief, unsuccessful stint with the Detroit Tigers in 1918, Bailey returned to St. Louis in 1921, this time with the Cardinals for a couple short terms.

In between all these stops on the major league circuit, Bailey was a minor league workhorse. In sixteen full or partial seasons in the bushes, Bailey won 242 games and lost 219. In 1925, his last professional season, the 36-year-old Bailey threw 307 innings for Omaha. In 1926 he was out of baseball for the first time in twenty years, and he died in November, 1926.

(—R.N.
Bailey's career records are included
in the SABR publication,
Minor League Baseball Stars.)

Bob Bailey, National League third baseman of the sixties and seventies.

Bailey, son of former minor league infielder Buck Bailey, was signed by the Pittsburgh Pirates in 1961 for what was then perhaps the largest bonus ever paid, reported between $135,000 and $175,000. He was the golden boy, a big, strong and handsome kid from Southern California with some obvious skills, and the scouts went wild over him. Everybody wanted him; the Pirates won. He made his professional debut with Asheville of the South Atlantic League, a tough place for an eighteen-year-old shortstop to start a career. Willie Stargell was the leftfielder for that team, and reflected in his autobiography on Bailey's season:

> As my teammates and I watched Bailey play, we wondered why he was given $150,000 while most of us received one seventy-fifth that amount. We never resented Bob as a person. He was a nice guy. But he hit only .220 at Asheville, which did make us resent the money he made, the publicity he received and the doors that opened so easily for him.

Susan McCarthy

Bob BAILEY

> What disturbed me most about Bob was his fielding . . . He didn't have much range, he had little speed and his arm was no better than average at best . . .

Despite Bailey's struggles at Asheville, the Pirates promoted him to Columbus, AAA, for the 1962 season. Still only nineteen years old, Bailey put together a brilliant year at the plate, hitting .299 with 28 homers, 108 RBI. Shifted to third base in mid-season, he led the league in errors, but *The Sporting News* named him the Minor League Player of the Year, and he was called to Pittsburgh for the last weeks of the season.

Don Hoak had been the Pittsburgh third baseman since 1959, one of the best in the league. While Bailey was tearing up the International League, Hoak hit .241 with 5 homers. Hoak was traded to Philadelphia in November, and Bailey opened 1963 as the Pirates' regular third baseman.

He would have the job for four years. After hitting .228 as a rookie (1963) he jumped to .281 in 1964, but his power was slow to arrive and his defense never ceased to be a problem. Sometimes he would play the outfield. Years later, Bailey liked to relate a conversation he once had with Pirate coach (and later manager) Harry Walker. Walker told Bailey that he was the worst third baseman in the league.

"No, I'm not," protested Bailey.

"Name a worse one," countered Walker.

Bailey thought about it for a long time. "I guess you're right," he told Walker.

In 1966 Bailey, still only 23, hit .279 with 13 homers despite missing some time with an injury, his best year yet with the bat. There was still a perception that he was destined to be a good hitter, and the Pirates decided to cash in that perception. Maury Wills was having conflicts with the Dodger management, and the Dodgers had decided to move him. On December 1, 1966, Bailey came home to LA.

He was a huge disappointment in Dodger Stadium.

In two years in blue Bailey batted 322 times each season and had 73 hits each year, a .227 average. The Dodgers, a powerhouse for 25 years, finished under .500 both seasons, and no one took more heat for that than Bob Bailey, who was as popular in LA as a drunken tanker captain. His perceived value dropped to zero. No longer young, he was now a veteran—slow, a poor fielder *and* he didn't hit.

The National League was ready to expand. On October 21, 1968, the new Montreal Expos purchased Bailey's contract from the Dodgers for an undisclosed sum, probably not in excess of five dollars.

Bailey broke an ankle during his first season in Montreal, but hit better. With Coco Laboy having a good year at third base Bailey played first. As mentioned in the article about Stan Bahnsen, after the 1968 season major league baseball made an effort to help the hitters. In addition, the Expos' first stadium, Jarry Park, was a converted minor league stadium, and a good place to hit. Things came together for him in 1970, and Bailey's career came back to life: he hit .287 with 28 homers in 352 at bats. It made a devastating APBA card—a slugging percentage near .600, an on base percentage over .400.

He didn't have a defensive position, and they used to call him "Beetle", because he fielded like a comic strip character. Gene Mauch was his manager. Mauch used to say, "Bailey means wood. Bailey doesn't mean leather."

He was the Expos' third baseman for four years after that, having consistently solid seasons. In 1973 he hit .273 with 26 homers, 86 RBI, the best of the four. In the spring of 1975 Bailey was hit by a pitch, and broke a bone in his hand. He was 32. The Expos had a new third baseman, Larry Parrish; within a couple of years they would have a new manager and a new ballpark. Bailey, by now the last original Expo, had no chance to get his job back.

He demanded a trade, and of course this was granted, although he had no more chance for playing time anywhere else. He hung on until 1978 as a pinch hitter for the Reds and Red Sox. In 1976 he was on the World Series roster for the Reds, but didn't play. The last game of his career was a forgettable appearance in an unforgettable game, the Yankees/Red Sox playoff on October 2,

1978. Bucky Dent hit a three-run homer to join Enos Slaughter, Lou Brock and Sparky Lyle in the pantheon of Red Sox tormentors. Bob Bailey pinch hit against Goose Gossage in the seventh inning, and took three called strikes. It wasn't the way he would have wanted his career to end, but there aren't too many guys who go out like Ted Williams. Bailey had been the most heralded prospect of his generation, and the biggest bust. He had played almost two thousand games in his career, and salvaged his respect.

(—R.N.
In addition to *Stargell*,
sources for this entry include
Dan Turner's *The Expos Inside Out*,
Peter Gammons' *Be6yond the Sixth Game*,
and *The Sporting News* articles of
April 23, 1965, and September 13, 1975.)

Ed Bailey, All-Star catcher for the Cincinnati Reds in the late 1950's.

Bailey, whose real first name was "Lonas", was born and raised in Strawberry Plains, Tennessee, a tiny town twelve miles from Knoxville. He made his mark early as a ballplayer, skipping his last two years of American Legion eligibility to play in three semi-pro leagues. In high school he earned all-state honors in baseball and basketball (the school was too small to offer football), and was ready to sign a professional contract upon graduation, but his parents, who ran a grocery store, insisted that he go to college. Bailey accepted a scholarship to the University of Tennessee for the fall of 1948. According to Bob Pille, in an article for the *Baseball Digest* in August, 1956, Bailey "chafed through five quarters at Tennessee" before his parents relented and allowed him to sign with the Reds. He was signed by Paul Florence for $13,000.

In his first year of professional ball he hit .313 with 87 RBI for Ogden of the Pioneer League, Class C. The Korean War began, so the spring of 1951 found Bailey at Fort Jackson, South Carolina, as a physical training instructor and special services operative. It was at Fort Jackson that he began to earn a reputation for insufficient seriousness. He joined the post football team as a linebacker, his career ending after only one game when a Reds representative ". . . told me they would appreciate it if I could see my way clear to retire," Bailey recalled.

Bailey spent two years in the Army, returning to spring training with the Reds in 1953. In his first appearance against major league pitching Bailey went five for five with two homers. Birdie Tebbetts, who would manage Bailey with the Reds from 1954 through 1958, told Pille it "could have been the worst thing that ever happened to him." Farmed to Tulsa of the Texas League for '53, he swung for the fences and produced 21 homers but an average of only .243.

Nevertheless, in 1954 the Reds kept him as a reserve catcher, behind veterans Andy Seminick and Hobie Landrith. He had 271 games of minor league experience. Neither Seminick nor Landrith hit, but Bailey, hitting .197, was unable to fill the void. "That was a wasted year," he remembered. "After a couple times around the league a guy can tell whether he's ready . . . and I knew I wasn't." He thought of requesting demotion, but "nobody wants to ask to leave the majors . . . you may get hurt, get forgotten, and never get back." In early 1955, with his average at .176, the Reds traded for Smoky Burgess, and sent Bailey to San Diego of the Pacific Coast League.

"They did me a favor," Bailey said later, and although it never showed up in any box score, he did them one during spring training, 1955. According to Jules Tygiel in *Baseball's Great Experiment*, one afternoon in Tampa:

> ". . . after being removed from a game, [pitcher Brooks Lawrence] and catcher Ed Bailey entered the stands to watch the remainder of the contest. A rope separated the black and white sections and while Bailey sat on the white side, Lawrence sat next to him on the black. "Boy, this is stupid," exclaimed Bailey, a Tennessean. "I'm gonna change this." The catcher removed the rope and, according to Lawrence, no one ever reattached it."

A million small victories over an ancient enemy, and then the rules changed and we haven't been able to figure out how to get the momentum back. Anyway, Bailey's batting average rebounded at San Diego, with the aid of some adjustments suggested by Tebbetts, and in the Venezuelan League that winter he was a dominant offensive player. When he reported to the Reds in 1956, Tebbetts noted later in his best Stengelese, "He was more serious, where in the past he had the tendency to be not serious enough when it hurt him."

Burgess hit .306 with 20 homers after joining the Reds in 1955, giving him a firm grip on the catching job. Bailey and Burgess were both left-handed hitting catchers. "I wouldn't have given you fifteen cents for my chances then," Bailey said later. The Reds stumbled out of the gate in '56. Bailey had three straight hits as a pinch hitter, and he had an edge over Burgess, in that he could throw and Burgess couldn't. When Tebbetts decided to shake up the line-up, Bailey began to play. This time he made the most of the opportunity, posting what were to be the best offensive numbers of his career, a .300 batting average with 28 homers in 383 at bats.

Bailey made the All-Star team. The Reds hadn't played .500 ball in ten years, but with Bailey and Frank Robinson, hitting 38 homers as a rookie, the 1956 Reds won 91 games, missing the National League pennant by just two. Tebbetts predicted greatness for him.

It didn't happen. Bailey was never able to match his 1956 offense, and the Reds were not able to contend from 1957 through 1960. Bailey was a solid and consistent player, hitting .250 to .264 every season and keeping his home runs between 11 and 20. He earned a reputation for defensive excellence. The *Historical Abstract* says he "blocked the plate as if a landmine was buried under it," and he made the All-Star team again in 1957 and 1960.

He'd become serious enough to suit Birdie Tebbetts, but his teammates were in no danger of mistaking him for Mr. Solemnity. Teammate and author Jim Brosnan was only half-kidding when he wrote that Bailey's nickname "Gar" was unquestionably short for "garrulous", and Frank Robinson, after pleading guilty to carrying a concealed weapon, had no doubt who was responsible when he discovered a water pistol in his locker shortly thereafter. In 1959, when Jim Bailey had a brief pitching trial with the Reds, the Baileys joined the select group of major league brother batteries.

In early 1961 the Reds traded Bailey to the Giants for Don Blasingame, Sherman Jones and Bob Schmidt. It was the oddest trade: the Reds, on their way to an unexpected pennant, actually weakened themselves behind the plate (the catcher obtained, Bob Schmidt, was hopeless) and Don Blasingame, expected to fill the second base hole for the Reds, had the worst year of his career. The Giants, expecting to contend, thought they had obtained a cannon arm to be the last piece of the puzzle, but found instead that, in the words of Charles Einstein: "There were times, as the season unfolded, when Bailey could not throw my mother out stealing." The Giants had his arm examined, but X-rays came back negative, and as the season wore on Bailey began to share playing time with Johnny Orsino and Hobie Landrith.

Bailey was never again a regular, but he staged a terrific comeback as a half-time player. In the spring of 1962 the Giants came up with another left-handed hitting catcher, Tom Haller. Haller and Bailey shared the position; between them they hit 35 home runs in 526 at bats (18 for Haller, 17 for Bailey). On the last day of the season Bailey hit a solo home run to help the Giants defeat Houston 2-1, forcing a three-game playoff with the Dodgers.

This was the year that Dodger shortstop Maury Wills ran wild on the basepaths, stealing a record 104 stolen bases. In the first playoff game, caught by Bailey, Wills made his job easy by going 0 for 4 as the Giants won. Haller caught the second game—won by the Dodgers as Wills scored on a sacrifice fly in the bottom of the ninth—but injured himself in the process, mandating that Bailey start the third and deciding game. In the seventh inning it appeared his arm would earn him goat horns as his wild throw to third on a Wills steal (his third theft of the game) enabled Wills to score an insurance run that gave the Dodgers the seemingly safe 4-2 lead they proceeded to fritter away so memorably, so agonizingly, in the ninth.

In the subsequent World Series Bailey managed only one hit in fourteen at-bats, a two-run pinch home run with two out in the ninth inning of the third game. Unfortunately the Giants were down three at the time, and the game ended with the next batter.

In 1963 the Bailey/Haller combination again hit 35 home runs, Bailey hitting 21 of those and making the All-Star team for the fourth and final time. On June 15, 1963, he caught Juan Marichal's no-hitter. One more strike was needed to seal the gem, and according to Marichal:

> Bailey came out to the mound again.
> "I think another screwball," he said. "What do you think?"
> "I think a fastball," I said. "What do you think?"
> "I think a fastball too," he said . . .

Bailey was traded to Milwaukee after the 1963 season. At first glance the trade is puzzling: several players of varying quality were exchanged, but each team included a veteran catcher, Bailey for Del Crandall. Crandall was essentially the same type and quality of catcher as Bailey, about the same age and a player who had made the All-Star team five times, most recently 1962. Why bother to trade them?

Each team gained a platoon edge. Each team had an outstanding young catcher, Haller in San Francisco and Joe Torre in Milwaukee, but San Francisco had two left-handed hitting catchers and Milwaukee had two right-handed hitting catchers. By exchanging Crandall and Bailey each team created the option of platooning.

Bailey had a respectable 1964 season in Milwaukee, but Joe Torre emerged as a star that year, and Bailey entered the nomadic phase of his career. He split the 1965 season between the Giants and Cubs, and after five pinch-hit appearances with the 1966 Angels his career was finished. Lee Allen reported in a 1968 *Sporting News* column that Bailey had found an interesting post-baseball occupation back in Knoxville:

> "What are you doing now?" was the obvious question to Bailey.
> "I'm a field representative for Congressman John Duncan."
> "What does a congressman's field representative do?"
> "Just takes care of the district—eight counties—when the Congressman is in Washington, that's all."
> "Don't you miss talking to the hitters? Earl Lawson always said you enjoyed talking to the hitters."
> "I'm talking to constituents," he replied.

It must be pleasant work. Presumably constituents don't have to be knocked down.

(—M.K.)

Fred Bailey, sometime outfielder for the Boston Braves in the late teens. Nicknamed "Penny", Bailey saw real action in just one season, 1917, when he got into fifty games but failed to hit two hundred.

Gene Bailey, semi-regular outfielder with the 1923 Brooklyn Dodgers.

The Red Sox tried Bailey in 46 games in 1920, but he hit just .230 and was back in the minors the next year. In 1922, by then 28 years old, he was the fourth best hitter on a bad Houston club in the Texas League.

Bailey must have been living right. When Wilbert Robinson decided he needed a veteran outfielder who couldn't hit (how else to explain it?), Bailey got the call, and broke camp in 1923 as the Dodgers' fourth outfielder. And when Zack Wheat injured an ankle on July 8, Bailey stepped into the lineup and spent the rest of the season playing left and center fields. He still didn't hit much, .265 with lousy peripheral stats, and after eighteen games in 1924 he was out of the league.

Bailey remained in professional baseball, and in 1930 managed Dizzy Dean for part of the season in St. Joseph, Missouri.

(—R.N.)

Harvey Bailey, who started eleven games for the National League Boston Beaneaters in 1899, and won six of them.

Howard Bailey, who won five games for the 1983 Tigers.

An undrafted free agent, Bailey went through the Tigers' farm system in two years, and vaulted from a spring training invitation in 1981 to a spot in the Tigers' starting rotation. He didn't get anyone out once the schedule started, and spent the better part of the year in Evansville, where he didn't fare much better.

In 1983 Bailey saw significant action as a long reliever. On April 20, 1983, George Brett was hitting .475 and had hit two homers and a single in the game when he came up in the ninth inning at Tiger Stadium, Tigers leading 7-6 with a man on first base. Although Sparky had been quoted as saying that he would never let George Brett beat him again, he was unwilling to put the winning run on base with an intentional walk, so he replaced Aurelio Lopez with Howard Bailey, giving him the platoon edge, and told Bailey to pitch to Brett. Brett hit his third home run of the game (5 3 4 7), giving Kansas City an 8-7 lead (and win). The fans chanted "Sparky Eats Shit, Sparky Eats Shit" for the rest of the game.

Jim Bailey, Ed Bailey's younger brother, who got into three games as a pitcher with the Reds in 1959, making one of the few brother batteries in major league history.

King Bailey, who won a complete game in his only major league appearance, on September 21, 1895, for the Reds. Bailey's birth and death dates are unknown.

Mark Bailey, semi-regular catcher for the Astros in the mid-eighties.

In April of 1984, the 6′5″, switch-hitting Bailey was a recently-converted catcher with Houston's double-A farm team. Due to a strange set of circumstances, including a broken foot suffered by Alan Ashby, Bailey shortly found himself in the majors. Installed as starting catcher, Bailey seemed over his head until mid-July, when he hit three home runs in three consecutive games. Bailey ended the season hitting just .212, though he did hit nine homers.

Given another shot as the more or less regular catcher in 1985, Bailey had a pretty decent year, hitting .265 and ten home runs, drawing 67 walks. That was to be Bailey's best season by far. In 1986 shoulder problems hindered both his offense (.176 batting average) and his defense, and his playing time dwindled. The next two seasons brought more of the same, and in 1989 Bailey began a new career as a triple-A catcher.

I'll tell you a story that I was told by a member of that Astros team. I said something about Bailey having an injury. "Shee," said the Astro. "He ought to have a lawsuit. He ought to sue the Astros for mental cruelty."

This was during the Hal Lanier era in Houston. According to this player, every time Bailey struck out or popped up Gene Tenace would get in his face as soon as he got to the dugout, yelling "What'd you swing at that thing for? How many times have we told you to lay off that guy's slider?" The player said he sat behind Bailey one time on a long flight. Tenace sat on one side of Bailey and Yogi Berra on the other, and they berated him for three hours. "Look at you. Don't you have any pride? This team spent a lot of money to send you to that fat farm, and you've just let yourself go. Why don't you get a haircut? Can't you at least trim your sideburns? You're such a slob. If you'd take a little pride in your appearance, maybe it would show up in the way you played." Bailey failed to respond to this intensive psychotherapy, and was out of the majors within a few months.

(—R.N. and B.J.)

Steve Bailey, long reliever with the 1967 Cleveland Indians.

Sweetbreads Bailey, relief pitcher with the Cubs and Dodgers from 1919 through 1921.

Bailey was apparently called "Sweetbreads" because he liked to eat them. His real name was Abraham Lincoln Bailey (he was from Illinois), causing us to wonder whether he ever relieved Cubs teammate Grover Cleveland Alexander. He did; on May 23, 1919, Bailey relieved Claude Hendrix, who had relieved Old Pete.

Prior to the July 4, 1919, heavyweight championship fight between Jack Dempsey and titleholder Jess Willard, who went about six-foot-six and 250 pounds, a Chicago sportswriter asked most of the Cubs for a forecast of the fight. Bailey predicted, "Willard can stand too much punishment to be bothered. Look at what he took from [Jack] Johnson, and the black man knew more about fighting than any of them." One hopes that Bailey was a better pitcher than he was a prizefight prognosticator. Dempsey broke Willard's jaw and a few teeth on the way to knocking the giant out in three rounds.

(—R.N.)

Bob Bailor, the first player taken by the Toronto Blue Jays in their expansion draft, and likely to be a major league manager within two or three years.

Initially an infielder in the Orioles system, Bailor won the Northern League batting title in 1971, hitting .340 for Aberdeen. He was with Rochester in 1975 when the May 31 *Sporting News* reported that though "Bailor is only 5-9, 160 pounds, [he] is becoming known for his fearless roll-block takeout slides at second base." Bailor had very brief trials with the Orioles in '75 and '76, but missed most of the latter season with a shoulder injury.

Despite the injury, that November the Toronto Blue Jays made Bailor their first pick in the expansion draft. Bailor, in his own words, babied the sore shoulder through spring training, sharing the shortstop job with Jim Mason as the Blue Jays opened the season, but became the regular shortstop as soon as he was ready to go. When a rash of injuries thinned the Blue Jays' outfield, Bailor moved to left field. He hit his first major league home run off of Steve Stone in his first game in the outfield, and in five games in the outfield had six hits including four doubles and the homer. He played in left field a while, then in center. Manager Roy Hartsield told Neil MacCarl that he thought Bailor could play any position on the field (*TSN*, May 21, 1977), but moved him permanently to center field after the All-Star break. Despite shifting positions and despite missing four weeks after he strained a knee in mid-August, Bailor hit .310 in 122 games in 1977, a record batting average for a player on a first-year expansion team.

Bailor spent three more years as a more-

or-less regular in Toronto, but never again approached the three hundred mark. In 1978 he batted 621 times, his best numbers being 29 doubles and 15 outfield assists. In 1979 he switched to right field and gunned down 16 more baserunners in 118 games, but hit only .229. After a trade to the Mets in December of 1980 he became a full-fledged utility infielder, a role he would play for the remainder of his career.

Bailor went to the Dodgers in 1984, his reputation for all-out play still intact. In the May 28, 1984, *Sporting News*, columnist Bill Conlin wrote:

> People close to the Mets last season were unanimous in deciding that no one played the game harder than utility infielder Bob Bailor. The Dodgers discovered Bailor's penchant for sticking his nose in there in the late innings of an exhibition with the Orioles in Miami. Bailor dived for a ball in the hole and suffered a shoulder separation. A lot of guys dive for balls; what set Bailor apart was that the Dodgers were losing, 14-2.

Bailor went hitless in one at-bat for the Dodgers in the '85 playoffs, his only taste of post-season play. He retired after that season, and spent 1986 helping his brother Jim operate a hunting guide service in Grand Junction, Colorado.

In 1987 Bailor was hired to manage Dunedin, Toronto's entry in the Florida State League. That team finished 76-64, earning Bailor a promotion to the Blue Jays' AAA team in Syracuse. The '88 Syracuse squad went 24-46 the first half of the season, but in what may end up the pivotal period in Bailor's managerial career, nearly reversed its record in the second half to finish at 70-71. In 1989 Bailor guided the Chiefs to the International League title and was named by *The Sporting News* as the Minor League Manager of the Year.

In the December 4, 1989, *TSN*, he outlined his managerial philosophy:

> I try to approach it the same way as when I was a player. I had to work to be average. So, what really bugs me is watching a guy with all the talent and potential in the world throwing it away by not working hard . . . If you get beat, you get beat. But if after the game you can say, "If only I'd run a little harder down to first, we would've won" . . . well, that's a little harder to live with. I don't think I'm a hard manager or anything like that. I just try to keep after them.

In a survey which appeared in the August 10, 1991, *Baseball America*, Bailor was named as the best managerial prospect in the International League. Following the 1991 season, the Blue Jays brought him up to Toronto to serve as first base coach, and he would appear to be next in line to manage the club.

(—R.N.)

Loren Bain, right-handed pitcher who appeared in three games with the Giants in 1945.

Harold Baines, contemporary outfielder and designated hitter.

Harold Baines grew up in St. Michaels, Maryland, the son of a stone mason named Linwood Baines. Linwood, who is said to look exactly like his son, was an excellent baseball and basketball player himself, but unable to pursue a professional career because of the need to feed his family. He had five kids, and he had them young, and he took damn good care of them.

Bill Veeck was out of baseball at the time, and living in the Baltimore area. Harold Baines was twelve years old, and playing little league baseball. Veeck would stop by the park to watch the kids play, and he noticed Harold Baines. He watched him for years, always impressed.

By 1977, when Baines was eighteen years old, Bill Veeck owned the White Sox again. As a senior in high school Baines hit .532. The White Sox had the number one pick in the draft. They chose Harold Baines. Paul Richards, working for the White Sox, said at the time that Baines was "on his way to the Hall of Fame. He just stopped by Comiskey Park for twenty years or so." No one could know at the time that Harold Baines would outlast Comiskey Park.

Baines reported to Appleton, and worked his way through the White Sox system in three regular steps. In 1979 at Iowa (AAA) he hit .298, with 22 home runs. Because he was the number one pick in the country he was under extraordinary pressure, which was intensified by the things which were said about him at the time. He never seemed to notice. He wasn't the first player from the 1977 draft to reach the majors, nor the first to become a star. Paul Molitor, the third player taken in that draft, hit .322 for Milwaukee in 1979, before Baines had played a major league game. People began to belittle Veeck's judgment in picking a kid he had seen in the little leagues.

Baines reached the majors in 1980. He wasn't the Rookie of the Year. The criticism intensified. Harold didn't seem to notice. In 1981 he hit much better, but missed some

Susan McCarthy

Harold BAINES

time with an injury, plus a third of the season was wiped out by a strike, so his numbers didn't get to be large and impressive.

In 1982 Baines hit .271 with 25 homers, 105 RBI. He's been good ever since, his only "off season" being 1988, when he hit .277 with 81 RBI. He has never been an MVP or a top MVP candidate; merely always good. Don Zminda described him as "the Charlie Gehringer of the nineteen eighties, a seemingly mechanical man who racks up great numbers every year without changing the expression on his face."

On July 7, 1982, Baines hit three home runs in one game. The first one went to dead center field, 420 feet, the second to deep right-center. The third was a grand slam.

On May 9, 1984, Baines hit a home run off Chuck Porter of Milwaukee to end the longest game in American League history, 25 innings.

In September, 1986, Baines hurt his knee, requiring arthroscopic surgery. He had been a fine outfielder, but after that he was unable to play the field, and became a DH.

On July 29, 1989, the White Sox traded him to Texas for three players. The next time he came back to Comiskey they had a ceremony for him, and retired his White Sox uniform, No. 3. They gave him a watch and some golf clubs, a necklace for his wife, a plaque that honored him as "one of the finest men and greatest players in the history of the White Sox." The gesture was excessive and slightly inappropriate—to retire the uniform number of a man you have just traded in mid-career—but the front office needed to tell him how they felt, to signal to their fans that they hadn't traded him out of any lack of personal respect. It was just business.

The Rangers, bailing out of the trade, sent him on to Oakland in exchange for two young pitchers. Tony LaRussa was glad to have him back.

He has played in five All-Star games and a World Series.

Despite his successes, Baines seems unchanged. He still goes home to St. Michaels in the winter, playing pool with the guys he grew up with. No one dislikes him, but few people know him well. Tony LaRussa, who managed him in Chicago and again in Oakland, speaks of him almost reverently, as does his longtime teammate Carlton Fisk.

One day, when Baines is old and things have happened to him outside of baseball and what happened to him inside of baseball has settled into perspective, we may have a little understanding of what makes him tick. No one is ordinary. There is no such thing as an ordinary man, and if there was he wouldn't hit .300, and yet he *seems* ordinary. Until we know more about him, perhaps the most interesting reflection comes from Fisk.

"Harold is almost incongruous with himself," Fisk told Phil Hersh in 1985. "As a hitter, he has to have an aggressive approach to face the challenge. To have him be the person he is, not to say six words all year, that is incongruous.

"Most of the best ballplayers in this game have been eccentric to a degree, some to a fault. With the exception of a few, star players are humble about what they do and not overly concerned about their greatness. I get a feeling that inside Bainsey there is a real exciting person."

Doug Bair, contemporary relief pitcher.

Bair, born in Defiance, Ohio, reached the major leagues at the age of 27 and defied the odds by having a fifteen-year career. Bair attended Bowling Green University before entering baseball, receiving a Bachelor of Science in industrial education. A second-round draft pick of the Pirates in 1971, Bair shot to the AAA level on the strength of a 15-7 record in the Carolina League in 1972, where he struck out 186 men in 180 innings. He was a teammate of Dave Parker's there; Parker was the Carolina League's Player of the Year, and Bair the Pitcher of the Year.

Bair reached the International League in late 1972 and stayed there, posting records of 0-1 (1972), 7-11 (1973), 7-16 (1974; he led the league in losses), 9-12 (1975) and 7-10 (1976). In 1976 he was converted to relief, and pitched better although it wasn't reflected in his won-lost record.

The Pirates suggested that it would help his chances of making the major league team in '77 if he would pitch winter ball in the Dominican Republic. He did; he went 8-0 with a 1.20 ERA. The Pirates traded for Rich Gossage and Terry Forster, relief pitchers.

Bair refused to sign his contract, and reported to spring training unsigned. He went in to see Harding Peterson, the Pirates' General Manager. Peterson told him that he had no chance to make the Pirates after the acquisition of Gossage and Forster. Bair told him there was no way he was going back to Charleston, where he had been for four full years. The Pirates saw his point, and included him in a package trade with the Oakland A's.

That finally got him to the major leagues—or actually, the A's sent him to San Jose of the Pacific Coast League, where he struck out 49 men in 33 innings, which put him in the major leagues in two months. He pitched fairly well for the A's, posting a 3.47 ERA in 45 relief appearances.

After the 1977 season Bair became a footnote to history. In December, 1976, the A's had tried to deal Vida Blue to Cincinnati for Dave Revering and $1.75 million. Commissioner Bowie Kuhn, using his power to prohibit actions "not in the best interest of baseball", voided the deal. Finley sued, seeking the right to dispose of his property as he chose. Finley lost, resulting in an important re-affirmation of the Commissioner's authority. When the lawsuit was finally resolved the deal went through with Bair substituted for Blue, and another dollar amount for $1.75 million:

> Asked if he knew how much money the Reds gave Finley, Bair replied: "Not quite as much as $1.75 million. Maybe it was $25."
>
> Bair was delighted to have traveled from one of baseball's weakest clubs to one of its strongest. However, he had only pleasant words for Finley, who had acquired him from Pittsburgh a year ago.
>
> "Before I left Oakland," Bair said, "I called Mr. Finley and told him I appreciated the opportunity he gave me last year. The A's gave me an opportunity to play."

In Cincinnati Sparky Anderson was looking for a relief ace to replace Rawley Eastwick, who had been exiled to St. Louis in a contract dispute a year earlier. Bair won the job early in the year, allowing no earned runs more than a month into the season. On June 13, 1978, Bair relieved Freddie Norman with one and runners on first and third, a 1-0 game in the ninth inning. Bair struck out Dave Kingman and Manny Trillo on six pitches. "If there had been a radar gun, I'll bet his pitches would have been clocked at 98 miles an hour or more," Sparky said after the game.

Bair never threw a 98 MPH fastball in his life, but in 1978 he pitched 70 times, saving 28 games for the Reds with a 1.98 ERA. Sparky said that Eastwick had never pitched so well. He said Bair threw harder than Eastwick and had a better slider. In one week, spanning late July and early August, Bair earned three saves and a win, pitched ten and two-thirds innings and struck out 14 men. He was the National League's Player of the Week.

That was to be by far his best week, and year. In 1979 Bair's ERA more than doubled, and he lost his closer role. In 1979 he threw his fastball for his out pitch almost exclusively, but in 1979 a tender elbow took something away from the fastball, and he had to begin relying on the curve. He struggled through 1980 and into 1981, his highlight of the 1981 season coming on May 20, when he hit a three-run homer in the ninth inning, giving the Reds (and himself) a 10-7 victory over the Cubs. It was the Reds' eighth consecutive win.

Continuing to pitch ineffectively, Bair was traded to St. Louis late in the year. Hub Kittle made some adjustments in his delivery, teaching him to step back toward second, rather than off toward first, which gave him better balance in his delivery. In 1982 he had a fine season as a setup man for Bruce Sutter; Sutter was kind enough to insist that Bair was just as important to the team as he (Sutter) was, and after the season he filed for $450,000 in arbitration. The Cardinals offered $325,000. Bair won.

Cardinal General Manager Joe McDonald ripped the arbitration process.

In 1983 Bair continued to pitch effectively but the Cardinals, coming up with younger pitchers who could play the same role, traded him to Detroit, where he rejoined Sparky Anderson.

Between 1983 and 1990 Bair was released or went through free agency eight times, or once a year, but was always able to get a job. He went to the minors in 1986, 1987, 1988, 1989 and 1990—but also spent part of each season in the major leagues. He began to throw a split-fingered fastball. In 1989 an entrepreneur started an old-timer's league, a "Senior's League". Bair was old enough to qualify. Receiving an offer to pitch in the league, Bair talked it over with his major league employer, the Pirates, and decided to accept, treating the Senior's League like winter ball. He pitched with the old guys, and then came back to pitch with the division champion Pirates in 1990. He was granted free agency by the Pirates after the 1990 season, and receiving no major league offers agreed to pitch for Toledo, the AAA team of the Tigers. He was released there after five innings, but signed with Syracuse (Blue Jays), where he pitched thirteen innings and struck out sixteen men. His major league career appears to be over, but you wouldn't want to bet too much on it. He waited a long time for his chance, and as long as somebody is going to let him pitch, he's going to pitch.

Al Baird, briefly a Giants infielder in 1917 and 1919.

On his debut the *New York Times* described Baird as "the Giants' sensational young infielder from the Univ. of Louisiana", but he lost the battle for a job to a sensational young infielder from Fordham.

Bob Baird, a phenom in the Senators' system in the early sixties.

Baird, a six-foot-four left-hander, went 13-3 for Pensacola in the Alabama-Florida League in 1962, striking out 207 men in 151 innings. He struck out twenty men in one game. Apart from his won-lost record it was almost a Dalkowski year; he gave up only 93 hits but walked 124 men and threw 34 wild pitches. The Senators, a second-year expansion team, vaulted him from Class D to the majors that September, giving him a start on September 3. In his column the next day, Shirley Povich commented that ". . . Baird was superb when he wasn't wild, with a fast ball that sang and hissed, and there was understanding why he was a whizbang at Pensacola."

Baird was never a whizbang at Washington, though he did reasonably well in two starts later that month. Another short trial in '63 ended his major league career with an 0-4 record.

Out of the majors by age 23, Baird was dead at 34. Late in the evening of April 11, 1974, Baird sat at a table in a Chattanooga bar with two women. Newspaper reports indicate that Baird was shot in the abdomen, "without warning and for no apparent provocation." One of the women at the table, Ruth Jean Lynn, calmly got up and walked away at that moment, and was later charged with his murder. The bullet lodged next to his spine. The encyclopedias list Baird's death date as April 11, which appears to be an error. Baird did not die until two weeks later.

(—R.N.
Sources for this article include
The Last Rebel Yell, Ken Brooks' history
of the Alabama-Florida League,
and the *Washington Post.*
Special thanks to Chattanooga
News-Free Press sportswriter
and SABR member David Jenkins,
who provided the information
about Baird's death.)

Doug Baird, National League third baseman from 1915 through 1920.

The Pirates' regular third baseman in 1915, Baird stole 29 bases while hitting just .219 and leading the league with 88 strikeouts. He had a similar season in 1916, and was released by the Pirates in June, 1917.

Baird was a native of the St. Louis area, and the Cardinals decided to give him a look. The *St. Louis Post-Dispatch* wrote that "He is fast, owns a great arm and needs to overcome only a batting weakness to become a major league star." He didn't, of course, and failed increasingly quick trials with the Cardinals, Phillies, Dodgers and Giants.

In 1921, playing for Indianapolis in 1921, Baird hit .310 and stole 72 bases, an American Association record at the time.

(—R.N.)

George A. Baird, who in 1908 invented one of the first electric scoreboards.

According to Harold Seymour's *Baseball: the Golden Age:*

> . . . George A. Baird of Chicago invented an electric scoreboard that instantly recorded balls, strikes, and outs. It was a simple, two-part contrivance: the display board itself and a little keyboard for running it that was set off to the side and behind the umpire. The section of the board showing the innings and score was still operated manually. Although players' names were not listed, numbers corresponding to the ones assigned to each man on the scorecard appeared on the board. The Boston clubs of each major league tried out the new electric board, and within a couple of years Shibe Park, in Philadelphia, had one that listed the names of the players in the batting order. Electric boards 50 by 24 feet could also be leased instead of purchased—at $2500 for the first year and $750 thereafter . . .

Tom Baird, co-owner or owner of the Kansas City Monarchs for a quarter of a century.

Baird, an Arkansas native, played semi-pro baseball until he was injured while working on the Rock Island Railroad. He then operated a billiard parlor in Kansas City, Kansas.

With the onset of the Great Depression in 1929, Monarchs owner J.L. Wilkinson concluded that for the team to remain profitable, a revolutionary step would have to be taken. Up to then, night baseball had been played only on an experimental basis. Wilkinson proposed an easily transportable system of lights which could accompany the barnstorming Monarchs from town to town. But Wilkinson could not afford the equipment himself, so he turned to Baird, and the two became equal partners in the ownership of the Monarchs.

From 1932 through 1937 Baird served as the booking agent for both the Monarchs and the House of David, a barnstorming team that featured long-bearded players and, for a while, Pete Alexander. The House of David used Wilkinson and Baird's lighting system, and when the two had saved enough money from the rental of the lights, they would start the Monarchs season. Sometimes he pitted the two against one another; Pete Alexander opposed Satchel in a long series of exhibitions.

The Monarchs joined the newly reformed Negro American League in 1937, and with outstanding players like Newt Allen, Hilton Smith, Willard Brown, Chet Brewer, Buck O'Neil, and Satchel Paige, dominated the league for half a decade.

In March of 1945, a new shortstop reported to the Monarchs' spring training camp. Baird and Wilkinson felt that the former college football star, "Jitterbug" Jackie Robinson, would be a good drawing card. Robinson won the job at shortstop, and played well enough to start in that summer's East-West all-star game.

On August 28, 1945, Robinson signed a contract with the Brooklyn Dodgers, who offered absolutely no compensation to the Monarchs. Robinson's signing remained a secret until October 23, when Brooklyn's Montreal farm club made the announcement.

Baird was livid, saying, "We won't take it lying down. Robinson signed a contract with us last year and I feel he is our property." Baird compared Rickey's "signing" of negro players to a man who found a rope, and when he got home discovered there was a horse on the end of it. Baird was careful to stress that he objected not to Robinson crossing the color line, but to the fact that it had occurred with no regard to his interests. Rickey's answer was that the Negro Leagues, with their informal contracts and frequent team-jumping, did not constitute a legitimate league and therefore were owed no compensation. "They're simply a booking agent's paradise," he said, "They are not leagues and have no right to expect organized baseball to respect them." Regardless, Baird threatened a lawsuit. Some of the major league owners opposed to the signing of blacks might have been willing to back his lawsuit, but Baird and the other Negro League owners were over a barrel, and Rickey knew it. As Jules Tygiel writes in *Baseball's Great Experiment:*

> . . . the Robinson signing posed a classic dilemma. For years they had decried the color line which provided the basis for their own existence. The spectre of integration threatened their interests, yet opposition to it would expose them to the wrath of their fans. By failing to reimburse the Monarchs for Robinson's services, Rickey had salted their wounds. With baseball integrated, the sale of their athletes to organized baseball represented the only hope of the Negro Leagues to offset their inevitable decline. Yet Rickey had declared all black players free agents and the owners dared not oppose him.

Baird, who was white, was in a particularly ticklish position with respect to his audience. On October 25 the Monarchs withdrew their claim to Robinson, Wilkinson declaring "I want to see Jackie make good. I would never do anything to mar his chances." That December the Negro Leagues adopted all the rules of organized baseball, opening the way for them to serve as a farm system of sorts for the majors.

In the spring of 1948 Baird bought out Wilkinson to become sole owner of the Monarchs. He continued until 1955, when poor attendance and inhospitable landlords (the recently-arrived Athletics) forced him to sell the team to black sports entrepreneur Ted Rasberry. In the interim, the Monarchs had produced more quality major league players than any other black team, including Willard Brown, Hank Thompson, Gene Baker, Ernie Banks, Bob Thurman, Elston Howard, George Altman, and Lou Johnson.

(—R.N.
A primary source for this entry was Janet Bruce's book, *The Kansas City Monarchs.*)

Jersey Bakely, who pitched for a number of teams in the nineteenth century.

Bakely pitched six seasons in the major leagues for nine different teams, never lasting more than a single season with one team. The reasons for his transience weren't much of a mystery. Bakely was a drunk, and not that great a pitcher besides. While with the Cleveland National League club in 1889, he missed a start due to intoxication, and was saved from suspension only by taking a temperance oath in front of a magistrate.

In *Baseball From the Newspaper Accounts* (the primary source for this article), author Preston Orem reports that Bakely

> was once a member of a variety theatrical troupe managed by Frank Bancroft, Cincinnati secretary. Bakely would go out on the stage and offer to meet all comers. Being then a good boxer and fighter, he generally won.

Anyway, Bakely began the 1891 season with the Washington entry in the American Association, but earned his release in June with a two and ten record. Signed by Baltimore, Bakely pitched very well for a while, but was suspended on or about July 12 for drinking, and 1891 was his last taste of the major leagues.

(—R.N.)

Dave Bakenhaster, who gave up nine hits in only three major league innings as a 19-year-old major leaguer.

In a 1964 *Baseball Digest* scouting report, it was written that Bakenhaster has a "good fast ball and had a good curve at times, but has a tendency to throw too many curves. Wild at times. May have chance."

The Baker, famous Cincinnati Reds fan of the early twenties.

As Ford Frick tells the story in *Games, Asterisks, and People,* The Baker somehow arranged it so that every time a Red hit a home run,

> an attendant was on hand with a big bouquet of roses to greet the successful hitter, compliments of "The Baker." The ceremony was always the same, and timed to perfection. Always the flowers were there before the hitter had reached the bench; sometimes the attendant was on hand to make the presentation almost before the runner had crossed the plate to register his run. Where the flowers came from, how and where they were kept fresh, how the delivery was timed so perfectly—these questions stumped all the boys in the pressbox.

According to Frick, no one ever discovered the identity of The Baker, though he always occupied a front row seat in the right field bleachers. Frick suspected that Reds owner Gary Herrmann was in on the mystery, but the magnate would never let on.

(—R.N.)

Al Baker, who pitched briefly for the 1938 Red Sox.

Bill Baker, National League backup catcher of the 1940s.

A native of Paw Creek, North Carolina, Baker signed with Greensboro in 1931 and spent nine years wading through the minor leagues, completing the journey with a .338 season for Indianapolis (American Association) in 1939. The Reds purchased him in 1940 to be their third-string catcher, behind Ernie Lombardi and Willard Hershberger, both .300 hitters.

Baker was Hershberger's roommate; the two had been teammates several years earlier at Newark. As I'm sure you know, Hershberger committed suicide on August 3, 1940. Baker apparently was the last person to see him alive, Hershberger telling Baker at the hotel that he wasn't feeling well and would be out to the park a little later.

Lombardi severely sprained an ankle on September 15, leaving Baker in a key role during the pennant race. Manager Bill McKechnie, however, had little confidence in Baker, and instead talked Jimmy Wilson, a 40-year-old coach, into coming out of retirement to be the starting catcher down the stretch and through the World Series, which the Reds won with Baker in a backup role.

Baker was sold to Pittsburgh in early 1941, and spent three years as a reserve catcher with the Pirates. After two years in the Army (1944–45) he came back in 1946 to resume the role. He was cut from the roster in 1947, 36 years old, but went back to the American Association and played well for a year and a half. In 1948 the Cardinals were trying to catch the Dodgers with a catching combination of Del Rice (.197), Del Wilber (.190) and Joe Garagiola (.107), while the 37-year-old Baker was hitting over .300 with Columbus. The Cardinals called up Baker, and he played a key role for them over the second half of the 1948 season, hitting .294 in 45 games. This experience also made him eligible for the player's pension program, which had commenced in the interim while Baker was at Columbus. He was released early in 1949.

Bock Baker, a pitcher whose major league career consisted of one start apiece with Cleveland and Philadelphia (AL) in 1901.

Baker started for the Cleveland Spiders on April 28, 1901, in Chicago. As John Phillips writes, "So many people turned out for the Sunday game that they were allowed to encircle the field, necessitating ground rules." Baker pitched a complete game. Unfortunately, he gave up 23 singles (an American League record which still stands) and thirteen runs, while his teammates scored just one. "Smiling Bock" also made a base-running mistake, being picked off first after reaching on an error. The Cleveland *Plain-Dealer* headlined its game story the next day, "SLAUGHTERED AND RELEASED", both words referring to Baker.

He was signed by Connie Mack on May 8, and on May 13, starting against Baltimore, Baker became the first American Leaguer to pitch for two teams in one season. This time out he allowed seven earned runs in six innings before being relieved for the major league debut of Eddie Plank.

Plank went on to a Hall of Fame career. Baker never appeared in another major league game, and the time and place of his death is unknown, as is whether he was right or lefthanded.

(—R.N.

Besides the *Plain-Dealer,* a source for this article was John Phillips' *Who Was Who in Cleveland Baseball 1901–1910.*)

Charlie Baker, a catcher who hit .140 in fifteen games with the Union Association Chicago Browns and Pittsburgh Stogies in 1884.

Chuck Baker, who served as a late-inning defensive replacement with the Padres in 1978 and the Twins in 1981. Baker received an engineering degree from Loyola Marymount University.

Dave Baker, a third baseman who got into nine games as a September call-up with the 1982 Blue Jays. He was the brother of Doug Baker.

Del Baker, manager of the 1940 American League champion Detroit Tigers, and the most famous sign stealer in baseball history.

Delmar David Baker was born in Sherwood, Oregon, in 1892. He signed with Helena (Montana) in the Union Association as a 19-year-old catcher, and within three years was in the major leagues, a backup catcher for the Tigers. He held that job for three years (1914–1916), and was sold to the San Francisco Seals of the Pacific Coast League. After a year in the Army during World War I he was traded to Portland, also in the PCL. It was there, Baker remembered,

> that I really started to learn what base ball was all about. I learned because I was in there every day . . . and never had so much fun in my life.
>
> Harry Wolverton, who earlier had been manager of the Yankees, was the boss at Portland. He taught me more about base ball than anyone else, before or since.

He spent the next decade catching in the minors: Portland, Mobile, Oakland, Fort Worth and Ogden, Utah. In Oakland he was assigned the job of tutoring Ernie Lombardi, with whom he shared the catcher's duties for two years. In 1930 the 38-year-old Baker was named player-manager of the Beaumont club in the Texas League; he retired as a player after that season.

The 1930 team wasn't very good, but in 1931–32 Baker managed successful teams littered with future major league stars. The 1931 Beaumont team, which finished 94-65 (second), included Jo-Jo White, Whitlow Wyatt and Luke Hamlin. The 1932 team, which won the Texas League with 100 wins, included Hamlin (20-10), Schoolboy Rowe (19-7), Art Herring (11-5), Pete Fox (.357, 19 homers and 78 RBI) and Hank Greenberg (.290, 39 homers, 131 RBI) as well as Skeeter Newsome, Flea Clifton and Izzy Goldstein, who pitched brilliantly at Beaumont, though not so well in the major leagues.

In 1933 Fox, Rowe, and Greenberg were promoted to the Tigers. Del Baker went with them, as the third-base coach. The Tigers won pennants in 1934 and 1935. In the '35 Series Baker was ejected in the sixth inning of Game Three after protesting vehemently when Pete Fox was picked off third base.

Tigers player-manager Mickey Cochrane suffered a nervous breakdown in June, 1936, and was absent from the team for a month. Though the reference books list Cochrane as manager for the entire season, in fact Baker managed the team for several weeks while Cochrane was recuperating in Wyoming. The Tigers lost seven in a row to drop below .500, but then captured fifteen out of twenty. Considering that the Tigers were missing their two best players (Cochrane and Greenberg, who was out with a broken wrist) it was generally thought that the team had played well under Baker. One of Baker's talents as a third base coach was a considerable ability to get under the skin of an opposition pitcher. It was during this stretch, while he was managing the team from the third base line, that Baker got Cleveland's Johnny Allen so riled up that Allen had to be restrained from attacking him (see entry on Johnny Allen, 1990 *Baseball Book.*) Cochrane returned on July 15.

Susan McCarthy

Del BAKER

In late May, 1937, Mickey Cochrane's skull was fractured by a pitch from Bump Hadley. Cochrane was hospitalized, lingering for several days in fear of his life, and his playing career was ended. Baker again took over the club while Cochrane recuperated, this time for two months, and again the Tigers played well.

On August 6, 1938, with Detroit in fifth place, Cochrane was fired, and Baker got the job. Baker had previously turned down offers from the Indians and the Browns, saying, "I don't want to be a manager. I'm satisfied with a job as coach." Nevertheless, Tigers secretary (and son of the club owner) Spike Briggs convinced him to take the reins, and the Tigers played extremely well at the tag end of the 1938 season, winning 37 of 56 decisions.

The Detroit team that Baker took over had fallen into confusion in the late thirties. The Yankees were *so* good, to begin with, that it was somewhat disorienting for the rest of the league. The Tigers had Hall of Famers at first base and second (Greenberg and Gehringer) and good players at third and short, but they had little power in the outfield, and with Bridges and Rowe not pitching particularly well they had no number one starting pitcher. The combination was pushing them further and further away from the mighty Yankees, and then to make it worse the fine third base/shortstop combination (Marv Owen and Billy Rogell) was beginning to grow old.

And then there was the catching situation. After Cochrane's career was ended by his injuries the Tigers tried several people—Birdie Tebbetts, Ray Hayworth, Cliff Bolton. In August, 1937, Rudy York had a phenomenal hot streak, hitting 18 homers and driving in 49 runs in one month. This left him in possession of the catching job, but he wasn't really a catcher. Although he was a part-time player until August, 1937, he wound up the season with 35 homers, 103 RBI, and he followed that up in 1938 with 33 homers, 127 RBI in 135 games. What to do? Live with his glove and admire his bat? Try to teach him to catch? Trade him for a starting pitcher? Move him to another position?

As life often is, the team was a mess.

Baker's challenge was to straighten it out.

The Tigers under Baker's leadership acted forcefully, making a long series of trades and adjustments over a period of two years. The major moves included:

• December 15, 1938, Eldon Auker traded to Boston for third baseman Pinky Higgins.

• May 13, 1939, Vern Kennedy, Roxie Lawson and others traded to St. Louis for starting pitcher Buck Newsom.

• December 6, 1939, Billy Rogell traded to the New York Giants for shortstop Dick Bartell.

There were several other trades that didn't lead anywhere. Detroit traded with Cleveland to get Earl Averill, but Averill didn't hit. The Tigers also were very active in attempting to strengthen their pitching staff by acquiring young pitchers, and within a period of two years came up with three very, very good ones—Dizzy Trout, Hal Newhouser and Fred Hutchinson. The system also produced a brilliant young outfielder, in Barney McCoskey.

In 1939 these moves didn't lead anywhere; the Tigers finished fourth, at 81-73.

In the winter of 1939–1940 the decision was made that Rudy York

a) wasn't going to make it as a catcher, and

b) was too valuable to be given away in trade.

In 1939, playing half-time because of his defensive problems at catcher, York had hit .307 with 20 homers, 68 RBI in 329 at bats. The Tigers decided to wedge him in at first base, moving Hank Greenberg to left field. Greenberg was given a sizeable bonus, reportedly $10,000, to become an outfielder.

Bingo.

Greenberg was great, the American League's MVP in 1940 with 50 doubles, 41 homers and 150 RBI. York, playing first base in every game, drove in another 134 runs, giving the Tigers the best offense in the league. Bobo Newsom, a practicing eccentric who had been winning around 20 games a year with bad teams, went 21-5 with the Tigers despite missing a month with a broken thumb. The Yankees cooperated, dropping to 88 wins, and the Tigers ended New York's four-year grip on the pennant by winning 90.

Now, we have to talk about the sign-stealing, because it's in the middle of everything. Whenever you read anything about Del Baker in an old baseball book, it will always focus on his ability to steal signs. This is omni-present, and Baker is unquestionably the most famous sign stealer in baseball history. Rudy York, discussing his 134 RBI, said that, "Del Baker was one reason I hit as well as I did. The guy is the greatest sign-stealer who ever lived, and he used to call the pitches for me."

While the Tigers won 90 games and the Yankees 88, the Cleveland Indians slipped in between them with 89. Bob Feller finished 27-11 that year—but lost five times to the Tigers. In *Strikeout Story*, Feller's first autobiography (1947), he mused on how he could have been beaten so regularly in 1940 by Detroit,

> The Tigers, whom I had beaten six straight times the year before, now had beaten me in three out of five games. I couldn't understand it as their lineup was much the same. [One] belief was that Baker, who coached at third, was tipping off my pitches to the batters. This was much more credible than . . . the other story [that someone with binoculars was stealing signs]. Baker was one of the better known pitching detectives. He studied a pitcher's throwing habits closely and soon discovered the things he did differently when he was going to throw a fast ball or a curve . . .

In Dick Bartell's autobiography *Rowdy Richard*, the Tigers shortstop confirmed Feller's suspicion, noting that Feller held the ball differently for the curve and fast ball, a flaw which he corrected in 1941.

The first volume of the *Fireside Book of Baseball* contains this anecdote in an article by Bob Deindorfer:

> Detroit's Del Baker had been reading Cleveland battery signs with great success most of the afternoon. Up stepped Greenberg to the plate and Baker called down to him "Hit it now" for a curve ball. Anticipating the curve, Hank spread his feet and leaned out over the plate. What neither one knew was that Cleveland, aware of too many interceptions, had just altered its code by interchanging the curve and fast ball signs. Hank sprawled in the dirt to escape a pitch whistling by at his features at roughly 90 mph. After the game he politely thanked Baker for all the help and said he'd blankety-blank steal his own signs in the future.

The exact role that Baker's ability to intercept a signal played in anything is of course impossible to know at this distance. Although Rudy York remained a fine hitter the rest of his career, it is true that he was never quite the same hitter after he and Baker parted company. On the other hand, I recently asked Feller his troubles with the Tigers in 1940, and he reverted back to the story that someone in the scoreboard with binoculars was stealing the signs. Anyway, the supposed sign-heist and the York/Greenberg maneuver came together beautifully in the season's final series, which happened to be against Cleveland. The Tigers began the three-game series with a two-game lead over the Indians. One victory would clinch the pennant. Feller would pitch the first game for the Indians, but who would the Tigers send to the mound?

On the advice of coach Steve O'Neill, Baker started thirty-year-old rookie Floyd Giebell. Rudy York hit a two-run home run off Feller, and Giebell pitched a six-hit shutout.

It was to be Giebell's only major league shutout. His career record was 3-1.

The off year by the Yankees and the tight three-way race allowed the Tigers to win the pennant with a winning percentage of .584, the lowest pennant-winning percentage in American League history at that time.

In the World Series the Tigers squared off against the Cincinnati Reds. In Game One Detroit scored five runs off Paul Derringer in the second inning, and Bobo Newsom went the distance for a 7-2 win. Lee Allen would later write that with Baker coaching third, he

> soon caught on to the messages signaled to Derringer. Whenever a curve was on its way, Baker would indicate the fact to the batter by calling to him by his first name.

Paul Derringer was the Reds' number two starting pitcher; why he had been selected to start Game One I'm not sure. Bucky Walters, the ace of the Reds' staff, pitched a three-hitter in Game Two, evening the series, but a seven-run outburst in Game Three made a winner out of veteran Tommy Bridges, putting the Tigers back on top, two games to one.

Buck Newsom's family was with the team for the series. His father had been ill, and in the excitement following Newsom's Game-One victory he suffered a heart attack, and died.

After three games the Tigers owned a one-game edge, and the biggest question facing Del Baker was, Who do I start in Game Four? Baker had used his #4 starter, Johnny Gorsica, to relieve in Game Two. Despite the death of his father and just two days rest, Newsom was eager to pitch, but Baker elected to go instead with Dizzy Trout, who had finished with a 3-7 record.

Trout lost to Derringer, and Baker of course was second-guessed for the decision to start him. Had Baker pitched Newsom the Tigers could have gained a commanding three-to-one advantage. Baker's reply was "if I had lost with Newsom, where would I have been?"

So the series was tied at two each, and Newsom was ready to go for Game Five. Dedicating the game to his late father, Bobo pitched a three-hit shutout. The Tigers were a game up after five.

Bucky Walters pitched a shutout in Game Six, sending the series to the limit.

Baker's pitching options for the Seventh Game were Bridges, 12-9 but working with three days rest, or Buck Newsom, 21-5 but working with only one day of rest. He chose Newsom, who was opposed by Paul Derringer. Both pitched seven-hitters, but Newsom allowed two runs in the bottom of the seventh inning and lost the game, 2-1. The Series belonged to Cincinnati.

Those criticizing Baker's strategy were apparently in the minority, if *Detroit News* columnist H.G. Salsinger's opinion is taken to be representative:

> It was agreed here, in the post-World Series comments, that Del Baker . . . did a perfect job of clinging to the percentages in seven straight games . . . It was an unhappy series for the second guessers. Baker did a perfect job in the World Series and he did a magnificent job during the regular season.

Well, maybe. The series was played in seven straight days, no travel days. Cincinnati manager Bill McKechnie had a huge advantage, in that he had *two* legitimate aces, Derringer and Walters, while Baker had only one. On the other hand, it seems fairly obvious that *if* you're going to start a pitcher three times in seven games, as Baker elected to do, the way to do it is Games One, Four and Seven, not One, Five and Seven. The selection of Trout for Game Four was like the selection of Floyd Giebell to start the first game of the Cleveland series: I'm the manager and I don't have to explain this. If it works we'll have a big edge. In the case of Giebell, it worked. In the case of Game Four, it didn't.

Lee Allen's comment about Baker picking up Paul Derringer's pitches also comes to mind. If Baker could read his pitches in Game One, why did he beat them in Games Four and Seven? According to Birdie Tebbetts in an article for *The Atlantic* in 1949:

> Our manager, Del Baker, one of the brainiest men in baseball, was a great sign-stealer. But in that World Series sign-stealing didn't help. We knew every pitch the Reds' pitchers were going to throw, yet lost. Catcher Jimmy Wilson was giving away the pitches by twitching his forearm muscles when he called a curve. When the muscles were still, the pitch was a fast ball.

As he says, it didn't help.

As manager, Baker was a low-key sort who once observed, "The fate of nations doesn't hang on the outcome of a baseball game." But he also said, "Give me a team that hustles all the time and I'll beat a team that is 20 percent better mechanically." That was why he wanted Dick Bartell, the most famous dirty-uniform player in the National League—but Bartell did not trust Baker as a manager. According to Bartell's biography, *Rowdy Richard:*

> I learned that you couldn't always believe what [Baker] told you. He would go behind your back, talking about you to other players. He asked me many times what I thought about somebody or some situation. I didn't like that.

Anyway, everything which had been so laboriously constructed fell apart in 1941. Greenberg was ordered into the military, gearing up for World War II. Gehringer grew suddenly very old. Bobo Newsom and Schoolboy Rowe slumped badly, and Bartell was traded away early in the year.

The Tigers finished fifth in 1941; Baker's job was rumored to be in danger. Tigers owner Walter O. Briggs responded by signing Baker to a new one-year contract for 1942. After another fifth-place finish in '42, however, the axe did fall, and Baker was replaced by Steve O'Neill.

Baker spent the next six years as a third base coach for Cleveland and the Red Sox. He went back to the Pacific Coast League to manage for three years, winning more games than he lost but no pennants. In 1953 the Red Sox brought him back as their third base coach.

In 1956, again because of his ability to swipe a sign, Baker became a footnote to one of baseball's most famous chapters. Don Larsen, starting for the Yankees against the Red Sox on September 20, decided to pitch the entire game without using a windup. As John Thorn writes in *Baseball's 10 Greatest Games:*

> The reason for this experiment was solely to foil Boston's third-base coach, Del Baker, who Don suspected was stealing his pitches and tipping the Boston

> batters. After the game, which he won 2-1, Don was delighted with his innovation. "I fooled the batters better," he said. "I had better control, and I fooled Baker. It's wonderful."

A couple weeks later, using that same no-windup delivery, Larsen threw his perfect game.

Baker retired from baseball after the 1960 season, ending his fifty-year career on the same day and in the same place that Ted Williams made his much more famous exit. He lived thirteen more years, and died in San Antonio on September 11, 1973.

(—Rob Neyer.

In addition to the sources listed within the article, Baker's obituary in the September 29, 1973 *Sporting News* was most helpful, as were a number of issues of *The Detroit News*.

Doug Baker, American League utility infielder of the 1980s.

Dusty Baker, who hit 242 home runs in a nineteen-year career, and is now a hitting coach.

Baker, a baseball, basketball, football and track star at Del Campo High School in Carmichael, California, was a 26th round draft pick in the June, 1967, amateur draft. He was undecided whether to play baseball or go to college, but a visit from Henry Aaron made up his mind:

> . . . when the Braves were in Los Angeles they sent Hank over to talk to me. I asked Hank if I should sign, and he said, "If you have confidence that you can make it, then sign." My mother made Hank promise to take care of me like a son, and he promised.

In 1968, his first full pro season, Baker hit .342 in the Western Carolina League, and was called up for five at bats with the Braves. The September callups became a regular part of his life, and gave him enough at bats that when he exploded on the league in 1972, hitting .321 with 17 homers and 76 RBI, he was not quite eligible for the Rookie of the Year Award.

Baker was 23 years old at that time, and a center fielder. That wonderful season created a widespread belief that Baker was destined to be a superstar, that he was destined to be Henry Aaron. It's an old story: everything he did from then on wasn't good enough. He hit .288 in 1973, and drove in 99 runs. Well, OK, Dusty, maybe you can have a good year *next* year?

So 1974 was a disappointment, and 1975. In retrospect these were solid seasons. In 1974 Henry Aaron broke Babe Ruth's record for career home runs:

> Hank would always take a big lunch early in the afternoon and after that, just eat light the rest of the day. Ralph [Garr] and I started doing the same thing. In the offseason, we would all go to the gym, and Hank would be running lap after lap around the track while Ralph and I played basketball. Hank would look at us and shake his head and say, "Get up here and run." He even told us how to act on the field. He'd say, "Now, don't be hotdogging around the bases. If you don't show up the pitcher, he might not have a vendetta against you the next time you bat. When you hit a home run, just run the bases. Then you can go into the tunnel and get happy.

After the 1974 season Aaron was traded to Milwaukee, and in 1975 Dusty had another disappointing season, hitting .261 with 19 homers and 72 RBI. The Braves finished fifth, and decided it was time to make some changes. On November 17, 1975, Dusty Baker and Ed Goodson were traded to the Dodgers in exchange for four players.

Baker hit a home run in his first at bat as a Dodger, and after that his first season in Los Angeles was a nightmare. Replacing the popular Jimmy Wynn in center field, Baker hit .242 with four home runs in 112 games. The public had no idea what the problem was until his season ended on September 12, and it was revealed that he had been suffering all season from the effects of a knee injury:

> I was out running my dog last winter and I just felt it give out on me. It was as simple as that.
>
> I didn't tell anyone about it except Al Campanis and Dr. (Frank) Jobe. I didn't tell the writers or anyone else . . . I didn't want to complain, especially since I was coming to a new team . . . Campanis and Jobe just told me to do the best I could.

Baker had knee surgery, and reported to Dodgertown in the spring of 1977 ready to play, although his speed was gone. The 1977 season was Tom Lasorda's first as manager, and one of his first projects was Dusty Baker, as Lasorda remembered in his book, *The Artful Dodger*:

> A lot of people were saying the trade had been a mistake, and that we needed an outfielder to take his place. "You haven't heard that from me, though," I told him, "and you won't, because you're gonna be my left fielder from the first game of spring training to the final game of the World Series" . . . I told reporters . . . I was confident he would be a great player for the Dodgers.

The Dodgers moved home plate out that winter, moving the plate closer to the fences. Four Dodgers hit thirty home runs, and the Dodgers won 98 games to give Lasorda the National League West. Baker was one of the four, hitting .291 with 30 homers, 86 RBI. He was the MVP of the 1977 League Championship series, driving in eight runs in a four-game rout of the Phillies, and followed that up with a good World Series (.292, a homer and five RBI).

Dusty would play regularly for the Dodgers for eight seasons, his best years being 1980 (.294 with 29 homers and 97 RBI) and 1982 (.300 with 23 and 88). On September 13, 1979, he drove in five runs in one inning. In the strike-shortened 1981 season he finished third in the batting race, hitting .320, and also won a Gold Glove. In four league championship series he hit .316 to .467 every time, overall .371. He became a favorite of the fans in Dodger Stadium; the left field area became known as "Baker's Acres." In the Dodgers' 100th anniversary celebration Los Angeles fans voted on the All-Time Dodger team. Dusty was voted to the team. He was both durable and consistent, and this too was at least partly the result of advice he had received from Aaron years earlier:

> Hank believed strongly that it was a ballplayer's duty to go out on that field. He preached that to guys like me and

> Garr. He'd say, "Now, you got to play a hundred and fifty games a year, so pick your spots. You can miss two games a month. Just two a month. So, pick the days you're gonna be hurt, or you're gonna rest, or you're gonna have a drink or two. The rest of the time, be out on that field.

Baker hit .260 in 1983, with 15 homers and 73 RBI. The Dodgers won the division title that year and Baker still had two years worth $1.4 million left on his contract, but Pedro Guerrero had been playing third base, and that wasn't working too well, and Dusty was almost 35 years old. In the spring of 1984 Dusty was given his release.

Baseball was having a drug problem, centered in Pittsburgh and Kansas City. When Dusty was released drug rumors were drawn toward him. Baker signed with the Giants. According to the April 16, 1984, *Sporting News*, the Giants put no stock in the drug rumors.

> "There was never any evidence to support those drug rumors," Owner Bob Lurie said. "We asked questions of a variety of people, and we didn't find anything that showed that Dusty is the type of guy to be involved with drugs. But when you're accused of something of this nature, it's difficult to erase the tag."

Baker was bitter about the Dodgers' treatment, but refrained from any serious blasts, and went along with the Dodgers' plans for Dusty Baker Night that April 13. He wanted to have a big year after the Dodgers released him to prove they were wrong, but never could. He played a year in San Francisco and two in Oakland.

Dave Stewart was released by Philadelphia in May, 1986, and Oakland decided to give him a shot. Stewart struggled at first, and he later remembered, "Dusty probably kept me from quitting the game . . . I talked to Dusty about it and he said, 'You never know, it could change for you. You owe it to yourself to stick around.' " Stewart, of course, hung around long enough to win twenty games in four consecutive seasons.

Baker was released after the 1987 season, and spent a year as an investment broker in Southern California. In 1988 he was invited to join the San Francisco Giants' staff as a first base coach. Later he was switched to the position of hitting coach, which he holds as of this writing. He is well thought of as a hitting coach, and may one day receive a chance to manage.

(—R.N.

In addition to those listed in the text, sources for this entry include *I Had a Hammer: The Hank Aaron Story* and *The Sporting News* articles of 5/1/76, 10/2/76, 10/15/79, and 10/23/89.)

Ernie Baker, who pitched in one game for the 1905 Cincinnati Reds.

Baker's lone appearance came in the middle of a twelve-nothing loss to Boston on August 18. It is not known with which hand he threw or how he batted. If he was your great-grandfather and you know, by all means write.

Floyd Baker, who was considered one of the top defensive third baseman of the post-war era.

Baker got his start in the St. Louis Browns system in 1937. As he later recounted,

> I was playing semi pro ball in Harrisburg Virginia and was scouted by a scout from St. Louis Browns. I went to Washington, D.C. and worked out with St. Louis for three days and then they signed me up giving me a bonus to sign.

Baker was a good hitter in the minor leagues, hitting .346 (Kitty League, 1938), .303 (Middle Atlantic League, 1940), .317 in the Three-I League (1941) and .326 in the Texas League (1942). He saw his first major league action with the Browns in 1943. About the time he reached the majors, however, he began to have a series of health problems, including ulcers, asthma and a hernia. He was classified 4-F, but hit .174 in 1943 and .175 in 1944. He appeared in the 1944 World Series, going oh-for-two, and was traded to the White Sox that winter.

To that point, Baker had been almost exclusively a shortstop. The White Sox needed help at third, and Baker moved to that position. He played better but not well, and went back to the American Association in 1946, when the returning major leaguers provided stiff competition for jobs.

Baker hit .287 at Milwaukee, and came to the major leagues to stay in 1947. Though he hit only .251 lifetime with one home run, his glovework bought him thirteen years in the major leagues. Sox manager Ted Lyons:

> In defensive skill, I refuse to give Kell the call over our own third sacker, Floyd Baker. Floyd has been making the most amazing plays at that position I have ever seen since I came into the American League.
>
> I told that to Ossie Bluege recently. I said, "Watch Baker for the best job since a guy named Bluege performed for Washington." I really had Ossie sobbing for his lost youth.

Dan Daniel, in a 1947 *World-Telegram* column, wrote that, "In so far as defensive pyrotechnics are concerned, there is no superior in either league to Floyd Baker, of the White Sox."

Here's a 1954 story from *The Sporting News*, which I'll repeat verbatim:

> PHILLIES BUY FLOYD BAKER;
> ALSO HUNT FOR A NEGRO STAR
>
> CINCINNATI, 0.—The Phillies announced the purchase of Floyd Baker, veteran infielder of the Red Sox, for an undisclosed sum, July 16. General Manager Roy Hamey also revealed that the Phillies were looking for "a good Negro player."
>
> "It is something we have needed for a long time and we have suffered because we haven't had one. We have had two or three in our farm systems but not good enough to bring up.
>
> "For the last three months, however, we have been industriously scouting the country for another Jackie Robinson, Willie Mays, or an outstanding boy."

Released in early 1955, Baker was hired by the Washington Senators as a scout in 1957, and became a coach with the team in 1961, when they moved to Minnesota. He coached with them for four years, and was known for never saying anything. In 1963 he was called upon to present Gold Glove awards to Jim

Kaat, Earl Battey and Vic Power. His presentations went like this: "Congratulations, Jim." "Congratulations, Earl." And for the finale, "Nice going, Vic." As *The Sporting News* put it, "Three speeches, seven words—including three names."

(—R.N.)

Frank Baker, a part-time outfielder with the Cleveland Indians in 1969 and '71.

Frank Baker, utility infielder with the Yankees and Orioles from 1970 to 1974. The 1970 *Baseball Register* lists his nickname as "Pancho", and says he got a degree in education from the University of Southern Mississippi.

Gene Baker, Ernie Banks' double play partner for three years, and the center of a discrimination controversy in the early fifties.

A native of Davenport, Iowa, Baker was signed by the Kansas City Monarchs in 1948, and was the starting shortstop for the Monarchs for two years. In 1950, he became the first black major-league prospect signed by the Chicago Cubs; the Monarchs replaced him with a kid named Ernie Banks.

After a three-game stint in Springfield and a third of a season in Des Moines, Baker ended the 1950 season with the Los Angeles Angels, the Triple-A affiliate of the Cubs. He would spend nearly four years with the Angels, playing himself into the middle of a controversy. Baker played consistently well at Los Angeles, hitting around .270 with some power and excellent defense, albeit many errors. According to Jules Tygiel in *Baseball's Great Experiment*, it was thought by many that Baker's color was all that prevented him from being promoted to the major league Cubs. As of 1953:

> For two years critics had demanded to know why black shortstop Gene Baker remained in the Pacific Coast League, while white players of lesser abilities inadequately manned that key position for the parent club . . . From the start Coast League observers hailed him as the best fielding shortstop in the circuit, if not the minor leagues. Yet during his first three seasons Baker received minimal attention from the Cub hierarchy.

According to Tygiel, the charges of discrimination grew louder in the spring of '53, when Baker again failed to stick with the Cubs. Black sportswriter Sam Lacy called Baker's demotion to Los Angeles "the prize stinkeroo of the 1953 spring training season." Roy Smalley and Eddie Miksis, who had hit .222 and .232 with no power in 1952, shared shortstop again, and six years after Jackie Robinson the Cubs still had no black players.

Finally, on September 14, Baker, now 28, was summoned to play for the Chicago Cubs. He had pulled a muscle in his side in his final PCL game, however, so was not the first black to play for the major league Cubs. That honor went to Ernie Banks. Banks, who had played shortstop for the Monarchs since Baker's departure, reported to the Cubs the same day Baker did. Banks played on September 17, Baker three days later.

While it is true that at the time of his call-up Baker was having his best pro season yet, just as important was the Cubs' signing of Banks a week earlier. It would be naive to think it coincidental that Banks and Baker, the first two black Cubs, just happened to report to the team on the same day. Baker and Banks were there to help each other out. In his autobiography *Mr. Cub*, Ernie Banks (and ghost-writer Jim Enright) wrote of Baker:

> Gene wasn't cocky, though he never lacked confidence in himself or his ability to help others. He helped me plenty . . .
>
> Before we arrived in St. Louis on that first road trip, Mr. Lewis, the Cubs' traveling secretary, reminded me several times to stick close to Gene Baker. I didn't understand why he was so worried until we walked through the big depot in St. Louis; there all the white players headed in one direction, to the Chase Hotel, while Gene and I took a cab to the Olive Hotel in the Negro section.

Many years later, Billy Williams would say that when he broke into baseball each team could have two black players, the star and his roommate. As Bill pointed out immediately afterward, this statement is nonsense; there was never any moment in baseball history at which more than three or four major league teams had exactly two black players, the star and his roommate. That image, however, is no doubt derived from the Cub experience. Banks was the star, Baker his roommate.

Of course, Baker and Banks were both shortstops, and if both were to play regularly for the Cubs, somebody would have to move. Management felt that Baker, with his experience, would more readily take to a switch, and after the '53 season he was sent south for the winter to learn to play second base.

So on Opening Day, 1954, Ernie Banks was at shortstop for the Cubs, and Gene Baker was at second. They would remain double play partners, and roommates, through 1956. Baker was not a star but a good player, good enough to play in the All-Star game in 1955. A trivia note: In a game against the Dodgers on May 10, 1955, Baker was the only Cub to reach base against Don Newcombe. Two years later he was the lone baserunner allowed by Von McDaniel. Ac-

Susan McCarthy

cording to an article by William Ruiz in the twentieth edition of SABR's *Baseball Research Journal*, Baker is the only player to twice break up a "near-perfect game", or NPG. For a while, Baker and Banks were hung with the nicknames "Bango" and "Bingo", respectively.

The names died out after May 1, 1957, when Baker was traded to the Pirates. Banks was sorry to see his friend leave, commenting at the time:

> I miss him. I miss rooming with him. Gene was a good ball player and a close friend. We had so many similar likes—movies, television, reading and cards. Lots of Gene's friends had us to dinner on the road. I wish he could have stayed, but the team had to make some trades . . .

The Pirates were set in the middle infield with Mazeroski and Groat, so Baker played third base for Pittsburgh. On July 13, 1958, while trying to field a hard-hit grounder off the bat of Curt Flood, Baker "came in fast, stumbled and went down hard, the ball getting away for a hit." Baker suffered a "ruptured knee cap tendon" on the play.

The injury effectively ended his career. He missed the rest of that season and all of 1959. Baker saw limited action in 1960, mostly as a pinch-hitter and runner, and appeared in three games of the wild World Series against the Yankees. He retired as a major league player early in 1961.

On June 20, 1961, Baker replaced James Adlam as manager of the Class D Batavia Pirates, and led them to a second place finish. He was the first black to manage a minor league team which had a major league affiliate. One thing that keyed the improvement of the team was that Baker himself played for them, hitting .387 and driving in 45 runs in 155 at bats. In 1963 he coached with the Pirates, becoming one of the first black major league coaches. Baker would remain with the Pirates for many years as a minor league manager, major league coach, assistant director of scouting, and special assignments scout.

Baker retired after the 1991 season, at the age of 66. He had served more than forty years in organized baseball.

(—R.N.

In addition to those listed above, sources for this article include Bill Libby's *Mr. Cub*—as distinguished from the *Mr. Cub* noted above, by Banks and Enright—and a *Sport Magazine* article by Jim Furlong, collected in *The Third Fireside Book of Baseball*, edited by Charles Einstein. Also consulted was the *Chicago Tribune* of September 1953, the *St. Louis Globe-Democrat* and the *Post-Dispatch* of July 1958.)

George Baker, regular catcher for the 1884 St. Louis Maroons, the Union Association champions.

Baker hit just .164 for the Maroons. When the Union Association folded after the one season, the St. Louis club transferred to the National League for 1885. Baker found National League pitching even more of a puzzle, hitting just .122, and the Maroons let him go.

Baker opened the 1886 season as one of four catchers on the Kansas City Cowboys' fourteen-man roster. In his first game, which also turned out to be his last, Baker allowed six stolen bases and was charged with six passed balls.

Little biographical information is known about him.

(—R.N.

The primary source for this entry is H.L. Dellinger's *One Year in the National League: An Account of the 1886 Kansas City Cowboys*.)

NOTES ABOUT OTHER PROJECTS

I work on a variety of projects with the Chicago company STATS, Inc. Three of these projects are:

Bill James Fantasy Baseball,

The **STATS Major League Baseball Handbook** and **STATS Minor League Baseball Handbook.**

The idea of the Major League Handbook was to do a book which was like *Who's Who in Baseball* or *The Baseball Register* or the annual updates to the *Macmillan Encyclopedia*, except that it was

a) much more comprehensive, and

b) available in November, rather than the following March.

Whereas the *Baseball Register* has nine categories of batting performance for each player each year (Games, At Bats, Runs, Hits, Doubles, Triples, Home Runs, RBI, Batting Average) and *Who's Who in Baseball* has ten (adding Stolen Bases), the *Handbook* has 24 categories, adding to those ten Walks, Intentional Walks, Strikeouts, Hit By Pitch, Sacrifice Hits, Sacrifice Flies, Caught Stealing, Stolen Base Percentage, Grounded Into Double Play, On Base Percentage, Slugging Percentage, Total Bases, Home Runs at Home and Home Runs on the Road.

The advantage for pitchers is about the same—we publish data on all of those stats like Wild Pitches and Balks which are left out of the other annuals. Of course, to get more things in you also have to take other things out. The *Handbook* doesn't included complete *minor league* statistics (we only run minor league stats for people who have been in the minor leagues within the last couple of years).

Anyway, the other advantage of the book is that it is available a month after the season ends, for those of you who don't want to wait all winter to see a summary of the season. Of course, this advantage is gone by now—you are reading this in a spring annual—but will return in the fall. This November, we'll be out with the 1993 edition. The book is popular with Strat-O-Matic players because it also includes platoon splits, plus there are some other features. We project the next-year stats for all hitters, which always gets more press attention than it deserves.

The *Minor League Handbook* is new in '92, and is a similar concept applied to the minor leagues: complete stats, early. The Minor League book has another "value" in that it includes the records of hundreds of players who won't be in any other spring annual, guys like (turning to a page at random) Al Liebert, Steve Lienhard, Chris W. Limbach and Orlando R. Lind. None of these players is on a major league 40-man roster, so they get left out of the other books, and sometimes you may want to look up somebody like that. The Minor League Handbook is the only place you can.

Bill James Fantasy Baseball is a game—you pay some money, you sign up, you draft players, get assigned to a league, try to work out trades, sign other players, release players, win, lose, etc. I made up the rules, and I play three teams. It's been three years and I have Dan Okrent's disease: I'm the only guy in my league who has never won the thing. Last year I dragged Jose DeLeon and John Smoltz both into mid-June, when they had a combined won-lost record of about 4-17. I decided I couldn't live with this, I had to do something, so I cut Smoltz. Don't ask me why—I guess I was thinking about the ballparks or something.

My goal in designing the game was **to get realistic values for players with simple rules.** I did not want the game to distort the values of the players by focusing on certain accomplishments or categories of accomplishment while ignoring other things. Everything is points; if a player hits a home run, that's four points. A win or a save by a pitcher earns six points, but also smaller stuff. A middle infielder gets a point if he turns a double play. A catcher gets a point if he throws out a base stealer.

There are a total of 28 things that a player can get points for—nine for hitters, nine for pitchers, four for defensive players and six "bonus" categories for things like throwing no-hitters. I wanted to evaluate talent in the same general way that it is evaluated by the press and public. One test of whether or not we are accomplishing that is whether *our* most valuable players, the most valuable players in the game, match the real-life award winners. Generally speaking, they do. Last year Cal Ripken was the most valuable American League player in our game, with the phenomenal total of 760 points, 83 more than Frank Thomas. Roger Clemens was the top American League pitcher with 612 points, ahead of Bryan Harvey with 557. Chuck Knoblauch was the top American League rookie with 429 points, and Bagwell the top NL rookie with 444. Tom Glavine was the top point-getting National League pitcher, with 553 points. The only award we "missed" was the National League MVP Award, which went to Terry Pendleton. Pendleton earned 536 points in our game, an outstanding total but ranking comfortably behind Ryne Sandberg (640) and Barry Bonds (603), and also behind a half-dozen other players. Cecil Fielder, the man who would be MVP, was the #10 point-earner in the American League, not that this proves anything.

It's a fun game, I think. If you're interested call STATS at 1-800-63-STATS; that's 1-800-637-8287. They'll send you more information and you can make a decision about signing up, and also they'll tell you how to order a copy of the STATS Handbooks. Well, they won't tell you unless you ask.

ROOKIE OF THE YEAR CANDIDATES

A couple of quick thoughts before I give you the lists:

1) I don't normally like to pick pitchers to be the Rookie of the Year because they usually need adjustment periods and don't win all that many Rookie of the Year Awards, but these lists are about 50% pitchers because that's what the talent is at this time, and

2) The lion's share of the best prospects this year are in the National League.

In last year's book I didn't list either of the actual rookies of the year, although I liked both of them a great deal, because I didn't think they would play regularly in 1991. Following Mark Twain's rule about the cold stove lid, I decided this year to list players that I like, like Matt Stairs of Montreal, even if I have no idea where they are going to play.

Here's my list of the top Rookie of the Year candidates for 1992:

National League

1. **Reggie Sanders, Cincinnati** If they trade Eric Davis so you can play, you'd better be good. I don't think he's Eric Davis, but he should hit .270 with some power and some speed.
2. **Mo Sanford, Cincinnati** Could strike out 225 men.
3. **Anthony Young, New York** He's not the best prospect in the world, but he has three things going for him:
   1) The team,
   2) The park, and
   3) Almost 50 innings of experience.
4. **Kyle Abbott, Philadelphia** A better pitcher than Young, but park and team provide less help.
5. **Matt Stairs, Montreal** Best hitting prospect among the National Leaguers. He doesn't have a job but he has four chances to get one—first base, second base, third base or left field.
6. **Todd Hundley, New York** Most people would place him higher, but I don't expect him to hit as well as a Rookie of the Year usually hits. He certainly *could* hit .265 with 16 homers, and if he does he'll walk off with the trophy.
7. **Lance Dickson, Chicago** It's tough for a pitcher to succeed in Wrigley, plus the Cubs don't seem to realize what they have. As an individual, his credentials couldn't be any better than they are.
8. **John Vanderwal, Montreal** Line drive hitter, should hit .270 with doubles and walks, secondary average over .300.
9. **Wilfredo Cordero, Montreal** On the basis of what he did last year at Indianapolis, I don't believe he's ready to play in the majors, but a 19-year-old player sometimes improves tremendously in one season. His long-range superstar potential is the best of any player on this list.
10. **Jeff Juden, Houston** In the Houston comment I said that at Tucson last year "he was working on controlling his curve and changeup, and not throwing his 90+ fastball much." That's the party line; the other possibility is that he just doesn't *have* a 90+ fastball any more. I still suspect he'll be pretty good.

Also keep in mind **Keith Mitchell, Atlanta** (.300 hitter with some power), **Carlos Hernandez, Los Angeles** (right-handed hitting catcher, would like him among the top five if it wasn't for Scioscia), **Royce Clayton, San Francisco** (I don't really like him but he does have a job, and any rookie who plays 150 games has got a good chance to win the Rookie of the Year award) and **Eddie Taubensee, Houston** (left-handed hitting catcher acquired from Cleveland).

Also, don't overlook **Donovan Osborne** of St. Louis, **Scott Servais** of Houston, and **Mark Wohlers** of Atlanta. All of those players (and others) are definitely capable of winning the Rookie of the Year award if they can get playing time early in the year.

American League

1. **Jim Thome, Cleveland** Ranks ahead of Bell only because his playing time is more certain. Should hit .270-.300, power uncertain, defense OK at third base, long-term growth potential outstanding.
2. **Derek Bell, Toronto** Could hit over .300 with power and speed. The Blue Jays have many options in the outfield and haven't traditionally played rookies much, but Bell could be good enough to earn immediate time.
3. **Luis Mercedes, Baltimore** Should hit .290-.300, no power, defense is suspect. If he hits .315 he'll probably win the Award.
4. **Denny Neagle, Minnesota** Has sensational minor league numbers, has to beat David West out of a job to be a starter. That seems plausible.
5. **Dave Fleming, Seattle** Injury to Brian Holman opens a spot in the rotation for Fleming, who pitched well in a late look. Left-hander, third round pick in 1990, struck out 125 in 156 innings in the minors, walked only 28.

6. **Cal Eldred, Milwaukee** I don't really like him but I don't hate him, either, and he's almost sure to be in the rotation in April. Should go 12-15; if he's lucky that becomes 16-11, and that's a Rookie of the Year.
7. **Rob Maurer, Texas** There's no job for him but he can hit. If playing time opens up with the release of Pettis or an injury to Reimer, Palmeiro or Gonzalez he'll step into the job.
8. **Eddie Zosky, Toronto** The last, best hope for a Toronto shortstop. If Walt Weiss won a Rookie of the Year Award, Eddie Zosky can win a Rookie of the Year Award.
9. **Roger Salkeld, Seattle** Probably won't be in the rotation before August, but one of the best pitching prospects in the minors today, and you never know what will happen with a new manager.
10. Or take a flier on: **Don Barbara, California** first baseman who can hit if he backs into a job with the absence of Joyner, or **Dave Nilsson, Milwaukee** catcher who will move up if the Brewers work out the long-rumored B.J. Surhoff trade, or **Jimmy Tatum,** a 200-pound shortstop from Double-A, given up on by the Indians, who could wind up with the Milwaukee third base job if Gary Sheffield continues to be Gary Sheffield.

Also capable of a Rookie of the Year season: **Domingo Martinez, Toronto; John Jaha, Milwaukee; John DeSilva, Detroit** and **Arthur Rhodes, Baltimore.**